Mac® OS X v. 10.2 Jaguar
Little Black Book

Gene Steinberg

PARAGLYPH
P R E S S

President *Keith* *Weiskamp*	**Mac® OS X v. 10.2 Jaguar Little Black Book** Copyright © 2003 Paraglyph Press, Inc. All rights reserved. This book may not be duplicated in any way without the express written consent of the publisher, except in the form of brief excerpts or quotations for the purposes of review. The information contained herein is for the personal use of the reader and may not be
Editor-at-Large *Jeff* *Duntemann*	incorporated in any commercial programs, other books, databases, or any kind of software without written consent of the publisher. Making copies of this book or any portion for any purpose other than your own is a violation of United States copyright laws.
	Limits of Liability and Disclaimer of Warranty
Vice President, Sales, Marketing, and Distribution *Steve Sayre*	The author and publisher of this book have used their best efforts in preparing the book and the programs contained in it. These efforts include the development, research, and testing of the theories and programs to determine their effectiveness. The author and publisher make no warranty of any kind, expressed or implied, with regard to these programs or the documentation contained in this book. The author and publisher shall not be liable in the event of incidental or consequential damages in connection with, or arising out of, the furnishing, performance, or use of the
Vice President, International Sales and Marketing *Cynthia Caldwell*	programs, associated instructions, and/or claims of productivity gains. **Trademarks** Trademarked names appear throughout this book. Rather than list the names and entities that own the trademarks or insert a trademark symbol with each mention of the trademarked name, the publisher states that it is using the names for editorial purposes only and to the benefit of the trademark owner, with no intention of infringing upon that trademark.
Editorial Director *Sharon Linsenbach*	Paraglyph Press, Inc. 2246 E. Myrtle Avenue Phoenix, Arizona 85202 Phone: 602-749-8787
Production Manager *Kim Eoff*	Paraglyph Press ISBN: 1-932111-72-7 Printed in the United States of America 10 9 8 7 6 5 4 3 2 1

PARAGLYPH PRESS

The Paraglyph Mission

This book you've purchased is a collaborative creation involving the work of many hands, from authors to editors to designers and to technical reviewers. At Paraglyph Press, we like to think that everything we create, develop, and publish is the result of one form creating another. And as this cycle continues on, we believe that your suggestions, ideas, feedback, and comments on how you've used our books is an important part of the process for us and our authors.

We've created Paraglyph Press with the sole mission of producing and publishing books that make a difference. The last thing we all need is yet another tech book on the same tired, old topic. So we ask our authors and all of the many creative hands who touch our publications to do a little extra, dig a little deeper, think a little harder, and create a better book. The founders of Paraglyph are dedicated to finding the best authors, developing the best books, and helping you find the solutions you need.

As you use this book, please take a moment to drop us a line at **feedback@paraglyphpress.com** and let us know how we are doing - and how we can keep producing and publishing the kinds of books that you can't live without.

Sincerely,

Keith Weiskamp & Jeff Duntemann
Paraglyph Press Founders

Paraglyph Press
2246 East Myrtle Ave.
Phoenix, AZ 85020

email:
feedback@paraglyphpress.com
Web: **www.paraglyphpress.com**
Phone: 602-749-8787
Fax: 602-861-1941

Look for these related books from Paraglyph Press:

Windows 2000 Security Little Black Book
By Ian McLean

Also Recently Published by Paraglyph Press:

Visual Basic .NET Programming with Peter Aitken
By Peter Aitken

Visual Basic .NET Black Book
By Steven Holzner

Mac OS X Version 10.1 Little Black Book
By Gene Steinberg

C++ Black Book
By Steven Holzner

C# Core Language Little Black Book
By Bill Wagner

I wish to pay special thanks to my "muse" (she knows who she is) for always helping me to find the right things to say and the means to say it.

About the Author

Gene Steinberg is an award-winning technology journalist. He is the author of more than 30 books on computing, the Internet, and telecommunications and he has written articles for such diverse sources as CNET, ZDNet, *MacAddict*, *MacHome*, and *Macworld*. His voice is heard weekly on the syndicated radio show, *The Mac Night Owl LIVE*, and his weekly column, "Mac Reality Check," is carried by Gannett News Service and published in many of the chain's newspapers and also at usatoday.com. Gene's Mac support site, The Mac Night Owl (**www.macnightowl.com**) is regularly visited by tens of thousands of Mac users each day. In his spare time, Gene and his teenaged son, Grayson, are developing a science fiction adventure series, *Attack of the Rockoids*.

Acknowledgments

Mac OS X is both a simple yet an extraordinarily complex operating system, and there is no way to a project of this scope without outside assistance. During the course of researching and writing this book, I've been pleased to receive the help of a number of folks who have made this daunting task far more pleasant.

First and foremost, I want to thank the folks at Apple's corporate communications department for letting me see the future of the Mac OS and answering all my questions, whether simple, complex, or just downright silly. I'm particularly grateful to Natalie Sequeira and Bill Evans for their able assistance. Apple's Director of OS Technologies, Worldwide Product Marketing, Ken Bereskin, was especially helpful in delineating the key aspects of Mac OS X for both this book and my ongoing online articles on the subject.

This book would not have been possible were it not for Joe Pedreiro, who took on the task as Technical Editor to make sure every single fact in this book was as accurate as possible. In addition, an author cannot work without a publisher and editors, and the terrific folks at Paraglyph Press were especially helpful in putting up with my quirks and demands without protest. I'm particularly thankful to Sharon Linsenbach, Editorial Director, for ensuring that the words I wrote were understandable to all of our readers, and for making this book look good.

Finally, I am especially thankful for the help and support from my little family, my beautiful wife, Barbara, and my brilliant son, Grayson, for putting up with the long hours I spent at the keyboard in order to deliver the manuscript for this book on schedule.

—*Gene Steinberg*

Contents at a Glance

Part I	Mac OS X Arrives
Chapter 1	The New Features from A to Z 3
Chapter 2	Upgrading to Mac OS X 21
Chapter 3	Mac OS X User Preferences 39
Chapter 4	Introducing the Mac OS X Finder 89
Chapter 5	Mac OS X Desktop Management 121
Chapter 6	Setting Up Mac OS X for Multiple Users 141
Chapter 7	Mac OS X's Search Feature 161
Chapter 8	Networking Overview 179
Chapter 9	The New AppleScript 211
Chapter 10	Installing Programs Under Mac OS X 227
Part II	Mac OS X and Hardware
Chapter 11	Hardware Management 247
Chapter 12	Hooking Up Accessories 245
Chapter 13	Taking Mac OS X on the Road 277
Part III	The Software Review
Chapter 14	Mac OS X-Savvy Applications 295
Chapter 15	Using Older Programs with Mac OS X 319
Chapter 16	Mac OS X Font Management 335
Chapter 17	Performing Backups 357
Chapter 18	Security and Mac OS X 379
Chapter 19	Troubleshooting Mac OS X 377
Part IV	Taking Mac OS X Online
Chapter 20	A Fast Introduction to Mac OS X's Unix Environment 421
Chapter 21	Surfing the Net 433
Chapter 22	Exploring Apple's Email Software 457
Chapter 23	Exploring Apple's Digital Hub Applications 491

Table of Contents

Introduction xxiii

Part I   Mac OS X Arrives

Chapter 1
The New Features from A to Z 3
    Apple Goes Operating System Shopping   3
    A Brief Look at the New Features   4
        Darwin   5
        Quartz   8
        Cocoa   9
        Carbon   9
        Classic   10
        Aqua   10
        The Mac OS X Finder   12
        The Dock   14
        Desktop   16
        Mac OS X 10.2 v. Mac OS X 10.1   16
    Are You Ready for Mac OS X?   18

Chapter 2
Upgrading to Mac OS X 21
    In Brief   22
        Preparing for Mac OS X   22
            Make Sure You Have Mac OS 9.1 or Later for Classic Applications   23
            Check Your Hard Drive   23
            Back Up Your Data   27
            Mac OS X: Hardware-Related Issues   28
    Immediate Solutions   31

Table of Contents

    Preparing for Mac OS X 31
    Installing Mac OS X 32
      Notes on Performing an Unsupported Installation 36

Chapter 3
Mac OS X User Preferences 39
 In Brief *40*
  Control Panel Settings: A Mixture of the Old and New 40
  Selecting Printers Without a Chooser 42
 Mac OS 9 Features: What Happened to Them? *44*
 Immediate Solutions *46*
  Configuring the Setup Assistant 46
  Setting System Preferences Under Mac OS X 52
    Setting Accounts Preferences 53
    Setting CDs & DVDs Preferences 53
    Setting Classic Preferences 54
    Setting ColorSync Preferences 55
    Setting Date & Time Preferences 56
    Setting Desktop Preferences 58
    Setting Display Preferences 59
    Setting Dock Preferences 65
    Setting Energy Saver Preferences 65
    Setting General Preferences 67
    Setting International Preferences 69
    Setting Internet Preferences 70
    Setting Keyboard Preferences 72
    Setting Login Items Preferences 73
    Setting Mouse Preferences 74
    Setting Network Preferences 75
    Setting QuickTime Preferences 77
    Setting Screen Effects Preferences 78
    Setting Sharing Preferences 78
    Setting Software Update Preferences 80
    Setting Sound Preferences 81
    Setting Speech Preferences 83
    Setting Startup Disk Preferences 84
    Setting Universal Access Preferences 84
  Configuring a Printer 86

Chapter 4
Introducing the Mac OS X Finder 89

In Brief 90
Additional Finder Navigation Features   93
Visiting the Finder's Toolbar   94
The New Finder Menus   96

Immediate Solutions   103
Setting Finder Preferences   103
   Keeping Folder Views Consistent   103
   Setting Viewing Preferences   105
   Changing Finder List View Columns   108
   Resizing Columns in Column View   109
   Customizing the Finder's Toolbar   109
Using the New Finder on a Day-to-Day Basis   111
   Moving a File   111
   Copying a File   111
   Making an Alias   111
   Finding a File   112
   Creating Favorites   112
   Accessing Contextual Menus   112
   Ejecting a Disk   113
   Using the Get Info Window   114
   Taking Screenshots   115
   Finder Keyboard Shortcuts   116
   Using the Finder to Burn CDs and DVDs   116
   Restoring Classic Mac OS Application Switching   118

Chapter 5
Mac OS X Desktop Management 121

In Brief 122
The Dock Dissected   122

Immediate Solutions   129
Setting Dock Preferences   129
Setting Desktop Preferences   132
Setting Finder Preferences   134
Using the Dock   135
The TinkerTool Alternative   138
Making Your Mac OS X Desktop as Cluttered as Ever   139

Chapter 6
Setting Up Mac OS X for Multiple Users 141

In Brief *142*

Mac OS X Multiple Users Features   142
Using Strong Passwords   146

Immediate Solutions *147*

Setting Up Multiple-User Access   147
Customizing a User Account   149
Editing a User Account   152
Setting Up Keychain Access   153
Checking and Using Your Keychain   155
Changing Keychain Settings   155
Running a Keychain on Another Mac   157
Coping with Problems Involving Keychains and Multiple Users   157
Suggestions for Setting Up Multiple Users for Use with Children   159

Chapter 7
Mac OS X's Search Feature 161

In Brief *162*

A Look at Apple's Search Utilities   163

Immediate Solutions *166*

Searching for Files on Your Mac   166
Advanced File Search Techniques   167
Searching Files for Content   167
  Using Advanced Criteria   169
  Setting Sherlock Preferences   171
Searching the Internet   172
  Customizing Your Sherlock Internet Search Request   174
Installing Additional Search Modules   177
Another Solution for Web Services   178

Chapter 8
Networking Overview 179

In Brief *180*

Accessing Networked Macs from Mac OS X   182
  A Different Way to Share Files   183
  A Look at Mac OS X's Networking Components   183

Immediate Solutions *186*

Sharing Files Under Mac OS X   186
  Accessing Shared Volumes with Network Browser   191
  Accessing Shared Volumes with the Chooser   192
Connecting to Shared Macs Under Mac OS X   193

Connecting to Shared Windows and
   Unix Servers   195
Using Internet Connect for Dial-Up Networking   197
Verifying Connectivity   202
Connecting Via a Virtual Private Network   203
Using Apple's Location Manager to Create Custom Setups   204
Setting Up a Web or FTP Server on Your Mac   206
Can't Access a Drop Box?   207
Correcting Network Access Problems   207
Protecting Your Network from the Internet   209

Chapter 9
The New AppleScript 211

In Brief   212
   What AppleScript Can Do   213
   Mac OS X Script Features   214
   The Tools for Using Scripts in Mac OS X   215
   AppleScript: The Future   216
Immediate Solutions   217
   Locating Mac OS X's AppleScript Collection   217
   Choosing Mac OS X's Sample Scripts   217
   Using Script Menu   219
   Making or Editing Your First AppleScript   220
   A Quick Primer on Folder Actions   223
   Running a Script from the Unix Command Line   224
   Using Toolbar Scripts   225

Chapter 10
Installing Programs Under Mac OS X 227

In Brief   228
   Introducing the Package   228
   The Microsoft Way   229
   Exploring New Application Features   229
Immediate Solutions   233
   Handling Complex Application Installations   233
      Using an Installer   233
      Using a Disk Image   233
      Making a Startup (Login) Application   234
   Using the New Open Dialog Box   237
   Using the New Save As Dialog Box   239
   Using the Services Menu   242
   Troubleshooting Software Installation Problems   242

Table of Contents

Part II Mac OS X and Hardware

Chapter 11
Hardware Management 247
In Brief 248
    Mac OS X's Special Hardware Features 248

Immediate Solutions 251
    Installing New Hardware 251
    Maintaining Your Mac on a Daily Basis 252
    Should You Buy a New Mac? 255
    Looking at Extended Warranties 256
    Solving Hardware and Software Problems 257

Chapter 12
Hooking Up Accessories 261
In Brief 262
    A Review of Mac Peripheral Ports 262
        Adding a Missing Port 265
    Peripherals Available for Macs 267

Immediate Solutions 272
    Installing a New Scanner 272
    Installing New Storage Devices 273
    Installing Digital Cameras, eBook Readers, Palm OS Handhelds, and Other Products 274
    Determining What to Do If It Doesn't Work 275

Chapter 13
Taking Mac OS X on the Road 277
In Brief 278
    Exploring Mac OS X Tools for Laptops 278
        Superior Power Management 278
        Integrated Mouse Preference Panel 279
        Superfast Sleep and Awake Features 279
        Editing Vacation Videos on the Road 280

Immediate Solutions 282
    Computing on the Road 282
    Checking Battery Life 283
    Getting the Maximum Amount of Battery Life 283
    Creating an Apple Laptop Travel Kit 286
    Getting the Most Efficient Online Performance 290
    Using FireWire Target Disk Mode 292

Part III   The Software Review

Chapter 14
Mac OS X-Savvy Applications 295

In Brief   296

The Two Forms of Mac OS X Applications   296
Key Mac OS X Software Profiles and Previews   297
- Microsoft   297
- Apple Computer   298
- FileMaker   309
- Adobe Systems   309
- Alias|Wavefront   309
- Corel   309
- Deneba   310
- Macromedia   310
- Stone Design   310
- AOL   311

Immediate Solutions   312

Introducing AppleWorks for Mac OS X   312
- Using AppleWorks Starting Points   312
- Using Tables in AppleWorks   313
Office v. X for Mac in Brief   315
- Profiling the Project Gallery   316
- Using Word X's Multiple Selection Feature   316
- Using Excel X's Auto Recover Feature   316
Introducing Create for Mac OS X   316
- Using the Inspector   317
- Starting a Web Page in Create   318

Chapter 15
Using Older Programs with Mac OS X 319

In Brief   320

Introducing the Classic Environment   320
- Classic Environment Limitations   321

Immediate Solutions   325

Launching Older Mac Programs   325
Running Classic as a Startup Application   326
Getting Reliable Performance from Classic Applications   328
Keeping Your Mac OS 9.x System Folder Safe and Sound   331
Solving Classic Environment Problems   332
Returning to Mac OS 9.x   334

Chapter 16
Mac OS X Font Management 335

In Brief 336

There Are Fonts and There Are Fonts   336
   Font Formats Defined   336
   Font Organization Under the Mac OS   337
   Mac OS X's New Font-Handling Scheme   339
   Introducing the Font Panel   341
   Special Font Features of Mac OS X   342

Immediate Solutions 344

Installing Fonts Under Mac OS X   344
Using the Font Panel   345
   Adding Font Favorites   346
   Using Favorites   347
   Creating a Font Collection   347
   Choosing Custom Font Sizes   349
Checking the Characters in a Font   349
Avoiding Too-Small Fonts in TextEdit   350
Using Font Reserve to Manage Your Mac OS X Font Library   351
Using Suitcase to Manage Your Mac OS X Font Library   354
Handling Mac OS X Font Problems   355

Chapter 17
Performing Backups 357

In Brief 358

A Survey of Backup Software   358
   An Overview of Retrospect   359
   An Overview of Intego Personal Backup X   360
   Other Backup Programs   362
An Overview of Internet Backups   364
An Overview of Backup Media   366

Immediate Solutions 371

The No-Frills Daily Backup Plan   371
The Special Software Backup Plan   372
Tips and Tricks for Robust Backups   374
Doing a Folder Backup via the Command Line   376

Chapter 18
Security and Mac OS X 379

In Brief 380

An Overview of Mac Viruses   381
   Types of Computer Viruses   381

           Viruses and Mac OS X   382
           Broadband Internet and Invaders from the Outside   382
    Immediate Solutions   384
       Choosing a Mac Virus-Detection Program   384
           MicroMat's TechTool Pro   384
           Intego's VirusBarrier   385
           Network Associates' VirexNetwork Associates' Virex   387
           Symantec's Norton AntiVirus   388
       Using Apple's Mac OS X's Built-in Firewall   390
       Choosing Personal Firewall SoftwareChoosing Personal
           Firewall Software   392
           Norton Personal Firewall   393
           Intego's NetBarrier X   393
           Intego's ContentBarrier   394
           Firewalk X   395
           BrickHouse   395
           Hardware Firewalls   396

Chapter 19
Troubleshooting Mac OS X 397
    In Brief   398
       Mac OS X's Crash-Resistant Features   398
       The Software Update Application   400
    Immediate Solutions   402
       Solving Mac OS X Installation Problems   402
       Solving System Crashes and Freezes   405
           The Application Won't Quit   405
           Applications Refuse to Launch   406
           The Classic Environment Fails to Run   407
       Solving Network Access Failure   408
       Login Window Shakes   408
       Desktop Folder Contents Aren't Visible Under Mac OS 9.x   409
       Mac OS X Can't Boot after You Deleted a File by Mistake   410
       Solving Other Common Mac OS X Problems   411
       Performing System-Level Disk Diagnostics   414
       Setting Root AccessSetting Root Access   416
       Monitoring System Use to Check for Conflicts   417

           Part IV   Taking Mac OS X Online

Chapter 20
A Fast Introduction to Mac OS X's Unix Environment 421

In Brief 422
- Looking at the Nuts and Bolts of Darwin 423
- Introducing the Autocomplete Feature 425
- Running Software from the Command Line 426
- Backing Up Files and Folders 427
- Suggested Reading 427

Immediate Solutions 428
- A Short List of Popular Command-Line Features 428
- Using Mac OS X's Command-Line FTP Software 431

Chapter 21
Surfing the Net 433

In Brief 434
- The Coming of Broadband Access 434
- Mac OS X Web Browsers Profiled 436
  - Microsoft Internet Explorer 437
  - iCab 439
  - Netscape 440
  - OmniWeb 442
  - Opera 443

Immediate Solutions 446
- Deleting Browser Caches 446
  - Killing the Cache in Internet Explorer 446
  - Killing the Cache in iCab 447
  - Killing the Cache in Netscape 448
  - Killing the Cache in OmniWeb 448
  - Killing the Cache in Opera 449
- Determining Whether a Larger Cache Is Necessary 449
- Using Bookmarks to Get There Faster 450
- Solving Internet Connection Problems 451

Chapter 22
Exploring Apple's Email Software 457

In Brief 458
- Reviewing Other Mac OS X Email Choices 460
  - Entourage X 461
  - Eudora Pro 462
  - Netscape 463
  - How Does Mail Rate? 464

Table of Contents

Immediate Solutions 467
   Setting Up Your User Account 467
   Importing Your Email Messages 471
   Customizing Mail's Toolbar 473
   Composing a New Message 473
   Responding to a Message 475
   Quoting Messages 476
   Spellchecking Your Messages 476
   Sending Email Attachments 477
   Forwarding Email 479
   Adding Email Signatures 480
   Formatting Email 481
   Blocking SPAM 481
   Setting Mail Rules 482
   Getting Your Email Automatically 483
   Using the Address Book 484
   Importing an Address Book 486
   Finding a Message 487
   Why Can't I Send My Email? 488
   Why Are Messages Scrambled? 489
   Why Doesn't Mail Check All My Accounts? 490

Chapter 23
Exploring Apple's Digital Hub Applications 491

In Brief 492
   An Overview of Apple's Digital Hub 493
      An overview of .Mac Features 495
Immediate Solutions 497
   Using iCal 497
      Creating New Calendar Events 497
      Creating a New Calendar 498
      More iCal Features Summarized 498
   Setting Up iChat 499
   Using iChat 501
   Using iPhoto 503
   Using the iDisk Feature 505

Glossary 507

Index 529

Introduction

Remember the story about the boy who cried wolf? Sure enough, if you were told for nearly a decade that a company was going to bring a product to market in the near future, you'd probably chuckle sadly and then get on with your business. Or just ignore it altogether.

This is, no doubt, the dilemma Apple faced when they first announced plans for Mac OS X. Apple's road for producing a modern operating system to replace the Mac OS was, for years, littered with failed projects, wrong turns, and missed deadlines. So it almost came as a relief when I attended a press briefing on Mac OS X Public Beta at the San Francisco headquarters of CNET, the online and broadcast technology news service, in September of 2000.

Within a few hours I was back at my home office, installing the future of the Mac OS on my computer. I examined the documentation, and checked my notes as the installation proceeded. Within less than fifteen minutes, my Mac restarted. A short trip to the Setup Assistant, and a second restart, and I was a believer!

Mac OS X was at last a reality, not vaporware to be touted strictly for public demonstrations.

However, that was only the beginning. By January 2001, Apple had poured through tens of thousands of feedback messages from devoted Mac users. In the Macworld Expo keynote, CEO Steve Jobs announced some important changes to the user interface to satisfy the clamoring of thousands to restore the Apple menu, restore disk icons to the desktop, bring back the menu bar clock and, if need be, allow the Finder to work just as the old "Classic" version did.

But that was only the beginning. By March, the first official release of Mac OS X hit the streets, but still wasn't quite a finished product. During Apple's rollout of what was dubbed "the world's greatest

Introduction

operating system," it had to admit that it was strictly a version for early adopters and systems administrators who wanted to test the new system for eventual widespread deployment.

After several bug-fix updates, Apple finally rolled out the "mainstream" version, Mac OS X 10.1, in September. The hallmark of the new release was a huge performance improvement, plus the addition of features missing from the original release, such as the ability to burn a CD or DVD from the Finder and DVD playback.

Eleven months later, and Mac OS 10.2, nicknamed Jaguar, came along, offering 150 new features, new""i" applications, such as iChat, and across-the-board performance enhancements.

The Mac OS X Version Little Black Book Jaguar Edition is designed to be your companion as you migrate to Apple's Unix-based operating system. From installation, to setup to troubleshooting, you'll find the information you need is readily available, all tested with the release version of the software for maximum accuracy.

The Bill of Fare

Since this book is part of The Little Black Book series, it covers the essential information you need to install, configure and use Mac OS X. There are no frills and no fluff. Useless tips and tricks that will satisfy one's intellectual curiosity or perhaps trigger a chuckle, but not enhance your productivity, aren't included.

The 23 chapters here are divided into four parts, each covering a particular area of your Mac user experience.

In "Part I: Mac OS X Arrives," I run through the important new features, and then help you plot installation strategies. You are then taken step-by-step through the actual installation and configuration. From here you'll be introduced to the new Mac OS X Finder, the Dock, multiple user features, search features, plus the big changes in the networking architecture. This part closes with information about AppleScript and how to install and use your programs. There's even a section covering the new Open and Save dialog boxes, which are sure to simplify file management.

Next there's "Part II: Mac OS X and Hardware." Are you planning to install Mac OS X on a new Mac, or just one you've upgraded with extra memory, drive space and other additions? These critical subjects are dealt with here. You'll also learn how to add peripherals, such as printers, scanners and removable drives, on your Mac. Finally, there's a section on using Mac OS X with one of Apple's iBooks or PowerBooks.

Moving on to'"Part III: The Software Review," you'll discover some of the new Mac OS X applications, how to run older "Classic" software on your Mac and how to handle fonts, perform backups, and check for computer viruses. Finally, there's a comprehensive section on troubleshooting, plus a visit to the Unix command line of the new operating system to perform a hard drive diagnostics and to navigate through the underbelly of the new operating system.

The last part of this book, "Part IV: Taking Mac OS X Online," covers Internet access from stem to stern. You'll have a birds-eye view of the newest Web browsers, Apple's Mail application with its terrific junk mail feature and other Apple digital hub applications, such as iPhoto.

How to Use This Book

The *Mac OS X v. 10.2 Jaguar Little Black Book* isn't designed to be read from cover to cover as you might read a novel, though I don't particularly mind it if you do it all in a single sitting. You'll probably just want to read the chapters that answer your questions about the new Mac OS.

As part of the Little Black Book series, each chapter is divided into two sections. The first,

In Brief, gives you the basics and theories about the subject. The second, *Immediate Solutions*, offers step-by-step instructions on how to accomplish tasks, along with guides on what to do if something goes wrong.

Although the Mac OS X user interface is ultra simple and smooth, it's a highly complex operating system, one that will be updated regularly as time goes by. If you were one of the early adopters to the new operating system, you can see the vast number of changes between the original release and the subsequent upgrades. As a result, a book of this sort is also a developing process, and future updates for this book will reflect those changes, plus what I've learned as I continue to use Mac OS X.

I also welcome your comments, questions, and suggestions for future editions. If you have a problem with the new operating system, or discover something totally unique and utterly cool, let me know. You can email me directly at the address below.

Gene Steinberg
Scottsdale, AZ
Email:
gene@macnightowl.com
www.macnightowl.com

Part I
Mac OS X Arrives

Chapter 1

The New Features from A to Z

Although the skeptics felt it couldn't be done, Apple has a history of confounding the skeptics. So when Mac OS X, a major upgrade to the aging Mac operating system, finally saw the light of day, Mac users were equally amazed and delighted. For years, Apple had tried and failed to provide a completely stable, robust operating system of a sort that would appeal to both newcomers and power users alike.

Apple's previous efforts to deliver a modern operating system were doomed to failure. In the most notable (and perhaps notorious) example, Apple spent tens of millions of dollars, thousands and thousands of man (and woman) hours, and several frustrating years developing an operating system (code-named Copland) that was designed to offer all the industrial-strength features needed to bring the Macintosh user experience into the twenty-first century. The project, though laudable in its intentions, fell apart when serious problems were encountered in such areas as offering backward-compatibility with older Mac software.

Eventually, the original expected shipping name for Copland, Mac OS 8, was used for a modest system upgrade that offered interface improvements but none of the under-the-hood features expected of a modern operating system. The upgrade and subsequent system versions through Mac OS 9 took advantage of some of the appearance features left over from Copland, but with only minor improvements in overall system reliability.

Apple Goes Operating System Shopping

When its own in-house talent was unable to finish the job, Apple went operating system shopping in 1996. According to published reports at the time, Apple flirted with acquiring a fledgling operating system called BeOS from a company run by a former Apple executive, Jean-Louis Gassée. The BeOS was briefly offered in a series of twin-processor computers, but the company soon abandoned the hardware and concentrated on the software.

Although the BeOS still works on the older PowerPC Macs, Apple would not deliver support for the G3 or G4 CPUs, and thus the company went to the Intel world in search of more enthusiastic support. However, the operating system never quite caught on as its developers hoped, and the BeOS was finally acquired by Palm; it may find its way into future iterations of Palm OS software for handheld devices.

Apple finally made what has become the decision that saved its neck. It agreed to spend some $400 million to acquire NeXT Inc., which was established by Apple cofounder Steve Jobs after he was ousted from Apple back in 1985, nine years after he and Steve Wozniak founded the company. The company's product, NeXTSTEP, was a Unix-based operating system that provided the basic underpinnings and technology Apple needed to develop its next-generation Mac OS. As soon as the former NeXT folks were on board, Apple began developing a new operating system bearing the code name Rhapsody, which would, in effect, merge NeXTSTEP with the Mac OS. In short order, Steve Jobs replaced Apple CEO Gil Amelio as head of the company, and went on to dice and slice both staff and products, finally bringing the company into sharp focus with a new line of striking consumer-oriented products.

Although Rhapsody's focus, direction, and release dates changed, the first iteration of the technology was delivered with the arrival of Mac OS X Server in 1999. It was a mixture of the old and the new, combining a large portion of NeXT Inc. core technology with elements of the traditional Mac user interface.

Once the server version was released, it was time to focus on a consumer version. The end result is Mac OS X, which first saw the light of day as a public beta in the fall of 2000, and as a release for early adopters the following spring.

A Brief Look at the New Features

The striking new look of the Mac OS X interface, called Aqua, is just a small part of the changes wrought by the new Mac operating system. Under the surface are a tremendous number of changes designed to provide improved support and make the Mac run more reliably than ever. Before we look at the new, however, it is fitting to examine where we've come from. For example, when the Macintosh first shipped in 1984, its graphical interface was unique for an affordable personal computer (see Figure 1.1). Instead of typing commands to make your computer perform a given function, you used a pointing

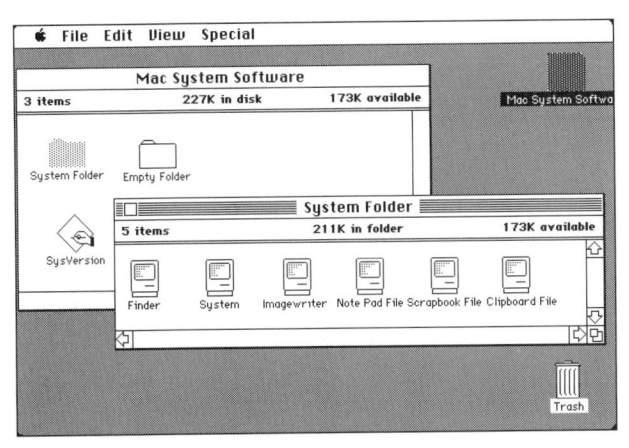

Figure 1.1 This is the Macintosh desktop that was introduced with the very first models.

device—a mouse—and you clicked on icons and command menus representing common functions, such as files, folders, and disks.

NOTE: It's fair to mention that the Mac wasn't the first Apple PC with a graphical interface. Prior to the Mac, Apple introduced a high-priced desktop computer, called Lisa, which never quite caught on. In those days, some firms who provided typesetting computers, such as Agfa CompuGraphic (now Agfa), were offering the Lisa as a simple-to-use front end for some of those systems.

Over the years, a number of changes have been made to the Mac. However, even the user interface of Mac OS 9, the last "Classic" or traditional Mac operating system version, bears a striking resemblance to the original, despite its more colorful, more delicately constructed desktop and icons (see Figure 1.2).

Now that you've taken a before-and-after look at the evolution of the Mac OS, the following sections detail what Mac OS X brings to the table.

Darwin

The open source core of Mac OS X, Darwin, is based on a Unix microkernel, consisting of the Mach 3 microkernel and FreeBSD. The Apache Web server, which powers a majority of Web sites, has been tamed and forms the basis of the new operating system's Web-sharing capabilities.

Chapter 1 The New Features from A to Z

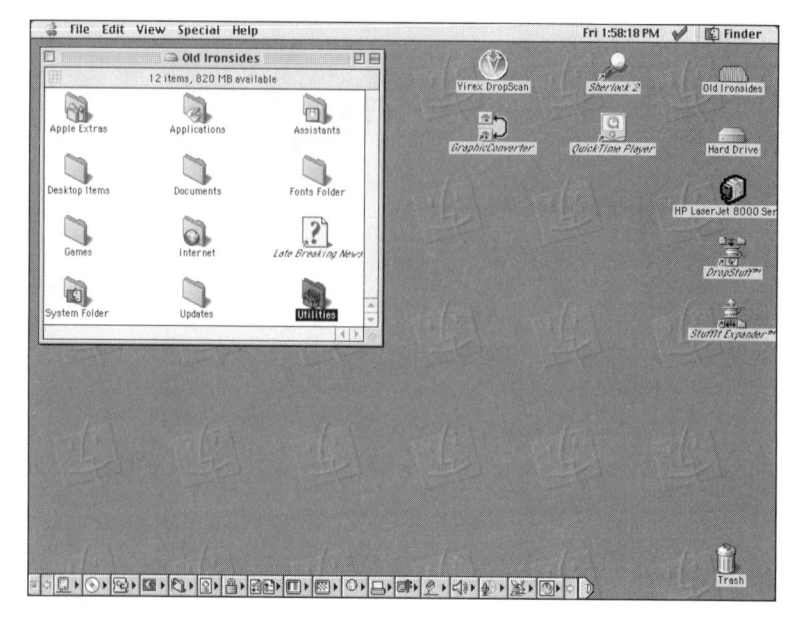

Figure 1.2 The traditional Mac OS has grown in complexity and size by quantum leaps, yet retains many of the core visual elements of previous versions.

> **NOTE:** Apple's Darwin is also an open-source project, where the core components of the operating system are made available free of charge to software developers, with Apple retaining full rights to the code. These developers can test and debug the software, and then make available bug fixes and enhancements to the entire developer community. For more information about this feature, feel free to visit Apple's Darwin Web site, www.apple.com/darwin.

Although its Unix underpinnings are well hidden beneath Aqua's striking user interface, they are not invisible. Power users can easily peer beneath the surface, bypassing the graphical user interface, and run regular Unix-based applications under Mac OS X via a command-line interface. Apple has even provided a Terminal application in the Utilities folder (see Figure 1.3), so power users can visit the command line and access the core Unix functions.

In addition, the new Mac operating system offers the same industrial-strength features that are the hallmark of Unix. These include the following:

- *Protected memory*—Each Mac OS X native program you run resides in its own address space, walled off from other programs. If a single program crashes, that application is shut down, along

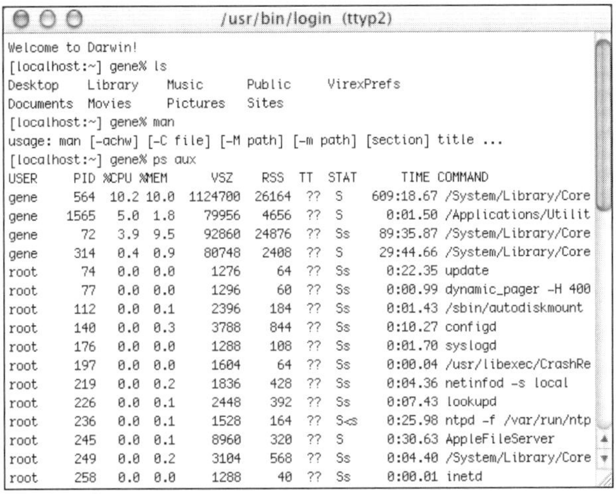

```
  ○ ○ ○                /usr/bin/login  (ttyp2)
Welcome to Darwin!
[localhost:~] gene% ls
Desktop     Library     Music       Public      VirexPrefs
Documents   Movies      Pictures    Sites
[localhost:~] gene% man
usage: man [-achw] [-C file] [-M path] [-m path] [section] title ...
[localhost:~] gene% ps aux
USER    PID %CPU %MEM    VSZ    RSS  TT  STAT    TIME COMMAND
gene    564 10.2 10.0 1124700 26164  ??  S     609:18.67 /System/Library/Core
gene   1565  5.0  1.8   79956  4656  ??  S       0:01.50 /Applications/Utilit
gene     72  3.9  9.5   92860 24876  ??  Ss     89:35.87 /System/Library/Core
gene    314  0.4  0.9   80748  2408  ??  S      29:44.66 /System/Library/Core
root     74  0.0  0.0    1276    64  ??  Ss      0:22.35 update
root     77  0.0  0.0    1296    60  ??  Ss      0:00.99 dynamic_pager -H 400
root    112  0.0  0.1    2396   184  ??  Ss      0:01.43 /sbin/autodiskmount
root    140  0.0  0.3    3788   844  ??  Ss      0:10.27 configd
root    176  0.0  0.0    1288   108  ??  Ss      0:01.70 syslogd
root    197  0.0  0.0    1604    64  ??  Ss      0:00.04 /usr/libexec/CrashRe
root    219  0.0  0.2    1836   428  ??  Ss      0:04.36 netinfod -s local
root    226  0.0  0.1    2448   392  ??  Ss      0:07.43 lookupd
root    236  0.0  0.1    1528   164  ??  S<s     0:25.98 ntpd -f /var/run/ntp
root    245  0.0  0.1    8960   320  ??  S       0:30.63 AppleFileServer
root    249  0.0  0.2    3104   568  ??  Ss      0:04.40 /System/Library/Core
root    258  0.0  0.0    1288    40  ??  Ss      0:00.01 inetd
```

Figure 1.3   Mac OS X brings something totally new to the platform: a command-line interface that allows you to make changes right in the underbelly of the system.

with the memory address space it occupies. You can continue to run your Mac without the need to restart. This feature will help to sharply reduce the Mac OS's tendency to crash at the least sign of a software conflict.

- *Preemptive multitasking*—Apple's previous multitasking method was cooperative, meaning that each application would, in effect, have to share CPU time with other programs. This meant that if you were working in a program, such as typing in a word-processing document, background tasks, such as printing or downloading a file, could come almost to a screeching halt, particularly if a program hogged processor time unnecessarily. With Mac OS X, the operating system serves as the traffic cop, performing the task management and allowing programs to run more efficiently and with fewer slowdowns when multiple processes are running.

- *Advanced virtual memory*—With previous versions of the Mac operating system, virtual memory meant slower performance, poor performance with multimedia programs, stuttering sounds, and other shortcomings. Under Mac OS X, virtual memory management is dynamic. Programs are automatically given the amount of memory they require, via either RAM or virtual memory disk swapping. Performance is optimized, so you get the maximum possible performance from your programs.

Chapter 1 The New Features from A to Z

> **NOTE:** Virtual memory in Mac OS X is super-efficient, but it can't perform miracles. To get the best possible performance, there is no substitute for having sufficient RAM to run your high-energy programs (such as Adobe Photoshop or Apple's Final Cut Pro). But you will no longer have to visit the Get Info window to constantly change a program's memory allocation to meet your needs (except, of course, for Classic applications).

Quartz

In previous versions of the Mac OS, Apple used an imaging model called QuickDraw to generate pixels on your display. For Mac OS X, Apple has given up this technology, moving instead to Adobe's Portable Document Format (PDF). As you probably know, most electronic documents are available in PDF format, which retains the exact formatting, fonts, pictures, and colors of the original.

Full system-wide support is provided for the major font formats—bitmap, PostScript, TrueType, and the new OpenType format. As a result, Adobe Type Manager (ATM) is no longer needed to render fonts crisply on the screen, although font management is not quite as extensive as the Deluxe version of ATM.

> **NOTE:** ATM will still work normally from Mac OS X's Classic environment, including the font-management features for the Deluxe version, but it will not be upgraded to Mac OS X. Chapter 16 covers the subject of font handling and includes information on the available options for font management.

The Quartz 2D graphics system is extremely powerful, with speedy rendering of images and anti-aliasing, providing sharp screen display. You'll see some of this elegance in the illustrations provided in this book, but you have to see the real thing to get the flavor of the effects of this unique technology.

There's also system-level support for PDF, which makes it easy for Mac software developers to provide built-in support to save documents in this format. In addition to PDF, Apple includes support for ColorSync to ease color management from input to display to output; the industry-standard OpenGL, which provides superlative performance for many 3D games and graphic applications; and Apple's famous QuickTime, used worldwide for generating multimedia content.

In addition, if you have the right video hardware on your Mac, when you upgrade to Mac OS X 10.2, code-named Jaguar, you'll experience the joys of Quartz Extreme, a souped-up version of Quartz that harnesses the power of OpenGL to offload 2D and 3D graphics to the video hardware. It's no free ride, though, as it requires a Mac with AGP-based graphics, using a graphic card from NVIDIA, or one of ATI Radeon products and a minimum of 16MB of video memory.

NOTE: If your Mac isn't equipped with the right video hardware, don't despair. Apple can also use the G4 processor's Velocity Engine, the chip's vector processing capability, to provide some performance improvement. There are also performance optimizations for Macs with a G3 processor, so older Macs, including those millions of vintage iMacs, aren't abandoned. I have personally verified speed improvements on all Macs capable of running Mac OS X, so don't feel you have to buy a new computer just to run Jaguar.

Cocoa

One of the technologies inherited from NeXTSTEP, which forms the basis for a large part of Mac OS X's capabilities, is Cocoa. This is the new name for an advanced object-oriented programming environment that's supposed to allow programmers to develop new applications much more quickly than with other programming tools. In one spectacular example, Stone Software's integrated illustration program, Create, which features drawing, HTML, and page layout capabilities, is largely the work of one programmer. With traditional programming tools, a large, highly skilled team would be required to perform the same work.

NOTE: If there's a downside to all this flexibility, it's that programs created in this fashion cannot run on older Macs. However, that situation may be of less significance as more Macs are shipped with or upgraded to Mac OS X in the years ahead.

Carbon

Once referred to by Apple CEO Steve Jobs as the "basis for all life forms," Carbon is, in fact, a new set of application programming interfaces, commonly referred to as API's. These interfaces are designed to offer software publishers a relatively easy upgrade path to deliver Mac OS X–savvy applications. Most major Mac developers, including such heavyweights as Adobe, Macromedia, Microsoft, and Quark, have worked long and hard porting their products to Mac OS X.

NOTE: Even though Carbon greatly simplifies conversion of software to Mac OS X, it's not a cakewalk. Microsoft Office 2001, for example, consists of millions of lines of computer code. Microsoft has the largest Mac programming team outside of Apple Computer, and yet it didn't complete work on the Mac OS X version of the application suite until late fall 2001. As this book is being written, Quark was still laboring over porting QuarkXPress to the new operating system.

The main advantage of an application that is "Carbonized" is that it supports the major features of Mac OS X, such as preemptive multitasking, protected memory, and advanced virtual memory, plus the eye-catching Aqua interface. In addition, when Apple's CarbonLib extension (which first appeared as part of Mac OS 9) is installed, many of these programs can run on older Mac operating system versions—though, of course, without the advanced features of Mac OS X.

NOTE: Not all Carbon applications have backward-compatibility. The Mac OS X versions of AOL's client software and Microsoft's Internet Explorer and Office run only under Mac OS X, but Adobe's and Macromedia's Mac OS X applications run fine with the older Mac OS. As with any development effort, there are trade-offs, and it's up to each company to decide how to address these issues.

Classic

Although thousands of Mac OS X–savvy programs have shipped since the release of the new operating system, you may still want to use some of the thousands of older programs. Fortunately, you can do so by virtue of the Classic feature.

Classic is, in effect, Mac OS 9.1 and later (9.2.2 is the version that was in use when this book was written) running as a separate application under Mac OS X. You can think of it as being somewhat similar to running Connectix Virtual PC to emulate the Windows environment on a Mac. But it goes further than that. Apple's Classic feature runs almost transparently under Mac OS X after a brief startup process. The feature lets you run most of your older applications with good performance and a high level of compatibility, but without taking advantage of the Aqua user interface or the robust underpinnings of the new operating system. It is designed to ease the transition to the new Mac computing paradigm.

NOTE: The Classic environment is not a panacea. Some cherished system extensions, particularly those that modify Finder functions and hardware drivers for such peripherals as scanners and CD writers, won't run. You'll need to get Mac OS X–compatible drivers for all these products.

Aqua

The Macintosh user interface is reborn with Aqua (see Figure 1.4). Although at first glance Aqua clearly comes across as eye candy—a software interface that is consistent with the striking industrial designs for Apple's latest computers—much more is involved here.

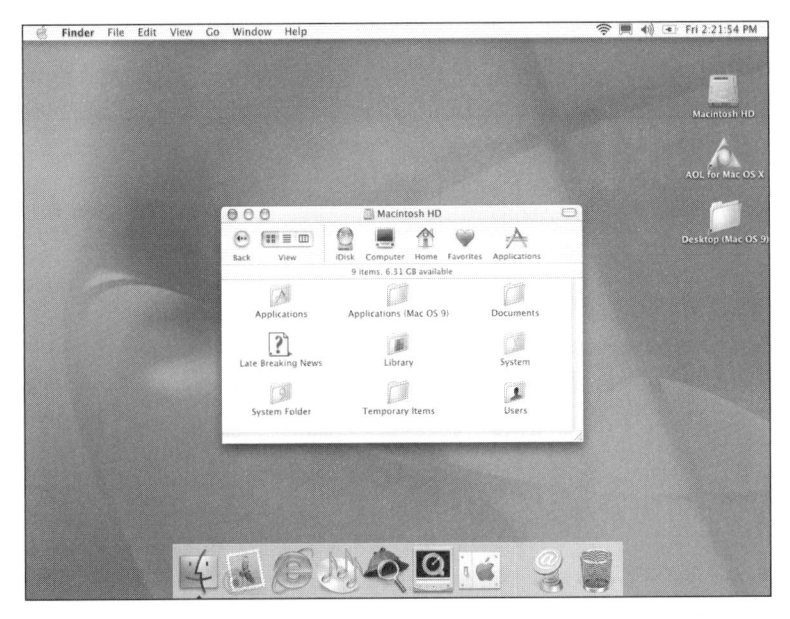

Figure 1.4 After you boot a Mac with OS X Jaguar installed, you will witness a bold, new, eye-catching user interface.

Aqua's translucent, shimmering, ocean-blue look is designed to address many of the usability problems with older graphical user interfaces (both Mac- and Windows-based). It is designed to be relatively easy for novice computer users to master; such users form a large percentage of purchasers of Apple's consumer-level products (the iBook and the iMac). But it's also intended to provide the power that will appeal to the sophisticated computer professional.

NOTE: Apple is also offering a slightly more subdued graphite version of its user interface as an appearance option, paying attention to professional users who might consider Aqua just a bit too imposing for an office environment. You'll learn more about setting this option in Chapter 3.

From large, photo-quality icons to translucent menus, drop shadows, and real-time object dragging (without a performance penalty), Aqua is designed to provide all Mac users, regardless of skill level, with a convenient, easy-to-manage user experience. The standard single-window mode, for example, which keeps Finder displays to one window, helps reduce the clutter and confusion of previous operating system versions. However, the new Mac OS X Finder has many adjustment options, so you can easily configure it to spawn additional Finder windows when you open a folder, just like the Classic Mac OS.

NOTE: *In prior versions of the Mac operating system, when you moved an object about the screen, you'd see its outline or bounding box rather than the object's contents. With Mac OS X, the power of the Quartz graphic layer allows you to see the actual object while it's moving (except for a few applications that do not support this feature). Although some third-party programs, such as Power Windows (a shareware utility), allow you to do this under prior Mac operating system versions, it requires a powerful Mac to avoid a serious performance penalty.*

One common interface problem addressed with the new operating system is the Save dialog box. Even experienced Mac users have sometimes had trouble navigating through complex folder hierarchies. Under Mac OS X, however, when you're ready to save an open document for the first time, the Save As dialog box opens as a sheet of paper right below the title bar of the document in question (see Figure 1.5). Unlike the present Mac operating system, you aren't prevented from doing something else while the dialog box is open. You can simply switch to another document window, and the Save As dialog box remains anchored to the document you want to save. Then, you just return to it when you're ready to save the document. In addition, the expanded column view arrangement provides Finder-like navigation of folder hierarchies.

The Mac OS X Finder

The core of the Mac user experience is the Finder, an application that runs full-time on a Mac, providing the desktop appearance as well as performing file- and disk-management chores. For Mac OS X, the venerable Finder has undergone a complete redesign (see Figure 1.6), ending up as a composite of technologies from the original Finder and from the NeXTSTEP file viewer. The combination is designed to make it possible to access your applications, files, and disks easily, without having to dig deep into numerous nested folders, scattered icons, and directory windows.

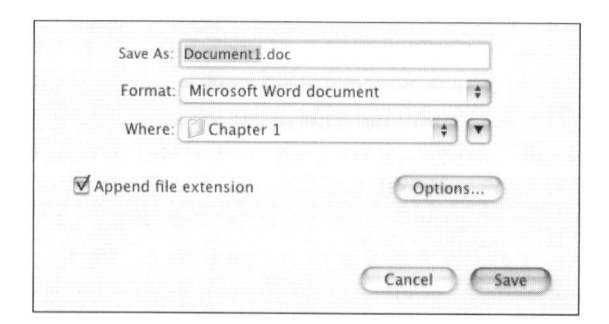

Figure 1.5   The new translucent Save As dialog box, known as a "sheet," remains hooked to the document window you're going to save.

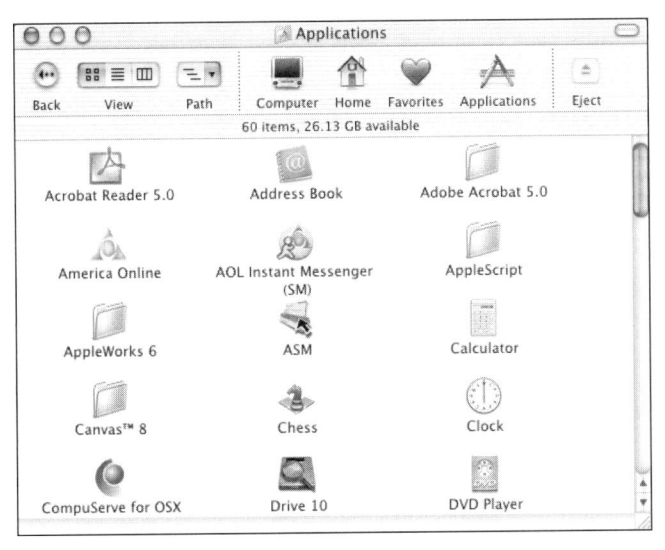

Figure 1.6 The new face of the famous Mac Finder has striking differences, yet retains some familiar elements.

At the top of the Mac OS X Finder are large, clearly labeled toolbar buttons that take you directly to the most frequently accessed areas on your Mac. The Computer button, for example, displays your mounted disks, those available for file access, and network connections. The Home button takes you to your main or personal Users directory or folder, regardless of whether it's on your Mac's hard drive or on a local or Internet-based network. There are also standard buttons for your favorites (files, folders, disks, and sites) and documents. New for Mac OS X 10.2 is a integrated Search feature, which allows you to locate the contents of a Finder window without having to launch Sherlock, Apple's search utility, which has become an Internet-only search tool. However, that is just the beginning. The toolbar can be customized with a variety of icons (see Figure 1.7) that can also be sized to your taste. You can even hide the toolbar altogether and have the Finder behave very much like the old Mac OS, despite the daringly different look.

TIP: Combining local, network, and Internet access in a single interface is part of Apple's Internet integration efforts. These also include the Mac feature at Apple's Web site, a subscription-based service that provides a set of Web-based tools for Mac users. I cover the subject in more detail in Chapter 23.

13

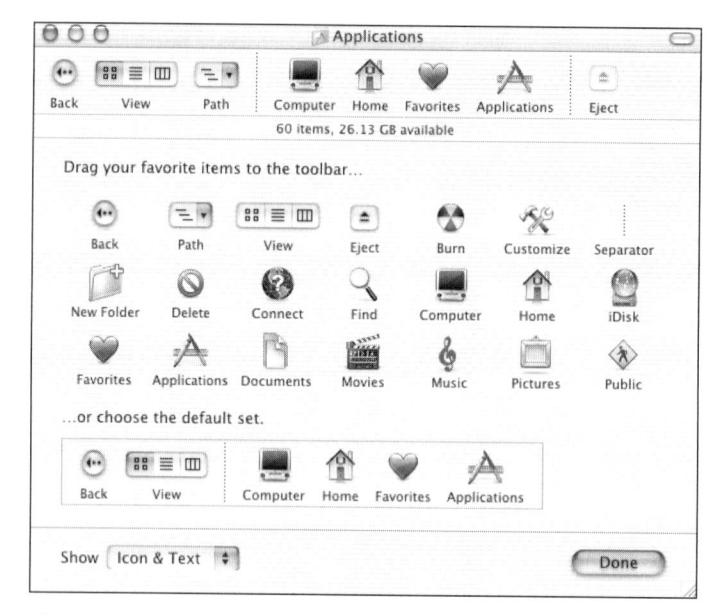

Figure 1.7 A wide range of possibilities is inherent in the new Finder toolbar setup window.

The Finder offers not only new, more colorful variations of the list and icon views that exist on the original Finder, it also offers a new column view that makes locating deeply nested items easier (see Figure 1.8). You single-click on a folder or disk, and the contents quickly display in the window at the right. Reminiscent of Greg's Browser, a popular Mac shareware program, this file-viewing feature allows you to more easily locate anything from a file to a networked drive.

TIP: A new feature of Mac OS 10.2 is spring-loaded folders. When you drag file atop a closed folder, it'll open, after a short delay, to reveal the contents; it even works on a Finder toolbar icon that represents a folder. This helps you more easily find the proper place to put that item. This is an enhanced version of a feature brought over from the traditional or Classic Mac OS.

The Dock

The Apple menu was once the principal repository on the Mac for your frequently accessed files, folders, and disks. Apple's Control Strip was a floating palette of control panels and other programs, offering one-click access. The latter is history, replaced (at least in part) by the Dock (see Figure 1.9). This picturesque taskbar puts a set of colorful, almost cartoonish icons at the bottom of your Mac's display (or

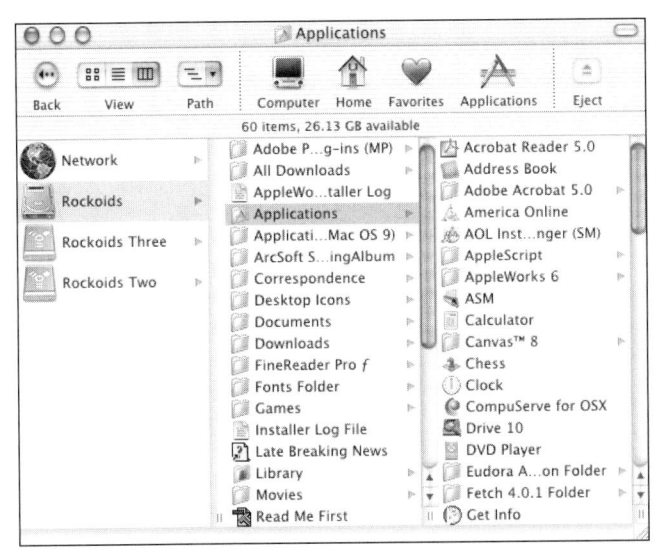

Figure 1.8   The Finder's column view option speeds navigation through even complex file directories.

at the side, if you prefer). It contains files, folders, disks, programs—whatever you choose to store there. The icons are designed to easily reflect their contents. For example, a picture file contains a preview of the image, so you can recognize it immediately. If you prefer to view titles, you'll be pleased to see the title of an item displayed as soon as the mouse passes over it.

To access an item on the Dock, just click once on it, and it will open in a new window. When you minimize a window, it transfers to the Dock in a flashy motion that looks like a sheet of paper being folded (in a sense, the end result is similar to the way a minimized window is moved to the Microsoft Windows taskbar). The motion is sometimes known as the *Genie Effect*. With the standard single-window mode, you'll find that your previous open window is closed and moved to the Dock. You can also use the Mac's drag-and-drop feature to add items to the Dock.

Figure 1.9 The Dock automatically resizes to accommodate additional items.

> **TIP:** If the Genie Effect is too distracting, Mac OS X 10.2 includes a scaling option that drops a minimized window to the Dock or returns it to full size with much less flourish.

Even the venerable Mac trashcan is now part of the Dock, although it performs precisely the same functions as in previous Mac operating system versions.

Desktop

The famous Apple desktop isn't left untouched by Mac OS X. Although on the surface it looks very different (again, see Figure 1.3), looks can be deceiving. The versions of Aqua that were first displayed showed a clear desktop, without even a disk icon to clutter the landscape. Apple answered the call of devoted Mac users and has restored much of the desktop behavior of previous versions of the Mac OS.

Mac OS X 10.2 v. Mac OS X 10.1

Mac OS X is extremely young as operating systems go, yet it has received numerous minor bug fix updates and two major updates since its release in March 2001.

The first version, 10.0, was primarily designed for early adopters who wanted to give the new operating system a try. By September, Mac OS X 10.1 came along, with speedier performance, interface improvements, better networking and expanded support for peripherals, such as external CD drives and so on.

Over the next few months, a torrent of new Mac OS X-savvy applications made their debut from the likes of Adobe, Corel, Macromedia and Microsoft, to name just a few of the major players.

Mac OS X reached its biggest milestone in August, 2002, with the release of Mac OS X 10.2 Jaguar, which offered over 150 new features and performance improvements over its predecessor.

If you gave up on earlier versions of Mac OS X, Jaguar may make you reconsider the new operating system. If you are already a user of the original version of Mac OS X, here are some of the most significant changes:

- *AOL-compatible instant messaging*—Apple's new instant messaging client, iChat, (see Figure 1-10) can be used to exchange messages with members of AOL, CompuServe, users of AOL Instant Messenger and subscribers to Apple's .Mac Web services. In addition, you can exchange messages with friends, family, and coworkers on your local network.

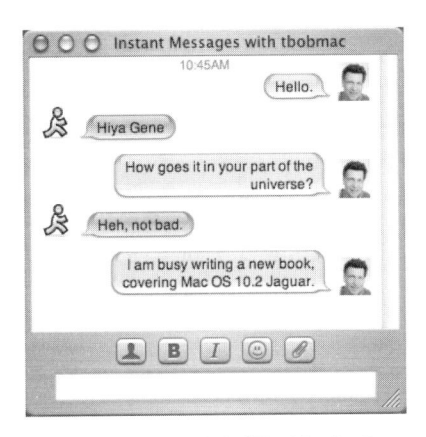

Figure 1.10 Apple's iChat instant messaging client can put text in fancy balloons or as simple text blocks. Take your choice.

- *Smart junk mail filtering*—The bane of every PC user's experience is junk mail, tons of it, and Apple's update to its Mail application ports a junk mail filter that checks the contents of a message, not just the subject line, for evidence that it fits into the SPAM category.
- *Improved system-wide Address Book*—The previous versions of this application were strictly bare bones, but the upgraded version in Jaguar is designed as a full-featured repository of contacts. In addition to Apple's own software, other programs can feed into this data if the software companies decide to add support.
- *Sherlock 3*—Apple's search tool no longer checks for files on your Mac and offers expanded Internet search features, bringing many of your search requests directly to its multipaned search window, without having to use a separate browser. Although the interface bears a striking resemblance to Watson, a shareware program, it's a totally separate application.
- *New, multithreaded Finder*—The centerpiece of the Mac user experience offers improved performance, an integrated Search feature, and spring-loaded folders.
- *Rendezvous*—Although it'll require support from third party publishers to fully implement, this is an automatic networking feature that allows your Mac to automatically detect devices on the network within seconds of the time they're connected.

Chapter 1   The New Features from A to Z

- *Quartz Extreme*—Apple's improved graphics engine is described in the section on Quartz, above.

- *New system preferences*—The System Preferences application, used to adjust all sorts of settings for your Mac, has been enhanced. New settings are provided for such functions as loading a CD or DVD and to activate Mac OS X's built-in firewall. You also have the ability to tailor screen antialiasing for a CRT or LCD display to provide less of that "smeared" look that makes text difficult to read in some situations. The Universal Access preference panel offers an expanded range of options to help the disabled have a more productive computing experience.

- *Enhanced networking*—Apple's built-in SMB/CIFS (SAMBA) software provides near seamless browsing of Windows file shares, access to your Microsoft Exchange Inbox and makes the Mac readily available for easy networking via a Windows PC.

- *Inkwell*—When Apple shut down its Newton personal digital assistant project several years ago, the technology wasn't abandoned. Inkwell offers system-wide handwriting recognition, using writing tablets, such as a Wacom, to input handwritten material.

- *More beneath the surface*—As you burrow deep into the operating system, you'll find enhanced support for multi-channel audio (including an Audio MIDI Setup application for simple configuration of musical hardware), overall performance enhancements that allow applications to launch and run faster, the ability to share USB printers across a network and many other features that'll be detailed throughout this book. If you have been on the fenceabout upgrading to Mac OS X, Jaguar may be sufficient reason to make the switch.

Are You Ready for Mac OS X?

If you're ready to take the plunge into a whole new world of ultra-reliable, speedy Macintosh computing, you should make sure that your Mac is ready for the upgrade.

Here are some points to consider when moving to Mac OS X:

- *System requirements*—Mac OS X will work on almost any Apple Macintosh computer that shipped with a PowerPC G3 or G4 CPU. This includes even the original Bondi Blue iMac. There is, however, one important exception—the first generation PowerBook G3, which was built on the original PowerBook 3400 chassis. In addition, Apple specifies a minimum of 128MB of RAM. If you don't plan to use Classic programs, you'll probably get away with 64MB of RAM; but it's highly unlikely you'll be able to avoid using such software, because it will take a while for most of the major programs to show up in Mac OS X trim. What's more, Mac OS X really does work better if you have 256MB of RAM or greater. You'll also want to allow 1.5GB of disk storage space for the installation.

NOTE: Although Jaguar doesn't include a copy of Mac OS 9, if you don't have a copy, you can use the "Proof of Purchase" coupon that comes with the package to order a copy at low cost via Apple's "Up-to-Date" program.

TIP: If you have a very large hard drive, you might want to consider making a separate partition for Mac OS X. Check the Mac OS X ReadMe that comes with the version you have to find out about any partition limits, such as putting it on the first 8GB of a drive on beige G3's and Rev. A through Rev. D iMacs.

- *Peripheral compatibility*—If your Mac has a non-Apple expansion card of any sort, such as a graphic card, SCSI accelerator card, or video capture card, contact the manufacturer about driver software that might be required for full compatibility with Mac OS X. Although the Classic feature lets you run older Mac software, it doesn't provide the hardware-level support you need for unsupported hardware.

- *Software compatibility*—Most older programs ought to run fine in the Classic mode under Mac OS X. You should contact the publishers directly, however, to be sure that the programs will run without a hitch. System extensions, for example, are not part of the Mac OS X architecture but might, within limits, work under Classic. However, programs that directly access the hardware, such as a CD writing program or hard disk formatter, will need an update to work properly—more than likely a Carbon version that's tuned to recognize Apple's updated hardware driver model.

- *Printer and serial devices*—Regular PostScript laser printers should work reasonably well under Mac OS X. Other printers, especially ink jets, will need driver updates to function with the new OS. Mac OS X printer drivers from such major companies as Canon, Epson, HP, and Lexmark are included with Mac OS X, but not all product lines are included. As far as other peripherals are concerned, in each case, you'll need to check with the

19

manufacturer about compatibility. Apple Computer has provided tools to help developers make its products Mac OS X–aware, but how quickly this is done depends on each particular company, its priorities, and the amount of work required.

- *Why you may not be ready for Mac OS X*—If you are perfectly happy with your Mac's performance now, and you are reluctant to spend a bundle on a new Mac, more memory and a speedier video card or, at the very least, Mac OS X native software updates, there is no need to rush headlong into a new operating system. While Mac OS X offers a host of compelling new features, you won't be able to take advantage of them if you are strictly using older software in the Classic compatibility environment. You may just want to wait until you are prepared to get the upgrades you need. In the meantime, let this book be your guide as to what to expect once you decide to move on to the next generation of Mac computing.

WARNING! Apple Computer doesn't officially support Macs or Mac OS clones upgraded from older PowerPC CPUs to G3s or G4s. If you decide to take the risk anyway and attempt to install Mac OS X on one of these unsupported models, you cannot depend on Apple for support. Be prepared to make a full backup of your data, in case you run into a disk-related problem or want to return to your previous Mac OS version. Some of the companies that make G3 and G4 upgrades promise to deliver Mac OS X support, but it won't come with Apple's blessings; you will have to depend on those companies to provide help if something goes wrong when you use the products. If you still want to experiment and accept the risks, be sure to back up your data before you take the plunge, in case something goes wrong.

Chapter 2

Upgrading to Mac OS X

If you need an immediate solution to:	See page:
Preparing for Mac OS X	31
Installing Mac OS X	32
Notes on Performing an Unsupported Installation	36

Chapter 2   Upgrading to Mac OS X

In Brief

Are you ready for the main event, the actual Mac OS X installation? Jaguar is a huge improvement over previous versions of the Mac OS. As explained in Chapter 1, there is really no comparison under the hood. Many of the familiar elements are no longer present. If anything, the new operating system, because it is Unix-based, has more in common with high-end workstations that are used to power Web and network servers around the world.

Don't be put off by all this sophistication. Despite the complexity of the underlying software, Apple has gone the extra mile to simplify installation. However, don't be lulled into a sense of complacency by the ease of the process. A lot of complicated things are happening very, very fast to install the new operating system as quickly as possible without undue delay. During that time, the Mac OS X installer is copying tens of thousands of new files to your Macintosh. It's not something to take lightly, and you should take a few precautions to make the process as seamless as possible.

Preparing for Mac OS X

Before you attempt to install Mac OS X, you should make sure that your Mac has been prepared for the installation. First, you should review Chapter 1 to see if your Mac can run the new operating system. Take the warnings about attempting an installation on unsupported hardware very seriously. If you want to take a chance, Ryan Rempel's XPostFacto is a good choice. You can find the latest version at **http://eshop.macsales.com/OSXCenter/XPostFacto/framework.cfm?page=XPostFacto.html**. I'd also suggest doing this sort of installation on a secondary machine, one you don't use for work or that contains important files. You'll learn the basics on how such an installation works at the end of this chapter, which was prepared with Ryan's assistance.

But don't say I didn't warn you.

In Brief

NOTE: *If you decide to take the chance and install Mac OS X on a Mac not supported for the installation, be guided by the instructions provided with the software you use, which are apt to change as Mac OS X itself is updated. The following information assumes you will be doing your installation on a Mac that is officially supported by Apple for Mac OS X.*

In the following pages, I cover the basics of getting ready for the installation. Once you're prepared, proceed to the "Immediate Solutions" section for step-by-step instructions that walk you through the entire installation process and let you know what to expect along the way.

Make Sure You Have Mac OS 9.1 or Later for Classic Applications

Despite the arrival of more Mac OS X software, a fair number of the Mac OS programs you'll be running may be of the older Classic variety; so, you'll need an installed copy of Mac OS 9 on your Mac. Since recent Macs include Mac OS 9.1 or later, you can feel confident that you can continue to use your older applications. You can keep your older Mac operating system version on the same disk volume as Mac OS X. If you choose to install it on a separate partition, be guided by the instructions later in this chapter in the section "Mac OS X: Hardware-Related Issues."

NOTE: *If you have Mac OS 9.1 installed, you aren't forced to upgrade to a later version for Classic to function. But the later versions of Mac OS 9 are more stable and offer better performance in the Classic environment, so you'll want to consider the upgrade seriously. In addition, Mac OS X will "suggest" you upgrade to a later version of Mac OS 9 the first time Classic runs. Jaguar users can order a copy from Apple at a special upgrade price.*

Check Your Hard Drive

During the installation process, the Mac OS X Installer has a lot of work to do. Whereas older versions of the Mac operating system generally consisted of hundreds of files, this time literally thousands of files (taking up nearly two gigabytes of storage space) are part of the agenda. All that work is done behind the scenes in minutes, which means your Mac and its disk storage system will be taxed to the limit to keep up.

As a result, you should make sure that the target drive for Mac OS X is working properly. Fortunately, this isn't hard to accomplish. Apple provides a free hard drive diagnostic and repair utility—Disk First Aid (see Figure 2.1)—in the Utilities folder of every Mac. This program, although not as full-featured as the commercial alternatives, should be able to do the job. Although it is true the Mac OS X Installer will also check the drive during the setup process, it doesn't hurt to run an extra verification.

NOTE: *One of the great features of Disk First Aid is its ability to repair directory damage to a startup drive without having to boot from a separate volume or system CD. Only Symantec's Norton Utilities (see below) can boast a similar capability.*

If you want to make doubly sure that your drive is in tip-top shape, however, you may want to look at one of these three commercial alternatives:

- *Norton Utilities*—This is the oldest existing hard drive utility package. The latest versions of the Disk Doctor application are, like Disk First Aid, capable of repairing drive directory problems on a startup disk. This ability saves trips to the program CD except when the startup drive won't boot or when you wish to optimize it. Norton Utilities, by the way, is also included as part of Norton SystemWorks (shown in Figure 2.2).

- *TechTool Pro*—MicroMat's upstart utility application (see Figure 2.3) performs many of the same tasks as Norton Utilities, plus the application can run an extensive set of hardware checks on your Macintosh, including several levels of RAM tests. In addition, beginning with version 3, virus protection capability is part of the package. A Mac OS X derivative of TechTool Pro called Drive 10

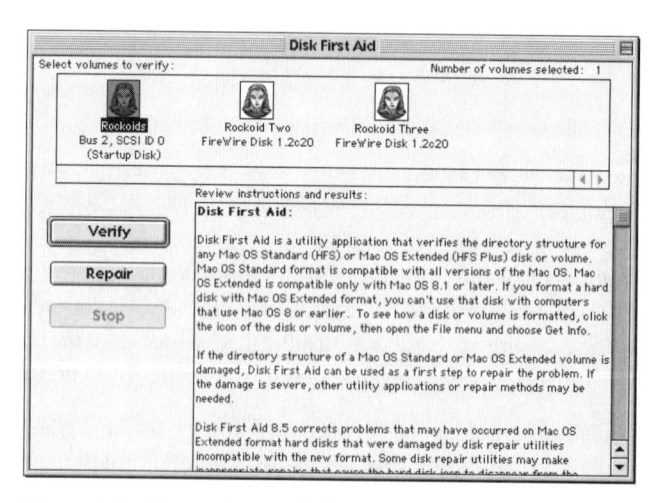

Figure 2.1   The best part of Disk First Aid is that it's free with every new Mac and included with every Mac OS installation.

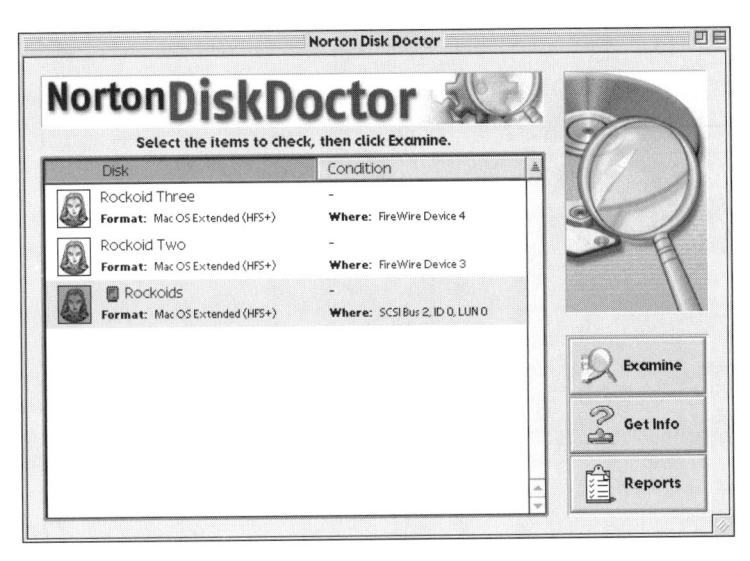

Figure 2.2   Norton Disk Doctor provides a far more comprehensive level of disk repairs than Disk First Aid.

(see Figure 2.4) is fully compatible with the new operating system, but must be run after booting from another drive or the application's CD to fix problems.

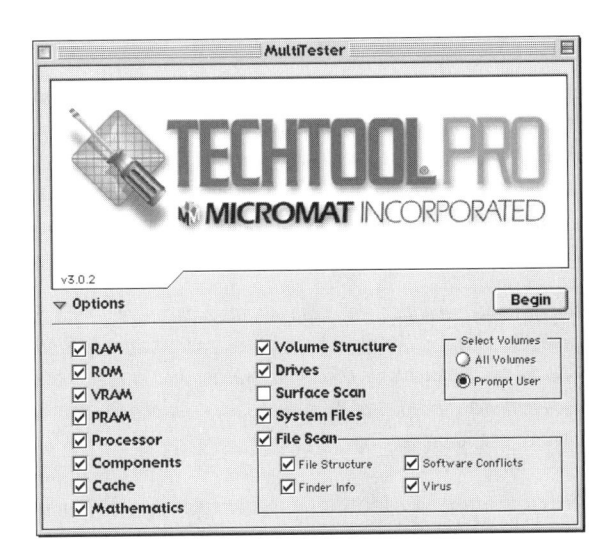

Figure 2.3   You can use TechTool Pro 3 to check a hard drive for directory damage prior to the Mac OS X installation.

Chapter 2 Upgrading to Mac OS X

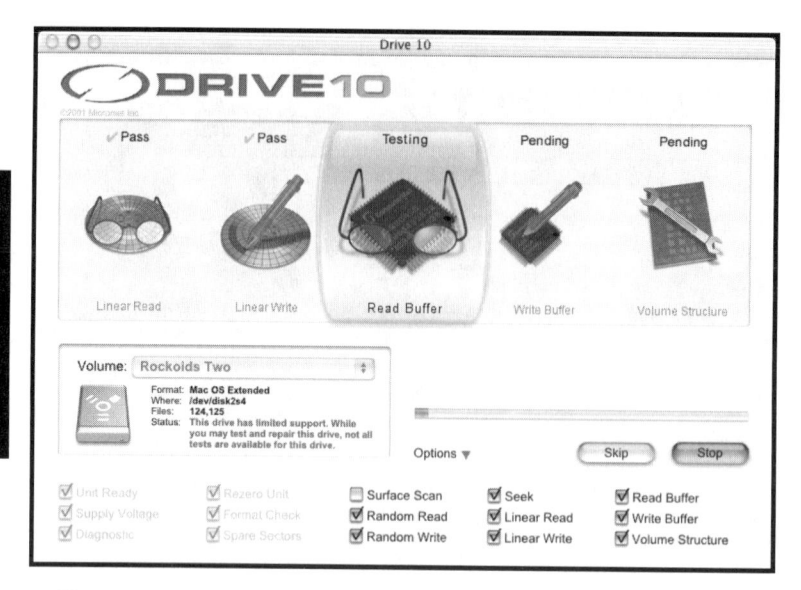

Figure 2.4 MicroMat's Drive 10 is a single-purpose utility designed to check and fix directory problems on your Mac's hard drive.

NOTE: *A limited-feature version of TechTool Pro—TechTool Deluxe—is provided under Apple's AppleCare extended service policy. However, that particular version of the program doesn't offer disk drive maintenance, nor does it offer virus protection.*

WARNING! *TechTool Pro is supported only under Classic Mac OS versions; it cannot repair directory problems on the startup drive, so you have to boot from the program's CD or another startup volume to handle those problems. However, the publisher assures me that current versions of TechTool Pro 3 can fix directory problems on a drive on which Mac OS X is installed.*

TIP: *Both Norton Utilities and Drive 10 are capable of doing surface scans of your hard drive (the option is to check for defective media in Norton Utilities). Whereas the scanning process takes longer, it will identify media-related problems that might present problems in copying data to the drive. If you do see a media-related error (bad blocks, for example), you will want to back up and reformat the drive before proceeding.*

- *DiskWarrior*—Reviewers call Alsoft's DiskWarrior (see Figure 2.5) a "one-trick pony" because it's limited to checking and replacing hard drive directories. However, it does that task extraordinarily well. Rather than just fixing damage found in a

26

In Brief

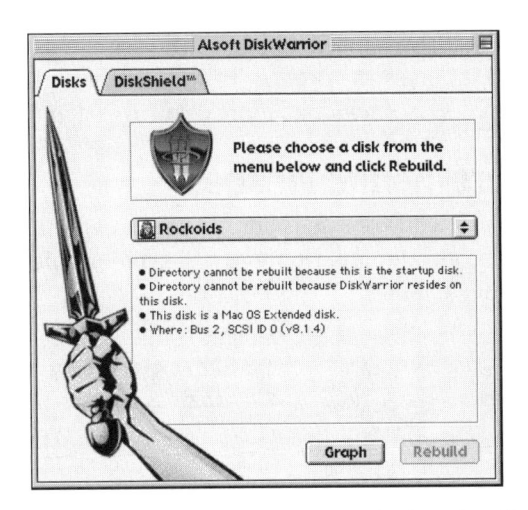

Figure 2.5 DiskWarrior performs its lone function so well that it merits a place in any Mac user's software library.

hard drive's directory, it prepares a new, optimized directory, delivering the promise of speedier performance. You need to boot from the CD or another volume to rebuild a drive's directory.

NOTE: *A Mac OS X version of DiskWarrior was under development when this book was written.*

WARNING! *You should try to restrict installation of Mac OS X to a hard drive formatted with Apple's Drive Setup. The installation makes major changes to the file structure, and although third-party disk formatting tools might be just fine, the safest course is to stick with the tried-and-true. If Apple's disk formatter won't work with your drive (and it doesn't support some older third-party SCSI devices), you should check with the manufacturer of the formatting utility you're using for compatibility information. At the time this book was written, the folks at FWB, publishers of Hard Disk ToolKit, had not yet delivered a compatible version of their hard drive formatting application.*

Back Up Your Data

Backup chores tend to be put off until the next day, but it is super-critical for any operating system installation. The most effective backup is complete, covering all your data. If you have backups of all your applications (such as the original CDs) and your original System Install or System Restore disks for your Mac, you can, as a time-saver, restrict the backup to the documents you've created with your software, along with critical program settings, such as your Internet preferences.

However, having your entire drive backed up on a single set of disks is far more convenient, and it makes the process of restoring your files much easier. I cover the subject of backups in more detail in Chapter 17.

Mac OS X: Hardware-Related Issues

You should consider some hardware issues and strategy suggestions before proceeding with the installation. Doing so will avoid problems and confusing performance later on.

NOTE: This information is based on the release notes for Mac OS X 10.2. As Apple updates its operating system, some of the limitations are apt to be addressed, and perhaps new ones will appear.

Here's a list of primary concerns:

- *Firmware*—You should make sure firmware is current. Many Macs produced since the summer of 1998 have firmware (a boot ROM) that can be upgraded by software. Because the updates enhance the boot process and stability of your Mac, you'll want to stay current for the best experience with your new operating system. The Mac OS X installer disk includes a selection of firmware updates for various Macs, but you'll also want to check Apple's support Web site (**www.info.apple.com/support/downloads.html**) to be sure that the firmware on your computer is up to date.

NOTE: Recent Apple firmware updates have also been known to prevent use of some third-party RAM in your Mac. Apple's reasoning is that the memory is out of spec and may cause performance problems or frequent system crashes. If you run a firmware update, and some of your memory isn't recognized, you'll want to contact the vendor about a replacement (most will replace memory disabled as a result of this update).

- *Beige PowerMac G3, PowerBook G3 (non-USB versions), and Rev A through D iMac (those with pop-up CD trays)*—For these models, if you choose to divide your hard drive into multiple partitions or volumes, make sure that the Mac OS X installation is performed on the first 8GB of the drive (it will appear first in your list of available volumes in the Mac OS X installer). Fortunately, the Installer will usually put up a warning message if the Mac has the wrong drive partitioning scheme.

NOTE: It is perfectly possible to install Mac OS X on a drive with a single partition and have it coexist with Mac OS 9.2.2. In fact, Apple ships all its new Macs this way. Partitioning a drive can be done for protection, as a way to start your Mac if the other partition goes down, or just to more easily organize the contents of your drive. However, it's not required.

- *FireWire and USB drives*—Most FireWire drives—from such companies as EZQuest, LaCie, Maxtor, Other World Computing, SmartDisk, and others—will work just fine under Mac OS X. However, don't think of using a standard USB (1.1) device, even if the installation takes, because it is just too slow. The newer, faster USB standard, 2.0, isn't supported without third party hardware and I'd urge caution.

- *Third-party SCSI cards*—If you can't boot your Mac after Mac OS X is installed, place a drive or terminator on one of the ports of your third-party SCSI card.

WARNING! Check your card maker's support Web site for information about compatibility between your SCSI card and Mac OS X. You may need to upgrade software, flash ROM, or a ROM chip, or perhaps even replace the card to avoid trouble with your new operating system. For example, Adaptec is not supporting many of its older cards with Mac OS X.

- *AirPort*—Apple's fancy wireless networking hardware, based on the 802.11b or Wi-Fi standard, works fine under Mac OS X. If you're using a third-party 802.11b wireless networking card, such as the Asante AeroLAN or the Farallon (now Proxim) SkyLINE, check with the manufacturer about updated drivers for Mac OS X. Central access points, which are similar to the AirPort Base Station, are configured via a browser interface and should work fine with Jaguar.

- *Third-party graphics cards*—Some third-party graphics cards aren't supported. Mac OS X only works with graphics chips and cards from ATI, IX Micro, and NVIDIA, all of which have supplied products for a number of Macs over the years. It's up to manufacturers of graphics cards to supply Mac OS X–compatible drivers for their own products. Formac informs us that its ProFormance3 graphic cards work in 2D mode under Mac OS X, but there is no official support for 3D graphics or games. With the departure of 3dfx Interactive from the scene in late 2000, it's not at all certain when, if ever, its products will become compatible, although a small number of third-party developers were trying to deliver updated drivers.

Chapter 2 Upgrading to Mac OS X

- *Processor upgrade cards*—Again, it's the responsibility of the manufacturers of these products to make a processor card function. Some of these products use special software to activate a G3's or G4's backside cache. Even if they worked otherwise, there might be a severe performance penalty. However, most existing products from such makers as PowerLogix, Sonnet Technology, and XLR8 (which is now out of business) do work fine under Mac OS X, although software updates may be necessary. In addition, the Sonnet processor cards designed for the Blue & White Power Mac G3 line do not require software.

NOTE: *Sonnet has included support for older Newer Technology MAXpowr products in its Mac OS X–compatible software updates. Also bear in mind that if you plan to boot your Mac under Mac OS 9, you should install the traditional Mac OS version of such software so your processor card runs at full efficiency in both environments. As this book was written, a resurrected Newer Technology was in the process of bringing out new processor upgrades for older Macs.*

Warning! Even though it includes a right processor, the original PowerBook G3, which used the same case as the 3400, doesn't support Mac OS X. According to Apple, the product model number includes M3553. You could, if you wish, attempt an unsupported installation, but nothing is guaranteed.

Immediate Solutions

Preparing for Mac OS X

Before you install Mac OS X, you'll need to make a few decisions about how to proceed:

- *Determine where to install*—You can install Mac OS X on the same drive partition as Mac OS 9 or on a separate partition. Be guided by the instructions in the previous section about partitioning and hard drive support on certain Macs. If you plan to install on a separate partition, the Mac OS X installer can handle the job of erasing the partition for you.

- *Install Mac OS 9.2 or later*—If you need to run Classic applications, you should install the Classic system first before proceeding with Mac OS X. That way, if something goes wrong with the Mac OS X installation, you can still return to the older operating system to remove Mac OS X files or just to use your Mac until you decide to reinstall the new system. A copy of the installation CD is available at a special "Up-To-Date" price directly from Apple for Jaguar users.

- *Copy Internet and networking setups*—During the installation of the Mac OS X, you'll need to enter information manually to get access to a local network or the Internet. This information is not cataloged during the Mac OS X installation process. You'll then need to copy all these settings from the Modem, Internet (see Figure 2.6), Remote Access, and TCP/IP control panels.

NOTE: If you are an EarthLink member, you can use the Mac OS X Setup Assistant, which appears right after the installation of Jaguar, to pick up your account settings. If you are upgrading from an older version of Mac OS X, you can pick up the previous settings by a simple upgrade installation or by one of the clean install options I'll detail in the next section. AOL members can simply install the Mac OS X version of the software, then use the Upgrade feature to pick up the settings from an any recent older version of the program.

Chapter 2 Upgrading to Mac OS X

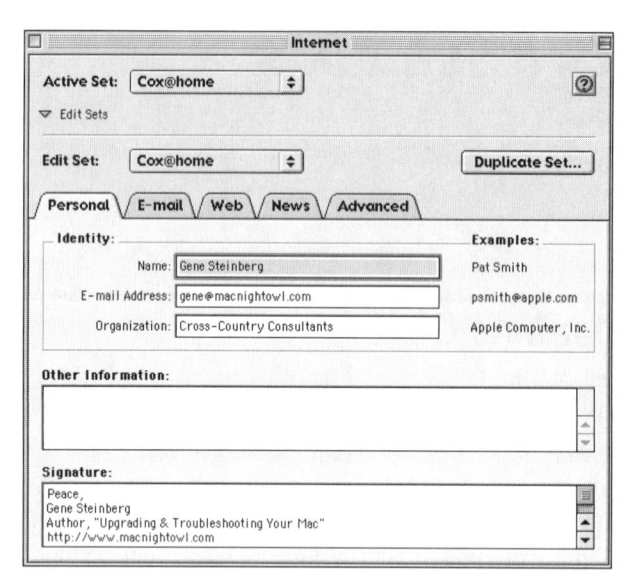

Figure 2.6 The Internet control panel has several tabs you need to check to pick up all your configuration information.

TIP: *You can quickly capture these settings with a screenshot. To take a picture of just the Control Panel window (rather than the entire screen), press Command+Shift+4+Caps Lock. Then, click on the window that you want to capture to complete the action. You'll hear the sound of a shutter clicking in confirmation. Each file will be identified by the name Picture plus the number (1, 2, and so on). You can then open these files in SimpleText and print them, so you'll have a copy to refer to when needed for Mac OS X's Setup Assistant.*

Installing Mac OS X

Now that you're ready to proceed, these instructions will take you through the entire installation process, including the actual restart:

NOTE: *These instructions are based on the installer screens used for Mac OS X 10.2. As the operating system is updated, the setup dialog boxes may change, but your basic choices will be essentially the same as described here.*

---

1. Insert Disk 1 from your Mac OS X 10.2 upgrade package into your Mac's drive.

32

Immediate Solutions

NOTE: *What's the second disk used for? It contains additional system software and applications for Jaguar and will be used after the first stage of the setup process is complete.*

2. Restart your Mac, holding down the C key, so that it boots from the CD. After you restart, the Installer will take several minutes to begin, so be patient. During each step of the process, you'll have to click a button or click a checkbox or pop-up menu to make a choice before proceeding. Therefore, read the onscreen instructions carefully, in case they've changed from those present when this book was written.

NOTE: *If you just double-click the Installer after the CD mounts., it will put up a prompt that lets you click the Restart button to automatically restart from the installer CD. There's no other way to do the installation.*

3. The first screen that appears, labeled Select Language, allows you to select the default language kit used for the installation. You're not restricted to English. After you've made your selection, click Continue to proceed. As you set up installer options, you'll see a Go Back screen that allows you to recheck settings. You can back out at anytime until you actually click Install on the final screen.

NOTE: *Because the Mac OS X Installer takes over a Mac during the setup process, I could not capture illustrations of the process in the usual way. If you follow the steps precisely as described, however, you'll get through the process like a champ.*

4. The Welcome to the Mac OS X Installer screen appears. All you'll find here is a message telling you to get ready for the main event. Click Continue to move on to the next step in the process.

5. The Important Information screen appears next. You should consult this ReadMe information to see if you must consider any additional factors before proceeding with the installation, or whether something in your setup might conspire to hurt the process. Spend a few moments reading this document. If it looks like you might have a problem, you can back out here and quit the Installer to restart; then, just hold down the mouse key to eject the CD and you'll reboot under your previous version of the Mac OS. If everything looks okay, click Continue to proceed, or click Go Back to review the previous screen.

2. Upgrading to Mac OS X

Chapter 2 Upgrading to Mac OS X

6. The next screen shows the License for Mac OS X 10.2 Jaguar. This is a fairly standard agreement covering Mac OS X. Click Continue after reviewing the information. You'll see a dialog box in which you must click the Agree button and accept the agreement to continue with the installation; if you click Disagree, you'll end the process then and there. You have no other choice. Click Agree to continue.

7. The Select A Destination screen appears, showing the available drive volumes that can support a Jaguar install. Click the icon representing the drive on which you want to place Mac OS X. The standard installation process will install a fresh copy of Mac OS X 10.2 or upgrade your existing installation, but you have other options worth checking, especially if you have an older Mac OS X version already present on your Mac. To see the choices, click the Options button, which gives you the following alternatives:

- *Upgrade Mac OS X*—As it says, it will simply replace all the updated components of your existing Mac OS X installation with the new versions. Under most circumstances, this choice should work fine. However, if you have run into trouble with a previous Mac OS X setup, you will probably want to consider the next option.

- *Archive and Install*—This is the Mac OS X equivalent of the clean installation. All your system files will be placed within a folder labeled Previous System and your new system will be installed fresh and clean. You'll have to reenter all your user settings, including your ISP access information, in the Mac OS X Setup Assistant. By leaving the old system around, you can access such things as third party peripheral drivers that may not have been picked up by the new installation, although it's better to install them from scratch.

NOTE: *Sorry, once the older system is archived, you cannot boot from it. It's doesn't work the same as it does when you do a clean install under Mac OS 9.*

- *Preserve Users and Network Settings:* **This is the most convenient clean installation because it picks up virtually all of your users and network settings, including application preferences. Even the extra items you added to the Dock will be there when you are finished with your Jaguar installation. Here you get the best of both worlds: A clean system installation, and little need to reconfigure your system and users settings.**

Immediate Solutions

TIP: When you are sure you don't need the components of your previous installation, it can be deleted, but you will have to use the Get Info window's Ownership & Permissions screens to give you, as systems administrator, the ability to remove those files. I'll explain more about the process of handling changed permissions in Chapter 6.

- *Erase and Install:* This option will erase your hard drive partition, first, before Mac OS X is installed. Don't forget that this will remove existing data, so make sure you have a backup if you need to keep any of those files.

NOTE: You can erase your drive and set up one of two file systems. The standard method, HFS+, allows you to use Mac OS 9 and Classic applications. The second, UFS (for Unix File System) is best for UNIX-based application development and is otherwise not really necessary.

WARNING! Formatting a hard drive can be a destructive process. If you select that option, all the data on the selected volume will be wiped out with little or no chance of recovery. Be certain that's the decision you want to make—there's no going back.

TIP: If you cannot locate the right startup volume on the Select A Destination screen, go to the Installer application window and quit the Installer so you can cancel the process and reboot your Mac. You should then verify that the drive on which you want to install Mac OS X is indeed available. After everything has been rechecked, you can attempt installation again by restarting from the CD.

8. After you click Continue, the Easy Install screen appears. If you click Customize, you'll see a dialog box where you can remove some of the Mac OS X installer components to save drive space, such as the extra printer drivers, applications, and unused foreign language kits. Usually it's best just to leave well enough alone, unless you are seriously storage space challenged, in which case you may want to consider putting Mac OS X on a larger drive or drive partition if one is available.

Once you click Install, you'll see a progress Install Software screen, where you'll observe the entire process, as various components of Jaguar are placed on your Mac's drive. You should expect the first part of the installation to take anywhere from 30 minutes to an hour, depending on the speed of your Mac's processor, the speed of your CD (or DVD) drive, and the speed of your hard drive. The time estimate in the progress bar will vary considerably until it settles down about halfway through the process. When the installation of the contents of CD 1 is complete, your Mac will restart automatically under its new operating system version, but you'll have more to do.

Chapter 2 Upgrading to Mac OS X

After the restart, an Additional Software screen will appear and your CD will be ejected. Put Disk 2 in the drive, and, in a short time, installation will resume. Once it's complete, you'll experience a brief multimedia presentation, and you'll be guided through the Setup Assistant, where you'll be asked to make some very basic system settings to get Mac OS X up and running to your satisfaction. These steps include registering your copy of Mac OS X, optionally registering Apple's iTools feature, plus setting up your Mac for Internet access. I cover these and other settings in Chapter 3.

NOTE: If you opted for an upgrade installation or a clean installation in which you choose the Preserve Users and Network Settings option, you won't see a Setup Assistant, as all the settings it requests will already be present and accounted for.

Related solutions:	Found on page:
Configuring the Setup Assistant	42
Configuring System Preferences Under Mac OS X	46

Notes on Performing an Unsupported Installation

Don't say I didn't warn you, but, yes, it is possible to install Mac OS X on a computer on which it wasn't designed to run, but it requires the clever efforts of third party programmers who know their UNIX and have managed to, shall we say, induce the installer to run.

One method that has proven successful for thousands of Mac users is Ryan Rampel's XPostFacto, which is being distributed by Other World Computing, a large Mac retailer. Although the program is free, the author requests a $10 goodwill donation if you get it to work.

When you download the software, you'll receive plenty of documentation that takes you through the process, but I want to cover a few of the basics here, so you know what you're getting into:

Immediate Solutions

- *Consider a new or refurbished Mac*—The easiest thing to do is just to buy a Mac that can run Mac OS X successfully without help. But if you have a large investment in a system and memory and want to save some cash, an unsupported installation is worth trying, with appropriate care.

- *Check the instructions before proceeding*—At the time this book was written, XPostFacto only worked on a Mac with a G3 or G4 processor upgrade if you want to install Jaguar, although the author was working on a way to get Macs with the original 603 or 604 processors to accept the installation. Also bear in mind, that performance on these older processors is apt to be rather slow anyway, so you may not want to proceed without a faster processor.

- *Expect less stable performance than a supported installation*—Some basic functions, such as the Sleep mode, may not be supported. The third party peripheral cards that don't officially work under Mac OS X will not operate under an unsupported installation either. So if you have a SCSI scanner or another older peripheral that is not likely to be upgraded for Mac OS X, expect to have to restart under Mac OS 9 from time to time.

- *Backup your files*—You should do it anyway, and I discuss the process in more detail in Chapter 17 [insert related solution????]. But if something goes wrong that affects your files, you'll need to consider reformatting the drive and starting over.

- *Some components won't run*—Although there is an unofficial driver for floppies from **http://www.darwin-development.org/floppy/**, there's no standard support for such drives, unless installed as a USB peripheral. In addition, not all serial modems will run, so you'll want to check the latest documentation from Ryan on supported devices.

- *What does it involve?*—In order to induce the Mac OS X installer to work on an unsupported Mac, XPostFacto places some kernel extensions on the drive on which you want to install Mac OS X, plus a modified version of BootX, which allows your Mac to restart with the Mac OS X Installer and put Mac OS X on that computer.

Warning: Since special files are required for the Mac OS X to be installed, do not erase the drive after running XPostFacto on it.

If you are willing to take the chance after knowing the risks, examine the instructions for XPostFacto or any other unsupported installation utility you try very carefully, especially the troubleshooting information. While

Chapter 2   Upgrading to Mac OS X

it does indeed work for many, don't be surprised if your specific installation doesn't take. At worst, consider the process a useful learning experience and perhaps a good incentive to acquire that new Mac you've been lusting after.

Chapter 3

Mac OS X User Preferences

If you need an immediate solution to:	See page:
Configuring the Setup Assistant	46
Setting System Preferences Under Mac OS X	52
Setting Accounts Preferences	53
Setting CDs & DVDs Preferences	53
Setting Classic Preferences	54
Setting ColorSync Preferences	55
Setting Date & Time Preferences	56
Setting Desktop Preferences	58
Setting Display Preferences	59
Setting Dock Preferences	65
Setting Energy Saver Preferences	65
Setting General Preferences	67
Setting International Preferences	69
Setting Internet Preferences	70
Setting Keyboard Preferences	72
Setting Login Items Preferences	73
Setting Mouse Preferences	74
Setting Network Preferences	75
Setting QuickTime Preferences	77
Setting Screen Effects Preferences	78
Setting Sharing Preferences	78
Setting Software Update Preferences	80
Setting Sound Preferences	81
Setting Speech Preferences	83
Setting Startup Disk Preferences	84
Setting Universal Access Preferences	84
Configuring a Printer	86

Chapter 3   Mac OS X User Preferences

In Brief

Once your Mac OS X installation hits the finish line, you'll be ready to take the setup process to the next level. As soon as the new Mac desktop appears, you'll be introduced to a pleasant multimedia presentation, providing a musical introduction to the new operating system, followed by the appearance of Apple's Setup Assistant. You use the Setup Assistant to register Mac OS X with Apple, and then configure a basic set of user and networking settings for Mac OS X. Typical of a Unix-based operating system, Mac OS X is designed for multiple users, allowing each person who works on the Mac to have a different level of access. If you're upgrading from Mac OS 9 or later, you'll find that this concept is nothing new. In almost every installation, more than one person is using a Mac. Even in a home setup, the family computer may be used by parents and children, each of whom may have a different set of requirements—and an equally diverse need to restrict certain elements of user access. (I cover the subject of configuring your Mac to work in such an environment in much more detail in Chapter 6.)

NOTE: *There's an exception to this rule. If you opted for an upgrade installation or used the "archive" or clean install option that picked up your previous network and users settings, the Setup Assistant will be bypassed, and you'll be greeted with the Jaguar Finder shortly after the installation process is over.*

This chapter first discusses the various preference settings you'll make right after installing Mac OS X using the Setup Assistant. In large part, these settings cover access to your Mac by you as administrator of the system. You'll also configure basic network setups, including your Mac's network name and various types of Internet access. In addition, time zone adjustments are necessary so that your Mac will put the correct time on your documents and email messages.

Control Panel Settings: A Mixture of the Old and New

After you've completed the basic setups, you can use your Mac and your favorite programs without altering anything further. However, to get the optimum performance from your computer, you'll also want

In Brief

to tackle the preference panels. Rather than offer each item as a separate control panel, Mac OS X merges them all into a single System Preferences application. This arrangement greatly simplifies the setup process, because you don't have to hunt down multiple applications from the Control Panel's submenu in the Apple menu or directly from that folder to enter the settings you want. For convenience, the preference panels are divided into four distinct categories: Personal, Hardware, Internet & Network, and System.

NOTE: Although the Apple menu is still present, it is a rather different breed from the one with which you're familiar from the Classic Mac OS. For one thing, it replaces the functions of the Finder's Special menu, and it adds a few elements from the original version. I cover that subject in more detail in Chapter 4.

In some ways, the new design is a throwback to the way system setups existed under older versions of the Mac operating system prior to System 7. Even though control panels were separate items then, they all displayed in a single window. Apple has apparently taken the simplicity of this design to heart, except for making the icons a horizontal Finder-like display rather than the vertical array of icons you clicked to get to a particular setting.

Click an icon to bring up the labeled function, which will launch essentially as a separate application within the Preferences window. You'll see how the System Preferences application is set up in the "Immediate Solutions" section of this chapter.

NOTE: Like the Classic Mac OS's Control Panels, the System Preferences application is open to third parties to configure their software. If you install a program that uses System Preferences, such as ASM or TinkerTool (two shareware utilities that enhance system setups), they will appear in a new System Preferences category called Other. In addition, if you install a Bluetooth wireless networking card on your Mac, the appropriate System Preferences icon will be added automatically.

Before I discuss the various preference settings, let's look at some new Finder-level features of Mac OS X. The rest are explained in Chapter 4. Unlike previous Mac OS versions, you don't click a square box to close, minimize, or maximize Finder windows. Instead, three separate traffic-light-colored buttons mounted at the left provide these functions:

- *Red ("X" symbol)*—Close the window. Clicking this button may or may not quit the application (in most cases, it won't).

- *Yellow ("–" symbol)*—Minimize the window. When you click this button, the window is collapsed and appears as an icon on the Dock.
- *Green ("+" symbol)*—Maximize the window. This command expands the window to the largest size necessary to encompass its contents, limited only by the size of your Mac's display.

NOTE: When you pass your mouse over any of these buttons, you'll see a symbol inside representing its function. If you choose the Graphite interface as a General preference, as described in the "Setting General Preferences" section later in this chapter, the button colors will all switch to the same color (graphite), but the symbols will still appear whenever the mouse is brought to the vicinity of these buttons.

Additionally, you no longer quit a Mac OS X application from the File menu (unless the publisher of that application defied convention, of course). Apple Computer decided to move that function to the Application menu (the one in bold at the left end of the menu bar, next to the Apple menu).

Selecting Printers Without a Chooser

In every version of the Mac operating system prior to Mac OS X, you used a somewhat clumsy little application—the Chooser (see Figure 3.1)—to both select a printer and connect to a Mac or PC with the proper networking software installed across a network.

TIP: To learn more about networking Macs and Windows-based PCs, check out a book that I wrote with networking guru Pieter Paulson, The Windows 2000 Mac Support Little Black Book. *This fairly technical instruction book covers networking Macs with Windows NT servers and Windows 2000 servers.*

For Mac OS X, Apple has moved to a more conventional solution called Print Center. As you will learn later in this chapter, this application can ferret out the printers on your network or directly connected to your Mac. You can then select the ones you want to use, configure custom features, and monitor and adjust your print queue while printing is in progress (in a fashion similar to the Desktop printer or regular PrintMonitor applications).

In Brief

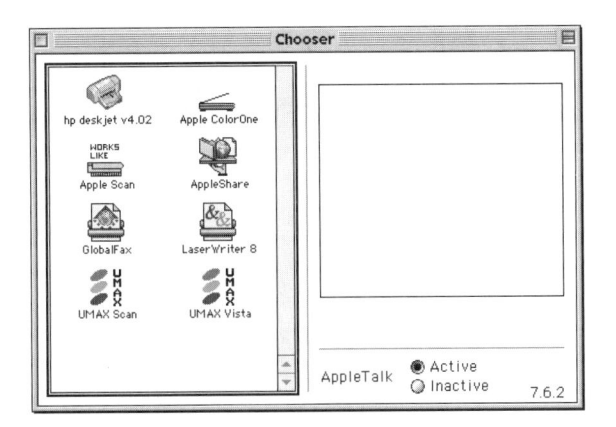

Figure 3.1 The venerable (and clunky) Apple Chooser is now history. Long live the Chooser.

NOTE: Another great feature of Jaguar, Rendezvous, is an open-source technology that allows your Mac to automatically recognize network devices as soon as they are connected. Once third party companies support the technology, network laser printers, handheld devices and other products will be discovered within just a few seconds of being attached to a wired or wireless network.

One big advantage over the older Chooser is that Print Center can search for any available printer, even if it's on a USB port or accessible via TCP/IP across the Internet, without having to fiddle with multiple network adjustments other than turning to AppleTalk (for a network printer). What's more, if you have a USB printer connected to your Mac and the correct drivers installed, Print Center automatically recognizes the device—no extra setup is needed. Once all your printers are configured, you can use the regular Page Setup and Print dialog boxes to switch among the available printers.

No more awkward visits to the Chooser, at least for Mac OS X applications. If you're using a Classic application, however, you'll still have to select your printer the old-fashioned way, in the Chooser. When a document is being printed, PrintMonitor (or the print driver's custom print window) will appear to show its progress.

NOTE: You will also have to install the Classic version of the driver software for your printer if you intend to use a Classic application. The Mac OS X printer drivers don't function in the Classic user environment.

ND
Mac OS 9 Features: What Happened to Them?

As much as Mac OS X resembles previous versions of the Mac OS, as you learn the lay of the land, it's clear some things are quite different. Functions that you expected to find in one place are performed differently, or not present at all. In some cases, preferences have been combined, so you no longer have to visit separate programs to perform a single set of settings. The International and Network preference panels are prime examples.

Throughout this chapter I will be covering many of those differences in more detail. But here is a table that lists the component of Mac OS 9 and where it went, using the most common equivalent. Features not specifically listed here are either not present in Mac OS X, or there are alternatives you'll want to experiment with.

Classic Mac OS Component	Mac OS X Solution
Chooser—setup printers	Print Center application (Utilities Folder)
Chooser—shared volumes	Connect to Server (Finder's Go menu)
Fonts folder (System Folder)	Fonts folder (Library folder and Library folder for each user, plus other locations)
Sounds	Sounds folder (Library folder within Home folder)
Utilities folder	Applications and Applications (Mac OS 9) folders
Apple Extras folder	Applications (Mac OS 9) folder
Internet folder	Applications (Mac OS 9) folder
Mac OS 9 applications	Applications (Mac OS 9 folder)
Desktop items (Mac OS 9)	Desktop (Mac OS 9) folder
Documents folder	Same location and Documents folder for each user
Sleep, Restart, Shut Down	Apple menu
Special menu	No longer needed
Finder preferences	Finder's application menu
Application preferences	Application menu within each application
Control panels	System Preferences
File Sharing	Sharing preferences (System Preferences)
Software Update control panel	Software Update (System Preferences)

In Brief

Classic Mac OS Component	Mac OS X Solution
SimpleText	TextEdit
TCP/IP control panel	Network preferences (System Preferences)
AppleTalk control panel	Network preferences (System Preferences)
Modem control panel	Network preferences (System Preferences)
Remote Access control panel	Network preferences (System Preferences)
Location Manager	Network preferences (System Preferences)
Multiple Users control panel	Accounts (System Preferences)
Numbers	International (System Preferences)
Text	International (System Preferences)
Startup Items	Login Items (System Preferences)
Extensions Manager	No longer needed
Disk First Aid	Disk Utility (Utilities folder)
Drive Setup	Disk Utility (Utilities folder)
Favorites in Apple menu	Favorites in Go menu

3. Mac OS X User Preferences

Immediate Solutions

Configuring the Setup Assistant

As you go through the setup screens in the Setup Assistant, check the instructions carefully. They will change from time to time as Apple updates Mac OS X. As you progress through the setup process, click the right arrow at lower right to move to the next setup screen, and click the back or left arrow to review or change a previous setting. At the top left of the screen, you'll see the title of the setup category you've entered.

NOTE: After the Setup Assistant runs during the initial Mac OS X configuration process, it is no longer needed. From here on, you can use System Preferences to configure your Mac; except for the initial registration process, you can configure all the same settings, and much more, as you'll see later in this chapter.

The introduction will consist of a short multimedia presentation, punctuated by music with a nice beat (as the music reviewers are apt to say), but you don't need to dismiss it. Soon, you'll see the message, "We'll have you up and running in no time." Follow these steps:

NOTE: Aside from the initial registration of Mac OS X, all user settings you make now can be changed in the System Preferences application as needed. Nothing is set in stone.

1. *Welcome*—When you see the Welcome screen (see Figure 3.2), select the country in which you're located from the list. Click Show All to see more options. After you've checked the appropriate country, click Continue.

2. *Registration Information*—There are several screens where you will enter the information needed to register your product with Apple Computer. The first screen asks for your name, address, phone number, email address, and so forth. The next screen inquires about some simple marketing information (you don't have to answer). Then, click Continue to receive an acknowledgement that your registration information has been recorded and will be sent to Apple when you have connected to the Internet.

Immediate Solutions

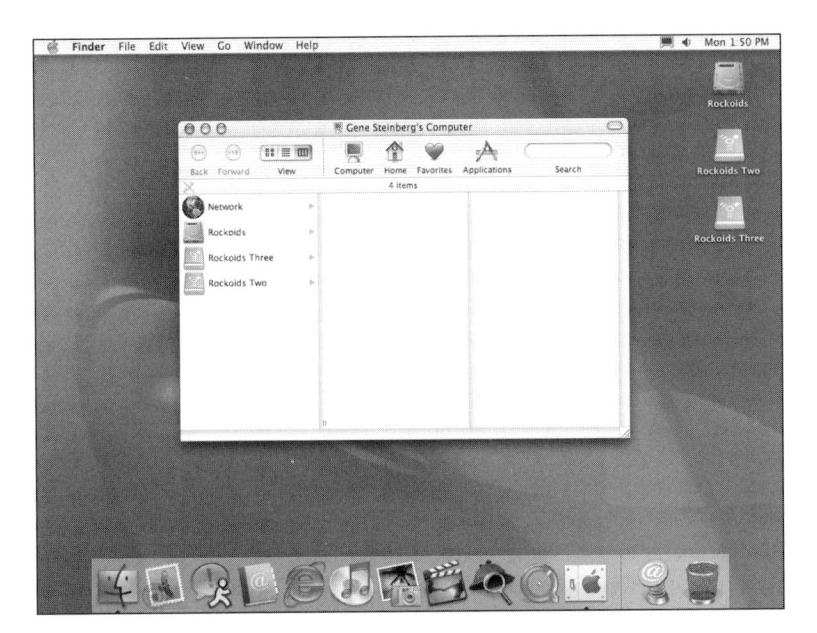

Figure 3.2 Get ready to set up your Mac OS X account and Internet access.

NOTE: *You won't have to toil through the registration process again if you reinstall Mac OS X, unless you've removed the original installed files (in other words, only if you're doing a clean installation).*

---

3. *Create Your Account*—Enter your username as owner or administrator of the Mac. For convenience, press the Tab key to move to the next text field; press Shift+Tab to return to the previous field. You also need to enter a short name or nickname for yourself containing eight lowercase characters; when you enter that text field, Mac OS X's Setup Assistant will create a shortened version of your name by default, but feel free to change it. In the next three text fields, enter a password, reconfirm your password, and enter a password hint—a word or phrase that will remind you of the password in case you forget it. You will also have the option to choose a picture for yourself that will appear at Jaguar's login prompt.

NOTE: *If you are using your Mac in a home or small office, a secure password probably doesn't matter. However, if you want the utmost in security, try to use what is considered a strong password: a password that consists of random numbers and mixed upper- and lowercase letters so that it cannot easily be guessed by anyone who might try to break into your computer. An example is 0Bfusc8. However, you should pick a password that is easy for you to remember (or at least write it down and put it in a safe place).*

47

4. *Get Internet Ready*—After you've created a username and password, you'll move on to a setup screen where you can configure your Mac for Internet access (see Figure 3.3). Click the button to indicate whether you already have an ISP or want Apple to set you up with an EarthLink account or retrieve your EarthLink settings from its servers. While you will enjoy more of the benefits of Mac OS X with an Internet account, such as the Sherlock 3 Internet services application, you aren't forced to establish an account here. You can make that decision later on. Assuming you are already connected and select the option to add your existing settings, you'll have the following options:

NOTE: *This particular range of settings can be separately duplicated in the Network preference panel later on, but doing so now is simpler, because you get the proper range of dialog boxes you need depending on the type of connection you specify. On new Macs with Mac OS X installed, you will usually find EarthLink sign-up software in the Utilities folder; otherwise you would need to install a copy from EarthLink's Web site or from an installation CD.*

- *Telephone Modem*—This option is for a standard, garden-variety, dial-up connection to an ISP. When you check this option and click Continue, you'll be greeted with a Your Internet Connection screen where you enter the basic login information required to connect to your ISP.

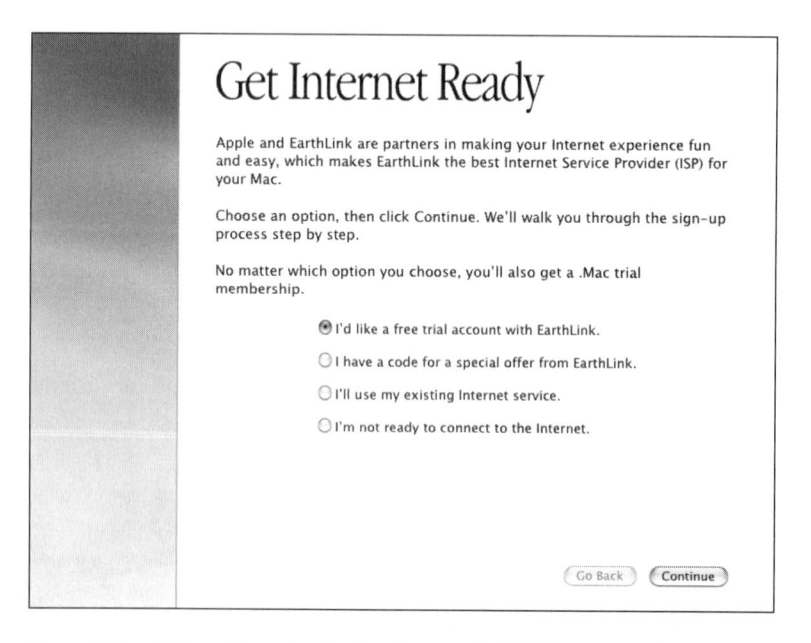

Figure 3.3 Follow this setup to handle your initial Internet settings.

Immediate Solutions

NOTE: *The Setup Assistant will not work with AOL or CompuServe 2000 because their client software must be separately configured to access these services. New Macs come with an AOL for Mac OS X setup program in the Installers folder, within your Applications folder. You can also download the latest versions from the ISP's Web sites, or from one of those ubiquitous AOL sign-up CDs.*

- *Local Area Network*—If you log on to the Internet via your local area network (perhaps using a server for the connection), choose this option. In the next screen you see, enter your network setup information.

- *Cable Modem*—This setting is used for high-speed Internet provided by a cable service. Click Continue to see a setup screen where you enter your setup information. You might have to put in a DHCP client ID number to allow your cable modem to connect, or PPP over Ethernet (PPPoE) settings, as required.

- *DSL Modem*—Another connection option for high-speed Internet service is accessing the Digital Subscriber Line broadband option. Again, if you click Continue after selecting this option, a setup screen will appear for you to enter the required information.

NOTE: *You'll need to check with your ISP for the specific settings you need, if you haven't recorded them from a setup book or your Mac OS 9.x installation.*

- *AirPort*—When you use Apple's AirPort wireless networking system, click this option to access the wireless network.

NOTE: *Because AirPort is based on an international standard known as 801.11b, or Wi-Fi for short, you can use your Mac's AirPort system to connect to a number of third-party wireless devices, which greatly increases your flexibility when it comes to connecting to a Mac or cross-platform network.*

5. *Get .Mac*—Depending on whether you want to pay the annual subscription rate, this may be one of Apple's better ideas to move the platform beyond the box. .Mac is a set of special features at the Apple Web site that enhances the user experience, including a mac.com email address, online disk storage and Web page publishing. The package also includes backup and virus protection software. In this settings screen, choose whether you want to set up a .Mac account (a free 60-day trial is offered for new subscribers) or use the one you already have, by entering the appropriate information.

49

Chapter 3   Mac OS X User Preferences

> **NOTE:** If you need to set up a new .Mac account, be sure your Mac has been set up to connect to your ISP so that Apple's Web site can be checked to establish your account and make sure your username hasn't already been taken (in which case you'll be given a chance to try a different one).

6. *Now You're Ready To Connect*—Click Continue to send your registration to Apple via your ISP and do the next stage of setups for your Mac. A progress screen indicates that you're connecting to Apple. Once you're done, continue to the next screen to perform the last setups.

7. *Set Up Mail*—Mac OS X includes a brand new email application called Mail that provides speed and reasonably powerful mail-handling features. Indicate whether you want to use your iTools account or choose the option Add My Existing E-mail Account. The setup screen will ask for your email address, incoming mail server, account type (POP or IMAP), user account ID, password, and outgoing mail server. These settings are the same ones you've always used for your email.

> **NOTE:** Don't have the settings? If you didn't follow my suggestions in Chapter 2 to copy your ISP settings from your Classic Mac OS, you'll need to refer to the documentation provided by your ISP or just ignore this setting right now. You can add them later on in the System Preferences application.

8. *Select Time Zone*—In order for such things as your email and documents to display the proper time, you first need to locate the part of the world in which you live on the map.. Then, choose the time zone or city nearest you from the pop-up menu if a special time setting is required (such as in Arizona, which doesn't observe daylight savings time).

9. *Thank You*—This final setup screen gives you one last chance to recheck all the entries you've made before they are stored in Mac OS X. You can use the back arrow to return to any setting and change it now. If you accept the setup, click the Go button to move on.

> **NOTE:** Once again, your setups aren't set in stone. Feel free at any time to change everything from networking to passwords in the System Preferences application. I explain how later in this chapter.

Immediate Solutions

10. *Logging In*—Once you're done, your Mac will proceed through the login process and finish the startup process. When you first see the Mac OS X desktop (see Figure 3.4), you'll feel for a moment as if you've visited an alien environment. The new Aqua interface has familiar elements, but there are unfamiliar elements as well. In the next few chapters, I cover every aspect of the revised look of the Mac OS. For now, get comfortable, and get ready to explore the system setup and printer setup options.

NOTE: This is the last time you'll need the Setup Assistant under Mac OS X, unless you want to reinstall the operating system on a different volume. If you launch the application again (it's located in a folder called Core Services, within the folder path System>Library), you'll return to your Internet setup screens, but you can configure the very same settings in the Internet and Network preference panels.

Related solutions:	Found on page:
Preparing for Mac OS X	31
Setting Up Multiple-User Access	147

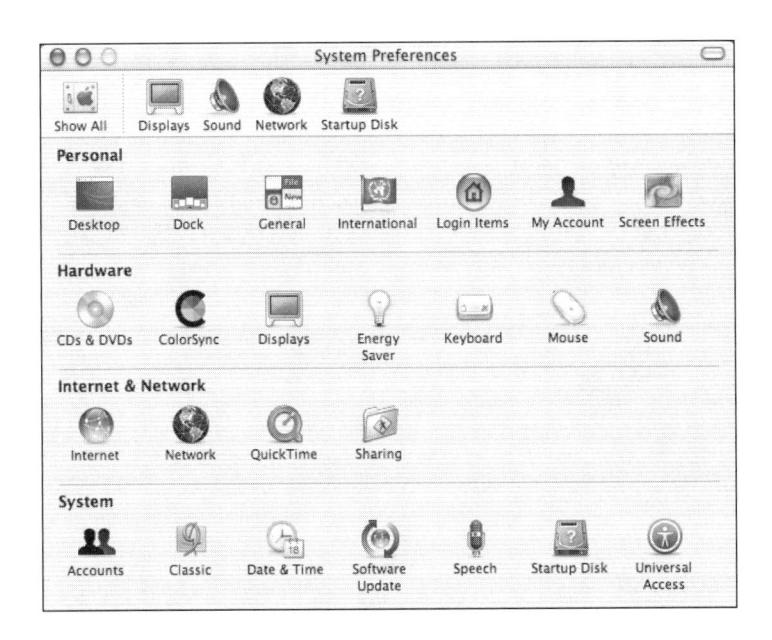

Figure 3.4 Your first exposure to Mac OS X, with your computer already given a name, based on your user name.

51

Chapter 3 Mac OS X User Preferences

Setting System Preferences Under Mac OS X

Once you've configured your basic Mac settings with the Setup Assistant, you can compute without having to change any other settings. However, if you want to make adjustments to the look and feel of your Mac, use the System Preferences application (see Figure 3.5).

You'll find the System Preferences application on the Dock when you've done a normal installation of Mac OS X. If for some reason the program isn't where you expect it to be, click the Applications button on the Finder's Toolbar (or use the same command in the Apple menu) to locate and launch the application.

TIP: If a program isn't already on the Dock, drag its icon to the left side, and the Dock will expand to accommodate it; icon sizes will be reduced as needed, should the Dock expand to the ends of your screen. Applications go on the left, and documents appear at the right, separated by a dark vertical line. Don't worry if you miss the separator line—sometimes you have to glance twice to notice it.

To switch from one program setting pane to the next, click the icon you want. If the icon isn't shown in the application's toolbar, click Show All to see the entire lineup. After making your settings, press Command+Q to quit the program. Depending on the settings you make, such as ones involving your network or ISP connection, you may see an additional confirmation dialog box with a Save button you have to click to store your settings. Some system-critical functions can be secured by clicking the padlock, in which case only users granted "administrator" status will be able to change those settings after entering the correct username and password.

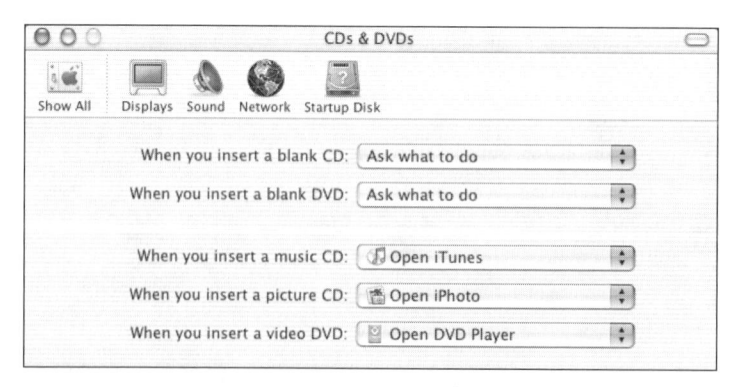

Figure 3.5 Click an icon to access a specific system setting.

Immediate Solutions

NOTE: If you've used previous versions of the Mac operating system, you'll find some of these preferences are quite familiar. Aside from the distinctive Aqua interface, they work pretty much the same as in the previous versions.

You do not have to set all the settings in the Preferences application right now. You can try each one for size, or experiment with one setting without changing any of the others. If the setting isn't what you like, you can quickly restore it to the previous one. In addition, depending on your specific Mac setup, you may find additional preference components to adjust.

Although System Preferences components are divided into categories, I've opted to put them in alphabetical order so that you can easily find the one you want without having to concern yourself over what category it's in.

TIP: To quickly bring up the settings pane you want, click the application's View menu and choose from the pop-up menu. That's the way I do it.

Setting Accounts Preferences

Bring up this screen to change your login password or add additional users to your Mac, to take advantage of its multiple-users features. To make the change, click your username, click the Edit User button, enter the new password twice in the appropriate text fields, and then enter the appropriate hint, if you want a reminder. Once you click the OK button, your new password goes into effect. The Cancel button undoes the changes you've made. You can also attach a picture for each user, and customize access for novice or younger users. Jaguar also includes a Simple Finder option that sharply limits access to various Mac features. Chapter 6 covers this subject in more detail.

Related solution:	Found on page:
Setting Up Multiple-User Access	132

Setting CDs & DVDs Preferences

Depending on what kind of Mac you have, it's equipped with an optical drive that reads just CDs or CDs and DVDs. Jaguar also includes software that allows you to burn optical discs. This preference panel, shown in Figure 3.6, is used to tell the operating system how to handle blank or recorded optical discs when inserted. By default, inserting a music CD will launch iTunes, a picture CD will deliver iPhoto and a

53

Chapter 3 Mac OS X User Preferences

DVD video will open Apple's terrific DVD Player application. You will be given a dialog box with options when blank optical media is inserted. Feel free to click on any pop-up menu to change the default selections (such as running a different jukebox application, such as MusicMatch, for music CDs), but they work quite well as they are.

Setting Classic Preferences

The Classic mode lets you use traditional Mac OS applications by opening the older version of the operating system within Mac OS X. In a sense, it's similar to running Windows applications on a Mac using Connectix Virtual PC. The major difference is that the Classic mode runs applications transparently, without inheriting the Aqua interface, using the Mac OS X Finder. What's more, performance is better than any of the emulation programs, because you're not emulating a foreign processor.

*NOTE: In order for you to use the Classic environment, you need to install Mac OS 9.1 or later, if you're not already using it on your Mac. While 9.1 is just fine, later versions offer better compatibility and performance. You can update from 9.1 via a free update from Apple's support Web site, at **http://www.info.apple.com/**. If you don't have Mac OS 9 installed, you can order a copy at a special price for Jaguar users from Apple's customer service or from its upgrade Web site, at **http://www.apple.com/macosx/upgrade/**.*

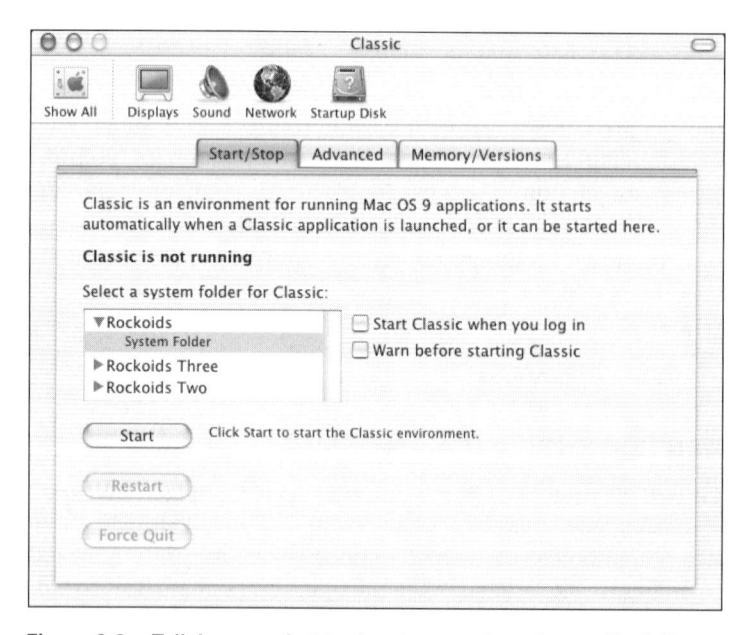

Figure 3.6 Tell Jaguar what to do when you insert an optical disc.

54

Immediate Solutions

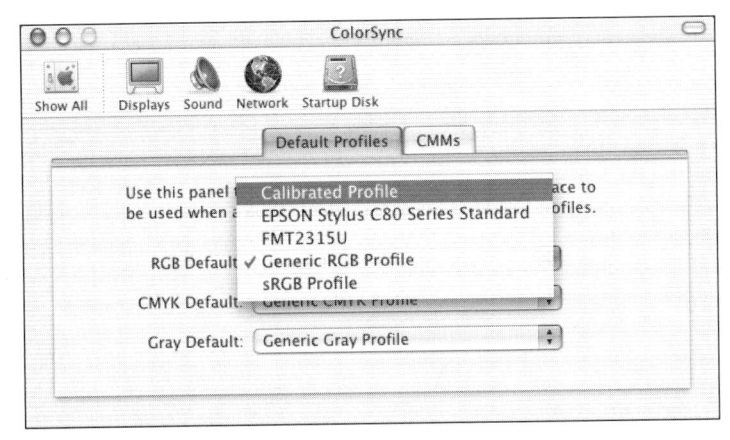

Figure 3.7 Choose your startup disk for Classic mode on this screen.

The Classic preferences panel (see Figure 3.7) lets you specify the startup volume for the Classic operating system, which is especially important if you have more that one volume with a System Folder installed. If your Mac has Mac OS 9.1 or later on another hard disk (or partition), you'll see the drive's name displayed in the list (drives without a 9.1 or later partition will be grayed out). You can click the disk from which you want to run the Mac in Classic mode, and then specify whether you want to have the Classic environment automatically start when you boot (log into) your Mac. This is not an essential selection unless you want to begin using Classic applications without having to wait for Classic to boot. You can also choose Restart or Force Quit Classic. The Advanced preference tab is used to configure additional options, such as whether to rebuild the Classic Mac OS system's desktop, restart with extensions off, or bring up Extensions Manager when Classic opens; I cover this subject in more detail in Chapter 15. You can monitor the amount of memory used by Classic applications by clicking the Memory/Versions tab.

TIP: If a preference panel is already open, you can access another panel by its icon on the top of the screen; if that icon isn't there, click the Show All button to see the rest of the list.

Setting ColorSync Preferences

Apple's ColorSync technology is tightly integrated into Mac OS X. You can use this settings pane (see Figure 3.8) to choose a ColorSync profile for input devices (such as a scanner), your Mac's display, output devices (a printer), or a proofing device. Click the pop-up menu to select the profile you want. To choose the color management method

55

Chapter 3   Mac OS X User Preferences

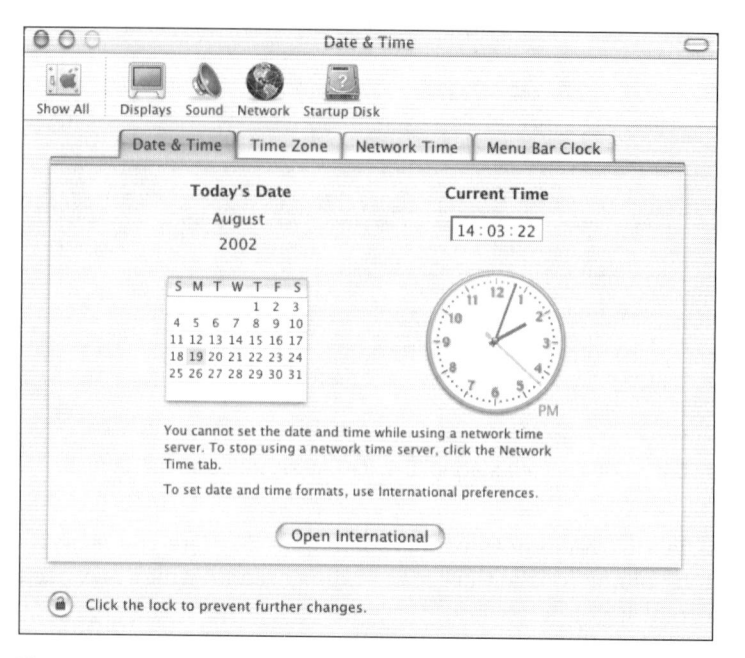

Figure 3.8   Select a ColorSync profile in this pane.

(CMM), click that tab in the ColorSync pane. The final tab is designed strictly for custom color workflow settings that may be required when you are working in an art department or prepress establishment.

NOTE: Many manufacturers of input and output peripherals provide their own ColorSync profiles. If one didn't come with a particular device, ask the manufacturer how one might be obtained or whether an existing ColorSync profile will do. In order to properly match up input and output devices, you must take a manual journey to this preference panel.

Setting Date & Time Preferences

In effect, the settings you create here (see Figure 3.9), in many respects, mirror the ones you've already configured in the Setup Assistant. However, these settings have a new wrinkle. At the bottom left of the settings screen, you'll notice a button labeled Click The Lock To Prevent Further Changes. You can protect this panel and any other panel with a padlock icon so that only users with administrator's permissions can access them.

TIP: If you plan to access a particular preference panel often, and it's not already part of the standard listing, simply drag its icon to the top of the System Preferences window.

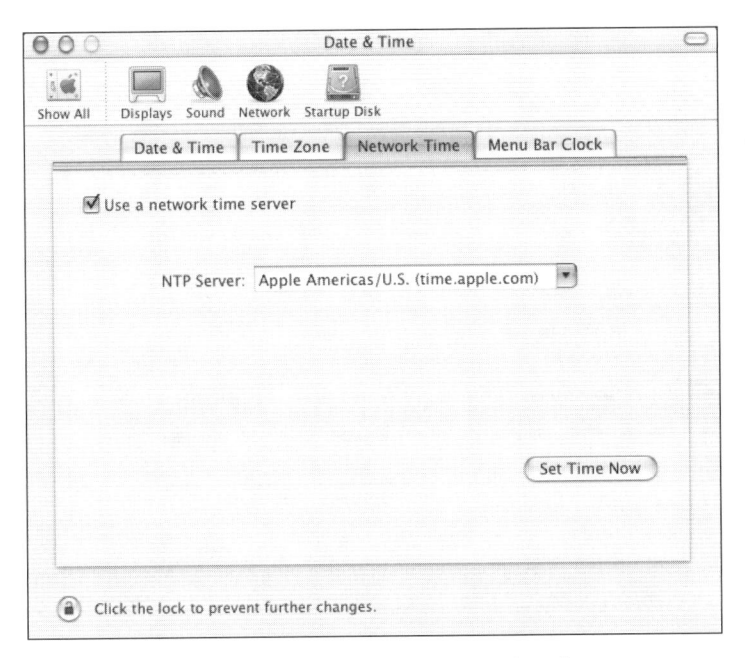

Figure 3.9 Make your various time-related settings here.

You can access any of the four settings categories by clicking on the appropriate tab:

- The first tab (Date & Time) and the second (Time Zone) offer the same settings you already performed in the Setup Assistant. You can leave them alone or make further adjustments now.

- The third tab—Network Time (see Figure 3.10)—allows you to have your Mac's clock synchronized to another computer on your network or to an Internet-based NTP time server (such as Apple's, which is offered by default) at the beginning of the startup process. The latter setting requires that you connect to the Internet to adjust the time, but when it's done, both the date and time will be configured automatically as needed.

NOTE: If you check Use A Network Time Server, Mac OS X will attempt to contact the server during the boot process to synchronize the clock. The only downside is that the boot process will be slower if you don't have a full-time ISP hookup or access to a time server on your own network. In addition, some network firewalls may prevent access to an Internet-based time server unless specially configured.

- The final tab—Menu Bar Clock—allows you to specify whether you want to show the clock in the menu bar (it's on by default) and whether you want it to display seconds, AM/PM, the date of

Chapter 3   Mac OS X User Preferences

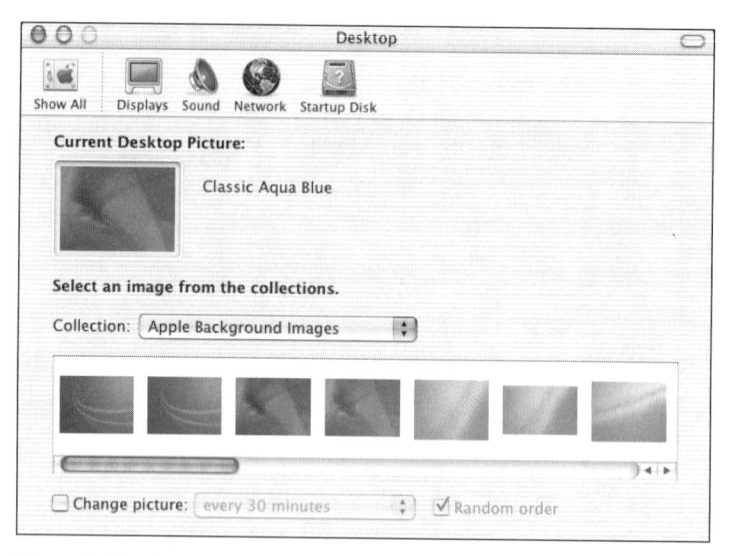

Figure 3.10   You can synchronize your Mac's clock via a network server.

the week, or flashing time separators. The settings are identical to those available under the Classic Mac OS, except for the inability to change the font and size of the menu bar clock's display.

*TIP: If you're not happy with the limitations of Apple's menu bar clock, check for a shareware alternative. One resource is **VersionTracker.com**, a popular Web site that includes information about software plus links to download sites.*

Setting Desktop Preferences

Don't like the default Aqua Blue ocean-blue backgrounds for Mac OS X? The Desktop preferences panel (shown in Figure 3.11) can be used to change it to your liking. I'll cover this subject in more detail in Chapter 5.

NOTE: If you used an earlier version of Mac OS X and want to restore the same desktop, choose the third option from the left among Apple's Background Images, which is known as Classic Aqua Blue.

Related solution:	Found on page:
Setting Desktop Preferences	132

58

Immediate Solutions

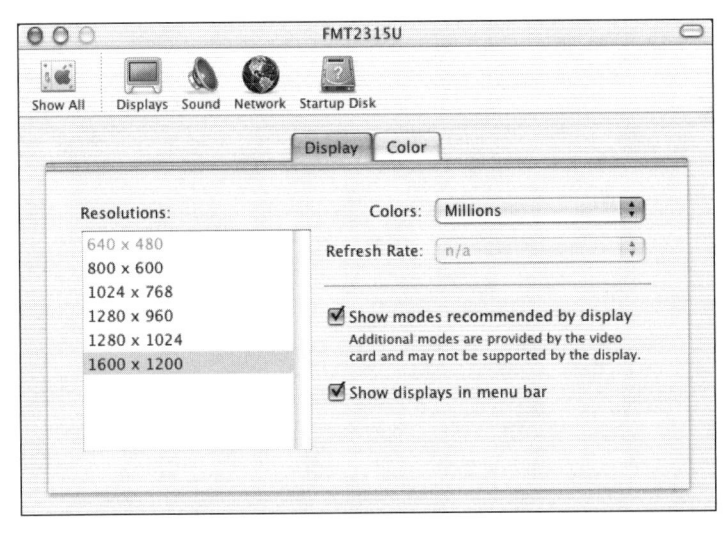

Figure 3.11   Pick another desktop backdrop from Apple's collection or yours.

Setting Display Preferences

The Display screen (see Figure 3.12) is used to configure the size (resolution) of the images on your Mac's display and the color depth setting. The Resolutions setting specifies the number of pixels that are shown on your Mac's display. When you make this adjustment, you should weigh the range of your Mac's desktop against the clarity of the items on it. To change the resolution, click the setting you want.

NOTE: On some Mac displays, you can configure contrast and brightness settings directly from the Display pane; on others, the settings will be grayed out. CRT-based iMacs, eMacs and some models equipped with an Apple display also have a tab labeled Geometry, where you can make sure your display's image is as wide as possible and that the shapes are straight and true.

To change color depth, click the Colors pop-up menu. For most purposes, the difference between thousands and millions is slight. But if you do graphics work, configure your Mac for the latter (unless you have a Mac with a slower graphics processor, such as a first-generation iMac, where the thousands setting will deliver noticeably better graphics performance).

NOTE: Click the checkbox to put a display system menu in your Mac's menu bar.

59

Chapter 3 Mac OS X User Preferences

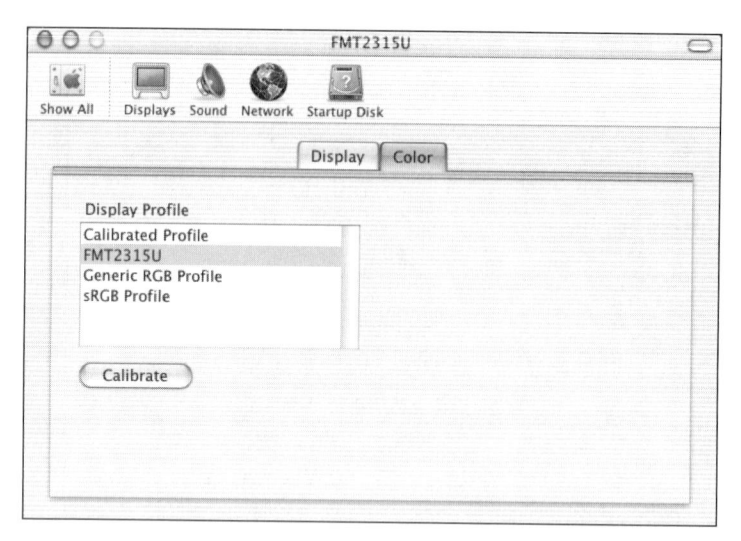

Figure 3.12 Choose your Mac's display preferences on this setup screen.

The Show Modes Recommended By Display checkbox restricts settings to the ones that the operating system expects your monitor to support. But if you uncheck it, you might gain additional choices, with which you can experiment (don't be concerned—if you pick one that can't be used, your Mac will revert within a few seconds to the previous setting).

Click the Color tab (see Figure 3.13) to adjust the color balance or calibration of your display. These settings take advantage of Apple's ColorSync technology so that your display more nearly matches the color balance of your printer or other output device.

NOTE: The model number of your display will be shown in this screen. If it's not one of Apple's, expect to see an arcane set of numbers that may not always be easy to decipher.

The settings on the Color tab are pretty much identical to those present in Mac OS 9.1 or later:

1. To establish a color profile for your Mac's monitor, select the model display you have or choose a generic profile from the Display Profile scrolling list. Then, click the Calibrate button. Apple's Display Calibrator Assistant (see Figure 3.14) will be launched.

60

Immediate Solutions

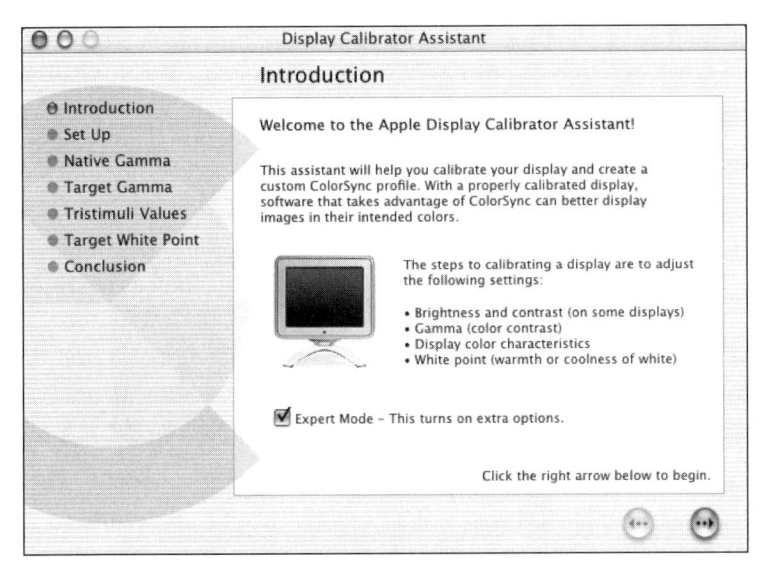

Figure 3.13   You can create a calibrated color profile to give your Mac a more accurate color balance.

NOTE: *You can also find the Display Calibrator Assistant application in the Utilities folder, inside the Applications folder, if you want to access it directly and bypass System Preferences.*

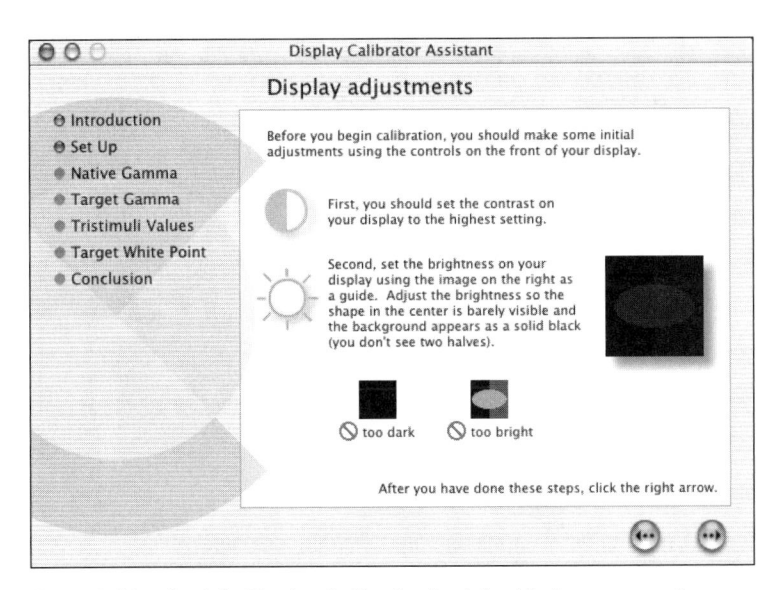

Figure 3.14   Apple's Display Calibrator Assistant helps you create a ColorSync profile for your monitor.

Chapter 3   Mac OS X User Preferences

2. Before proceeding, take a quick look at the introductory text in the Assistant's dialog box. For the most accurate color calibration, click the Expert Mode checkbox, if it's not already selected. Click the right (forward) arrow to proceed, and the left (back) arrow to review a setting. When you click the right arrow, you'll move to the Set Up screen (see Figure 3.15).

3. Use your display's brightness control to increase the brightness so that the center shape is visible but the two halves of the background square appear as one.

NOTE: If you have a regular CRT display, you'll need to redo brightness as the unit ages. Users of LCD displays shouldn't have to revisit these settings unless lighting conditions change substantially or you move the unit to a different working environment.

4. When you click the right arrow, you'll see the Native Gamma screen (see Figure 3.16). This setting lets you calibrate the gamma (center point) for the three RGB (red, green, blue) colors of your display by moving the slider back and forth. At the proper setting, the color of the Apple picture within the squares will seem to almost disappear into the background.

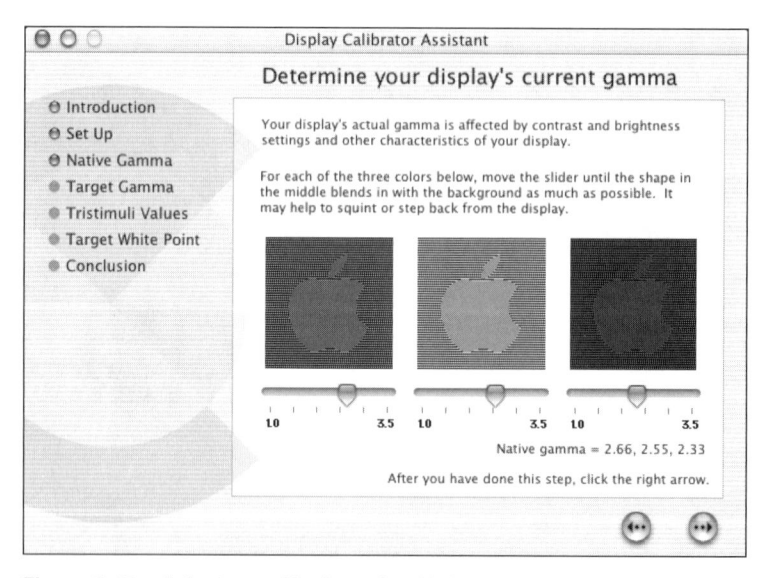

Figure 3.15   Adjust your Mac's optimal brightness here.

Immediate Solutions

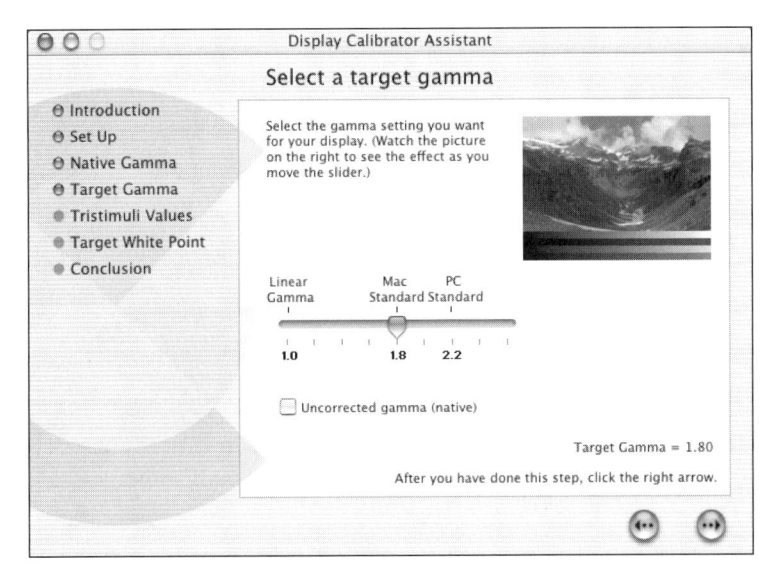

Figure 3.16 The gamma settings for each color are made here.

TIP: *It's a good idea not to sit too close to your display when making these adjustments. You get the most accurate view of gamma settings if you sit back from the display as far as possible. Otherwise, you might find that the inner and outer portions of the square never seem to merge.*

NOTE: *A number of Apple's own displays, including those in the iBook and PowerBook, have an automatic ColorSync capability built in, where settings are adjusted as the display ages. Thus the gamma settings windows will not appear. No, there's nothing wrong with your setup; this is the way it's supposed to work.*

---

5. A click of the right arrow brings up the Target Gamma setting (see Figure 3.17). Move the slider to configure the setting and observe the picture in the preview screen to see the end result. If you work in a mixed-platform environment, you might want to choose the PC Standard setting. Otherwise, use Mac Standard.

6. You are near the finish line. Click the right arrow to see the Target White Point screen (see Figure 3.18). The slider will set white point (or color temperature) for your display. D65, or 6500 degrees Kelvin, is normal. A setting of 9300 will brighten the display somewhat.

Chapter 3   Mac OS X User Preferences

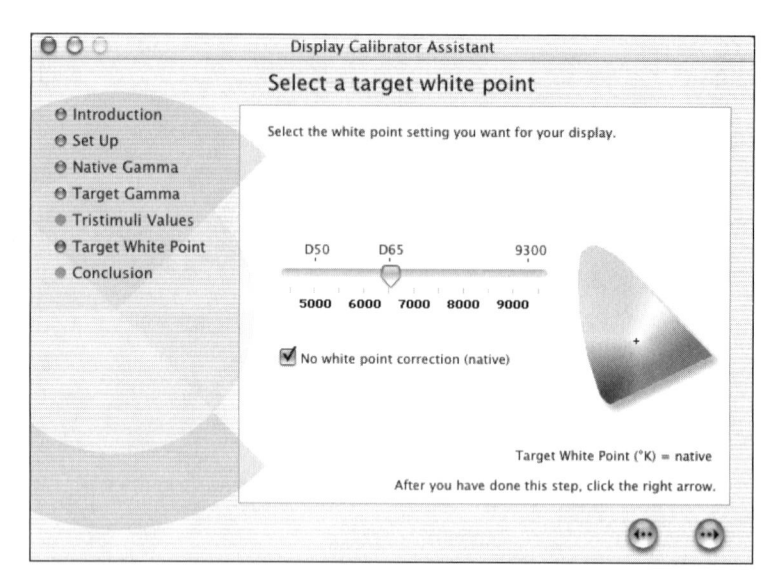

Figure 3.17   When Native Gamma is done, Target Gamma is next.

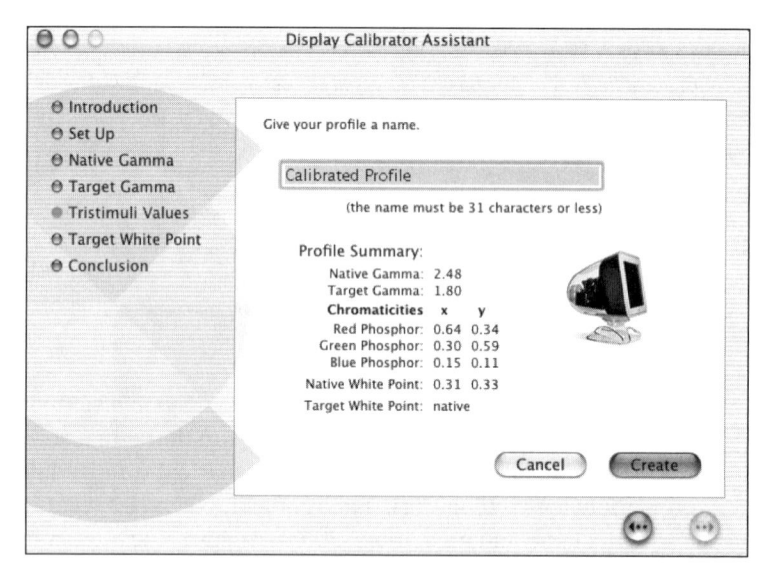

Figure 3.18   Choose the white point setting and you're almost finished.

NOTE: You may find that some displays benefit from one setting as opposed to another, depending on their design characteristics. Apple's LCD monitors, for example (such as the 17" and 22" models), seem to provide a brighter, more brilliant picture at the 6500 settings, as does a Planar WS231, 23-inch display I've reviewed for my "Mac Reality Check" column. Other LCD displays I've used, such as the ViewSonic ViewPanel VP181 (18.1-inch) and the Sony SDM MD-81 (also 18.1") work best at 9300. Feel free to experiment.

Immediate Solutions

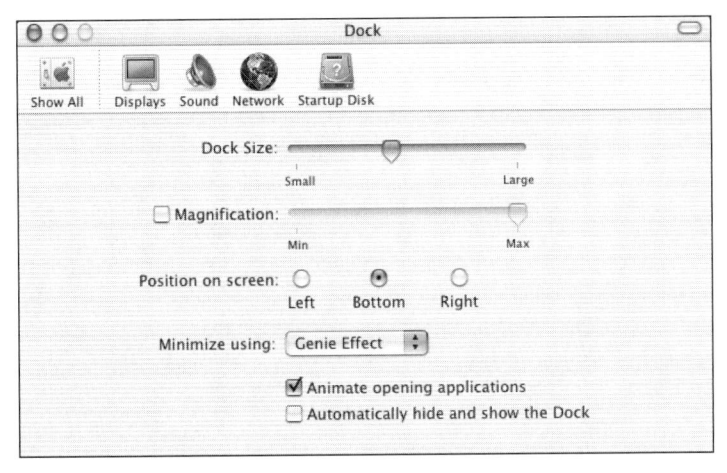

Figure 3.19 Name your calibration profile and click Create to wrap up.

7. Click the right arrow to reach the final stage of the process (see Figure 3.19). Name your profile (Calibrated Profile is the default). Then, click Create to finish and close the Display Calibrator Assistant.

NOTE: By default, the Display Calibrator Assistant will simply overwrite a previous setting with the same name without warning. So, be careful about naming your profile.

Setting Dock Preferences

Apple's Mac OS X taskbar (see Figure 3.20) can be configured in several ways to adjust the display. I'll cover these settings in more detail in Chapter 5.

Related solution:	Found on page:
Using the Dock	135

Setting Energy Saver Preferences

The Sleep settings screen (shown in Figure 3.21) will be the same regardless of which desktop Mac you're using, but it will be collapsed on an Apple laptop. The following adjustments are offered:

- The first setting puts the system into sleep mode after it's been idle for the preset period of time. The most recent desktop Mac models, beginning with the Power Mac G4, are designed to operate most efficiently by leaving the unit in sleep mode rather than shutting it down (in fact, they use hardly more current than

65

Chapter 3   Mac OS X User Preferences

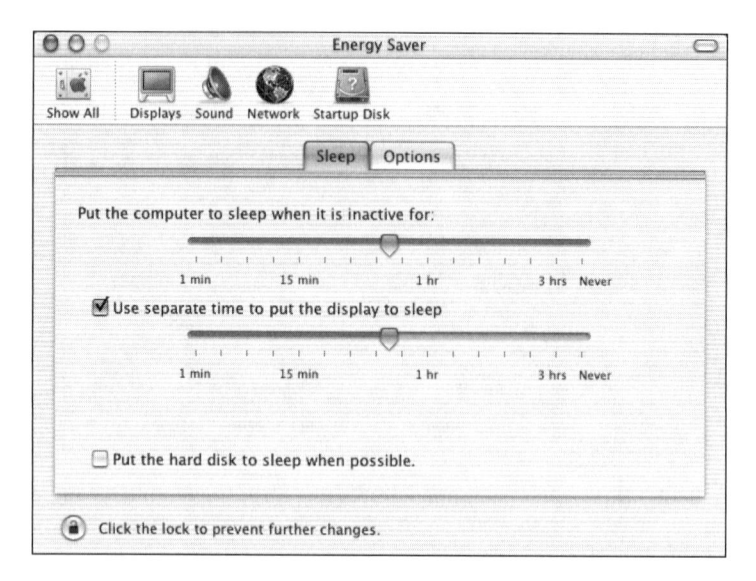

Figure 3.20   Adjust how you interact with the Dock here.

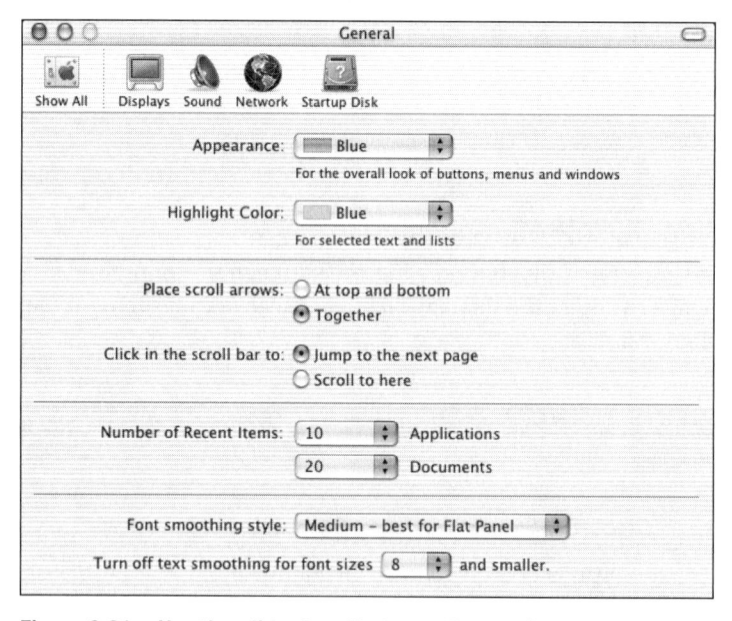

Figure 3.21   Use the slider to adjust your Energy Saver options here.

a small light bulb). Move the slider to change the idle time from the minimum of 30 minutes to Never (which deactivates the function).

Immediate Solutions

- The second setting lets you establish separate adjustments for your display, to preserve screen life and put it into sleep mode when not in use for a specific interval.
- The final setting puts the hard drive to sleep when possible. To activate this or the previous option, click the checkbox.

WARNING! Some older displays are not Energy Star–compliant and will not go into sleep mode, even though you've activated that setting. If you're not certain whether your display supports the feature, check the manufacturer's documentation, the shipping box, or the manufacturer's technical support division. Some displays ship with front panels peppered with all sorts of compliance information, but most users rip off these decals before putting the products into use.

NOTE: Some programs make continuous demands on the hard drive, and thus putting the drive into sleep mode won't work efficiently. The best time to use this feature is when you do not intend to work on your Mac.

The second set of preferences appears when you click the Options tab. The first choices, Wake Options, will awaken your Mac when the modem detects a ring (useful if you use your Mac for faxing) or when a network administrator needs to access it.

The Other Options choices depend on the kind of Mac you have. The first, Restart Automatically After A Power Failure, is useful if you need to keep your Mac on all the time (otherwise you can uncheck it and not worry over it). If you have an iBook or PowerBook, there will also be an option labeled Show Battery Status In Menu Bar on both screens, which is enabled by default if you install on an Apple laptop. You will also have the option to reduce processor performance on some models to conserve battery life. Such differences will be described in more detail in Chapter 13, where you'll learn about the Automatic option, where Mac OS X figures the best settings based on whether you're using AC power or the battery.

NOTE: Whenever you see a lock icon at the bottom of a preference panel, as you do with the Energy Saver preferences, it requires administrator access to change.

Setting General Preferences

If you thought you'd see the Mac OS X equivalent of the General control panel from previous versions of the Mac OS, think again. What you see is the Aqua equivalent of the Appearance control panel, at least part of it, along with a pair of settings for the Apple menu. So much for consistency.

67

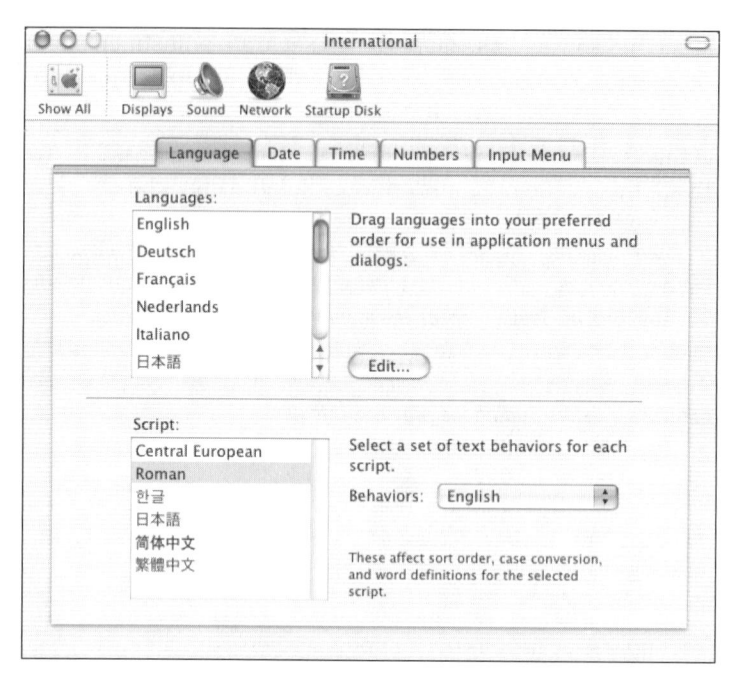

Figure 3.22 Choose your Mac's appearance settings on this panel. In this picture, I've increased the number of recent items and configured smoothing to support my digital flat panel monitor.

You have seven sets of appearance-related settings in the General pane (see Figure 3.22) from which to choose:

- *Appearance*—If the default Blue (or Aqua) color isn't to your liking, click the pop-up menu to choose the Graphite setting to adjust the look of buttons, menus, and windows.

NOTE: When you switch the appearance to Graphite, the colorful buttons at the left of a Finder or document window become gray when they can be used. The only visual indication of what they do is a symbol within each clear button when the mouse is brought near it.

- *Highlight Color*—This option sets the color you see when you select text. Feel free to experiment with different settings to see which colors set off highlighted text to your liking.

- *Place Scroll Arrows*—How would you like it? At the top and bottom, or all together at the bottom (this option may be easier on the mouse)? Take your pick.

Immediate Solutions

- *Click In The Scroll Bar To*—This setting is supposed to direct how far a screen jumps when you click in the scrollbar (to the next page or to the point at which you click). For most programs, however, there will be no difference, so the setting is best left at its default.
- *Number Of Recent Items*—This is, in a small part, the Mac OS X equivalent of the Apple Menu Items Control Panel under the Classic OS. Click a pop-up menu to pick the number of applications and documents displayed in the Apple menu's Recent Items list. The default is 10, and I'd suggest you increase the number of documents to, say, 20, since you're more likely to open lots of documents than lots of applications.
- *Font smoothing style*—Apple offers four options from the pop-up menu. The first and default setting, Standard, is recommended for a CRT display. The second choice, Light, is for folks who don't like the smoothing or anti-aliased effect. The third, Medium (the one I use) is optimized for flat panel displays. The final effect, Strong, may be too much of a good thing. But the differences are really subtle and you may have to blink twice to see the differences.
- *Turn Off Text Smoothing For Font Sizes*—Choose the threshold at which smoothing is activated, in one-point jumps from 8 point to 12 point. If you find that smaller type is hard to read with smoothing on, you may want to choose 9 point or larger.

NOTE: It's a good idea to check a few programs when you switch the text smoothing starting point. You may find, for example, that the text with smoothing disabled may be poorly spaced and look worse than with smoothing on. This is particularly true of Carbon-based rather than Cocoa-based applications, which do not yet have Quartz text rendering.

Setting International Preferences

Mac OS X is designed to be a worldwide operating system, with built-in support for some of the major languages. Under older system versions, you had to install separate modules for different parts of the world or buy a different product and use the Keyboard, Numbers and Text control panels to configure the settings. But Apple has moved to selling a single operating system version, and the preferences available (see Figure 3.23) are designed to localize keyboard and language settings as needed. You have settings for Language, where you can move a language to a different position by dragging and dropping it to set its priority. Separate tabs also let you adjust display formats for

69

Chapter 3 Mac OS X User Preferences

Figure 3.23 Choose your language settings on this screen.

Date, Time, and Numbers. The final tab—Input Menu—lets you choose whether to put up a menu bar label from which you can quickly switch from one keyboard layout to another.

NOTE: *If you opted not to install some of the language packages during the initial installation of Jaguar, you may find fewer options than I've shown here.*

Setting Internet Preferences

This settings pane (see Figure 3.24) is reminiscent of the Internet Control Panel from the Classic Mac OS, with the notable addition of a category for Apple's .Mac feature. Click a tab to enter a particular setup screen. Four are available:

- *.Mac*—Put in your iTools member name and password. If you don't have an account, click the Sign Up button; you'll be connected to Apple's Web site to set up your account.

NOTE: *Although you get a free .Mac trial with Jaguar or a new Mac, after that you will have to pay an annual subscription fee to continue use of any of the .Mac services.*

- *iDisk*—Examine the status of your iDisk, which is the online storage feature offered by Apple's .Mac service. You can use this preference screen to order up additional storage space or set access privileges to the files you have posted.

70

Immediate Solutions

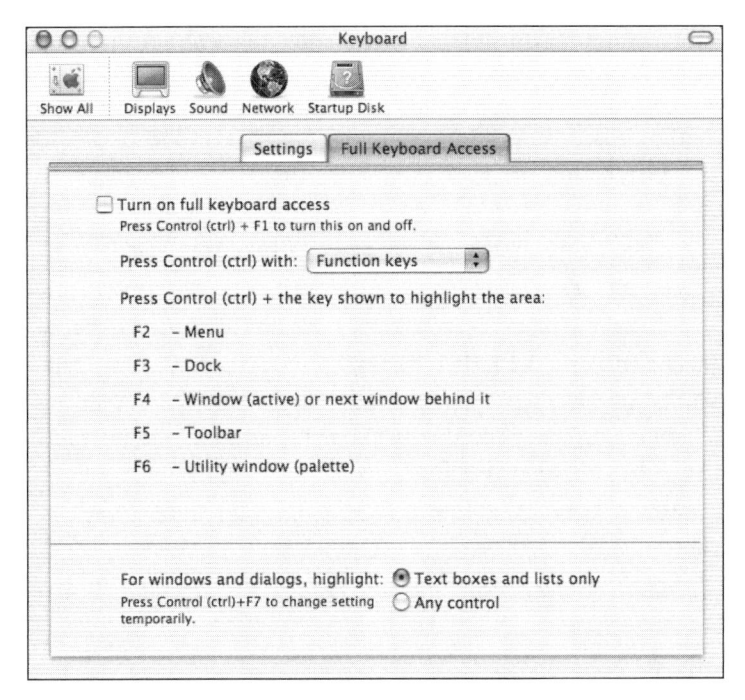

Figure 3.24 Configure your Internet application settings here.

- *Email*—These are settings you would have retrieved from your Classic Mac OS's Internet Control Panel. Specify which email program you want (Mail is the only Mac OS X–savvy program shipping with Mac OS X, but others are available, as you'll see in Chapter 22), the incoming and outgoing mail servers used by your ISP, the type of account, and the username and password required to log in.

TIP: *If you failed to write down this information from your Classic Mac OS installation, you can launch any Classic application to bring up the Classic environment. After you switch to that application, use the Apple menu to view the settings from the Internet Control Panel.*

- *Web*—Pick a browser, a home page, and a default search page. You can also select a default location on your Mac's drive where downloaded files are placed; the default, and probably the best locale, is your Mac's desktop.

In case you're wondering, no there is no Advanced setting panel, as you'd find under the Classic Mac OS version of the Internet Control Panel. Mac OS X sets most settings behind the scenes, though individual applications may overwrite them. In addition, Internet Explorer

71

and other programs do let you control some of these settings, such as helper applications. Settings for proxies, required by some ISPs and network administrators, are moved to the Network preference panel. In addition, the option to choose a default newsgroup reader didn't make the transition from Mac OS X 10.1 to 10.2.

Related solution:	Found on page:
Setting Up Your User Account	467

Setting Keyboard Preferences

You can configure two types of settings here. The first, under the Repeat Rate tab, affects your Mac keyboard's Automatic Repeat modes. Here's the list of the available choices:

- *Key Repeat Rate*—Specifies the time you hold down a key before it repeats.

- *Delay Until Repeat*—Specifies the speed at which a key repeats.

Move the sliders to make the needed changes. You can also enter text in the text box to get a feel for the changes you'll be making.

The second set of preferences can be accessed by clicking on the Full Keyboard Access tab (shown in Figure 3.25) and is used to give you more control of Finder functions via the keyboard. When you click the Turn On Full Keyboard Access checkbox, you'll harness the power of the seldom-used function keys.

TIP: Full Keyboard Access can also be activated (or deactivated, if it's already on) by pressing Control+F1.

The end result? When you activate these functions, you'll switch the focus to a specific area of your Mac's desktop. With the menu bar selected, for example, the Apple menu will drop down, and the left and right arrow keys can be used to move through the menus. Up and down arrows will travel up and down the commands, and the Return or Enter key will activate the functions.

Once Full Keyboard Access is working, you can do the following:

WARNING! Individual programs have keyboard shortcuts that might work in place of the various Full Keyboard Access shortcuts. This is especially true if the program has its own brand of function key support, such as the various applications in Microsoft Office.

Immediate Solutions

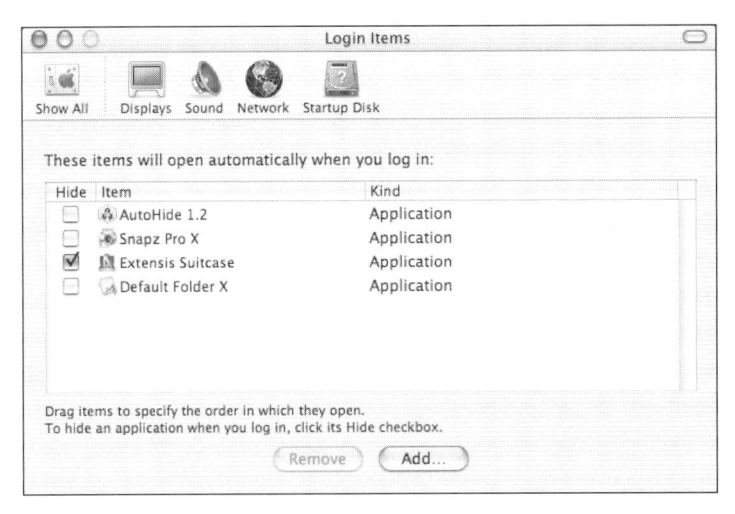

Figure 3.25 Full Keyboard Access gives you the ability to access certain functions via keyboard.

- *Press Control With*—This option lets you choose whether the function keys or other keys activate the various features.
- *Keyboard focus*—When you press F2, it points to the menu bar. F3 focuses on the Dock, F4 the active window or the one behind it, F5 focuses on a toolbar, and F6 focuses on a utility window or palette. Try it; you might find that changing focus via keyboard is a faster way to go.
- *For windows and dialogs, highlight*—By default, the emphasis is on text input fields and lists, but the Any Control option switches the emphasis. Pressing Control+F7 switches the setting from what you've checked.

NOTE: If you've used Windows, you might find that Full Keyboard Access has some familiar elements.

Setting Login Items Preferences

You use these settings (see Figure 3.26) in a fashion similar to the Startup Items folder under previous versions of the Mac OS. The programs that appear in this window launch when you log in. Click the Add button to locate and select startup applications, documents, network shares and other items that will open when you boot or log into your Mac, and click the Remove button to delete a selected item. Doing so, of course, won't delete the actual file itself.

73

Chapter 3 Mac OS X User Preferences

Figure 3.26 Add the programs that will launch when you boot your Mac.

NOTE: Items added as Login Items apply strictly to a single user. If you want more than one user to be able to access a particular startup item, the best way to apply it is in the StartupItems folder inside the Library folder at the top level of your hard drive. If such a folder isn't there, just create one.

Setting Mouse Preferences

Most Macs ship with the Mouse speed in the middle setting, and that can be somewhat slow. However, the middle setting can be helpful for those new to personal computing and pointing devices and who need to get accustomed to a mouse's feel and movement. Generally, though, you will find that the standard speed setting is just too slow, especially if your Mac has a large screen display. The Mouse Speed slider adjusts the tracking speed; the Double-Click Speed setting is used to configure the ideal interval for a double-click to activate a Mac OS function. There is no correct setting. It's entirely up to your taste, and you can experiment with different adjustments to see which are most comfortable. You'll also find that the ideal settings change as you move from one Mac to another, or to a different brand of pointing device. If you have an iBook or PowerBook G4, the Mouse panel

Immediate Solutions

window provides direct support for your trackpad rather than the mouse. On some older Apple laptops, however, a separate Trackpad tab controls these settings.

NOTE: *Some non-Apple input devices, such as those from Kensington and Microsoft, come with special software to allow you to access extra button features plus custom tracking routines. For such products, the Mouse panel probably will not work.*

Setting Network Preferences

This configuration screen has four tabs (see Figure 3.27) that control various aspects of your network settings, including those connected with access to your ISP. As you saw above, in the section entitled "Mac OS 9 Features: What Happened to Them?," earlier in this chapter, this preference panel replaces the functions of several in your Classic Mac OS, which should make your configuration go faster and easier. You can make two types of settings. One is for your internal modem, used for connecting to your ISP. (I cover those in more detail in Chapter 8.) The other, under the Built-in Ethernet category, includes four tabs to configure different settings (these are mirrored in the settings panels for an AirPort card, if one is installed):

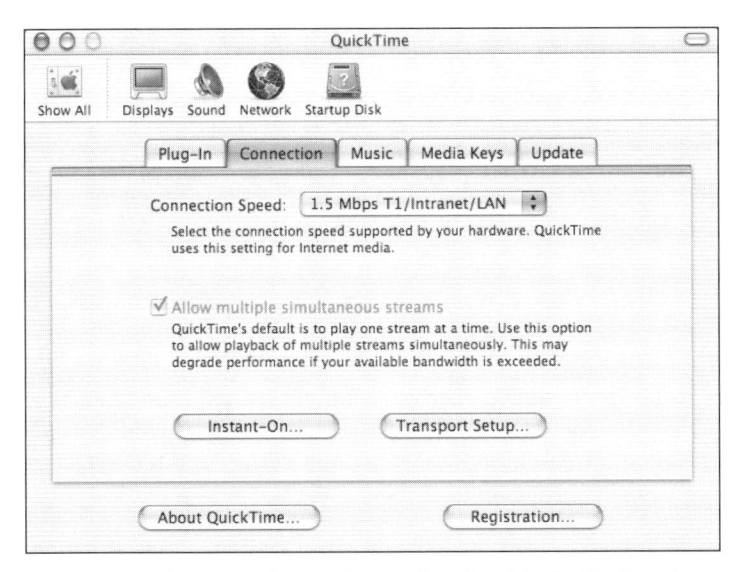

Figure 3.27 Select a tab to make a network-related adjustment on your Mac.

Chapter 3   Mac OS X User Preferences

- *TCP/IP*—The settings you make here, labeled Manually using DHCP Router, BOOTP or DHCP, are for TCP/IP-based connections, if you have one. They activate these services for a local network, cable modem, or DSL. They're very similar to those used in the TCP/IP control panel of older Macs. The required settings will come from either an ISP or network administrator.

NOTE: To access a dial-up connection to the Internet, you'll make your settings in the Internal Modem category, available from the Show pop-up menu. AirPort users will find a category devoted to that product (with settings pretty much the same as the Built-in Ethernet category) if an AirPort card is installed on your Mac.

- *PPPoE*—Some broadband ISPs, such as those using cable modems or DSL, use PPP over Ethernet (PPPoE) software or settings. When you click this tab, you'll be able to enter information for Service Provider, PPPoE Service Name, Account Name, and Password. You can also save your password and click the PPPoE Options button to make settings that might be required by your ISP.

NOTE: Your ISP is the source for updated information about the settings required for the PPPoE panel. The settings will vary from service to service. In addition, before installing anyone's software to make this connection, try the settings screen in the Network preference panel. It should accommodate the needs of the vast majority of ISPs that require this setup. You may have to argue the point with your broadband ISP's technical people, but you can definitely do it yourself in just a few minutes, tops, once you get the setup information.

- *AppleTalk*—To access Macs and network printers on a standard AppleTalk network, select the checkbox to activate AppleTalk.

NOTE: On or off? On some Macs with Jaguar installed, it's turned on automatically, sometimes it isn't. It never hurts to double-check.

- *Proxies*—Depending on the requirements in your network or for your ISP, you might have to enter proxy settings to access the Internet. Contact your network administrator or ISP for the appropriate settings information.

After you've made your changes to your network services, click Apply Now to store your settings. If you quit System Preferences without saving your settings, you'll see a prompt asking if you want to save your settings before you move on. If you don't click Save, the network changes will be discarded.

Immediate Solutions

Related solution:	Found on page:
Using Internet Connect for Dial-Up Networking	197

Setting QuickTime Preferences

Apple's QuickTime is a multimedia standard around the world. Use this settings pane (shown in Figure 3.28) to establish five sets of user preferences:

- *Plug-In*—These settings determine how your Web browser works with the QuickTime plug-in. The Play Movies Automatically checkbox turns on a QuickTime movie as soon as it's downloaded. Save Movies In Disk Cache stores a movie in the browser's Web cache (not a good idea if it's a big file). Enable Kiosk Mode turns on Kiosk mode, which allows you to save movies and adjust your QuickTime settings from within the browser.

- *Connection*—Click this tab to optimize QuickTime to work best with your specific ISP connection. Choose the speed at which you access your ISP and whether to allow multiple streams of net traffic (this option is best only with broadband Internet access). The Transport Setup button should be left to network administrators.

NOTE: By default, the Connection settings are configured for a 56K modem. Although QuickTime Player will remind you to change the settings if you activate that program with a faster network hookup, it's better to save a little time and do it now.

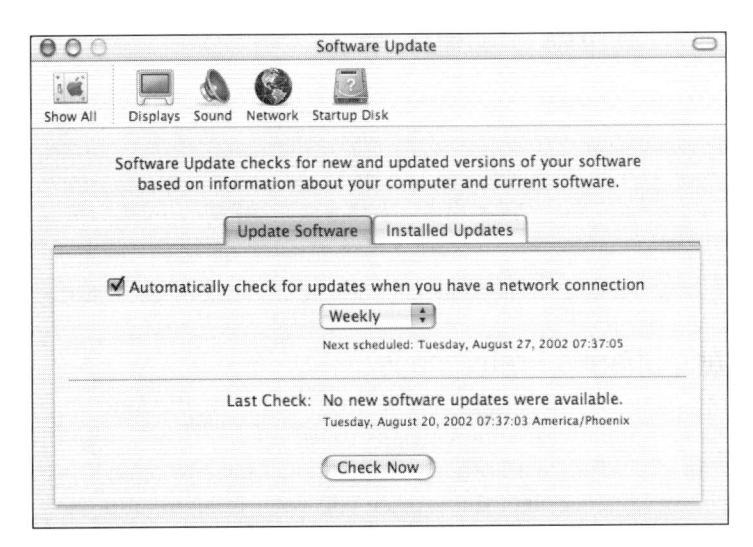

Figure 3.28   Choose your QuickTime user preferences from this pane.

- *Music*—Use this setting to choose a music synthesizer package. You don't need to use it unless you've added such a package from a music program.
- *Media Keys*—Use this setting to store passwords to access secured multimedia files. Specify the fashion in which Mac OS X's built-in QuickTime features are used.
- *Update*—The final tab lets you check for updates to QuickTime from Apple's Web site. You can also enter your registration information, in the event you've opted to purchase QuickTime Pro (and get rid of those annoying messages about doing so when you try to view multimedia content on the Internet).

NOTE: *The upgrade to QuickTime Pro, which costs $29.95 in the USA, gives you more options with which to edit and export movies in the QuickTime Player application. It also allows you to save at least some of the movie trailers that you download from the Internet. In some cases, you may not be able to access a larger movie trailer without buying the Pro license. This was true, for example, with Star Wars: Episode Two.*

Setting Screen Effects Preferences

If you've used Microsoft Windows, no doubt you've discovered that it has a built-in screen saver. Apple has finally delivered one of its own. The setup screen is ultra-simple. Pick a module, and then click the Activation tab to set the idle time before the screen saver activates. The intervals are in 5-minute jumps up to 60 minutes. The Hot Corners option lets you automatically activate a screen saver when moving the mouse to the selected corner.

NOTE: *By default, the screen saver interval is activated when you install Jaguar, but you can change the interval or switch it to Never if you're not a fan of screen savers. On the other hand, you can also opt to password-protect your screen saver in the Activation pane, using your regular username and password to unlock it and dismiss the display. You will also want to coordinate this setting with your Energy Saver settings, so your Mac doesn't drift into sleep mode, when you really want to see a fancy screen effect.*

Setting Sharing Preferences

Peer-to-peer file sharing is one of the delights of the Mac OS. You don't need a network administrator to set up a network over which you can share files with other users. You just have to open this pane (see Figure 3.29), select the service you want to share and click the Start button to activate the feature. The display at the top shows your

Immediate Solutions

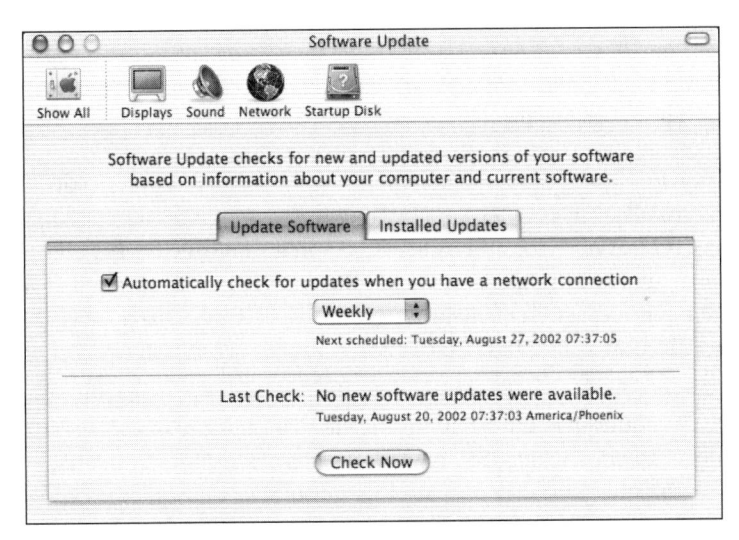

Figure 3.29 Choose whether file sharing and some sharing services will be available on your Mac.

Computer Name, which is used to identify your Mac on the network, and the corresponding name used for Apple's Rendezvous networking technology, along with its IP address for TCP/IP connections. I'll cover this subject in more detail in Chapter 8.

The following sharing preferences are available, selected just by clicking the appropriate tab:

- *Services*—Use this to turn on sharing for Personal File Sharing, Sharing with Windows (which allows a Windows PC to see your Mac as just another computer in the network), personal Web sharing, Remote Login (allowing connection from a program that takes over your Mac, such as Timbukto, FTP Access, Remote Apple Events (used for Apple Scripts and Printer Sharing (for personal or USB printers).

NOTE: You do not have to turn on Sharing with Windows to access files from a Windows PC. It's only required to allow the Windows user to access the files from your Mac. You will also have to engage the option to allow Windows logins for a specific user in the Accounts preference panel.

NOTE: If you want to network with an older Mac that cannot share files via TCP/IP, you'll need to turn on AppleTalk in the Network preference panel before activating file sharing here.

79

Chapter 3 Mac OS X User Preferences

WARNING! *The FTP sharing feature is, like Web sharing, a potential security hole, so use this feature with caution. If you must share files in this fashion, be sure to turn on the Firewall feature to protect your Mac.*

- *Firewall*—Click the Start button on turn on this feature. If you need to allow access to specific network communication ports, click the service from the Allow list. You'll find they mirror all the sharing features in the Services preference pane. If you need to add other services, such as instant messaging or Timbukto access, click the Edit button and choose the services you want to allow).

- *Internet Sharing*—With the exception of AOL and CompuServe, which require a separate login for each account, you can use this feature to share your ISP over your network connection. Just click the checkbox to activate this feature.

NOTE: *Your Mac must be on whenever another computer on your network attempts to access the shared connection. You may be better off checking into a separate ISP router, such as Apple's AirPort Base Station, which allows any connected computer (be it wired or wireless) to share an ISP without requiring any specific Mac to be left on.*

Related solution:	Found on page:
Setting Up a Web or FTP Server on Your Mac	206

Setting Software Update Preferences

Starting with Mac OS 9, Apple offered a Software Update option. It's intended to provide an effective way to check Apple's Web site for the latest Mac OS X software updates (see Figure 3.30 for Mac OS X's version).

You can opt to update your software manually whenever you want, or select the Automatically option to have Apple's Web site checked on a daily, weekly, or monthly basis for needed updates. The status display will show the last time you attempted the update. Click Update Now whenever you want to recheck for updates. When an update is available, a separate Software Update application will launch, and that's where you can select the updates you want to install from the list (yes, sometimes there's more than one). If you want to see the list of previously received updates, click on the Installed Updates tab.

Immediate Solutions

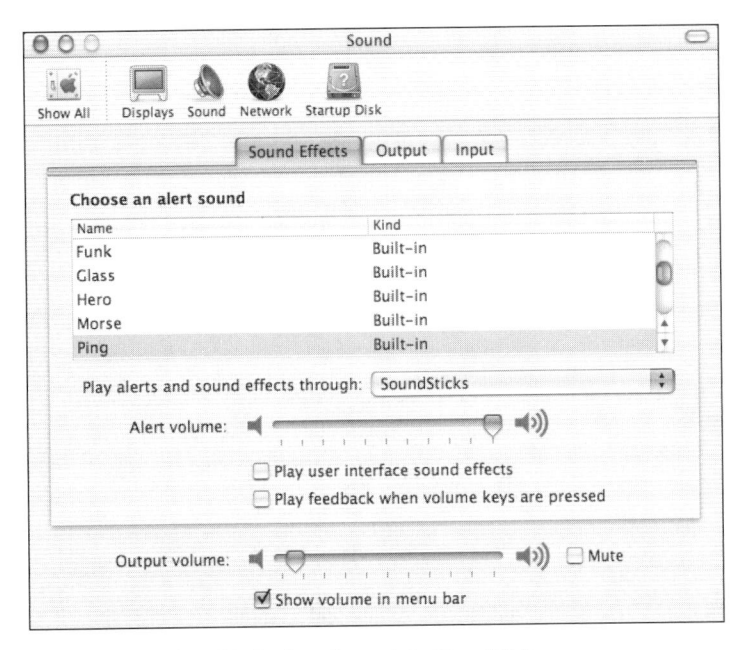

Figure 3.30   Use this feature to update Mac OS X.

NOTE: *The Software Update feature is not always as effective as it should be. However, Apple assures us that the version used for Mac OS X will deliver the goods. Regardless, you may want to check the VersionTracker.com Web site periodically to see if you missed a needed update for your Apple system software. Also bear in mind that Software Update only works for minor maintenance updates for Mac OS X. Complete or reference updates, such as the upgrade from Mac OS X 10.1 to 10.2, are only available as retail packages, not as downloadable files.*

TIP: *When you access the Software Update application, choose Save As from the Update menu to store a copy of the update on your drive right after the updates are installed. This is a great way to ensure that the update is available should you need to reinstall it later (perhaps after reinstalling Mac OS X), without having to access the Internet to retrieve it again.*

Setting Sound Preferences

Your Mac is, at heart, a multimedia computer with the ability to create and play audio and video productions (with the right additional software for making such productions, of course). There are several categories of settings. Alerts (see Figure 3.31) perform the following:

- *Choose An Alert Sound*—Select the audible warning you get when an alert is displayed. When you pick a sound from the scrolling list, you'll hear it played in your Mac's speaker.

81

Chapter 3 Mac OS X User Preferences

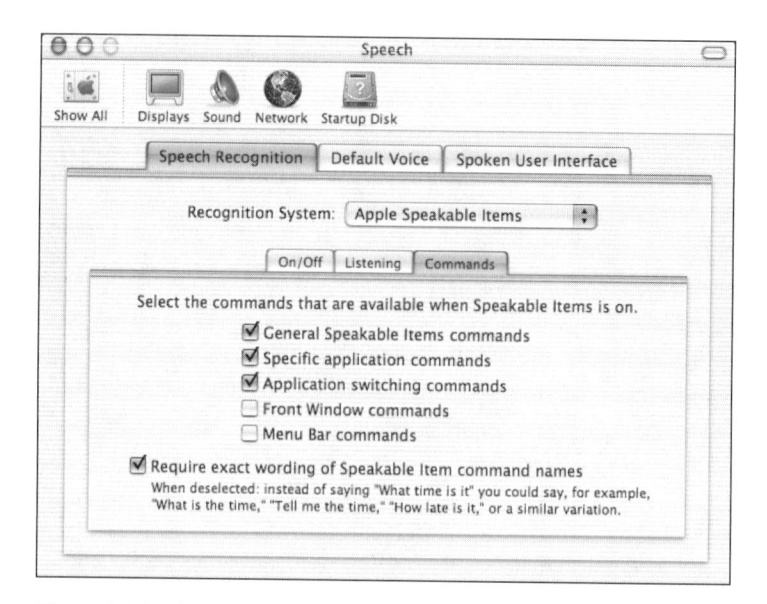

Figure 3.31 Set your volume and choose alert sounds in this pane.

- *Play Alerts Through and Sound Effects Through*—Do you have an extra set of speakers on your Mac? In the example shown in Figure 3.31, I had a set of Harman Kardon SoundSticks attached to my Power Mac G4, which is why SoundSticks is shown. Otherwise, the choice would be confined to Built-in Audio Controller.

- *Alert Volume*—Choose the level at which the Mac plays alert sounds, such as those warning you of a problem with your Mac. If the little beeps and blurbs irritate you, you can make them lower than the overall volume.

- *Checkboxes*—This is the Mac OS X 10.2 equivalent to the system sounds you could activate under Mac OS 9. I disabled both checkboxes after they became a little annoying (they are activated by default), but the first plays a sound when you access a different element of the Aqua interface, such as the Finder or Dock. The other checkbox adds a little click or thumping sound when you press the volume keys on the Apple Pro keyboard.

- *Output Volume*—This setting controls the system volume. The checkbox puts a system menu volume control on your Mac's menu bar.

When you click the Output tab, you'll be able to pick a device for audio (assuming you have a second choice) and also choose Balance, moving the slider to match up the levels between your left and right

Immediate Solutions

speakers. The Input function is active if your Mac has an input jack or a separate audio input adapter, such as the Griffin Technology iMic.

NOTE: *The Sound preferences you see also depend on the kind of Mac you have. For example, if you have a slot-loading iMac, you may see additional adjustments for use if you're using Harman Kardon's iSub, a woofer module that enhances the sound reproduction on these models.*

Setting Speech Preferences

Some Mac programs support Mac OS X's Speech Manager, which allows you to activate Mac functions via spoken commands and have text read back to you. In the first Speech settings pane, Speech Recognition (see Figure 3.32), you can decide whether to activate the speech recognition feature. Turn Apple Speakable Items on to specify whether to activate the feature. The standard setup calls for saying "computer" prior to a command. With recognition turned on, you'll be able to access the Speakable Items folder to see the available commands. The Listening and Commands tabs allow you to configure speech recognition options to tailor the feature to your needs.

NOTE: *It's not a good idea to be overly dependant on Apple's speech features, unless you have a handicap that makes manual labor difficult. The "recognition" feature won't support all possible Mac commands and doesn't work terribly well in a crowded room. The Text-to-Speech feature works after a fashion, but many words simply are not pronounced correctly. To use speech recognition for dictation, you may want to look for a separate program, such as the Mac OS X version of IBM's ViaVoice, which also allows you to verbally access some of your Mac's commands—but it's still a far cry from the way it is done on Star Trek.*

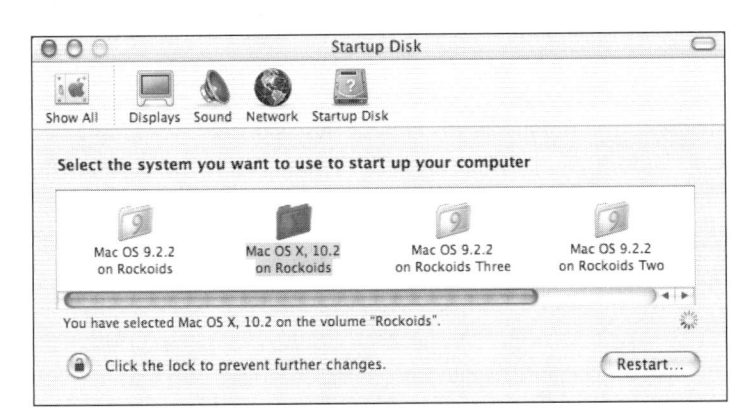

Figure 3.32   Speak to me. Activate your speech recognition preferences here.

83

Chapter 3 Mac OS X User Preferences

The Default Voice and Spoken User Interface tabs allow you to specify the voice for text-to-speech and whether talking alerts will be allowed. Again, this is a personal preference, and most Mac users prefer to leave the features off unless absolutely needed.

Setting Startup Disk Preferences

This setting lets you switch startup disks, if you have additional volumes with system software on them on your Mac. In Figure 3.33, you can see selections representing the names of the volumes connected to my Mac when I wrote this book and the system versions they contained. For most of you, the option will be to switch from Mac OS X back to Mac OS 9. To change the startup disk, follow these steps:

1. Click the icon representing the name of the volume from which you want to boot your Mac.

2. Click the Restart button.

3. You'll see an acknowledgement prompt; click Save and Restart to boot from a different startup volume. Click Cancel to simply save your settings, in case you want to restart at a later time. This choice will produce a dialog in which you'll be asked if you want to save the new settings (even they are the old settings).

4. If you opt to restart later, choose Restart from the Apple menu to boot your Mac from the previously selected startup volume.

WARNING! For your Mac to boot properly from another startup volume, it must contain system software that's compatible with your computer. The Startup Disk preferences screen only displays the disks on which a Mac OS System Folder is present; it won't always know whether your Mac can run from it. Should your Mac not be able to boot from the specified volume, it will, instead, boot from another volume with a compatible version of the Mac OS (perhaps the one from which you just switched).

5. When you're finished setting your Mac's preferences, choose Quit from the application menu. The changes you make go into effect as soon as you apply them.

Setting Universal Access Preferences

This settings panel (see Figure 3.34) is a direct descendant of the EasyAccess feature of the Classic Mac OS. It's designed for those who are physically disabled, or anyone for whom the keyboard and mouse are difficult to use. The Seeing panel, shown in the figure, activates the Zoom feature, which blows up lettering for easier reading.

Immediate Solutions

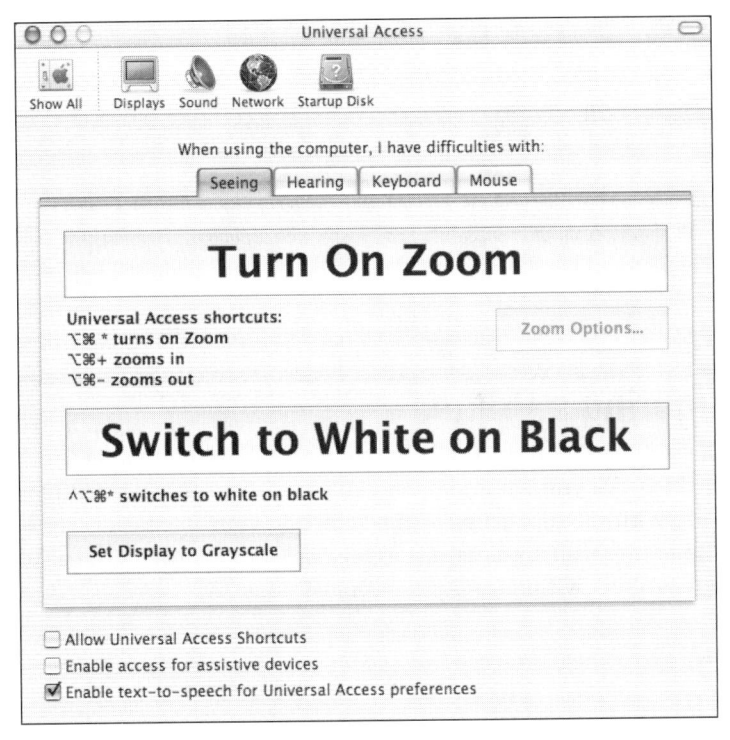

Figure 3.33 Click a System Folder icon to select another startup disk.

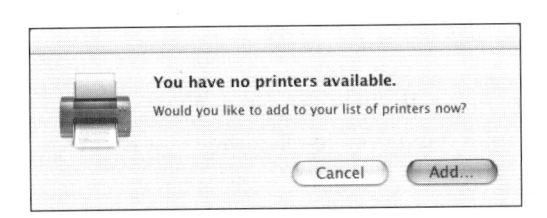

Figure 3.34 For those with visual or hearing disabilities, or for whom mouse and keyboard movement is painful, Mac OS X has a possible solution.

The Hearing tab activates a visual alert, for those who are hearing impaired. Click the Keyboard tab to access a sticky keys feature, to make it easier to handle sequential keystrokes, such as Command+S for Save. You may also choose to play a beep sound when you type the modifier key and see visual confirmation. The Mouse tab allows you to use the numeric keypad on your keyboard to emulate the functions of the mouse, using just the number keys to control mouse action.

TIP: To quickly access the Sticky Keys function, press the Shift key five times in a row (repeating the action turns the function off). The Mouse Keys function is activated by pressing the Option key five times in a row (repeat the action to turn the feature off).

NOTE: According to Apple, the accessibility features provided in Jaguar meet or exceed the requirements of the U.S. government's Section 508 Accessibility statute.

Configuring a Printer

As mentioned at the start of this chapter, under all previous versions of the Mac OS, you would use the Chooser to select and configure a printer. With the departure of the Chooser, your printer choices are now made with an application called Print Center. You'll find it in the Utilities folder, within the Applications folder.

NOTE: If you're using a printer hooked up to your Mac's USB port, and drivers are available, you don't need to use Print Center except to set a default printer (the one listed first in your Page Setup and Print dialog boxes). Once the drivers are installed, the printer is automatically recognized as soon as it's connected and turned on. The following steps, however, are needed if you want to connect a network printer. Once network printers support Apple's open-source automatic networking technology, Rendezvous, these printers will be automatically discovered too.

After you've located the application, follow these steps:

1. Go to the Utilities folder and double-click the Print Center application icon to launch it.

2. If you have no printers selected, you'll see a dialog box (see Figure 3.35) asking if you want to add a printer. Click the Add button.

WARNING! What happened to your networked printers? Before you can check an AppleTalk network, you need to make sure AppleTalk is turned on. It's a setting in the Network pane of the System Preferences application.

3. On the next screen, click the Connection pop-up menu and select the network or peripheral connection on which you want to check for printers. Depending on the kind of Mac you have, you can choose from AppleTalk, LPR Printers Using IP, or USB. Additional ports that support specific makes and models, such as network models from Epson and Lexmark. The Directory

Immediate Solutions

> **You have no printers available.**
>
> Would you like to add to your list of printers now?
>
> [Cancel] [Add...]

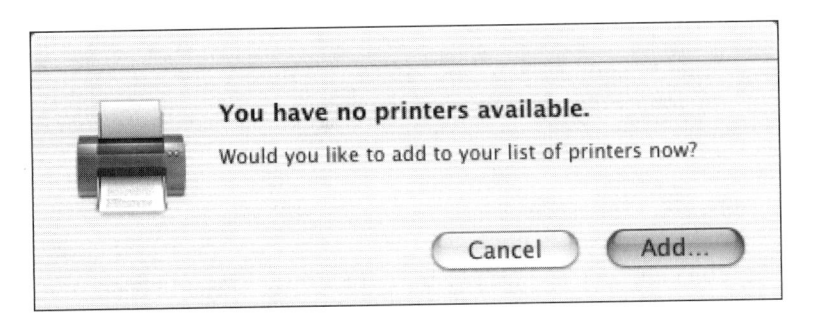

Figure 3.35 This dialog box comes up if no printer has been configured.

Services option can locate an enterprise printer located on your network. In the example shown in Figure 3.35, I chose AppleTalk to locate a printer on my Ethernet network.

4. If your printer is located in another AppleTalk zone, click the second pop-up menu to pick that zone.

5. Continue browsing for printers until they are all displayed.

6. Under Printer Model, leave the Auto Select option selected, or pick a printer from the list of PostScript Printer Description (PPD) files to provide maximum support for your output device. A PPD file will recognize the custom features of your network printer, such as extra paper sizes, extra trays, custom resolutions, and, if available, the ability to duplex or print on both sides of the paper. If you don't have the right PPD file available, your selections will be limited to the standard paper tray and a limited range of paper sizes.

NOTE: Mac OS X 10.2 shipped with files for a number of printers, including those from Apple, Hewlett-Packard, Lexmark, Tektronix, and Xerox. To install a PPD file, just drag it to the proper folder. You'll find it via the following hierarchy: Library>Printers>PPDs>Contents>Resources> en.lproj (for the English language version). You can obtain PPD files from the manufacturer, sometimes using a special installer provided by the manufacturer, or from Adobe's Web site at: www.adobe.com/products/printerdrivers/macppd.html.

7. Click the red button to close the window. At this point, all your available printers should appear in the main Printers window.

8. To select a default printer (the one normally selected when you want to print a document), click the name of the printer to select it, and then choose Make Default from the Printers menu (or press Command+D). The name and icon of the default printer will be listed in bold and will be the first item shown in

3. Mac OS X User Preferences

Chapter 3   Mac OS X User Preferences

printer dialog boxes. However, you'll still be able to pick other printers connected to your Mac or your network directly from the Page Setup and Print dialog boxes.

NOTE: *Jaguar will always make the last printer you selected the default, so you may have to switch the settings if you prefer another to be your default.*

9. You can remove a printer from the Printers window at any time by selecting the printer's name from the list of available printers and clicking Delete.

10. Depending on the make of your printer, you may be able to configure other options by selecting it and choosing Configure from the Print Center toolbar, or Printer Info from the Printers menu. In the case of a PostScript laser printer where several versions of a particular model are available, you can tell Mac OS X whether your unit has such things as extra paper trays, the ability to duplex or print on both sides of the page, or a built-in hard drive on which to store fonts.

11. After you've completed setting your preferences, click the close box or choose Quit from the application menu to close the program.

If you have no more printers to add, you will not see Print Center again until you print a document. Then, its icon will show up in the Dock. Click the Dock to bring up a status display of your printer queue, where you can monitor your print jobs and remove or stop processing of specific documents. This window is very similar to the one shown in Apple's desktop printer window from earlier versions of the Mac OS.

NOTE: *When a job is being printed from a Mac OS X application, Print Center's Dock icon will display the number of pages remaining to be processed in the current document. If there's a problem with a job, you'll see an onscreen prompt and an exclamation point within the Printer Center icon.*

Chapter 4

Introducing the Mac OS X Finder

If you need an immediate solution to:	See page:
Setting Finder Preferences	103
Keeping Folder Views Consistent	103
Setting Viewing Preferences	105
Changing Finder List View Columns	108
Resizing Columns in Column View	109
Customizing the Finder's Toolbar	109
Using the New Finder on a Day-to-Day Basis	111
Moving a File	111
Copying a File	111
Making an Alias	111
Creating Favorites	112
Accessing Contextual Menus	112
Ejecting a Disk	113
Using the Get Info Window	114
Taking Screenshots	115
Finder Keyboard Shortcuts	116
Using the Finder to Burn CDs and DVDs	116
Restoring Classic Mac OS Application Switching	118

Chapter 4 Introducing the Mac OS X Finder

In Brief

Although the Mac OS has been upgraded time and time again since it debuted in 1984, there has been one constant—the Finder, Apple's famous file-access and management software. Although it has been enhanced and refined over the years, its basic look and goals have persisted substantially unchanged.

Not so with Mac OS X. The Finder (shown in Figure 4.1) has metamorphosed into a totally new application, bearing more than a passing resemblance to the file viewer for the NeXT operating system and even some of the Mac shareware programs that have been introduced over the years. In fact, it can even find the stuff on your Mac without launching a separate program. At the same time, however, it retains characteristics of the Finder you know and love, although some contents appear in a very different form.

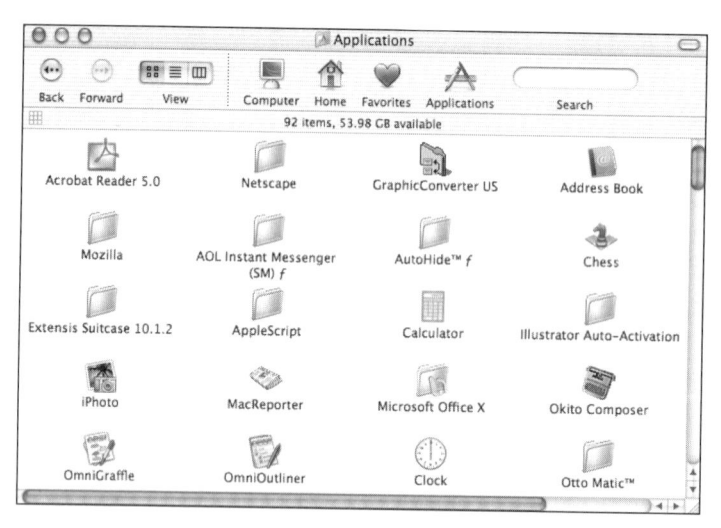

Figure 4.1 The Mac OS X Finder, the 10.2 edition, retains basic elements from the original Mac Finder, but in an entirely new uniform complete with a search field.

In Brief

NOTE: *Greg's Browser is another application that offers a similar look in some respects. This file-viewing or browsing program is produced by the folks responsible for Kaleidoscope, a popular shareware program that alters the entire appearance of the Mac with various themes. However, neither Greg's Browser nor Kaleidoscope are Mac OS-bound as of the time this book was written, though you can continue to run the former from the Classic environment. The authors of Kaleidoscope won't have an easy job migrating to Apple's newest operating system, saying, "We intend to make a version of Kaleidoscope for Mac OS X. However, unlike applications which can be Carbonized, low level hacks like Kaleidoscope need to be completely rewritten for Mac OS X."*

Aside from the function of the new Finder, there's plenty to be said about its form. Using Apple's Quartz imaging technology, as enhanced by Quartz Extreme on Macs with high-energy graphic cards, the new Finder is carefully crafted from an artistic standpoint. You can drag it Finder windows across the screen in real time; the image is anti-aliased, with clearly defined corners that cast a shadow behind them as the image is dragged across the desktop.

NOTE: *In moving from Mac OS X 10.1 to 10.2, Apple has refined the interface somewhat. Buttons appear thinner, more sharply defined, and drop shadows surrounding Finder and document windows are slimmer. Pull-down menus are no longer quite as translucent, so items behind them don't intrude near as much.*

Despite the surprisingly new look and feel, however, you'll see more than a passing resemblance to the traditional or Classic Mac OS Finder. The basic functions—viewing the contents of a hard drive, as well as opening, copying, and moving files—are, of course, little different despite the highly changed Aqua interface. But in some respects, the way you look for files may be substantially changed; and, as you'll see later on in this chapter, you have more options with which to customize the Finder's look and feel. To start with, look at the ways in which you can now view your files with Mac OS X's Finder. To change the display motif, simply click one of the three small View buttons at the left end of the Finder window. Here's what they do, from left to right:

- *Icon View*—This is familiar territory again (see Figure 4.1); it's quite similar to the way you examine files with the original Mac Finder. Each Finder item is identified by a unique icon, ranging from the simple folder picture to a far more complicated rendering for some applications. You just double-click any item to open it.

- *List View*—The icons in List View (see Figure 4.2) are small (unless you change the Finder option to make a larger icon, as explained in the "Immediate Solutions" section titled "Setting Viewing Preferences," later in this chapter). As with previous

4. Introducing the Mac OS X Finder

Chapter 4 Introducing the Mac OS X Finder

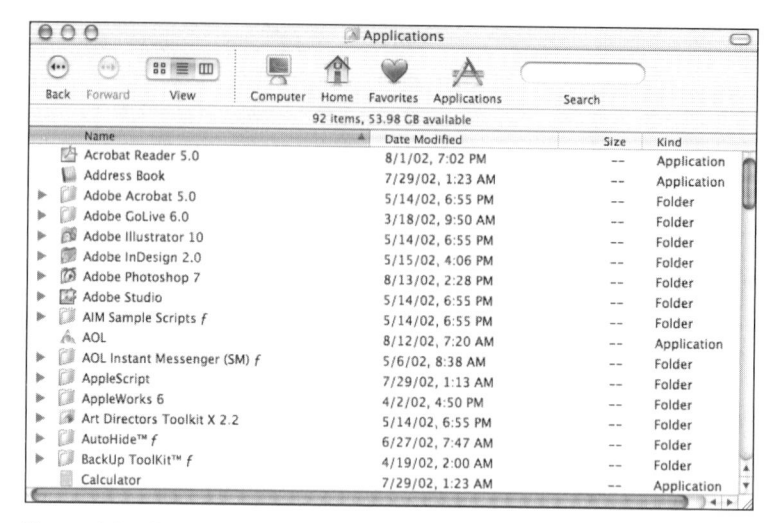

Name	Date Modified	Size	Kind
Acrobat Reader 5.0	8/1/02, 7:02 PM	--	Application
Address Book	7/29/02, 1:23 AM	--	Application
▶ Adobe Acrobat 5.0	5/14/02, 6:55 PM	--	Folder
▶ Adobe GoLive 6.0	3/18/02, 9:50 AM	--	Folder
▶ Adobe Illustrator 10	5/14/02, 6:55 PM	--	Folder
▶ Adobe InDesign 2.0	5/15/02, 4:06 PM	--	Folder
▶ Adobe Photoshop 7	8/13/02, 2:28 PM	--	Folder
▶ Adobe Studio	5/14/02, 6:55 PM	--	Folder
▶ AIM Sample Scripts f	5/14/02, 6:55 PM	--	Folder
AOL	8/12/02, 7:20 AM	--	Application
▶ AOL Instant Messenger (SM) f	5/6/02, 8:38 AM	--	Folder
▶ AppleScript	7/29/02, 1:13 AM	--	Folder
▶ AppleWorks 6	4/2/02, 4:50 PM	--	Folder
▶ Art Directors Toolkit X 2.2	5/14/02, 6:55 PM	--	Folder
▶ AutoHide™ f	6/27/02, 7:47 AM	--	Folder
▶ BackUp ToolKit™ f	4/19/02, 2:00 AM	--	Folder
Calculator	7/29/02, 1:23 AM	--	Application

Figure 4.2   You see more items in a Finder window when you choose the List View option.

versions of the Mac OS, the contents of a disk or folder are displayed as a list, in four distinct categories: Name, Date Modified, Size, and Kind. You can use the Finder List View preferences to add or remove categories. To open an item, just double-click it.

TIP: It's easy to change the sorting order in List View. Just click the title of the category under which you want the listings sorted. Normally, items are sorted by name; but if you click Date Modified, Size or another category, the list will be organized in that fashion. Click the arrow at the right of the Name or Date Modified category to reverse the sorting order.

- *Column View*—This choice is new for Mac OS X, although as mentioned, it is not unfamiliar to users of the NeXTSTEP operating system or some shareware file-browsing programs (such as Greg's Browser, mentioned earlier). It gives you a full hierarchical view of the contents of a folder, from left to right (see Figure 4.3). Just click an item to see its contents, which are displayed at the right. If you click a file or application icon, a graphic preview describing the item you selected is displayed. This viewing method is ideal for navigating deeply into nested folders without having to produce endless numbers of open folders on your Mac. In addition, if you click a folder in one of the two rightmost columns, the view shifts to the left.

In Brief

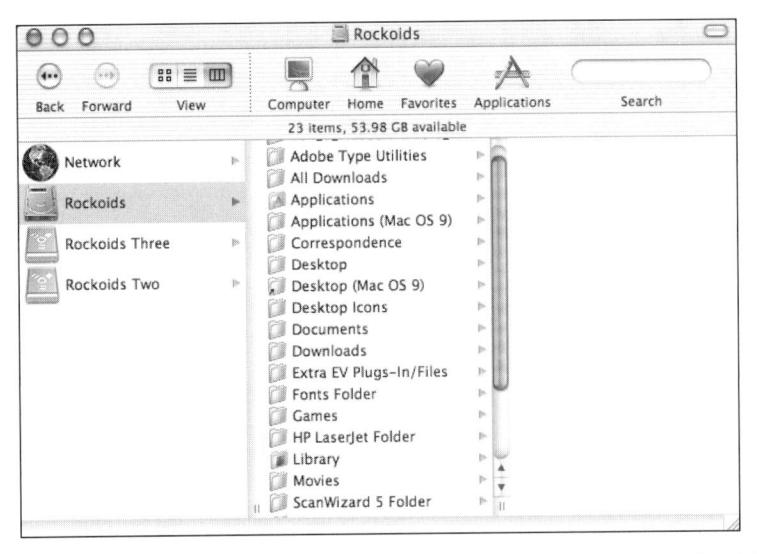

Figure 4.3 Click once on an item at the left to see the contents at the right.

> *TIP:* There are other file browsers available, if you decide the Finder's not your cup of tea. Among the selections, SNAX offers an enhanced viewing interface. Macintosh Explorer X more or less mimics the file viewing features of Windows. You can find these and other offerings at versiontracker.com.

Additional Finder Navigation Features

After you've opened a folder, you can Command+click the title bar to produce a pop-up menu to see the direction (path) of your folder navigation and access the higher-level folders through which you've traveled. This feature is a carryover from earlier Mac OS versions. You can also move back through previous folders one at a time (regardless of path) if you click the back arrow. In that sense, it works similarly to the back arrow of a Web browser.

> *TIP:* Just like a Web browser, the back arrow takes you to the previously viewed window, and the forward arrow to the next one, and like a browser, it is grayed out if there is no next window. If you prefer the Classic Mac OS Finder, just click the little rectangular button at the upper right (or press Command+B) and the toolbar will vanish and the Finder will spawn new windows whenever you open a disk or folder.

Chapter 4 Introducing the Mac OS X Finder

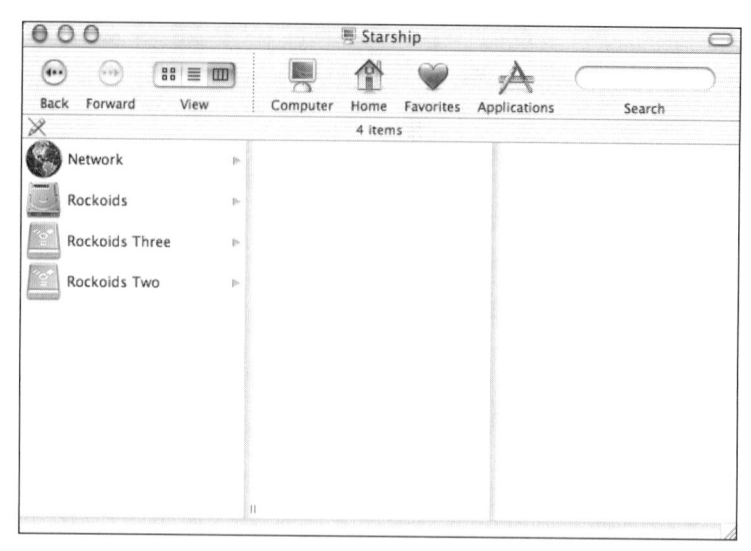

Figure 4.4 The Computer toolbar button takes you directly to your disks and servers.

Visiting the Finder's Toolbar

Another highly useful feature of the Mac OS X Finder is a colorful customizable toolbar, which gives you one-click buttons (or icons) to provide fast access to specific folders, files, or other features (depending on what choices you make). Let's start with the four icons at the right of the separator bar, because the other two were explained earlier:

- *Computer*—This is the Mac OS X Finder's display for the disk icons that also inhabit the desktop (see Figure 4.4). When you click this button, you'll see icons for available drives and a Network icon, to access network or Internet-based services. Disk icons will differ, depending on the type of drive, such as a fixed drive, FireWire drive, or CD. The iPod, for example, when the cute little jukebox player is put in FireWire disk mode, has a typically unique icon that's instantly recognizable. The name on the title bar will reflect the name you've given your Mac (a name that can be changed in the Sharing preference panel).

- *Home*—The Home folder is part of the multiple-user feature of Apple's operating system, which is designed for multiple users. When you click this button, you'll see the directory that contains your personal file folders in your User's folder. Figure 4.5 shows the standard layout, neatly categorized for convenient organization of your stuff. In the Shared folder, you place files that you want to share across a network when file sharing is activated.

In Brief

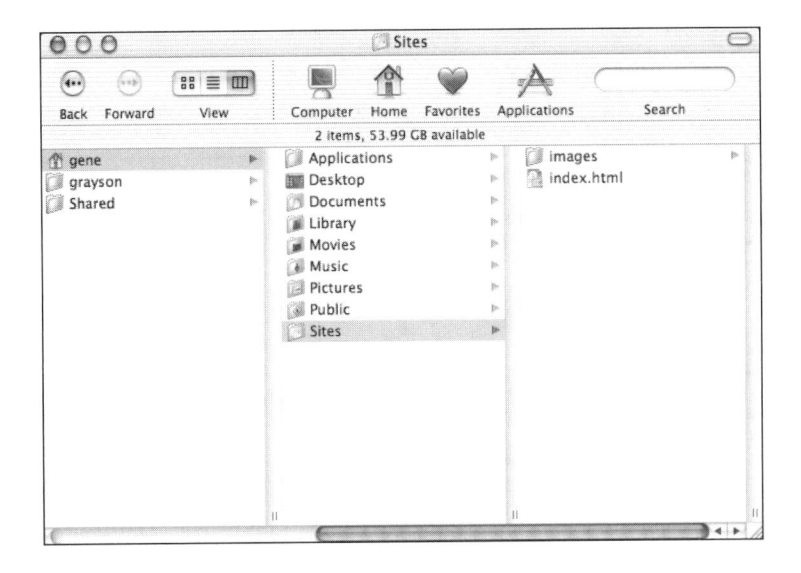

Figure 4.5 Several folders make up a user's personal Home directory under Mac OS X.

Each user of your Mac gets a separate set of folders for their personal settings and files

NOTE: The desktop you create and the preferences you make apply strictly to your session. If another user creates an account on your Mac and logs in, that user will have a separate set of user preferences, their own desktop and even personal files.

- *Favorites*—Probably the closest equivalent of what you could do with the Classic Apple menu, this locale can be used as a repository for items you want to access again and again. By default, it has aliases to your personal Documents folders, but you can easily add more. I cover this topic in more detail in the "Immediate Solutions" section of this chapter.

- *Applications*—This folder, shown in Figure 4.6, is meant to be the repository for all your installed Mac OS X programs (although they can run if put elsewhere). This rigidity is useful from an organizational standpoint, because you don't have to hunt all over your Mac's drive for a specific program.

TIP: Don't want the Finder's toolbar to intrude on your Mac's desktop? No problem. Just choose Hide Toolbar from the View menu, press Command+B, or click the little oval icon in the upper-right corner of the Finder window. If the toolbar has already been hidden, the View menu displays Show Toolbar instead; the keyboard combination stays the same. When you hide the toolbar, the Finder acts like a Classic Mac OS Finder, and double-clicking on an item

95

Chapter 4   Introducing the Mac OS X Finder

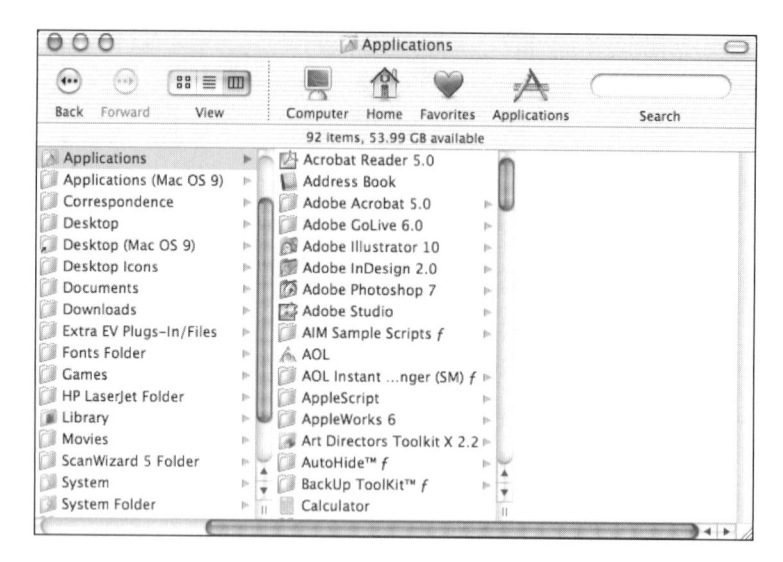

Figure 4.6   This Applications folder includes the standard applications that are distributed with Mac OS X, plus a number I've installed.

spawns a new Finder window rather than showing everything in one window. Double-clicking with the Command key pressed produces the same result.

The New Finder Menus

The Mac OS Finder has had essentially the same display options from day one. But certain elements have changed with Mac OS X, and in some respects, the changes are drastic. In this section, I cover the new menu bar commands and how they differ from the previous versions of the Mac OS.

There is, for example, an Apple menu (shown in Figure 4.7). However, the application menu is now situated at the left side of the menu bar rather than the right.

Although the Apple menu looks the same, you'll notice some big changes in the contents. Part of this is the result of the elimination of the Finder's Special menu. All those commands, and some extras, are now available system-wide in the Apple menu. So, you don't have to return to the Finder to activate these functions.

NOTE: If you use a Classic application, the Apple menu you see is the old one, from your Classic Mac OS System Folder. And it can be configured just as before, by dropping items into the Apple Menu Items folder, within that System Folder. But those tools aren't available, as you'll see for the Jaguar variant.

In Brief

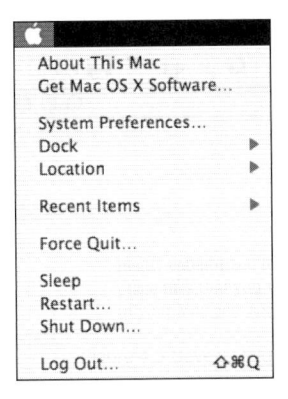

Figure 4.7 A familiar menu, but in a new guise.

Here's the list of the Apple menu features:

- *About This Mac*—Very little is different here. Choose this command to see a window displaying the Mac OS X version you are using, the amount of memory installed, and the kind of processor your Mac has. The big change is that the amount of virtual memory is no longer listed, because virtual memory is a full-time function and is never turned off. If you click the More Info button, it'll launch Apple System Profiler (see Figure 4.8), an application that can display all of your installed hardware and software.

TIP: *Mac OS X version numbers are also classified by build numbers, which are used by Apple's Mac OS X development team to catalog the process. Just click the version number in the About This Mac window to see the actual build number. On some Macs, a third click will produce your computer's serial number. Either way, once you've gone through the options, the next click takes you back to where you started.*

- *Get Mac OS X Software*—Select this command to be taken to a page on Apple's Web site where you can order new programs for your Mac. This is one of the few concessions to commercialization in Mac OS X (as distinct from Microsoft Windows XP, which includes a number of links to sites where you can take advantage of commercial offerings for specific features, such as working with digital photos).

- *System Preferences*—Access the System Preferences application from here.

- *Dock*—Configure the settings for the famous Dock, such as whether you'd like to hide it, magnify the icons when you pass the mouse over them, anchor the Dock in a different position, and so on. Chapter 5 covers this subject in more detail.

4. Introducing the Mac OS X Finder

97

Chapter 4 Introducing the Mac OS X Finder

		Apple System Profiler					
	System Profile	Devices and Volumes	Frameworks	Extensions	Applications	Logs	

▼ Software Overview

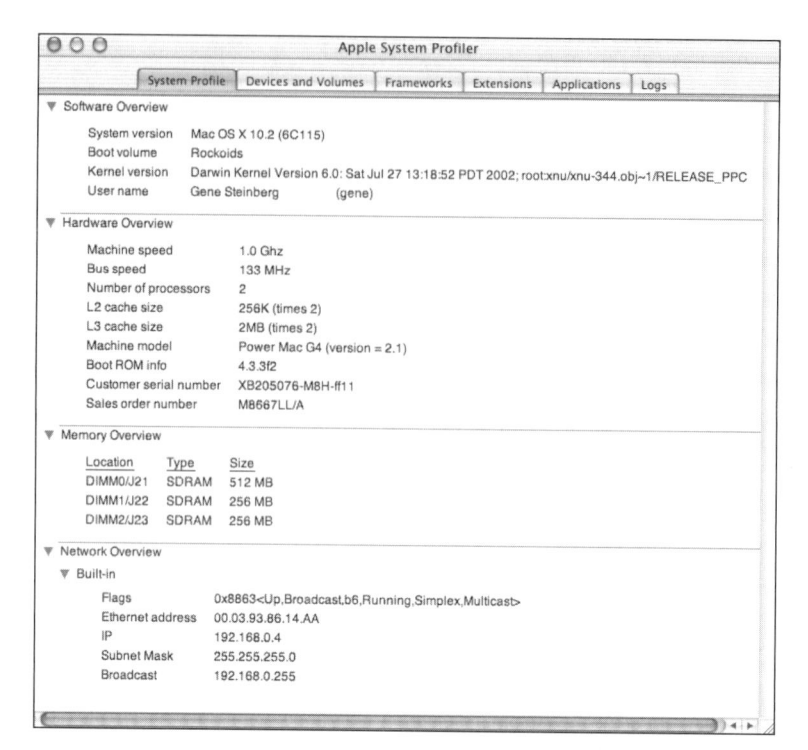

    System version   Mac OS X 10.2 (6C115)
    Boot volume   Rockoids
    Kernel version   Darwin Kernel Version 6.0: Sat Jul 27 13:18:52 PDT 2002; root:xnu/xnu-344.obj~1/RELEASE_PPC
    User name   Gene Steinberg   (gene)

▼ Hardware Overview

    Machine speed   1.0 Ghz
    Bus speed   133 MHz
    Number of processors   2
    L2 cache size   256K (times 2)
    L3 cache size   2MB (times 2)
    Machine model   Power Mac G4 (version = 2.1)
    Boot ROM info   4.3.3f2
    Customer serial number   XB205076-M8H-ff11
    Sales order number   M8667LL/A

▼ Memory Overview

Location	Type	Size
DIMM0/J21	SDRAM	512 MB
DIMM1/J22	SDRAM	256 MB
DIMM2/J23	SDRAM	256 MB

▼ Network Overview

    ▼ Built-in

        Flags   0x8863<Up,Broadcast,b6,Running,Simplex,Multicast>
        Ethernet address   00.03.93.86.14.AA
        IP   192.168.0.4
        Subnet Mask   255.255.255.0
        Broadcast   192.168.0.255

Figure 4.8   Click a tab to bring up a display for that category of information. The first screen focuses strictly on the overall system profile, from serial number to hardware address.

- *Location*—Location may be the watchword for realtors, but it's also a feature of Mac OS X that lets you customize network and Internet setups for different locales. It is especially helpful if you move your Mac from place to place (invaluable with an iBook or PowerBook). Chapter 8 covers this feature in more detail.

NOTE: By default, Mac OS X is multihoming, which means it can automatically switch between a single set of network and ISP hookups, including an AirPort network, Ethernet network, and dial-up connection.

- *Recent Items*—A carryover from the Apple Menu Options software of previous Mac OS versions, this feature displays up to 10 recent applications and documents in the submenu by default, or up to 50, each, courtesy of the General preference panel in the System Preferences application.

- *Special menu items*—The remaining five items—Force Quit, Sleep, Restart, Shut Down, and Log Out—are Special menu–type commands moved to the Apple menu for convenient access

98

without returning to the Finder. You can also access the Force Quit dialog box via the Command+Option+Esc keystroke.

TIP: Commands with one or more letters beginning with the Command (or Apple) key are keyboard shortcuts you can use to access a feature without using the mouse.

Following is a list of how the remaining menus have changed:

- *Application menu*—As mentioned, the application menu has been moved. In addition, the name of an application is now in bold (see Figure 4.9) for clear identification. When you click the application menu, you'll see commands that apply to that program. Another new feature of Mac OS X is the Services submenu, which gives direct links to programs that extend the features of the one you're using; you can, for example, take a selected text passage that's actually a URL and open the site in a Web browser window. You can use the various hide options to hide the program in which you're working or to hide other programs for a cleaner desktop. The biggest change is the Quit command; it has now moved from the File menu to what Apple feels is a more logical location—the application menu. Empty Trash is also found under the Finder's application menu.

NOTE: Older, Classic Mac applications will still have their Quit commands in the File menu, and their application menus will still appear in the accustomed spot at the right side of the menu bar.

TIP: If you hold down the Option key while selecting another application's window, all windows for other programs are hidden from view; the exceptions are applications that run in the Mac OS 9 or Classic environment. The Show All feature in the application menu reverses the effect. This feature works the same as in earlier versions of the Mac OS.

- *File menu*—The Finder's File menu (see Figure 4.10) isn't much different from the one in Mac OS 9. The big change is the modification

Figure 4.9 The Finder's application menu has new features for Mac OS X.

of the Get Info window to provide a far greater range of settings and an Open With command that allows you to select a different application to open a specific document. It has some of the same functions, plus some new ones I'll get to shortly. The other notable changes include: Command+N now produces a new Finder window, and the keyboard command for a new folder is Command+Shift+N. To make an alias, you press Command+L (Command+M previously). You now use Command+M to minimize a window and consign it to the Dock. (Don't ask me to explain the wisdom of changing things in this fashion; I just work here.)

> NOTE: Some of the readers of the previous editions of this book suggested that the Command+L combination also signifies the fact that, under Unix, what we call an alias is referred to as a link. Makes sense.

- *Edit menu*—Some things have remained nearly the same. The Edit menu, shown in Figure 4.11, is functionally identical to the Edit menu of older versions of the Mac OS, except for one big addition: You can actually copy a file or folder from the Finder in addition to text or a picture object. You do so in the same way you would in Windows. This technique lets you copy these items without having to navigate or manipulate Finder windows to allow for a normal drag-and-drop operation. What's more, the Undo command also affects the last copy or move operation.

- *View menu*—The first three options (see Figure 4.12) simply mirror those available in the Finder itself. You can select to view items as icons, as a list, or as columns. The other choices let you hide a Finder window's toolbar, customize the Finder's toolbar, or set view options. I explain the latter in detail later in this chapter.

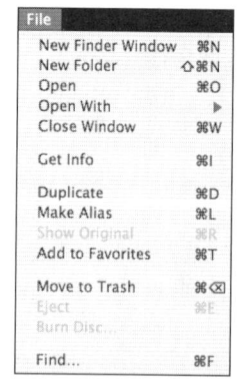

Figure 4.10   New keyboard commands and a new Get Info window highlight major changes to the Finder's File menu.

In Brief

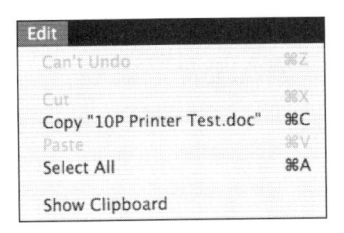

Edit	
Can't Undo	⌘Z
Cut	⌘X
Copy "10P Printer Test.doc"	⌘C
Paste	⌘V
Select All	⌘A
Show Clipboard	

Figure 4.11 The contents of Mac OS X's Edit menu have not changed from the menu in Mac OS 9.

- *Go menu*—This menu inherits at least some elements of the original Apple menu in Mac OS X (see Figure 4.13). Four of the first five choices mirror the standard toolbar options in the Finder, plus add the ability to bring up your iDisk, part of Apple's Mac suite of online subscription services. The Recent Folders option provides a submenu of recent Finder folders you've accessed. Another new command to the mix—Go To Folder—lets you type the actual path of a folder in order to bring it up. An example would be "/users/<your username>", which would immediately transport you to your Home directory. The Connect To Server option accesses a shared volume (Mac OS, Windows, and Unix, courtesy of built-in SAMBA and NFS support), whether it's on a local network or on the Internet.

- *Window menu*—This menu is found in many applications. It first appeared in Mac OS 9.1 and has been carried over to X's Finder (see Figure 4.14). The second option—Minimize Window—shrinks an application or Finder window to the Dock. Bring All To Front makes all open Finder windows accessible (you'll use this option if the windows were previously hidden from view). The items at the bottom of the display are the names of the Finder windows presently open. Select the one you want to bring to the front.

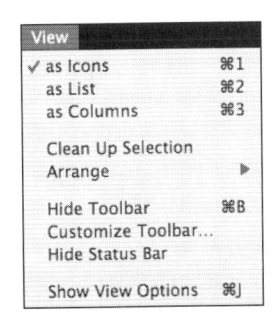

View	
✓ as Icons	⌘1
as List	⌘2
as Columns	⌘3
Clean Up Selection	
Arrange	▶
Hide Toolbar	⌘B
Customize Toolbar...	
Hide Status Bar	
Show View Options	⌘J

Figure 4.12 Choose the manner in which Finder contents are displayed from this menu.

Chapter 4 Introducing the Mac OS X Finder

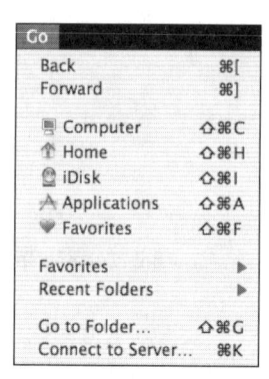

```
Go
Back                ⌘[
Forward             ⌘]

💻 Computer         ⇧⌘C
🏠 Home             ⇧⌘H
💿 iDisk            ⇧⌘I
📂 Applications     ⇧⌘A
⭐ Favorites        ⇧⌘F

Favorites           ▶
Recent Folders      ▶

Go to Folder...     ⇧⌘G
Connect to Server... ⌘K
```

Figure 4.13 The Forward and Back features shown in the Go menu operate in the Finder's Column View mode.

NOTE: If you click Mac's desktop, the Zoom Window and Minimize commands will be grayed out so don't get alarmed.

- *Help menu*—This menu is just what the name implies. Most of the information that Apple provides about Mac OS X is available here, brought up in a convenient browser window, rather than in a printed document and a lot of it requires knowing the right material to search. (But at least you have this book to learn the rest.) In addition, just about every Mac application has some sort of Help support.

NOTE: The original documentation for the Mac OS that Apple provided in the 1980s consisted of large books. When Mac OS X first came out, the basic information was distilled to a booklet of less than 32 pages. It shrunk to just 19 pages, plus the cover, for Jaguar.

```
Finder Preferences

Show these items on the Desktop:
  ☑ Hard disks
  ☑ Removable media (such as CDs)
  ☑ Connected servers

New Finder Window shows:
  ○ Home
  ● Computer

  ☐ Always open folders in a new window
  ☐ Keep a window's view the same when
    opening other folders in the window

  ☑ Show warning before emptying the Trash
  ☐ Always show file extensions
```

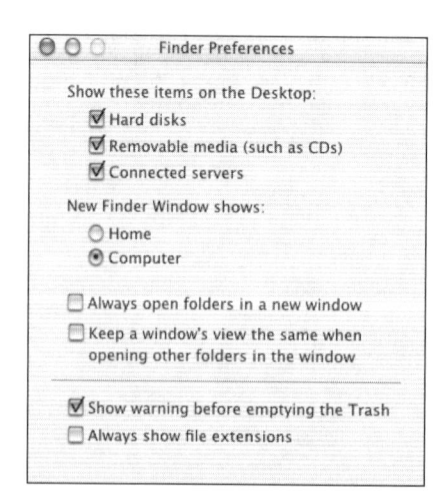

Figure 4.14 Adjust the display of Finder windows from this menu.

102

Immediate Solutions

Immediate Solutions

Setting Finder Preferences

As with any feature of Mac OS X, there's no need to customize or alter the new Finder. You can continue to use it in its pristine form if you prefer, running applications on your Mac, surfing the Net, and so on, without needing to alter its appearance. But there are many ways to customize its look and feel.

By default, the Mac OS X Finder displays its contents in single-window mode. You open the contents of a folder in the Finder, and the Finder replaces the contents in the window with the contents of the opened folder. If you want to change this functionality to the way it worked with the previous Mac OS, where opening a folder opened a new Finder window, you can take any of the actions described in the following sections.

Keeping Folder Views Consistent

This preference setting establishes the default behavior when you double-click a folder icon to open it. Just follow these instructions:

1. Choose Preferences from the Finder's application menu to bring up the Finder Preferences window shown in Figure 4.15.

NOTE: I will cover the desktop-related preferences in Chapter 5, so don't be concerned that they aren't all tackled in this chapter.

2. If you need to change a Finder preference, click on the appropriate checkbox to select or unselect an item. The following Finder preferences are available:

    - *Show these items on the Desktop:*—Do you want to see the icons for mounted disks or network shares or not? Its up to you.

    - *New Finder Window shows:*—Choose Home directory or Computer (which displays available drives and network shares if you decide to turn that item off for desktop display).

103

Chapter 4 Introducing the Mac OS X Finder

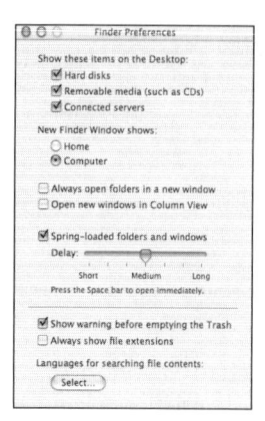

Figure 4.15 Select the way the Finder displays the contents of an opened folder.

- *Always open folders in a new window*—This option makes Finder behavior similar to what you had in the Classic Mac OS. Opening a new folder will spawn a new Finder window. Although you will probably prefer the Mac OS X way of doing things when you get used to it, you aren't forced to stay with single-window behavior.

- *Open new windows in Column view*—Take your choice. Leaving this box checked supports the new viewing option available in Jaguar, but you can stick with icon or list view like the Mac OS of old if you prefer.

- *Spring-loaded folders and windows*—Move the slider to adjust the delay. When you drag an item over a folder, it'll open after a short delay, allowing you to see the contents. Holding the item over a folder within the parent folder will soon open that as well. Regardless of the interval you set, and it's a matter of personal taste, you can use the spacebar key to open it immediately.

- *Show warning before Emptying the trash*—This setting mirrors what you could do with the Classic Mac OS. When you uncheck this box, there will be no warning when you attempt to empty the trash from the Finder's application menu. If you want a second chance before deleting, you may want to leave this option checked.

Immediate Solutions

TIP: *Another way to avoid the Finder's warning about emptying the Trash is simply to click the Trash icon in the Dock and, while it's held down, choose Empty Trash from the pop-up menu. There will be no backing out here and the only wait to avoid removing something is in the event you do not have permission to trash that file.*

- *Always show file extensions*—By default, Mac OS X will hide file extensions unless you specifically add them to a file name (except for some applications that do it anyway regardless of how the Finder is configured). However, the file extensions will always be present for cross-platform compatibility, except for older Classic applications that do not offer the option to put a file extension at the end of a file name. For a simpler Finder and desktop, you may want to leave this option unchecked, as it is by default.

NOTE: *Languages for searching file contents is only useful if your needs for Jaguar extend beyond your default language selection.*

---

3. When you're finished configuring the Finder, click the red light button to close the window and save your preferences. From here on, all folder windows opened within a Finder window will inherit the same view setting, whether Icon, List, or Column View.

NOTE: *No, I didn't skip the other preference settings. I discuss the rest of the Finder Preferences options in Chapter 5, because they relate to how the desktop is displayed.*

If you don't want to make a permanent change in the way an opened folder displays, just hold down the Option key to reverse the behavior when you double-click a folder icon. That way, you can decide on the fly whether a new Finder window is opened.

Related solution:	Found on page:
Setting Finder Preferences	103

Setting Viewing Preferences

As with the previous Mac OS Finder, you can set the way items appear in the Finder, but your options are far more extensive under Mac OS X. Settings can be made on a global basis, so they apply to all open Finder windows and all display categories, or to a specific Finder window. The options you have depend on the view setting, so each will be explained separately:

105

1. With a Finder window with Icon View selected open, go to the View menu and choose Show View Options, or press Command+J. The window shown in Figure 4.16 appears.
2. Click the All windows if you want all Finder windows to inherit your changes, or This window only to affect just the selected Finder window. You can choose from the following changes:

   - *Icon Size*—By default, icons are fairly large—at least compared to older versions of the Mac OS. You can move the slider to change their size as you look on.

   - *Text size*—Is 12 point too large for you? You can select from 8 point to 16 point.

   - *Label position*—At the bottom or to the right of the icon? Your call.

   - *Icon Arrangement*—Whether you like your desktop automatically arranged or not, the choice is yours. Just click the appropriate radio button. The default—None—means you can place your disk, file, and folder icons as you wish, anywhere in a Finder window. The Always Snap To Grid option is similar to what you find in some drawing programs. The icons are spaced by an invisible grid, at fixed distances apart. The Show item info option will display the size of a picture file and the number of items in a folder. Show icon preview does what the name implies, providing preview images of picture files. The final option—Keep Arranged By—gives you a pop-up menu of sort sequences: Choose from Name, Date Modified, Date Created, Size, and Kind.

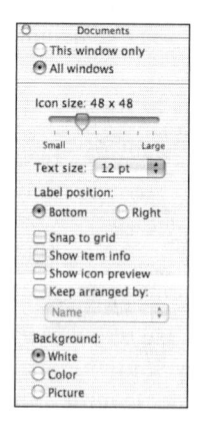

Figure 4.16   Choose a global or individual preference here.

Immediate Solutions

NOTE: Is something missing? Well, in the Classic Mac OS, you could also view by Label and apply a specific color to an item for convenience or appearance. However, as you'll see in the next section, you have another option in the Finder's List View that may be a suitable replacement.

- *Background*—This Finder feature is new for Mac OS X. You can leave it set at White if you prefer the default background. Otherwise, you can give your Finder background a unique color by clicking the Color radio box, then on the box at the right to bring up an Apple Color Picker (see Figure 4.17). After you click the kind of color adjustments you want, moving the sliders with the mouse changes the selected colors. When you click the final Background option—Picture—you'll see a Select button that you click to bring up the Open dialog box. There, you can choose a picture.

After you've made your settings, you can click the close button to activate the changes. Or, go to the next section if you want to make further Finder changes.

NOTE: Remember that a background color or picture you select will apply only to the selected Finder window unless you click All windows.

3. If you prefer the Finder's List View, the View Options window is different (see Figure 4.18). You can, as you did with the Mac OS 9 Finder, choose an icon size, and, beginning with Jaguar, a text size, just as in Icon View. Under Show Columns, choose which categories you want displayed. The most interesting option here

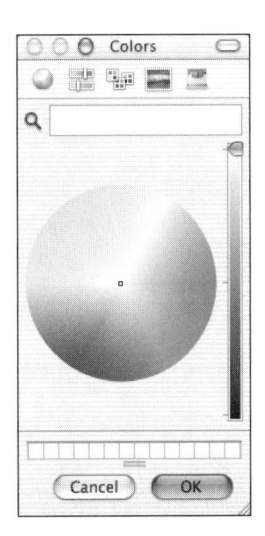

Figure 4.17 Drag sliders to produce a color scheme that suits your taste.

107

is Comments which allows you to sort by the Finder comments you place in the Get Info window, a useful way to keep tabs on documents that require special priority or are needed to meet a deadline. The Use Relative Dates option gives you such selections as Yesterday and Today (but never Tomorrow—that was a bad joke!). As with the Classic Mac OS, Calculate All Sizes will give you the size of items in a folder, but at the expense of slowing down performance. The final option is Icon Size. Make it small or make it large—those are all the choices you have.

TIP: You can still view the size of an item without checking it in the View Options window. Instead, select a folder and choose Get Info from the Finder's File menu, and you'll see a visual display of the size in the first or General category.

4. When you're finished setting Finder preferences, click the close button.

Changing Finder List View Columns

To change the sort order, simply click on a column title; when an arrow appears, you can reverse the sort order. The Jaguar Finder can be customized extensively in List View. In addition to adjusting preferences as to which categories are displayed, you can further modify it in two ways:

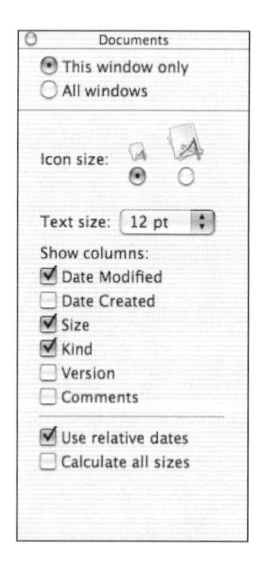

Figure 4.18 A new variation of View Options shows up in List View.

- *Resize Category Lists*—Move the mouse between the columns, and you'll see the cursor change to reflect two opposite pointed arrows. Then, simply click and drag the column to resize it. The change you make is reflected in all new Finder windows.
- *Change Order Of Categories*—You can also move an entire category into a new position in the Finder window. Just click and drag the Finder category to its new location, and let go of the mouse button. This change can be made in all categories except Name. After a category is in a new position, the change is reflected in all new Finder windows.

Resizing Columns in Column View

If you opt for the Finder's Column View, you aren't locked into the default size either. Just click the two vertical lines at the bottom in the space between columns and drag back and forth to resize the columns. If you hold down the Option key, the change is confined to the column at the left.

The changes you make in this fashion will affect all the new Finder windows you open in Column View.

TIP: Want to see how much disk space is left on a drive or removable disk? Choose Show Status Bar from the View menu. From here on (until you select the option again—it's now labeled Hide Status Bar), you'll see a display showing both the number of items in a Finder window and the amount of available disk storage space.

Customizing the Finder's Toolbar

You can simply hide the Finder's toolbar, if you prefer the old ways of the Mac OS—the ability to open a folder and spawn a new Finder window. If you decide to keep the toolbar open, you can customize it in a variety of ways. Here's how it's done:

1. Choose Customize Toolbar from the Finder's View menu to bring up a convenient window displaying lots of cool icons (see Figure 4.19).
2. To add an icon, drag it to the toolbar. You can use the Separator icon to categorize your selections.

NOTE: If you add too many icons, you can drag the resize bar to the right to make the Finder window wider; otherwise, you can click the arrow at the end of the toolbar to access the remaining icons.

Chapter 4   Introducing the Mac OS X Finder

[screenshot of Customize Toolbar window]

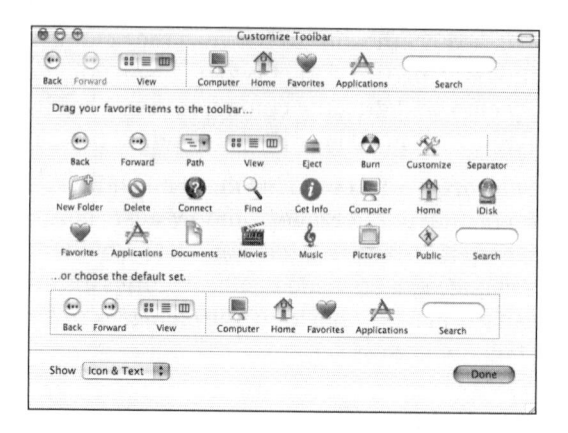

Figure 4.19   Go ahead and drag icons to the toolbar.

3. To limit the toolbar icon to either the icon or the text, make your choices from the Show pop-up menu at the bottom of the screen.

TIP: *If you make a mistake and put the wrong icon in the toolbar, you can click and drag it to a new position.*

4. Click the Done button to complete the process.

TIP: *To restore the toolbar to factory issue, click the default set on the Customize Toolbar screen and drag it to the toolbar. It will replace the contents.*

NOTE: *Don't fret if the icon you want to add isn't shown. You can drag and drop any application, file, or folder icon onto the Finder's toolbar, and it will be added immediately.*

After you've changed the toolbar, you can remove an icon by holding down the Command key and dragging the icon off the toolbar. The default toolbar icons, however, cannot be removed this way. They can be removed only when you bring up the Customize Toolbar screen.

TIP: *The Path icon in the Customize Toolbar screen is useful. When you add it to the toolbar, clicking it will show the folder path of the item you've selected, which lets you quickly move to higher folder levels. Of course, holding down the Command key and clicking the title of a Finder window gets the same result.*

Immediate Solutions

Using the New Finder on a Day-to-Day Basis

After you have configured the Finder the way you want, you'll find that it's easy to get accustomed to the new way of handling your Mac's files and even the somewhat restricted organizational requirements. In the next few pages of this chapter, I discuss basic file management techniques. For the most part, you'll see they aren't terribly different from earlier versions of the Mac OS.

Moving a File

To move a file from one folder to another, simply click to select the file, and then drag it to the new folder. You might need to open another Finder window to move between widely disparate folders.

Copying a File

To copy a file from one folder to another, hold down the Option key as the file is being dragged to its new location. This copying function is automatic if you are moving an icon from one drive's folder to a folder on another drive.

TIP: *If the folder to which you want to copy a file is buried deep and not easily accessed, just use the Copy command in the Finder's Edit menu to copy the entire file or folder. Now open the folder into which you want to copy the item, and then choose Paste from the Edit menu to put a copy there. This is, of course, similar to the way it happens in the Windows platform. You can also simply drag the file atop a folder or Finder toolbar icon, and hold it, and it'll spring open. Then you can place it inside or put atop another folder within the parent folder.*

Making an Alias

An *alias* is a pointer to the original file that aids in file navigation (it's similar to a shortcut in Windows or a symbolic link under other Unix-based operating systems). You can put the alias where you want without having to depend on Mac OS X's organizational structure for applications and other files. Many Mac users place aliases for files on the desktop, putting them a double-click away from launching without having to burrow deep through nested folders.

To make an alias, simply select the item, and then choose Make Alias from the Finder's File menu or press Command+L. The alias can then be moved or copied to your preferred location.

TIP: *To make an alias of an item and move it at the same time, simply drag it to its new location while holding down the Command and Option keys.*

4. Introducing the Mac OS X Finder

111

Finding a File

Why call it Finder if you don't use it to find something? That's an old argument, since the search tools were always available as a separate function. However, with Jaguar, there's an integrated Search function in the toolbar (you can remove it if you customize the toolbar icons, of course). To locate an item in the folder or disk you've opened, just enter its name or part of the name, in the search field. A list of likely candidates will appear (see Figure 4.20) in a browser window, labeled by relevance.

NOTE: You can still bring up a search screen via Command+F, with more elaborate searching options. I'll cover that topic, plus Apple's redesigned version of the Sherlock search application, in Chapter 7.

Creating Favorites

The Favorites folder is a great place to keep the documents you use over and over again. To make an item appear in that folder, select it and then choose Add To Favorites from the Finder's File menu or press Command+T. Favorites are available as a default Finder toolbar item, or via the Go menu.

Accessing Contextual Menus

This feature, which debuted with Mac OS 8, produces a pop-up menu related to the item selected. It's quite similar to the right-click feature

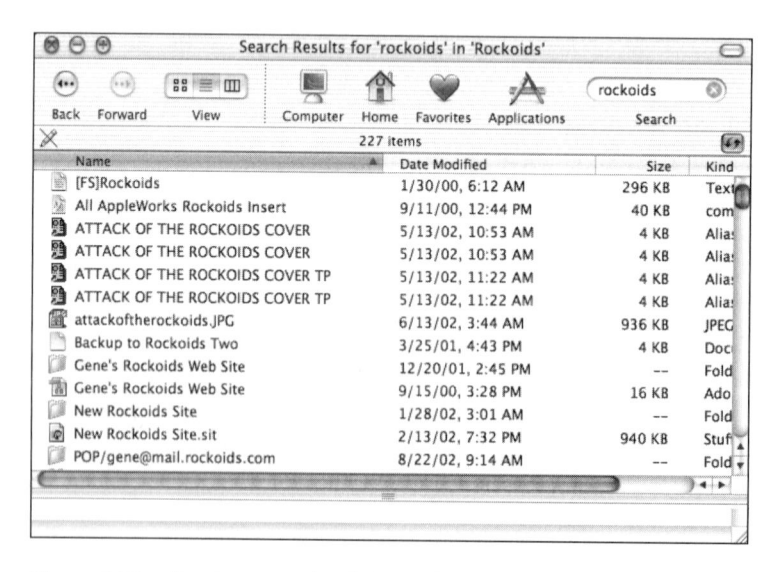

Name	Date Modified	Size	Kind
[FS]Rockoids	1/30/00, 6:12 AM	296 KB	Text
All AppleWorks Rockoids Insert	9/11/00, 12:44 PM	40 KB	com
ATTACK OF THE ROCKOIDS COVER	5/13/02, 10:53 AM	4 KB	Alias
ATTACK OF THE ROCKOIDS COVER	5/13/02, 10:53 AM	4 KB	Alias
ATTACK OF THE ROCKOIDS COVER TP	5/13/02, 11:22 AM	4 KB	Alias
ATTACK OF THE ROCKOIDS COVER TP	5/13/02, 11:22 AM	4 KB	Alias
attackoftherockoids.JPG	6/13/02, 3:44 AM	936 KB	JPEG
Backup to Rockoids Two	3/25/01, 4:43 PM	4 KB	Doc
Gene's Rockoids Web Site	12/20/01, 2:45 PM	--	Fold
Gene's Rockoids Web Site	9/15/00, 3:28 PM	16 KB	Ado
New Rockoids Site	1/28/02, 3:01 AM	--	Fold
New Rockoids Site.sit	2/13/02, 7:32 PM	940 KB	Stuf
POP/gene@mail.rockoids.com	8/22/02, 9:14 AM	--	Fold

Figure 4.20 Here's a search window with likely responses to your search request.

Immediate Solutions

of Windows. To access the contextual menu, select an item and hold down the Control key.

NOTE: Some third-party input devices, from such companies as Kensington, MacAlley, and Microsoft, have extra buttons that you can program to access the contextual menus. This will be familiar territory for Windows users.

Ejecting a Disk

This function works the same as in previous versions of the Mac OS, with a small exception. The normal behavior is to drag the disk icon to the Trash. You can also press Command+E after the drive has been selected. The Put Away command (Command+Y) has been removed. When you drag a disk icon to the Trash, the icon for the Trash changes to an eject symbol, no doubt a response to complaints from user interface experts that you aren't trashing a disk when you eject it.

TIP: If you have an Apple Pro keyboard, you can also use the Eject key or F12 to remove a CD or DVD from the desktop and eject it in a single operation. Having a drive access key on the keyboard is especially useful for many Apple computers that do not have CD eject buttons on the drives themselves.

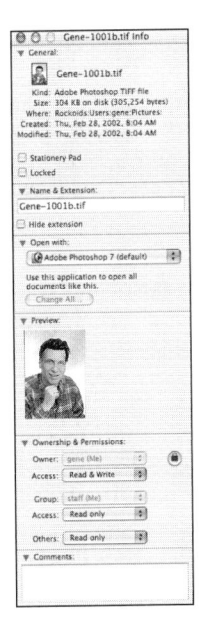

Figure 4.21 The Get Info window, with all categories expanded, lets you access information about a file, change the application that will automatically open a document and fix permissions.

113

Using the Get Info Window

In older versions of the Mac OS, you'd use the Finder's Get Info window to adjust a program's memory allotment and get information about a program's version. The Mac OS X variation (see Figure 4.21) adds a host of new features, but eliminates one, at least with native software: the ability to change the memory given to a program. You no longer need to do so under Mac OS X, because the operating system dynamically allocates the memory a program requires. What you see depends on the kind of item selected. A document will provide one set of options, an application another. Here are the basic features, each disclosed or hidden by a click of the triangle:

> **NOTE:** When you use the Get Info command with a Classic application, you will still see a Memory option, which you can use to control allocation of memory for that application. Mac OS X's superior memory management doesn't help your older Mac applications.

- *General*—Expanded by default, it displaysThis screen presents general information about a selected item, including its location and size. If you've selected an application, it shows the version information.

- *Name & Extension*—For documents, this option lets you change the file's name and specify whether the file extension that applies to that document will appear.

> **NOTE:** The Get Info window is context sensitive, and will have options that depend on the kind of file that's selected. For example, if you bring up a Get Info window for a folder or disk, you'll have a Content index option with an Index Now button that will catalog text for the Finder's search feature.

- *Open with*—If you've selected a document, this option lets you change the application that launches that document, or all documents of the same type.

- *Languages*—This window (available for Mac OS X applications only) shows the languages supported by an application. You can uncheck some of them, if you wish; doing so might improve performance at the expense of limiting the application's ability to handle multilingual material.

- *Preview*—This feature appears only when you select a document icon. You can use it to view a preview image of the document.

> **NOTE:** If the icon you've selected belongs to a Classic application, all you'll see is an enlarged picture of its icon.

- *Ownership and Permissions*—Use this window to set access privileges to the selected item. That way, you can extend the range of users who can view that item via file sharing. You have three categories of users. One is the Owner (you), the second is the Group, and the third is Others. In each case you can set privileges for Read & Write or Read Only access to a disk, folder or separate file.

NOTE: On some items, such as files reserved for the system or that belong to another user, you will have to click the lock and enter an administrator's password into a prompt to change privileges.

TIP: You can easily change the icon for an item. Just select the item, bring up the Get Info window, and paste the new icon atop the previous icon in the General Information window. This is best done for drives and folders. Changing a file icon may make it difficult to visually identify which application opens the file.

- *Comments*—Like the Classic Mac OS Finder, you can place comments here that can be used to identify a file, or specify a priority. Although it doesn't quite replace Finder Labels from Mac OS 9 and earlier systems, you can use this feature, along with the ability to sort by Comments in List View, to keep tabs on important files.

Taking Screenshots

In previous versions of the Mac OS, you could take a screenshot of the contents of your desktop or a selected item via simple keyboard shortcuts. Most of theses features are present in Jaguar. Here's a brief run-through of the built-in screen capture capabilities:

- *Command+Shift+3*—This is the original shortcut. When you press this combo, a picture of your entire screen is captured and saved as a PDF (Adobe Acrobat) file. The file itself will be named Picture 1, Picture 2, and so on, and placed on your desktop.

- *Command+Control+Shift+3*—This awkward combination also captures the entire screen, but puts the data in the clipboard, so you can paste it within an open document window via the Paste command.

- *Command+Shift+4*—This combination changes the cursor to a crosshair. Just drag the cursor across the area you want to capture. When you release the mouse, the area is captured as a screenshot and also saved as a PDF file on your desktop, named Picture 1, and so on.

TIP: *Press a spacebar after typing this combo and you'll be able to automatically select a specific window to capture without having to manually drag the cursor around it (a process very easy to do incorrectly). The cursor will take on the image of a camera, and when you click on a window, only that window will be captured.*

- *Command+Control+Shift+4*—This combination also lets you select an area for capturing. The saved area is stored in the clipboard for pasting into another application.

TIP: *Mac OS X includes Grab, in the Utilities folder, which can also do timed screen grabs and save the results with the file name you choose. However, if you do lots of screen captures, my personal recommendation is Snapz Pro X, a shareware application available from Ambrosia Software (www.ambrosiasw.com). I used this program to capture all the illustrations in this book.*

NOTE: *If you want to convert your screen shot to a different format, just use Apple's Preview application, in the Applications folder, to convert to any of the popular image formats, such as JPEG and TIFF.*

Finder Keyboard Shortcuts

You don't have to mouse around in Mac OS X. A liberal number of keyboard shortcuts can help you navigate without a mouse click. Some of these, in fact, will work in many of your Mac programs. The shortcuts listed in Table 4.1 will work in the Finder as listed.

Using the Finder to Burn CDs and DVDs

When Apple got the message and added built-in CD burners, it also added a feature that lets you burn your CDs from the Finder. Under Mac OS X, it works essentially the same as in your Classic Mac OS:

1. Insert a blank CD, CD/RW, or DVD-R disc into the drive. After a short time in which the optical media is analyzed, you'll see a screen prompt where you can prepare the media for copying data (see Figure 4.22).

NOTE: *If you need to format the CD/RW, Disk Utility will open to the proper screen, where you can erase it.*

WARNING! *The Finder's CD burning feature works primarily with Apple's built-in CD and DVD burners (DVD-R support requires the SuperDrive), and a moderate selection of supported third-party devices. If you want to see the current supported list, check with Apple's iTunes site at www.apple.com/itunes. Whatever drives are supported by iTunes will, in large part, work with Finder-level disk burning as well.*

Immediate Solutions

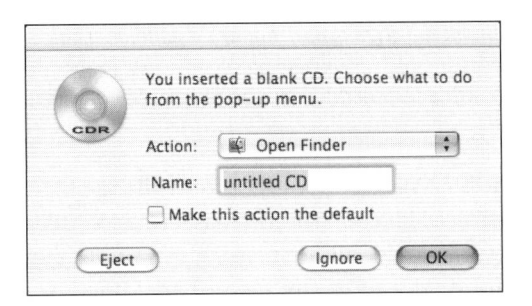

Figure 4.22 What do you want to do with the blank optical media you inserted?

2. Name your CD or DVD and then choose what you want to do next from the pop-up menu. For data CDs, you'll want to open the Finder, so you can move files to the CD icon that will be created. If you want to make a music CD, you can select the option in the menu to open iTunes.

3. With your selections made, click OK to complete the initial setup process. In a few seconds, you'll see an icon on your Mac's desktop identified by the type of media you prepared.

4. Drag the files you want to copy to the optical disc's icon.

WARNING! Depending on the kind of media you use, you'll be limited to 700MB for an 80-minute CD, 650MB for a 74-minute CD, and 4.7GB for a DVD-R. You will receive a Finder warning if you attempt to copy over too many files.

5. If you want to organize the layout of the optical media before it's burned, open its window and reorder the icons as you like and the position of the window. This will simplify locating the material on the disc later.

6. After the layout is set up, choose Burn Disc from the Finder's File menu to begin the process. You'll get a final warning from the Finder to confirm that you really want to burn a disc.

7. After you OK the prompt, the disk burning process will begin, followed by a verification procedure in which the data will be read back to make sure that the data is good.

8. When the disc burning process is complete, you can insert more media and continue to create CDs or DVDs.

WARNING! Not all optical media work with all drives, even if the labels say they're compatible. If you run into consistent problems with a specific brand, where burning is halted or the media isn't successfully verified, try another brand. If you're using a

4. Introducing the Mac OS X Finder

117

third-party CD or DVD burner, contact the drive manufacturer for additional help, because Apple won't provide direct support for its disc burning feature except with an Apple computer that shipped with a factory CD or DVD burner.

Restoring Classic Mac OS Application Switching

When Mac OS X was first unveiled, sharp criticisms were leveled at the disappearance of the oh-so-useful application-switching menu, which was located at the right end of the menu bar. Although the Dock (see Chapter 5) is meant as a substitute, there is another alternative, in the form of a donationware (meaning you send a voluntary donation) utility. ASM (see Figure 4.23) is installed as a System Preference component. Once installed, it can be configured to restore an application-switching menu in its accustomed spot.

Two of the most interesting features of ASM are the ability to hide other applications automatically courtesy of its Single Application Mode, so you see only the active application. This is a sure way to reduce screen clutter and confusion, especially if you have a smaller display on your Mac. The other key feature is Classic Window Mode, in which all windows in an open application come forward, rather than just the one you select (the Mac OS X way).

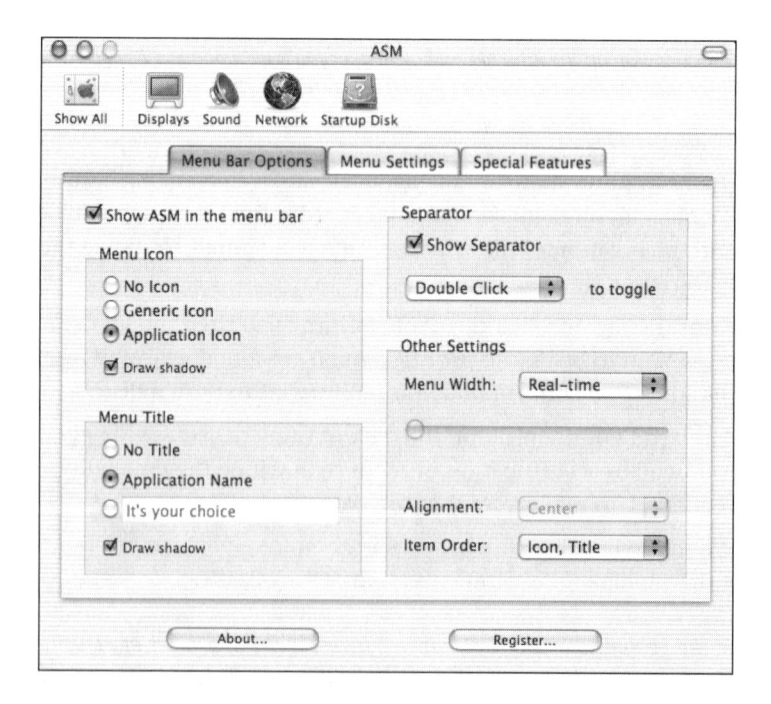

Figure 4.23   This handy utility, one regularly used by the author, restores a cherished Mac OS feature.

Immediate Solutions

ASM also sports an extensive array of adjustments to the way the application menu looks, from icon size to whether labels and icons appear, or just one or the other. You can also suppress application hiding for individual programs, in case you need to see both applications at the same time (or even use a modifier key such as Shift to suppress the feature altogether).

Related solution:	Found on page:
Using the Dock	135

Chapter 5

Mac OS X Desktop Management

If you need an immediate solution to:	See page:
Setting Dock Preferences	129
Setting Desktop Preferences	132
Setting Finder Preferences	134
Using the Dock	135
The TinkerTool Alternative	138
Making Your Mac OS X Desktop as Cluttered as Ever	139

In Brief

Ring out the old, ring in the new, the old saying goes. But Mac OS X is a bit of both. For example, the Mac OS X desktop looks very similar to the one from previous Mac OS versions. It has a decorative background pattern and, unlike the versions of the new operating system that were shown during the initial development process, the familiar icons for your hard drive are present and accounted for. But something appears to be missing. Where's the trash? As you've probably noticed, it's migrated to the Dock, which, in part, forms the main subject to be dealt with in this chapter.

The pristine desktop is part of the normal behavior of Mac OS X, but as you'll see in this chapter, it's not necessary to keep things neat and clean. One of the rights of the Mac user is to arrange, even clutter, a desktop to suit your taste, and the new Mac operating system, as with the Classic Mac OS, gives you lots of freedom to change background images and clutter it with icons to a fare-thee-well.

The Dock Dissected

Previous versions of the Mac OS gave you several ways to access a file quickly, whether a document, a folder, or a program. Apple has merged a number of these functions into a single taskbar—a colorful, almost cartoonish, and almost infinitely resizable palette of icons that resides at the bottom of your Mac's display (or elsewhere if you prefer, as you'll see shortly). It's called the Dock (see Figure 5.1).

NOTE: Although it's easy to find the Dock's roots in Windows, actually the Dock is more closely aligned to the original application-launching palette used for the NeXT operating system, on which Mac OS X is based.

Here's what the Dock replaces:

- *Apple menu*—The original Apple menu (see Figure 5.2) was the former repository of frequently used items and Control Panel access. It was immensely customizable, but doing so required a trip to the System Folder and then to another folder called Apple Menu Items. For Mac OS X, the Apple menu has gotten an overhaul, after disappearing entirely in prerelease versions (see Figure 5.3). It now incorporates the functions of the Finder's

In Brief

Figure 5.1 The Dock is a single location where you check and open applications, documents, and folders. Note the white separation line to divide the Dock into two usually unequal parts.

Figure 5.2 The original Apple menu was infinitely customizable and was easily set to reflect the tastes of its user.

Special menu, system-wide customization, and just the core of the recent items features of the previous version. The list of recent folders has been moved to the Go menu, as explained in Chapter 4. Control Panels have been replaced by the System Preferences application, which consolidates the various system settings into one program; it gets a featured spot in the Dock. I discussed setting your Mac OS preferences in detail in Chapter 3.

- *Control Strip*—Some Control Panel functions and settings for a number of applications were put in the Control Strip (see Figure 5.4), a floating palette that first debuted as a feature on the Apple PowerBook. It later spread to all Macs. Some of the functionality has been rolled into the System Preferences application, and other functions for a handful of preference panels, such as Airport, Display, Internet Connect and Sound, can be placed as system menu items on the menu bar.

Chapter 5 Mac OS X Desktop Management

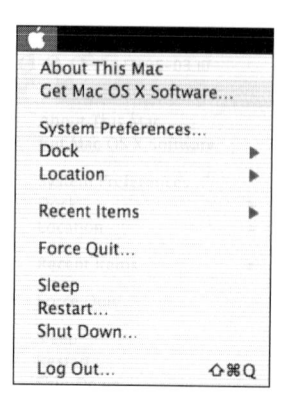

Figure 5.3 The new Apple menu is designed in a more rigid fashion, merging the old and the new and replacing the functions of the Finder's Special menu.

Figure 5.4 Depending on the programs you have installed on your Mac, the contents of the Control Strip will change; this version has lots of extras.

- *Application menu*—Part of the function of working with open applications stays in the menu bar, with the bold application menu now at the left of the screen. The ability to switch between open applications is now a function of the Dock.

NOTE: *If you prefer something more akin to the Control Strip of old, don't despair. Independent programmers have plenty of opportunities to get in the game. The OpenStrip shareware program is meant to replace some of the functions of the original Mac OS Control Strip. One popular application menu replacement is ASM, which deposits the same sort of application menu on the right side of the menu bar that you'd see in the Classic Mac OS. As with all such useful Mac OS X enhancements, you can find a good collection at the **VersionTracker.com** Web site (www.versiontracker.com/macosx).*

The Dock is divided into two parts, separated by a thin vertical line, and some of the icons have clearly identifiable functions. Here's a description of how they work:

- *Left side*—Application icons, including those representing open programs, stay here (see Figure 5.5).

- *Right side*—Icons representing documents, folders, servers, Web sites, QuickTime TV channels, and the Mac OS Trash exist on the right end of the Dock (see Figure 5.6).

124

In Brief

Figure 5.5 The items at this end of the Dock consist strictly of applications. Icons with the triangles beneath are open.

Figure 5.6 The rest of the icons you put in the Dock reside at the right, regardless of content.

Figure 5.7 This icon represents the Finder.

- *Finder*—Click this icon to open a Finder window (see Figure 5.7).
- *System Preferences*—As part of the Dock when you install Mac OS X, this icon allows you to set your Mac's preferences (see Figure 5.8). It replaces the Control Panels, at least in part.

TIP: Missing an icon? Although several application and document icons are part of the standard installation of Mac OS X, it's easy to drag them off the Dock. If you want an icon back, just locate the original icon for that item, which will usually be in the Applications or Documents folder, and drag it to the Dock.

- *Mail*—This icon represents Apple's powerful new email software (see Figure 5.9). When you receive email, you'll see a display on the Mail icon indicating the number of unread messages waiting for you. I'll cover this program in detail in Chapter 21.

Figure 5.8 Click this icon to launch the System Preferences application.

5. Mac OS X Desktop Management

125

Chapter 5 Mac OS X Desktop Management

Figure 5.9 This icon represents Apple's Mac OS X-exclusive email software.

NOTE: *The ability to display messages about an application in the Dock is something you'll find in many applications. If you're an AOL member and you're using the latest Mac OS X version, for example, you'll see numeric displays of the number of email and instant messages waiting. Mac OS X's Print Center will show you an icon indicating the number of pages waiting to be processed, or a warning exclamation mark if there's a problem with the print queue.*

- *Document*—This icon represents a document that's been placed in the Dock (see Figure 5.10).
- *Web Sites And Servers*—Another great feature of the Dock is the ability to store icons that link you to your favorite Web sites or provide direct access to a networked server (see Figure 5.11).
- *Minimized window*—When you click the Minimize icon in an open document window, the document shrinks to the Dock (see Figure 5.12). It remains there until you click it to restore or maximize the document window. This is a difficult effect to capture, and it took a clever little application, Andrew Welch's Snapz Pro X (shareware from **www.ambrosiasw.com** that is bundled with some new Macs) to capture it for posterity. Pressing Command+M, by the way, will also minimize a window.

Figure 5.10 When you add documents to the Dock, they'll look something like this.

In Brief

Figure 5.11　Whether a networked server or a favorite Web site, it's just a click away in the Dock.

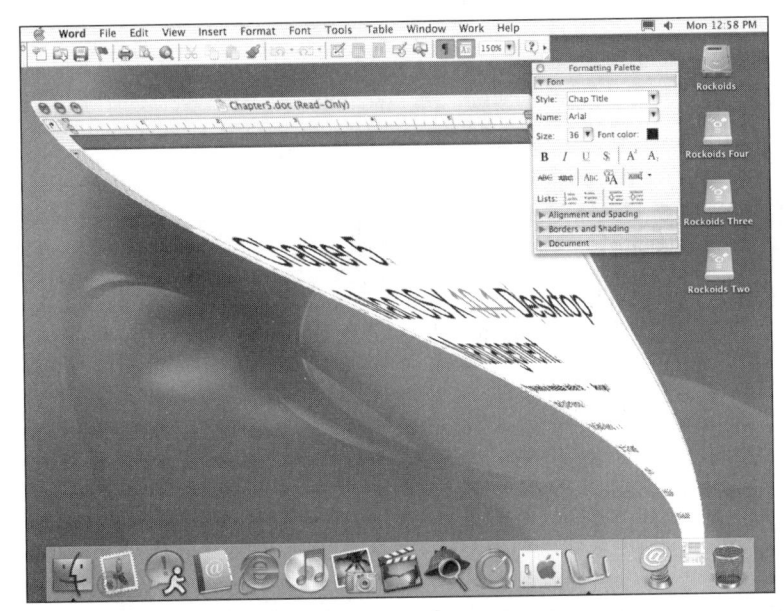

Figure 5.12　The Genie Effect ends with the icon lodging itself in the Dock.

TIP: *If you want to see the ultraslow Genie Effect demonstrated at Macworld Expos by Apple CEO Steve Jobs, hold down the Shift key when minimizing a document. You'll see the reverse effect with the same keyboard shortcut when you click an icon representing a minimized document in the Dock.*

- *Trash*—The Mac OS Trash is no longer a resident of the desktop (see Figure 5.13). It now always sits at the right end of the Dock.
- *Pop-up menus*—Click any item in the Dock and hold down the mouse button to see a pop-up menu related to that item; this is not the same as the contextual menus you see when you Control+Click an item. With a word-processing program, such as Word X, for example, you'll be able to directly access an open application window. The best effect occurs when you click a disk

127

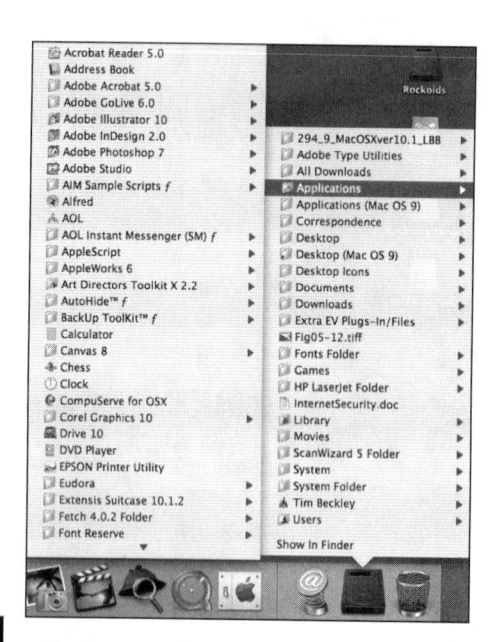

Figure 5.14 Up to five levels of pop-up menus can be displayed when you click and hold a folder or disk icon in the Dock.

or folder icon (see Figure 5.14). The end result is a menu with lots of submenus, similar in scope to what you used to see in the Apple menu. The display for a regular application is more pedestrian. Click the icon to access a Show In Finder command. If the application is open, you'll be able to quit it from the pop-up menu.

TIP: Some applications, such as Apple's iTunes, display application controls in the Dock-based pop-up menus. That way, you can access functions without going to the program itself. Apple has opened the programming interface for this feature, so you can expect to see a number of programs supporting it over time.

NOTE: The pop-up menu you see when you click a Dock item is similar to what you get when you command click an item to see its contextual menu, but it doesn't require a modifier key and it's strictly limited to items placed in the Dock.

Immediate Solutions

The Mac OS X desktop is ripe for change, and you'll be pleased to know it's quite possible to organize it in many ways depending on your particular needs. In the following pages, I'll describe the various desktop preferences and then cover how you can tailor your Mac's desktop to resemble the one used in prior versions of the Mac OS, or in ways you might not have imagined before. You'll also get a look at a third-party utility or two that will take the desktop farther than you might have expected.

Setting Dock Preferences

In Chapter 4, I discussed the Finder preferences, one type of preference you can establish under Mac OS X that may impact your desktop. Now I'll give you, as long-time radio broadcaster Paul Harvey says, the rest of the story. You can follow these steps to change the way your Mac's desktop and the Dock function:

1. To change Dock settings, choose Dock from the Apple menu and select Dock Preferences from the submenu. Doing so brings up the Dock settings pane from the System Preferences application (see Figure 5.15).

2. Set all or some of the following six Dock preferences:

    - *Dock Size*—This setting lets you configure the size of the icons by moving the slider. You're apt to find that the Dock is just too imposing on your Mac's screen unless you have a very large display, so you'll probably want to make it smaller.

    TIP: You can also resize the Dock by clicking the bar on the Dock that separates applications from documents and dragging it up or down. If you hold down the Option key while resizing the Dock, the Dock will default to fixed-sized icons, such as 32 pixels, 64 pixels, and 128 pixels. Otherwise, the adjustments are infinitely variable. When you Control-click the Dock, you'll have immediate access to its preferences.

    - *Magnification*—Select this checkbox to make the Dock magnify the icons as you drag the mouse over them (see Figure 5.16). It looks flashy, but it may be a little bit much after you use it for a while. The slider bar lets you decide how much the icons will expand.

129

Chapter 5   Mac OS X Desktop Management

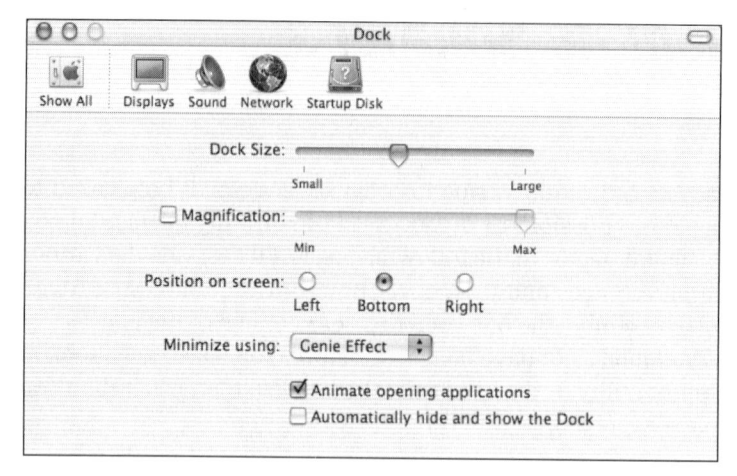

Figure 5.15   Change the look and actions of the Dock here.

Figure 5.16   The Dock's icons magnify when you drag your mouse over them.

- *Automatically Hide And Show The Dock*—The Dock sits above your open application windows, and you cannot grab anything beneath it, so this adjustment may be a great convenience. It's also a good way to save screen real estate. The Dock stays hidden unless you drag the mouse to the bottom of the screen to make it visible. You'll find this adjustment particularly useful for a smaller Mac's display.

TIP: You can also make the Dock hide itself when the mouse isn't near by pressing Command+Option+D. Repeating the command will undo the change. This shortcut won't work if you're in a Classic application or in a program that has a keystroke that duplicates this one.

- *Position On Screen*—This is the answer to many requests to move the Dock from its bottom position. You can center it at the left or right end of your screen, if you prefer (see Figure 5.17).

130

Immediate Solutions

Figure 5.17 Right or left—make the Dock go where you want.

NOTE: As you'll see later in this chapter, you can pin the Dock at the end of the screen or even at the top, courtesy of a third-party utility such as TinkerTool. This handy System Preferences add-on also can change other Dock settings, such as the one that follows.

- *Minimize Using*—The Genie Effect is regarded by some as totally cool, but others regard it as totally annoying. This setting lets you choose a scaling effect instead, which rapidly reduces an item in size and puts it on the Dock. You may prefer this option if you have a slower Mac and the Genie Effect slows things downeven more.

- *Animate Opening Applications*—When this feature is shown at a presentation, it looks cool; but the idea of having an application's icon bounce up and down in the Dock may grow tiresome. You can switch off the option here and wait for programs to open for you without warning.

NOTE: The Dock provides another level of animation, where an icon bounces up and down to alert you that another application is calling for your attention. It may mean there's a problem with the application or, for example, that a Web site opened in Internet Explorer cannot be retrieved. This option can't be switched off (although some programs, such as Print Center, manage to limit alerts to an icon that doesn't bounce).

131

3. After you've set your Dock preferences, you can quit the System Preferences application or make further settings, such as the one that comes next.

Setting Desktop Preferences

In addition to modifying the Dock in various ways, you can change your Mac's desktop backdrop or control a handful of Finder preferences to make your desktop take on more of the look and feel you like. To begin with, let's change the desktop pattern:

1. To change your Mac's desktop settings, launch System Preferences and click the Desktop preference panel. The dialog box shown in Figure 5.18 appears.

2. Select a picture from those displayed in thumbnail form at the bottom of the dialog box (use the horizontal scrollbar to see more).

3. Drag the image into the well or double-click it and, within seconds, your background image will change to the one selected.

TIP: If your new background doesn't appear right away, log out and log in again. This time, the changeover should work as you expect.

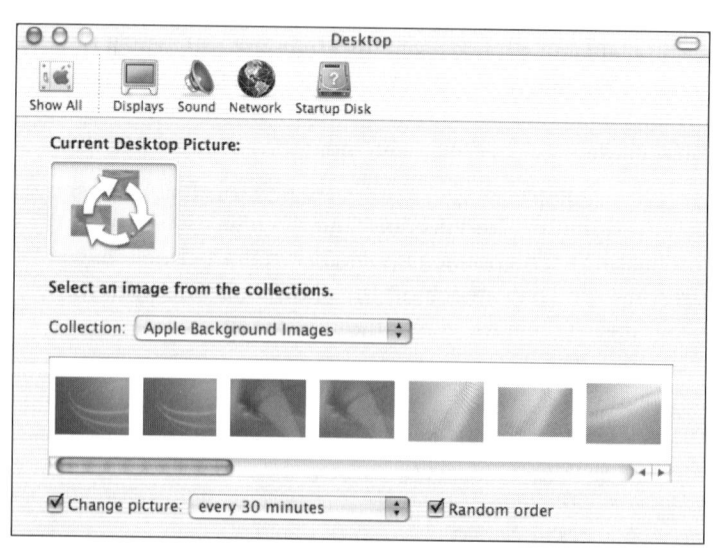

Figure 5.18 Alter the Mac's desktop backdrop here.

Immediate Solutions

4. If you don't see a background image that suits your taste, or if you want to use one of your own photos, click the Collection pop-up menu (see Figure 5.19) to see additional choices. The pictures in the folder you choose will appear in the Desktop preference dialog box in thumbnail form.

5. When you've made your selection, you can quit System Preferences or choose another preference icon for further changes.

NOTE: *You should be able to use just about any JPEG or TIFF image file as a background, but remember that a large or complicated image may take longer to display on your screen, particularly if you don't have the latest and greatest Mac with the fastest graphics accelerator. Should screen refresh slow down, pick a simpler image (or just try a few and see which work best).*

Can't settle on a single background picture? You can configure your desktop to automatically change at fixed intervals, when your Mac awakens or when you log in. Just click the Change picture checkbox and choose the interval from the pop-up menu (the default is every 30 minutes).

When you activate this option, the pictures from the selected collection will be used. Click Random order if you want pictures selected out of sequence.

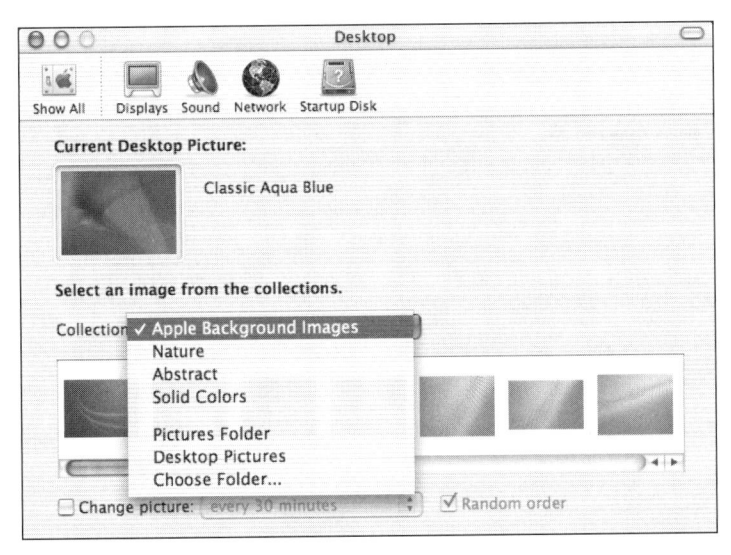

Figure 5.19 Pick a suitable source for desktop patterns from the ones on display.

133

Chapter 5 Mac OS X Desktop Management

Related solution:	Found on page:
Setting Desktop Preferences	58

Setting Finder Preferences

Once you've established the way you want the Dock to look and the desktop background that meets your needs, setting Finder preferences is the final step of the equation. Here's how it's done:

1. Click the Finder.
2. Choose Preferences from the Finder's application menu to bring up the dialog box shown in Figure 5.20.
3. Click a checkbox or button to establish your personal settings. Here are the changes you can make:

   - *Show These Items On The Desktop*—One of the controversial features of prerelease versions of Mac OS X was the fact that drive icons didn't show up on the desktop automatically. Now a clean desktop is an option. If you don't want certain items to appear automatically on the desktop, just uncheck the options for hard disks, removable media, or connected

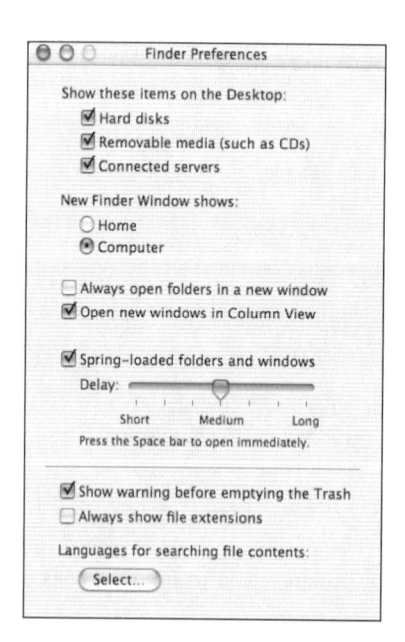

Figure 5.20 Click a checkbox to change your preference.

134

Immediate Solutions

servers. Even if you turn them all off, you can click the Computer icon in the Finder to show a display of available disks and servers.

- *New Finder Window Shows*—Choose whether a new window will go to your Home or Computer directory (Computer is the default).

- *Always Open Folders In A New Window*—When you check this option, Finder behavior is changed to that of the Classic Mac OS, in which opening a folder spawns a new Finder window, rather than display the contents in the existing Finder window. Checking this option is a sure way to increase desktop clutter, if that's what you want.

These options control how your Mac's desktop is populated under Mac OS X. If you want to go further and set the entire range of Finder preferences, including those nifty spring-loaded folders, refer to Chapter 4 for more information. When you're done, click the Close button to dismiss the Finder Preferences screen.

Related solution:	Found on page:
Setting Finder Preferences	103

Using the Dock

In day-to-day use, the Dock is highly intuitive. It provides clear status messages about your open applications and documents, and it can be, as explained previously, customized in many ways for your convenience. Here are some basic hints and tips for getting the maximum value out of the Dock:

- *Adding icons*—Because the Dock expands dynamically to accommodate the number of icons you've added, all you need to do is drag an icon to the Dock to have it display (the actual file, of course, remains where it was). The left side of the Dock carries your application icons. The right side handles the rest, such as documents, folders, links to servers and Web sites, and QuickTime channels. You can't put the wrong icon in the wrong side; the icon will only be accepted in the proper side of the Dock.

135

Chapter 5 Mac OS X Desktop Management

> **NOTE:** Icons in the Dock are not automatically sorted for you. You can click and drag them to new positions, depending on whether you prefer alphabetical order or some random sequence.

- *Application switching*—As explained earlier, open applications are indicated by a black triangle below the application's icon in the Dock. Click the icon of any opened application in the Dock to move directly to that program.

> **TIP:** To hide all other open application windows when opening a new one from the Dock, hold down the Command+Option keys while clicking any application icon. Hold down the Option key to hide just the application window from which you're switching (but not all windows opened with that application). The Show All command in the Desktop application menu brings back the windows.

- *Single-click access*—Just like the Launcher in older versions of the Mac OS, you can access any item in the Dock with a single click.

> **TIP:** You can use the keyboard to switch between open applications. Press Command+Tab to open the next application icon, as shown from left to right. Repeat the action to select other applications. To reverse the process, press Command+Shift+Tab.

- *Reordering icons*—To change the order of an icon in the Dock, click and drag it to its new position. You cannot, of course, put application icons on the right end of the Dock; but otherwise, feel free to reorder items as you prefer.

> **NOTE:** Did the application icon disappear? Some applications, such as Mac OS X's Print Center, stay open only as long as the print queue has a job being processed. After the processing is finished, the application automatically quits (except, however, if you double-click the print queue, in which case it stays open until you quit Print Center). It may take a few moments, however, for the actual document to finish, depending on the speed and the need for extra processing by the output device itself. The same vanishing effect holds true for the Classic environment; the Mac OS 9 icon vanishes when Classic has loaded (even though it remains active).

- *Removing icons*—Did you change your mind? You can discard a Dock icon you no longer need. Just click and drag it away from the Dock. In just a second, it will disappear in a puff of smoke, like magic.

> **NOTE:** You cannot remove the icon for an open application.

Immediate Solutions

- *Pop-up menus*—When you click and hold a Dock icon, you'll see a menu related to the contents of that icon. For Mac OS X applications, you have the option to jump to an open document window, to display the folder in which the item is located in the Finder, or to quit the application. In addition, some applications, such as Apple's iTunes, let you access additional control functions courtesy of the Dock, such as playing a song from your playlist or moving to other tracks on the list. This feature is optionally available to program developers, and you may see it in a specific application from time to time.

- *Dock notifications*—Are you trying to access a Web site while working in another program, and the browser needs to tell you the site can't be found or you have to OK a security window? Or, is there a problem with an application you need to know about? If you see a bouncing icon from an open application, click the icon to see what's up. Some applications, such as AOL, Mail and Print Center, will simply alter the Dock icon to present a notice, such as the number of messages waiting to be read in your mailbox or how many pages are still to be processed in a job queue.

NOTE: *Sorry, you cannot turn off the bouncing icon feature, even if you switch off the Dock preference to animate the process of opening applications.*

- *Dock icon shortcuts*—The Dock gives you a fast way to gain access to your hard drive. Drag a drive icon to the Dock and then click the Dock to see a hierarchical menu of the drive's contents. If that seems to be overkill, just drag a folder's icon to the Dock (such as your Favorites folder in your personal Users directory). The contents of that folder, up to five levels deep, are now just a click away from fast access.

TIP: *Another way to speed access to the Dock is to use the Full Keyboard Access feature, which is an option in the Keyboard panel of the System Preferences application. With this feature enabled (see Chapter 3 for details), the Control+F3 command will highlight the Dock for instant access to any Dock icon.*

Related solution:	Found on page:
Setting Keyboard Preferences	72

5. Mac OS X Desktop Management

137

The TinkerTool Alternative

If Apple hasn't implemented a feature, you can bet a third party will find a way. TinkerTool is a useful alternative (see Figure 5.21); it's a shareware utility that can configure a whole range of default preferences for Mac OS X. When installed, TinkerTool occupies the Others category in the System Preferences application.

The Desktop settings in TinkerTool include the following features that will enhance your desktop control far beyond the standard range of Mac OS X settings:

NOTE: *As with most System Preferences settings, TinkerTool can be configured to offer a separate set of options for each person who has a user account on your Mac.*

- *Finder Options*—The option to Show Rectangle Effect When Opening Files may make things slower on an older Mac, so you may want to turn it off. Other useful options include the ability to display hidden and system files normally invisible to the Finder, although Jaguar's clean install option minimizes its usefulness. The other feature, the ability to set a maximum number of label lines from two to three, helps in displaying lengthy Finder labels.

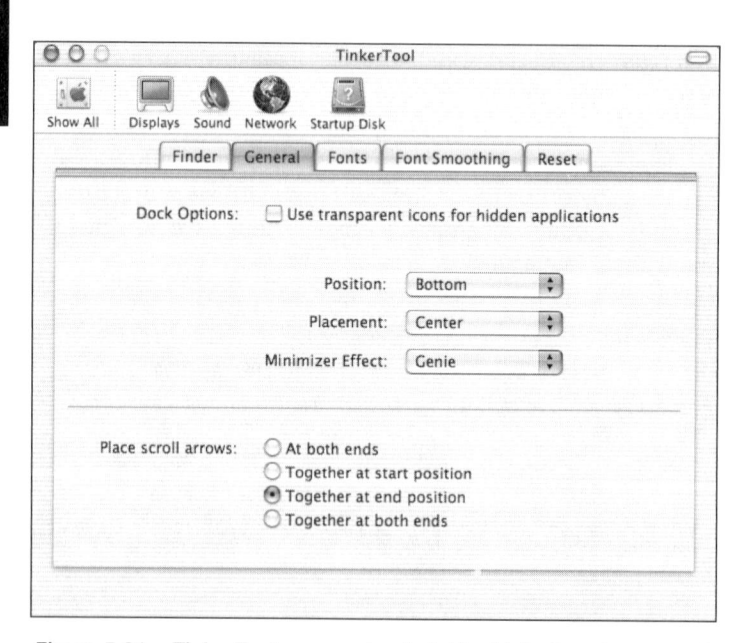

Figure 5.21 TinkerTool uses a simple tabbed interface to access its powerful features.

Immediate Solutions

- *Dock Options*—Even though Apple allows you to place the Dock at the left or right sides of your screen, TinkerTool adds the ability to place the Dock at the top or at any corner of the screen. In addition, a new Minimizer Effect called Suck-In displays a rapid shrinking motion when an open window is minimized. The Use Transparent Icons For Hidden Applications option will make it easier to see background applications that may be open on your Mac. You can also configure scrollbar arrangement beyond the two choices available in the General preference panel (at top and bottom and together).

NOTE: Many TinkerTool settings require a logout and a login (or a regular restart) to take effect. You'll see a message at the bottom of a TinkerTool settings window if this is required.

- *Other TinkerTool options*—Click a tab to see additional settings for TinkerTool. Other available options let you choose different default system fonts and sizes (another feature that not all applications support) and configure font smoothing beyond the 8 to 12 point range offered in Jaguar.

Warning: Don't assume your Mac OS X system enhancer is compatible with Jaguar simply because it worked in 10.1. Such utilities as ASM, Default Folder, an Open and Save dialog box utility, Mac Reporter and TinkerTool were all modified for Jaguar as a result of various incompatibilities. You'll always want to be sure you have the latest versions, especially after a major system upgrade.

Making Your Mac OS X Desktop as Cluttered as Ever

One of the good or bad features of Mac OS X, depending on your point of view, is the new desktop. It can be clean and uncluttered when you remove the disk and network volume icons. However, if you leave them intact, you are well on your way toward producing the requisite degree of disorder.

Under Mac OS 9.2.2, my Mac's desktop traditionally had about 100 items on it, ranging from mounted drives and available desktop printers, to files I need to send to my son's computer for our joint writing projects, to folders containing recent downloads, to files I need to access... well, one of these days. Every so often, I put most of these

139

Chapter 5 Mac OS X Desktop Management

files in another folder called, with no attempt at originality, Desktop Icons. The desktop is clear, at least for a few days, after which it becomes just as cluttered as before.

Apple has made a concerted effort to organize your desktop and file organization patterns under Mac OS X. The desktop is clear as water, unless you decide to pollute it with some icons. Here's how to return your Mac's desktop to its former glory:

1. In Mac OS X's rigid organizational system, applications are meant for the Applications folder and documents for the Documents folder. Mac OS X–savvy applications are meant to stay put, but if you hold down the Command+Option keys and drag the icon to the desktop, an alias is placed there.

NOTE: *The Command+Option shortcut also works with all files and Classic applications.*

2. After your application icons are on the desktop, go ahead and locate your favorite document files and place them there as well. A few minutes of clicking and dragging and, presto (see Figure 5.22), your Mac OS X desktop can be as cluttered as you wish, precisely as it was in previous versions of the Mac OS.

Figure 5.22   If your taste is for a busy Mac desktop, don't worry. Mac OS X will not prevent you from organizing it the way you want.

Chapter 6

Setting Up Mac OS X for Multiple Users

If you need an immediate solution to:	See page:
Setting Up Multiple-User Access	147
Editing a User Account	152
Setting Up Keychain Access	153
Checking and Using Your Keychain	155
Changing Keychain Settings	155
Running a Keychain on Another Mac	157
Coping with Problems Involving Keychains and Multiple Users	157
Suggestions for Setting Up Multiple Users for Use with Children	159

Chapter 6 Setting Up OS X for Multiple Users

In Brief

While it's true most Mac users are individuals, it has long been recognized that more than one person might use a single computer. Thus, beginning with Mac OS 9, Apple introduced a Multiple Users feature. It was an outgrowth of AtEase, a no-frills security program that allowed the owners of Macs to create a simplified user environment for children and inexperienced users. The program was popular in the educational environment because it gave teachers and system administrators the ability to restrict student access to certain files and disks on the Macs in their classrooms and computer labs.

NOTE: *In addition to being offered in workgroup form for network use, AtEase was bundled as standard equipment on many of Apple's mid-1990s consumer computers in the Performa series and used extensively at schools with Mac systems installed.*

Mac OS X extends the Multiple Users feature on a more professional level, allowing any Mac user with appropriate access privileges to easily configure his or her computer to offer a customized user experience. The great value of this feature is to give each user a personal workspace. As a result, those who work on your Mac can customize their Mac's desktop and Finder appearance to their needs without impacting the settings made by other users. They can also have a separate set of applications, documents, fonts, and other items, plus their own user settings, from mouse tracking speed to Dock location and keyboard options.

Mac OS X Multiple Users Features

Because it is based on Unix, Mac OS X is, at heart, a multiple-user system in its own right. Although it inherits some of the features that were first introduced in Mac OS 9, Mac OS X has its own unique variation. However, once you get used to its simplified user interface, you'll find that Mac OS X provides a fairly secure working environment with lots of options to help you set it up for all the people who will use your Mac.

Here are some of the basic features of Mac OS X that provide customized user environments and security:

- *You are administrator*—When you first install Mac OS X, you'll establish your user account as the administrator or owner of the computer. After you've set up your username and password, you

In Brief

can add users to and remove users from your system, and you can unlock and use certain system-wide preferences that are available only to the administrators (see Figure 6.1). These preferences include Accounts, Date & Time, Energy Saver, Login Window, Network, Sharing and Startup Disk. Chapter 3 talks more about using these preference settings.

NOTE: Items in the System Preferences application that can be accessed only by the administrator are always identified by a padlock icon. In large installations, it is usually recommended that a dummy account, separate from the administrator's real user account, be created for systems administration. Doing so provides even greater security.

- *Keychains*—If you use a number of different passwords to access your Internet accounts, online ordering and banking services, and various applications and server connections, no doubt you have to keep a record or memorize many passwords. It's easy to forget those passwords and thus lose your access to programs and services. With Apple's Keychain Access application (see Figure 6.2), located in the Utilities folder, you can store all those disparate passwords in a single location—called a *keychain*—and enter a single password to access all of them. Only you or someone with your password can unlock those passwords. When the

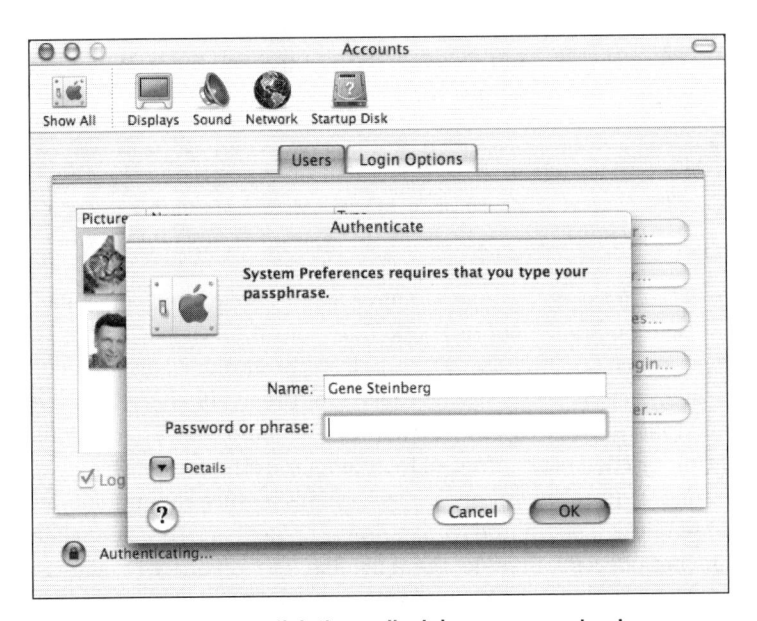

Figure 6.1 When you click the padlock icon, you must enter your administrator's username and password to gain access to certain Mac OS X features and System Preferences settings.

143

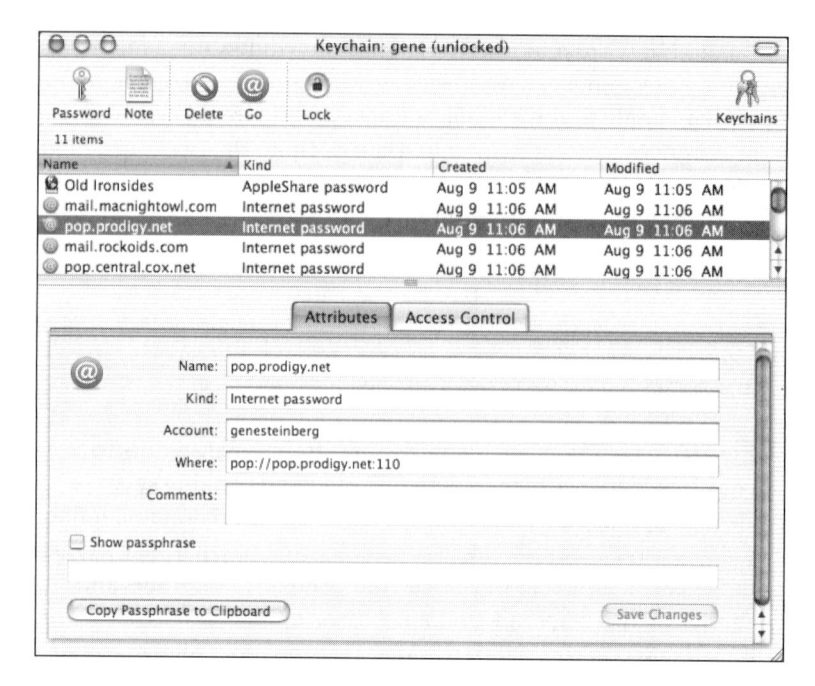

Figure 6.2 You can use the Keychain Access application to set up your personal account and store all your user passwords.

passwords are unlocked, applications and services that need them can get them, but casual users cannot see them. When you finish using them, you just lock your keychain.

NOTE: *In order for a keychain to work, the application for which you want to store a keychain must support that feature. Not all do, so you'll want to check the appropriate documentation to see which Mac OS X features are supported before you attempt to use passwords stored in a keychain.*

- *Shared folders*—All users who have accounts on your Mac have their own personal user or Home folder for their own sets of applications, documents, system-related preferences, fonts, Internet accounts, and so on. These files are available only to the individual user who logs in to that user account, unless additional sharing privileges are granted by that user or the administrator courtesy of the Ownership & Permission's feature of Finder's Get Info window. The Shared folder, however, serves as a place where you can put files and make them available to anyone who accesses your Mac. That way, those users do not need special access privileges. You can also create a Drop Box folder, where other users can place files, but only the individual user (who created the Drop Box) or the administrator can access the files inside.

In Brief

NOTE: *The Shared folder is also used as a reasonably safe location where users who access your Mac from across a network can send and receive files. You'll want to read Chapter 8 for information on how to configure network file-sharing privileges so that access to your Mac is restricted.*

- *System logins*—When you log out, only a user with a valid username and password can use your Mac. That rule provides the maximum possible degree of security for system-related access. However, if you are usually the sole user of the Mac and you have no qualms about letting others—perhaps family members or coworkers—work on your Mac, you can continue to bypass the Login prompt at startup. This is the default setting, so nothing need be changed.

WARNING! *Although you need the proper password to access a Mac under Mac OS X, nothing prevents you from restarting your computer under Mac OS 9, or with a Mac OS 9 or Mac OS X startup disk, and then gaining access to files in that environment. If maximum security is important to you, you'll want to set up the Multiple Users feature of Mac OS 9 as well so that users cannot casually access your Mac. It would also be a good idea to store system startup CDs (and third-party utilities, such as Norton Utilities, that come with bootable CDs) in a safe place, so that access cannot be gained in that fashion.*

- *Dedicated security software*—Under previous versions of the Mac OS, a number of dedicated security programs were available from such publishers as Intego and Power On Software. Although these programs have not yet been updated for Mac OS X, Intego, which took over the products from ASD Software, was working on Mac OS X upgrades for DiskGuard and FileGuard when this book was written. In addition, Power On Software was still considering whether to upgrade DiskLock and On Guard to the new operating system. Another workable solution is Apple's free Open Firmware Password application, available from Apple's support Web site. You can use this program to prevent startups from any volume other than the one set as a Startup Disk, even from a CD, unless the user enters the appropriate password. It works with the iBook, slot-load iMac and flat-panel iMac, eMac, PowerBooks with FireWire ports, the Power Mac G4 (except for the version that has PCI graphics) and the Cube.

WARNING! *Because of changes in the file structures of Mac OS X, do not even consider using a Classic security program with the new operating system. If you must secure your Mac to a level beyond what is available via the combination of Mac OS 9 and Mac OS X Multiple Users settings, you may want to delay deploying Mac OS X until dedicated security software is available for the new environment.*

6. Setting Up Mac OS X for Multiple Users

145

Using Strong Passwords

If you are running your Mac in a family environment or in a small office, you might not have to be overly concerned about your choice of passwords, because it might not be a critical issue if another user in your environment works on your Mac. But if you need the maximum amount of security, you'll want to use a password that is difficult for others to guess. The best password is a random combination of upper- and lowercase letters intermixed with numbers. Such a password is extremely difficult for anyone to guess, and thus you have the maximum level of security. An optimal password should contain at least eight characters to provide a good level of security.

WARNING! Once you set up your Mac with Mac OS X, there is no way to gain complete user access without the proper password. Even if you use the Login preference panel to bypass a password request at startup, some features, such as the ability to install some new applications, will not be available to you until you can manually enter that password. Should you forget it, you will have to reset your password using the Password Reset utility available in the Mac OS X Installer application. Chapter 19 explains how, and this is why you should also keep your Mac OS X installer CD in a safe place.

Immediate Solutions

Immediate Solutions

Setting Up Multiple-User Access

Each user of your Mac can be given his or her own personal password and user environment, which allows each user to set, within the guidelines you establish, a custom font collection, user preferences, desktop layout, applications, and documents.

Follow these steps to create a new user account:

1. Launch the System Preferences application. You'll find it on the Dock or in the Applications folder.
2. Click the Accounts icon to bring up the settings panel (see Figure 6.3).
3. If the padlock is closed, click the padlock to open it, and enter the username and password for your administrator account.

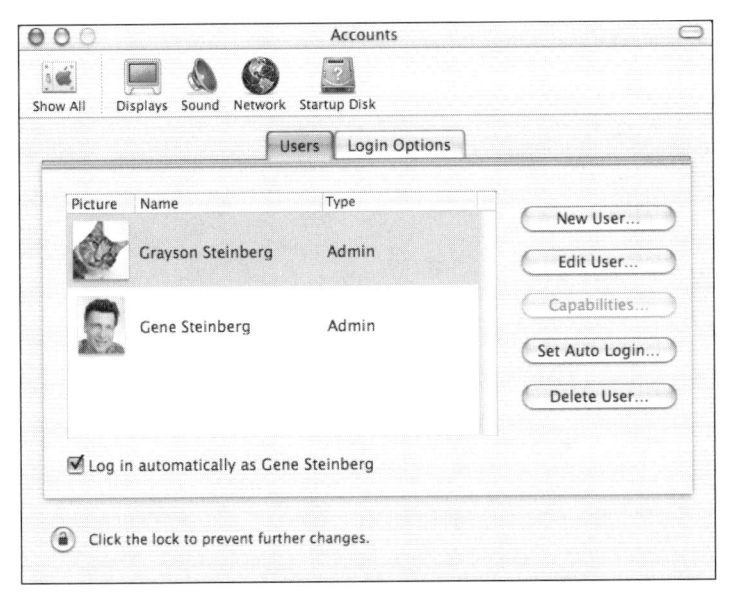

Figure 6.3 You can establish a new user account from this dialog box.

Chapter 6 Setting Up OS X for Multiple Users

NOTE: If you are logged in under your administrator account, the padlock is normally open. You might want to consider closing it in various system settings until you can establish separate user accounts for others who are going to use your Mac.

---

4. With the padlock open, click the New User button to open the New User dialog box shown in Figure 6.4.
5. In the Name field, type the actual name of the new user.
6. In the Short Name field, type a username (nickname). By default, Mac OS X will suggest an alternate username that usually consists of the same name in lower case, minus the word spaces. Feel free to shorten it further to just your first name, or a totally different name, if you prefer.
7. In the New Password field, type a password containing at least four letters. Then, retype the password in the Verify field. If the password isn't accepted, retype it again. It must be entered the same way (both upper- and lowercase letters) in both places.
8. If you want a helpful reminder about a forgotten password, enter a question in the Password Hint text field (but don't make it so obvious that a third party can guess the answer).
8. Choose a Login Picture from those provided and drag it into the picture well. You can also click Choose Another and select a JPEG or TIFF picture in an Open dialog box from among the ones you might have on your Mac.

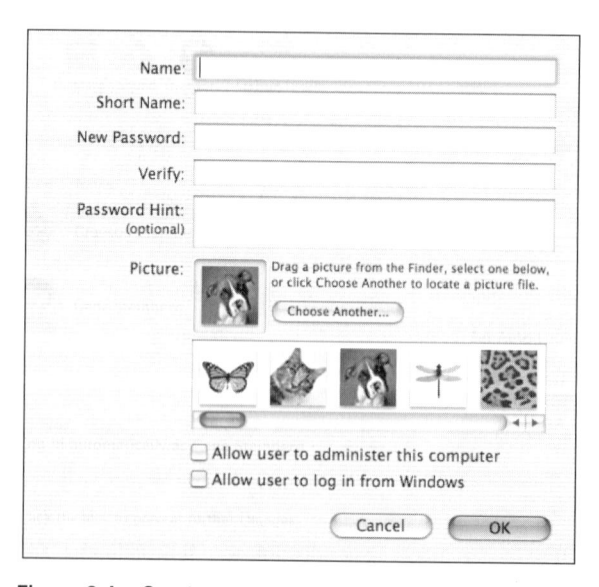

Figure 6.4 Create a new user account on your Mac here.

148

Immediate Solutions

9. If you want to give the user the authority to act as administrator for the Mac, select the checkbox at the bottom of the dialog box. You can at this point also access the second checkbox, which allows you to log in from a Windows PC.

10. Click the OK to finish.

WARNING! Before allowing another user to act as administrator for your Mac, consider carefully whether you really want to grant those access privileges to someone else (other than a family member, of course). Remember that any user who can log in as administrator will have the same authority that you do as owner of the Mac.

11. When you create your initial administrator's account when setting up your Mac, Auto Login is set by default. If you want to change that setting, select the account name, click the Set Auto Login button in the Users window, and enter your password when the prompt appears.

12. Click OK to store the change, or Cancel to keep things the way they were.

NOTE: You can turn off the automatic login by deselecting the Log in automaticallyÖ checkbox on the Users screen. When this feature is turned, you'll see a prompt whenever you boot your Mac where you can select the account for logging in. If you have no qualms about an automatic login, however, there's no reason to uncheck that option.

13. Repeat Steps 4 through 12 to add more user accounts.

14. Quit the System Preferences application by choosing Quit from the application menu or by pressing Command+Q.

Related solution:	Found on page:
Setting System Preferences Under Mac OS X	52

Customizing a User Account

If your children are using your Mac, or you simply want to restrict access to certain files and features for other users at your office, you can use the Capabilities feature (see Figure 6.5) to simplify the user environment or set access.

NOTE: The Capabilities feature only functions with accounts that do not have administrator's access. So if you want to change the user's rights, you'll need to use the Edit User feature (see the next section) to turn off the ability to administer your Mac.

149

Chapter 6 Setting Up OS X for Multiple Users

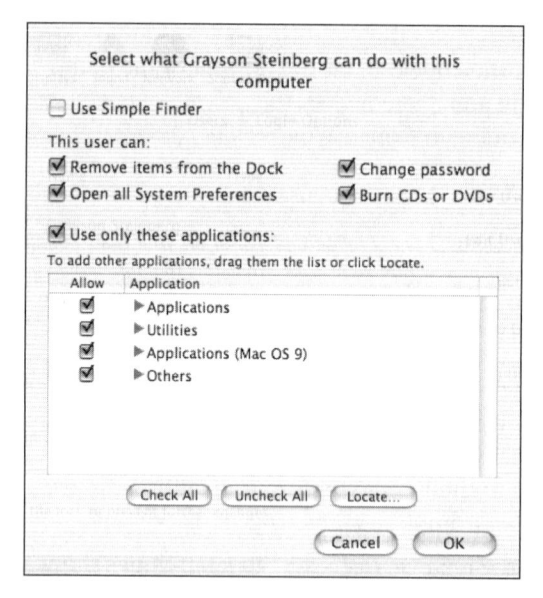

Figure 6.5 Customize the user environment extensively with this simple setup window.

1. To customize the user, launch System Preferences from the Dock or Applications folder.
2. Click the Accounts icon to launch the settings panel.
3. Click the padlock (if it's not already open) and enter the username and password for your administrator account.
4. With the padlock open, click a user's name and click Capabilities to bring up the settings screen.
5. For children or other users who haven't mastered your Mac, click the Use Simple Finder option, which will, when that user logs in, create an ultra simple environment (see Figure 6.6), where only a small number of Mac OS X features can be used.
6. To keep the standard user interface, and just customize individual features, select one of the options in This user can category. These include the following:

    - *Remove items from the Dock*—When this option is unchecked, Dock configuration functions in one direction, and that is to add new items to it.
    - *Open all System Preferences*—Unchecked, and the user cannot use the System Preferences application.
    - *Change password*—This one speaks for itself.

150

Immediate Solutions

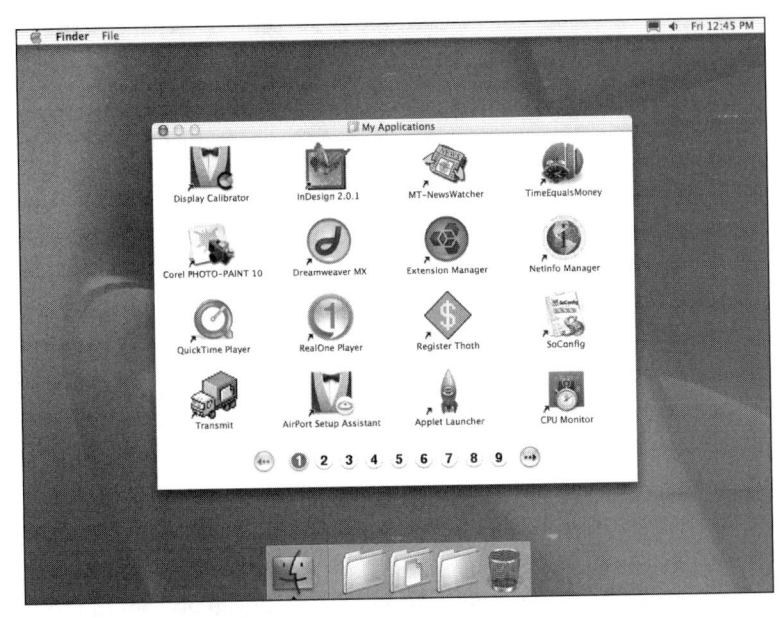

Figure 6.6   For young ones or others who aren't ready to enjoy the full Mac experience, here's the Simple Finder, with applications just a click away.

- *Burn CDs and DVDs*—Important for educational or office environments where you want to prevent users from copying files or applications to optical disks.

- *Use only these applications*—Click the disclosure triangles under each category to bring up a list of applications in that category. You can allow all applications, or just the ones that are checked, separately. This way, for example, if you don't want someone to use your financial management software, you can leave it unchecked.

NOTE: The buttons at the bottom of the Capabilities window can be used to check or uncheck everything in a single operation, and you can use the Locate button to select an application that is not listed or just drag the application icon to the list.

7. Click OK to store the settings and, if you wish, quit System Preferences. The next time that user logs in, the privileges you established will be honored.

151

Editing a User Account

A user account can be changed easily at any time. If you need to reset a password or change other user information, follow these steps:

1. Launch the System Preferences application from either the Dock or inside the Applications folder.
2. Click the Users icon to launch the settings panel.
3. Click the padlock (if it's not already open) and enter the username and password for your administrator account.
4. With the padlock open, click a user's name. Then, click the Open User button or press Command+O to access the user account information.
5. Make the appropriate changes to the user's name and password information and enter a password reminder question if you wish.
6. If you intend to grant this user the authority to act as administrator for the Mac, select the checkbox at the bottom of the dialog box.
7. Click Save to save the edited user account.
8. Exit System Preferences by choosing Quit from the application menu or pressing Command+Q.

If you need to remove a user account, follow these steps:

1. Launch the System Preferences application.
2. Click the padlock if it's closed and enter the username and password for your administrator account.
3. With the padlock open, click the name of the user account you want to delete.
4. Click the Delete User button, and then click Delete to respond to the acknowledgment prompt (see Figure 6.7). (Or, if you change your mind, click Cancel instead to leave the user account.)

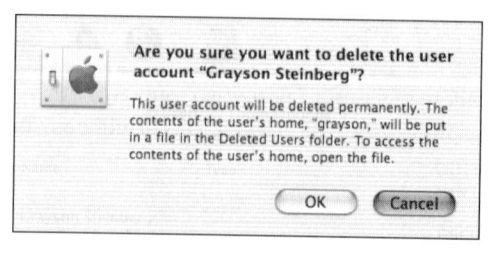

Figure 6.7 Are you sure you want to remove that user account?

Immediate Solutions

NOTE: When you delete a user, the Home folder for that user will still be present and will inherit the label Deleted. The administrator(s) of your Mac will have control over the material inside that folder.

5. Quit the System Preferences application by choosing Quit from the application menu or by pressing Command+Q.

Setting Up Keychain Access

The keychain, first introduced in Mac OS 9, is a valuable feature that helps simplify management of all your passwords by storing them in a single place.

NOTE: To be precise for the sake of Mac historians, the keychain feature appeared previously in System 7.1.1, commonly called System 7 Pro, but that system version didn't quite catch on (it was a failure in the marketplace). It was several years before the feature returned.

Here's how to use the feature:

1. You need to create a keychain so you have a place to store all those passwords. To do so, locate the Keychain Access application, which is located in the Utilities folder inside your Applications folder.

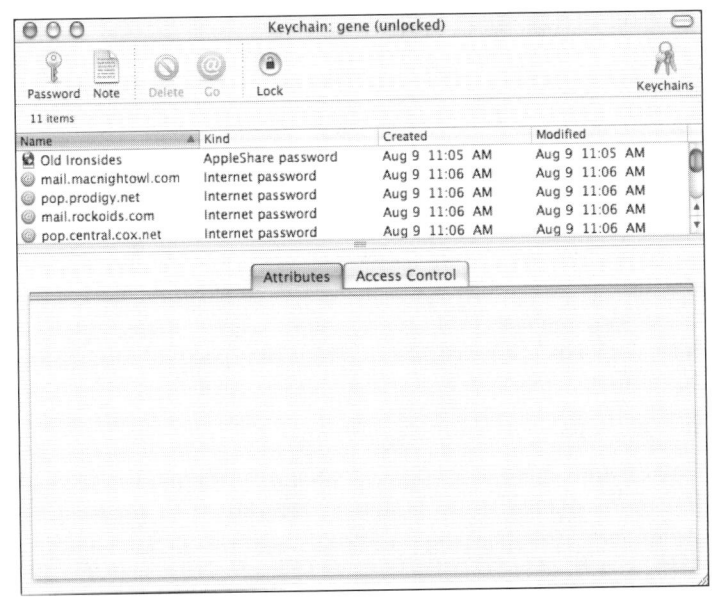

Figure 6.8 Here's your existing keychain.

153

Chapter 6 Setting Up OS X for Multiple Users

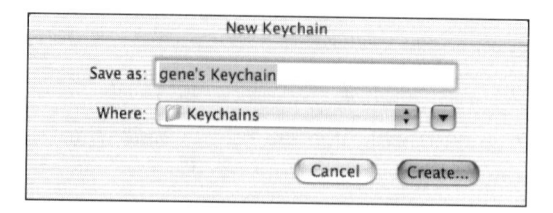

Figure 6.9 Give your keychain a name.

2. Double-click the Keychain Access application to launch it and display the screen shown in Figure 6.8.

NOTE: When you set up a username, a Keychain under that name is already made for you.

3. Choose New from the File menu and New Keychain from the submenu to name your new keychain (see Figure 6.9).

4. Type a name for your keychain, and then click the Create button.

5. On the next screen, type a user password, and then retype the password to confirm it. Use a strong password, as explained earlier in this chapter.

6. Once you've created a keychain, it's time to populate it. If you have several keychains, there will be a Keychains menu; otherwise, your new keychain will be displayed. Click Add and type a name for the item you want to add. (Use a name that identifies the item's contents.)

NOTE: If you are entering a Web site, be sure you include the exact access URL in the Name field. Otherwise, you won't be able to use that password to access the site.

TIP: A quick way to enter a complicated password is simply to access it via your Web browser and then copy the address in the URL field. You can then paste it into the Keychain Access application.

7. Type the user password you need for that particular program or service.

8. Repeat Steps 6 and 7 for each password you want to enter.

9. When you're finished using Keychain Access, quit the application by choosing Quit from the application menu, pressing Command+Q, or clicking the Close button.

Immediate Solutions

NOTE: *You can easily create multiple keychains, each of which stores a different set of user passwords. This method may help you from an organizational standpoint.*

With your keychains active, the first time you use a keychain, you'll see a prompt asking whether using the keychain should be allowed for this one time only or in all situations (Always Allow). If others are using your Mac under your account, you may prefer not to use that option.

NOTE: *Access to each entry in the keychain can be configured separately. Just click the entry, and then the Access Control tab, and you can confirm whether you will always allow access to an item when your keychain is unlocked, or require confirmation.*

Checking and Using Your Keychain

Once you've configured Keychain Access to store your user passwords, it's very simple to launch the program and check or use your passwords. Just follow these steps:

1. Locate Keychain Access in the Utilities folder, inside the Applications folder, and double-click the program to launch it.
2. If you have more than one keychain, select the Keychain Access menu and choose the keychain you want to open. If you have only one keychain stored, there will not be such a menu.
3. To unlock a keychain, click the Unlock button, and then enter your keychain password.
4. To learn about a specific password, click Get Info and then click View Password.
5. Click Allow Once to see the password.
6. Keep your keychain unlocked if you want to use it with your applications or services.
7. When you're finished working with your keychains, choose Quit from the application menu, press Command+Q, or click the Close button to close the program.

Changing Keychain Settings

The Keychain Access application has just a few settings, but you'll want to consider all the options to see what fits your work environment. Here's how to change the settings:

6. Setting Up Mac OS X for Multiple Users

155

Chapter 6 Setting Up OS X for Multiple Users

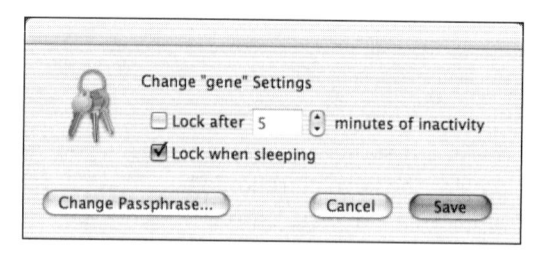

Figure 6.10 Choose your keychain settings here.

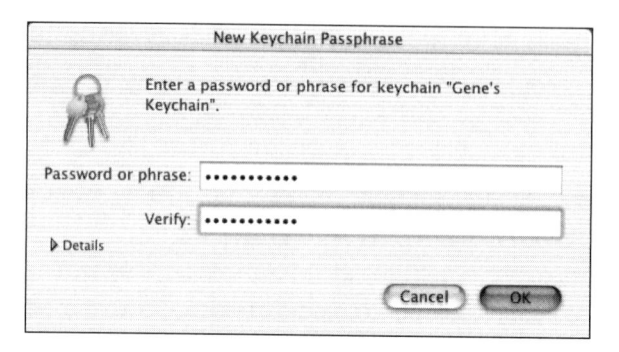

Figure 6.11 You can alter your password from this dialog box.

1. Launch the Keychain Access application.
2. Choose My Keychain Settings from the Edit menu (the words *My Keychain* will reflect the actual name of the keychain you want to configure). Doing so opens the dialog box shown in Figure 6.10.
3. If you want to change your password, you can do so now, by clicking the Change Passphrase button (see Figure 6.11). You'll have to confirm your password to make it active.

NOTE: If you use a password that the software thinks isn't secure, such as a simple word or recognizable name, you'll get a warning prompt. If you need a strong password, I suggest you heed the warning and create a new password, preferably one with mixed upper- and lowercase letters and numbers to make it more secure.

4. Once your password is changed (assuming you want it altered), you can also have your keychain lock automatically after a specified period of inactivity (you set the number of minutes) or when your Mac slips into sleep mode. Go ahead and check the settings you want.
5. To change the name of a keychain, choose Keychain List from the Edit menu, and then select the name of the keychain.

Immediate Solutions

6. Type a new name for the keychain.

7. When you're finished making your changes, quit Keychain Access by choosing Quit from the application menu or pressing Command+Q.

Running a Keychain on Another Mac

When you create a keychain on your Mac, the keychain is not limited to that one computer. You can easily access the very same keychain on another Mac, which is quite convenient if you need to run the same applications and services on home and office computers or on an Apple laptop. Here's how to work with a mobile keychain:

1. Locate your personal keychain file. You'll find it in the Your Keychains folder, inside the Library folder, within your Users folder. Your keychain file will be stored using the name you specified when you set it up.

2. Drag the file to a mounted disk to make a copy, or make a copy in your Public folder by holding down the Option key when you drag the file to that folder.

3. On the other Mac, you can access the keychain file from across the network or from another drive simply by locating the file and double-clicking it.

4. If you want the keychain to appear in another Mac's Keychain List, drag the other keychain file into the Keychain List you have open to place the file on the other Mac as well.

5. Once the keychain is available, you can open it by entering the proper username and password.

6. When you're finished using the keychain, close the application by choosing Quit from the application menu, pressing Command+Q, or clicking on the Close button.

Coping with Problems Involving Keychains and Multiple Users

The Users features of Mac OS X are quite straightforward and usually work without a hitch. They just require a little attention to detail. But if you run into trouble, here are some likely problems and solutions:

Chapter 6 Setting Up OS X for Multiple Users

- *Password isn't recognized*—Are you sure you entered the password correctly? Did you leave the Caps Lock key engaged by mistake? If you followed my suggestions about using a strong password, the keyboard combination might not be something you readily remember. It would be a good idea to write it down somewhere and put it in a safe place. Type the password again, just in case you made a mistake the first time (which you wouldn't see because the only feedback on your screen are the bullets in place of the characters you type). If you cannot get your keychain or multiple-users password to work, you'll have to consider reinstalling Mac OS X and starting again, unless you can delete the individual keychain file or user account via your administrator's access using the Reset Password feature of the Mac OS X Installer (it's in the Installer's application menu when you restart from the installer CD).

WARNING! Being able to reset a password via the Mac OS X installer CD represents a potential security issue. If you are in an office environment, you may want to keep this CD under lock and key and accessible only if you need to reinstall Mac OS X or reset a password. The other issue, of course, is that individual users can bring in their own CD and do the deed, but this is an issue between you and your employees and beyond the scope of this book.

- *Keychain doesn't work with a program*—Not all applications support keychains or other multiple-user features. Check with the software publishers about their plans to support these features.

- *User forgets password*—Log in as administrator and recheck the user's account. You should keep a written record of all user accounts in a safe place, so you can access the users' computers whenever necessary or simply give them a lost password. As administrator, you can easily log in via the Multiple Users feature, open the user's account, and reset the password with a new one, if necessary.

NOTE: You cannot readily reset a password for your keychain. The best solution is just to trash it and start again if you forget the password.

- *User doesn't have permission*—If you used early releases of Mac OS X (such as 10.0 through 10.0.4), perhaps you ran into a problem with not having permission to access, copy, or move a file. One sure way to fix this problem is to modify the permissions via the the Owners & Permissions feature of the Finder's Get Info window. The options are described in more detail in Chapter 4. If you prefer to do it via the command line, simply launch Terminal from the Utilities folder. With Terminal open, type "sudo chmod –R u+rw nameoffile". Press Return, and then enter your password at the password prompt, followed by another press of the Return key. In this command, **sudo** calls up your super user access. The **chmod** command and the subsequent instructions tell Mac OS X to give you both read and write access to the named file.

NOTE: In testing Get Info while writing this book, I never ran into a file that I couldn't fix in this fashion. If you still have problems, you might try a third party permissions altering utility, such as GetInfo, or BatChmod, Both programs are available via versiontracker.com.

WARNING! From a security standpoint, when you set up an administrator's account, it's never a good idea to leave a password setting blank. If nobody else will access your Mac, or only friends and family, you can just as easily create a password identical to your username.

Suggestions for Setting Up Multiple Users for Use with Children

Many new Macs are purchased for home or small business use, where they'll be used frequently by children, ranging from those barely out of the toddler stage to those in the teen years. Parents are often surprised that young people take to personal computers far more easily than they did. My son, for example, was actively trying to trash all my files from my Mac's desktop when he was three or four years old. But more seriously, they learn mouse skills and develop good typing skills (with a little parental or school-based direction) far more speedily than the older generation. As a result, they can get on the Internet more easily and perhaps get into trouble more easily, as well.

Here are some considerations for setting up Mac OS X for use with children:

- *Keep passwords hidden and hard to guess.* Just as you would hide your password from outsiders, consider making your user password difficult for children to detect. Today's kids have a remarkable ability to figure out such things, if you make your password too easy to guess. Make sure they cannot log on to your administrator's account and do mischief (even if unintended). That way, they will be limited to system preferences that are padlocked or secured.

159

Chapter 6 Setting Up OS X for Multiple Users

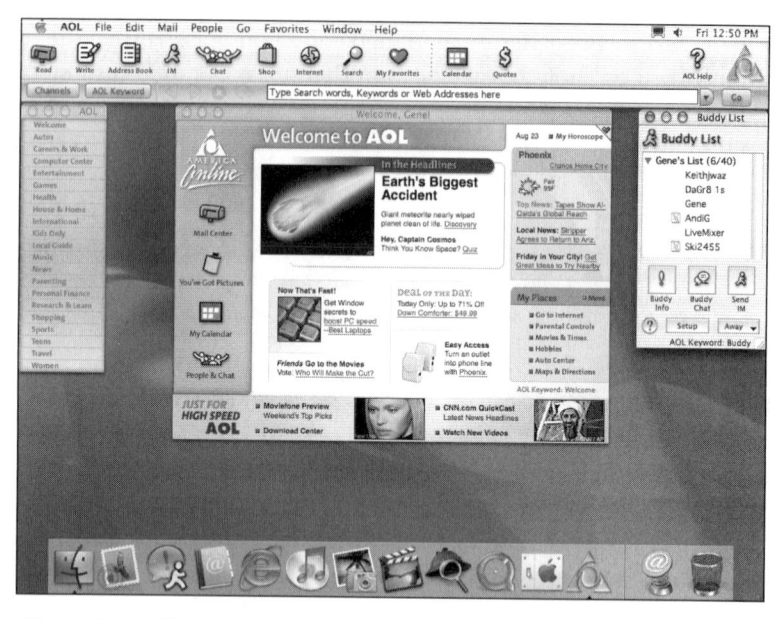

Figure 6.12   Here is AOL for Mac OS X.

- *Consider AOL or CompuServe 2000 for a kid's Net access.* Both AOL and CompuServe have Mac OS X–savvy software available (see Figure 6.12). AOL, for example, has a powerful set of Parental Controls that allow you to restrict your child's access to various features of the service, such as instant messages, email from strangers, and various Web sites. This family-friendly approach is one reason AOL has risen to the top of the heap in terms of online services (not to mention its hugely successful promotional campaigns).

- *Use email filtering.* Apple's Mail application and the other alternatives have filtering options that let you prevent email from specific locations from arriving. The junk filters in Mail, however, are first-rate and, with a little time in the "Training" mode, can catch more than 99 of your junk mail. In addition, when you use custom rules in your e-mail software, , you can restrict a user to receiving email only from approved locations, such as family members or friends. That way, unacceptable material will be blocked entirely. Another ISP that will help you in this regard is EarthLink, Apple's default ISP partner. It inherited a feature called Spaminator when it merged with MindSpring. This feature automatically blocks email from known purveyors of junk mail. That, plus careful filtering, will go a long way toward protecting children from unacceptable email solicitations.

Chapter 7

Mac OS X's Search Feature

If you need an immediate solution to:	See page:
Searching for Files on Your Mac	166
Searching Files for Content	167
Setting Sherlock Preferences	173
Installing Additional Search Modules	177

Chapter 7 Mac OS X's Search Feature

In Brief

"Where did I put that file?" That's a common refrain when you're trying to locate a missing file. Hard drives are constantly getting cheaper and bigger, which means you can store more of your stuff on them. However, with so much data (and some new drives with capacities greater than 120GB), it gets increasingly difficult to find the files you want. In addition, the World Wide Web contains literally millions of sites, with content that dwarfs the largest libraries in the world. With so much material out there, what can you do to find the information you want without spending endless amounts of time in the process?

For Jaguar, Apple has two different search tools. One is a Finder-level search feature, which allows you to find the stuff on your drive, any drives connected to your Mac or accessed via a network. In addition, there's an enhanced Sherlock search utility (see Figure 7.1), which has become a powerful tool to provide Web services, such as business phone numbers and movie listings, in a single application, often without the need to jump to a separate browser. This approach makes it much easier to find the information you want without having to know special search techniques or arcane instructions.

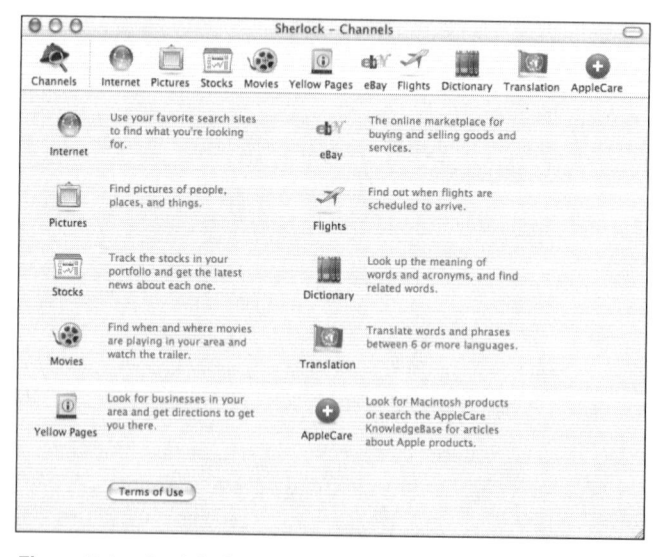

Figure 7.1 Apple's fancy search utility handles Internet searching with aplomb.

162

A Look at Apple's Search Utilities

Last night you finished an important document for your business, but today you just can't recall where you placed it. Or perhaps you recall writing material on a specific subject, but the content is buried in a document and you can't remember its title.

What to do?

The Mac OS X 10.2 Finder's toolbar includes a Search field. You can search the contents of whatever folder or disk to which the open Finder window applies by word or phrase. Press Return or Enter and, in seconds, the Finder window is updated with a screen showing the (see Figure 7.2).

However, searching the files on your drive is only part of the question. What if you need to find information that isn't saved

on your Mac? How about a news story about your favorite movie star? Are there online resources where you can search for new homes in the city to which you've been transferred?

Before Apple created its highly flexible Internet search tool, Sherlock, no central resource existed to access these kinds of information. The Internet has a number of popular and powerful search engines, but knowing which one will work for your specific range of requests is a matter of trial and error. In addition, you have to learn the right search syntax for any but the most simple information requests.

For Jaguar, Apple has overhauled Sherlock extensively, so it not just presents links to Internet content, but some of it is presented in a convenient multipaned interface, so you can see the information without having to jump to your browser.

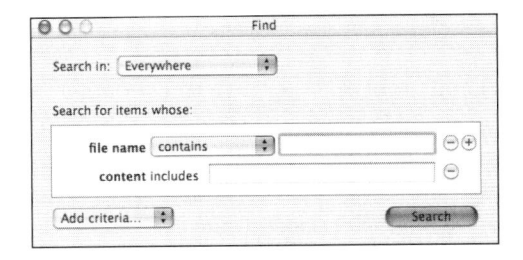

Figure 7.2 Click in a Search field and enter your search request.

Sherlock divides its search feature into channels, each of which accesses content in a specific category or from a specific resource. Here's a brief description of what they do; I'll cover all these features in detail later in this chapter:

- *Internet*—Use the resources of popular Web-based search sites (see Figure 7.3) to search for almost any accessible Internet-based content.

- *Pictures*—Are you looking for photos of a particular person, place or object? This feature brings up a window with thumbnails of pictures that match your description, and it requires double clicking on the image to see the result in your browser.

- *Stocks*—Find out how the companies that move and shake our economy are faring. You'll not only see the recent price, delayed by up to 15 minutes during the trading day, but links to the latest news about a company and its stock price history.

- *Movies*—One of my favorite features. You can check by movie or theater in your area, get a list of when it's playing along with a brief description of the plot. In most cases, you can even check out a movie trailer (see Figure 7.4) and order your tickets.

- *Yellow Pages*—You can look up a business phone number anywhere in the USA and, in most cases, see a map and get driving directions from your home, office, or whatever location you specify in Sherlock's preferences (I'll get to this in the Immediate Solutions section).

- *eBay*—Whether you want to participate in an online auction, or just check out the prices for a product of interest, this is going to be a very useful component of Sherlock.

- *Flights*—No, it's not a reservation's tool. It's a way to check on flight arrivals and departures.

- *Dictionary*—Check spelling and definitions, and consult Roget's Thesaurus to find the right word.

- *Translation*—Use this handy tool to do a rough translation in a number of major languages, including Chinese to English. To use, just write the text, or copy and paste it from its source into the top or Original Test pane, select the language from the pop-up menu, and, in seconds, you'll see the result in the bottom pane.

- *AppleCare*—Need more help with your Mac? Or, do you just want to check out the latest models? This channel has direct links to several of Apple Computer's Web sites.

In Brief

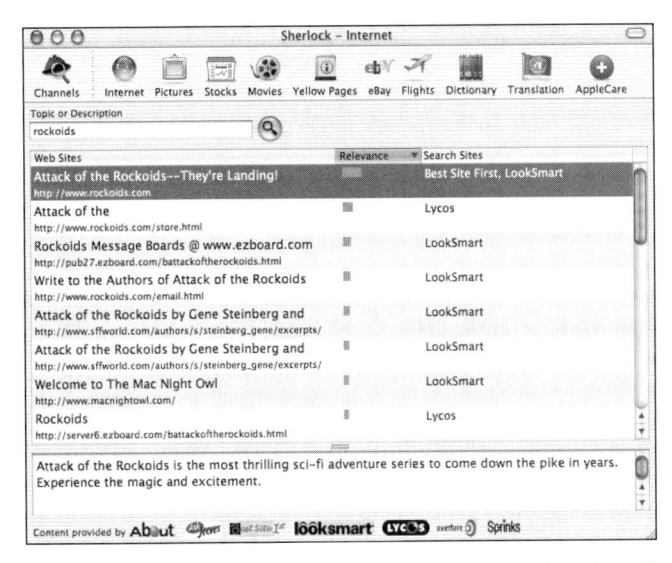

Figure 7.3 Check a number of Internet search engines in a single step.

Figure 7.4 If you're not sure what to see, check the trailer first..

You can launch the Sherlock application, choose a category or channel, and then enter your search request. Sherlock will go to work finding the information you want. Whether you are searching for information already stored on your Mac or you want to check out the Internet, you'll learn how to tailor Jaguar's search tools for your needs in the next section.

7. Mac OS X's Search Feature

165

Immediate Solutions

Searching for Files on Your Mac

In seconds, you can easily locate a file on any drive connected to your Mac or accessed across a network. Whether you're looking for a document, application, or folder, the finder's convenient Search feature can handle the job for you. There are two ways to seek information, depending on the scope of your search:

1. If you want to search for something within a folder or drive, just open up a Finder window.
2. Click on the Search field and enter the name of the file or folder you want.
3. Press Return or Enter. Within seconds a list of files or folders matching your request will appear in the same Finder window in list view, sorted by title (see Figure 7.5).

TIP: If you want to sort your search results differently, just click on a title, such as Date Modified, and it'll be resorted. If there's an arrow in a title field, clicking on it will reverse the sorting order.

NOTE: No search field? If you've collapsed the toolbar, click the little rectangle at the upper right of a Finder window to bring it back. If you don't see the Search field in a toolbar, choose Customize Toolbar from the Finder's View menu, and add the icons you like, or just drag the Default Set to the toolbar window to bring it back to factory condition. Click Done when you've finished your setup.

4. To actually use the file or folder, just double click on it from the search window.

TIP: To actually see the location of the item, look at the bottom pane of the search window. If the window is too small, just click on the bar above the bottom pane and drag it upward to expand its size.

Immediate Solutions

Advanced File Search Techniques

The Finder's built-in search field is strictly limited to the name of the file in the folder or disk you've selected. However, there are more powerful weapon's in the Finder's search arsenal, including the ability to actually search out the text in a file.

Here's how to harness these features:

1. Return to the Finder by clicking on the desktop, clicking on the Dock's Finder icon or any visible Finder window.
2. Press Command+F to bring up the search window. Click the Search in pop-up menu to indicate where you want to search (see Figure 7.6).
3. If you don't need to customize any further,
4. Click on the Search field and enter the name of the file or folder you want.
5. Click Search or press Return or Enter. Within seconds a list of files or folders matching your request will appear in the same Finder window in list view, sorted by date to your search request. The bottom pane will show the file's location.
6. To actually view the file, double-click on it to launch its creator application and the file itself.

TIP: To delete selected items from the Finder's Find window, press Command+Del. This action moves the selected item to the Trash, but the Trash won't be emptied until you either perform that action in the Finder's application menu or click and hold the Trash icon in the Dock and select Empty Trash from the menu.

Searching Files for Content

It's not enough to simply find a file by its name. Sometimes, you need to find files that contain a specific word or phrase. Fortunately, the Finder's search utility can handle that chore just about as easily as any other search routine. But first you have to index the folder or disk so the words can be found. When a drive is indexed, keywords to locate the text strings are all placed in a special file so Sherlock can access the information quickly. Here's how to perform the indexing process:

167

Chapter 7 Mac OS X's Search Feature

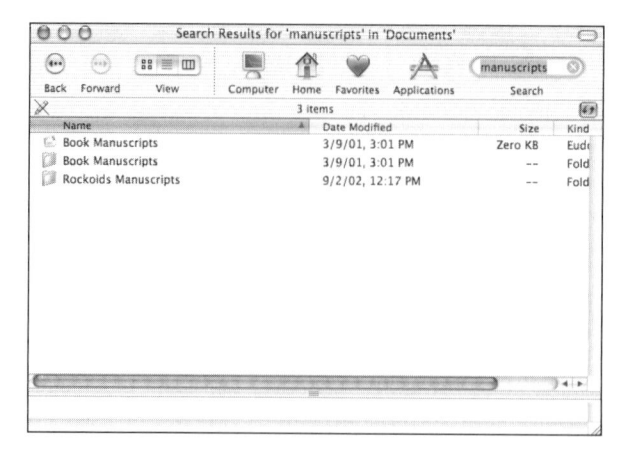

Figure 7.5 All the information the Finder locates appears in this convenient window.

1. Select the folder or disk you want to index.
2. Go to the Finder's File menu and choose Get Info or press Command+I.
3. Click the Content Index disclosure triangle and then the Index Now button. With the progress indicated by a progress bar and numeric display, the contents of the selected item will be indexed (see Figure 7.7).
4. Repeat the process for each drive or folder you want to index.

WARNING! *Because a new index procedure can take a long time, as will an index of a drive on which lots of changes have been made, you might want to schedule the process for times when you're not using your Mac. Even though Mac OS X's preemptive multitasking feature can handle multiple tasks at the same time (more so if you have a dual-processor Power Mac), you should do the indexing when you're not apt to be changing the files that are being indexed.*

Once you've indexed the item to be searched for content, here's what to do next:

1. Press Command+F to bring up the Find window.
2. Under the Content includes category, enter the word or phrase for which you want to search.

NOTE: *No field for content? Just click the Add criteria menu at the bottom of the Find screen, and choose Content to add that field. I'll cover the other options*

Immediate Solutions

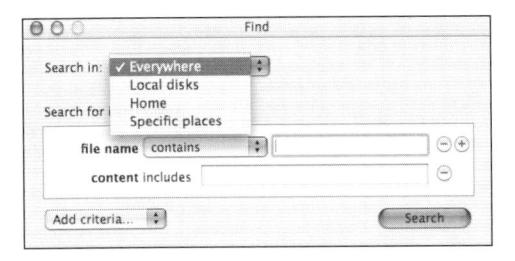

Figure 7.6 You can search your Home folders, local drives or network volumes here. Or choose Everything to cover all these categories.

3. Click Search to start the process. Your search results will appear in a new Finder window, sorted by relevance. The bottom pane will show the folder hierarchy, displaying where a selected file actually resides.
4. To change the sort order, you can click on a title field, such as Name or Date modified.

NOTE: The text-parsing process isn't perfect. Jaguar's find feature should be able to search for the text in most documents from word processor, page layout, graphic, and Internet applications, but the possibility always exists that a program will encode text in a manner that Sherlock can't read.

5. To actually read the file, double click on its title.

NOTE: If your file and text search doesn't yield results, you might want to refine your request still further. Read the section "Customizing Your Information Request," later in this chapter.

Using Advanced Criteria

Still unable to find the information you want? You can add criteria to the Finder's search field to customize the process. Just click on the Add criteria button to bring up a pop-up menu where you can add additional search options (see Figure 7.8).

Here are all the name search options available, but each can be customized still further by clicking on the pop-up menus at the right of a specific category.

- *File Name*—Click the pop-up menu to decide whether the file name begins or ends with the word or phrase.

NOTE: You can add more File Name categories by clicking the Plus symbol at the right of the field, and remove a field by clicking on the Minus icon.

169

Chapter 7 Mac OS X's Search Feature

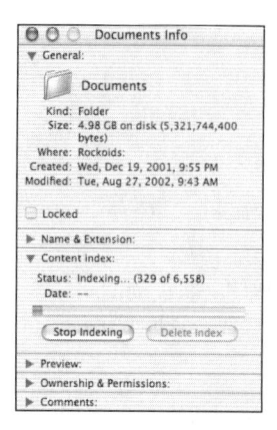

Figure 7.7 In this example, an entire drive with a ton of files is being indexed.

- *Content Includes*—Refine your file search by making sure that a certain bit of text (a word or phrase) is included. This topic is covered in more detail in the previous section.

- *Date Modified*—When was the file last changed? You can specify whether the date is "Today," or choose another option and specify a specific date.

- *Date Created*—Decide how closely the search will look at file creation dates in making your request.

- *Kind*—Is the file an alias, a document, or a font, or does it fit into a wide range of categories? Choose the one you want from the pop-up menu.

- *Size*—This option limits or includes files of a particular size. It's especially helpful for content searches—particularly if you want to look at text in a small document but don't want to wait until large documents are also searched.

- *Extension is*—Mac OS X supports the same file naming conventions as windows, which means a Word document has a .doc extension, for example. You can search documents this way if you're just trying to find the ones made in a specific program.

- *Visibility*—Is the file invisible? Some files are declared invisible by the Finder because they are system-related and not intended for general access. You can specify whether a file is visible, invisible or both.

Immediate Solutions

Figure 7.8 In this illustration, I've selected all the major search categories. Or can click the Plus sign on some of them to refine your choices.

WARNING! *A number of system-related files under Mac OS X are set in a specific way or located in a specific place because they are required for your Mac to run properly. Don't attempt to seek them out and manipulate them with Sherlock, or you might find that your Mac fails to run properly or will not even boot when you try to restart.*

After you've fine-tuned your information request, click Search to make your request. The modification you make to the Find screen remains in place until you change it.

Setting Sherlock Preferences

The Sherlock Preferences dialog box, available from the application's menu, gives you a limited number of ways to configure the program, as you'll see in Figure 7.9.

- *Locations*—When checking local movie times or using the map feature in the Yellow Pages channel, you'll want to be about to select your home or office location. You can click Add to include extra locations.

- *Countries*—Specify which parts of the world you want to include in your search.

Chapter 7 Mac OS X's Search Feature

Figure 7.9 Click a tab to change or check a setting.

- *Subscriptions*—You can use the standard, Apple Channels, or specify whatever group of channels may be available from a third party company.
- *Security*—Since Sherlock is acting as a Web browser, you'll want to specify whether to accept Web cookies or not. It's just fine to keep this selected.

Once you've changed or viewed Sherlock's preferences, close in the close box to dismiss the dialog box.

Searching the Internet

The first, core, feature of Sherlock is Internet searching. Sherlock uses a number of popular search tools to locate the information you want.

Here's how to use Sherlock for this function:

1. Log on to your ISP. (See Chapter 8 for information on how to configure Mac OS X to make your Internet connection.)
2. Launch Sherlock, and then click the Internet channel icon (see Figure 7.10).

Immediate Solutions

3. Make your search request. Enter the word or phrase that best describes what you're searching for in the Topic or Description field. For example, if you are interested in buying a new Ford, enter "Ford" or, more specifically, the model, such as "Ford Taurus".

4. Click the magnifying glass to start the process.

5. Sherlock produces a list of items that match your search request. Depending on the number of sites you've activated and the speed of the connection to your ISP, this process may take anywhere from a few seconds to several minutes. A progress bar indicates the status of your search. By default, items are listed in order of relevance (how closely they match your search query). When Sherlock is done, click any item in the search list to see more information in the results pane at the bottom of the Sherlock application window (see Figure 7.11). This information will only appear if the selected Web page has meta tags that provide a description of its content.

NOTE: *Not all search requests will yield a response. If you don't receive any matches to your request, try refining the request a bit, perhaps by using a more descriptive phrase. I'll get to the process of customizing your search requests later in this chapter.*

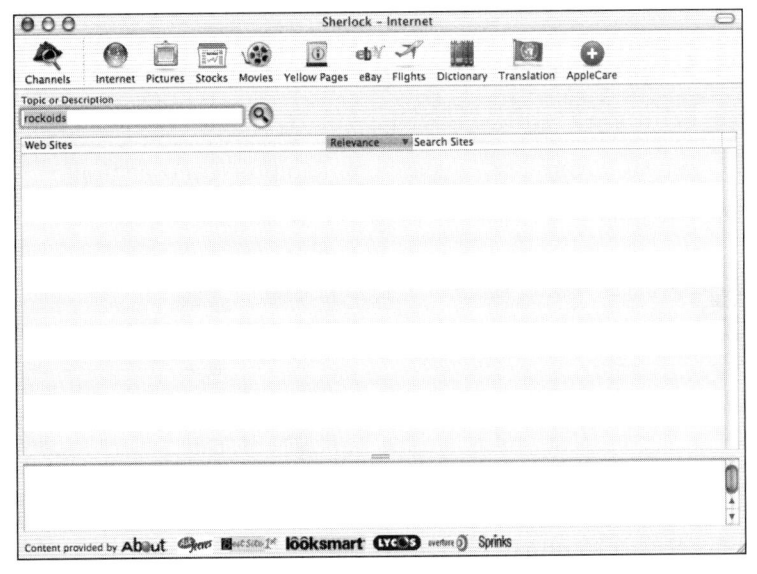

Figure 7.10 Enter your search request in the Topic or Description field.

173

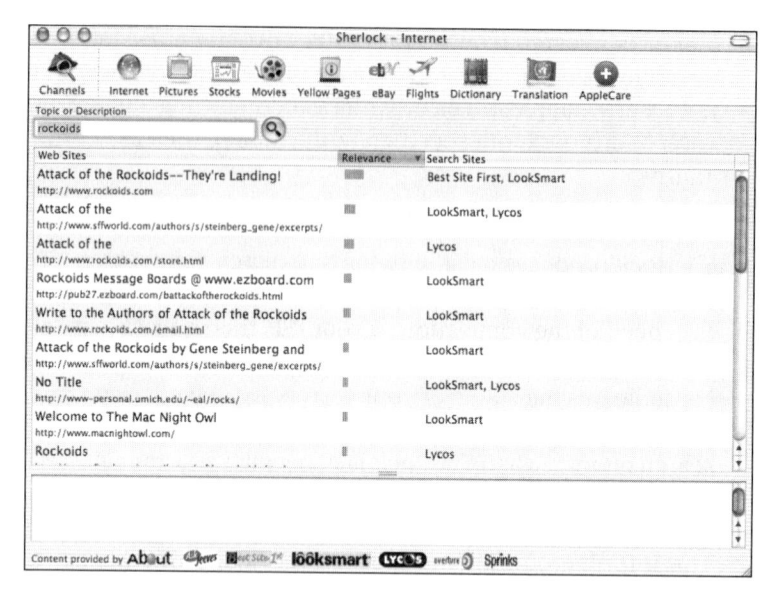

Figure 7.11   The bottom pane tells you something about a selected Web site.

6. If you've found an item you want to know more about, double click on the item. Your default Web browser will be launched and you'll be taken directly to the page you've selected (see Figure 7.12).

NOTE: Even if a Web site is shown in Sherlock, it doesn't mean it's still available. Search engines don't always remove obsolete links.

7. Repeat the process to search for additional information.
8. Quit Sherlock when you're done using it.

Related solution:	Found on page:
Using Internet Connect for Dial-Up Networking	197

Customizing Your Sherlock Internet Search Request

Not every request you make for Internet information in Sherlock's request will be successful, and it's not always because you've done something wrong. There is so much information available that sometimes you must fine-tune your request or try a few different ways of asking.

Immediate Solutions

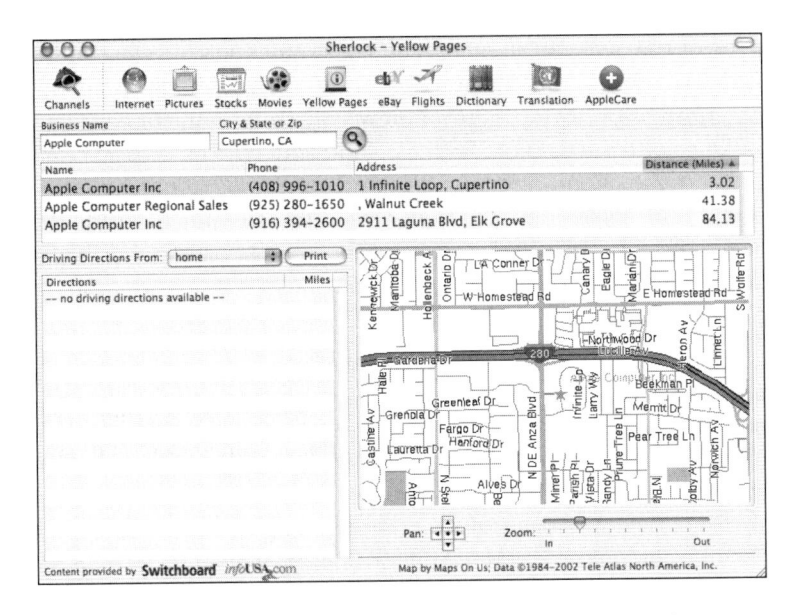

Figure 7.12 Your browser opens and the page you've selected appears.

As mentioned, Sherlock works with plain English to send your requests, whether they're made locally, on a network, or on the Internet. However, you can narrow the information so you get what you need. Here are some suggestions:

- If you want your search request to include all the words of a phrase, type a plus (+) character between each word. So, if you're looking for a Ford Taurus, try "Ford+Taurus" if the original request isn't specific enough.

- To exclude a word, you'd think you'd type a minus sign, right? Well, no; you need to use an exclamation point (!). To refine that request on Ford products to exclude the Taurus from the search, use "Ford!Taurus".

- Now we get a bit more complicated. If you'd like to search for a group of items, use parentheses. You can even group items, yet exclude specific categories in this fashion: "(cars|Ford)! Taurus". Again, this request excludes the Taurus.

NOTE: That vertical bar character, described above as a means to group items (which looks like a slash in some typefaces), is accessed by pressing Option+Shift+1.

7. Mac OS X's Search Feature

175

In the old days, if you wanted to find out someone's physical address, you had to check a phone directory or call the telephone company for the information. Now, there's a new way to let your fingers do the walking, with the help of Sherlock—and you don't have to go hunting for the right phone directory or pay your phone company a fee to look it up for you. You don't even have to call your roadside assistance company for directions, because, in most cases, Sherlock will give you driving directions. To find businesses on the Internet, just follow these steps:

1. Log on to your ISP in the usual fashion.
2. Launch Sherlock, and then click the Yellow Pages channel icon.
3. Enter the business's name, as exactly as you can recall it, and the city, state and/or zip code.
4. Click the magnifying glass. Sherlock goes to work searching the Internet Yellow Pages for the business you want to contact. A progress wheel indicates the search is still in progress.
5. After you see a list of likely candidates, if any, click the item to bring up a map in the results pane of the Sherlock application window (see Figure 7.12). If the location is within reasonable driving distance, directions from the selected location will appear.
6. If you don't find the right company the first time, continue to select likely candidates from the list.
7. Should your initial request not be successful, recheck the spelling of the name. Try without the "Inc." if necessary.

NOTE: *Don't expect miracles with Internet-based mapping services. In many cases, recently built roads won't be reflected, and sometimes directions will be more convoluted than necessary to reach a specific location.*

8. If you want a hard copy of the address, map and directions, click the Print button.
9. When you're finished with the search request, make another or quit Sherlock.

Immediate Solutions

NOTE: The above directions give you information on how to use two of the popular channels of Sherlock. All the rest have a similar range of text entry and information fields that make them easy to follow. Over time Apple will be adding different changes to expand your range of options.

Installing Additional Search Modules

Apple signs new partnerships with content providers, it will automatically send you the channel updates, so you don't have to do anything to configure Sherlock to receive them.

Over time, other Web sites will be supplying their own search components for Sherlock that can be downloaded, automatically, in the same fashion. When they show up, you'll simply have to click a link at the Web site to start the process.

However, it is also possible to manually install a component for Sherlock manually in your own user's folder.:

1. Download the module to your Mac's drive.
2. Make sure the file is not compressed. It will be named with an .nib extension if it's ready to use. Go to your Home directory by clicking on the Home button in the Finder.
3. If it's running, quit Sherlock and then locate the Cache folder. It's located in the Library folder in your Home directory Open the folder labeled Sherlock, where you'll find a folder labeled Channel Nibs.
4. Place the new module within the Channel Nibs folder.

Once installed, the new channel will appear when you launch Sherlock again.

NOTE: Modules can be removed simply by taking them out of the folder in which they were installed, but you'll want to do it after you quit the Sherlock application. The changes will appear the next time you launch the program.

7. Mac OS X's Search Feature

177

Another Solution for Web Services

Before Apple's Sherlock 3 appeared, a shareware application, inspired by the original Sherlock, offered a wide range of Web services. Known, appropriately, as Watson, Dan Wood's highly acclaimed application (see Figure 7.13) offered, in the release shown in this book, a larger and more expansive range of channels.

Fortunately, you can use both, and benefit by the different selection of services. To get a copy of Watson for evaluation, visit the publisher's Web site at: **http://www.karelia.com/watson/**.

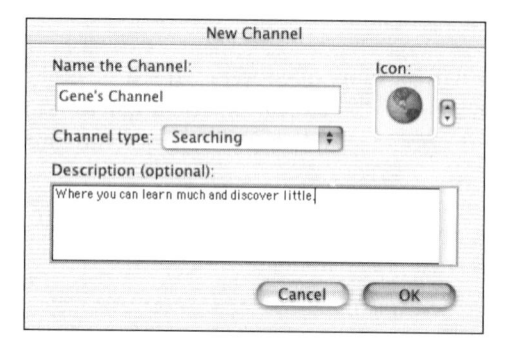

Figure 7.13 Some say Watson inspired Sherlock 3, but they continue to exist as separate programs.

Chapter 8

Networking Overview

If you need an immediate solution to:	See page:
Sharing Files Under Mac OS X	186
Accessing Shared Volumes with Network Browser	191
Accessing Shared Volumes with the Chooser	192
Connecting to Shared Macs Under Mac OS X	193
Connecting to Shared Windows and Unix Servers	195
Using Internet Connect for Dial-Up Networking	197
Verifying Connectivity	202
Connecting Via a Virtual Private Network	203
Using Apple's Location Manager to Create Custom Setups	204
Setting Up a Web or FTP Server on Your Mac	206
Can't Acces a Drop Box?	207
Correcting Network Access Problems	207
Protecting Your Network from the Internet	209

179

In Brief

Networking is often thought of as an arcane realm of confusion and frustration. But when you use a Mac, you don't have to contend with setup wizards or complex configuration to join a network. Although the Macintosh was originally designed as a computer that empowered the individual, easy networking was always a part of the picture. The first example of simple networking was the ability to set up a network-capable laser printer in just a minute or so simply by plugging it in, turning it on, and selecting the driver that worked with the output device in the Chooser. The same easy networking extended to more powerful printers. Even an imagesetter, used in the printing industry for high-quality output, could be hooked up to a Mac just as easily as the cheapest laser printer. If you wanted to network Macs with each other, however, you needed special software.

NOTE: There was one no-cost exception to the rule of having to buy commercial sharing software, such as Apple's own Mac OS X Server, both of which are used for larger networks. A free program, produced but unsupported by the former Claris division of Apple, allowed for limited file sharing. It was called Public Folder, but its value ended when Mac users moved past System 6.

When Mac OS 7 came around in 1991, Apple made a logical extension of networking by offering built-in support for personal file sharing. This support allowed Mac users on a small network to activate peer-to-peer file transfers without special software by attaching cables among the computers and turning on file sharing. In minutes, the shared Mac's drive was visible in the Chooser as an AppleShare volume available on your network (see Figure 8.1).

For larger setups, it was easy to use the Get Info window to set user access privileges for file sharing. Using this limited set of user controls, you could restrict the ability of those connected to a Mac to see or modify files. As file sharing evolved, Apple also added the capability of sharing a Mac across the Internet with almost the same ease as connecting to a Mac on a local network.

For Jaguar, Apple has advanced its networking architecture, using industry-standard technologies to provide faster performance, greater reliability, and better cross-platform compatibility. The Darwin core

In Brief

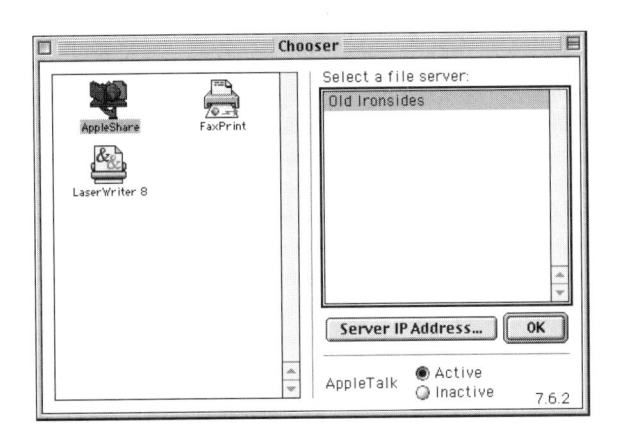

Figure 8.1 The late and definitely not lamented Mac Chooser is still required to configure printers from the Classic environment.

of the new operating system includes the BSD networking stack, which includes TCP/IP, the protocol used to power the Internet. You don't have to abandon your existing techniques for getting connected, either; there's native support for Point-to-Point Protocol (PPP) connections, so you can access your ISP as easily as before—perhaps more easily. (I'll cover the subject of Mac OS X's Internet features in Chapter 21.) AppleTalk is also supported, so you don't have to do anything extra to access your existing Macs and printers. In all, Mac OS X includes built-in network support for such file services as AFP (AppleShare), Server Message Block / Common Internet File System (SMB/CIFS), WebDAV, and Network File System (NFS), which means you can mate not only with a Mac, but also with computers running Linux and other Unix operating systems, Novel NetWare, Windows 3.1, Windows 95, Windows 98, Windows Me, Windows NT, Windows 2000, and Windows XP. All of this is accomplished under Mac OS X without your having to learn special skills or trip through a complicated series of dialog boxes and interpret arcane commands.

Even better for a cross-platform network, with a couple of simple settings on your Mac, it'll show up on a Windows PC as just another member of the "network neighborhood." That mean that file transfers can work both ways.

NOTE: Apple's open source automatic network technology, Rendezvous, based on standard internet protocols, allows for automatic discovery of network devices. Although Mac's running Jaguar have this capability out of the box, other products, such as printers and handheld computers, will have to add support of their own to allow those products to be automatically recognized.

8. Networking Overview

181

Chapter 8 Networking Overview

Accessing Networked Macs from Mac OS X

When you look over your new operating system, you'll see that something's missing. Where's an application for accessing networked computers?

The method for accessing shared volumes is closer in concept to the Network Browser application that first appeared under Mac OS 8.5 (see Figure 8.2). Networked computers appear in the Connect To Server dialog (see Figure 8.3), available from the Mac OS X Finder's Go menu. Your network installation, whether local or Internet-based, is divided into *neighborhoods*, each of which consists of a set of networked Macs.

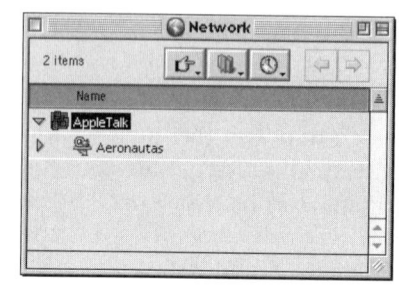

Figure 8.2 The Network Browser application could access local and Internet networks.

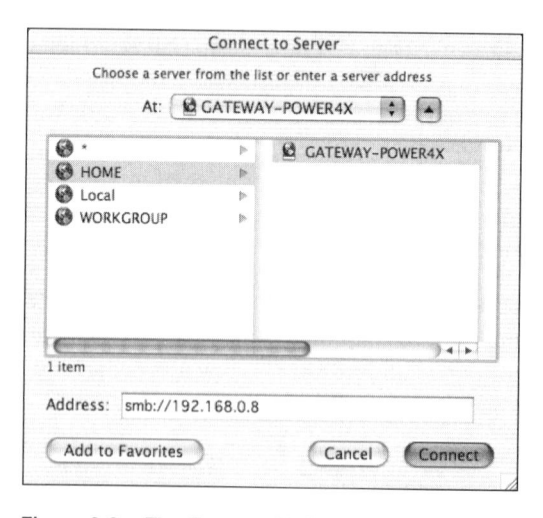

Figure 8.3 The Connect To Server feature in Mac OS X's Go menu is the new method of taking advantage of file-sharing features.

In Brief

A Different Way to Share Files

With older versions of the Mac OS, the normal situation was to share an entire disk or folder. For Mac OS X, the safest routine is to place items you want to make available to others on your network in your Public folder. That way, everyone who uses your computer can have access to the files without having to log in via any of your user accounts. That folder can also be used as a repository for the files you want to share or to receive across your network. In the "Immediate Solutions" section of this chapter, I'll explain how to establish access privileges so that only the users you specify can connect to your Mac without going through a login process.

TIP: To share a large number of files in other parts of your Mac's drive and see other files on your Mac's drive, without having to provide access to the rest of the volume, create an alias for each of those items and place them in your Public folder. Doing so will provide easy access to these items for users who connect to your Mac directly or across a network.

You can limit file access even further by using the Drop Box folder, which is located within your Shared folder. The Drop Box folder can be used to receive files, but those who network with your Mac will not be able to see any files in that folder or anywhere else on your Mac other than in the Shared folder.

A Look at Mac OS X's Networking Components

The tools to network your Mac require settings in two System Preferences panels and a dialog box. I'll describe them here, and then, in the "Immediate Solutions" section, I'll discuss how they're used:

- *Network*—This settings pane (see Figure 8.4) is used to configure your AirPort, Ethernet, and modem connections, all from a single set of screens. It replaces several control panels in the Classic Mac OS. This tool helps ease the setup process. Moreover, most of the setups are essentially the same as the ones you used in the Classic Mac OS. There's even a Location Manager feature, which can automatically switch network settings when you move your Mac to different locales.

NOTE: If you are working in an organization where a systems administrator handles network-related issues, you should consult with that person before you attempt to change any of the existing network settings on your Mac.

Chapter 8 Networking Overview

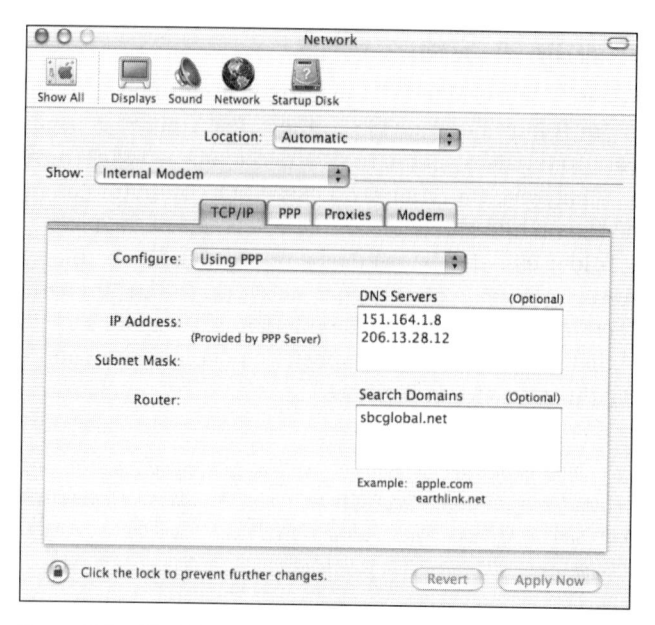

Figure 8.4 The Network settings pane is used to configure all your modem and network hookups.

- *Sharing*—You'll use this settings pane (see Figure 8.5) to activate Mac and Windows file sharing and other services. Web sharing uses the features of the Apache Web server software to let you run an Internet site from your Mac. You can also allow others to access your Mac via FTP or Telnet (remote login)—an option that adds to the flexibility of the new networking features. The Firewall tab activates built-in protection for your Mac, and the Internet tab is used to share your online connection across your network. Another option, available from the Internet tab, allows you to set up your Mac as a router to share your Internet connection with other Macs. When you choose the option to share the connection with others on your network, your Mac will distribute IP addresses across the network, and all the other computers have to do is use the DHCP option to hook up.

NOTE: Sharing a connection this way has its disadvantages. You need to keep your Mac on while the connections are being shared, and performance may take a hit as the Mac is doling out the shared hookup. Also, it won't work with AOL or CompuServe connections, which use a proprietary dialing program and require a separate account for each login. You can, though, use Apple's AirPort for an AOL login within these limitations.

In Brief

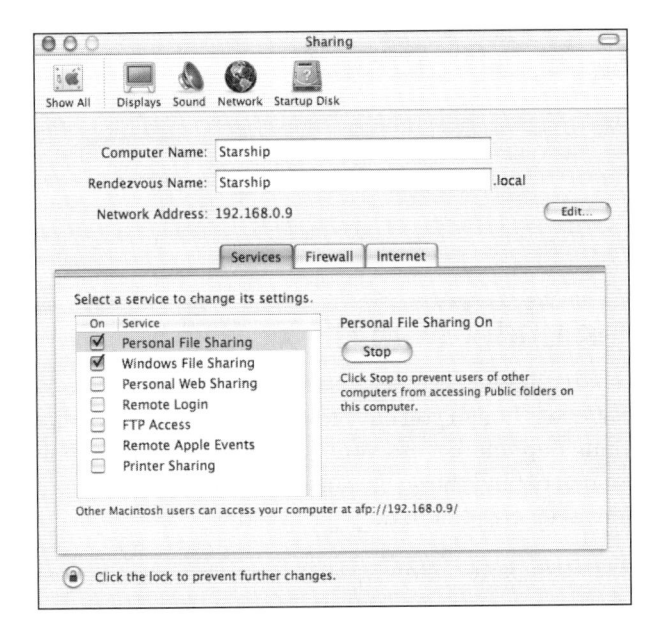

Figure 8.5 The Sharing settings pane is used to switch sharing services on and off.

- *Connect To Server*—This dialog box, available from the Go menu, is used to access all shared volumes (again, see Figure 8.3). You'll notice that aside from the Aqua user interface and a few additions, it bears a striking resemblance to the Network Browser application from the Classic Mac OS.

Immediate Solutions

Sharing Files Under Mac OS X

If you want to share files with a Mac running Mac OS X, you'll find the process familiar, even though you have to use a different set of dialog boxes to set things up and access your shares. The really sophisticated stuff happens behind the scenes, as Mac OS X's highly flexible network services are activated to do your bidding.

Here are the basic steps to follow to activate file exchanges using Mac OS X:

1. On the OS X Mac, open the System Preferences application, click the Network pane, and choose Built-In Ethernet from the Configure pop-up menu (see Figure 8.6). I'll discuss the modem option in the section entitled "Using Internet Connect for Dial-Up," later in this chapter.

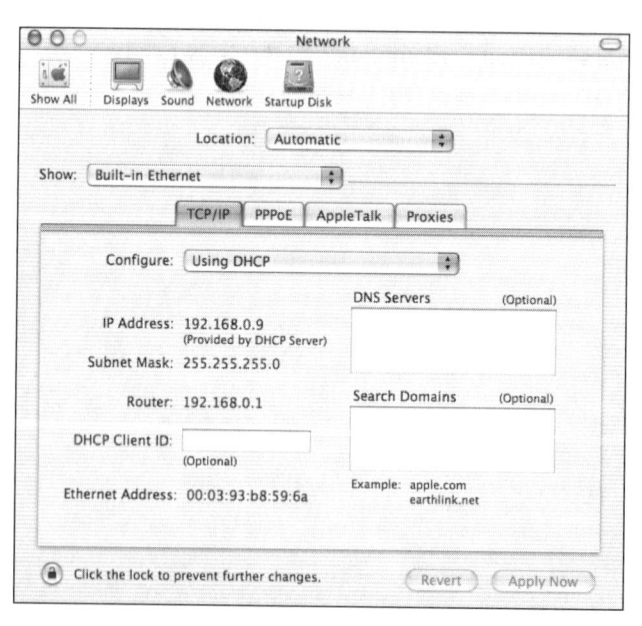

Figure 8.6 Change your network setups here.

Immediate Solutions

2. If the padlock is locked, click its icon, and then enter your administrator's username and password. If the login window shakes, it just means that you entered the wrong username and/or password—try again.

NOTE: If you do not have the username and password handy, please consult with your network administrator, if applicable. There's no way to access the protected features of Mac OS X without entering this information. The padlock remains open whenever you log in with an account that has administrator access.

3. If you're going to share files with an older Mac running a Mac OS version prior to 8.5, you'll need to network via AppleTalk (it's also required for many network printers). In this case, click the AppleTalk tab and click the Make AppleTalk Active checkbox (see Figure 8.7). To change the name of your Mac for network access, you'll need to move on to the Sharing pane.

NOTE: If you need to split up your AppleTalk connection to specific nodes, click on the Automatically pop-up menu, choose Manually and enter the appropriate network information required in your installation.

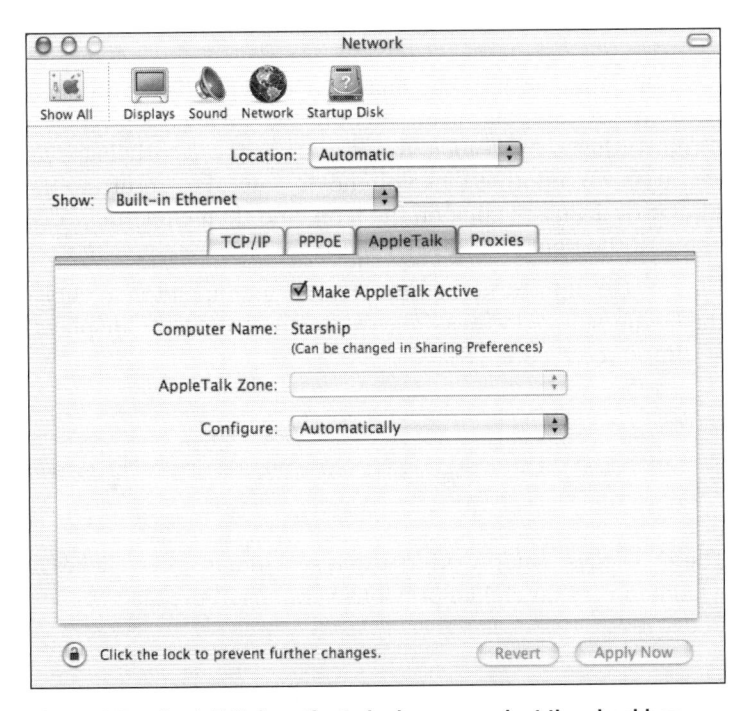

Figure 8.7   AppleTalk is activated when you select the checkbox.

8. Networking Overview

187

4. Click the Apply Now button to store your settings. If you forget, you'll see a reminder prompt in which you can click the Save button.

5. Click Show All at the top left of the System Preferences application window to display the other settings panes in System Preferences.

6. Go to the Sharing pane, and select the service you wish to share, which in this case would be Personal File Sharing (I'll get to the other options, such as Windows File Sharing, later in this chapter). This is the equivalent of selecting a service and clicking the Start button, but you save a keystroke. Note the Computer Name and Network Address of your Mac, either of which will be used to connect to your computer from elsewhere on the network. You can change the name of your Mac before sharing is activated, by the way. Once sharing is activated, it may take a few minutes to start up.

NOTE: Even though Mac OS X will use a computer's IP address, in addition to its name, to configure it, if you have five Macs at hand all named something like "Gene Steinberg's Computer," it would make sense to give each a unique identity, so you know which is which without having to remember which IP address is right, ask someone at the other end of the office or make a good guess.

7. Only the administrator can change access privileges for an entire drive. A regular user can only change access privileges for his or her users folder. To set custom access privileges for that folder or another disk volume on your Mac, return to the Finder or desktop, click on the icon, and then click on the name of the item you want to share.

8. Choose Get Info from the Finder's File menu, and then click the Ownership & Permissions disclosure triangle to display the settings (see Figure 8.8).

NOTE: If your Mac is accessed by a user who has administrator's privileges, the entire drive will be available for sharing, with the exception of another user, unless privileges for that user are changed.

9. The Privileges window offers three sets of access privileges, in a fashion very much like previous versions of the Mac OS. These are:

Immediate Solutions

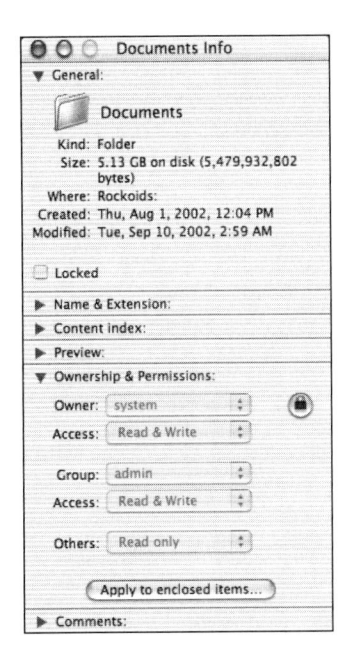

```
●  ○  ○              Documents Info
▼ General:
              Documents
       Kind: Folder
       Size: 5.13 GB on disk (5,479,932,802
             bytes)
      Where: Rockoids:
    Created: Thu, Aug 1, 2002, 12:04 PM
   Modified: Tue, Sep 10, 2002, 2:59 AM

   ☐ Locked
▶ Name & Extension:
▶ Content index:
▶ Preview:
▼ Ownership & Permissions:
     Owner: [ system        ⇕ ]   🔒
     Access: [ Read & Write  ⇕ ]
     Group: [ admin          ⇕ ]
    Access: [ Read & Write   ⇕ ]
    Others: [ Read only      ⇕ ]

          ( Apply to enclosed items... )
▶ Comments:
```

Figure 8.8 Set file access and sharing privileges in this window.

- *Owner*—This is the name of the owner or administrator of the files on this Mac. The normal access setting is Read & Write, which gives the owner the ability to access and modify files. By design, you can restrict your own access to files, but I'm not sure why you'd want to do that.

- *Group*—Each selected user of your Mac can be given a specific set of access instructions. Click the pop-up menu to change privileges, choosing Read & Write, Read Only, or Write Only. The Write Only setting lets the user place files in a Drop Box folder within the Shared folder but not see any other files. Files or folders "admin" group, such as your Mac's hard drive, are accessible by anyone with administrator's privileges.

- *Others*—These settings are identical to those for a group, except that when you set them here, anyone who connects to your Mac as a guest can have that level of access—even if they haven't been given specific user privileges.

Set your access privilege settings. They are activated as soon as they are changed. To keep the same settings for all the files and folders within a folder, click Apply to incorporate the settings.

Chapter 8 Networking Overview

NOTE: *Depending on your needs, you may prefer to establish separate settings for individual files and folders. So, use the Apply function with caution, because it will only duplicate the permissions you've established for the main folder or file. In addition, copying privileges to a folder with lots of files (or en entire drive) can take several minutes.*

10. If you have Macs on your network that are not using Mac OS X, and you want them available file sharing, the users of those Macs need to launch the File Sharing Control Panel (see Figure 8.9) or, as it's known on older Macs, Sharing Setup.

11. With File Sharing open, make sure the Network Identity fields are filled in with Owner Name, Owner Password, and Computer Name.

12. Click Start to activate file sharing.

NOTE: *The Network Identity is automatically configured when you use the Mac OS Setup Assistant to configure your Classic operating system. However, it's not uncommon for folks to change the settings; if your new Mac was pretested before delivery (perhaps to install a RAM upgrade due to those prevalent free RAM offers), you may find that the Assistant doesn't launch when you boot your Mac and thus no computer name was selected.*

13. Once sharing has been activated (it can take a few minutes, particularly on a Mac with several large drives attached to it), click the Close box to dismiss the File Sharing Control Panel.

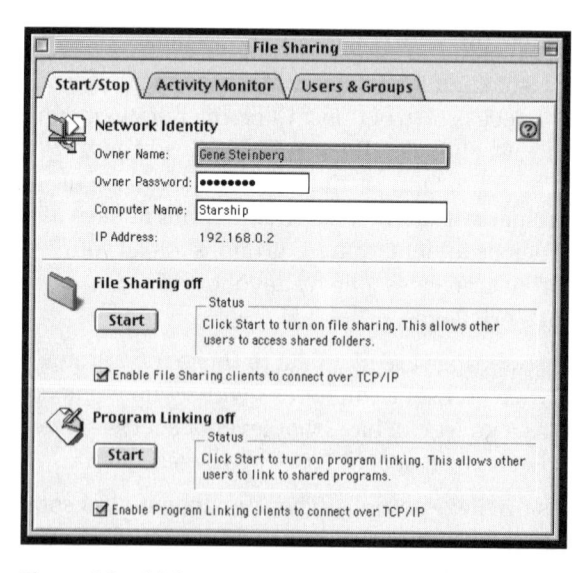

Figure 8.9 Make sure File Sharing is set up for your Classic Mac OS computers.

Immediate Solutions

NOTE: If your Mac supports TCP/IP-based file sharing and you have an always-on Internet connection, you'll see the IP address of your computer displayed. If you are using an AirPort or compatible 802.11b wireless network, you should use TCP/IP file sharing, where possible, for maximum performance in file transfers. AppleTalk file sharing with a wireless network can be mighty slow. In addition, for security reasons, you'll want to enable the maximum level of encryption supported by your wireless network. Otherwise even folks driving past your home or office will be able to access your computer network; a practice some call "drive-by hacking."

Accessing Shared Volumes with Network Browser

Depending on the Classic Mac OS version you're using, you can access shared volumes two ways: with Network Browser or the Chooser. These techniques are described in this section and the next.

Follow these steps to use Network Browser to access a shared volume:

NOTE: These file-sharing tools work only when you boot under a Classic Mac OS. If you are accessing shares under Mac OS X, you'll need to use the Connect To Server feature from the Finder's Go menu, described in the next section.

1. To access the Mac OS X computer from the other Mac (if it's running Mac OS 8.5 or later), launch the Network Browser application (it should be in the Apple menu), as shown in Figure 8.10. For earlier Mac OS versions (or as an alternative), you can also use the Chooser to access shares (see the next section).

NOTE: Be patient here. Each step might take up to a minute to complete, because the Mac takes a while to find that other computer with Network Browser.

2. Click the right arrow next to Network to display the name of your Mac OS X computer.

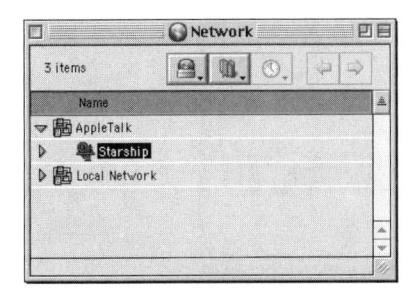

Figure 8.10 You'll see your shared Mac listed here.

191

3. Double-click the other Mac's name in the list to display the standard file-sharing login dialog. After you enter the proper user name and password and click Connect, you'll see a list of shared volumes that are just a double-click away from access.

4. When you've mounted the share volumes, you can quit Network Browser.

Accessing Shared Volumes with the Chooser

The other way to access a shared volume with the Classic Mac OS is with the famous (or infamous) Chooser. Follow these steps to use that feature:

1. Launch the Chooser from the Apple menu.
2. Click AppleShare to bring up the list of available file shares (see Figure 8.11).
3. Click the name of the share, and click OK.

NOTE: To access the shared volume via TCP/IP (which is available only for Macs running Mac OS X or Mac OS 8.5 through Mac OS 9.x on which the option to enable file sharing via TCP/IP is checked), click the Server IP Address button and enter the IP address of the computer you want to access in the text field.

4. Enter the user name and password in the login dialog box, and click Connect. You'll see a list of available shared volumes. Choose one or more to mount on your Mac's desktop. If you want to have those shares mount automatically at startup, check the appropriate boxes at the right of the volume's name.

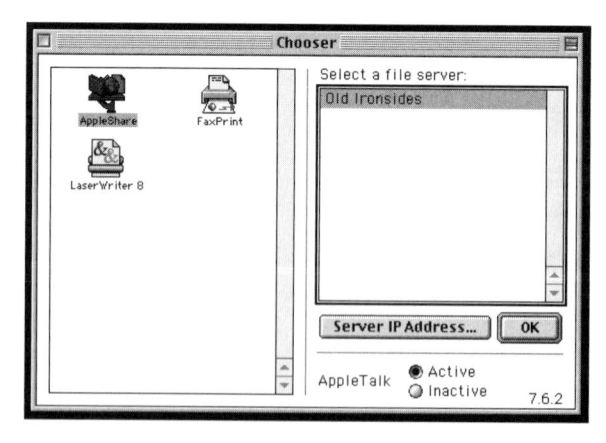

Figure 8.11   Select a networked computer from the list.

Immediate Solutions

5. Click the close box on the Chooser when you've finished mounting file shares.

Connecting to Shared Macs Under Mac OS X

For Mac OS X, the Go menu becomes a neat substitute for the Chooser and the Network Browser application. To access other shared computers, follow these steps:

1. Click on the Mac's desktop or the Finder icon in the Dock.
2. Choose Connect To Server from the Go menu to open the dialog box shown in Figure 8.12. Or just press Command+K.
3. From the pop-up menu at the top of the screen, choose the server you want to access. Or just browse the list for the ones to which you want to connect.
4. Unless you have a network with several zones, however, only a single list will be provided. Otherwise click on the name of the network connection or zone to locate the computers you want to access.

NOTE: If the computer you want to connect to isn't displayed, enter its IP address in the Address field and click Connect. If the computer is on your network or accessible via the Internet, the login window should appear in a few seconds. See the next section for information on accessing Windows or Unix file shares; the differences are slight, but there are differences.

Figure 8.12 Your available network shared volumes are shown here.

6. Double-click the name of the networked computer you want to access.

7. In the login window (see Figure 8.13), enter the username and password needed to access the Mac's shared volumes. When you choose guest access, your choices are usually limited to the Shared folder.

NOTE: *You may need to check with your systems administrator to get the login information for the other computers on the network. The Options button also lets you attach a password to your Mac's keychain. Chapter 6 covers this subject in more detail.*

8. In the next dialog box, double-click the name of the volume you want to access or just select it and click the OK button. You'll see it mounted on your Mac's desktop momentarily. It's also added to the Finder's display when you click the Computer icon in the Finder's toolbar (see Figure 8.14).

The shared volumes can be handled just like local volumes on your Mac's desktop, and can be accessed by the Mac OS X Finder in the same fashion. The only significant difference is when you trash a file from the shared volume. If you drag the item to the trash, you'll see a prompt notifying you that the file must be deleted immediately (you can't leave it in the trash and decide later whether to zap it from your computer).

NOTE: *If the shared volume is no longer accessible because either sharing has been turned off on the other Mac or there has been a system crash or restart, you'll see a prompt saying the file server has closed and when it happened.*

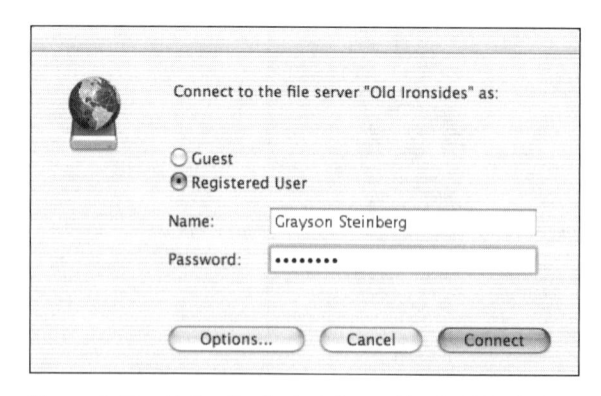

Figure 8.13 Enter the login information in this dialog box to bring up a list of available shares.

Immediate Solutions

Figure 8.14 Once a volume is shared, its icon appears on your Mac's desktop and the Finder (note the special globe icon).

Related solution:	Found on page:
Setting Up Keychain Access	153

Connecting to Shared Windows and Unix Servers

In addition to providing easy access to Macs on your network, Mac OS X also makes it possible to access Windows and SAMBA Unix file shares, via the Connect To Server feature. For the most part, access and the end result is identical to a Mac, but the access screens will look different.

Here's how it works:

1. Click on the desktop or click the Finder icon in the Dock.
2. Choose Connect To Server from the Go menu.
3. Locate the name of the computer you want to access. In the example shown in Figure 8.15, you see a Gateway desktop computer, running Windows XP, on the list.
4. Click Connect to access the login prompt.

195

Chapter 8 Networking Overview

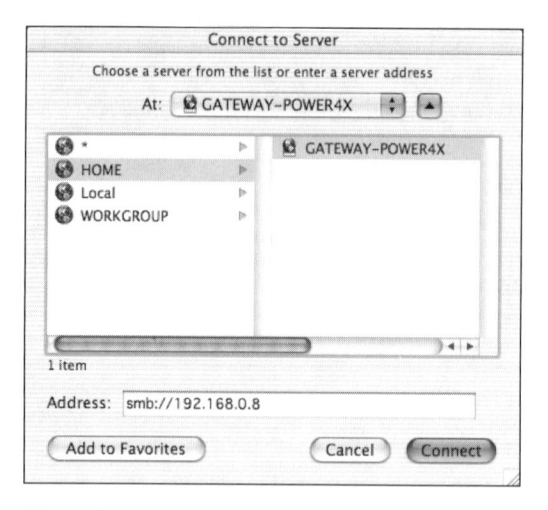

Figure 8.15 The Gateway Profile 4 on my home office network is listed among the network shares.

5. In the login prompt, enter the Workgroup/Domain name, your username, and your password.

NOTE: *Normally a Windows PC is listed under WORKGROUP unless this has been changed during the network setup.*

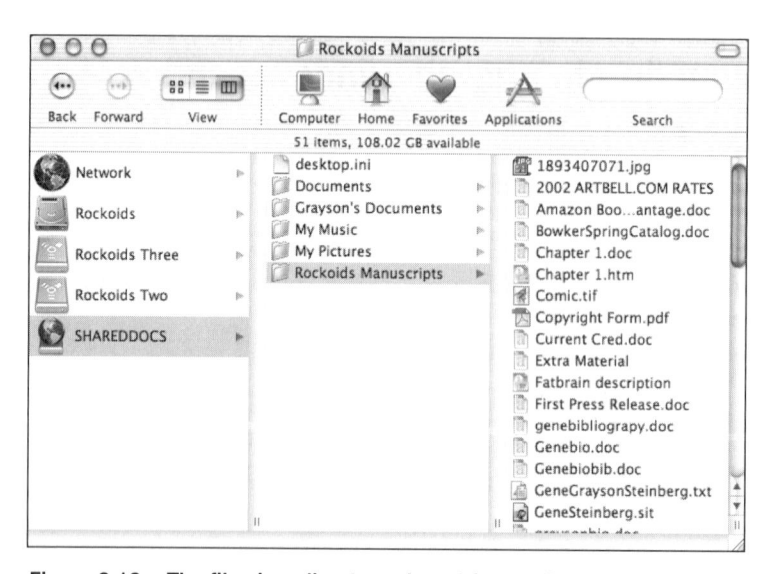

Figure 8.16 The files in a directory shared from a Gateway PC appear on my Mac is just another set of documents.

Immediate Solutions

6. Click the OK button to bring up the shared volume. As with Mac volumes, the ones you access from a Windows or Unix network will appear just like any drive on your Mac's desktop and the files will appear just as other files in the Finder (see Figure 8.16)s. The main difference is that the list of shared volumes or directories will appear in a pop-up menu.

NOTE: Like your Mac, you will need to set sharing privileges on your Windows PC to make specific portions of a drive available. It's usually best to restrict the sharing to the My Documents folder or a similar locale for files to be shared. The main directory for your Windows hard drive consists largely of system or application-related files that you will not wish to share.

Using Internet Connect for Dial-Up Networking

In the days of Apple Remote Access, you could call up your Mac from a remote location in order to access or send files. Your modem was used to hook up to the other computer's modem, and then—within the limits of dial-up file transfers, of course—your remote Mac was as easy to access as one connected to your local network. Mac OS X has no Remote Access Control Panel. Instead, you make your connection with the Internet Connect application, with more than a little help with the settings you make in the Network pane of the System Preferences application.

NOTE: Depending on your ISP, these settings might be made courtesy of an installer. You had the chance to install them when you ran the Setup Assistant right after you installed Mac OS X. I'm covering the process here in case you didn't enter the settings then or you want to change them now.

Here's how it's done:

1. Launch System Preferences from the Dock or from the Applications folder.

2. Click the Network pane and make sure the Internal Modem (or Modem) option is chosen from the Configure pop-up menu (as shown in Figure 8.17).

8. Networking Overview

197

Chapter 8 Networking Overview

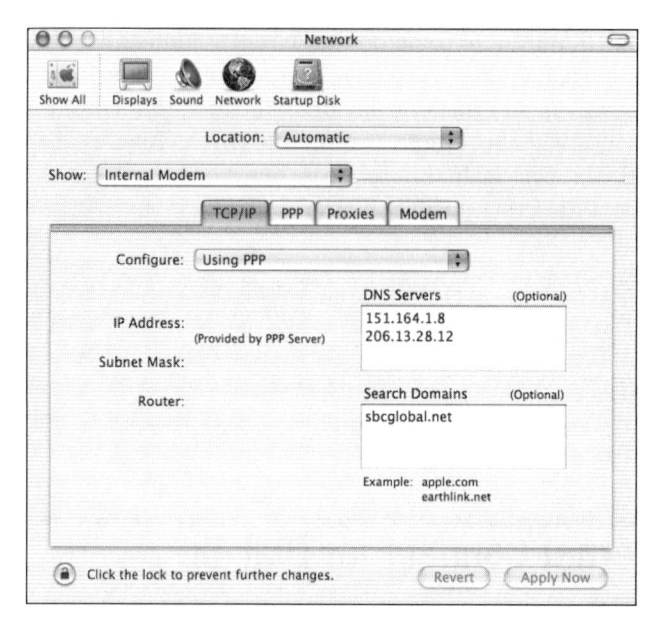

Figure 8.17 Enter your ISP's settings here.

NOTE: *One of the reasons for being able to enter separate settings for your AirPort, Ethernet, and dial-up TCP/IP access is to allow you to access any available network via Mac OS X's multihoming feature. Working with the built-in Location Manager software, you can automatically switch from AirPort to Ethernet to dial-up, depending on which port is available and which provides the speediest access.*

3. If it's not already selected, click the TCP/IP tab.
4. Make sure the Using PPP option is shown in the pane's Configure menu. The second setting, Manually, is used only for specialized situations that may be required by your network setup.
5. If required by your ISP, enter the correct numbers in the Domain Name Servers field.

Immediate Solutions

6. Under Search Domains, input the proper information. Again, your ISP may not need this setting. The example shown in Figure 8.17 has the regular settings for making a dial-up connection to Prodigy Internet (now going under the name SBC Yahoo Dial).

NOTE: *Where did these settings come from? In Chapter 2, I suggested that you obtain your setup from the Remote Access and TCP/IP Control Panels. Here's where they go. If you don't have the information, contact your ISP directly.*

7. Click the PPP tab to enter your dial-up information (see Figure 8.18).

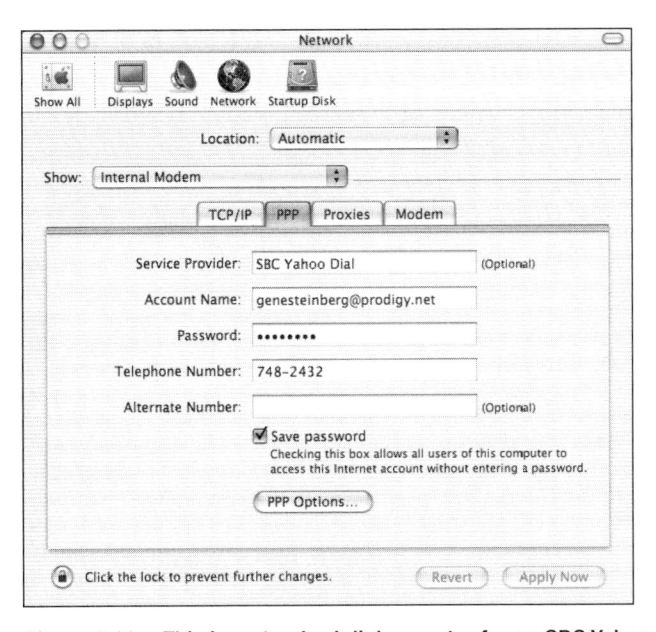

Figure 8.18 This is a standard dial-up entry for an SBC Yahoo access number in Tempe, Arizona.

199

8. Enter the telephone number, account name, and password for your account. When you click the Save Password checkbox, the password will be stored, but you can skip this process and enter it manually if others may have access to your Mac.

NOTE: You don't have to enter an alternate number, but it's a good idea, because then you have a choice if the first number is busy. You should put the name in the Service Provider field for identification in the event you use more than one, or to help you choose the proper option if you've created multiple Location setups (that's coming in the next section).

9. To fine-tune your online session, click the PPP Options button and enter the appropriate information in the dialog box (see Figure 8.19). All the items shown are defaults, except Connect Automatically When Starting TCP/IP Applications, which you may want to activate. This option will log you in to your ISP whenever you launch applications such as your browser or email client. Here are the options from which to select:

NOTE: If you have both cable modem and dial-up access to an ISP at your location, it's a good idea not to enter the option to connect automatically, because it will result in an attempt to dial up your ISP, rather than use your network-based Internet access.

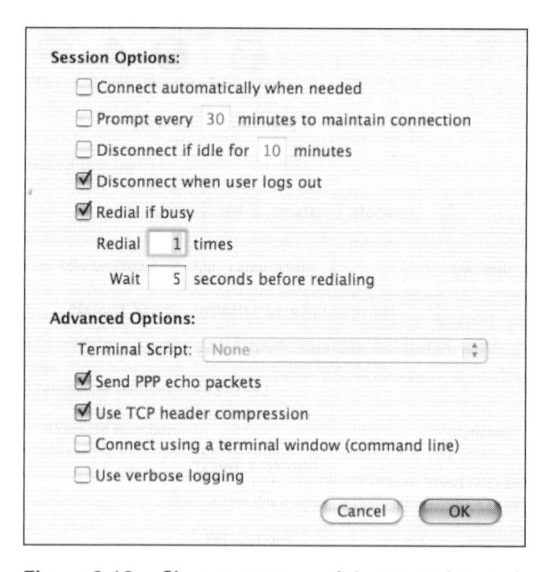

Figure 8.19 Choose your special connection options here.

Immediate Solutions

- *Session Options*—In addition to making your connection when you launch your Internet application, you can also get a warning prompt if you've been idle for a while, or automatically disconnect after a selected interval. This is especially helpful if you have a basic ISP account, which is billed by the hour if you exceed the monthly allocation. Another option, which is checked by default, redials your ISP in the event of a busy signal.

- *Advanced Options*—Depending on the needs of your ISP, you may have to select one or more of the options beyond those already checked. Your ISP or network administrator can give you this information.

10. When your settings are made, click the OK button.
11. To double-check your modem setup, or if you're not using a standard Apple Internal Modem, click the Modem tab (see Figure 8.20). You can select from a wide variety of modem scripts by clicking the Modem pop-up menu.

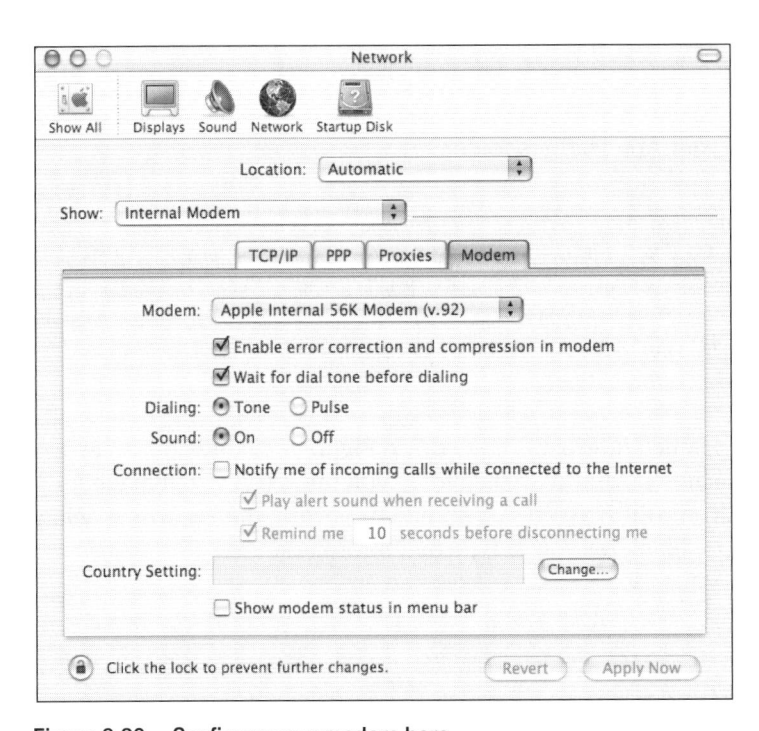

Figure 8.20   Configure your modem here.

TIP: *Although Mac OS X has built-in support for most popular modems, if you don't find any from the manufacturer of the one you own, try a Hayes or Apple model and see which provides the best connection. You can ask the company that makes your modem for a modem script, which would be installed under Mac OS X via the following folder path: Library>Modem Scripts.*

12. When you're done, click Apply Now to store your setup. Now you're ready to get connected.

Related solution:	Found on page:
Preparing for Mac OS X	31

Verifying Connectivity

Once you've established your dial-up settings, you should try logging on to your ISP and making sure everything works properly. Here's where you'll see Apple's replacement for the Remote Access Control Panel. To get connected, follow these steps:

1. Locate the Internet Connect application, which you'll find in your Applications folder.

TIP: *If you intend to use Internet Connect frequently, check the option labeled Show Modem Status In Menu Bar, available in the Network preference panel, at the bottom of the Modem tab. To access your ISP, click on the modem icon in the menu bar and choose Connect (it becomes Disconnect when you're logged in). The status of your connection will be displayed graphically. In this sense, the function is essentially the same as the Remote Access Control Strip under the Classic Mac OS.*

2. Launch Internet Connect (see Figure 8.21). It will display the name of your modem, along with the settings you made for your ISP. If you didn't enter a password, the Password field will be blank for you to type that information.

NOTE: *You can redo the settings from the Internet Connect application simply by clicking the Edit button, which launches the Network pane in the System Preferences application for you to reconfigure your setup.*

3. Click the Connect button to establish your connection. A status window will appear, indicating when your connection is established.

Immediate Solutions

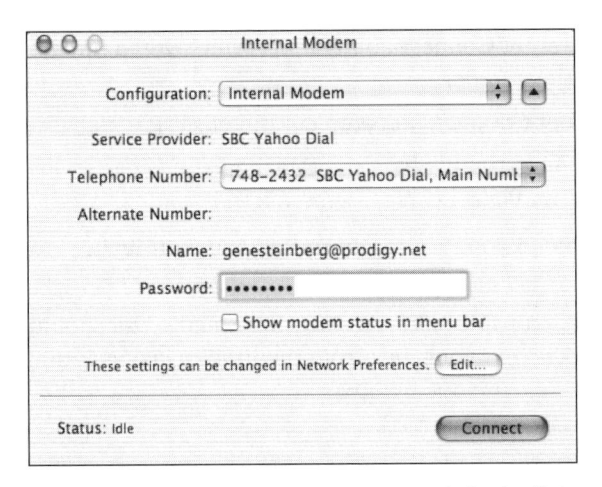

Figure 8.21 The settings previously made in the Network pane are duplicated here.

4. When your online session is done, click the Disconnect button (which toggles to Connect). The process is no different from the way it was done under the Classic Mac OS.

NOTE: Internet Connect will work even if your Internet application runs from the Classic environment, but it doesn't support the ability to connect with an application that uses its own dialing method, such as AOL or CompuServe.

Connecting Via a Virtual Private Network

Are you away from the office but need to hook up to the corporate network to check e-mail or access your files. Jaguar includes support for connecting to a Virtual Private Network (VPN). Such a network can be accessed over your online connection as easily as connecting to a local network. You don't need special software or a complicated configuration to stay in touch.

NOTE: Compatibility with a VPN requires that your corporate network system supports PPTP (Point-to-Point Tunneling Protocol). If in doubt, contact your systems administrator if you run into connection troubles.

Here's how to make that connection:

1. Locate the Internet Connect application, which you'll find in your Applications folder.
2. Launch Internet Connect, and connect to your ISP.
3. Once you're logged in, click on the File menu and select New VPN Connection Window (see Figure 8.22).
3. Enter the name of your corporate server, and your login information.
4. Click Connect and your connection will be made. You should not be able to access your files from the Finder, just as if they were on your Mac or a local network.

NOTE: *Unless you have a high-speed connection to the Internet, however, don't expect blazing speeds when trying to retrieve files. It is, however, useful for simple documents.*

Using Apple's Location Manager to Create Custom Setups

As with the Classic Mac OS, sometimes you want to move your Mac to different places, particularly if it's an iBook or a PowerBook. Apple's location feature lets you create custom AirPort, modem, and network setups for each particular location. That way, you can easily connect to the right local network and access the proper ISP without having to redo the settings. As you move from one place to another, just choose the correct location from the Network pane in the System Preferences application. Frequent travelers will treasure these features. Here's how it's done:

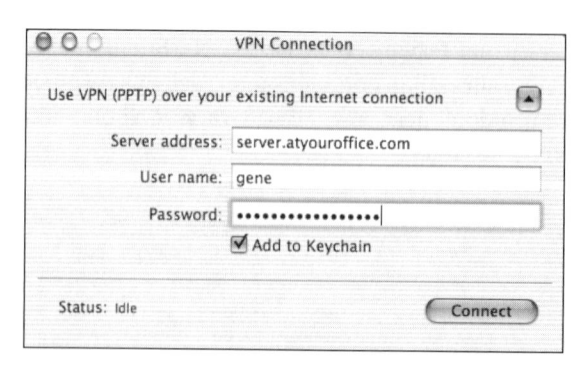

Figure 8.22   Enter your corporate hookup information here and Connect.

Immediate Solutions

1. Launch the System Preferences application and click the Network pane.
2. Click the Show menu and select the Network Port Configurations option, which brings up the display shown in Figure 8.23. You will see your present setup.
3. To create a new location, click the New Location button.
4. Type the name for your new location and select a port from the pop-up menu.
5. Click the OK button.
6. Make the Ethernet, modem, and connection settings for that location, and click the Apply Now button to store them.
7. Repeat this process for each location you want to create.
8. To switch locations, choose Location from the Apple menu and select the name of the location you want to use from the submenu. The default is Automatic, which simply accesses whatever available network service is required for a particular purpose.

NOTE: *The default setting is smart enough to sort out most routine differences in network setups as you move from location to location.*

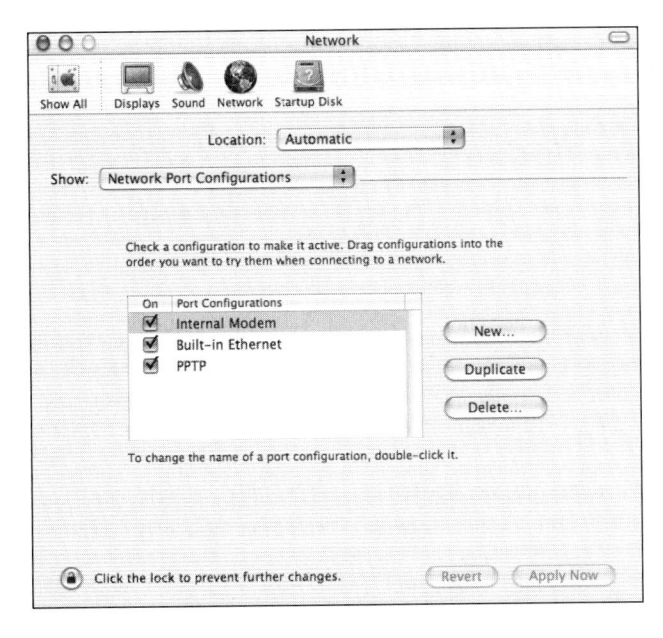

Figure 8.23   This is the standard setup for a typical Mac.

Setting Up a Web or FTP Server on Your Mac

One of the extra networking features afforded by Mac OS X is the ability to run your Mac as a Web server or to allow others to access files via FTP, which greatly expands your ability to make files available to others—with proper security precautions, of course (such as having a strong password).

Here's how to turn on Web sharing:

1. Launch System Preferences from the Apple menu, Dock, or Applications folder.
2. Click the Sharing panel.
3. Under Select a Service or Change Its Settings, click Personal Web Sharing.

NOTE: To allow FTP access to your Mac, click the Allow FTP Access button located just below the Web Sharing access control.

4. Check the bottom of the Sharing panel to see your Mac's IP number. Once activated, other users can connect to your Mac via this URL: **http://[computerIPaddress]/~[shortusername]/**. An example, to use a typical IP number, might be **http://192.168.123.254/~gene/** to access a site I might make available under Web sharing (the IP number is actually the default number of an Asante cable/DSL sharing router).

NOTE: When you turn on Web sharing, the files placed in the Sites folder in your Home or Users folder will be available for Web access. The default index.html file that's already present in that folder includes more information about using the Web Sharing feature; you might want to print this file or save under a different name if you want to refer to it later on.

WARNING! Some ISPs prohibit Web sharing as part of the end-user agreement, and they will cancel your account if you violate their terms. Before setting up your Mac for full-time duty as a Web server, you may want to contact the ISP first. Just making your Mac available for a short time to share files or information with another user probably will be all right. If you want full-time access, consider one of the free Web spaces provided by your ISP or consider subscribing to Apple's .Mac service. For business use, you may want to contact your ISP or a third-party hosting service to set up a Web server.

Immediate Solutions

5. If you want to allow other users to access your Mac and transfer files via an FTP client, such as Fetch or Interarchy, click Allow FTP Access. This setting is helpful if those with non-Apple operating systems are going to be connecting to your Mac.

6. To allow remote login to your Mac via a terminal application, click the Remote Login option in the Sharing preference panel. To send Apple events to your Mac (required for using AppleScript across the network), click the checkbox labeled Remote Apple Events.

WARNING! I mention this feature for your information only. You should use this feature with extreme caution, as it allows your user name and password to be clearly transmitted over the Internet, and thus make your Mac vulnerable to access by hackers. If you want to set up this sort of tool, you might consider downloading an SSH program instead. Check versiontracker.com for some choices for Mac OS X users. In the meantime, you'll also want to click on the Firewall tab and enable the feature for ports that are not being activated for sharing. This will provide an added measure of safety until better tools are secured.

7. Quit the System Preferences application after you've set your Web and FTP sharing options.

Can't Access a Drop Box?

Here's the problem. You attempt to copy or write files to the Drop Box folder on an AppleShare IP Server. But instead of seeing a progress bar to indicate that the files are being copied, you see a warning: "The operation cannot be completed because you do not have sufficient write privileges." The solution is to make sure that you attempt to send files only to a shared volume that has read/write privileges established. If you cannot change access privileges, contact your network administrator.

Correcting Network Access Problems

One of the hallmarks of the Mac operating system is easy networking. You plug one Mac into another, or into a printer, network hub, and so on, and with a few simple setups, you are sharing files and printing

207

without any great difficulty. Should your network installation not work, however, you should look into these possible solutions to the problem:

- *Recheck your settings.* Your first troubleshooting step should be to verify your setups in the Network pane of the System Preferences application. Remember that you will need to click the Apply Now button for changes to become effective (fortunately you'll be reminded by a Save prompt if settings are changed and not stored). One common problem is the failure to turn on AppleTalk, which means that standard network printers may not be available.

NOTE: *Don't assume Mac OS X is at fault. You should also recheck the settings on the other computers involved in the network connection. If the setup is good, see if your Mac OS X computer can work with a different computer or printer. By checking this, you will be able to isolate a probable source for your problem.*

- *Examine your networking hardware.* Consider rechecking the networked cables and your hubs. Whenever there's a complete connection to the network hub or switch, one or two green lights will appear on that jack on a hub to indicate a proper connection is being made. If there's no activity or connection light, consider swapping cables to see if the problem transfers itself to the other computer or printer to which the cable was connected. If the problem travels, replace the cable. If networking still doesn't work, consider whether your hub itself might be defective.

- *Use the Network Utility application.* Mac OS X supplies a handy tool that can help you examine the condition of your network in a more sophisticated fashion. You'll find the application in the Utilities folder, inside Mac OS X's Applications folder. After you launch the application, click a tab to access your network scouring features. Ping is the most common utility to check whether a network connection is being made; it sends a signal to the target Mac and then records whether the signal has been returned to you. Just enter the IP number of the Mac, click Ping, and see if you get a result on repeated probes. Click the Stop button when you're finished. Another useful feature is Traceroute, which displays the path packets take during their travels. It's useful in locating the source of a possible network problem. If these probes don't yield successful results, you should return to your network hardware and configuration to be sure you didn't miss anything.

- *Be careful about naming files copied to a Windows PC.* If you try to copy files to a PC on your network and keep getting error

Immediate Solutions

messages, make sure the file names are "legal." Under Wndows, a file name cannot contain any of following characters: \ / : * ? " < > " You may also run into trouble using extended characters. Visually inspect and change the names as needed, or just take a few precautions when you first name the files.

- *What if Windows File Sharing Doesn't Work?* Be careful about doing custom installs when you upgrade to Jaguar. If you are having a problem getting Windows File Sharing to work, it could be because you did a custom installation and deselected BSD Subsystem. This is the danger of being too creative. The only solution is to reinstall Mac OS X and keep this option selected. Fortunately, a simple "Upgrade" installation should not damage your settings or your Mac's reliability, but it's the only solution.

Protecting Your Network from the Internet

More and more folks these days have high-speed Internet connections. From cable to DSL, homes and businesses are joining the fast lane. (I discuss these and other fast access options in Chapter 21.) However, an always-on connection doesn't just deliver convenience; it also means your Macs are vulnerable to attack from Internet vandals who might want to play pranks with your computers, or attempt to retrieve passwords and other personal information. Nobody is immune from such intruders. Even Microsoft has been victimized of highly publicized network attacks on the secured servers that contain the source code for some of the company's software. Here are some ways to protect your network:

- *Use a hardware router to share connections.* Several companies manufacture Internet router products that will feed your Net connection across an Ethernet network to other computers (Macs and PCs). They include Apple's AirPort Base Station, plus products from Asante, Proxim (formerly Farallon), LinkSys, and MacSense, to name just a few. These products are all designed to distribute the connection, and some include a hub or network switch. Most of these products also offer a built-in firewall, which sets up a secured barrier to prevent outsiders from entering your network. The common form of security employs a network address translation (NAT) feature that, in effect, manages requests to and from the network and hides the true IP numbers of your workstations. As a result, network intruders will find it far more difficult to invade your systems.

- *Set up software firewalls.* Apple's built-in firewall will provide a good level of protection, but if you have a lot of critical data to secure, you may want to get something more full-featured. Current commercial entrants in the Mac marketplace include Symantec's Norton Personal Firewall (based on another program called DoorStop from Open Door Networks) and Intego's NetBarrier X. Both programs will help to block unauthorized traffic from reaching your Macs and can be adjusted to selectively allow certain traffic, as needed.

NOTE: Symantec has also bundled Norton Personal Firewall with Norton AntiVirus and Aladdin's iClean (which deletes old cache files and other items) to form an integrated package called Norton Integrated Security. A shareware alternative, FireWalk X, also offers a high level of protection.

- *Restrict distribution of administrator passwords.* Many of you have heard horror stories about vengeful former employees of a company stealing confidential files and other proprietary information. Although you may have legal remedies to get this material back, the cost in manpower and legal action can be tremendous, with no guarantee of success. The best approach is to be careful who gets access to passwords in your company, and perhaps to consider a non-disclosure agreement if employees have access to company secrets that could give a competing company an advantage. You should also follow through with my suggestion to use strong passwords when setting user accounts to further protect your network.

Related solution:	Found on page:
Choosing Personal Firewall Software	392

Chapter 9

The New AppleScript

If you need an immediate solution to:	See page:
Locating Mac OS X's AppleScript Collection	217
Choosing Mac OS X's Sample Scripts	217
Using Script Runner	219
Making or Editing Your First AppleScript	220
A Quick Primer on Folder Actions	223
Running a Script from the Unix Command Line	224
Using Toolbar Scripts	225

Chapter 9 The New AppleScript

In Brief

Hard to believe, but true. Despite a powerful operating system and incredible processing power courtesy of the Mac's G3 and G4 processors, or whatever might come in the future, a lot of the work you do on your Mac is manual. Every step requires an operation of keyboard and mouse. You locate a document in a specific folder with the Finder, and then double-click on the document to open it in the appropriate application. You then examine or edit the document. As necessary, you save it, print it, and proceed to the next document.

When you navigate the World Wide Web, you might enter a site's address or select one from your list of Favorites. During the course of a day, you carry out a number of repetitive steps.

What if you could make your Mac perform a complex set of repetitive steps just by running a single application or by accessing a simple command within a program? What if the tools to provide all that complex functionality didn't cost an extra cent and didn't require installing additional software? A dream? Something only a skilled computer programmer can do? Read on.

For years, the Macintosh operating system has had a built-in feature that lets you automate complex tasks. This capability is not reserved for computer programmers and highly technical power users. It's in use today in the graphic design departments of major companies around the world. This feature is used for creating print publications, editing videos, producing Web content, and automating everyday tasks, such as copying and printing files.

Did I say it was free? In fact, its origins can be traced way back to Mac System 7 in 1991. It's called AppleScript, and this powerful feature is already on your Mac and has no exact equal in the Windows world.

NOTE: To be perfectly technical, you can use Visual Basic for automating tasks in a number of applications from Microsoft and other companies. But AppleScript is far more user-friendly, and it's a standard part of the Mac OS.

In Brief

What AppleScript Can Do

The word *script* connotes an arcane language that is apt to confound and befuddle all but the most experienced Mac users. Yet AppleScript, although not quite plain English, is close enough to make it possible for folks like you and me to create scripts. What's more, using the scripts already available, you might be able to get all or most of the desktop automation you want without having to make anything at all.

In effect, AppleScript lets Mac programs communicate with one another and with the operating system. The scripts you make tell these programs what to do. For example, you might want scripts to automatically copy a file from one disk to another, to batch-process a series of images and apply certain Photoshop filters to them, and to save and print documents. And that's just the beginning. Many popular Macintosh productivity programs depend on AppleScript to exploit some of their most useful features.

NOTE: *To learn what sort of support an application has for AppleScript, check the application's documentation. AppleScript's uses range from the simple to the complex, and all variations in between.*

In the "Immediate Solutions" section of this chapter, you'll discover some of the tools Apple has already provided to let you exercise AppleScript. For now, here's a brief idea of what you can do with AppleScript:

- *Automate use of the Mac OS X Finder*—Many common Finder functions can be scripted. That means you can harness complex file-management features by launching a single script.

- *Automate Mac OS system functions*—From searching the Internet, to querying and directing XML-aware applications, to automatically adjusting a specific set of settings, AppleScript can handle operations that require repeating steps.

- *Automate workflow*—This is where AppleScript comes into its own in a working environment. Users of the popular desktop publishing application QuarkXPress, for example, can create scripts that access specific templates for pages, flow in text, import images, and scale and crop the images. In Adobe Photoshop, a script can be used to open all the images placed in a single folder, apply a specific set of program filters to them, and then save the images in a specific file format. Canvas 8 for Mac OS X can perform such functions as activating any of its extraordinary range of tools and functions, or preparing Web graphics without direct user intervention. Imagine if you had to do all this work manually, one step at a time, every time you needed to handle these chores.

- *Folder Actions*—This is a feature that originally made its debut in Mac OS 8.5, but was missing in the first two releases of Mac OS X. It allows a script to be connected or attached to a folder. The script is activated whenever a folder is opened, closed, moved, or items are placed within or removed from the folder. Even better, a combination of these actions can be configured to make for some pretty complicated operations with these folders, which one might call "drop boxes" or "hot folders."

- *Record your actions*—You don't have to write all your scripts from scratch. Many programs let you record a series of actions, using Apple's Script Editor application. After the steps have been recorded, you can save them as a script, and then have them run the same as any other AppleScript.

NOTE: *Which programs support the record function? In most cases, check the program's documentation. Sometimes it's not documented, and you have to open the application in Apple's Script Editor to see which functions are supported. One notable, undocumented example, is AOL for Mac OS X, which has a fairly wide range of scripting options, but doesn't mention the feature anywhere in its Help menu.*

AppleScript, however, is not the only desktop automation feature. Some commercial programs, such as CE Software's QuicKeys, perform similar functions, but have the added advantage of working with all Mac software, not just programs that can be specifically scripted. QuicKeys for Mac OS X (see Figure 9.1) includes the ability to record mouse actions and multistep actions (formerly called sequences), so that you can script complicated procedures.

Mac OS X Script Features

When you get started with AppleScript, you'll find that a number of Mac applications support this feature and thus will provide quite a bit of exposure to what this valuable tool can do. These include such standard applications as the Address Book, Finder, DVD Player, iCal, Image Capture, Internet Connect, iPhoto, iTunes, Mail, Print Center, QuickTime Player, Terminal, and TextEdit. In addition, AppleWorks 6.2x, which has been rewritten to support Mac OS X, can be scripted, as can Microsoft Entourage X, Stone Studio (a set of graphic applications and tools), and lots more.

In Brief

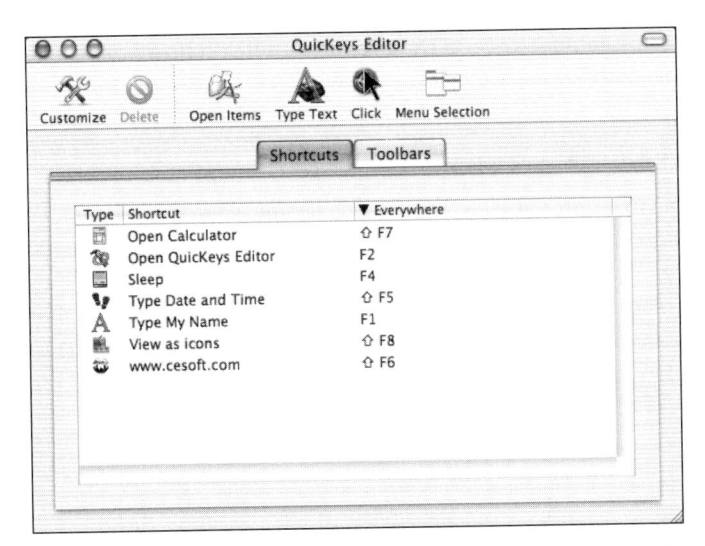

Figure 9.1 A long-time favorite of many Mac users, QuicKeys is making the migration to Mac OS X.

The Tools for Using Scripts in Mac OS X

Aside from the built-in functions of some programs that use AppleScript behind the scenes, an AppleScript can come in several forms—as an applet, as a fully compiled script, or as a text file containing the script commands. Which form to use depends on the program you're running, but the most common form of script is the applet. An *applet* is a small application; you can double-click it to start it, or you can drag and drop onto it an item that is subjected to the scripting action.

> **NOTE:** *In addition to double-clicking and dragging and dropping, you can place an AppleScript applet in the Dock so that it can be activated with a single click, use a toolbar script that is identified by a Finder icon, or use a handy utility Apple has placed in the AppleScript folder, in your Applications folder. The utility, Script Menu, puts up a menu bar icon to access your scripts. Script Menu. To activate Script Menu, just drag the little application to the menu bar and it will show up automatically.*

In addition to double-clicking and dragging and dropping, you can place an AppleScript applet in the Dock, so it can be activated with a single click. But one of the best ways to activate a script is to use a neat little menu bar add-on, Script Menu, which can put your scripts

9. The New AppleScript

215

in a set of submenus, divided by category. I tell you how to set it up in the "Immediate Solutions" section of this chapter.

AppleScript: The Future

The future of AppleScript is vast. Apple has made no bones about the fact that the present iteration of its system-wide scripting language works fine with both the Carbon and Cocoa environments, so it doesn't matter whether software developers use either. In addition, AppleScript continues to function with Classic applications, so there's no fear of losing the functionality of scripts made with such programs as QuarkXPress.

NOTE: Quark has committed to bringing its flagship desktop publishing application into the Mac OS X environment. You'll want to check with the company for the timetable. At the time this book was written, QuarkXPress for Mac OS X was expected to appear in early 2003. The existing versions, however, should operate fine in the Classic environment.

NOTE: If you are intrigued with Mac OS X's UNIX core, you'll be pleased to discover that Apple has incorporated a "Do Shell" script that allows you to script various actions. This is something you'll want to experiment with over time.

Immediate Solutions

Immediate Solutions

Locating Mac OS X's AppleScript Collection

Before you get started making a script of your own, you might want to try using the ones Apple has provided. You'll get a good idea of what an AppleScript can do, and by examining the script in the Script Editor application, you'll learn the scripting language; this will go a long way toward helping you develop your scripting skills. To locate the scripts, follow these steps:

1. Open the Applications folder.
2. Double-click on the AppleScript folder.
3. Open the Example Scripts folder, and then open the folder that contains scripts in the category you want to try.

After you've located the scripts you want, you can open them and see how they strut their stuff. You'll find, by and large, that the lingo is clear enough for you to understand how they accomplish the various actions.

Choosing Mac OS X's Sample Scripts

As explained in the previous section, Apple has assembled a small collection of useful scripts that you can use to learn how AppleScript works. Here's a list of the script folders and some of the scripts provided:

- *Basics*—These scripts are designed to help you discover the fundamentals of preparing your own AppleScripts. The scripts provided will transport you to the AppleScript pages at Apple's Web site, launch the Script Editor application, and give you a tour through the handy Help menus on the subject.

217

- *ColorSync Scripts*—Apple's built-in ColorSync technology allows for superior color calibration and the ability to match up the colors you see on your monitor with the colors from a scanner or other input device and a printer or proofing device. This folder contains a number of scripts that allow you to handle color profiles, including one that will mimic a PC monitor. This particular script is useful if you exist in a cross-platform environment.

- *Finder Scripts*—These scripts are designed to direct the Finder to perform various functions. They can alter file and folder names in various ways, from changing case to searching and replacing the names of files in a folder. In addition, file and folder names can be trimmed to look more readable in a Finder window.

- *Folder Action Scripts*—Actually Jaguar has two folders devoted to scripts that turn this nifty scripting feature on and off and add to its functionality. The first, Folder Actions, contains the scripts that turn the feature on or off or allow you to add or remove an action from a selected folder. The second, Folder Actions Scripts, is only available once you run the script to Attach a Folder action.

- *FontSync Scripts*—A boon for those with huge font libraries. The two scripts available with Jaguar let you create and match up your FontSync profiles.

- *Info Scripts*—One lets you change your Date & Time setting, and another produces a font sample sheet in TextEdit with all your installed fonts.

- *Internet Services*—These scripts exploit AppleScript's XML capability to query Web sites. They provide the current temperature in any USA location and retrieve stock quotes (assuming you want to know whether your favorite stock has gone up or down).

- *Mail Scripts*—One entrant in this folder can be used to set an address and a subject line for an email message. Once you enter these values (you have to set a default address first), the script will automatically open the Mail application and then populate a new message window with the information. Other scripts include such features as enhanced import from other e-mail programs and address book import.

- *Navigation Scripts*—These scripts are designed strictly to work with the Finder. They will activate a new Finder window pointing directly to a specific folder. There are scripts for the Applications, Documents, Favorites, and Home folders.

Immediate Solutions

- *Script Editor Scripts*—These all have a single purpose—to help you write a script that runs properly. Each is designed to test a particular script function, such as checking for syntax errors. They are all useful if you want to hone your AppleScript skills.
- *Sherlock Scripts*—The sole entrant when this book was being written allowed you to use Sherlock's handy Internet searching features. I discussed Apple's search application in Chapter 7.
- *URLs*—The scripts in this folder are designed to access specific Web sites. These scripts contain the examples I use when I show you how to modify or create your own scripts.

NOTE: One odd entrant in the URLs folder is a relic of the past, a script that connects to MacWeek's Web site. Curiously, MacWeek ceased publication several years ago, before Mac OS X appeared on the market..

Related solution:	Found on page:
Searching the Internet	172

Using Script Menu

To get started with AppleScript in Mac OS X, you'll want to set up Apple's Script Menu, a useful system menu add-on. You can use this program to both organize and run your scripts (see Figure 9.2). Here's how to work and add scripts with Script Runner:

NOTE: By default, Apple installs its sample collection of scripts for you. So, when you click the Script Menu, it's ready to roll with a decent number list of scripts to try.

1. Locate your copy. Script Menu is in the Applications folder.
2. Drag Script Menu to the left side of the menu bar, where an AppleScript icon will suddenly appear.
3. To access a script, click on the icon, which will bring up a list of available scripts, all neatly sorted into categories.
4. If you want to add some scripts of your own, click on Choose Scripts folder, and place the scripts inside..

9. The New AppleScript

219

Chapter 9   The New AppleScript

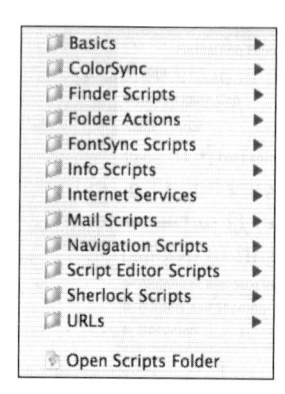

```
Basics               ▶
ColorSync            ▶
Finder Scripts       ▶
Folder Actions       ▶
FontSync Scripts     ▶
Info Scripts         ▶
Internet Services    ▶
Mail Scripts         ▶
Navigation Scripts   ▶
Script Editor Scripts ▶
Sherlock Scripts     ▶
URLs                 ▶

Open Scripts Folder
```

Figure 9.2   Script Menu is a convenient way to access all your scripts from a single, simple interface.

5. Removing a script is a simple matter of dragging it from the Scripts folder or whatever folder it's located in. The next time you invoke Script Menu, the script will no longer be available.

Making or Editing Your First AppleScript

Although AppleScript is a plain-English language, you need to use some basic commands to make your scripts work. In this section, I'll show you how to create your first script, just to give you an idea of how it's done. Using these techniques, after you learn the syntax, you'll be able to make scripts as easy or complex as you want.

NOTE: *I am not trying to minimize the learning curve for AppleScript. It takes time, study, and some practice to become flexible in writing reliable scripts. To learn more about the subject, visit the AppleScript Web site at www.apple.com/applescript. There, you'll discover sample scripts and online tutorials that will help you learn both simple and complex scripting skills.*

In this script, you will tell Microsoft's Internet Explorer to access a Web site—in this case, mine. Here's how to make your first script:

1. Locate the Script Editor application, which is in the Utilities folder inside the Applications folder.

2. Double-click the program to launch it (see Figure 9.3).

3. When the program is running, a blank script window should be on your screen. If it's not, choose New Script from the program's File menu.

Immediate Solutions

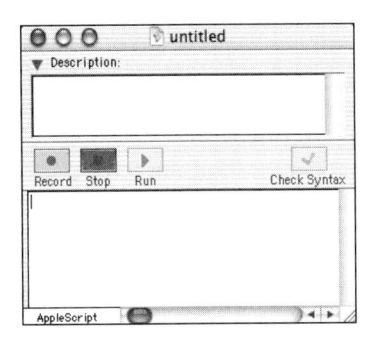

Figure 9.3 Creating an AppleScript starts here.

4. In the Description field, enter a sentence or two that describes the purpose and function of your script.

5. The first element in your script is a property. The property defines the item you will be acting on in the script. In this case, the URL **www.macnightowl.com** will be accessed. So, type the following text and then press the Return key (don't worry about writing commands in bold as you see them in a completed script; it's not necessary):

    ```
    property target_URL: "http://www.macnightowl.com/"
    ```

6. Type the following command, which tells the script to ignore how an application responds to the command:

    ```
    ignoring application responses
    ```

7. In the next set of commands, specify the application that you want to script, tell it what action to perform, and then close this set of commands:

    ```
    tell application "Internet Explorer"
    Activate
    GetURL target_URL
    end tell
    end ignoring
    ```

NOTE: *You don't use Internet Explorer? No problem. You can put the name of the browser you prefer, such as Netscape or OmniWeb, in its place.*

9. The New AppleScript

221

8. You are almost at the finish line, and your Script Editor window should look much like the one in Figure 9.4. The next step is to make sure the script was written properly. Click the Check Syntax button. The script you just wrote will be checked for errors. AppleScript is very literal-minded, so if a single letter in a command is wrong, you'll see what it is and what you need to do to fix it.

NOTE: *When a script is examined for syntax, it will take on the text formatting shown in Figure 9.4, with bold commands. Before you check the syntax, the script is all straight text; you don't have to format any of it manually.*

---

9. If the script has an error, now's the time to recheck the script and fix the problem. If the script checks out, choose Save As from the File menu.
10. Type a name for your new script that corresponds to its purpose, choose Compiled Script as the format, and specify the location where the script will be saved. The best place to save the script is in the URLs folder, under Example Scripts, so that it will be recognized by Script Menu in the appropriate folder.
11. Click the Save button.
12. To make sure your script truly does what you want, go ahead and run it via Script Menu. Launch Internet Explorer. If the script to access a specific URL was compiled correctly, it will access the Web site you specified (see Figure 9.5).

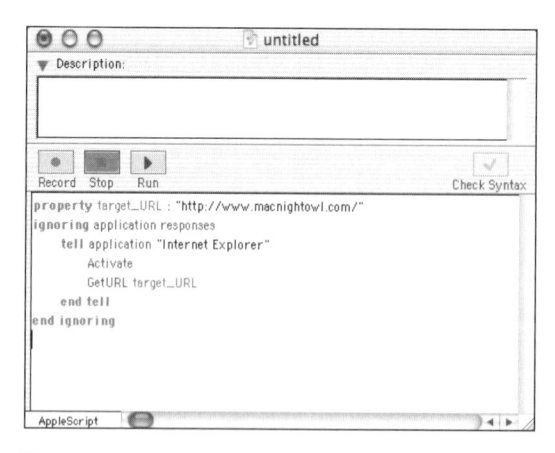

Figure 9.4 Here's the completed script, already formatted.

Immediate Solutions

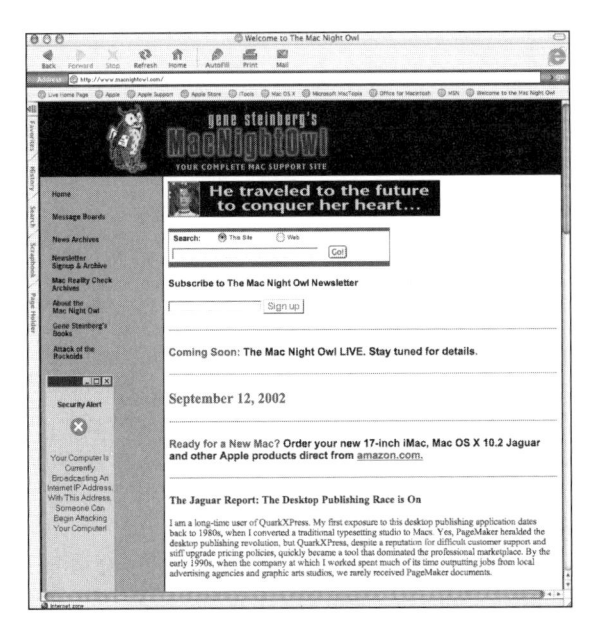

Figure 9.5   Success! The author's Web site was opened, courtesy of the script you created.

A Quick Primer on Folder Actions

Once you have a chance to give Folder Actions a try, you'll wonder how you lived without it. From backing up critical files, to performing batch processing actions, this can be a powerful tool.

Here's how you use it:

1. First you'll want to make sure Script Menu is installed. Click on Script Menu, and choose Enable Folder Actions from the Folder Actions sub-menu.

*NOTE: If you're adept at AppleScript, you can select from one of five Folder Action "handlers" that are located in the Standard Additions dictionary. You'll find a few examples of cool Folder Actions at Apple's Web site, at **http://www.apple.com/applescript/folder_actions/**.*

2. Return to the Script Menu, and this time choose Attach Folder Action from the Folder Actions sub-menu.

3. In the dialog box that appears, as shown in Figure 9.6, select a Folder Action and click OK.

223

Chapter 9 The New AppleScript

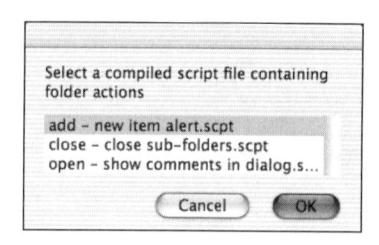

Figure 9.6 Choose a Folder Action from this dialog box.

4. Once a folder is selected, you'll see a standard Open dialog box in which to select the folder to which the script is attached. Once the folder is selected, click Choose. From here on, performing the specified action on the folder, such as adding or removing an item, or just opening or closing the folder, will trigger the script.

5. If you no longer want to use the script, return to Script Menu and choose Remove Folder Actions, and, in the next dialog box, choose the folder from which you want to deactivate the Folder Actions.

6. You can turn off Folder Actions entirely, if you feel the need to, simply by selecting Disable Folder actions from Script Menu's Folder Actions sub-menu.

Running a Script from the Unix Command Line

To try running an AppleScript from Mac OS X's Unix command line, here's what to do:

1. Locate the Terminal application in the Utilities folder, within the Applications folder.

2. Double-click the Terminal application to launch it.

3. In the command line, type "osascript" and then type the name of the script.

4. Press Return to activate the script. If you enter the correct file name, the script should run precisely the same as if it were accessed via Script Menu.

Using Toolbar Scripts

Another way to access a script is via the Finder's toolbar. Apple has provided a set of scripts that perform a variety of Finder-related functions, such as opening and closing folders and hiding open applications. You can find these and more at the AppleScript Web site, at **http://www.apple.com/applescript/toolbar/**.

To use one of these scripts, just follow these steps:

1. Open any Finder window.
2. Drag the script you want to the Finder's toolbar.
3. To use the script, just click its icon.

TIP: If you would also like to use these scripts via the Script Menu application, place them in the Scripts folder, within the Library folder. The advantage of the Script Menu is that it's available from all Mac OS X applications (no, you won't see it when you run a Classic application).

Chapter 10

Installing Programs Under Mac OS X

If you need an immediate solution to:	See page:
Handling Complex Application Installations	233
Using an Installer	233
Using a Disk Image	233
Making a Startup (Login) Application	234
Using the New Open Dialog Box	237
Using the New Save As Dialog Box	239
Using the Services Menu	242
Troubleshooting Software Installation Problems	242

In Brief

The more things change, the more they stay the same. Way back when, you could install an application on your Macintosh simply by dragging the application's icon from a floppy disk to your hard-drive icon. In a few moments, the program would be on your Mac, a double-click away from running.

Over time, however, things became a lot more complicated for the Classic Mac OS. A single application might consist of hundreds of files, and not all those files are placed in the same folder. Some go into disparate locations inside the System Folder. More often than not, it isn't even readily apparent which file belongs to what program. So, the installation is handled by an installer that is designed to sort out all these files for you and, if necessary, to restart your Mac.

Removing an application can be totally frustrating unless the installer has an Uninstall option. There's even a third-party program—Spring Cleaning, from Aladdin Systems—that is designed to remove all vestiges of a program. I'm reminded of the Add/Remove feature of Windows (which persists even in Windows XP) as an example of how complicated a program installation can get; some Windows software installations require multiple restarts.

NOTE: *Yes, there is indeed a Mac OS X version of Spring Cleaning, but as you'll see shortly, the need for uninstalling an application is sharply reduced.*

Introducing the Package

Beginning with Mac OS 9, Apple came up with a better idea for Mac users (although it's not unique to the Mac)—the *Package*. A Package is simply a folder that contains an application and all its support files, whether 1 or 1,000. But all these elements are hidden from the end-user. The Package appears on your Mac as a single icon that you can double-click to launch the application located within the Package folder.

Installing is a dream—a throwback to the earliest days of the Macintosh. Just drag the application's package icon to the appropriate folder (usually the Applications folder) and launch it.

In Brief

Removing an application involves the same process. You drag it to the trash and empty the trash, and all elements of that program (except for preferences files) are removed. It's remarkable that the best way to install and remove a program was the way it was done originally, back in 1984 when the first Mac appeared on the scene.

The Microsoft Way

Microsoft, which has paid more attention to the Mac platform in recent years, has been featuring drag-and-drop installation of its software since Office 98 came out in 1998. The process involves dragging a folder to your Mac's hard drive. However, you still have a visible folder containing loads of separate files, and you still must open that folder to run any of the applications you've installed.

Also, when you first launch any recent Microsoft application, it will populate the older Mac OS Extensions folder with a bunch of files, and these must be manually removed if you decide to uninstall the software. So, Microsoft's drag-and-drop installation is only part of a solution—but it's a step in the right direction.

NOTE: *To be perfectly fair, there is an installer on the Office v. X CD. But it's designed for optional installs of fewer or extra components, and isn't needed just to install the software in its standard form.*

Exploring New Application Features

As I explain throughout this book, any application written to support Mac OS X inherits a bevy of beautiful interface features and Unix-based reliability. In addition to preemptive multitasking and protected memory, you'll see visible differences to enhance your computing experience. These differences include:

NOTE: *Although older, Classic Mac applications can run under Mac OS X, they do not inherit any of the features about to be discussed. These are all the province of programs developed for the Carbon or Cocoa programming environments.*

- *Services*—Available in the Applications menu of many applications, the Services command produces a submenu that makes it possible for you to access the features of another application. This feature allows you to select text or a picture in your document and then go to the Services menu, choose a command from another application, and have that command executed in that program. In effect, you can send the text from one program to another without having to launch the second application, drag text between them, or use Export and Import features.

NOTE: *Although Services is available for both Carbon and Cocoa applications, it's up to Carbon application developers to add specific support for its powerful features.*

- *Open dialog box*—The venerable Mac Open dialog box has been one of the most confusing features of the operating system. It can be difficult for folks to navigate through large collections of nested folders and various disks to find a file. Although the Open dialog box was updated in Mac OS 8.5 with a new scheme, called *navigation services*, this was only part of what needed to be done. For Mac OS X, Apple has redesigned this dialog box yet again, and the new version, affectionately called *sheets* (see Figure 10.1), simplifies navigation tremendously. In addition, it's non-modal, which means that it doesn't prevent you from doing something else on your Mac until it's dismissed. You can bring up the Open dialog box and then switch to another application, and the Open dialog box will still be there when you return; the operation of your Mac is not affected.

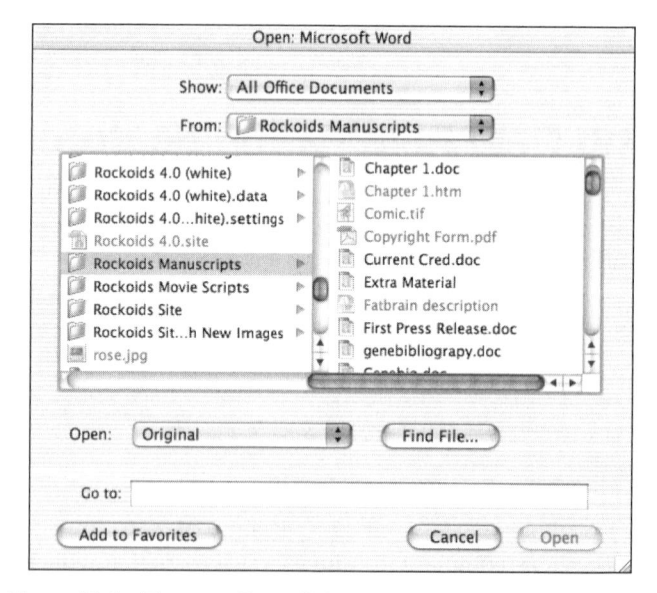

Figure 10.1 The new Open dialog box makes it easier for you to locate the file you want to use.

In Brief

TIP: *Users often overlook the Open dialog box. A prime example is the common practice of many Mac users to double-click a file's icon to open it, even if the application used to make the file is already open. Apple has had to do its homework here, and it has made things somewhat better for Mac OS X.*

- *Save As dialog box*—Another bugaboo of the older versions of the Mac OS was the Save As dialog box. When you wanted to save your document, where were you putting it? How often did you waste time figuring out the correct place (if there was one) to put a file? The Mac OS X version of the Save As dialog box opens as a sheet in the document window in which you're working (see Figure 10.2). There's no question about what you're saving, and the simple elegance of its interface makes it easy for you to specify precisely where your document is going so you can easily locate it later—without a headache or constant use of the Finder's file-search utility.

- *New location for the Quit command*—This is a logical issue rather than a critical one. Instead of putting the Quit command in the customary place in the File menu, Apple put it in the application menu. The logic is that the command affects the application, not the file (except indirectly, because files are closed before an application is closed). If nothing else, logic wins here.

TIP: *Regardless of the location of the Quit command, pressing Command+Q still activates this feature. Some things never change, thank heaven.*

- *Font panel*—Not all applications designed for Mac OS X will inherit this feature (just those programmed in the Cocoa environment, unless Apple changes it), but those that do use the Font

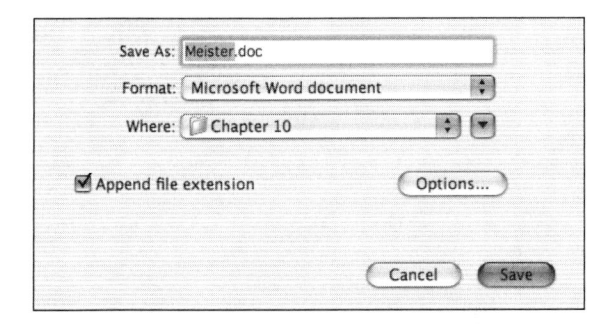

Figure 10.2   A new way to simplify the process of saving your document; this is the version you see in Word for Mac OS X.

231

panel will enjoy enhanced abilities to access fonts and manage a font library. As described in Chapter 16, Mac OS X has native support for PostScript, TrueType, and OpenType fonts, plus all those bitmap fonts that date back to the original versions of the Mac OS. With the Font panel (see Figure 10.3), not only can you select your fonts, but you can preview them in the sizes you want and create special collections to ease font management.

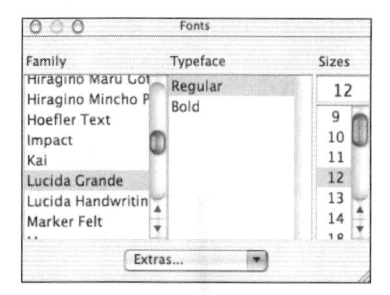

Family	Typeface	Sizes
Hiragino Maru Got	Regular	12
Hiragino Mincho P	Bold	
Hoefler Text		9
Impact		10
Kai		11
Lucida Grande		12
Lucida Handwritin		13
Marker Felt		14

Figure 10.3 The Mac OS X Font panel, when available in your application (at least the ones developed via Apple's Cocoa API), eases font handling.

Immediate Solutions

Handling Complex Application Installations

Mac OS X's Package feature greatly simplifies the installation and removal of applications, but some programs, such as those from Adobe and Symantec, require more complex installation processes. This can also happen when you're trying to install a Classic application. The following sections describe some of the installation options.

Using an Installer

The normal way to install an application—when you're not using Mac OS X's new techniques—is to load a CD and double-click an installer application. After an installer is launched, read the prompts and other on-screen instructions. Should the installer application ask for a location for the application, specify the Applications folder for ease of organization.

At the end of the installation, you might see a Restart prompt. Click it to restart your Mac. After the restart, you'll be able to use the application normally.

NOTE: In my experience, Restart prompts are quite rare in Mac OS X installations. You usually see them only if the installer needs to install certain system-related software (or one of Apple's own Mac OS X updates), such as Norton SystemWorks or Norton Utilities. An example is MouseWorks, which is used to provide custom scrolling, mouse movement, and direct access features for Kensington's line of input devices.

Using a Disk Image

Another way to distribute software is to use the disk image. The disk image has the virtue of being a carbon copy of the original distribution disk for the software, so you can use it without needing to have the disk media present. A disk image can consist of just the installation files or the full installation CD.

233

> **NOTE:** Just about all of Apple's software files are distributed in disk image form for convenience. Many other publishers (and even shareware developers) are using a similar technique for efficient transfer of their products.

To use a disk image, follow these steps:

1. Locate the disk image file. It will usually be identified by a file name with the extension .img or .smi and an icon that looks like a small hard drive embedded into a document. Double-click the file's name. Over the next few seconds, the file will be checked to make sure it isn't damaged. If it turns out to be damaged, you will have to get another copy (download it again, for example).

> **TIP:** If the file was compressed for distribution to save download time from the Internet, the file may come as a compressed archive, which sports a .sit or .hqx extension. If you have a file of this sort, double-clicking it ought to be sufficient to activate the decompression software (StuffIt Expander, which comes with Mac OS X). If you want to be able to compress documents yourself, considerStuffIt Deluxe 6.5 and StuffIt Expander 6.5, available from Aladdin Systems. The latter is free, so you should consider downloading it from the publisher's Web site at **www.aladdinsys.com**. The installation process fully supports Mac OS X.

2. When the file opens, it will put a disk image icon on your Mac's desktop. Double-click the icon to reveal its contents (see Figure 10.4).

3. If the file contains an installer, double-click the installer to proceed.

> **NOTE:** When you open the contents of a disk image file, you'll want to see if they include any ReadMe files. If there are ReadMe files, open them to see if you need to follow any special instructions to install the application or prepare for the installation.

4. Should the disk image contain the actual file or files to be installed, look for instructions on how to proceed. Microsoft's Office v. X (see Figure 10.5) and some Internet applications might even include a text description on the disk image or on the CD itself explaining what to do (usually just drag the installation folder to your Mac's hard drive).

5. When the installation is done, you can proceed with using the new software.

Making a Startup (Login) Application

To have your application launch as soon as you boot your Mac, follow these steps:

Immediate Solutions

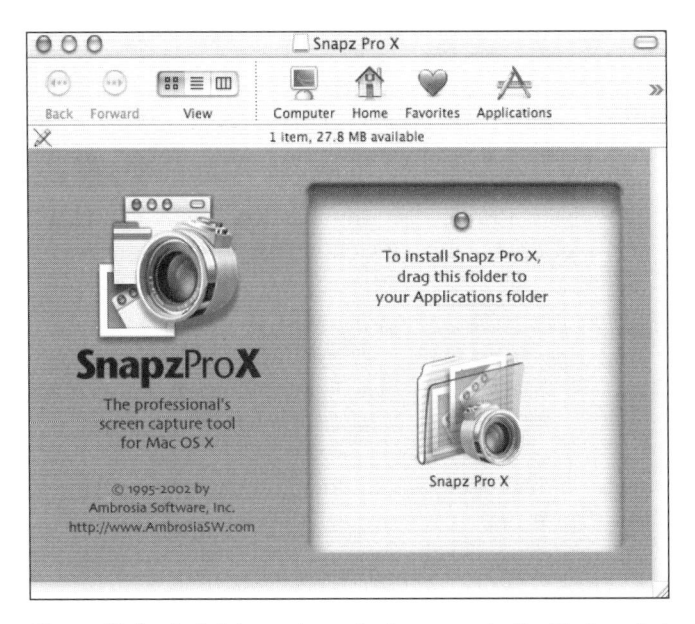

Figure 10.4 A disk image's contents appear in the Finder window, but sometimes have custom backgrounds tailored to a specific software product.

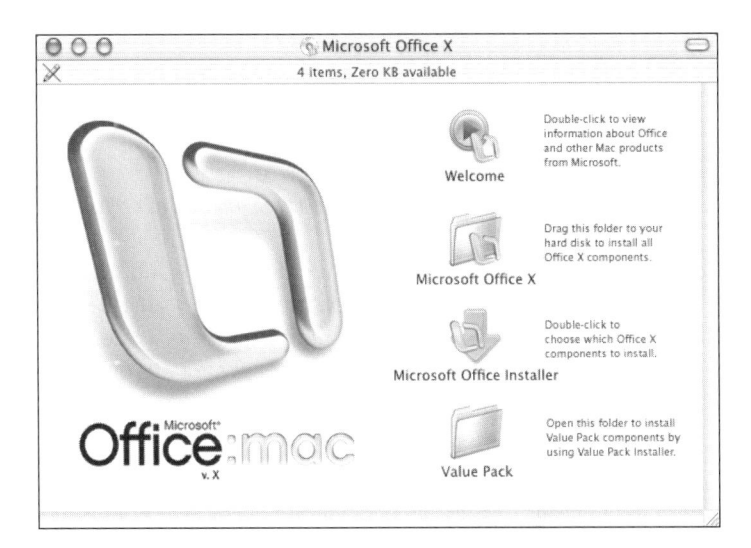

Figure 10.5 As you see from this Microsoft software disk, the installation file consists of a single installation folder, a Welcome message a custom installer and a folder of extras.

235

Chapter 10   Installing Programs Under Mac OS X

NOTE: *Mac OS X uses no system extensions in the traditional sense (although there are kernel extensions that run at the core of the operating system). The alternative is to run your program as an application that starts up with your Mac. Some installers might set this up for you behind the scenes. These instructions tell you how to do it yourself.*

1. Locate the System Preferences application icon in the Dock and click it, or double-click its icon in the Applications folder.

TIP: *Startup applications apply strictly to a single user's account. Each user of your Mac can select from a different range of startup applications. If you want to make a system-wide startup application, place an alias to it in the StartupItems folder inside the Library folder at the root level of your hard drive. If such a folder isn't there already, just create one.*

2. Click once on the Login pane to open the Login Items window, shown in Figure 10.6.
3. Click the Add button.
4. In the Open dialog box that appears next, select the application, file or network server that you want to open when you log in as a user on your Mac (see Figure 10.7).
5. Click the Open button to store the file in your Login Items window.
6. To hide the application (so its window is available only from the Dock), click the Hide checkbox.

TIP: *Some applications, particularly those providing system-wide enhancements may include a preference to automatically make the program a login application. That can be a time-saver.*

7. Choose Quit from the application menu or press Command+Q to quit System Preferences (or click the close button). The next time you boot your Mac and log in under that username, the selected application will launch. If the item is a network share, you'll have to respond to a separate login dialog for each server.

TIP: *If you decide you don't want to have your login applications launch during a work session, you can use a shortcut that's reminiscent of how you avoided Startup Items under Mac OS 9. As soon as you see a startup progress bar on restart or login, hold down the Shift key. Release the key when the Finder appears and the startup process is finished. This process will prevent the startup applications from launching.*

Immediate Solutions

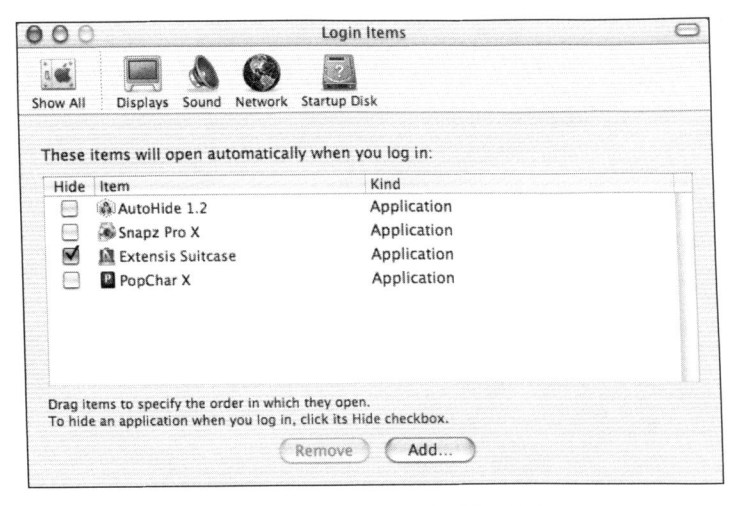

Figure 10.6 Add startup applications in this window.

Using the New Open Dialog Box

If you're used to double-clicking a document to open it, rather than going through the Open dialog box, here's Mac OS X's better way:

1. Launch the application in which you want to open the document.

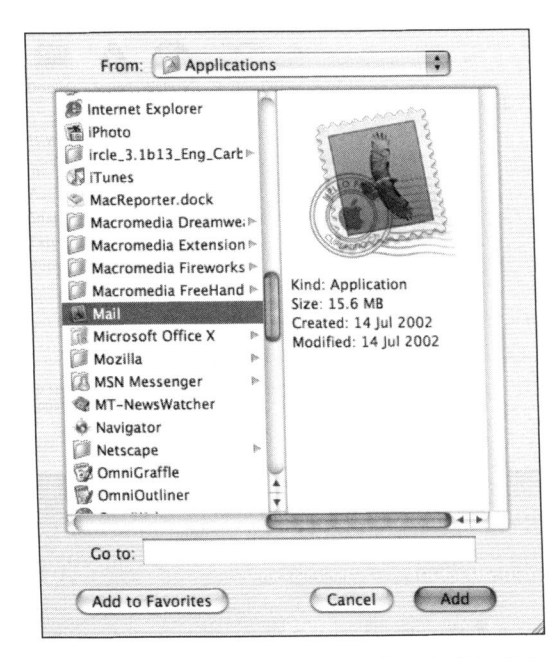

Figure 10.7 Select your startup item in this dialog box.

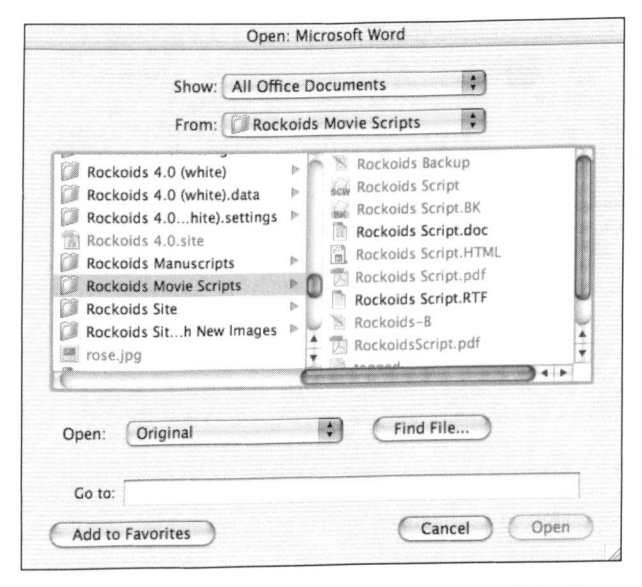

Figure 10.8 Easily locate the document you want to open.

2. Choose Open from the File menu or press Command+O, which produces a dialog box much like the one shown in Figure 10.8, featuring a Finder-type column display. The pop-up menu lists the folder hierarchy from bottom to top, also easing navigation.

NOTE: Open dialog boxes include options that apply to a specific application. I used Microsoft Word X for this illustration. You will find that some choices are different for other Mac OS X applications.

3. Click a folder's name to reveal its contents.
4. Should you want a folder or document added to your Favorites, select its icon and click the Add To Favorites button before opening the document.
5. If the document you want doesn't appear, see if your application's Open dialog box has a pop-up menu listing alternate file formats supported. Use them to see if the document appears.

TIP: If a document's name is grayed out, the program you're using cannot open it.

6. When you locate the document you want to open, either select it and click the Open button, or double-click the document's name.

TIP: If a document you open is a template or was created in an older version of a program, you might see a new, untitled document on your screen, rather than the name of the document you selected. If this is the case, you can simply save the document with the original name to replace it, or give it a new name and store it in a new location, if necessary.

7. If the document you wanted to locate isn't shown, click the Cancel button or press Command+. (period) or the Esc key to dismiss the Open dialog box. Then, use Apple's Sherlock search application to find the document. You'll find more information about Sherlock in Chapter 7.

Related solution:	Found on page:
Searching Files for Content	167

Using the New Save As Dialog Box

On the surface, saving a new document ought to be an especially easy process, but it hasn't always been thus in the Mac OS. The new Save As dialog box for Mac OS X offers both basic and advanced options to help you quickly find a place to put your document, so you can easily locate it later. Here is how to use this feature to its best advantage:

1. When you're ready to save your new document for the first time, choose Save As from the File menu. On some applications, a virtual sheet will drop down from the document's title bar (see Figure 10.9). With others, it'll appear as a separate dialog box, but will function in essentially the same fashion.

NOTE: When the Save As dialog box is displayed, you can move on to another document in the active application or to another application on your Mac. The dialog box will stay put, anchored to the original document's title bar, so you can return to it later without storing the wrong document by mistake.

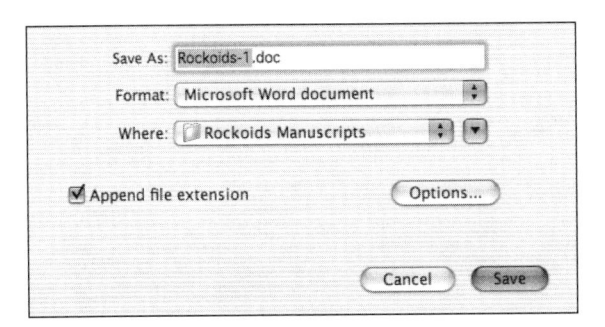

Figure 10.9   Where do you want to put your document?

239

Chapter 10   Installing Programs Under Mac OS X

2. Type a name for your document in the Save As text field. It's always a good idea to be as clear as possible when creating a name, so you can easily recognize the document when you need to open it again.

NOTE: Although, in theory, Mac OS X supports file names with a total of 256 characters, you should keep a file name to a reasonable length. Some applications, such as Word, did not, at the time this book was written, support the expanded character set.

3. To select a location for your document, click the pop-up menu to the right of the Where field. The default location is your Documents folder, inside your personal user's folder, but you can click the menu and specify another location.

TIP: The most logical place to put your file is in the Documents folder, which is where the Save As dialog box will usually point by default. But if you plan to generate lots of documents for a single category or a single business contact or friend, you should consider making a separate folder within the Documents folder, to avoid having to comb through long lists of files to find the ones that apply.

4. To see more locations and additional choices, click the down arrow at the right of the Where pop-up menu. You'll see the expanded view reminiscent of the Finder's column view (see Figure 10.10).

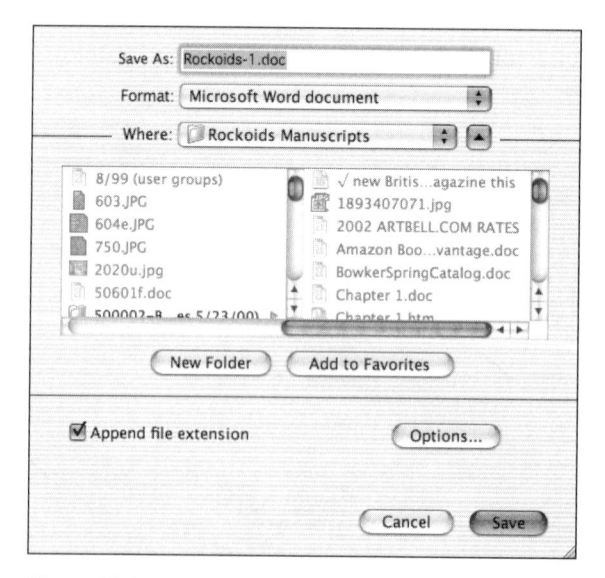

Figure 10.10   You have additional choices as to how to handle your new document.

Immediate Solutions

NOTE*: When you choose an expanded Save As dialog view, the selection will usually stick for that particular application until you switch to the standard, simplified display by clicking on the up arrow to the right of the Where field.*

5. Click a folder in the left column to see the contents in the right column.
6. To put your file in a new folder, choose the location for the folder from the column display, and then click the New Folder button to open the New Folder dialog box (see Figure 10.11).
7. Type a name for the new folder.
8. Click the Create button. The new folder will be placed in the location selected in the Save As dialog box.
9. You can also make the document a favorite so that it will appear in your Favorites folder for fast access. To do this, click the Add To Favorites button.
10. When your save options are selected, click the Save button to store the file. If the document name you selected is already in use, you can either replace the document with the duplicate name or give your new document a different name; the document you are replacing must be closed for this to work.

NOTE*: Depending on the application you're using, there may also be an Options button, which gives you access to program-specific features related to the Save As function.*

WARNING! *Once you replace a document with the duplicate name, the replaced document is history. Consider carefully which choice to make if you run into this situation.*

TIP: *If the column display isn't big enough to show a thorough view of the contents of your Mac's drive, click the resize bar at the bottom-right corner and drag to expand the Save As window.*

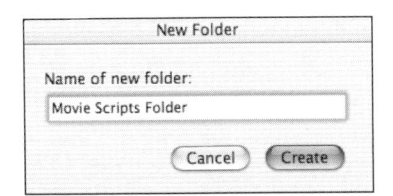

Figure 10.11   Name your new folder.

Using the Services Menu

Wouldn't it be nice if applications could communicate with one another easily without your having to go through the confusing processes of cutting and pasting and dragging and dropping? The Services menu for Mac OS X helps to minimize this problem. Here's an example of how it can be used to make two programs work together:

NOTE: This example is for demonstration purposes only. I used TextEdit and OmniWeb, a Web browser described in Chapter 21, but any Web browser that accesses the Services feature can accomplish the same task. You can download a copy of the latest version of OmniWeb from www.omnigroup.com.

1. Open a word-processing or text-editing program. For the sake of this exercise, I'm using TextEdit, the replacement for Apple's SimpleText.
2. Type the URL for your favorite Web site.
3. Select the URL.
4. Go to the application menu, choose Services, and scroll to OmniWeb, where the submenu will read Open URL (see Figure 10.12).

When you select this option, the selected URL will open in OmniWeb (see Figure 10.13). Depending on the program you're using and the kind of text or picture objects you've selected, the Services menu will display different choices, and different commands will be available to apply to the selected material.

Troubleshooting Software Installation Problems

Mac OS X makes software installation easy, but sometimes things simply won't work. Here are some common problems and solutions:

- *The application won't launch.* Is it a Mac OS X application? If the program is Mac OS X–savvy, consider restarting your Mac to see if doing so makes a difference. If it doesn't, look for the application's preference files, in the Preferences folder within the Library folder of your Users directory. As with previous versions of the Mac OS, a corrupted settings file can definitely cause

Immediate Solutions

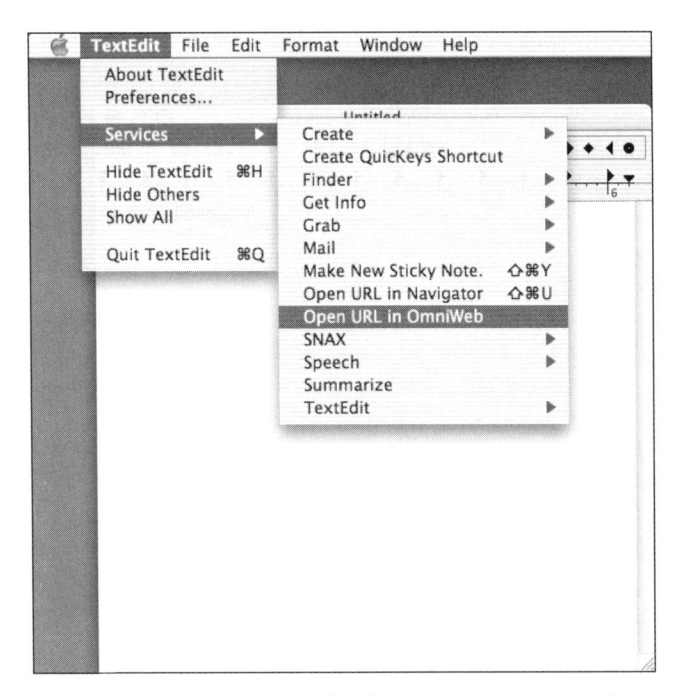

Figure 10.12   This feature takes longer to describe than to show.

Figure 10.13   OmniWeb displays a Web site whose URL was selected in TextEdit.

performance problems or the failure to run. If it still doesn't work, reinstall the application. If this final step fails, contact the publisher about possible compatibility problems.

NOTE: *Most applications designed to work with specific hardware, such as scanning software, may have a problem working in the Classic environment of Mac OS X. You may need to wait for a genuine Mac OS X version.*

- *The application keeps quitting.* Usually, this is an installation or compatibility problem. Your first line of attack is to try launching the application again. Mac OS X's protected memory will close down the memory space with the application (unless it runs in the Classic environment). If that doesn't work, restart your Mac. You might also want to consider following the remedies in the previous paragraph, by deleting the preference files and reinstalling the program. Otherwise, consult the documentation or the publisher's support department or Web site for information about possible bugs.

Warning: Some applications, such as Apple's Mail and Microsoft's Entourage, store saved messages in a database file. If you remove the file, the material is gone (unless you have a backup copy, of course). So it's best to stick with an actual application preference file when looking for the cause of a performance problem.

NOTE: *In the scheme of things, Mac OS X is quite new. So, don't be surprised to find applications failing from time to time. You should check with the publishers about possible updates. In particular, you'll find that the Classic environment sometimes won't quit or will quit very slowly.*

- *The application is installed in the wrong place.* Drag the application icon or folder to the Applications folder. Although this shouldn't make a difference, there may be other support files in a separate folder in the Applications folder that the program needs to run. It never hurts to try.

If you continue to run into problems with an application, whether newly installed or not, check Chapter 19 for more information about troubleshooting Mac OS X.

Related solution:	Found on page:
Solving System Crashes and Freezes	405

Part II
Mac OS X and Hardware

Chapter 11

Hardware Management

If you need an immediate solution to:	See page:
Installing New Hardware	251
Maintaining Your Mac on a Daily Basis	252
Should You Buy a New Mac?	255
Looking at Extended Warranties	256
Solving Hardware and Software Problems	257

Chapter 11   Hardware Management

In Brief

Mac OS X may be a blessing when it comes to handling your Mac's system and application software. Ease of installation, simplified file management, and improved performance and reliability are hallmarks of the new operating system and the programs that come with it.

Most of the other chapters in this book deal primarily with the software, except for those devoted to adding new hardware accessories and using a Mac on the road. But another factor is important on the road to setting up and maintaining a Mac system: the Mac itself. In this chapter, I cover the basics of surviving a new Mac hardware installation, some of the special features Mac OS X provides to support that hardware, and some of the problems you may encounter and their solutions.

Mac OS X's Special Hardware Features

It's not just the system software that provides the performance advantages and reliability for Mac OS X. The new operating system includes special support to harness powerful features you might already have on your Mac.

Here are some of the main capabilities that can make your Mac more powerful and productive:

NOTE: *To fully exploit these powerful technologies, you need to run Mac OS X–savvy applications. Your older programs will run with good performance in the Classic compatibility environment, but no faster (except in a few rare circumstances) and no more reliably than they did before. If any of these applications crashes, it will bring down the entire Classic environment, although the crash won't affect the rest of the system. In some cases, you could experience a performance hit, particularly if you're using programs heavily dependent on 3D graphics.*

- *Advanced graphics management*—The Quartz imaging layer has built-in support for technologies such as PDF, OpenGL, and QuickTime. The superlative visual display of the Aqua interface, with shadings, shadows, transparency, and real-time object dragging, is one of the features that maximizes the potential of the graphics chips in your Mac. Even the first-generation iMac with a 233Mhz processor (the original Rev. A model) and the entry-level graphics chip from ATI Technologies can provide decent performance, but these work best in the thousands-of-colors mode. Of course, if you have a top-of-the-line Power Macintosh computer with an NVIDIA GeForce 4 Titanium or ATI Radeon 9700 graphics card, you will realize the maximum possible benefit from the new features, regardless of resolution settings. Apple's enhanced imaging technology, Quartz Extreme, will work with an AGP graphics card and 16MB of video RAM or greater, and supports any NVIDIA card or the ATI Radeon family.

WARNING! *If you do not have a Mac with a graphics chip from ATI, IX Micro, or NVIDIA, you will have to contact the manufacturer about driver updates to address Mac OS X compatibility. This problem could be difficult if you have a graphics card from a defunct maker, such as 3dfx Interactive (although a third party has been trying to build Mac OS X–compatible drivers for these cards). Check such software information sites as VersionTracker.com to see if any outside parties will provide updates.*

- *Symmetric multiprocessing*—Some Macs come with more than a single processor chip. Although previous versions of the Mac OS and a very few applications (such as Adobe Photoshop) offer limited support for multiprocessing, as a practical matter, the extra brainpower doesn't do much good, except to help Apple's marketing department push new Macs. This situation changes, however, with Mac OS X, which has built-in support for multiprocessing and can efficiently parcel out tasks between processors to speed up performance. Any multi-threading application can also take advantage of multiprocessing, so that you get the maximum level of performance from the extra processors.

NOTE: Multiple threading *means simply that a program can handle more than a single chore at the same time.*

- *Preemptive multitasking*—The original Mac version of multitasking was cooperative, which meant that the programs themselves were designed to play nicely with one another. Under Mac OS X, the operating system is the traffic cop, parceling out tasks at a system level, providing better management of multiple applications.

Together, these features can make the same Mac that served you well under previous versions of the Mac OS behave almost as if you bought a new computer. Your Mac will start faster, will launch applications

Chapter 11 Hardware Management

more quickly, and won't bog down at inopportune times when you're trying to make it do two things at once.

NOTE: *Multiprocessing isn't a panacea. Other systems on your Mac, such as your graphics card and hard drive, can conspire to put limits on overall performance.*

With preemptive multitasking, the operating system parcels out the tasks among programs (rather than the programs themselves divvying things up), so your Mac will be able to play a QuickTime movie, download software from the Internet, and print documents without slowing down or coming to a screeching halt.

TIP: *One way to test the effect of Mac OS X on your Mac is to pull down a menu while performing all the functions I just listed and see if performance changes. Then, try doing the same thing under Mac OS 9, one of the more reliable Mac operating system versions, and see how long it takes for the multiple processes to stop.*

Immediate Solutions

Immediate Solutions

Installing New Hardware

The arrival of a new Mac in your home or office can be a special event. It may be your first Mac or your tenth, but you'll want to get it up and running right away. The promise of getting on the Internet in 10 or 15 minutes flat is tempting. But here are some things to consider before you deploy that new computer in a production setup:

1. Check the Mac for obvious damage. Macs are packed pretty carefully by Apple and its dealers, but sometimes they don't survive the trip to your home or office. If the box has severe visible signs of damage, let the shipper or dealer know right away. Then, open the box carefully and see if the computer also seems damaged. If so, don't use it. Wait for a thorough diagnosis or replacement.

NOTE: In early 2000, I was assigned to review a snow-white iMac DV SE for CNET, a large online tech news resource. When the computer arrived at my home office via overnight carrier, the box was a mess. I opened it, and the top of the case was cracked. Such a thing has happened to me only once, but it was a jarring experience.

2. Assuming your computer looks fine, carefully follow the instructions to hook it up. If you intend to connect it to a network and/or hook up a bunch of peripherals, it's a good idea to first run the new Mac system all by itself, with just mouse, display, keyboard, and a modem or other Net connection to handle registration.

NOTE: On a rare occasion, a Mac with no visible damage will be dead on arrival. If the Mac refuses to boot properly or crashes constantly even before you can perform simple functions, you should stop using it and contact your Apple dealer or Apple Computer about repair or replacement. Although Mac dealers usually will not exchange a Mac for another unit or give you a refund, most (even The Apple Store) will replace a DOA unit.

11. Hardware Management

251

3. Turn on the Mac and follow the setup prompts to store your user settings and register the product. Registering from the Mac requires that you connect to Apple's Web site to send the information.

NOTE: *If you don't have ready Net access, check the documentation with the new Mac for a registration card that can accomplish the same task via the post office.*

4. Once the Mac is registered, try running a few programs and see if everything works.
5. If the Mac is running all right, connect your peripherals and/or network connections and see if everything functions normally.
6. If the computer seems to work, but you run into problems with one accessory or another, be sure you have installed the latest drivers for those products. I cover the subject of adding extras to your Mac in Chapter 12.

If your Mac comes through like a champ, you're ready to deploy it for production purposes.

Related solution:	Found on page:
Determining What to Do If It Doesn't Work	275

Maintaining Your Mac on a Daily Basis

If your Mac runs fine, you may be tempted to use it day in and day out and never concern yourself about proper hardware maintenance. Although a personal computer is nowhere near as sensitive to lack of proper care as the family car (where a missed oil change or two, or the failure to change worn brakes or tires, can be catastrophic), you should periodically give your Mac a once-over (or two or three) to keep it purring. Here's a simplified maintenance schedule:

- *Check the hard drive regularly.* Every week or so, use the First Aid component of Apple's Disk Utility or your favorite hard-drive diagnostic program to check all the drives connected to your Mac. Directory damage has a habit of creeping up on you: You'll receive reports of simple problems, and then they'll grow worse, until finally you lose files or the drive can't mount. But if you perform regular diagnostics, you'll be able to fix problems before they become too serious.

Immediate Solutions

NOTE: *You cannot use Disk Utility to check your startup drive, but you can run Disk Utility after booting from another drive, or you can access it from the Mac OS X Installer CD, in the Installer application menu, once you boot from that CD.*

TIP: *You can't use Disk Utility to check your Mac OS X startup drive. Drives are scanned at each startup; so, even if your Mac has been running fine for days or weeks without a restart, it wouldn't hurt to restart occasionally to allow the disk scans to run.*

WARNING! *Many older hard-drive diagnostic programs are not designed to work with Mac OS X, even if you restart your Mac from the Mac OS 9 environment. You should check with the publisher directly about compatibility issues. The file structure under Mac OS X is different enough to cause bogus reports of disk problems, and attempts to fix those problems could create real ones.. There are, however, Mac OS X savvy versions of such disk diagnostic programs as Norton Utilities and Drive 10 (derived from MicroMat's TechTool Pro), and, as of the time this book was being written, a native version of Alsoft's DiskWarrior was under construction.*

- *Keep it clean.* I live in a Southwest desert state, so I have a chronic problem with dust buildup. In just a few weeks, the surface of the Macs in my home office can become dusty, and don't ask about the interior of the computers. On a regular basis, it's a good idea to dust the case with a soft cloth (not abrasive). Stay away from caustic cleaning solutions, but sometimes a light dose of a window-cleaning solution on a soft cloth is useful. If your display has become dusty, check the manufacturer's instructions about cleaning. Be especially careful with the soft surface of an LCD display—damage can be mighty expensive. Every few months, you might want to open your Mac (powered off, of course) and blow out the dust. Excessive dust buildup could affect the integrity of the items, such as RAM, connected to the logic board or the expansion bus (PCI or AGP). It can also hurt the performance of a cooling fan, or block the convection cooling vents on the iMac and PowerMac G4 Cube.

NOTE: *Excessive dust inside your Mac can cause performance anomalies. I once visited a client who had chronic crash problems. His software seemed up-to-date, and he had recently reformatted the drive, yet the problems persisted. Before sending him to the repair shop, I opened the Mac. A cloud of dust filled the room (and I suppressed a cough). A dose from a compressed air canister, placed just close enough to do some good, cleared out the Mac in short order. After removing and reseating the RAM and expansion cards, I closed the Mac. It ran perfectly; no more chronic crashes.*

253

- *Optimize sparingly.* The process of optimizing (or *defragging*) a hard drive rewrites all the files and puts them adjacent to each other, rather than spread across the drive as they are normally (although Mac OS X's advanced file system handles the process of writing files more efficiently). In theory, sufficient fragmentation might cause performance to suffer. In practice, it takes a lot to make a difference. Besides, Mac OS X's improved file handling can reduce the problem. However, if you remove and reinstall huge numbers of files, which is common in the graphic arts industry, you might experience a slight speed boost if you optimize. Video capture performance can be especially affected by such problems.

NOTE: *The ultra-efficient nature of the Unix File System (UFS) option means you shouldn't have to optimize your drive if it's formatted that way. The downside is that you can't run Classic from a UFS volume, nor can the UFS volume be seen if you restart from your Classic Mac OS.*

- *Check for driver/software updates.* Software and device drivers are all in a constant process of evolution and change. You should stay in contact with the manufacturers about needed updates for better support of Mac OS X. A good resource for such information is the **VersionTracker.com** Web site (see **www.versiontracker.com**).

- *Check your Mac after a power failure.* If a weather or power company problem has resulted in loss of power at your home or office, you should check your computers carefully when power is restored. Normally, when you restart or shut down your Mac, a "housecleaning" process writes cached files to the drive and updates the drive's directory. If the process is interrupted, files could be damaged, and drive directory problems might occur. Your hard drives will be scanned when you restart your Mac, but you may also want to use your favorite commercial hard-drive program (such as DiskWarrior, Drive 10, or Norton Utilities) to make sure everything is all right before you get back to work.

- *Shut down everything before you install something inside your Mac.* The delicate electronic components in your Mac, from the logic board to the processor, can easily be damaged by static electricity or a short circuit. If you need to add or remove a peripheral card or RAM, touch the power supply (with the plug in) to get rid of any static charge you might have and then pull the plug. Some of the better memory and peripheral card dealers will supply a wrist strap to help with the process. You may feel like a surgeon beginning an operation while thus equipped, but the

Immediate Solutions

benefit is that your installation can be done with the maximum degree of safety and the maximum protection to the delicate internal workings of your computer.

NOTE: *If you remove RAM or a peripheral card from your Mac, try to store it in a static-resistant bag. You may want to keep them around for warranty service or for storing old hardware.*

Should You Buy a New Mac?

You've probably been to someone's home or office and seen an original compact Mac still purring away in the corner, working almost as reliably as the day it was purchased. Although it's possible to keep a Mac for many years without encountering more than the customary range of system crashes and reinstallations, sometimes you might just want to give the old computer to the kids, or donate it to your favorite charitable institution.

Here's what to consider when you're deciding if your Mac should be retired:

- *It's too expensive to fix.* You've encountered problems that appear to be hardware related. Although there are dealers who can supply used or reconditioned logic boards, RAM, graphics cards, and hard drives, do the addition before you take this route. It could be time to give your Mac a well-deserved permanent vacation.

NOTE: *One of my clients has an older Mac (a Mac OS clone computer from Motorola) upon which he has lavished attention and considerable expense. Between paying my fees for troubleshooting and installation, and buying parts, he has long since exceeded the cost of a new computer. He still persists; however, the arrival of Mac OS X, with its great user interface and promise of greater performance and reliability, is tempting him to upgrade so that he can run the new operating system. That is, unless he attempts to do an unsolicited installation of Mac OS X on his older Mac, using one of those third party installer packages that induces Mac OS X to run on such hardware.*

- *It won't run Mac OS X.* This is a judgment call. Just because you can't run the latest and greatest doesn't mean your Mac will stop working and play dead. It could take years before most major applications are updated for Mac OS X. Even the initial updates will probably be Carbonized, which means the application may (but not always) work under both Mac OS X and the Classic Mac operating systems from 8.6 or 9.0 and on. That means you can use

255

the updated program now on the older Mac, and it will also work great with Mac OS X when you buy a new computer. You can compare this situation to the so-called "fat" applications of the early PowerPC Mac era. Such programs contained both the older 680x0 Mac code and PowerPC code, and thus could be transported easily from a computer with one processor to the other and work fine. That's why software publishers are taking Carbon so seriously.

- *It's slow and won't run the latest software.* Do you really need to use AppleWorks 6 if ClarisWorks 3 works all right? That's just one example, and it's significant. You may find that you're perfectly happy with the older version of a program and you don't want to learn new tricks. Although older software will work on a newer Mac, if you're happy with your old computer and applications, don't let this book or the flashy "Think Different" ads you see from Apple deter you.

- *You just have to have Mac OS X.* All right, that's a good reason to upgrade; but before you do, consider whether you'll also have to update your favorite programs before you make the jump and how much those upgrades will cost. If the applications you want are not yet Mac OS X–savvy, you won't get much advantage from the new operating system, because you'll still see the old interface much of the time in the Classic environment and not experience the joys of Aqua. On the other hand, Mac OS X includes programs you can use to surf the Internet, so that may be partial compensation. In addition, although new Macs or recently discontinued models are much cheaper than the older models, you should consider what you'll do with the computer to see if the upgrade is justified.

NOTE: *One of my clients, a semiretired hairdresser, restricts his first-generation Power Mac to sending and receiving email and occasionally surfing the Net. However, he finally decided to buy a new Power Mac G4, and when I set it up for him, I took him on a tour of Mac OS X. Because all the software he needed was native, he happily switched to the new operating system without any regrets.*

Looking at Extended Warranties

Whether you buy a new Mac from a local store or a mail-order house, before you finish your order, the salesperson probably will ask you to consider just one more purchase—an extended warranty. Apple's computers, as of the time this book was written, had a one-year limited warranty on parts and labor, with just 90 days of free telephone support. If you plan to keep your new Mac for a while, the prospect of extended support might be tempting.

Consider this, though: Dealers often rely on the sale of extended warranties to shore up their profit margins, particularly in these troubled times when sales of new computers have stalled. More often than not, a hardware failure will occur early in an electronic component's life, during the warranty period. As with any insurance policy, you need to weigh the possible expense of an out-of-warranty repair against the certain expense of the extended warranty.

If you are using an Apple iBook or PowerBook, however, such a warranty might be a good idea. Laptop computers are potentially subject to far greater abuse than desktop computers, because they are dragged around so frequently. Having that extra protection might be worth the expense.

WARNING! If you opt to buy an extended warranty, double-check with the dealer to find out whether the warranty is Apple's (known as AppleCare) or comes from another company. I have seen instances where customers ordered AppleCare and got something else. When checking into such a program, compare the cost and benefits before signing on the dotted line—and look at the actual policy information (don't just depend on what the salesperson tells you).

Solving Hardware and Software Problems

This is an eternal difficulty. Your Mac crashes constantly, and you've gone through all the possible software troubleshooting you can, following the steps outlined in Chapter 19. But still your Mac misbehaves. Here are some additional choices to consider, along with cases when you might want to have the Mac's hardware serviced:

- *Chronic hard-drive errors*—Every time you check your hard drive with the First Aid component of Disk Utility or one of the commercial hard-drive programs, it comes back with reports of directory damage that needs to be fixed. Sometimes, you'll even see a message that the repairs can't be performed. Should this happen, first try restarting your Mac with a System CD or one of the CDs provided with the commercial drive utility. If you continue to run into problems that recur or can't be fixed, back up your data and reformat the drive. Leaving directory damage unfixed can eventually result in a loss of files or the inability of your Mac to recognize your drive.

TIP: It's a good idea to back up your important data regularly, not just in response to a report of a drive directory problem. Not all drive problems announce themselves in advance; sometimes the drive just fails.

WARNING! If you see a prompt on your Mac's display offering to initialize your hard drive, don't do it! This destructive act will erase the data. Although it sometimes may be possible to restore a drive with a program such as Norton Utilities or with an expensive trip to a drive recovery service, you should try other diagnostic methods before going this route.

- *Hard drive doesn't work properly after it's reformatted*—You bit the bullet and reformatted your hard drive, but problems still occur. You continue to get reports of hard-drive directory errors, or the worst happens and the drive doesn't appear on your Computer directory in the Finder or the desktop. You should have both the drive and your Mac checked by a technician. It's possible one or the other has failed.

- *Mac makes a startup sound, but the screen is dark*—If you just installed Mac OS X and you're using a graphics card that isn't from ATI, IX Micro, or NVIDIA, you should consult the manufacturer about Mac OS X support. You may need to restart with an Apple-approved graphics card to install updated software.

NOTE: At press time, one or more independent programmers were at work trying to develop Mac OS X drivers for the Voodoo graphic cards produced by the now-defunct 3dfx Interactive. If you still have a Voodoo card, there may be hope; otherwise, you should seriously consider retiring it to an old Mac that will not be upgraded to Mac OS X.

- *Mac with an upgrade card fails to boot*—Mac OS X requires a Mac that shipped with either a G3 or G4 processor. If you have an older Mac and upgraded the processor, don't expect it to work or to receive support from Apple. However, you may want to check with the manufacturer of the upgrade card to see if it has a way to make it run. Such companies as PowerLogix and Sonnet Technology have special software that will allow some of their cards to run under Mac OS X (some of Sonnet's upgrade cards don't need software), but you must depend on these companies for support for installations not supported by Apple Computer.

Immediate Solutions

- *Mac fails to boot and doesn't make a startup sound*—Recheck the power cord, the power strip, and the devices attached to your Mac. If you recently installed a new peripheral card or RAM upgrade, remove each item in turn (closing the Mac each time) and see if you can get the Mac to run. If removing one fixes the problem, reinstall the item and try again. If you have a Mac that's more than a year old, consider replacing the lithium backup battery, which, when spent, can affect the startup process. Should the problem persist, contact the manufacturer of the peripheral product for repair or replacement. If you cannot get the Mac to run, it's time for a trip to the dealer's service department.

NOTE: Another potential cause of a Mac's failing to boot is a defective peripheral card, particularly the graphics card. Shut down, and then remove and reseat the video card, and see if doing so brings your Mac back to life.

- *Mac fails to boot with peripheral device attached*—The blame should be placed on the device. If it's a SCSI device, make sure it's powered on before you boot your Mac. One key test is to remove the device (after powering down); if your Mac then works all right, you have a good idea as to the culprit.

NOTE: If your Mac has a SCSI adapter card, you should check with the manufacturer about Mac OS X support for its products. As this book was written, Adaptec had released drivers for some of its newer cards, while retiring some older models. Orange Micro was still at work developing Mac OS X–savvy firmware for its SCSI cards.

- *Mac crashes constantly early in the startup process or right after restart*—Follow the software diagnostics covered in Chapter 19. If a reinstallation of Mac OS X fails to fix the problem, consider backing up and reformatting your hard drive. From here, continued problems could be traced to bad RAM, a faulty hard drive, or your Mac's logic board. Take it to your dealer for diagnosis.

NOTE: Can you do your own hardware diagnostics? Possibly. MicroMat's TechTool Pro (and the TechTool Deluxe application that comes with Apple's AppleCare service warranty) can test the various systems on your Mac. A number of new Macs also include an Apple Hardware Test CD that can be used to perform a basic set of hardware tests. However, if you see a report of a potential problem, let a technician make the final call. In general, some motherboard and RAM defects would result in a Sad Mac, but sometimes they'll just result in more system crashes or the failure to complete a startup process.

Chapter 11 Hardware Management

- *You smell smoke or see a spark from your Mac*—What can I tell you? Although laser printer toner can sometimes smell a little smoky, if you see symptoms of this sort, don't try to use your Mac. Unplug it immediately and move away from any flammable material. Let a dealer's service representative do a diagnostic first.

NOTE: *A slight spark could just be static electricity. If you have thick carpeting or you're in a particularly dry climate, walking around may build up static electricity. If you touch a metal object, you may see a slight spark.*

Related solution:	Found on page:
Solving Other Common Mac OS X Problems	411

Chapter 12

Hooking Up Accessories

If you need an immediate solution to:	See page:
Installing a New Scanner	272
Installing New Storage Devices	273
Installing Digital Cameras, eBook Readers, Palm OS Handhelds, and Other Products	274
Determining What to Do If It Doesn't Work	275

In Brief

Macs are not designed to exist in a vacuum. Although the original compact Macintosh may have started out as a device with just an internal floppy drive, a keyboard, and a mouse, your Mac isn't an island. Even if you have an iBook or PowerBook (especially the flashy Titanium G4 version), sometimes you'll want to add extra devices to enhance its capabilities. Fortunately, the promise of the Macintosh operating system that has endeared it to millions upon millions of customers is easy (well, fairly easy) plug-and-play ability. That means you can attach a peripheral device and have it function with the absolute minimum of fuss.

Mac OS X expands on this promise. When you install the new operating system, you'll find built-in support for a huge number of devices, including ink jet printers from Canon, Epson, HP, and Lexmark; laser printers from a number of major companies; third-party CD burners and input devices; and most digital cameras. If you install any of these devices, you'll find that they just work without your having to do a special software installation (beyond a visit to the Print Center application for networked laser printers). If you've just migrated from the Windows platform, where some things and some things call for a trip to the aspirin jar, this may seem a revelation.

However, peripheral support isn't 100 percent. If drivers aren't included with Mac OS X, you will have to look to the manufacturer of the product for the drivers you need (this is especially true for scanners, which were slow to receive support for the new operating system). However, when the drivers are all in place, the combination of easy installation and the powerful system management of Mac OS X makes it possible to get the maximum value from any peripheral you want to buy.

In this chapter, I cover many of the types of devices you can buy and how to install and use them as speedily and efficiently as possible.

A Review of Mac Peripheral Ports

In the old days of the Macintosh, you attached your input devices to an ADB port, a printer to the printer port, a modem to the modem port, and an external storage device to the SCSI port. All that changed, however, with the 1998 arrival of the computer credited with Apple's resurgence—the iMac.

In Brief

The iMac begat a new peripheral standard on the Mac (although it wasn't new in the personal computing world) and eliminated some of the ports that were considered standard issue. Here's a brief rundown of the various peripheral standards present on Macs that can run Mac OS X and where they fit in the overall picture:

- *Apple Desktop Bus (ADB)*—This was an early standard input port for input devices, such as the keyboard and mouse you use on your Mac, a trackball, and joystick, and such extras as digital cameras. Even some modems use this port. However, it can only support a very few devices, performance tends to be slow for demanding accessories, and the plug-and-play aspect is a little murky. You have to shut down your Mac to remove and add devices, or you risk damage to the computer's logic board. The ADB port vanished with the arrival of the iMac and later new models, both desktop and laptop; it was replaced with Universal Serial Bus (USB), a much more flexible standard. If you have an older device you need hooked up to a newer Mac, consider an ADB to USB adapter, such as the Griffin Technologies iMate. Yes, it is compatible with Mac OS X, and, in fact, with Windows.

- *Serial port*—Some Macs had two serial ports, and some PowerBooks had just one. A regular desktop Mac had one port for printers (it doubled as a LocalTalk port) and another for modems. PowerBooks combined the two and added built-in modems so that there was no conflict or need for a switch to allow you to use an extra device. These ports are, in theory, plug and play. You can usually switch devices without a restart, although it's recommended you restart when you can. As far as performance is concerned, a serial port is more than adequate for printing and for modems. But networking speed is a fraction of that available for Ethernet, and thus the process of transferring files can be cumbersome if the files are too large.

NOTE: *The original Mac serial ports simply are not supported for Mac OS X. If you have a LocalTalk printer, then the iPrint from Proxim (formerly Farallon) or the AsanteTalk will convert to Ethernet. But serial printers, such as the Apple StyleWriter, should be replaced with USB versions even if you must use a USB adapter on your Mac, because driver support is not likely to be offered; a simple serial-to-USB converter isn't enough.*

- *SCSI port*—Except for the very first Mac (which used the floppy drive port to add a hard drive), the SCSI port was the original standard for adding storage devices, scanners, and some specialty printers to your Mac. This is the closest thing to plug and *pray* on your Mac, because SCSI can be problematic, especially when the

12. Hooking Up Accessories

263

SCSI chain is large. For regular SCSI, you can connect up to seven daisy-chained devices. Each device has a unique ID number, from 0 through 6 (up to 15 for some high-speed SCSI cards), and the last physical device on the chain (regardless of ID number) must be terminated. With large SCSI chains, sometimes devices won't work properly or your Mac will crash frequently. The diagnostics include reordering devices (observing proper ID numbering and termination), swapping cables, taking two aspirins, and trying again. With millions of SCSI devices out there, Mac users still need to employ this peripheral standard, although better ones are available.

- *Ethernet*—This high-speed networking standard is in use in homes and both large and small offices. The standard Ethernet protocols in use on Macs are 10Base-T and 100Base-T, and recent generations of desktop Power Mac G4s and the fall 2001 version of the PowerBook G4 include Gigabit Ethernet. At its maximum speed, Ethernet can deliver networking throughput nearly as fast as a big hard drive. This is a true plug-and-play standard. You can connect multiple devices to a central connecting point, such as a hub or switch, and remove and reconnect as needed. Ethernet devices aren't limited to computers and printers. You can also add network routers and special modems for broadband Internet, such as cable and DSL.

- *Universal Serial Bus (USB)*—This low- to medium-speed serial port is standard issue on all shipping Apple computers. Most Macs, except the iBook, have two USB ports (the iBook has just one). To add more devices, you need hubs. In theory, you can connect up to 127 devices with full plug and play, but to do so you must install driver software for many products and unmount a storage device first before removal. Up to 12 megabits per second speed is shared on a single USB bus, which is enough for input devices, low-cost scanners, digital cameras, and storage devices where speed is not a concern.

NOTE: An updated USB standard, version 2.0, promises speeds that exceed those of FireWire. However, as of the time this book was written, support on the Mac platform was reserved to third-party adapters and peripherals. . In addition, actual tests of USB 2.0 hard drives showed performance to be no better than comparable FireWire products, although prices can be a little cheaper.

- *FireWire*—This is an Apple invention, a high-speed peripheral port that puts the kibosh on SCSI for all practical purposes. It delivers up to 400 megabits in performance, coming closest to all

In Brief

but the fastest SCSI standards. Newer FireWire standards were on the horizon when this book was written. Devices can be daisy chained, and there's a high level of plug-and-play compatibility, including hot-plugging. Drivers are needed on some devices, and storage devices must be dismounted from the desktop, but that covers most exceptions. FireWire devices include digital camcorders, which makes all recent Macs ideal desktop video-editing computers. FireWire storage devices and scanners are available, and Apple's stylish music player, the iPod, uses the FireWire port to update the music on its internal drive or to serve duty as a regular storage device.

NOTE: *This is not to say that FireWire is free of conflicts. I once installed a FireWire scanner, and it had to be the last item on the peripheral chain. Otherwise, weird startup problems, problems copying large files to FireWire storage devices, and occasional system crashes resulted. The file-copying problems persisted after I installed Mac OS X, so it wasn't a driver issue (no drivers were available at the time). So, I never say never.*

Adding a Missing Port

What do you do if you want a peripheral, but your Mac doesn't have the correct port? For desktop Macs with expansion slots, you can get relief in the form of PCI-based peripheral adapter cards. They come in many shapes and sizes, offering the following:

- *FireWire*—Two or more FireWire ports can be found on a single expansion card. Best of all, such cards usually don't need any special software (aside from Apple's FireWire extensions for Mac OS 9) and can cost less than $50.

- *USB*—With so many USB products available, it would be nice if older Macs could use them. All it takes is a peripheral card that costs less than $20. Make sure Apple's USB extensions are installed if you're using Mac OS 9.x (USB support is standard issue under Mac OS X).

NOTE: *When you're buying a FireWire or USB adapter, check the documentation that comes with the product closely. Some companies bury the Mac OS compatibility information on the back of the box. I ran across a $20 Belkin USB adapter at Wal-Mart that was labeled in this rather confusing fashion.*

- *High-speed Ethernet*—Although the newest Mac desktops offer Gigabit Ethernet, you don't have to feel abandoned with an older Mac. Expansion cards fill this gap as well, but they're costly.

265

- *Combo cards*—If you don't have enough slots, take heart. Combination cards offer both FireWire and USB. Now, you don't have to choose just one.

- *SCSI cards*—If you need to find a home for your existing SCSI devices, a ready collection of SCSI cards are available with various price points and speeds. The cheapest cards, at roughly $50, are up to twice as fast as the built-in SCSI on most Macs, and they get much faster as the price increases.

> **NOTE:** Before buying a SCSI card, make sure it supports the devices you already have and, just as important, Mac OS X, which may leave out some products from the used parts bin or a garage sale. For a scanner, removable drive, and a regular SCSI hard drive, the cheaper cards are fine. But some external drives and even backup drives require cards with "wide" SCSI ports.

- *SCSI-to-FireWire converter*—This is another way to have the best of both worlds. Several brands of such converters are available that allow a single SCSI device to connect to the FireWire ports on your Mac. Because they're single devices, you don't have to consider issues of termination and ID.

- *Serial-to-USB converters*—These modules let you attach products that work on regular Mac serial ports, such as older ink jet printers and modems, to a newer Mac's USB port. The major limitation is the occasional software conflict and the inability to work with LocalTalk devices, such as AppleTalk printers that attach to a standard Mac printer port.

- *SCSI-to-USB converters*—This type of product would appear to be a blessing, because it lets you continue to use those old SCSI products on a Mac that has only USB, such as the iMac. However, because the older USB standard is slower than SCSI, the conversion works best for a scanner or low-speed storage device (such as a Zip drive or tape drive). As of the time this book was written, I did not see any SCSI-to-USB 2.0 adapters, which should, in theory be plenty fast.

- *LocalTalk-to-Ethernet bridge*—If you have an older Mac where Ethernet is an option or a network printer that only has a LocalTalk port, this device allows you to continue to use these products on your Ethernet network. You won't get any faster speed, but you won't have to buy a new printer or spend extra money on a peripheral card for an old Mac that is near the end of its useful life.

In Brief

Note: *Yes, you can share files with on a Mac running Mac OS X with a Mac running an older version of the operating system. Just remember to turn on AppleTalk in the Network preference panel of Mac OS X's System Preferences application.*

- *ADB-to-USB adapter*—If you still cherish that old keyboard, mouse, trackball, or similar input device, fear not. You can still use it on your new Mac with this type of adapter. On the other hand, many terrific input devices are available for Macs these days—particularly Apple's new Pro Keyboard and Pro Mouse (I love these and use them all the time), which ship standard on new Macs and are available from the Apple Store for older models. You may find the money better spent acquiring something new.

WARNING! *Not all peripheral cards work seamlessly with Mac OS X. Before you purchase one of these products, contact the manufacturer or check its Web site directly to see its plans. For example, older SCSI cards and none of the DOS cards that put an AMD or Intel inside your Mac will probably never run with Mac OS X and don't hold out much hope for driver updates. If you have an older product, other than these two categories, you can try it at your risk, and keep your fingers crossed.*

- *Expansion cards for PowerBooks*—PowerBook users shouldn't feel abandoned by the new peripheral buses. Both USB and FireWire PC cards are available that will add this capability to just about any PowerBook that can run Mac OS X.

NOTE: *Unfortunately, the iBook and the iMac were conceived as inexpensive consumer computers and thus lack extra expansion slots and the ability to add them (except for FireWire on later models of both). So, you must live with the ports you have, should you be using one of these models.*

Peripherals Available for Macs

What do you need? Although some folks decry the limited availability of products for Macs, they aren't really paying attention to the lists in today's Mac mail-order catalogs or the shelves in Apple's own retail outlets and other stores that specialize in the platform.

Literally thousands of Mac products are available. Many, in fact, are cross-platform—the same product is available for both Mac and Windows users, with the sole difference being the driver software or the label on the box.

NOTE: *Some companies with cross-platform products will, for some unaccountable reason, put their software drivers only on their Web sites, rather than on the CD that comes with the product.*

If a product seems to work only under Windows, check the box and the manufacturer's Web site, in case you get lucky.

Here's a short list of the kinds of products you can add to your Mac to help harness the power of Mac OS X:

NOTE: *This list is meant for information only, to give a sampling of the sort of products you can connect to your Mac. Check with a particular manufacturer to find out whether a special upgrade is needed for Mac OS X. Some of these products will plug in and run, regardless of whether you have Mac OS X or Mac OS 9.x.*

- *Scanners*—Once, desktop scanners were the province of professional graphic artists. They were expensive, with color models of reasonable quality running from one to two grand. Although there are still products in that price range, literally dozens of models are available from less than $100 to around $200. A scanner allows you to capture and digitize artwork and photos and even convert printed material to text that you can edit in your favorite word-processing program (with special optical character-recognition software). Once the artwork is scanned, you can convert it into a format that you can use on your Mac for word processing or desktop publishing, or send to your friends and business associates. Scanners are available in FireWire, SCSI, and USB form; some models support more than one peripheral standard.

TIP: *Is the manufacturer of your scanner late to the party in developing Mac OS X drivers? Try VueScan, a clever third-party solution. I used this demoware scanning application (you need to buy a user license to get it to scan without a watermark on your image) until Microtek was able to deliver drivers for my scanner. Available as a download from the publisher's Web site at **www.hamrick.com**, VueScan supports a huge number of flatbed and slide scanners. It's also updated almost weekly, so if your scanner isn't working with it when you try the program, just be patient or write to the publisher and see if support is coming.*

- *Digital cameras*—Is film obsolete? Perhaps not, but digital cameras offer a convenient way to take a picture and not have to wait for it to be developed by a processor lab. Although the cheapest models provide pictures that hardly rate in comparison with those offered by even a low-cost film camera, a few hundred dollars can now get you a digital camera that compares favorably to traditional models. Some of the more expensive models match film cameras with special features, such as single-lens reflex viewfinders (where you see the same image picked up by the

In Brief

camera's lens), and even the ability to do limited motion videos. Most of these products store data on small memory cards. Best of all, Apple's Image Capture and iPhoto applications provide built-in support for most available digital cameras. Just plug the camera into your Mac, and either of these programs will launch to download your pictures.

- *Hard drives*—This type of device can be essentially the same as the one in your Mac now, except that it's in an external case. Hard drives come in FireWire, SCSI, and USB formats (both 1.1 and 2.0, but the latter requires an adapter of course); the first two and USB 2.0 provide the highest degree of performance. In terms of speed, there should be no difference between external and internal drives. The Power Macs, except for the Cube, sport extra drive bays for additional internal storage devices, in case you want to put everything on one case.

- *Removable drives*—As I explain in Chapter 17, backing up your data is critically important. Even though Mac OS X is a superbly stable, industrial-strength operating system, problems can happen to a drive's directory, and individual applications can still fail. That, plus the possibility of external dangers, such as a burglary, natural disaster, or weather-related problems, makes it imperative that you keep regular backups of your most valuable material. A removable drive is a convenient backup tool and just as handy for moving files to another location—particularly files that are too large to send online. Two removable formats are the venerable Zip drive, which has found its way into millions of computers, and the Imation SuperDisk, which also reads older-style floppy disks.

NOTE: *Although the SuperDisk drive is quite handy and the technology seems robust enough, such drives are usually found in the closeout bins these days. The primary manufacturer, Imation, gave up competing with the Zip drive, but still makes regular floppy drives. QPS Inc. also makes a SuperDisk drive, as well as a big line of CD burners and FireWire hard drives.*

- *CD writer (or burner)*—This type of product became standard equipment on a Mac only in early 2001. The closest equivalent is the DVD-RAM drive on some older Power Macintosh G4 models, which records on a special DVD-based medium with a capacity of up to 5.2GB. A CD writer, or *burner*, lets you make a CD of data or music. Such devices are ubiquitous and available in FireWire, SCSI, and USB trim (also ATA for use in a present-day desktop Mac's internal drive bay). There are two basic types of CD formats for writing data: CD-R, which can be recorded only once, and CD-RW,

269

Chapter 12 Hooking Up Accessories

which can be rewritten up to 1,000 times (but the disk can't be read on all drives). Although a CD drive is slower than a regular removable hard drive, a CD has the added benefit of permanence. A CD can last for many years without suffering damage or possible loss of data, unless given ultra-severe abuse. In addition, you can buy a DVD-R burner, similar to the one used for the SuperDrive on the flat-panel iMac and G4 desktop computers, from such companies as LaCie and Que. These drives not only make DVD movies, but they can also be used for data storage via the Finder's Burn feature (check with the manufacturer about support for Mac OS X).

NOTE: There are two basic types of CD-R media. The data type is designed to record any kind of data from a computer. The music CD consists of the same media, but higher priced, to cover the royalty paid to artists whose material you are copying.

- *Graphic cards*—Is your desktop Mac's bundled graphic's card a little slow in rendering 3D games? Do you have a first generation Power Mac G4 with AGP with a card from the ATI Rage family that doesn't support the ultra-fast Quartz Extreme? Or just a beige or Blue & White Power Mac G3 with one of those early-generation ATI cards? Either way, there are options. ATI has several products in its Radeon series that will provide better graphics acceleration in almost all respects. If you have a recent G4, you might also be able to get a high performance NVIDIA graphic card from Apple's own retail outlets or its Web site. All of these products will also support two displays, which is a boon for graphic artists and other content creators who need extra desktop space.

- *Wireless networking*—Apple's AirPort wireless networking modules are available for all new Macs. They allow Macs to network with each other at near standard Ethernet speeds at distances of up to 150 feet. The AirPort Base Station lets you share an Internet connection.

NOTE: If you have an older Mac without AirPort capability, other choices are available for wireless networking. Among these choices are the SkyLINE from Proxim (formerly Farallon) and Asante's AeroLAN, both of which use the same industry standard protocols as AirPort (802.11b or Wi-Fi) and can function as part of the same network. Both firms also offer Wi-Fi base stations that work on both Macs and Windows-based PCs.

- *Loudspeakers*—Yes, most loudspeaker systems you add to a computer plug in to your audio output or earphone jack, but

In Brief

some speakers connect directly to your USB port. These include the Harman Kardon iSub and SoundSticks. They take advantage of the Mac OS's own sound control features to adjust volume, balance, and tone.

- *Handheld computers*—These devices include the popular Palm OS products from Handspring and Palm, as well as dedicated electronic book readers, such as the Rocket eBook. They aren't designed to be attached to your Mac all the time, but they need to interface with your computer for installing and removing software, or for just synchronizing information. You'll need special software to allow this connection to work.

- *Digital music players*—MP3 has taken the music world by storm. Millions of PC users have assembled music libraries, and these little devices allow you to collect your tracks on a memory card or storage device. They work in the fashion of the famous Sony Walkman, letting you take music with you. Apple's iPod, a tiny, steel-clad player the size of a deck or cards, mates seamlessly with Apple's iTunes 3 software to sync the music library on your Mac with the one on the player.

NOTE: *I'll avoid the issues of the copyright disputes involving the recording industry and certain MP3-related Web sites. But I will mention in passing that Apple's iPod lets you share music only with a single Mac when run in its standard, or automatic mode, so you can't copy music from the player onto other computers.*

Although installing an accessory on your Mac is fairly easy, you should always take a few extra precautions to make sure everything is set up properly. This is particularly important if you are setting up a complicated peripheral device, such as a scanner, and some extra steps might be necessary. In addition, because many products come with very sparse documentation, these steps will help you get things working without extra fuss or confusion.

In the next section, I cover some basic recommendations for installing a peripheral device on your Mac and how to cope with problems, should they arise.

12. Hooking Up Accessories

271

Chapter 12 Hooking Up Accessories

Immediate Solutions

Installing a New Scanner

After unpacking the device, check the manual or installer card for basic setups and follow these basic guidelines:

1. Locate the lock on the scanner. It might be identified by a padlock icon, and unlocking can be done with a screwdriver or just by turning a latch. This is critical, because you risk damaging a scanner if you attempt to run it while the optical mechanism is locked. Some scanners, however, especially lower cost products, don't come with locking mechanisms. If in doubt, check the installation instructions.

NOTE: *If you plan to move your scanner to a new location outside your workplace, remember to lock the optical mechanism first to protect the unit. Also, not all scanners have locks. If there's no indication of one on the unit, check the setup documentation. If it's not there, you may be lucky (although only really cheap scanners seem to lack those locks).*

2. If another user has logged in to your Mac, you'll need to use your administrator's account. Installing anything that requires system-wide access can be done only in this fashion. If the installer requires a login, you'll see a prompt at the beginning of the installation process.

WARNING! Before you install any software for new hardware, be sure to consult the documentation or contact the publisher about Mac OS X compatibility. Even if you bought the product long after Jaguar was released, don't assume the unit is compatible unless the package or the product's label provides specific information about the subject such as a "Built for Mac OS X" label. If you can't find this information, check with the publisher.

3. Install the software. It should be on a CD that shipped with the scanner. Some scanners include an integrated installation process, which handles the scanner drivers, image-editing software, and other extras. Others offer each element as a separate, clickable install. Follow the prompts about selecting installation options. Depending on the installer, you may have to restart your Mac (usually you don't).

Immediate Solutions

WARNING! If, for some reason, the scanner uses an old-fashioned floppy disk installer, you can be assured the scanner drivers aren't compatible with Mac OS X. Contact the manufacturer about this problem, or try to use it under the Mac OS X Classic environment until a new version of the software is available (but success isn't guaranteed).

4. Connect the scanner to your Mac. If it's a SCSI product, shut down your Mac and attach SCSI devices first, then restart after the hookup. For FireWire and USB, shutting down isn't necessary, because of the plug-and-play nature of these two peripheral standards.

NOTE: If you are installing a SCSI device, make sure there are no duplicate ID numbers and that termination switches on the product are turned on or off as needed for your installation. If you're using a third-party SCSI card, verify its compatibility with Mac OS X before attempting to install devices on it.

5. Launch your scanning software and run the scanner through its paces for scanning and processing images. If you have problems, consult the documentation (it might be on the CD) for further assistance.

NOTE: Some scanner drivers don't work separately from a photo-editing program. So, you'll need to see if a copy of Adobe Photoshop or a similar program is on your Mac and use that program's Acquire feature to activate the scanning driver.

Installing New Storage Devices

Depending on the sort of storage device you have, you may not need to add any extra software. Here are the basic steps to follow:

1. Consult the documentation or look for a CD to see if special software needs to be installed.

NOTE: Mac OS X has built-in support for a number of popular removable devices, such as Imation SuperDisk drives, Iomega Zip and Jaz drives, and a large number of FireWire storage devices. You can run them without adding any extra software, and they will function normally. If you are installing a device in the same category, you may, as an experiment, want to hook it up and try to make it run before you attempt to use the software, because it's possible the drivers aren't updated for Mac OS X.

273

Chapter 12 Hooking Up Accessories

2. If software is required, make sure it's Mac OS X compatible. You will see a login prompt for your administrator's password if required for the installation.
3. Launch the installer application and follow the prompts.
4. If necessary, restart your Mac (this step is necessary only for devices that load as part of the Mac's startup process).
5. Connect the drive to your Mac. If you're hooking up a SCSI device, make sure that your Mac and attached SCSI devices are turned off first; you can safely restart after hookup.

NOTE: Don't forget to check for SCSI ID and termination settings before powering up.

6. Verify that the drive works properly. If it's a hard drive, copy files to and from it. For a removable device, insert the removable media and run it through its paces.

WARNING! On a CD burner, it's worth trying one CD-RW disk just to be sure that you can copy data satisfactorily; the benefit of using a CD-RW disk is that you can reuse it after determining the drive is all right. You do not want to back up critical data and then find out, too late, that there was a problem reading the CD.

Installing Digital Cameras, eBook Readers, Palm OS Handhelds, and Other Products

The process of setting up a device that's not connected full time to your Mac is essentially the same as connecting a device that's always hooked up. Here are the steps to follow:

1. Unpack the device and check for interface plugs. If there's no USB or FireWire cable, check to see if a serial cable is available. Depending on the kind of Mac you have, you might need an interface adapter, such as a serial-to-USB converter, to make it run.
2. After verifying Mac OS X compatibility, locate the installer CD and install the software. In many cases, you'll have to enter your administrator's password in the login prompt.
3. Check the device for proper operation, and then attach the unit to your Mac as instructed.
4. Consult the instructions about synching or interfacing with your Mac.

Immediate Solutions

5. If the product doesn't run as expected, check manuals or the manufacturer's support Web site or telephone support line for further advice.

NOTE: *Most digital cameras mate perfectly with Apple's Image Capture software out of the box. So before you install anything, just take a few shots, attach the camera to your Mac, and see if Image Capture or iPhoto application loads. This application will appear only if the camera is supported.*

Determining What to Do If It Doesn't Work

Despite some of the concessions to mass production and competition to keep prices low, it's a rare product that will fail out of the box. Usually, when something doesn't work, you can take steps to address the problem.

Here are some items to check in case the accessory you've bought for your Mac isn't working as you expected:

- *Is the device compatible with Mac OS X?* Even if the box or documentation says it is, don't expect seamless compatibility in every case. You may need to double-check with the manufacturer to see if additional updates are required. If the box or documentation doesn't specifically address the issue, assume the product won't run unless there's built-in support under Mac OS X. Except for a limited number of products, the answer is probably no.

NOTE: *The promise and non-delivery of Mac OS X–compatibility information was brought home to me shortly after I first installed the new operating system. I bought a new software product whose box had a sticker promising details about a Mac OS X upgrade inside. I checked thoroughly, and no information whatsoever was provided. A call to the manufacturer yielded the worst news of all—the label was a mistake. The company hadn't made any decisions about when such an upgrade would be available and in what form.*

- *Have you installed the wrong software?* New products are apt to have different installers for Mac OS X and for the Classic Mac OS. Double-check to make sure that you ran the correct installation. You might want to do it again and see.

- *Did you forget to restart?* It may or may not be necessary, but if a product won't work, this step is worth taking just to make sure the proper drivers load.

- *Are you experiencing peripheral application crashes?* Even though the Darwin core of Mac OS X is highly robust and crash resistant, individual programs still may crash from time to time. Fortunately, protected memory means that even if an application quits, you can continue to use your Mac. Should the program continue to quit or freeze, contact the manufacturer about needed updates.

- *Is the device plugged in?* Even if the AC adapter is connected to the wall socket or a power strip, you may have to tear through a spaghetti-like maze of cables to see if everything is hooked up properly. Cables sometimes separate during spring cleaning.

NOTE: This issue isn't as obvious as it seems. I once got a frantic call from a client who wondered why her printer had stopped working. I asked her to double-check her cables, and she assured me everything was plugged in. But when I visited her office to check, I discovered the loose printer cable lost behind a mass of similar-colored wiring that was extremely difficult to sort out. Apparently, a cleaning person had mistakenly pulled the cable from a USB hub in a futile attempt to make the wiring mess look neat.

- *Is a cable bad or broken?* It's not always easy to see such a problem, because of the sometimes thick shielding on a cable. Try another cable, if you have one, as a test. Frayed or otherwise damaged cables should be replaced right away. Naked wires could cause a short circuit, which would fry the delicate electronic circuitry in the component.

- *Is the device faulty?* Perhaps the problem isn't your Mac or something you did. Sometimes, new products just fail out of the box or shortly after they're placed in service. That's the purpose of the new product warranty, and don't hesitate to read the fine print and find out what you need to do to get the unit repaired or replaced. Some companies will replace a product that's dead on arrival, by the way.

Although you may prefer to work work full time in Mac OS X, it's not always possible. Situations will do doubt arise where a product just won't run under Mac OS X, even if the manufacturer claims compatibility. If this is the case, bite the bullet and return to your old operating system.

Chapter 13

Taking Mac OS X on the Road

If you need an immediate solution to:	See page:
Computing on the Road	282
Checking Battery Life	283
Getting the Maximum Amount of Battery Life	283
Creating an Apple Laptop Travel Kit	286
Getting the Most Efficient Online Performance	290
Using FireWire Target Disk Mode	292

Chapter 13 Taking Mac OS X on the Road

In Brief

The rise of mobile computing means that you can truly take it with you—your laptop, that is. That way, you can join your fellow road warriors and sit on the beach and finish that business proposal, or write your great American novel while on a Caribbean cruise. Apple Computer even ships some iBooks and PowerBooks with DVD drives, so you can catch your favorite flick on that cross-country or cross-continent flight and not have to depend on the often-mediocre fare the airline selects for you.

With Mac OS X, Apple Computer has made your portable computing experience even more pleasant, with clever touches that will make your iBook or PowerBook run faster and more efficiently.

Exploring Mac OS X Tools for Laptops

Laptop computers nowadays are extremely powerful, in many respects on a par with desktop computers. A notable example is the striking Titanium PowerBook G4, which offers a brilliant 15.2-inch LCD display and great processor performance. In addition, using the built-in peripheral ports, you can easily attach a regular keyboard and mouse and, on some iBooks and a PowerBook, an external display, and use the laptop for double duty as a stationary desktop computer. If you need to take your work on the road, disconnect the laptop, pack it in a case, and you're ready to roll.

NOTE: *Some recent model PowerBook G4's also include a DVI port for a digital flat panel display. With an external adapter, they can also support Apple's own line of monitors, including the 23-inch Apple HD Cinema Display.*

Superior Power Management

Year after year, as computer processors get more powerful, they also require less power. Today's iBook and PowerBook can crunch numbers with the best of them, yet the low power requirements of their microprocessors and Mac OS X's power-management features allow you to maximize the amount of time your computer can run without requiring a battery recharge or a nearby AC outlet.

In Brief

Integrated Mouse Preference Panel

Under Mac OS X, a separate system setting for trackpad speed is usually not present on newer Apple laptops (you might find it on older PowerBooks). When you launch the System Preferences application and click the Mouse settings pane (see Figure 13.1), you'll be able to adjust trackpad speed and double-click speed directly. With some models (such as various PowerBook G3s), you'll see a separate Trackpad tab, similar to the one in Mac OS 9.x.

Superfast Sleep and Awake Features

In the old days (before Mac OS X), when you put your PowerBook to sleep, your Mac would take a few seconds to do its disk drive and network housecleaning chores before going into idle mode. The reverse process could take even longer; it might take up to a minute for your Mac to return to normal operating mode after being brought back to life.

NOTE: *The process of awakening from sleep mode is quicker for Mac OS 9 and later, but it's still not as fast as in Mac OS X.*

For Mac OS X, Apple has made both processes ultra-efficient and superquick. Just choose Sleep from the Apple menu, and your iBook or PowerBook will close almost immediately. Best of all, you can bring it back to life almost instantaneously by pressing any key on the keyboard

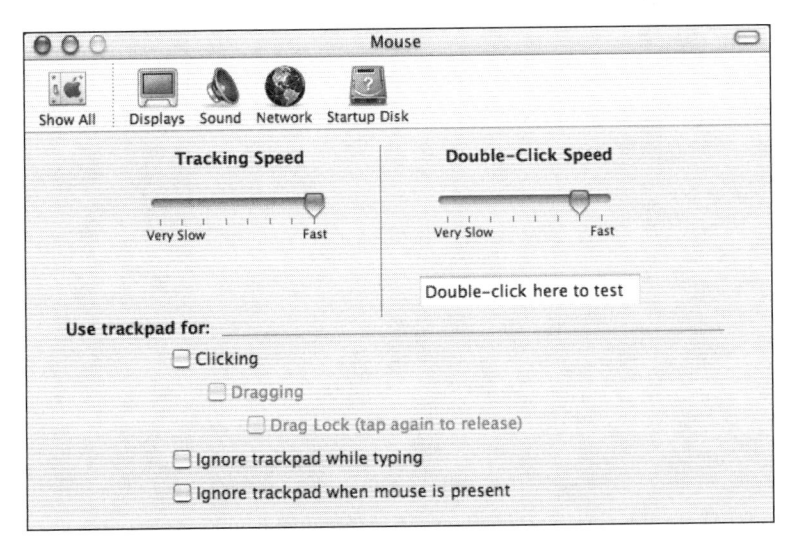

Figure 13.1   The Mouse settings pane handles trackpad settings for your Apple laptop.

279

or, with most models (check your documentation to be sure), opening the case. It almost seems as if it was never placed in sleep mode to begin with. This side effect can help speed your passage through airport security when they ask to see the computer's desktop to confirm it's really a laptop.

Editing Vacation Videos on the Road

If your iBook or PowerBook has FireWire capability (and all the recent models do), you'll be able to edit videos of the family vacation or presentation on the road, using Apple's iMovie software (see Figure 13.2) or any video-editing tool you prefer.

NOTE: It's not just videos. When the sound editors for the last Star Wars movie, Attack of the Clones, wanted to capture sound at remote locales, they used a PowerBook G4 running Mac OS X.

After you have shot your videos, you can easily copy them to your iBook's or PowerBook's hard drive and then edit the footage the way you like, adding special effects and sound effects. Then, after the movie has been prepared, you can save it in a variety of formats, including QuickTime, which allows for easy online distribution.

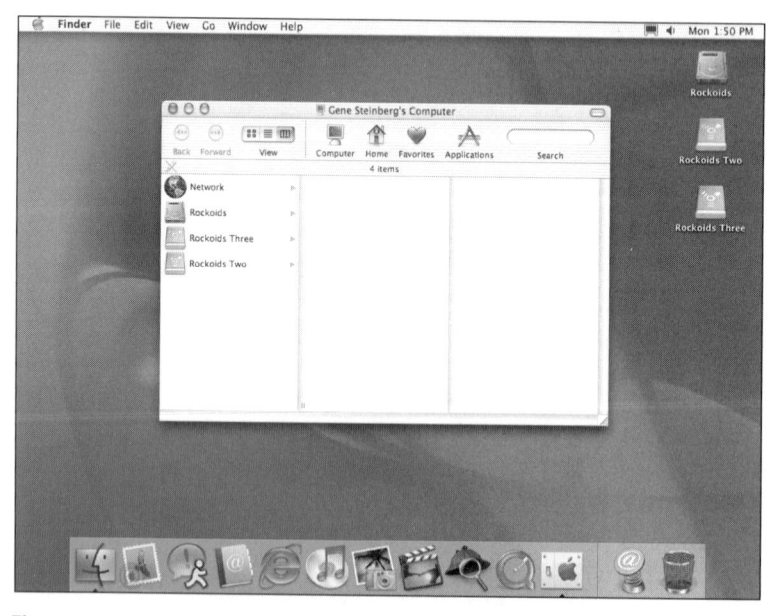

Figure 13.2   iMovie is the flexible yet super-simple desktop video-editing software that's included with Mac OS X 10.2.

Immediate Solutions

In addition to making and editing videos, you can also use programs such as AppleWorks 6 and Microsoft PowerPoint X for Mac to make slide shows. After you're finished, you can attach your Apple laptop to a TV or projector and use it for a portable presentation.

TIP: Apple iBooks equipped with FireWire have an AV output port that you can use to attach these cute laptops to a regular TV with composite video or camcorder ports. The PowerBook's output capabilities include S-video.

NOTE: Because video fills a large amount of drive storage space, consider bringing an extra drive with you if you intend to capture a large video. Remember that USB-based drives are very slow and absolutely unsuitable except for lower-resolution video capture and playback. Expansion bay, FireWire, and SCSI-based devices can provide sufficient speed for good performance.

Chapter 13 Taking Mac OS X on the Road

Immediate Solutions

Computing on the Road

Some day in the future, it's possible that most computers will be mobile devices, designed to work efficiently on the road, yet ready to plug into a desktop docking system at a moment's notice. Apple flirted with this sort of setup some years back with the Duo system, but the product never caught on as expected. In the meantime, you can enjoy a flexible Mac computing experience with the iBook, the PowerBook, and, of course, Mac OS X.

An Apple laptop comes complete with all the ingredients for performing the computing tasks you need when you're not at your home or office. The latest models include a built-in modem and Ethernet networking ports, and most models have a reasonable array of expansion ports so you can add extra devices to fill the gaps. Only the later models (the iBook and Titanium PowerBook G4) lack such niceties as a high-speed expansion bay for storage devices.

NOTE: Why would newer Apple laptops make do with less expansion? In the drive to make them ultra thin, a few compromises were necessary, so you are left with an appendage if you want to connect an additional drive, even if it's the cool little iPod, which does double duty as a FireWire hard drive.

Before you take your iBook or PowerBook on a trip, however, you'll want to be prepared for the worst and for the most effective computing experience, whether you're visiting someone's home, staying in a hotel, or camping out. With a little advance preparation, you can get the most value from your Mac computing experience regardless of your destination.

Immediate Solutions

Checking Battery Life

With older versions of the Mac OS, you could check the state of your laptop's battery courtesy of a Control Strip module or an optional icon on the menu bar clock. For Mac OS X, Apple's new solution is a menu bar status display.

Where is it? You can enable this feature (if it doesn't already appear by default) in the Energy Saver preference panel (see Figure 13.3).

Once you check the Show Battery Status In Menu Bar item, you'll see a graphical display of estimated battery life. You can use it to keep tabs on how much juice your battery has left.

Getting the Maximum Amount of Battery Life

Whatever you do, your iBook or PowerBook won't run forever before the battery is spent. If you have an AC outlet and your power supply nearby, this may be a minor inconvenience at most. But if you're in a plane or power is otherwise unavailable, you'll want to stretch your battery as far as you can.

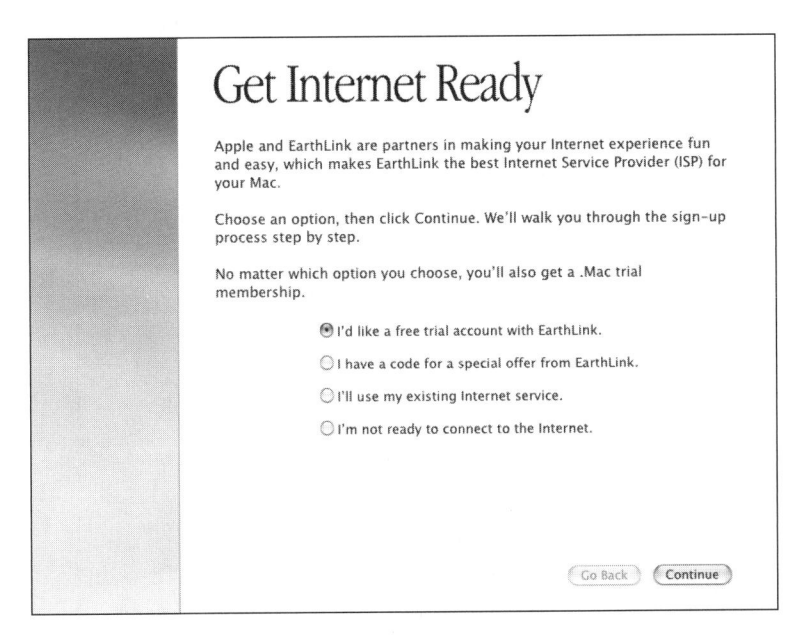

Get Internet Ready

Apple and EarthLink are partners in making your Internet experience fun and easy, which makes EarthLink the best Internet Service Provider (ISP) for your Mac.

Choose an option, then click Continue. We'll walk you through the sign-up process step by step.

No matter which option you choose, you'll also get a .Mac trial membership.

- ● I'd like a free trial account with EarthLink.
- ○ I have a code for a special offer from EarthLink.
- ○ I'll use my existing Internet service.
- ○ I'm not ready to connect to the Internet.

(Go Back) (Continue)

Figure 13.3 Activate the battery status display from this settings panel, which is collapsed unless you click Show details.

283

Here are some suggestions to get the most from your Apple laptop's battery power:

- *Let it sleep.* When you're not using your laptop, let it drift into sleep mode. Mac OS X will bring it to life in just a second when you're ready to use it again. While in sleep mode, all your applications remain open with your settings intact. Only your online or network connections will be deactivated.

WARNING! *Sleep mode doesn't last forever if you're not near AC current. Over time, possibly a week or two, or maybe a bit more, battery power will be spent and when you fire up your Apple laptop, you'll have to recharge the battery. So it's worthwhile hooking up your baby to its power adapter from time to time during a long period of sleep, or just turn it off altogether if you're not going to use it for a while.*

- *Use the Energy Saver preference panel.* Launch System Preferences and open Energy Saver. Choose Automatic to let it sort it out for itself, or just click the Show Details button to see the entire display (see Figure 13.4). You'll be able to adjust the intervals for system, display, and hard drive sleep. Because the hard drive can use a lot of extra juice, letting it go to sleep after a brief period of inactivity might conserve battery life far beyond the normal level. If you want to sacrifice a little power, click Options (see Figure 13.5), and click on the Processor Performance pop-up menu. The Automatic mode will cut processor power slightly on supported models

Figure 13.4 Use Energy Saver to give your battery greater longevity.

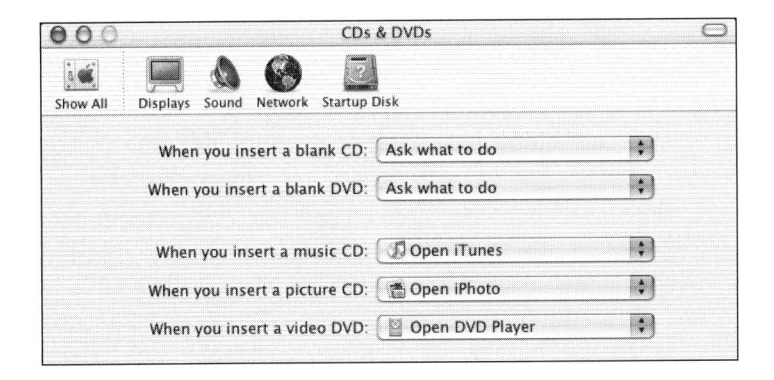

Figure 13.5 The Options panel has addition choices to optimize battery performance.

when the battery is in use. But you can choose your performance option manually if you prefer.

NOTE: Some applications cause a lot of hard-drive activity when running, so a sleep setting won't save battery life. In addition, if your Apple laptop doesn't have a large amount of RAM, Mac OS X's advanced virtual memory feature will swap data to and from the hard drive frequently, again limiting the effectiveness of this setting.

- *Turn down the brightness.* You probably like a brilliant picture, but the brighter the setting, the more power is required. If you can reduce brightness and not suffer too much from the dimmer screen, you might buy some extra time from your battery power.

- *Don't use the modem.* If you don't have to surf, your iBook or PowerBook won't need to draw as much current from the battery. Hence, you'll get longer life.

- *Remove expansion bay devices.* These devices are powered by your PowerBook's battery and thus will reduce battery life. Just remember, if it's a storage device, you need to eject the disk icon first by dragging it to the trash before you disconnect the device itself.

NOTE: The Titanium PowerBook G4 and iBook lines do not have expansion bays.

- *Remove FireWire and USB devices.* Some FireWire devices, including Apple's ultra-cool iPod jukebox player, draw current from your Apple laptop to run. Others, such as USB devices, just get trickle current. Regardless, unplug these devices if you don't need them and want to get maximum battery life.

285

- *Avoid PC Cards.* Don't use a PC Card expansion module if you can help it, because it will require additional juice.
- *Use headphones for audio.* Headphones draw less power, and you can turn the volume lower and save on precious battery life. The side benefit is that bystanders won't be annoyed if your sound, game, or musical preferences differ from theirs.
- *Forget the DVD.* If you have a model with a DVD player that's supported under Mac OS X, it's nice to be able to watch your favorite flick on the road, but doing so can sharply reduce battery life. It's a trade-off, but you might find the entertainment value to be worth the sacrifice.

Creating an Apple Laptop Travel Kit

When you take your iBook or PowerBook and Mac OS X on your next trip, you should consider adding a few items to your packing list so you can get the maximum level of convenience that portable computing has to offer. Here's a short list of items to take with you and the preparations to make:

- *Traveling bag*—You can pack your iBook or PowerBook into a suitcase, well cushioned with clothing, and it should survive the trip just fine. But you should consider buying a dedicated laptop travel bag. Such products usually have extra pouches and special storage compartments for removable media, extra drives, batteries, cables, software, and other items you might need for your work. There's also usually a shoulder strap in case the entire package gets a little heavy for you. When buying such a bag, consider a product that has a well-cushioned area to protect your laptop from the rigors of such things as airline turbulence and driving on rocky terrain in a sport utility vehicle.

WARNING! Some older laptop cases aren't large enough to contain the first-generation iBooks or PowerBook G4s comfortably. Although the new Apple laptops tend to be lighter than many older models, they may be physically wider or deeper. I ran into this problem when trying to fit an original iBook into my favorite carrying case, although the ultra-wide Titanium PowerBook G4 fit perfectly.

- *Protection from the elements*—As rugged as laptops are in normal use, if you're going to be outside in a damp environment or you're at sea, make sure your computer is well protected. Check with your dealer about getting a case that can protect your

Immediate Solutions

laptop, particularly in a damp environment. You might want to check into some moisture-absorbing gel packs, like the ones that sometimes ship with consumer electronics, as they can help keep your computer dry in humid climates.

NOTE: This may seem at odds with a book about Mac OS X and Apple computers, but if you do travel to extreme environments, you may want to consider a notebook computer that's designed to withstand the elements. Called ruggedized notebooks, such products as the Itronix GoBook (a Windows-based notebook that can cost upward of five grand) and similar notebooks from such makers as Panasonic, are designed to withstand treatment that would cause any normal notebook computer to break or at least fail to run.

WARNING! Don't expect your iBook or PowerBook to run perfectly on your favorite ski slope or in the midst of a blizzard. According to Apple's spec sheets, the normal operating temperature is 50 to 95 degrees Fahrenheit. If you bring your laptop in from the cold, be sure to give it enough time to warm up before you use it.

- *Backups for key files*—You plan to get some work done on the road, but your laptop's hard drive fails. Although these little computers are built to survive a reasonable amount of abuse, the fact is that storage devices fail at unexpected moments. It's easy for a repair shop to replace the drive, but recovering data from a defective drive can be costly, with no guarantee of total success. In addition to taking backup media for your most important files, you may want to include a copy of your laptop's system installer and restore disks in case you have to replace everything on a new hard drive.

TIP: You might also want to take with you a backup for your home or office system. That way, should something happen at either location during your trip, you'll still be able to get up and running again upon your return.

NOTE: Having a hard drive fail on a notebook computer isn't as unusual as you might think. Just before I left to attend the Macworld Expo in San Francisco in January 2001, the drive on my nearly new iBook Special Edition began to make a frightening clicking sound and quickly failed. Fortunately, I made a CD of the files I needed to continue working, and I was able to borrow another laptop from a colleague and continue working with minimal delay.

- *Extra storage devices*—Whether your Apple laptop has a built-in expansion bay port or not, plenty of convenient storage devices are small enough to pack in a PowerBook case. A number of external FireWire and USB storage devices, from such companies as Iomega, LaCie, and SmartDisk, are *bus powered* (meaning they are powered by your Mac's ports). As a result, you don't have to deal with power bricks and finding extra AC outlets in your hotel room. If you can put up with the little appendage, you can even use these devices during airline travel.

TIP: If you have an iPod, you can also use its built-in FireWire drive for backups.

- *Diagnostic or repair CDs*—In addition to a Mac OS system disk, you might want to bring along an emergency CD for such programs as Alsoft's DiskWarrior, Symantec's Norton Utilities, or MicroMat's TechTool Pro or Drive 10. These programs offer an extra measure of protection against drive directory problems and, in the case of TechTool Pro, potential hardware issues.

WARNING! Some disk diagnostic programs won't work properly under Mac OS X, but they will function properly when you boot under Mac OS 9.1 or later. Before using any of these programs to diagnose a possible disk-related problem, check the compatibility information from the publisher.

- *Extra input devices*—Not everyone loves the feel of a laptop's keyboard; I have been hot and cold about the PowerBook G4 (the second generation model with gigabit Ethernet is a little better), although the iBook seems nice for my purposes. Such a keyboard might be fine for occasional use, but if you have to pound a keyboard or do lots of mousing around during your trip, you might want to pack a full-sized keyboard and mouse in your carrying bag. If you're into computer games, or the kids are part of the trip, consider buying a trackball or joystick, both of which are recommended for superior computer gaming.

- *Patch cables*—Need to hook up to a network, a phone jack, or an external drive or scanner? Don't forget to bring the proper cables, along with your laptop's AC power supply. Even if you're not 100-percent certain you'll need a specific cable setup for a specific purpose, having an extra cable isn't likely to weigh down your carrying bag much.

TIP: Don't assume that the phone in your hotel room is in a convenient location. It might be next to the bed, but you want to work on a table. It's a good idea to get a long telephone cable for just this purpose. Another good addition to your packing list is an Ethernet crossover cable, in case you need a direct connection (without a hub or switch present) to another Mac, network printer, or cable/DSL modem.

Immediate Solutions

- *Consider a wireless connection*—Apple makes it possible to network or explore the Internet with the iBook and recent PowerBooks without a direct connection cable using its AirPort wireless networking system. You can install the AirPort module in your laptop and attach a base station to a phone. Then, you can stay connected for a distance of up to 150 feet (sometimes more). You can lounge on a patio or a beach, and surf the Net with your Apple laptop without having to run a long cable.

- *Special connection cables*—For trips overseas or when you are staying in a hotel or other locale where a convenient modem data port isn't available, you'll have to be creative to find a way to get connected. One useful resource is a company called TeleAdapt (**www.teleadapt.com**), which makes connection cables and power adapters for a variety of installations around the world. You'll be able to cope with foreign power connections, portable power supplies, and various forms of telephone hookups with the right connection kit. Although nothing is perfect, if you need to stay in touch, this is an option to consider.

- *Portable printer*—The major manufacturers of ink jet printers, such as Canon, Epson, and HP, all have smaller models that are designed for travel. What they lack in terms of print quality and speed is more than made up for in size and convenience.

- *Insurance*—Laptop computers are theft magnets. The convenient carrying handle of the first-generation "clamshell" iBook, for example, may tempt you to just carry it in your hand and leave the rest of the accessories in your suitcase or laptop accessory bag. But it can also attract thieves who'd love to separate you from your computer. Be wary of tight crowds at the airport and deliberate distractions—especially in light of the increased security since the September 11, 2001 terrorist attacks—and definitely don't put down your computer, even for a moment. Professional thieves know all the tricks. The best preparation you can consider, however, is simply to get a good insurance policy so you can replace the computer in case the worst happens. Some major insurance companies offer computer coverage, including units taken on the road, as part of homeowner's and small-business policies.

13. Taking Mac OS X on the Road

*TIP: If your insurance agent can't cover your computers, consider Safeware (see **www.safeware.com**). It has been in business for years, it's listed favorably with the Better Business Bureau, and many PC and Mac laptop owners swear by it. Remember, however, that insurance will cover only the cost of replacement hardware and software, but not your data. So have a backup ready in another location (at home or a bank vault, or both) if something goes wrong.*

289

- *Airport X-rays*—Through the years, I've dutifully put my iBooks and PowerBooks under the airport security X-ray machines and haven't suffered any losses of data or computing power. Just let them do their job; the enhanced security at airports often requires a personal inspection of your computer. Just remember to put your laptop in sleep mode rather than shut it down, to speed up the inspection process. The security personnel primarily want to see the computer's desktop display so they know it's really a computer. Imagine their surprise when they see how quickly Mac OS X starts up.

- *Games for the kids*—If you are taking your clan on a long trip, you may want to bring along some of their favorite computer games for relaxation. Games can keep them from getting into your hair, plus they can help you get the most value out of your iBook or PowerBook. The latest generations of both products are, in fact, decent game machines, with fairly good performance on high-action 3D games.

TIP: If games are your "bag," or your children are picky, consider the PowerBook G4s released in the fall of 2001, or the iBooks released in the Spring of 2002, both of which include an ATI Mobility Radeon graphics chip for superior 3D graphics and improved frame rates for more fluid gameplay.

Related solution:	Found on page:
The No-Frills Daily Backup Plan	371
MicroMat's TechToolPro	384

Getting the Most Efficient Online Performance

Today, it's getting increasingly difficult to stay away from your email, unless you can afford to let the mail sit unopened until your return. Fortunately, if you must keep up with the messages, there are ways to stay in touch even if your ISP isn't available in the area you're visiting.

Here are some considerations to help you track your email in the event you need to surf the Net:

- *Check your ISP's access.* Such services as AOL, its sister service CompuServe, EarthLink (Apple's recommended ISP), Prodigy Internet (now in the process of being renamed Yahoo Internet), and other large services have access numbers in many major cities around the world. Before leaving, you should retrieve and print out a listing of the phone numbers in the cities you plan to visit. If your itinerary changes along the way, you can usually go online and look for additional numbers. If you're using a local service, however, you may have to consider other options. One possible solution is the EarthLink Mobile Broadband service, which uses a special high-performance wireless model to deliver speeds of up to 128KBps. Many services, such as AOL and EarthLink, also offer Web-based email options to retrieve your messages, or you can sign up for a free email account from such services as Microsoft's Hotmail or Yahoo. That way, if you can get online from, say, a public library, you can still retrieve your email. If you intend to travel to an out-of-the-way locale without convenient online access, check with the hotel or airline or travel agent for suggestions. On the other hand, it was once possible to survive on a trip without cellular telephones or email, so you may find that you can live without the luxury.

TIP: *You may want to check whether your hotel offers high-speed Internet access. Some hotels offer DSL for a daily surcharge in some rooms, but you must make sure you reserve a room that's prewired for the Internet. Although you may have to redo your ISP settings (usually outgoing, rather than incoming mail), this is a way to speed up your on-the-road computing experience and have more time for rest and relaxation. The hotel should have an instruction booklet from the broadband ISP about how to access its services and your existing email.*

- *Send messages to yourself for backup.* If you plan to get some work done on the road, consider sending copies of your documents via email so you can retrieve them at your home or office. That way, if something happens to your laptop during the trip, you'll still be able to get the files when you return.

NOTE: *Some ISPs have strict limits on the size of file attachments you can send with your messages. For AOL, it's 2MB outside the service and 16MB within the service. Other online services limit the size to 5MB or 10MB. If you need to handle larger files, consider compressing them, or bring along extra disks and a removable device for storage. Another possibility is to subscribe to Apple's .Mac service, which includes 100MB of storage space on your personal iDisk. Since you can password protect your iDisk, this may be an ideal spot for sending big files, so you don't overwhelm your ISP's limited storage space.*

- *Use a fax machine for a printer.* You can use your computer's fax modem to print a document by sending a fax to yourself. If you're using the hotel's fax machine, check the hotel's fees beforehand, because some charge several dollars per page. Or, perhaps you can find a local business or travel office that will

Chapter 13   Taking Mac OS X on the Road

lend a hand. Another way to get printed pages is to visit a print shop that can provide output for your files.

TIP: Some upscale business-oriented hotels even place fax machines in some rooms, but check the price list to see if there's a daily or per-page charge. You may also find a small business center at the hotel, where you can plug in your iBook or PowerBook to a networked printer. Again you'll want to know the costs of this service before outputting those pages.

Using FireWire Target Disk Mode

Once you return to your home or office, or you need to set up shop at another office, you'll be pleased to know that FireWire-equipped iBooks and PowerBooks offer a speedy way to retrieve files without having to concern yourself with a new network setting. The feature is called FireWire Target Disk Mode. Here's how to set it up:

TIP: Target Disk Mode isn't reserved for late-model Apple laptops. The feature is also available on any PowerMac G4 with AGP graphics, the PowerMac Cube, and slot-load iMacs with FireWire ports.

1. Shut down your Apple laptop.

WARNING! *Target Disk Mode is best used while your iBook or PowerBook is connected to AC current. Running out of juice during a copy operation may result in missing or damaged files.*

2. Take a regular FireWire cable and attach your iBook or PowerBook to the host computer (which can be a desktop Mac or another Apple laptop).

NOTE: Because FireWire is a hot-pluggable technology, it's not necessary to turn off the other computer when you make the connection.

3. Boot your Apple laptop and hold down the T key. Keep pressing the key until you see a FireWire icon on the laptop's display. Wait a few seconds, and the laptop's drive icon should show up as another FireWire device on the host computer.

4. When you're finished transferring files, you can remove or dismount the drive icon from the desktop by selecting it and pressing Command+E or by choosing Eject from the Finder's File menu.

Part III
The Software Review

Chapter 14

Mac OS X-Savvy Applications

If you need an immediate solution to:	*See page:*
Introducing AppleWorks for Mac OS X	312
Using AppleWorks Starting Points	312
Using Tables in AppleWorks	313
Introducing Office v. X for Mac	315
Profiling the Project Gallery	316
Using Word X's Multiple Selection Feature	316
Using Excel X's Auto Recover Feature	316
Introducing Create for Mac OS X	316
Using the Inspector	317
Starting a Web Page in Create	318

Chapter 14 Mac OS X-Savvy Applications

In Brief

Mac OS X has a host of new interface elements and features that can provide a more productive, enjoyable, and reliable computing experience. But to be able to use those features, you have to run software that is specifically compiled to run under Mac OS X.

The situation is similar to what prevailed back in 1994 when Apple moved to PowerPC processors from the 680x0 processor family. An emulation mode let you run older software at reduced speed, but it took months and in some cases a few years for most Mac software companies to move their products over to the new architecture. Some applications never made the switch, but emulation was there to fill the gap.

The Two Forms of Mac OS X Applications

Back in the days when the first iteration of Mac OS X was announced (it was then known as *Rhapsody*), Apple announced that it expected software publishers to totally rewrite their products in a new programming language to be compatible. This requirement, of course, fell on deaf ears in the major companies, who didn't want to invest years and millions of dollars in the effort to rewrite millions of lines of computer code (over 30 million in Microsoft Office). So, Apple went back to the drawing board.

The company came up with two ways to provide programs that are compatible with Mac OS X:

- *Carbon*—This is Apple's trump card. Carbon is a special set of application programming interfaces (APIs) that can be used to modify an existing Mac program and make it support all or most of the features of Mac OS X. Rather than having to do all the work from scratch, only 10 to 20 percent (on average) of the program's code must be updated to support the new system architecture. Even better, most of these same applications can run normally on Macs equipped with Mac OS 8.6 through the various versions of Mac OS 9, by virtue of a system extension called *CarbonLib*. Depending on the program, the update could take days or months, so check with specific publishers about their plans.

296

In Brief

NOTE: *By "all or most of the features of Mac OS X," I mean that some capabilities, such as the Font Panel (described in Chapter 16) were still unavailable in the Carbon environment as of the time this book was published. Check with specific publishers about which features they choose to support and which they do not. Also, to be fair, not all Carbon applications are designed to also run in a Classic Mac OS. Microsoft Office v. X and AOL for Mac OS X are two examples of such applications, because they run strictly under Mac OS X.*

- *Cocoa*—A native Mac OS X application can also be developed using either Sun Microsystems' Java programming language or one descended from the original NeXT-based Objective C. These programs will yield full support for all the core features of Mac OS X, but they won't run under the regular Mac OS. For new programs, it's a lot faster to build a program from scratch this way, but this isn't the best alternative for existing publishers that have to rewrite up to millions of lines of code.

The best thing about the way Mac OS X is set up is that you don't have to concern yourself with the choices publishers make to achieve product compatibility with Mac OS X. You can just install and use the program and take advantage of the features and improved performance and reliability.

Key Mac OS X Software Profiles and Previews

As of the time this book went to press, thousands of new or updated applications had been announced for Mac OS X. Some were out, and others were promises of what was to come. The initial releases of Mac OS X included several offerings to sample the possibilities.

This section profiles some of the significant programs. In the "Immediate Solutions" section, I describe some useful features you'll want to try from three of the available Mac OS X-savvy programs—AppleWorks 6, Microsoft Office v. X, and Stone Design's Create suite.

Microsoft

One of the first publishers to declare support for Mac OS X was, believe it or not, Apple's former adversary, Microsoft. The original Public Beta of the new operating system included a Carbonized version of Microsoft's Internet Explorer browser (see Chapter 21), and the final version was bundled with Mac OS X. A Mac OS X version of Office 2001 for the Macintosh was announced in January 2001 and released in November of that year as Office v. X (see Figure 14.1).

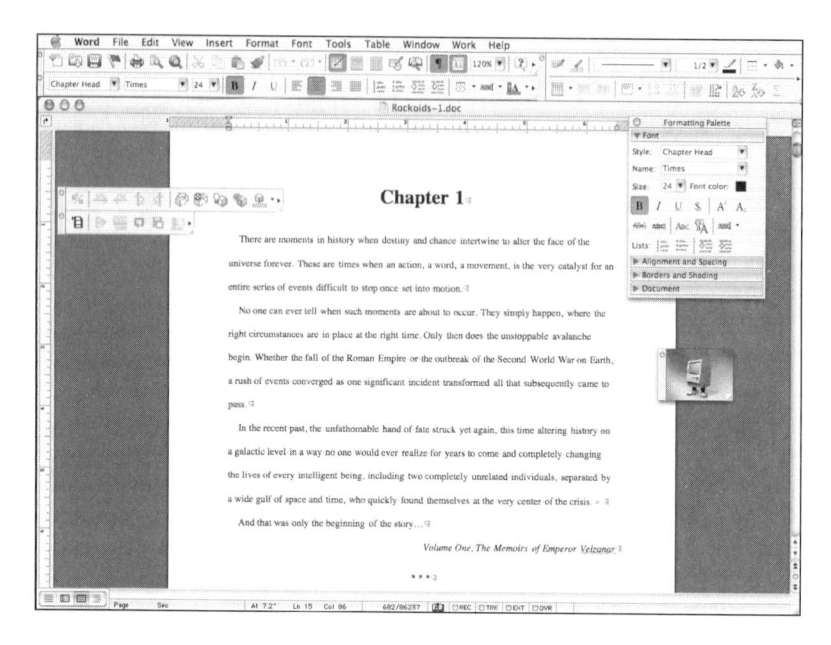

Figure 14.1   Dubbed Office v. X for Mac, the Carbon version of Microsoft Office takes special advantage of the Aqua interface.

The Mac OS X version of Office includes extensive revisions for Entourage, Microsoft's new email client and personal information manager, in addition to support for Mac OS X's robust features. A handful of minor features are spread across the remainder of the suite (Excel, PowerPoint, and Word). Microsoft boasted in the product's rollout that over 700 icons and numerous dialog boxes were carefully redesigned to take best advantage of Aqua.

NOTE: This book was written using Word X, and it was a joy to write and edit..

Apple Computer

The standard installation of Mac OS X includes a number of utilities for you to try. These include the Mail application described in Chapter 22, plus revised versions of old standbys such as the Calculator, Disk Utility (a combination of Disk First Aid and Drive Setup), Key Caps, QuickTime Player, Script Editor, Sherlock, and Stickies. In addition, Aladdin's StuffIt Expander is along for the ride, so you can open compressed files created in a variety of formats (even those from the Windows and Unix environments).

The installation includes quite a few new contenders, as well, Apple's famous "i" applications, designed as part of its digital hub strategy. Following is a brief description of a number of the most interesting programs included with Mac OS X, in the Applications and Utilities folders:

- *Acrobat Reader*—Adobe's popular application reads the many electronic documents that software publishers include in place of printed manuals these days.

- *Address Book*—This Rolodex-like application works with Apple's Mail application (described later in this list) to keep tabs on your personal and business address books.

NOTE: *Address Book is set up so other applications can hook up to it. IChat, Apple's instant messaging software, supports it as do such third party programs as SmithMicro's FAXstf X.*

- *Bluetooth File Exchange*—Bluetooth is another wireless networking technology, suited for communication between your Mac and printers, handheld devices and cell phones. If your Mac is equipped with a Bluetooth adapter, you can use this utility to configure how networked devices are handled. When a Bluetooth adapter is installed (the external adapters fit in the USB port), you'll see a Bluetooth preference panel pop up in the System Preferences application.

- *Chess*—Pit yourself against your Mac's G3 or G4 processor and see how well you can do in an interactive Chess game (see Figure 14.2) designed to exploit the ultra-crisp graphics of Mac OS X.

- *Audio MIDI Setup*—Are you a professional musician, or are you just "messing around" with a keyboard to have a little fun with friends and family? Apple's Audio MIDI Setup software offers a convenient, flexible front-end to attach and configure MIDI devices to your Mac. It's a convenient method to harness the powerful audio features of Mac OS X, which include multichannel sound, support for 24-bit/96kHz audio and more.

- *Clock*—This program is intended as a replacement or supplement for the popular menu bar clock. It can also put a floating clock palette on your desktop. You have a choice of analog or digital clocks.

TIP: *If you prefer the menu bar clock, no problem. You can continue to use both. But if you prefer to eliminate the one on the menu bar, launch System Preferences, click the Date & Time pane, and click the Menu Bar Clock tab. Uncheck the option Show The Clock In The Menu Bar.*

Figure 14.2 A grayscale picture doesn't really do justice to Mac OS X's interactive chess game.

- *ColorSync*—Mac OS X 10.2 comes with ColorSync 4.1 (in the Utilities folder), which provides automated support for color calibration between your Mac's display and an input or output device (such as a scanner or color printer). The ColorSync utility also includes a special First Aid feature that verifies a color profile against ICC specifications and repairs such problems, to ensure the best possible color matching.
- *Console*—As you use your Mac, you might, from time to time, see some strange error messages because of a printing problem or system-related issue. The Console application (see Figure 14.3) keeps a log of those messages. They may not be directly useful to the average Mac user, but you can use the information to help a software publisher figure out what went wrong with its product; you don't have to remember the arcane messages or prompts. This utility resides in the Mac OS X Utilities folder.
- *CPU Monitor*—Get a visual indication (see Figure 14.4) of how your Mac's processor is being accessed by Mac OS X. If you have a Mac with two processors, as I do, CPU Monitor (available in the Utilities folder) provides a separate display for each, so you can see how both are handling the load. This utility is proof positive of the operating system's built-in support for symmetric multiprocessing.

In Brief

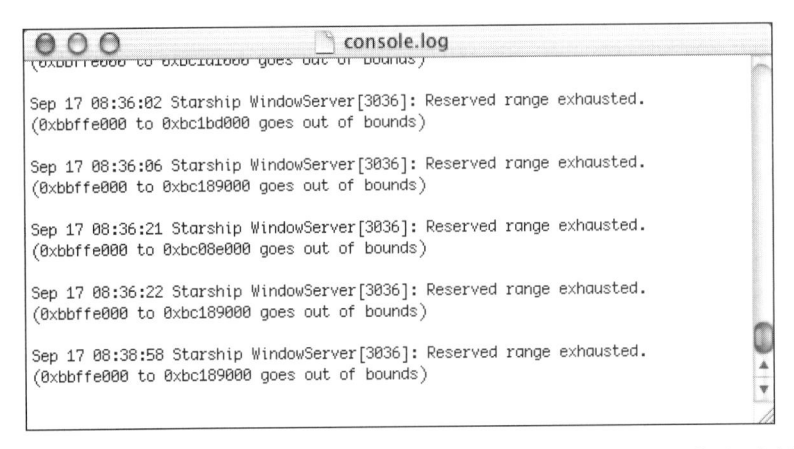

```
○ ○ ○                    console.log
(0xbbffe000 to 0xbc1d1000 goes out of bounds)

Sep 17 08:36:02 Starship WindowServer[3036]: Reserved range exhausted.
(0xbbffe000 to 0xbc1bd000 goes out of bounds)

Sep 17 08:36:06 Starship WindowServer[3036]: Reserved range exhausted.
(0xbbffe000 to 0xbc189000 goes out of bounds)

Sep 17 08:36:21 Starship WindowServer[3036]: Reserved range exhausted.
(0xbbffe000 to 0xbc08e000 goes out of bounds)

Sep 17 08:36:22 Starship WindowServer[3036]: Reserved range exhausted.
(0xbbffe000 to 0xbc189000 goes out of bounds)

Sep 17 08:38:58 Starship WindowServer[3036]: Reserved range exhausted.
(0xbbffe000 to 0xbc189000 goes out of bounds)
```

Figure 14.3   The log can display system-related error messages that might help you troubleshoot a problem on your Mac.

- *Disk Utility*—Take one part Disk First Aid and one part Drive Setup, and the result (in the Utilities folder) is an application that will check and format a drive. The sole limitation of the First Aid component of Disk Utility is its inability to check a startup drive for directory problems (but that's already done during the Mac OS X boot process). However, it does have the ability to repair permissions, which can fix situations where you find you don't have access to some of your files even though you have administrator's access.

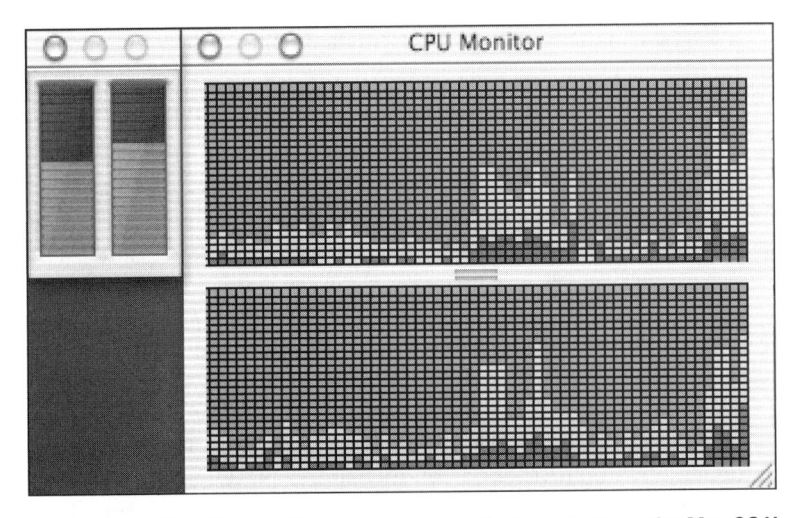

Figure 14.4   Yes, it's true. Two processors really share tasks under Mac OS X, and these little windows show what they're up to.

NOTE: Another useful feature of Disk Utility is its ability to format IDE and SCSI (FireWire isn't supported in the 10.2 release) drives in Redundant Array of Independent Disks (RAID) format, for the highest possible performance for content creators.

- *DVD Player*—If you have a Mac with DVD drive (and it's supported by Mac OS X), you can watch your favorite flick at home or on the road. DVD Player's controls mimic what you find in a home DVD player.

NOTE: By default, DVD Player is installed only on Macs with supported DVD drives. The version shipping with Jaguar works with Macs that feature AGP graphics capability and a handful of other models. Check your Mac's spec sheet to see what sort of graphics system it has, although the presence of the DVD Player is usually the best clue.

- *Display Calibrator*—This application (in the Utilities folder) works directly with the Displays preference panel in the System Preferences application to calibrate your Mac's display.

NOTE: When you calibrate your display, you give it the best possible color balance within its design limitations. A calibrated monitor along with color calibrated scanners or printers yields the best possible match between input and output. Although Apple's calibration process is not quite as perfect as a separate outboard calibration unit, it will suit for all but the most critical graphic artists and printers.

- *Grab*—So, what does this utility grab? A screenshot of your Mac, useful in providing illustrations for documentation. Although Command+Shift+3 (for a whole screen) and Command+Shift+4 (for a selected area) still work, Grab (in the Utilities folder) adds one interesting variation. You can also perform a timed capture, which gives you 10 seconds to set things up before the shutter goes off.

TIP These aren't your only screen-capture options. I used a shareware utility, Snapz Pro X (from Ambrosia Software, www.ambrosiasw.com), to deliver all the illustrations in this book. This application can capture whole screens, selected areas, or objects (a single window, dialog box, or menu), and can save in a number of different formats. If you upgrade to the "Pro" version, you can even capture QuickTime movies. This utility is included free of charge, by the way, with the PowerBooks and PowerMacs.

- *iChat*—Tens and tens of millions of online visitors communicate via instant messaging. Apple's iChat (see Figure 14.5) takes the concept a step further. It not only supports AOL's sprawling instant messaging system with a spiffy new interface, but allows you to send messages to fellow Mac OS X 10.2 users on your local computer network, courtesy of Apple's Rendezvous technology.

In Brief

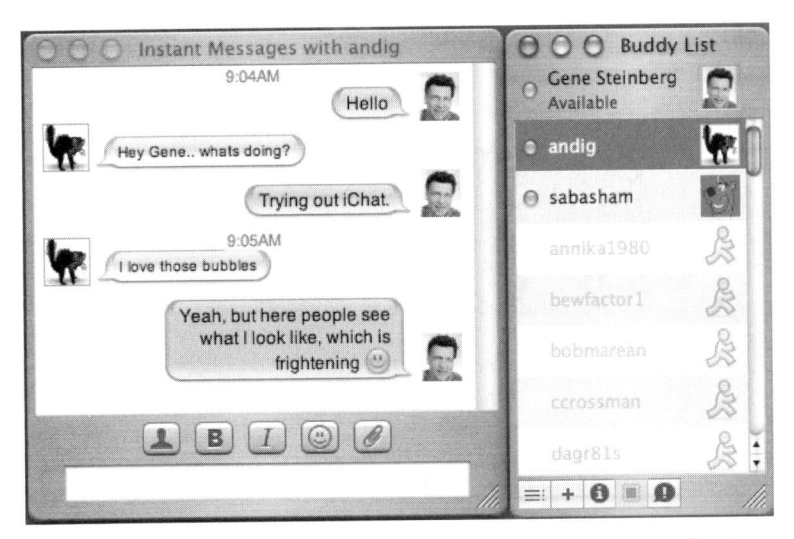

Figure 14.5   Your chat message can include your photo too. Here I took a calculated risk, as I didn't want to frighten away my friends.

NOTE: *One of the cool features of iChat is the ability to use your actual photo when sending a message to an iChat or AOL Instant Messenger user. That assumes, of course, that you feel comfortable displaying your photo.*

- *Image Capture*—Found in the Applications folder, this application launches automatically whenever you hook up a supported digital camera. It can then download files from the camera; you don't need any extra software to get pictures. You can even use it for a limited number of supported scanners (see Figure 14.6).

NOTE: *The original shipping version of Jaguar included support for several popular Epson scanners, but support for other products was expected to be added over time. In addition, Image Capture can be set to automatically launch the manufacturer's TWAIN drivers for supported scanners, rather than display its own simple user interface. This is a program preference.*

- *iMovie*—Apple's great video-editing application is standard issue with Mac OS X. It will capture video from a DV or Digital8 camcorder via your Mac's FireWire port, or edit video files you already have on your Mac's hard drive.
- *Internet Connect*—This application (see Figure 14.7) incorporates some of the elements of Remote Access, with a direct link to the Network pane of the System Preferences application to help you set up your dial-up access. You can also use it to establish a VPN (Virtual Private Network) with your company, if it has such a system. Chapter 8 discusses the subject in more detail.

Figure 14.6   Dozens of digital cameras and several scanners work with Image Capture to bring digital images over to your Mac.

- *Internet Explorer*—For several years, Microsoft's browser has been included with new Macs. For Mac OS X, Microsoft has made it look good for the Aqua environment, but the features are the same as those in the Classic version. They include the Auction Manager, Scrapbook, and the ability to change the theme color to suit your taste.
- *iPhoto*—What good is the hub of your digital lifestyle, which is supposedly what the Mac represents, if there's no way to organize your digital photo library? iPhoto combines simple management of pictures from digital cameras and scanners with basic retouching. Removal of the red eye look is done in a flash, so you don't have to worry about your friends thinking you may have been burning the midnight oil the previous night, or perhaps had an

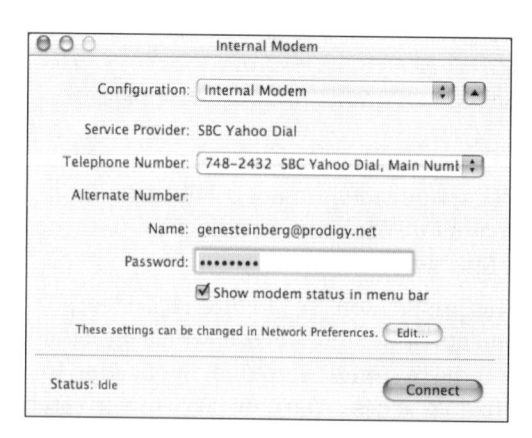

Figure 14.7 Use Internet Connect to dial up and log in to your ISP.

In Brief

extra cocktail or two. You can also use iPhoto to post your album to your .Mac Web site or order up a high-quality printed version.

- *iTunes*—Apple's popular jukebox program already sported an Aqua-inspired interface in its initial Classic Mac OS version. The version that comes with Mac OS X has hardly changed. It works with Apple's built-in CD drives and a host of third-party devices so you can burn music CDs containing your personal playlists.

NOTE: *iTunes also mates seamlessly with Apple's iPod, the ultra-slick jukebox player that keeps my son occupied when he's not doing his homework (or is that instead of doing his homework?).*

- *Key Caps*—This utility is an update of the Classic Mac program for checking obscure characters on your Mac's keyboard.
- *Keychain Access*—Beginning with Mac OS 9, Apple incorporated a keychain feature that lets you manage all your user passwords from a single application. This application, in the Utilities folder, is used to configure keychains. You can also do so automatically via such features as the Finder's Connect To Server function for accessing network shares.
- *Mail*—Email is often the most-used feature on the Internet, and Apple has delivered a brand-new application for the purpose (see Figure 14.8). Mail will handle most of your email accounts. It provides a bevy of features, including the ability to import your messages from several other email programs, multiple signatures,

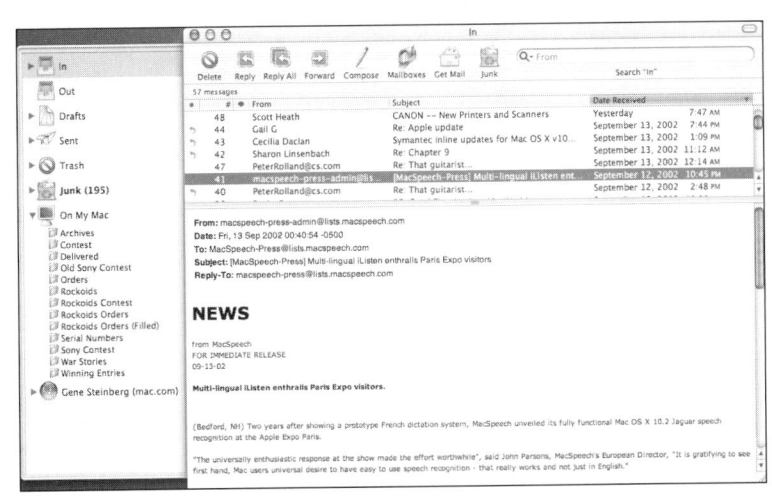

Figure 14.8 Manage a full range of email features, including junk mail filtering, with this speedy little application.

305

Chapter 14 Mac OS X-Savvy Applications

email rules, scheduled retrieval of messages, and a Finder-like interface where you can change the toolbar icons to meet your needs. Even better, it has a superlative junk mail filter that, when activated, can catch the vast majority of those annoying unsolicited messages. Chapter 22 discusses the subject in more detail.

- *NetInfo Manager*—This application, in the Utilities folder, is a valuable tool for system administrators to manage Mac OS X users and directories. At the basic level, you can use it to create root access to your Mac (a kind of super-user). You can get a fairly extensive and technical explanation of how this powerful application is used from Apple's Web site at **www.apple.com/macosx/server/pdf/UnderstandingUsingNetInfo.pdf**.

- *Network Utility*—What's happening on your network? Are you encountering a problem connecting to a shared computer or printer, or is your Net access not functioning as you expect? This application (see Figure 14.9) can be used to perform such functions as **ping** (contact and return, like sonar) or **trace** to find the source.

- *Preview*—This application can read both PDF files (and convert documents to that format as well) and pictures in such popular formats as GIF, JPET, PICT, and TIFF.

- *QuickTime Player*—This is yet another program that inherits nothing more than a new look for Mac OS X. It's used to play QuickTime movies from your Mac or from the Internet.

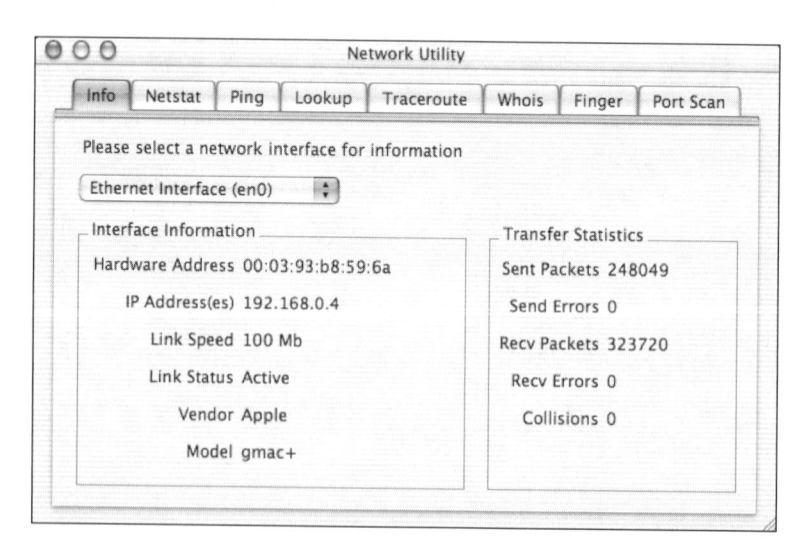

```
┌─────────────────────────────────────────────────────────────┐
│  ● ○ ○                  Network Utility                      │
│  ┌──────┬─────────┬──────┬────────┬────────────┬───────┬────────┬──────────┐ │
│  │ Info │ Netstat │ Ping │ Lookup │ Traceroute │ Whois │ Finger │ Port Scan│ │
│  └──────┴─────────┴──────┴────────┴────────────┴───────┴────────┴──────────┘ │
│                                                              │
│   Please select a network interface for information          │
│                                                              │
│   [ Ethernet Interface (en0)     ▼ ]                         │
│   ┌─ Interface Information ─────┐  ┌─ Transfer Statistics ─┐ │
│   │                              │  │                       │ │
│   │  Hardware Address 00:03:93:b8:59:6a │  Sent Packets 248049 │ │
│   │                              │  │                       │ │
│   │  IP Address(es) 192.168.0.4  │  Send Errors   0       │ │
│   │                              │  │                       │ │
│   │  Link Speed 100 Mb           │  Recv Packets 323720    │ │
│   │                              │  │                       │ │
│   │  Link Status Active          │  Recv Errors   0       │ │
│   │                              │  │                       │ │
│   │  Vendor Apple                │  Collisions    0       │ │
│   │                              │  │                       │ │
│   │  Model gmac+                 │  │                       │ │
│   └──────────────────────────────┘  └───────────────────────┘ │
└─────────────────────────────────────────────────────────────┘
```

Figure 14.9   You can use this application to test the condition of your local network or Internet connection.

In Brief

- *Stickies*—What's a Mac without Stickies, your personal post-it note system? For the Mac OS X version, Apple has taken the basic features of the Classic version, added some additional text formatting and import features, and put them into a familiar package. You can import all your Stickies from your Classic Mac System Folder, so you don't lose a thing in switching over.

NOTE: *Of course, nothing prevents you from running the Classic version of Stickies, but because the conversion is completely accurate, doing so shouldn't be necessary.*

- *System Preferences*—Apple's replacement for Control Panels, System Preferences is used to configure most of your system settings. This application is alsos extensible, so third-party software companies can put their own material in System Preferences (it will appear in a category labeled Other).

- *Terminal*—Apple has gone to great lengths to bury the native Unix command line for Mac OS X. As a result, Mac users can continue to use the new operating system without taking a gander at the core; but Terminal (see Figure 14.10) gives Unix mavens full access to the command line and a chance to explore the underpinnings.

WARNING! *Unix is not a tool for the casual user. The wrong commands can get you in trouble and invoke the wrong functions or cause performance problems. Unlike most graphical software, there's no opt-out provision or Are You Sure message if you do something destructive, like trashing files by mistake or removing a directory the operating system needs in order to run. Before you explore the ins and outs of the command line, you should read Chapter 20, where I introduce you to this new element of the Mac OS. For additional information, visit the Web site http://public.sdsu.edu/Docs/unixf/basic_unix_f/basic_unix.html.*

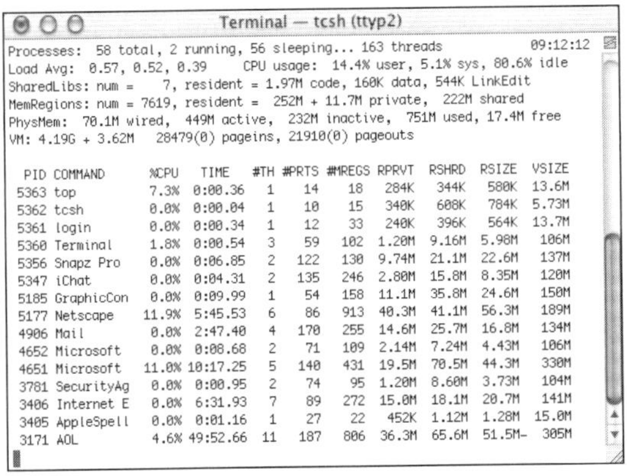

14. Mac OS X-Savvy Applications

Figure 14.10   Experience the guts of Unix with this application.

307

Chapter 14   Mac OS X-Savvy Applications

Just to give you a gander at what Terminal does, launch the application (it's in the Utilities folder) and then type the command **ls**. This command will list the contents of your Mac's drive. To move to an individual folder, type the command **cd <name of folder>**, which switches you to the specified folder. Now, an **ls** command will list the contents of the folder. All those text listings, even if they don't really change the way your Mac works, will look impressive to your friends.

- *TextEdit*—The Classic Mac OS had TeachText and later SimpleText, to open and view short text files, such as the ReadMe files that come with new computer products. TextEdit can view ReadMe files, but it's also a simple word processor complete with spell checking and a basic level of document formatting capabilities. It can create and open documents in Rich Text Format (RTF), so you can see files created in a wide variety of software.

NOTE: *Am I missing something? Well, there are so-called "i" applications that weren't included with the original release of Jaguar, such as iCal and iSync. The former sets up a system wide calendar that you can use to keep yourself organized, and it can also be published on the Internet to share with friends and business contacts. ISync allows you to automatically synchronize data with your handheld computer or mobile phone.*

One interesting Mac OS X application, however, is not one of the handy utilities or nifty "i" applications bundled with the new operating system, but an upfront and personal example of the potential of Carbon. This program was originally released for users of Mac OS 8.6 or later, but when the Public Beta came out, Mac users learned that the popular software suite had built-in support for Mac OS X. The program? AppleWorks 6 (see Figure 14.11), a major upgrade to the venerable program suite from Apple. I cover AppleWorks in more detail later in this chapter.

NOTE: *If you bought an iMac or iBook released since the Spring of 2000, a copy of AppleWorks 6 is already present in your Applications folder at no extra cost. A version that's more compatible with Mac OS X (the latest was 6.2.4 when this book was being written) is available in free update form from Apple's Web site. If you didn't get a copy with your new Mac, you can order one from your favorite Mac dealer.*

Although its interface seems simple and uncluttered, a lot of power is packed into this program. I tell you more about it in the "Immediate Solutions" section.

FileMaker

Apple's spin-off, which handles development of FileMaker Pro, was one of the early applications to move to Mac OS X. FileMaker Pro is a cross-platform database program (available in both Mac OS and Windows versions) that has existed since the early days of the Mac.

Adobe Systems

When Apple CEO Steve Jobs first demonstrated Mac OS X's Aqua interface in January 2000, he produced an early development version of Adobe Photoshop to show the potential of Carbon. The unique aspect of this application was the fact that it was all developed by a single Adobe programmer, working in his spare time, without actually seeing what Aqua looked like. The end result was rough, but functional. Adobe has committed to bringing all its current graphics programs to the new operating system. As of the time this book has appeared, all of Adobe's flagship applications, such as Go Live, InDesign, Illustrator and Photoshop, have made the Mac OS X transition. The only notable exceptions are PageMaker and FrameMaker.

Alias|Wavefront

One of the most significant developments for Mac OS X users is the arrival of new programs on the Mac platform. The $1,999 3D animation program Maya is a prime example. Although the program isn't quite a household name, the work done with Maya has been prominent in a number of popular movies. Maya has been used to create spectacular effects for films such as *Star Wars Episode I and Episode II*, *Hollow Man*, and *The Perfect Storm*. A number of the major production houses have this application doing duty in their special effects labs.

Corel

This Canadian software publisher is best known for CorelDRAW, which has always been more popular on the Windows than Mac platforms. Even worse, the Windows version managed to arrive months earlier than the Mac equivalent. For version 11, the Mac version Corel Graphics Suite came out pretty near the time of its Windows equivalent, and runs only in Mac OS X. In addition to CorelDRAW, a host of useful applications are provided for additional content creation capabilities, including Corel PHOTO-PAINT 11. The bundle also includes a Mac OS X version of DiamondSoft's Font Reserve for native font management, tons of clip art, and 1,000 PostScript and TrueType fonts.

Chapter 14 Mac OS X-Savvy Applications

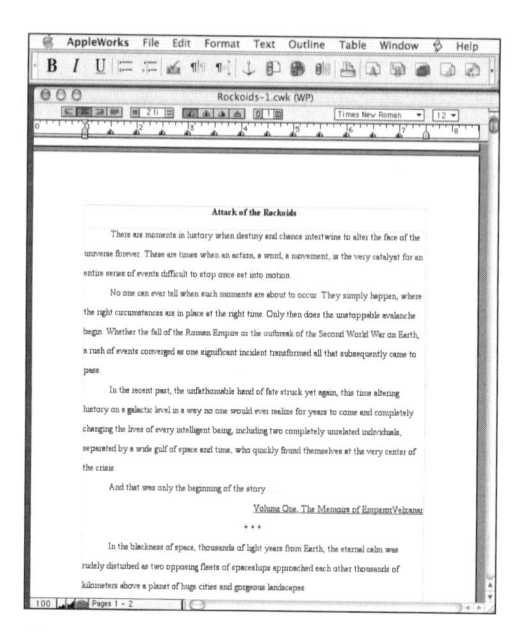

Figure 14.11 AppleWorks shows off the flexibility of a Carbon application.

Deneba

From sunny Florida comes Canvas 8, an application that combines superior graphics, page layout, and HTML tools in a single application. The feature-set is huge and not easily summarized. To make the package more compelling, Deneba bundles the collection with a healthy set of clip art and over 2,000 PostScript and TrueType fonts. Even if you buy it for the extras, you might find value in Canvas once you give it a workout.

Macromedia

Program for program, a number of Macromedia's offerings are in direct competition with those from Adobe. It comes as no surprise, then, that Macromedia is also in the forefront of Mac OS X development, offering native versions of its flagship software, such as DreamWeaver MX and FreeHand.

Stone Design

This publisher has migrated from the NeXT world and has embraced Mac OS X. Among its most useful applications is Create (see Figure 14.12), an integrated illustration program that also incorporates elements of HTML authoring and page layout. Create treats every element, from text to pictures, as an object, which can then be dragged and dropped onto other objects to create sophisticated illustrations.

In Brief

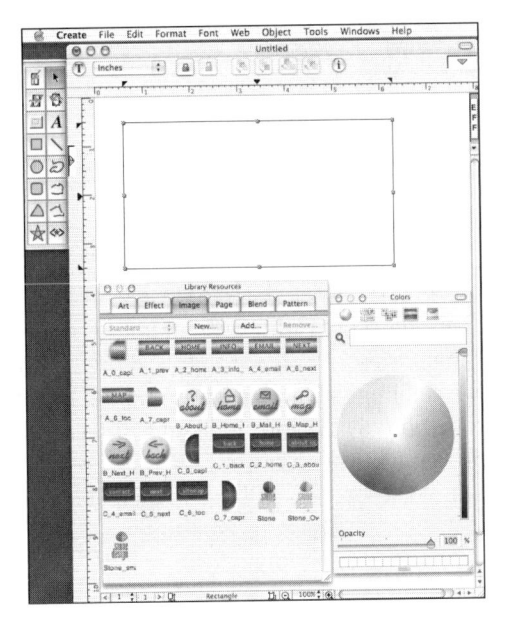

Figure 14.12 Create is the centerpiece of Stone Design's Mac OS X product line.

NOTE: *The various Stone Design applications stand as evidence of the power of Apple's Cocoa development environment. Considerable work on these programs was done by one person, Andrew Stone. Using traditional developer tools, it would have taken a programming team to create software of this level of sophistication in a reasonable amount of time.*

AOL

The world's largest online service has committed itself to fully support Mac OS X. The second Mac OS X release of its client software, version 10.2.1 as of the time this book was written, not only fully supports Mac OS X's Aqua interface, but, at least for a while, leapfrogged the Windows version in some respects. This is the first time in years that AOL has delivered Mac software first.

Chapter 14 Mac OS X-Savvy Applications

Immediate Solutions

Introducing AppleWorks for Mac OS X

What's the good of having a modern operating system if no programs exploit its wide-ranging capabilities? Apple's integrated application suite, AppleWorks, underwent a huge change with version 6. But the biggest change of all was only hinted at if you checked a file placed in the System Folder after the installation—CarbonLib. This file allows Mac OS X applications that use the Carbon API to run on a Mac using Mac OS versions 8.6 through 9.1.

Here's a brief run-through of this cleverly designed program—the first Carbon application from a major publisher (which is fitting).

NOTE: *Starting Points has had its influence in big places. The Project Gallery featured in Microsoft Office 2001 and Office v. X is highly reminiscent of this feature.*

Using AppleWorks Starting Points

When you first launch AppleWorks, you'll be greeted by the program's Starting Points (see Figure 14.13), a floating tabbed palette. From here you can create new documents or open recent ones. Here is a brief description of what you get when you click each tab:

NOTE: *The following information applies strictly to version 6.2.4 of the program. If you're using an earlier revision, access the latest from Apple's Web site.*

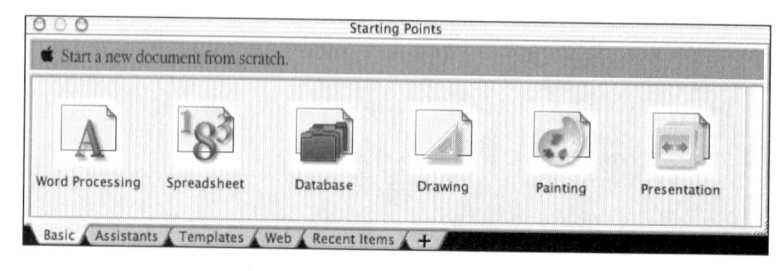

Figure 14.13   Use Starting Points to originate or open documents in AppleWorks.

312

- *Basic*—Access any of the six AppleWorks modules by clicking once on the kind of document you want to make. Depending on what you select, the user interface will vary in terms of menu bar commands, toolbars, and features.

TIP: Where's Starting Points? If you don't see it, choose Show Starting Points from the File menu.

- *Assistants*—AppleWorks is designed for users of all skill levels, from novices setting up their first Mac to power users. The Assistants palette provides step-by-step guidance in setting up a new document in several useful categories, from a business card to an envelope.

- *Templates*—To help get you started with a new document, you can choose from a collection of document templates. Click a preview icon to bring up a blank document with the template ready to roll.

- *Web*—Apple keeps an updated collection of clip art, templates, and tips about AppleWorks 6 at its Web site. When you click this tab, you can access a current list of what's available. If you're logged on to your ISP, a single click in the listing automatically downloads the templates to your Mac.

- *Recent Items*—This tab provides a fast way to open a document you've worked on previously. When you click here, you'll see a list of dozens of documents you've created in the program, sorted alphabetically.

- *+*—You can use this tab to make your own custom palette, and then drag and drop items to fill it in.

Using Tables in AppleWorks

One of the most important new features of AppleWorks 6, aside from the user interface and Mac OS X support, is the Table tool. You can easily add tables to any AppleWorks document and resize the tables to fit your needs. To use this handy feature, follow these steps:

1. Launch AppleWorks 6.
2. Start a new document.
3. Make sure the program's toolbar is open. If it's not visible, go to the program's Window menu and select Show Tools (see Figure 14.14).
4. Locate the Table Frame tool (see Figure 14.15) and select it.

Chapter 14   Mac OS X-Savvy Applications

Figure 14.14   The toolbar you see in AppleWorks changes depending on the kind of document you're creating.

Figure 14.15 Easy table creation in AppleWorks starts here.

5. Place the cursor in the location in your document where you want to put a table, and then drag the mouse in a diagonal direction to set the approximate size of the table. The size can be changed easily.

6. In the Insert Table dialog box that appears (see Figure 14.16), type how many rows and columns you want to put in the table. These values can also be changed easily.

7. Click OK to finish the table setup process.

Immediate Solutions

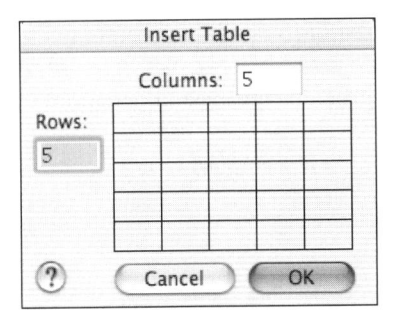

Figure 14.16   Choose how many rows and columns with which to populate your table.

After you have set up the raw essentials of your table, you can easily adjust the table as you see fit. The entire table or rows and columns can be resized by clicking and dragging. When you're working in a table, a new Table menu appears on the menu bar; you can use it to add or delete rows and columns.

Office v. X for Mac in Brief

When you first take a gander at any of the Office v. X applications, it's hard to get beyond the luscious Aqua interface; but some new features

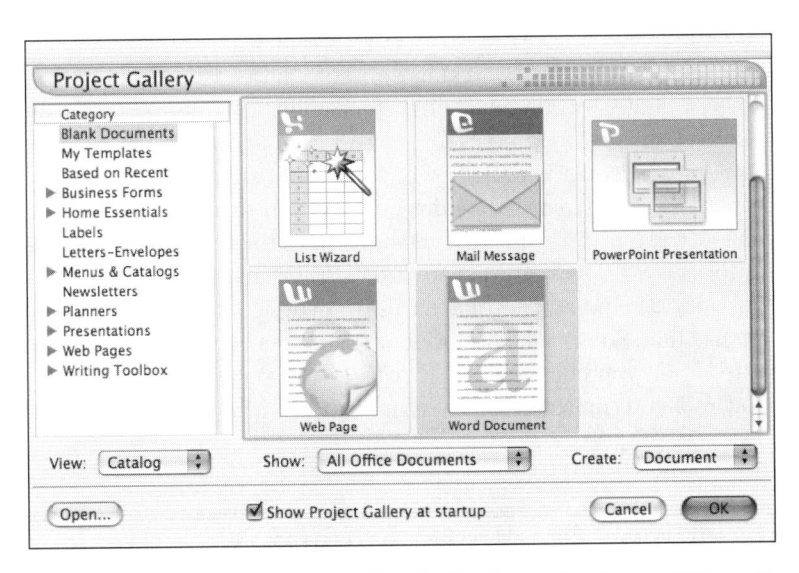

Figure 14.17   The Project Gallery is a flexible beginning for any Office v. X document.

315

are particularly useful. I'll cover three of the highlights here, features new to the Mac OS X version. It would take a large book to even scratch the surface of what's offered in this sprawling business application suite.

NOTE: Although Office v. X may seem an awkward name for this product, that's the way Microsoft refers to it, and that's the way I'll refer to it also.

Profiling the Project Gallery

When Microsoft introduced the Project Gallery (see Figure 14.17), some people thought it was the company's answer to AppleWorks' Starting Points palette. But it does offer some neat features. One of them is the new Based On Recent feature, which is a super Save As capability that lets you automatically open a new document with all the formatting and content of the original.

Using Word X's Multiple Selection Feature

This isn't an original feature (such Mac word processors as Mariner Write and Nisus Writer already have it). But in practice, it's both simple and useful. When you want to select more than a single item in your Word document, hold down the Command key and click and select each item, in succession. Once you've done that, all you have to do is apply updated text formatting to these items. Or, just cut and paste or drag and drop into a new location.

Using Excel X's Auto Recover Feature

Suppose you are busy working on a long spreadsheet, and there's a power outage (I won't dwell on the possibility of a system crash, but it can happen, even in Mac OS X). You restart your Mac and find that your Excel spreadsheet is damaged beyond recovery or doesn't reflect all the changes you made since the last time you saved. Mimicking a feature already present in Word, you don't have to change anything to use AutoRecover. It's already in your Excel Preferences box under the Save category. The default setting is to save every 10 minutes, but you can change that. So, even if your original document is damaged or not up to date, when you launch Excel, you'll see the version automatically recovered; you can save and use that version without missing a beat.

Introducing Create for Mac OS X

Stone Design's clever illustration suite, Create, is an all-purpose illustration program that has elements of several applications rolled into

Immediate Solutions

one. In addition to being able to produce simple or highly complex drawings in its uncluttered interface, you can create special effects, manage complex text stylings, and build your own Web site.

Using the Inspector

A lot of the work you do in Create is directed by the Inspector window. It's a mélange of buttons, checkboxes, sliders, and text entry points where you can originate the look and feel of your document.

NOTE: The Inspector feature available with Create is not the same as the Finder's Inspector. It provides services strictly for the application, and not for the rest of the Mac OS.

To access the Inspector, follow these steps:

1. Launch Create.
2. Go to the Tools menu and choose Inspector (see Figure 14.18).
3. Click the tab that represents the type of project you are working on.

With the Inspector active, you'll find an easy way to manipulate your artwork, configure Web pages, and apply and change color selections.

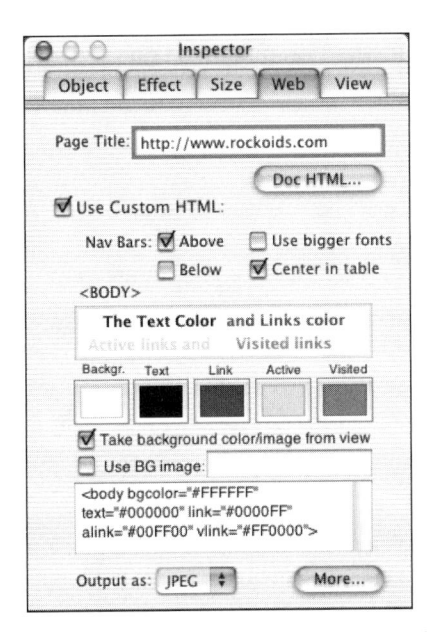

Figure 14.18 The Inspector has many faces, depending on the tab you select.

317

Chapter 14   Mac OS X-Savvy Applications

> **TIP:** *You can use another terrific feature of Create—the Resources palette—for clip art and document templates. If the Resources palette isn't present, choose Library Resources from the Tools menu to bring it up.*

Starting a Web Page in Create

In addition to being a flexible object-oriented illustration environment, Create lets you generate a fully professional Web page. Here's how to get started setting up a Web page in this program:

1. Launch Create. A new Untitled document window appears, along with, by default, the Resources and Inspector windows.
2. Type your text and place your pictures in the document.
3. When you're ready to enter URL links to other pages or sites, click the area of your document where you want to place the link.
4. Click the Web tab of Inspector, as shown in Figure 14.19.
5. Enter the URL. To specify special options for this link, click the Use Custom HTML option.
6. When your Web page is finished, choose Create Web Pages from the Web menu and name your file. When you click Save, you'll see the page opened in the Web browser set as an Internet preference in the System Preferences panel, so you can check to see how it will look when it's published on the Web.

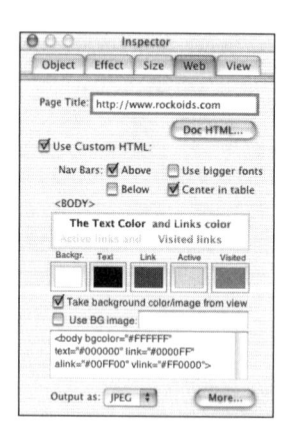

Figure 14.19   The multipurpose Inspector lets you configure your Web page. It is shown here with the Use Custom HTML option selected.

318

Chapter 15

Using Older Programs with Mac OS X

If you need an immediate solution to:	See page:
Launching Older Mac Programs	325
Running Classic as a Startup Application	326
Getting Reliable Performance from Classic Applications	328
Keeping Your Mac OS 9.x System Folder Safe and Sound	331
Solving Classic Environment Problems	332
Returning to Mac OS 9.x	334

Chapter 15 Using Older Programs with Mac OS X

In Brief

How time flies. When Apple Computer released the first Macintosh computer with a PowerPC processor in the early part of 1994, the landscape was quite lonely. Although these computers offered the promise of far greater levels of performance, it would only happen when programs were ported (or updated) to support the new chip architecture.

However, thousands of Mac applications were designed to run on the older 680x0 Motorola processors. With this in mind, Apple devised a plan to allow Mac users to continue to use the vast majority of these programs with decent performance, and then gradually migrate to the PowerPC versions as they were released. The ROMs for PowerPC Macs came with an emulator (extensively updated via patches to the system software). The emulator, shorn of the complex programming techniques involved, would, on the fly, emulate a 680x0 processor. It would thus allow those programs to run with good compatibility—except for software that required a Mac with an FPU chip for special math-related functions. At first, the speed of the emulator barely kept up with 68030 processors, let alone the fastest 68040 processors that were produced before the PowerPC took over. But as the emulator got better and the new chips got faster, performance of the older programs was so good, it was sometimes hard to see a significant difference.

Introducing the Classic Environment

For Mac OS X, the changes are far greater than the switch to the PowerPC's RISC code. The underlying structure of the operating system would seem, in comparison, to be from an alien world. It's Unix-based—the same operating system that powers some of the most powerful Internet servers—and thus the situation is rather more complex.

However, Apple has an inventive solution: the Classic Compatibility environment (see Figure 15.1). It's not an emulator, such as the one used for PowerPC Macs, nor is it in the tradition of software that emulates Windows on a Mac, such as Connectix Virtual PC.

The closest description would be that Classic runs as a sort of virtual machine in which Mac OS 9 runs as a separate process or application within Mac OS X, but without inheriting the Aqua user interface or the robust operating system features of the Darwin core. Basically,

320

In Brief

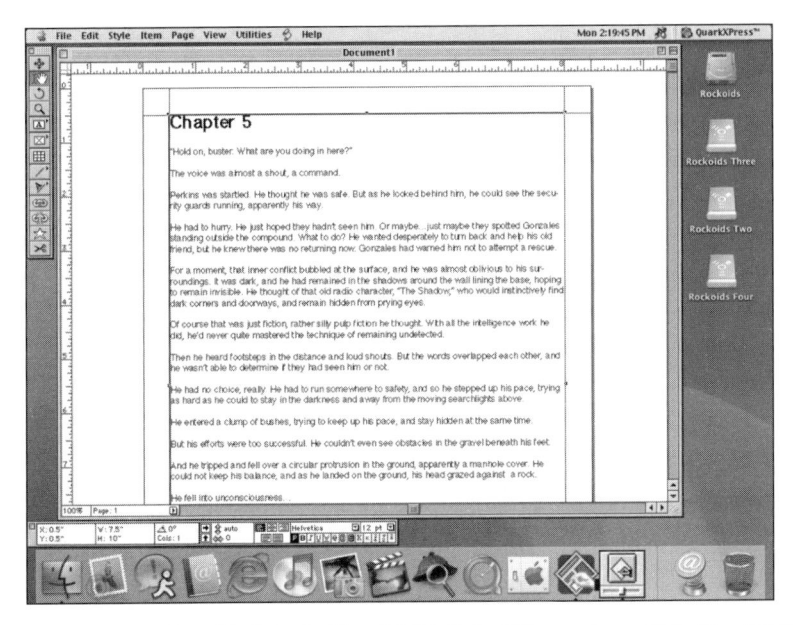

Figure 15.1 Yes, this is truly Mac OS 9.2.2, but it's running within Mac OS X.

when you run a Mac OS 9 program, the old menu bar, Apple menu, Control Strip, Launcher, and most features of the older operating system take over your screen (see Figure 15.2). However, when you switch out of a Classic application, you're back in Aqua.

NOTE: The real version of Office v. X came out in November 2001. But if you haven't upgraded to that version yet, you can continue to use the Classic version with good performance and compatibility. Although the native version looks a lot better, it only offers a handful of new features.

Classic Environment Limitations

As seamless as switching to a Classic application may seem (and I'll explain the best ways in the "Immediate Solutions" section of this chapter), there are limits to compatibility, more so than with the switch from 680x0 to PowerPC. Although you can run most of your applications with good performance, some programs just won't run until updated for the new operating system. Here's the short list of potential problems:

- *It still crashes a lot.* The Classic environment doesn't inherit the robust features of Mac OS X, such as preemptive multitasking and protected memory. It has the same limitations as the original Mac OS, which means that if a single application crashes, you will need to restart Classic. However, because it operates in its own protected memory space, that memory is walled off from the rest

321

Chapter 15 Using Older Programs with Mac OS X

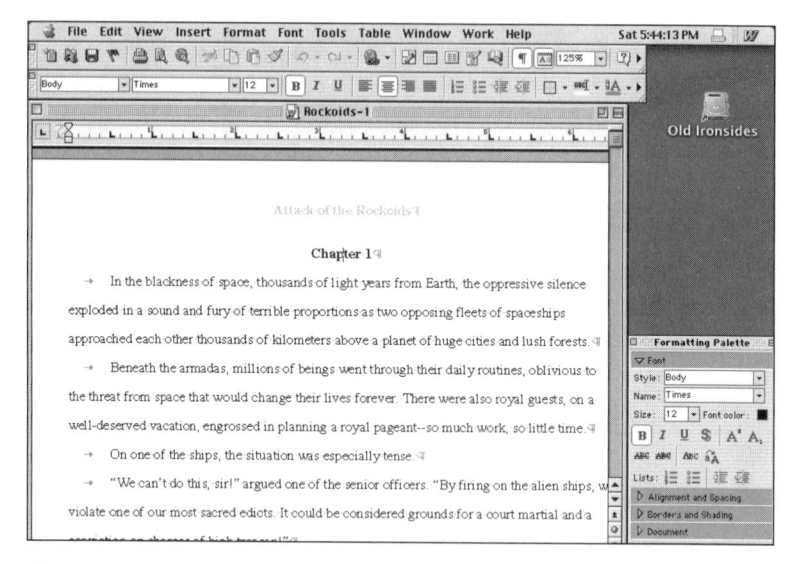

Figure 15.2 This is the Classic version of Microsoft Word 2001 running under Mac OS X, but with the Mac OS 9 look.

of the system, so you can continue to use your Mac OS X applications without a problem. If Classic crashes, just run it again.

- *Many system extensions don't run.* Mac OS system extensions that access hardware functions will probably fail, or will run only with limited compatibility. I'll explain ways to clean out your Mac OS 9 user environment for best performance in the "Immediate Solutions" section of this chapter.

- *CPU-intensive applications are slower.* Adobe Photoshop and other programs that tax the Mac's processor to the limit may run somewhat slower in the Classic environment. The amount that the performance suffers depends largely on the speed of your Mac's processor, hard drive, and graphics hardware. However, other functions, such as launching and screen refreshing, will seem not much different from a regular Mac OS 9 Mac.

NOTE: *Some Photoshop 6 filters, such as the processor-intensive Gaussian Blue, run slightly faster in the Classic mode on faster Macs with a G4. However, since there is a Mac OS X-savvy version of Photoshop available, which offers some nifty new features, it may be worthwhile to upgrade anyway, even though the older version still runs at a decent clip.*

- *Certain Mac peripherals fail.* Any product that requires special drivers to run will probably fail under Mac OS X, even if run from the Classic environment. Although it's possible that some of these

322

In Brief

devices will work after a fashion, don't expect consistent compatibility. Among the affected products are CD burners, DVD-RAM burners, removable storage devices (except for Imation and Iomega products), scanners, tape backup drives, and peripheral cards that provide such features as extended audio editing or video capture. Even graphics cards that were not provided by Apple's graphics chip partner, ATI Technologies, IX Micro (which is now defunct), or NVIDIA won't function unless the company that makes the product has produced drivers for Mac OS X. The best source of information about what works and what doesn't is the manufacturer of these products.

NOTE: Formac, a German-based manufacturer of high-performance graphics cards for Macs, indicates that its ProFormance 3 products will run under Mac OS X, but that 3D acceleration isn't supported. Formac is no longer manufacturing graphic cards, and further driver enhancement of its older products isn't expected. 3dfx Interactive, which went out of business in late 2000, never updated drivers for its Voodoo cards for Mac OS X, though some third parties are looking for a solution. Fortunately, most digital cameras work fine under Mac OS X and the Image Capture application without the need for special drivers.

- *Some printers won't work.* You can continue to use most laser printers by using the Print Center application of Mac OS X. But some special laser printers that do not have Adobe PostScript installed or that use the USB rather than Ethernet ports may not work without driver updates, except from the Classic environment. The same holds true for those ever-popular ink jet printers that have captured a large portion of the printer market. A core selection of printers from such companies as Canon, Epson, HP and Lexmark work just fine. But you'll need to check with the manufacturer directly (probably at its Web site) for drivers that aren't supported by Mac OS X out of the box.

- *Third-party hard drive formatters won't work.* Any device that provides low-level support to storage devices probably won't work until a special Mac OS X version is delivered. Apple's own Disk Utility can handle most—probably all—ATA drives and many recent SCSI drives. Otherwise, you have to wait for the third-party manufacturer to come through for you.

NOTE: As of the time this book was written, the only Mac OS X-savvy hard drive formatter was Apple's Disk Utility. If you've been using such applications as FWB's Hard Disk ToolKit to prepare your drives, you'll want to contact the manufacturer about Mac OS X compatibility.

323

Chapter 15 Using Older Programs with Mac OS X

- *Some Windows emulators are not compatible.* Although Connectix released Virtual PC 5.0, which supports Mac OS X, there's no solace for users of the rival product, SoftWindows. FWB has made it clear that it won't update the product, and the chances of the Classic Mac OS version running under Mac OS X aren't terribly high. Ditto for PC processor cards from such companies as Orange Micro.

- *Internet software compatibility is a mixed bag.* If you have a high-speed (broadband) Internet connection, you may be all right, but dial-up connections that require a custom dialing program (rather than just a straight PPP connection that can be configured via the Network preference panel), have problems of one sort or another. Although a shareware program, PortReflector, may help resolve some dial-up problems, programs with their own dialers, such as AOL and CompuServe, must be updated to the Mac OS X versions.

- *Some classic games won't work.* Although Mac OS X is designed to be a gamer's paradise, the realization of that promise won't happen until games are truly ported to the new operating system. In the meantime, you can run many older games in the Classic environment, but do not expect stellar performance. Frame rates, for example, will not be quite as high as you experienced under Mac OS 9, because of less complete support for graphics acceleration.

Immediate Solutions

Immediate Solutions

Launching Older Mac Programs

You don't have to do anything special to run your Classic Mac applications within Mac OS X. The operating system is clever enough to sort it all out for you and give you the proper environment for the program you run. To launch an older Mac program and have it work, just do the following:

1. Locate the document or program on your Mac's drive.

TIP: Have both a Classic and Mac OS X version of a program, such as Microsoft Word? In theory, the Mac OS X version should launch, but in practice, the Classic version may run instead. Should this happen, use the Finder's Show Info command on the document and use the Open with: option in the Finder's Get Info window to make the Mac OS X version the default (it won't affect how the document opens if you restart under Mac OS 9.x, when the available Classic application will launch).

2. Double-click the application icon or a document created with the application.
3. If the Classic environment isn't running, it will go through its regular boot process (see Figure 15.3).
4. The first time you launch Classic from Mac OS X, you'll see a dialog box notifying you that some resources (extensions) need to be added to the Classic System Folder to continue the startup process. You must click OK to accept the installation and continue running Classic. Otherwise, click Quit, and the process will stop.

NOTE: Mac OS 9.2.2, the most recent version available when this book was written, included several Classic-related extensions to run under Mac OS X's Classic environment. However, the Mac OS X 10.2 upgrade uses later versions of these utilities, so don't be surprised if you see that message anyway and if it returns as more updates to Mac OS X arrive.

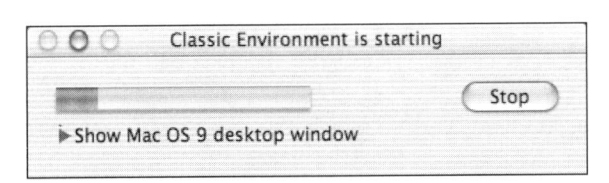

Figure 15.3 This progress bar shows that the Classic environment is starting up.

15. Using Older Programs with Mac OS X

325

Chapter 15 Using Older Programs with Mac OS X

5. If you click the disclosure triangle in the Classic window, you'll see a standard Mac startup screen (see Figure 15.4), but it happens within an application window within Mac OS X. Clever! Once the Classic environment is running, the application you launched will be opened as well. Then your document will appear on the screen, surrounded by a user interface that is essentially the same as what you experienced under Mac OS 9.x.

NOTE: *When Classic is launching, its icon will appear in the Dock and will (assuming you haven't changed the option) bounce up and down rhythmically as the environment is loading. You'll also see an icon representing the Mac OS 9.x application you opened. However, once Classic is open, its icon will no longer be present, so do not get concerned. You can easily verify Classic's presence in the Classic preference pane of System Preferences.*

Running Classic as a Startup Application

It's highly likely that, if you haven't yet upgraded your applications to Mac OS X native versions, you'll have to spend plenty of time in the Classic environment to run your older programs. Therefore, it may be a good idea to have Classic as a startup application so that

Figure 15.4 If you click the disclosure triangle, you'll see the standard Mac OS 9 startup screen.

Immediate Solutions

you don't have to wait for it later when you're running those programs. Here's how to make it a startup program:

1. Launch the System Preferences application (it's normally in the Dock).
2. Click the Classic icon. The Classic preference pane, shown in Figure 15.5, appears.
3. Choose the startup volume that contains the Mac OS 9.x System Folder you want to use from the scrolling list.

NOTE: *Which to use if you have several? Well, you might want to have a backup System Folder on another partition or drive in case something happens to your Classic System Folder, or perhaps you have one with a lean set of system extensions for best Classic performance. So long as it's 9.1 or later (and the later the better), any of these will work.*

4. Click the Start Classic when you log in checkbox. Whenever you log in to your Mac OS X user account, Classic will be launched. You can still quit the environment in the normal fashion later, but you'll be all set when you're ready to run your older software.
5. If you want to begin Classic right away, click the Start button.

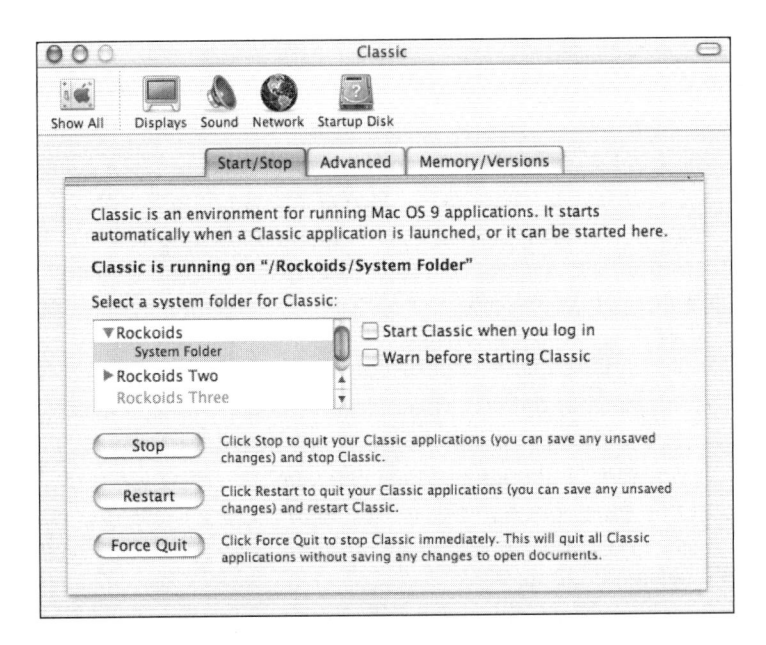

Figure 15.5 The Classic preference pane is used to set up the environment as a startup process.

Chapter 15 Using Older Programs with Mac OS X

6. Choose Quit from the application menu or type Command+Q to leave the System Preferences application.

NOTE: *The next section discusses the settings found in the Advanced Classic settings pane, which will help you tailor Classic performance and reduce potential system hang-ups or performance problems.*

Getting Reliable Performance from Classic Applications

Making it possible to run older Mac programs under Mac OS X is one of the main factors that will ease migration to the new operating system. Rather than fret over what works and what doesn't, the most efficient way to run Classic right now is bare bones. Here's the ideal way to set it up for maximum compatibility:

1. Launch the System Preferences application (it's probably in the Dock unless you removed it).
2. Click the Classic pane.
3. Click the Advanced tab (see Figure 15.6).
4. Click the Startup Options pop-up menu and select one of the configuration options you want. They are as follows:

    - *Turn Off Extensions*—When you select this option and click the Restart Classic button, Mac OS 9.x will reboot with extensions off. This step offers maximum compatibility at the risk of losing access to system extensions needed to run specific programs (such as Microsoft's). Video acceleration in Classic mode is also turned off, so screen refresh of your older applications will slow considerably.

    - *Open Extensions Manager*—When you select this option and click the Restart Classic button, the Extensions Manager application will open as Mac OS 9.x boots, giving you a way to fine-tune your extensions lineup to remove items that may cause performance hits or incompatibilities. I'll cover this in more detail shortly.

    - *Use Key Combination*—When you select this option, you'll need to enter a keyboard combination in the data field that will appear below the pop-up menu to trigger Classic with System Preferences open.

Immediate Solutions

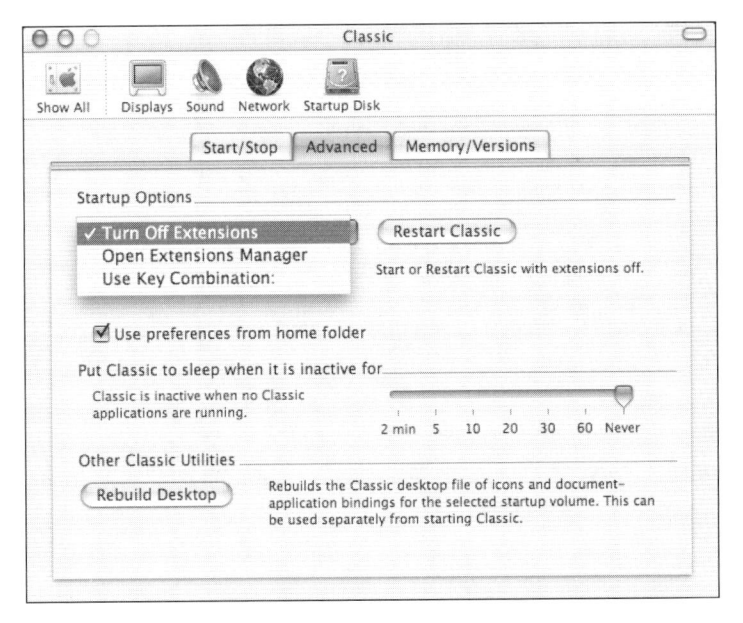

Figure 15.6 These Advanced settings help you tailor Classic performance and compatibility.

5. The easiest management technique is to select the Open Extensions Manager option. When Classic starts, this option acts as the equivalent of holding down the spacebar at startup under Mac OS 9.x. The Extensions Manager window appears, as shown in Figure 15.7.

6. Choose the Mac OS 9.x Base set from the Selected Set pop-up menu.

7. Go to the File menu and select Duplicate Set. A window appears allowing you to name the set, as shown in Figure 15.8. This simply makes a copy of the Base set you've already selected.

8. Name the copy of the Base set something that will identify it for the purpose, such as "Mac OS X Classic Set."

NOTE: If you run any recent Classic version of Microsoft's Internet programs or any Microsoft Office application while using this Mac OS X set, a number of system extensions required by these programs will be installed the first time any of those programs are launched. There's no reason to be concerned; the installation is normal. This is why I am not recommending you run a Base set, because those sets cannot be modified; that is extensions such as those from Microsoft can't be added.

9. Close Extensions Manager to save your set. From here on, whenever you want to start your Mac under Mac OS X, make sure you activate this special "lean and mean" set for Mac OS X.

329

Chapter 15 Using Older Programs with Mac OS X

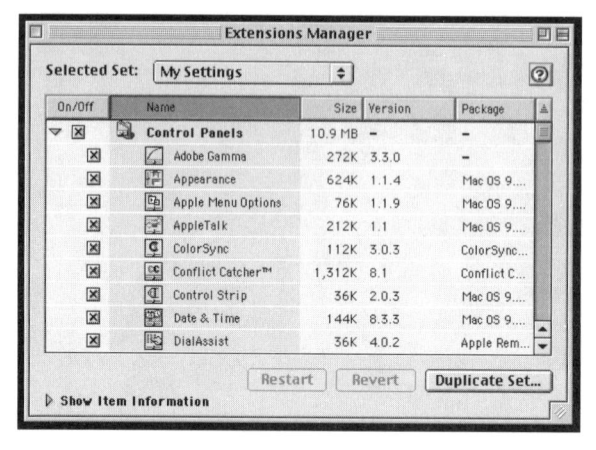

Figure 15.7 Apple's Extensions Manager helps you set up Classic for the best performance.

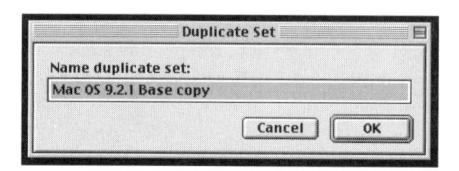

Figure 15.8 This is a copy of the extension set you selected.

NOTE: You can perform essentially the same operation if you use Casady & Greene's Conflict Catcher to manage your Mac OS 9.x System Folder. However, you should use version 8.0.9 or later. Earlier versions of Conflict Catcher had a peculiar bug when they interacted with the Classic environment, with recurring requests for the program's serial number. Free updates to any Conflict Catcher 8 version are available from the company's Web site, **www.casadyg.com**.

After this special set has been created, you might want to consider adding a few of your cherished extensions and see if Classic continues to run efficiently. There's no reason to abandon your normal extensions set; just switch over before you install or run Mac OS X.

In my experience, a lean and mean Classic environment is a good way to get the most out of Mac OS X without a wasting a lot of time seeking out possible extension conflicts. If you need to return to Mac OS 9.x after restart (see "Returning to Mac OS 9.x" later in this chapter), hold down the spacebar until the Extensions Manager (or Conflict Catcher) window appears. Then switch back to your regular extension set (which will probably bring up a dialog from Conflict Catcher stating that it will restart your Mac yet again). That way, you can enjoy the best of both worlds.

Immediate Solutions

TIP: If your Classic application runs very sluggish, check the Memory/Versions tab of the Classic preference panel and see how much RAM the program is using. If the dark bar is close to the end, you'll want to quit the application and use the Finder's Get Info feature to increase application memory. Click the Memory disclosure

NOTE: If you switch extension sets with Conflict Catcher, on occasion you'll see a prompt indicating that you need to restart your Mac again. This happens if some of the extensions that were activated must boot before Conflict Catcher. It is normal behavior.

Keeping Your Mac OS 9.x System Folder Safe and Sound

You can also protect your Mac OS 9.x System Folder by using another startup drive for your regular setup when you're not using the older operating system. This way, you don't have to fret over special startup sets, extra extensions in the System Folder from Mac OS X, or other possible problems that might result from the switching process (although it should, in theory, work all right). Here's how to get the most value out of this multiple System Folder scheme:

1. Before you install Mac OS X, back up and reformat your Mac's hard drive into at least two partitions. After restarting with your first Jaguar installer CD, you can use Apple's Disk Utility, available from the Mac OS X Installer menu, to handle this task. Just click the Partition tab, select the drive, and bring up the Volume Scheme pop-up menu to choose from default partition methods.

WARNING! If you have a PowerBook G3, beige Power Macintosh G3 or an early version iMac, you must put Mac OS X on a partition occupying the first 8GB of space on the drive. When you use Disk Utility to reformat a drive on one of these models, make sure the first or top partition is no larger than 8GB. It doesn't matter how big the second partition is, so long as Mac OS X isn't placed on it.

2. Install the version of Mac OS 9.x you want to use with Mac OS X on your first partition.

3. Install the System Folder you want to use for regular work on the second partition.

4. Proceed with your standard installation of Mac OS X, as described in Chapter 2.

331

5. When the installer proceeds to the dialog box where you select a disk for installation, choose the one on your first boot partition. Be sure not to check the box to erase the partition; otherwise, you'll wipe out the data on that drive.

6. Continue with the Mac OS X installation. For now, whenever you wish to use Classic, you'll choose the Mac OS 9.x System Folder on the first partition. When you want to work full-time in the older operating system, you'll simply select the System Folder in the second partition.

TIP: If one or the other System Folder isn't recognized for startup or by the Startup Disk pane in the System Preferences application, open that folder and then close it again. This action has the effect of "blessing" the System Folder, making it possible to boot your Mac from it.

NOTE: Some folks feel that putting Mac OS X on a separate partition from the Classic Mac OS might improve performance and compatibility. Apple installs both operating systems on a single partition on all new Macs. My personal experience with a single partition and dual-partition setup yielded no significant differences. If you want to go through the trouble to back up your data and reformat your drives, it may be worth trying, at least as a measure of protection in case something goes wrong with the partition on which Mac OS X is present. Consider, however, that this might be best done on a new Mac, where you can partition the drive during the initial setup process and just restore all the standard files to one of the partitions.

Related solution:	Found on page:
Installing Mac OS X	32

Solving Classic Environment Problems

If you follow the steps in the previous sections, you should be able to continue to use your Classic Mac OS applications with decent performance and the maximum level of compatibility. However, if you choose to abandon the simple setup to add extra extensions, you may encounter some troubles along the way. Here are likely causes and solutions:

- *A slow startup of the Classic environment*—If it seems to take a long time to access a Classic application, consider this remedy: Pare down Mac OS 9.x system extensions to the Base set, and then create a new Mac OS X set from it. The startup process should be much faster, and your problems fewer.

Immediate Solutions

- *Classic startup applications switch back and forth*—I have observed this phenomenon when the Launcher and Spell Catcher played a game of dueling launches (but it can happen whenever there are multiple Classic startup programs). The immediate solution is to click the menu bar and quit the Spell Catcher application, but the long-term remedy is to disable one or the other. Spell Catcher's compatibility under Mac OS X is questionable.

NOTE: *Spell Catcher is a terrific interactive spell-checking and thesaurus utility. It runs in virtually all programs and will flash warnings if you make an error. Its Ghostwriting feature stores keystrokes, in case you lose a file as a result of a system crash. It would be nice to see this program continued under Mac OS X, but author Evan Gross told me wasn't certain if he'd do it; it would have to be rewritten from scratch as a Cocoa-based application, because the tools he needs to make it work aren't supported in Apple's Carbon APIs.*

- *A nasty startup crash when returning to Mac OS 9*—More than likely, you will need to restart under Mac OS 9.x for one reason or another, unless the Mac on which Mac OS X is installed is devoted to testing and nothing else. Shortly after the startup process begins, before extension icons appear, all or part of a blank bomb screen may bring the whole process to a halt. One of the causes could be a corrupted TCP/IP Preferences file. The solution is to restart with system extensions off (hold the Shift key down at startup), and then trash this file, which is located in the Preferences Folder inside the System Folder. Then it will be safe to restart normally. You'll need to re-create the settings (or keep a backup around, just in case).

TIP: *One way to avoid this annoying file corruption is to remove your standard TCP/IP Preferences file and keep it for safekeeping. Upon restart, a new, empty file will be created. With no data entered, it is less apt to become corrupted when you try to run your old Mac Internet software from the Classic environment. Another way is to lock your settings, so that they cannot be modified. You do so by changing the user mode to Administration (via the File menu). Once you're in Administration mode, you can lock down any setting.*

- *Launching Internet programs doesn't get you connected*—If you have dial-up access to the Internet, you need to launch the Internet Connect application first and then connect. You can then use any Carbon or Cocoa Internet application. If you're trying to use a program that does its own dialing, such as AOL or CompuServe, you'll need to check for Mac OS X updates to their client software.

Returning to Mac OS 9.x

There is no reason not to switch back to Mac OS 9.x to run programs and hardware that aren't ready to work under Mac OS X (that's why it's part of the Mac OS X package). To return to your former environment, do the following:

1. Launch the System Preferences application.
2. Double-click the Startup Disk pane (see Figure 15.9).
3. If you are not using an administrator's user account, click the padlock icon (if it's closed) and then type your username and password to get access to changing the startup disk.
4. Click your Mac OS 9.x startup disk.
5. Click the Restart button that appears at the bottom of the Startup pane in System Preferences and then in the confirming dialog box to save your settings and restart. In a few moments, your Mac will restart under Mac OS 9.x.

NOTE: If you followed my recommendation to establish a special set in Extensions Manager or Conflict Catcher to use when running Mac OS 9.x in the Classic environment, be sure to hold down the spacebar when starting under Mac OS 9.x. Doing so will bring up your startup manager's screen, and you can then switch to your preferred Mac OS 9.x startup set for regular use and enjoy all your favorite system extensions. Apple calls your default extension setup My Settings unless you've renamed it.

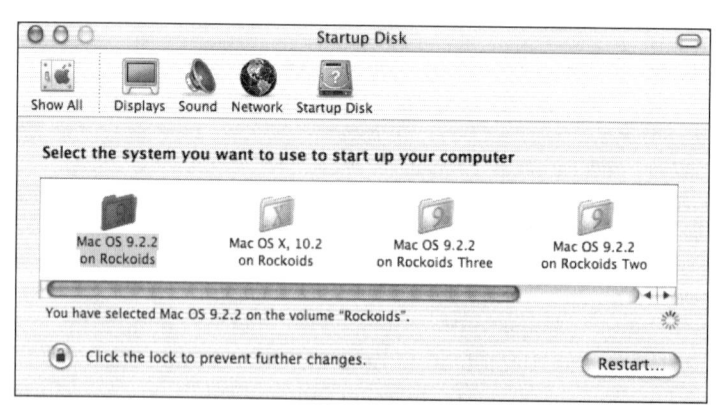

Figure 15.9 Choose your startup disk from this screen.

Chapter 16

Mac OS X Font Management

If you need an immediate solution to:	See page:
Installing Fonts Under Mac OS X	344
Using the Font Panel	345
Adding Font Favorites	346
Using Favorites	347
Creating a Font Collection	347
Choosing Custom Font Sizes	349
Checking the Characters in a Font	349
Avoiding Too-Small Fonts in TextEdit	350
Using Font Reserve to Manage Your Mac OS X Font Library	351
Using Suitcase to Manage Your Mac OS X Font Library	354
Handling Mac OS X Font Problems	355

In Brief

You can't compute without fonts. The desktop publishing revolution is credited with giving the Macintosh platform credibility. Where you once had to use an artist's table, dedicated typesetting computers, and high-cost output devices to produce artwork for a brochure or publication, the Mac made it possible to do it all on your desktop at relatively low cost, even in your own home. Page layout applications, such as Adobe PageMaker and QuarkXPress, low-cost fonts, and relatively high-quality laser printers combined to bury much of the traditional typesetting industry, except for extremely specialized work.

However, the availability of thousands of fonts has proven to be the bane of the Mac user's experience, because it creates new concerns and sources of confusion.

There Are Fonts and There Are Fonts

It would be nice if fonts all came in just one format and were easy to install, but the situation has been otherwise. There are multiple font formats, and fonts of different types with the very same name. Where do you begin?

Font Formats Defined

Before you even select a font to use in your document, you are faced with choices of installation and organization. Here's a list of the types of fonts commonly used on Macs:

- *Bitmap fonts*—The original Mac font format, bitmap fonts are designed for printing and display in a single size. If they are scaled to one size or another, the quality of the image deteriorates in proportion to the size difference; the image can become an almost unreadable collection of pixel shapes when printed or viewed at a very large size.

- *PostScript fonts*—This scalable font format was developed by Adobe Systems in the 1980s and quickly came to dominate the printing and publishing industries. See the next item for a full description of what such fonts do.

- *Scalable fonts*—Whether PostScript or TrueType, these fonts can be printed in any available point size at the full resolution of the printer or other output device. However, the fonts come in a form that confuses many Mac users. The scalable fonts, called variously *outline fonts* or *printer fonts*, are separate from the fonts that generate images on your Mac's display, the *screen fonts*. This arrangement is a carryover from the way fonts were organized in the days of traditional typography, when font sets were divided into two parts for width or space values and for output. But it causes confusion because the lack of the screen font means your font won't show up in a Font menu, and the lack of a printer font means it won't print at full quality.

- *TrueType fonts*—In 1990, to avoid having to pay license fees for use of PostScript fonts, Apple (with a little help from Microsoft in its later stages) developed a new scalable font format. TrueType fonts include the screen font and outline font in a single file. For that reason alone, they are easier to handle. However, they have downsides. One is that you should not try to use a PostScript and TrueType font of the same typeface family. At worst, printing of the document will be inconsistent or output in the wrong font. Or, letterspacing may be distorted. The other problem with TrueType is that printers and service bureaus with high-resolution output devices may not fully support the format, particularly if they are using older hardware.

NOTE: *Although originally introduced on the Mac platform, TrueType fonts are the standard font format for Microsoft Windows. On the Mac platform, however, PostScript remains the font format of choice for the publishing industry, because the high-resolution output devices used may not always support TrueType (a situation that has been largely fixed with newer devices). New Macs and the Mac OS ship with TrueType fonts.*

- *OpenType fonts*—A recent entrant in the font arena, the OpenType font format can combine elements of PostScript and TrueType fonts in a single file, along with more extensive character sets, including decorative characters and such. It's fully supported by Mac OS X and more and more font makers, such as Adobe, are coming around to supporting the format. Someday maybe it'll replace those old fashioned PostScript fonts.

Font Organization Under the Mac OS

Before Mac OS X arrived, Mac users had to rely on extra software for flexible font handling and, in fact, to use fonts with some printers. These programs would allow you to store fonts in places other than the Fonts folder and only activate them when needed. That and various degrees of font organizational capability made these programs essential for handling large font libraries. Even better, most of these

Chapter 16 Mac OS X Font Management

applications, with only one notable exception, are available in native Mac OS X versions, and as you'll see Jaguar takes the world of font handling to a new level of complexity.

Here's a list of the font management options and what they did:

- *Adobe Type Manager (ATM)*—Originally introduced in 1989, this program is designed to provide clear screen display of PostScript fonts in all available sizes. It also has the side effect of allowing non-PostScript printers, such as ink jet printers, to use PostScript fonts and deliver the maximum quality they were capable of. An enhanced version of ATM, ATM Deluxe (shown in Figure 16.1), also allows you to activate and deactivate fonts that are not installed in the System Folder, check for duplicates and damaged fonts, and print font samples.

NOTE: *Although a Mac OS X version of ATM will never be produced, according to Adobe, you should still keep it at hand for clean display of PostScript fonts used in the Classic environment. This is the only program in this list that will probably never be updated for the new operating system.*

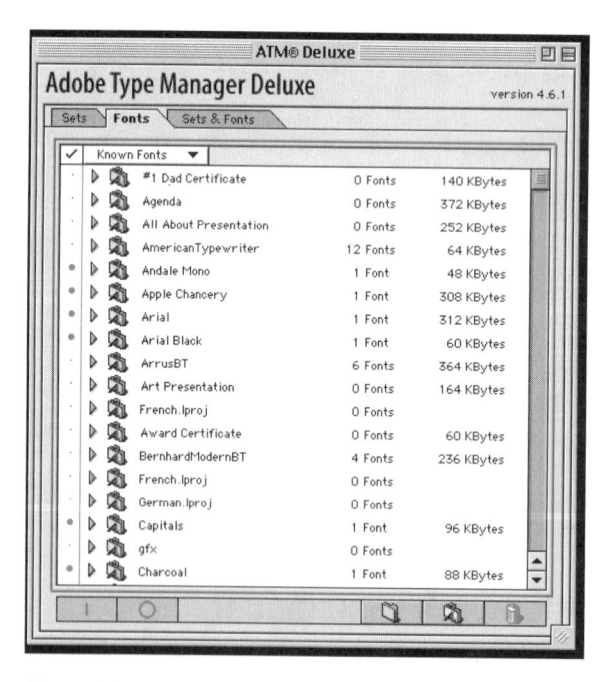

Figure 16.1 ATM Deluxe manages your font library and provides clear display of fonts, all in the same program.

338

- *Alsoft's MasterJuggler*—MasterJuggler is one of the early font management programs. As with ATM Deluxe, it's used to activate and organize a font library. It does not, however, do anything about font rendering, so you still need the basic version (now free) of ATM for that purpose. A Mac OS X version is expected to be out by the time this book appears.

- *DiamondSoft's Font Reserve*—This program provides a unique way to store and manage fonts. It places all fonts outside the System Folder in a database file, so you don't have to concern yourself with placing them in any particular location. It offers various sorting features, as well as the ability to print samples of your library. Again, ATM is needed for font rendering in the Classic environment. Otherwise, Font Reserve can work seamlessly with both Classic and Mac OS X applications, and automatically activate fonts in both environments in many of your favorite programs, such as Adobe InDesign, Microsoft Word and QuarkXPress. You'll learn how to set it up for best efficiency in the "Immediate Solutions" section of this chapter.

- *Extensis Suitcase*—This is the original font manager, which has passed through several software publishers (such as the late Fifth Generation Systems and Symantec) before finding its current home with the popular publisher of add-on graphics utilities. It is somewhat similar to MasterJuggler in terms of its focus and features, but you still need ATM for clean display of PostScript fonts. A Mac OS X–native version of Suitcase was released in the fall of 2001 and is discussed later in this chapter.

Mac OS X's New Font-Handling Scheme

When developing Mac OS X, Apple Computer realized that font management was confusing for many Mac users and often the source of trouble in preparing and outputting documents. The response is the Apple Type Solution (ATS). This mechanism, which works with the Quartz 2D imaging layer of the new operating system, delivers system-wide handling of all the major font formats—PostScript, TrueType, OpenType, and even the original Mac bitmap fonts.

ATS handles font rendering of all the formats using Mac OS X's Portable Document Format (PDF) mechanism (which uses Adobe's popular open standard for creating electronic documents), so you don't need ATM for PostScript font display. In addition, built-in tools organize font collections and display samples, which may, to some extent, reduce or eliminate the need for a font management program.

Mac OS X applications can use fonts stored in all the Mac OS X Fonts folders (yes, there are several), plus the Fonts folder in your Mac OS 9.x System Folder. Classic applications are restricted to the contents of the Classic Mac OS Fonts folder; that is, unless you install a font management program to manage your library (as described earlier).

NOTE: *As you'll see in the pages that follow, the ATS font system isn't a panacea, and it doesn't work with all programs; nor will its font-handling features appeal to everyone. This is apt to leave plenty of room for third-party publishers to update existing font managers or develop new programs to provide needed features lacking in the core operating system.*

Additionally, fonts are available in two ways to users of Mac OS X:

- *System-wide*—Fonts can still be placed in a Fonts folder, but several Fonts folders are in use under Mac OS X. The one you'll be using most often for system-wide fonts is in a new location, but it is used in a fashion similar to the Fonts folder under the Classic Mac OS. You'll find it in a folder labeled Library, where a number of folders related to system settings and preferences are located. Fonts in this folder are available to all users of that computer. Changing fonts or anything else on a system basis, of course, requires that you log in using an administrator's account name and password, unless you log into that sort of account by default.

NOTE: *Is that all? Not quite. Within the Mac OS X System Folder, in a folder also labeled Library, is yet another Fonts folder. However, you cannot normally add or remove files to this folder, because it's protected. Another Fonts folder is located in another Library folder, located inside the Network folder (as accessible via the Computer directory). This font library is designed to be shared across a network and may be a useful alternative if you plan to use your Mac as a repository for fonts throughout your network (although a dedicated network server would be a more useful alternative if you want to divvy up files to lots of users from a single source).*

- *User-specific*—Each user can have a separate library, stored in the Fonts folder, in his or her personal Library folder. The Library folder is located within the Home or Users folder, which bears the user's name. Those fonts are available only to that user, but they behave transparently to Mac OS X otherwise and are indistinguishable in the Font menu.

NOTE: *Another advantage of Mac OS X is the number of fonts you can use. Under Mac OS versions prior to 9, the limit was 128 font resources, meaning bitmap and suitcase files. Some users would drag and drop font suitcases atop one another to combine them and get around this limitation. The limit went to 512 fonts under Mac OS 9, but Mac OS X has no limit to how many fonts you can install, other than the size of your Mac's drive and the agony you want to experience in looking at an endless font display.*

In Brief

Introducing the Font Panel

Apple has made a significant stride toward more efficient font management with Mac OS X's Font panel (see Figure 16.2). This handy feature not only simplifies selection of fonts, but also allows you to organize your collection, regardless of size, according to your needs.

The Font panel may even partially replace the need for a separate font management program—except that it has a serious limitation. When software publishers Carbonize their applications to work under Mac OS X, they must make a number of choices. One is to make the program run in the new environment and be compatible with the basic features, such as preemptive multitasking and protected memory. This option entails less work on the part of a publisher's programming team. Apple also provides tools to exploit the features of Carbon, should the publisher undertake the extra work. However, at least with the version of Mac OS X covered in this book (Jaguar), Font panel support wasn't available. As a result, an application that otherwise fully supports Mac OS X will have a plain-Jane Font menu (see Figure 16.3). Unfortunate, but true.

NOTE: Something else you may miss under Mac OS X is a font menu modifier, such as Adobe Type Reunion, Action WYSIWYG or Menu Fonts. Such programs would group fonts into families, to keep font menus shorter, and also provide WYSIWYG display of fonts, meaning they appear in the actual typeface. Some programs, such as AppleWorks and Word, do provide the option to display this way, but only Adobe, so far, groups fonts by family in its font menus. Perhaps someone will develop a Mac OS X variation of one of those font menu modifiers by the time you read this book, although I did not hear of any firm plans while writing it.

However, if the publisher has developed a Cocoa application, you'll find the Font Panel to be a flexible way in which to manage your font collection.

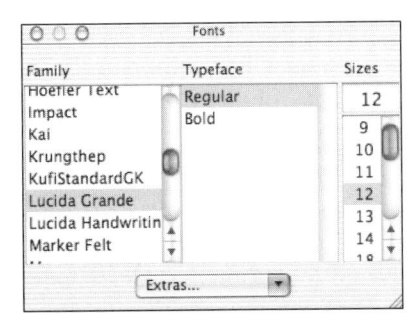

Figure 16.2 Choose, sample, and organize your font library here.

16. Mac OS X Font Management

341

Chapter 16 Mac OS X Font Management

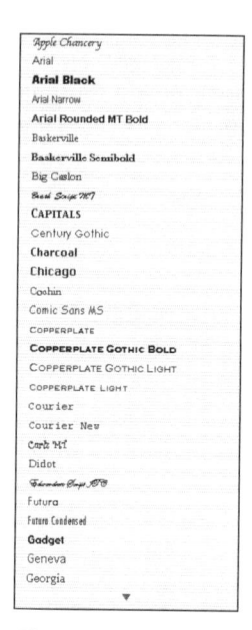

```
Apple Chancery
Arial
Arial Black
Arial Narrow
Arial Rounded MT Bold
Baskerville
Baskerville Semibold
Big Caslon
Brush Script MT
CAPITALS
Century Gothic
Charcoal
Chicago
Cochin
Comic Sans MS
COPPERPLATE
COPPERPLATE GOTHIC BOLD
COPPERPLATE GOTHIC LIGHT
COPPERPLATE LIGHT
Courier
Courier New
Curlz MT
Didot
Edwardian Script ITC
Futura
Futura Condensed
Gadget
Geneva
Georgia
```

Figure 16.3   This particular application, although Carbonized for Mac OS X, yields only an old-fashioned Font menu.

TIP: *One quick way to see whether a program was developed for the Carbon or Cocoa environment is to see whether it has a Font panel. However, regardless of which environment was used for developing the application, it should work fine under Mac OS X, with full support for its industrial-strength operating system features.*

Special Font Features of Mac OS X

If an application supports the Font panel, it also inherits some additional system-wide font features that used to be available only in separate programs. When you call up a Font menu in a Mac OS X program that offers the expanded font capability (see Figure 16.4), you'll see a number of those additional features (some will vary from program to program) in addition to the normal range of font formatting choices. They include the following:

- *Kern*—Used by graphic artists, *kerning* is the process of adjusting the spacing of letter combinations that would otherwise be wide apart visually. For example, in the word *To*, kerning tucks the lowercase *o* closer to the letter *T* for a more pleasing appearance and better readability. Mac OS X lets you use the kerning features of a font. You can also adjust the overall spacing between characters, which is sometimes called *tracking* or *range kerning*.

In Brief

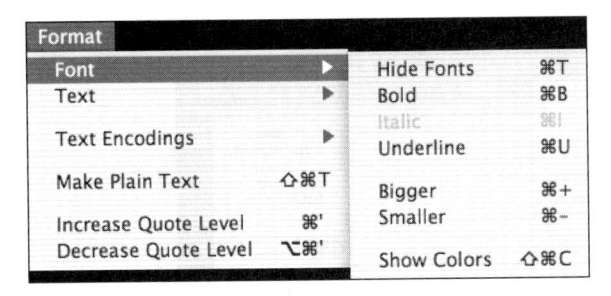

Format			
Font	▶	Hide Fonts	⌘T
Text	▶	Bold	⌘B
		Italic	⌘I
Text Encodings	▶	Underline	⌘U
Make Plain Text	⇧⌘T	Bigger	⌘+
Increase Quote Level	⌘'	Smaller	⌘-
Decrease Quote Level	⌥⌘'	Show Colors	⇧⌘C

Figure 16.4 This submenu shows only some of the additional font management options for Mac OS X.

- *Ligature*—In high-quality books and ads, *ligatures* create single, integrated characters of such combinations as *fi* and *fl*, by joining the tops of the characters, such as ° and °. The conversion is done automatically when you type a character.

NOTE: Such programs as QuarkXPress and Adobe InDesign, two popular page-layout applications, can convert ligatures on the fly. Mac OS X lets you do it with all programs that support its font-handling features. In addition, automatic kerning is also supported by the major desktop publishing applications, and, to some extent, in graphics software.

With all the great font-handling features of Mac OS X, you may begin to cherish the ease with which you are able to manage your library, whether it includes a few dozen or a few thousand fonts. In the "Immediate Solutions" section, I'll cover the ways you can install or use fonts under the new operating system.

Chapter 16   Mac OS X Font Management

Immediate Solutions

Installing Fonts Under Mac OS X

As explained at the beginning of this chapter, fonts can be installed on a system for everyone who uses your Mac or on an individual-user basis (so only that user can access them). Here's how to install a font on a system-wide basis:

1. Log in as the administrator of that Mac or a user with administrator's rights, if that's not your normal mode of operation. If another user has logged in, use the Log Out command in the Apple menu, confirm the logout and then enter your username and password in the Login prompt.

2. Locate your Mac's Library folder, which is located on the startup drive and locate the Fonts folder within it.

3. Copy the fonts directly to the Fonts folder. The fonts will be recognized by your newly opened applications. If they don't appear right away, restart your Mac (this shouldn't be necessary, however).

The other way to install fonts is for the individual user only. Here's how it's done:

1. Log in under the individual user's or an administrator's account.

2. Locate the Home or Users folder, and then the folder with that user's name.

3. Locate the Library folder and copy the fonts directly to the Fonts folder located within it. Fonts installed in this fashion should show up immediately in your Font menu. If they don't, follow the steps in the preceding list and restart your Mac.

WARNING! Fonts installed under a user's account are available only to an individual user. If you expect more than one user will work with a font, it's better to install the font on a system-wide basis.

Immediate Solutions

NOTE: *Am I missing something? I didn't mention the Mac OS X System folder and its Fonts folder, located within the Library folder. You normally cannot copy or remove any files from this folder with a couple of exceptions. One is to gain root access or just restart under Mac OS 9, if you feel you want to touch those fonts. Best thing is to leave them be, since most are required for various system display functions.*

Using the Font Panel

Mac OS X's Font panel provides a feature-laden way to organize and access the fonts in your library, regardless of its size. Here's how to use the Font panel:

1. From within an application that supports the feature, go to the Format menu and choose Font. Select Font Panel from the submenu. The window in Figure 16.5 appears. To open it more quickly, press Command+T.
2. Under Family, select the font you want to use.
3. If the font has several styles, choose the one you want from the Typeface column.
4. Pick the size you want from the Sizes column (or type the size in the text field at the top of the column to get a size not listed in the display).

TIP: *If the Font panel is too large to fit comfortably on your Mac's screen in addition to your document window, resize it by moving the resize bar. Fonts are also organized into*

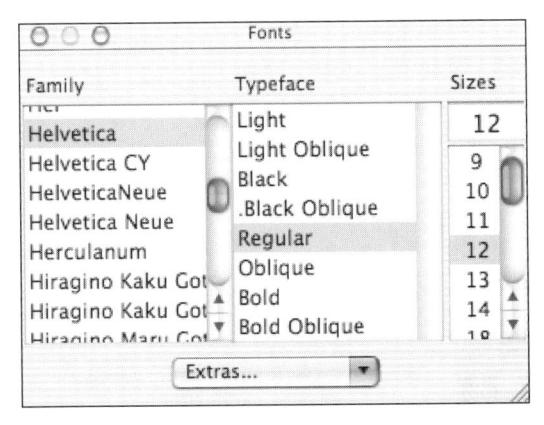

Figure 16.5 Many Mac OS X—savvy applications support the Font panel.

345

collections. If you expand the width of the Font panel, you'll see one more column, Collections, from which you can select a different group of fonts.

5. Close the Font panel screen and continue to work in your document.

TIP: If you plan to switch fonts back and forth from among your font collection, feel free to keep the Font panel window displayed so that you can return to it quickly from your document. Unfortunately, the Font panel doesn't have an active minimize function, so you can't leave it on the Dock for quick access.

NOTE: Commonly available weights of a font, such as bold or italic, can be selected directly from the Font menu without invoking the Font panel, although purists say you'll get better printing results if you choose the correct font weight from the panel itself.

Adding Font Favorites

Another great feature of the Font panel is the ability to store fonts as favorites for fast retrieval. Here's how to set them up:

1. From within an application that supports the feature, activate the Font panel.
2. Select the font family, style, and size you want.
3. Click the Extras pop-up menu (see Figure 16.6) and select Add To Favorites.
4. Repeat the process for each font you want to use as a favorite. Favorites will list not just the typeface, but also the exact size you specified.

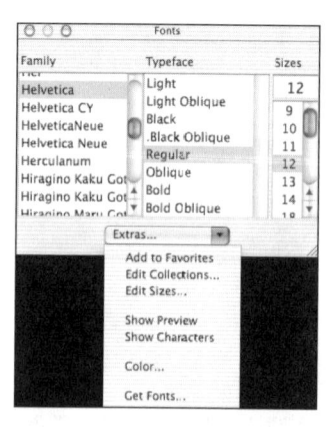

Figure 16.6 Additional commands are available for you to organize your font collection.

Immediate Solutions

Using Favorites

To access a font from your Favorites list, follow these steps:

1. Activate the Font panel. Click the resize bar and extend it to the right, to expand the width of the Font panel.

2. From the Collections column, click Favorites to see the display in Figure 16.7. The Favorites list will show the selected fonts in their actual size and style.

TIP: *If you want to check on how the font looks, click the Show Preview option in the Extras pop-up menu. The preview will display the actual face in the actual size you select. The Show Characters option will produce a convenient palette showing optional characters available in a font.*

---

3. To remove a font from your Favorites list, select it and choose Remove From Favorites from the pop-up menu.

Creating a Font Collection

One of the more useful features of Mac OS X for managing a large font library is the ability to create a custom collection to match your specific needs. That way, you can have one font collection for personal use and another for business. If you're a business user, you can subdivide fonts by the name of your client, your document, or the type of fonts you're using, such as serif and sans serif, or title and text, to name a few.

The Collections feature of the Font panel makes easy work of this process. Just follow these steps:

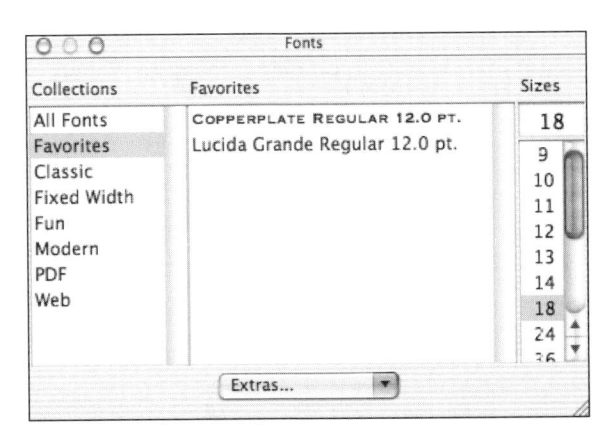

Figure 16.7 Choose your favorites from this list.

347

1. Activate the Font panel.
2. Click the pop-up menu below the font sample area and choose Edit Collections to open the window shown in Figure 16.8.
3. In the Collections column, click the plus (+) symbol to produce a brand-new collection with the name New-1, New-2, and so on, depending on how many you've made.
4. Click the Rename button to give the collection a more appropriate name, if you wish.
5. With the new collection selected, locate the font you want in the All Families column and click the left-pointing arrow to add it to your collection.
6. Repeat the process for each font you want to add to that collection.
7. To remove a font collection, select the item you want to delete and click the minus (–) button.

WARNING! *There is no warning prompt if you click the minus button when selecting a font collection. So, be certain you want to remove that collection before clicking the button. This feature may or may not be fixed in the final release of Mac OS X.*

8. Click Done when you're finished making your collections.
9. To add that particular font collection as a favorite, choose Add To Favorites from the Font panel's pop-up menu.
10. When you're finished creating font collections, close the Font panel.
11. When you need to use a specific collection, access the Font panel and click the collection's name in the Collections column.
12. Select your font in the same fashion described at the beginning of this section.

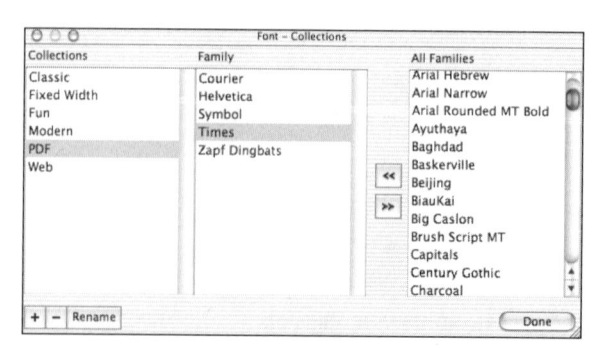

Figure 16.8 Manage and create new font collections from this window.

Immediate Solutions

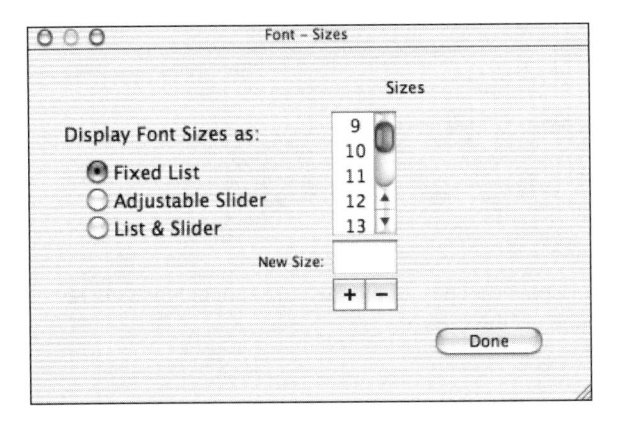

Figure 16.9 Add new font sizes here.

Choosing Custom Font Sizes

The Font panel includes a standard set of popular display sizes, but if your needs require more fine-tuning, follow this process:

1. Activate the Font panel from a program that supports the feature.

2. With the Font panel on display, choose Edit Sizes from the pop-up menu to bring up the screen shown in Figure 16.9.

3. In the New Size box, enter the size you want to include in the Sizes list, and click the plus (+) button. Alternatively, you can choose the Adjustable Slider button and move a slider to select the various font sizes.

4. To remove a font size, select it and click the minus (–) button.

5. Click Done when you're finished. You'll be returned to the Font panel.

Checking the Characters in a Font

Some things never change, and the way you look for the extra characters in a font under Mac OS X is the same as in previous versions of the Mac OS: you use Key Caps (see Figure 16.10).

To use Key Caps, follow these steps:

1. Locate Key Caps in the Utilities folder, and double-click the program's icon.

2. Go to the Font menu and select the font you wish to use.

Chapter 16   Mac OS X Font Management

Figure 16.10   Key Caps is still part of the Mac OS, and its functions remain essentially the same.

3. The keyboard layout displays the characters available. Press the appropriate modifier key, either Option or Option+Shift, to see the character you want.

4. Type the character by clicking on the key with the mouse or pressing the appropriate key on the keyboard. That character shows up in the display window above the keyboard layout.

5. To use this special character, select it, and then copy it. You can then paste it into the text-entry point in your document.

TIP: There's another way to display a character map. Go to the International preference panel in the System Preferences application. Click on the Input tab and check the Character Palette box. When this setting is activated, a tiny palette icon will appear in the menu bar, at the right of a program's or whatever the rightmost menu bar label is. Choose Show Character Palette to bring up a cool display of all the characters available in a selected font. Another option is PopChar X, a shareware utility that also provides a convenient character palette. You can check out a copy at http://www.macility.com/products/popcharx/.

Avoiding Too-Small Fonts in TextEdit

Apple's replacement for SimpleText, TextEdit (shown in Figure 16.11), can be used as a simple word processor, with full management of fonts with the Font panel. However, it can be quirky in an important respect, because you cannot specify an exact line width in the same fashion as a regular word-processing program. Instead, it uses the width of your document window to determine the size, and the line breaks made in the document on your Mac's display will match those in your printout.

Immediate Solutions

Avoiding Too-Small Fonts in TextEdit

Apple's replacement for SimpleText, TextEdit (shown in Figure 16.11), can be used as a simple word processor, with full management of fonts with the Font panel. However, it can be quirky in an important respect, because you cannot specify an exact line width in the same fashion as a regular word-processing program. Instead, it uses the width of your document window to determine the size, and the line breaks made in the document on your Mac's display will match those in your printout.

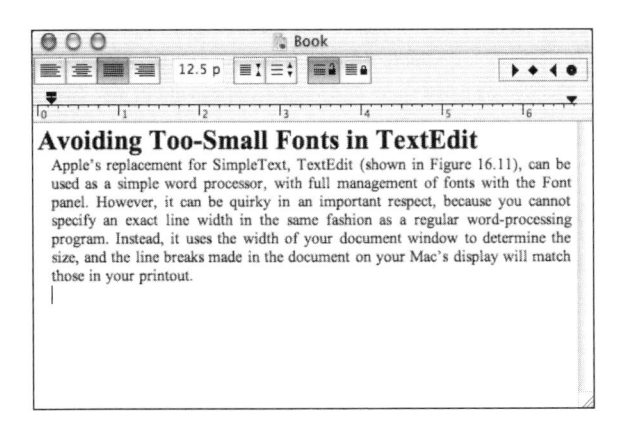

Figure 16.11   TextEdit is meant to be a less modestly featured replacement for the famous SimpleText application.

However, if your printout uses a page width smaller than the screen, the font's size will be scaled down in proportion, and under some circumstances, it can get downright small. However, a simple solution to this dilemma exists:

1. Go to TextEdit's Format menu.
2. Select the Wrap To Page option. When this feature is active, lines will wrap on the basis of the page size selected in the Page Setup box. No more ultra-small (or ultra-large) letters, and the size that's printed will be the exact size you selected in the document itself.

Using Font Reserve to Manage Your Mac OS X Font Library

Because most of the applications you are likely to use under Mac OS X that require extensive font handling are Carbon-based rather than Cocoa (such as the popular graphic applications from Adobe, Macromedia, and Quark), you'll appreciate the ability to use software that can manage a huge font library. The first available solution to hit the marketplace was DiamondSoft's Font Reserve; here's how to use it for maximum flexibility.

Begin by installing the software. The installer disk will usually include both the Mac OS 9.x and Mac OS X versions and runs the same as any other installation program.

351

Chapter 16 Mac OS X Font Management

TIP: *You can get a free limited-edition version of Font Reserve for Mac OS X as part of the Corel Graphics Suite 11 package. The sole limitation is the number of fonts you can use: 2,000. But that isn't an issue unless you expect to use more than that many fonts.*

After performing the installation, here's how to set up the program to recognize your library. The first consideration, of course, is that for maximum efficiency, the program should manage all but your very basic operating system fonts:

1. Make sure none of your applications are running. Quit any that are still active (using the Dock as the guide to see which ones are open).

NOTE: *What's a system-related font? Keep such fonts as Charcoal, Chicago, Courier, Geneva, Lucinda Grande, Monaco, Times, and Symbol where they are. You can safely move the rest.*

---

2. Locate the Font Reserve application in your Mac OS X Applications folder and launch the Font Reserve Settings application (see Figure 16.12).

3. Click the On button at the top of the application window to make Font Reserve active.

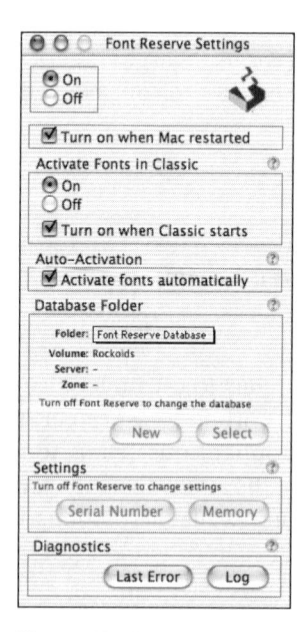

Figure 16.12 Activate Font Reserve from this application.

352

Immediate Solutions

4. To avoid having to launch the application each time you log in or restart your Mac, click the Turn On When Mac Restarted checkbox, which will make the program a login or startup application.

5. Quit the Font Reserve Settings application and then launch the Font Reserve Browser application (see Figure 16.13), which you'll use on a regular basis to manage your fonts.

6. To add fonts to Font Reserve, they need to be placed in the Font Reserve Database, the program's font storage area, located in the Font Reserve Browser application window. Drag and drop the Temp Fonts folder you made into the lower pane of the Font Reserve Browser window.

NOTE: The first time you add a fonts folder or set of files to Font Reserve, you'll see a Preferences dialog box in which you tell the program how to handle the fonts. The best option, Copy Into Font Reserve Database, will simply make a copy rather than put the original fonts in the database. This option leaves the fonts intact and will consume extra storage space, but it's useful if you need to install and use both the Classic and Mac OS X versions of Font Reserve and want to make duplicate Font Reserve Database files.

After your font library has been compiled into Font Reserve, you can use the Font Reserve Browser application's toolbar to activate or deactivate fonts as needed. Font Reserve supplies plug-ins that can be used with such programs as QuarkXPress to provide automatic activation of fonts stored in an opened document, or when fonts are activated with Font Reserve.

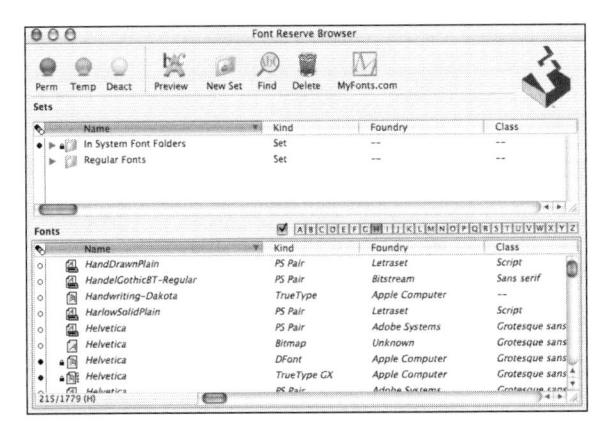

Figure 16.13 This application is used to locate, sample, and manage your Mac's font library.

353

Chapter 16 Mac OS X Font Management

Using Suitcase to Manage Your Mac OS X Font Library

While it may not have been the first out of the starting gate, Suitcase 10 for Mac OS X was long-awaited and highly praised by folks looking for an easy font management solution. In this section, I'll give you a brief look at how you manage your fonts with Suitcase.

NOTE: It's interesting to note that some users of Extensis Suitcase actually began working with the program in the late 1980s, while using Mac System 6. A lot has changed since then, but the program continues to be an important tool for graphic artists who need to handle large numbers of fonts with relative simplicity.

Since it works in both the Classic and Mac OS X environments, there's an installer to sort things out. Once the program is installed, you'll find an Extensis Suitcase folder in your Mac OS X Applications folder and several system extensions in your Classic Mac OS System Folder. The latter are used to allow Suitcase to bridge both environments and let both Classic and Mac OS X folders access your entire font library.

When you first launch Suitcase (see Figure 16.14), you'll see a simple interface with intuitive controls. If you want to have the program recognize fonts stored outside of your Classic and Mac OS X Fonts folders, click on the Add Fonts button on the program's toolbar to locate and incorporate those fonts in its database.

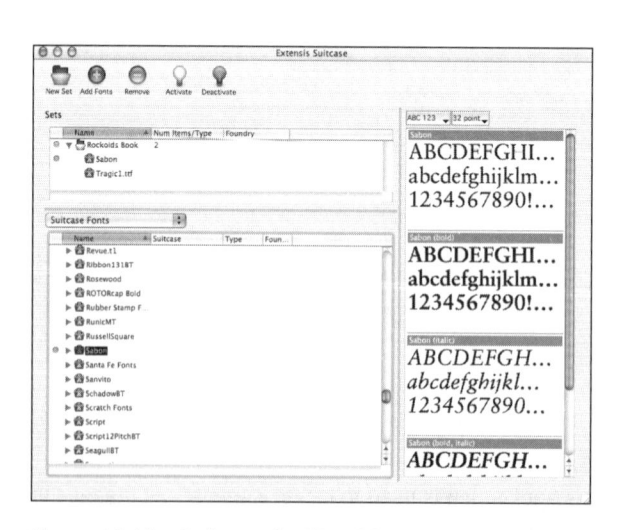

Figure 16.14   Suitcase for Mac OS X lets you do your font management from a single window.

Immediate Solutions

Fonts can be organized as sets (see the top pane), which allows you to activate a group of fonts in a single operation, and, in the lower pane, you can display fonts in different categories, from the entire library, to just the fonts stored in individual Fonts folders. The pane at the right lets you easily preview a font before you use it.

TIP: *Suitcase also lets you print a sample page for the fonts in your library, so you can keep a convenient font book at hand for personal reference or to help your clients select the right fonts for a particular job. To print the samples, first select the fonts in the Suitcase pane, and choose Print Sample Pages from the File menu and then select your printer's options in the Print dialog box.*

To activate a font, simply click at the left of its name. The font will be activated on a temporary basis, until the next restart. To keep a font activated all the time, hold down the Option key when you click the font to activate it.

Is that all? Mostly. Fonts can be autoactivated when you launch a number of Classic programs that contain those fonts. Autoactivate support under Mac OS X was, at press time, limited to Illustrator 10, so long as a special plug-in module is installed. This support may be expanded by the time you read this book.

Handling Mac OS X Font Problems

The new, more robust font-handling features of Mac OS X usually make it far easier to handle a font library, whether small or large. But because of the interaction between Mac OS X and the Classic environment, for example, you may still run into problems.

Here are some common Mac OS X problems and the standard range of solutions:

- *Fonts not in the Font menu*—If a font was installed in a user's folder, it won't be available to any other user on your Mac. If you want more than a single user to access a font, install it under that user's account as well, or system-wide. If you did install the fonts in the proper fashion, try restarting your Mac just to make sure they are recognized by the operating system.

- *Fonts appear in some applications but not in others*—If you're using a Classic Mac application, only fonts installed in the Fonts folder within the Classic System Folder are recognized, unless you use a font-management program to handle additional fonts. Depending on whether you're using Font Reserve or Suitcase, you may have to have separate versions installed in both environments.

- *Garbled or bitmapped font output*—This is probably a font conflict, similar to those that afflicted earlier versions of the Mac OS. The best way to handle this problem is to make sure you have installed only one version of the font, and not both PostScript and TrueType versions. Another possible cause is installing two or more fonts of the same name from different sources. If you buy fonts from different collections, you may run into a problem of multiple versions of Futura and other typefaces. You'll want to recheck your fonts to make sure you have only activated the correct one. Font manager programs can help you by providing previews of a selected font before it's actually turned on. The operating system won't be able to sort them out.

- *Poor letterspacing*—Check the previous item to be sure you do not have fonts that are in conflict. Another possible problem is a damaged font suitcase or TrueType font, which may not provide the right letterspacing information.

- *Missing font collection*—Are you sure you didn't delete it by mistake? You get no acknowledgement if you click the minus button by accident. Otherwise, make sure the fonts added to a collection were not part of another user's account. That would explain why the collection isn't there when you try to access it.

- *Font menus too long?*—The reason font managers are useful is because they allow you to deactivate fonts you aren't using. The best way to control the symptom of the mile-long font menu is just to turn on the fonts you need, other than the standard ones used by Mac OS X. Do not place the fonts you only use occasionally in the standard Fonts folders. Use the instructions provided with the font manager program for guidance on organizing a font library.

Chapter 17

Performing Backups

If you need an immediate solution to:	See page:
The No-Frills Daily Backup Plan	371
The Special Software Backup Plan	372
Tips and Tricks for Robust Backups	374
Doing a Folder Backup via the Command Line	376

In Brief

Yes, it's a good idea to take a hint from that old TV commercial with the motto "nobody can eat just one." Although the comment originally applied to potato chips, the same theme can be carried over to the files you create on your Mac. Nobody should depend on just one.

There is no telling what might happen to your files during your day-to-day Mac computing experience. Although Mac OS X offers a robust computing environment, about as free of potential system crashes as the state of the art allows, both the operating system and application software can still fail under normal use. When the software fails, it could conceivably harm the document you're working on. In addition, hard drives, being mechanical devices, can fail unpredictably, even though they are supposed to have lengthy mean times between failures (sometimes 500,000 hours or more).

All sorts of potential issues beyond your Mac and computing environment could also conspire to cause data loss. They include weather-related problems such as hurricanes or tornadoes, natural disasters such as earthquakes and floods, and potential disasters like fire, theft and, heaven forbid, a terrorist act. In addition, any factor that might cause a power outage or power spike, even if caused by a problem at the power company, can result in a damaged file or hard drive directory damage if it occurs at the wrong time.

Even if all your computing equipment is protected by insurance (and it should be, especially if used for business purposes), insurance cannot re-create the files you lose. However, if you have recent backups of all your critical data, you will be able to resume operation without having to re-create the material.

A Survey of Backup Software

Depending on your setup and requirements, different methods are appropriate to perform backups. The easiest is just to copy your critical files to another drive by dragging the files or folders to that drive's icon. If you don't have a lot of files to handle, this may be the perfect and highly practical solution, as long as you remember to do so on a regular basis.

In Brief

NOTE: *All Macs of recent vintage have one or more Software Restore CDs that allow you to return the Mac to its shipping condition (minus the files you've added, of course). In addition, the vast majority of software shipped nowadays comes on a CD. So, even if you only back up the documents you create, you can restore your Mac's hard drive without a full backup, although at the expense of losing your user settings, such as those required for Internet access, and any applications you've added.*

The other method is probably more reliable, because you don't have to remember to make those backup copies. It's done for you on a more or less automatic basis, and it involves using dedicated backup software.

I'll list several of the popular backup applications here. No doubt, as Mac OS X continues to gain in popularity, additional backup options will be available to suit a variety of needs.

An Overview of Retrospect

Most people regard Retrospect from Dantz Development as the most popular backup program for the Mac (check **www.dantz.com** for more information). This program is bundled with a number of backup drives, which makes the choice automatic. It's also sold separately and is available at most Apple dealers. Besides its market share, the various forms of Retrospect routinely get top reviews from the Mac magazines.

Depending on your needs, there are three versions of Retrospect to consider:

- *Retrospect Express Backup*—Consider this the no-frills version of the program, although it doesn't scrimp on important features that you need for regular, robust backups. You can use its EasyScript feature to create a custom backup routine by simply answering a few basic questions about the sort of backups you plan to do and how often you want to do them. Based on this information, Retrospect Express will build an automated backup routine that suits your needs. Say, for example, you want to back up your Mac at 4:30 P.M. each afternoon, using your Jaz 2 drive. You just place your backup disk in the drive and leave the drive and your Mac on. At the appointed hour, Express will launch itself, and then run your scripted backup precisely as you specified. You can backup a group of files or folders, or your entire hard drive, and the program has its own compression feature to reduce the size of backup sets. Hundreds of fixed and removable storage devices are supported, including CD-R/RW and DVD-RAM. Backups are stored in

17. Performing Backups

359

Chapter 17 Performing Backups

sets, which are special files containing all the data you've backed up. You can perform full backups and incremental backups (just the files that have changed). The Express version of the software only lacks support for networking backup and tape drives. It may be all the backup software you need, however, for a small home or business office setup.

> **TIP:** *A particularly useful feature of Retrospect is multiple snapshots, which are, in effect, backups of your Mac taken at different points in time. Snapshots give you the power to restore your drive to the state it was in at a given point in time. Another program, Rewind from Power On Software, allows you to revert your Mac to an earlier configuration in case of a problem, by taking a snapshot of your drive's contents. However, it had not been updated for Mac OS X as of the time this book was written.*

- *Retrospect Desktop Backup*—This version of Retrospect (see Figure 17.1) has all the features of Express, including EasyScript. It adds support for a large variety of tape drives (including the hardware compression offered by these drives) and the ability to expand support to networked Macs and Windows-based PCs via Retrospect Client. These programs allow the files on each Mac on a network to be backed up to the same set of storage devices, in a single or separate backup session. Because Retrospect is also available for the Windows platform, cross-platform backups are possible. This version of Retrospect can also be configured to send backup status reports to you via email.

> **NOTE:** *All versions of Retrospect include a robust security option. This allows the backup sets to be encrypted, so only those with the correct username and password can access and decrypt the backups or retrieve files from them. When I tested this feature with a security expert several years ago, efforts to crack the password encryption scheme proved unsuccessful. It doesn't mean it's perfect, but the results should deliver a greater feeling of confidence.*

- *Retrospect Workgroup Backup*—This is a fully packaged solution for automatic backups. The program comes with the standard Retrospect application and thus supports the entire set of features. You also get Client software (see Figure 17.2) for a number of networked computers.

An Overview of Intego Personal Backup X

ASD Software (see **www.intego.com**), publisher of several popular Mac security products, targets Personal Backup for single users or small offices (see Figure 17.3). The program supports standard removable media, but it doesn't work with tape drives. In addition, it has no network client option.

In Brief

The following are Personal Backup's features:

- The program's features can be accessed from a single, simple application. Just drag and drop the drive icons to the Source and Destination locations in the application window, and click on a pop-up menu to select backups, clones, restores, or create scripts.

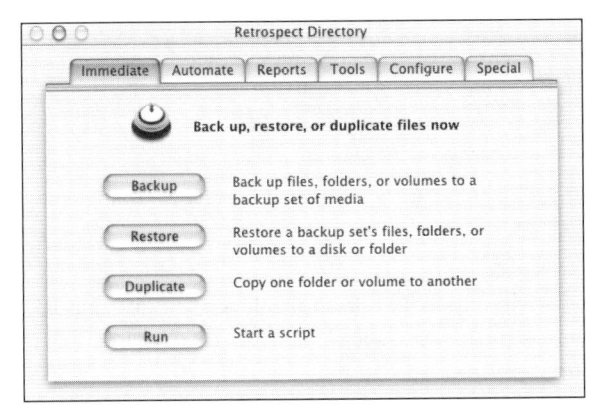

Figure 17.1   Retrospect Desktop Backup is bundled with a number of backup devices and is also sold separately.

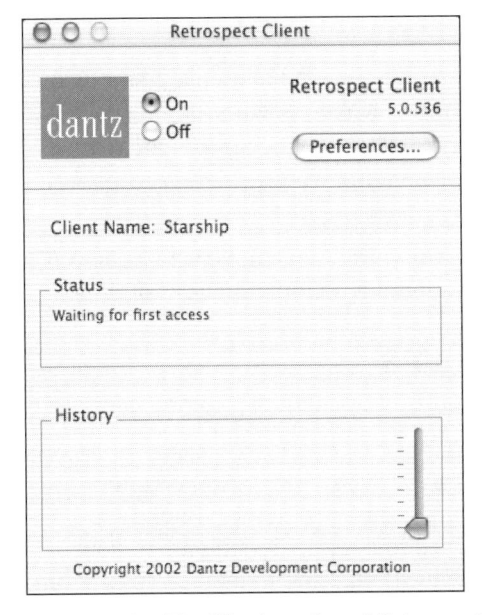

Figure 17.2   The Client version of Retrospect offers a simple interface that displays backup status.

17. Performing Backups

361

Chapter 17 Performing Backups

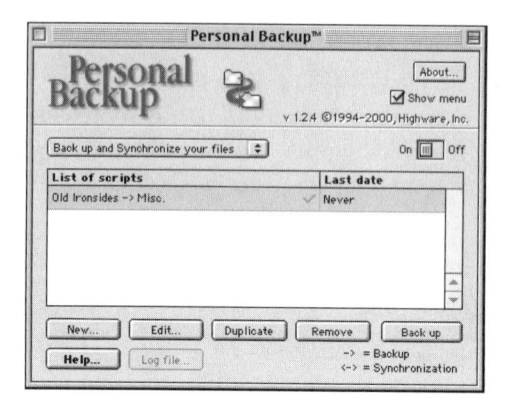

Figure 17.3 All of Personal Backup's features are available from a simple application window.

- *Easy scripting*—You can schedule multiple sets of automatic backups without scripting knowledge simply by clicking the dates, times, and options you want.

- *File synchronization*—You can compare the files you create on your desktop Mac with the ones you make on your iBook or PowerBook (or any other Mac you use to work at a different location), so that you always have the latest versions on both systems.

- *Finder format backups*—The files you back up are simply copied in regular Finder format for easy access without your having to use a special restore feature. This may be an advantage over Retrospect, which puts files in its own proprietary format, thus requiring the program to restore the files.

- *Full Volume Clones*—Personal Backup can be set to backup and restore an entire volume, not just an individual set of files.

Other Backup Programs

The choices listed in the preceding sections are not the only ones available. Here are some other backup programs:

- *Apple's Backup*—If you opt to subscribe to Apple's .Mac program, one of the features that's included is Backup, a simple application that can be used to backup documents to your Mac's CD or DVD drive, or to your iDisk. Among its features are drag and drop backups and a QuickPick feature, which guides you through the sometimes confusing process of finding files in multiple locations.

In Brief

- *Iomega's QuikSync 3*—This program is easy to set up for on-demand or scheduled backups. The new version overcomes the limitation of the previous edition, by supporting storage devices not manufactured by Iomega. Among the features of QuikSync 3 are:

  - *Easy setup*—A convenient setup wizard guides you through the process of setting up an unattended backup without your needing to understand scripting or complicated setups.

  - *Automatic copying*—You can specify certain folders on your Mac's hard drive for automatic backup. Files that are copied or moved to those folders will be duplicated automatically in the "sync" location, which is usually an external storage device.

  - *Multiple revisions*—By being able to save more than a single revision of an individual file, you can view documents in progress at different stages and restore the ones you need to use.

  - *Enterprise implementation*—As with Retrospect, QuikSync 3 can be administered from a central location, making it easy for IT managers to set up the program on a network system.

NOTE: *QuikSync 3.1 and later will run native under Mac OS X. Another program that was useful for backups, Connectix's CopyAgent, will not be developed for Mac OS X, according to the most recent information available from the company.*

- *FWB Backup ToolKit*—The publisher of Hard Disk ToolKit, a popular disk formatting utility, released a Mac OS X version of its Backup ToolKit software in the Fall of 2001. This application has three basic modes and does all its work via a simple application interface. The Automatic Backup feature performs your backups at regular intervals. An Incremental Backup feature, like the one in Retrospect, backs up only the files that have changed. For road warriors, a Synchronization feature eases the task of making sure both your Mac and your iBook or PowerBook have the same sets of files. Like Retrospect's EasyScript feature, a Configuration Wizard makes fast work of setting up your backup regimen. The notable missing feature is the ability to work with tape drives.

- *Power On Software's Rewind*—Suppose you install something new on your Mac, and suddenly the computer behaves like it's possessed. You can, of course, troubleshoot the problem and perhaps remove the application. But wouldn't it be easier just to turn back the hands of time? Rewind does that, by keeping a reference file of changes you've made to your Mac. Then, when called into action, it restores your Mac to the condition that existed before the event that triggered your problem. You can

17. Performing Backups

also use this clever application to recover a lost file, by going back in time to the point before you deleted the file. Although file recovery utilities are available, this may be a more robust way to regain lost ground.

> **NOTE:** At the time this book was being prepared, Power On Software was committed to updating several of its programs, which include security and personal information managers, to Mac OS X. An updated version of Rewind wasn't available for me to examine, however, so I'm summarizing the features of the Classic Mac OS version (based on the assurance from the publisher that features will be similar).

In addition to the commercial programs, several freeware and shareware offerings promise many of the basic features of the commercial options. These include such entrants as FoldersSynchronizer, Gemini, Project Backer, Revival, SwitchBack, and Sync X. You'll want to check out the feature sets at VersionTracker.com (**www.versiontracker.com**) and see which ones might be worth a second look.

When you decide which program to deploy in your environment, consider the features offered and how they fit your situation. A simple file synchronization utility may be all you need if you just need to back up document files.

> **WARNING!** Don't even think of trying to back up system files and applications with software that isn't Mac OS X compatible. The file system changes will conspire to give you nothing more than a set of damaged files. If you aren't ready to upgrade your backup software, consider copying your critical documents manually

An Overview of Internet Backups

Beginning with Mac OS 9, Apple attempted to make Internet networking as transparent as connecting to a local area network (LAN). Mac OS X's user interface is designed to further blur the differences between the location of shared volumes, so it no longer makes a difference whether they're located at the other end of your room or at the other end of the world (except for file transfer speed, of course).

The ease of Internet networking and the lack of standard backup drives on some new Macs have resulted in a search for other backup methods. One of those methods harnesses the power of the Internet as a repository for your backed up files. Following are descriptions of two Internet-based backup resources. Both are extra cost services:

In Brief

- *iDisk (www.mac.com)*—Apple's .Mac subscription service offers backup software and virus software, a custom mac.com email address, the ability to create a personal home page, and iDisk (see Figure 17.4), which sets aside 100MB of storage space for your files. iDisk is easily accessed as a disk icon, which you can use in the same fashion as a volume connected directly to your Mac or your local network. iDisk is useful as a limited, fairly robust backup solution. It allows you to store your files in a private area, free from public access.

NOTE: When you install Mac OS X 10.2 or set up a new Mac, you get a 60-day trial membership to give .Mac a whirl. The trial iDisk storage space is limited to 20MB until you upgrade.

- *BackJack (www.backjack.com)*—This Canadian-based company claims top ratings from Mac support Web sites. It offers a dedicated program that will provide automatic, unattended backups to its 128-bit secured Web servers. It also uses StuffIt compression technology to maximize the number of files you can send in a given amount of storage space. Pricing plans depend on the amount of storage space you need.

Although Internet backups are a reliable method of backing up critical files, and they offer the added benefit of being offsite, they have

Figure 17.4 Apple's iDisk feature gives you online storage to use for backups or to make files available to your Internet contacts.

17. Performing Backups

365

some decided disadvantages. Chief among them is throughput and capacity. Transferring even a few megabytes of files via a standard 56Kbps modem connection can be a tedious process. Worse, if you are disconnected during the transfer process (a fairly common occurrence), you must go through all or most of the process again to make sure all your files were sent. Consider broadband access, such as a cable modem or DSL (if available in your area), should you choose this backup solution.

> **TIP:** Even if you have broadband Internet service, don't be surprised if your upload speed is throttled to a level far below that of download speed. Typically, cable modems limit uploads to 256Kbps (often less), even though they promise download speeds from 1 to 2Mbps or greater. The reason cited by some of these providers is to give maximum emphasis on downloads, and to limit use of their services by PC users who want to set up personal Web servers.

The other shortcoming is capacity. iDisk limits you to 100MB total storage. Commercial Internet backup resources such as BackJack offer standard plans with fixed storage capacities (BackJack's are 40MB and 100MB) and additional per-megabyte charges for larger storage capacities. Even if you could send large amounts of data in a speedy fashion to such a service, the cost of backing up a fairly full hard drive in a new or recent Mac (with several gigabytes of files) on a regular basis can be considerable.

An Overview of Backup Media

A number of storage media are useful for backups—some more robust than others. When choosing a product, you should consider your specific needs, such as the amount of data you wish to back up and how robust the medium is for long-term storage, if that's one of your requirements. Here are your choices:

> **NOTE:** I have made no attempt to cover older, discontinued removable devices, such as SyQuest drives. Any of these products can be judged compared to the products mentioned here in terms of speed, capacity, and reliability. You should consider, however, whether it's a good idea to trust your backups to an obsolete product with little or no customer support.

- *Floppy drive*—This was the original backup medium, not offered on Macs in several years. It isn't terribly robust; floppy disks are known to develop disk errors after being used just a few times. Worse, capacity is extremely limited. Even if you have an older Mac with a floppy drive, or you're using HD-style floppy disks on a SuperDisk drive or external floppy drive, you'll find this medium works best for small documents or pictures, when transferring them from one location to another.

NOTE: Worse, the standard floppy drive on older Macs isn't supported unless you're willing to install a third-party patch that recognizes those old devices. One such driver is available from this site: http://www.darwin-development.org/floppy/.

- *SuperDisk drive*—This product was a would-be floppy drive replacement, but never managed to catch on (although some dealers still sell the product from such makers as QPS Inc.). It has the benefit of reading and writing to HD floppy disks at a speed greater than a standard floppy; it's most noticeable if you have the "2X" SuperDisk product. It allows support for legacy media (except for 800KB and 400KB floppies, of course). The SuperDisk medium is a 120MB disk that, at first glance, looks very much like a floppy (there's also a 250MB version). The media appears to be robust and relatively inexpensive. Such drives are not particularly fast, however, which makes them less efficient for larger files, and the user base is still relatively small, despite the relative popularity of such devices as accessories for the iMac and other USB-based Apple computers.

NOTE: Let me emphasize that the SuperDisk drive isn't the same as the SuperDrive, the Pioneer-built drive that is available in some Mac desktop computers, including Power Macs, the eMac and the flat-panel iMac. The SuperDrive can play and record to both CD and DVD media.

- *Zip drive*—This is Iomega's most popular product; Zip drives are found in many business environments. The medium resembles a fat floppy disk, and it uses a mixture of floppy- and hard-drive technologies to provide storage capacities of 100MB, 250MB and 750MB. Zip drives have been standard issue on many of Apple's desktop models, and millions of drives are out there, so it's easy to find compatible drives at other locations. The drives and media are considered quite robust, standing the test of time beyond some early reliability concerns about the mechanisms.

NOTE: One particularly vexing problem that still occurs sometimes is the so-called "click of death"—an annoying sound that emanates from the drive when you're using defective media or when the drive is poised for failure. Should you encounter this problem with a Zip drive, remove the disk and see if the sound persists when you insert another one. Should it still occur, have the drive serviced or replaced. It appears more recent Zip drives are far less vulnerable to such ills.

- *Jaz drive*—The Iomega Jaz drive is, essentially, a portable drive using traditional hard drive technology. It comes in 1GB and 2GB formats (the latter product is called the Jaz 2), with media to match. It has the benefit of being relatively fast—about the equivalent of a slower hard drive. Long-term reliability of the media is something of a question, although the drive seems solid enough for part-time use and archiving.

- *Iomega Peerless drive*—This is an interesting variation of the removable drive scheme, brought up to date for the needs of twenty-first century PC users. A Peerless Storage System, to use the official term, consists of two parts. It starts with a Base Station, which works with a Mac's FireWire or USB port (the former is best to access this product's performance potential). Then there is the actual disk, which comes in 10GB or 20GB form. The product is sold as a bundle, with Base Station and disk, and separately (but why?), and is a clever way to handle the diverse needs of high capacity, good performance, and removable storage.

- *Castlewood ORB drive*—This product has superficial similarities to the now-departed SyQuest drives, perhaps because the founder of Castlewood was also the founder of SyQuest Technologies. The standard drive uses low-cost 2.2GB cartridges and employs a variation of standard hard drive technology called *magneto-resistive*, now standard on modern fixed drives. Its long-term robustness is not known, because the product has been on the market only a relatively short time at this writing. A review in *Macworld* magazine, however, suggested there might be some reliability concerns with the product. At the time this book was written, Castlewood had announced a 5.7GB version of the drive, using the same form factor (so older media can be read). But the initial release of the product didn't include a Mac OS version (although one might be available when you read this book).

- *Portable hard drive*—Because this standard hard drive is in a small case, it is suitable for easy transportation. Such drives are available in all the popular storage technologies, including FireWire, SCSI, and USB. Some notable examples include a FireWire product line from SmartDisk (see **www.smartdisk.com**), which uses the FireWire bus for power. That and its Hot Plug feature make such drives easy to set up and move from workstation to workstation.

- *CD-R/CD-RW*—These products use special CD-based media, offering a high degree of longevity. The standard recordable CD technology is write-once, meaning that you cannot erase or replace the data already recorded. However, the medium is very cheap, so this isn't a serious problem. The more expensive CD-RW products let you rewrite data up to 1,000 times, but the discs themselves do not work on some regular CD drives, particularly older models. The shortcoming is speed, although newer 12x and 16x CD recorders promise to record a complete 650MB CD in just a few minutes. Optical media are great for archiving files for an extended period of time.

NOTE: *The figures 12x, 16x, and so on refer to multiples of the normal CD record speed, which takes approximately 74 minutes to write to a 650MB disc. In addition to the basic speed in recording data, you have to add the time it takes to read back the completed CD for verification (although that process is much faster, because standard CD readers on the Mac reach and exceed speeds of 32x, and third-party drives are even faster). Apple no longer ships the high-end PowerMac G4 with a DVD-RAM drive. In addition, a number of third-party peripheral companies, such as LaCie and QPS, offer drives using this format. However, the format is unfinished enough that the media recorded on one drive may not work on another brand.*

- *DVD-R/DVD-RW*—Still another variation of DVD technology is supported by the SuperDrive on Power Mac G4 and some eMacs and flat-panel iMacs, and a number of third-party products incorporate the same Pioneer drive and similar products. Under Mac OS X, you can create movie DVDs using Apple's iDVD software, or store your data files via the Finder's disc-burning feature.

NOTE: *As of the time this book was written, iDVD did not support third party external DVD writers.*

- *Tape drives*—Such drives come in several forms, using tapes that are roughly similar in setup to a cassette deck. Tape drives are not cheap, but the media are. You can buy DDS tapes for around $10 apiece or more, with storage capacities of up to 40GB (depending on the ability of the tape drive or software to compress data). Larger capacities are available for some tape drive formats, such as AIT. Tape drives tend to be slower than the other media, except for CDs, and the technology doesn't offer random access.

Therefore, restoring files in different locations on a tape can take a while. In addition, although tapes are subject to wear and tear, the medium is easily and relatively cheaply replaced.

- *Network volume*—You can also back up your data to a drive on another computer (a Mac or a Unix- or Windows-based server), located on your local network. Such techniques are useful for each individual workstation, but the volume to which you are backing up should also receive a regular backup routine to ensure the highest amount of protection for the files. Consider the network backup, then, as just an intermediary to a full backup solution. At the other end of the equation, the system administrators should be using one of the previously described media for backup and archiving.

Immediate Solutions

The No-Frills Daily Backup Plan

This plan doesn't require special backup software. All it requires is a commitment to a regular program so you don't face the loss of crucial files in an emergency.

Before you begin your backup, you need the following elements:

- *Backup media*—Use a separate drive or networked volume (local or Internet-based). The "In Brief" section covers a number of backup products you might want to consider. You should also make sure you have backup media with sufficient capacity to store all the files.

- *A plan*—Create a small word-processing document listing the files and folders you want to back up on a regular basis.

TIP: To keep track of your backups, you might want to include a list of dates and times on your backup list, along with an underscore or checkbox where you can easily mark your backups as you complete them.

- *Logically named folders*—Create folders on the backup drive to easily identify the files you are backing up. If you plan to keep separate copies of each generation of your backup files, consider putting a date on each folder or other identification information that will help you quickly locate the files you need at a later time.

- *Reminder device*—It will help to have an alarm clock, clock radio, reminder program, or other means to notify you of the time of the scheduled backup.

- *Easy access to your original system or application CDs*—As mentioned earlier in the chapter, new Macs come with a Restore CD (or set of Restore CDs for the latest models), which can put the computer back in the form in which it shipped (at the expense of losing application and system updates and preferences).

TIP: The standard user license for most every program allows you to make a single backup copy. It is a good idea to make a backup of your software CDs and store them off site, in the event of theft or damage at your original location. Remember that if you are backing up a bootable CD, follow the instructions in the CD software to make your copy bootable as well.

371

Chapter 17 Performing Backups

After you've got the raw materials set up, follow these steps:

1. Make sure you set your notification device to alert you of the appointed time for the backup.
2. Have your backup medium ready. If you're using a removable drive, such as a Zip drive, be sure that a disk is in the drive, ready to roll.
3. Refer to your backup list for the files and folders you need to copy.
4. Drag the files to the appropriate folders.
5. After the files are copied, put a note on your backup list confirming the day's backup is complete.

NOTE: *If your Mac is set up for multiple users, you may want to establish a single backup folder to which all users have access, such as a Shared folder. That way, each user does not have to run separate backup sessions (a potentially confusing, awkward process).*

These steps allow you to easily keep track of your daily backups, to make sure that you or one of your employees has performed the task as scheduled.

TIP: *If you are working on a mission-critical document that will take you a long time to re-create in the event of loss or damage, you may also want to perform frequent backups of the files throughout the workday. I do this regularly when I'm writing a book, because re-creating even a single chapter or portion can be an annoying, time-consuming process. It only happened to me once, and that was quite enough.*

The Special Software Backup Plan

The following steps are based on using one of the backup programs described in the earlier section, "A Survey of Backup Software." I'm assuming you will be installing the software according to the publisher's instructions and that you will be setting up your backup media as indicated.

First, take steps to prepare for your regular backup regimen:

- If you're using a removable device, be sure the disks or cartridges are inserted into the drive and ready to run at the appointed time.

Immediate Solutions

NOTE: If you expect your backups to fill more than a single disk or tape, you should have spares available in case additional media are requested. You may, of course, recycle media if you want to discard older backups that are no longer useful. For tape-based media, however, you should replace the cartridges every year or two; they do wear out.

- Make sure that the backup software is properly installed.
- Use the program's scheduling features to create a regular backup routine that meets your needs. You may schedule full backups once a week and incremental backups (which cover only the changed files) each day.
- If your backups are likely to consume more than a single disk or tape, be sure someone is available to insert extra media, if necessary.
- If your backup software includes automatic notification of problems via email, such as Retrospect offers, be sure the program is configured to contact you or your systems administrator at a location where they're likely to be at the time the backups occur. This may, for example, include the email address you use at home. If you have email service on your pager or mobile phone, that might be a convenient option to use for offsite notification.

WARNING! If your Macs are located in an office, take the time to explain your backup schedule to your staff. Advise them to try not to use their Macs while files are being backed up, or to leave them on at the end of the day for after-hours backup duty. Files created or left open during the backup process may be copied in an incomplete form or not at all.

After your backup program is in place, here are the steps you'll follow to make sure the process is done correctly:

1. Schedule your backups to occur at least once every workday, usually at a time when your Macs are not in use, so as not to interfere with your work schedule.

TIP: Although some firms run backups at the end of the day or during the early morning hours, backups can also be conveniently done during lunchtime (which is when I do mine) or any time when all or most employees aren't present, if the backups can be completed within that time frame.

2. Before the scheduled backup is to begin, be sure the backup drive or drives and media are ready so that the process can occur (where possible) unattended.

373

3. Make sure that the backup drive and all the computers from which files will be retrieved are left on and ready to run at the appointed time.

4. If the backups are unattended, check your software to see if it produces a log of the backup (Retrospect offers this feature). If a log is available, consult it regularly for information about possible problems with your scheduled backup.

Tips and Tricks for Robust Backups

Once you get accustomed to a regular backup routine, you'll appreciate the added security it offers. Consider the following additional procedures to customize your backups:

- *Store additional backup disks off-site.* Financial institutions, ISPs, and other companies store backups at other locations. That way, if something damages or destroys equipment and media at the original location, the valuable files are still available to be copied onto replacement equipment. A bank vault is one possible location. Although it may not be convenient to store all your files off-site, those most valuable to you should be considered as candidates for such storage.

NOTE: *Particularly tragic examples of lost data occurred during the bombing of the World Trade Center some years ago and the September 11, 2001 terrorist attack that destroyed the Twin Towers. Even if a firm managed to stay in business after this disaster, only an offsite backup would restore operations to a reasonable degree.*

- *Test your backups.* Don't assume you will be able to restore your files, even if the software reports the backups were successful. From time to time, do a test run to make sure you can easily retrieve files if necessary.

WARNING! *Tape drives need to be cleaned at regular intervals, because clogged read/write heads can result in premature wear of a drive or incomplete backups. Low-cost cleaning cartridges are available for such drives. The manufacturers of the mechanisms usually recommend cleaning them every 15 or 30 hours (check the documentation to determine the correct interval).*

- *Use the automatic backup or autosave features from your software.* A number of Mac programs include the ability to save documents at a regular interval or make extra copies. Check a

Immediate Solutions

program's preference dialogs or documentation for information about these features. Among the programs that offer one or both of these features are AppleWorks 6, Microsoft Word, and QuarkXPress. Financial programs, such as Intuit's Quicken 2002, also can create backup files of your financial records.

- *Perform extra backups of work-in-progress.* Whether you are compiling a financial profile, writing a novel, or creating an illustration for an important ad, it's a good idea to create extra copies from time to time. You can simply drag a copy of your document to a backup location, so there's always an extra one in case the original is damaged.

WARNING! *Although using the Save As feature is a possible method of making an extra copy, the end result is that you will end up working with the new document rather than the old, which means the original won't be updated.*

- *Save often.* The best protection against loss of a document in case of a crash or power outage is to have a copy on disk. Consider saving the document each time you make an important change and certainly after you create a new document.
- *Get file recovery software.* Even if you take extra steps to make sure you do regular backups, it's always possible you will trash a necessary file by mistake. Programs such as MicroMat's TechTool Pro, and Symantec's Norton Utilities are able to restore files you delete by mistake. They work best when you install them first, because they are able to track files as you trash them.

TIP: *If you delete a file by mistake, try to recover it right away with one of the programs mentioned. When a file is trashed, it is not actually erased. The portion of the drive on which the file is located is simply marked as available, meaning new data can be written there. If you don't create new files, there is a greater possibility you'll be able to recover the file.*

- *Use a program's incremental backup feature.* Backup software will handle a backup in two ways: a full backup, in which all of your files are copied; and an incremental backup, in which only the files that have changed are added to your backup. The most effective, time-saving routine is to use a mixture of both. The initial backup should include all the files that need to be backed up, and the subsequent backups should be limited to changed files until the backup medium is filled. Then you should begin from scratch. In either case, you will probably want to do a complete backup once a week if you have a steady flow of files, or once every two weeks otherwise.

17. Performing Backups

Chapter 17 Performing Backups

> **WARNING!** Backup programs that use tape-based media may restore files much more slowly if they have to check for a large number of new or changed versions of files when retrieving files. You should use this feature judiciously at best, particularly with tape media.

- *Double-check your network setups.* In order for a networked backup to work, you need to make sure that your networked volumes are accessible when the backup is being performed. Pay particular attention to such issues as access privileges and whether your backup software is properly installed. Also make sure that your media are large enough to handle the available files. If not, an unattended backup won't be a good idea. If you run into problems in getting a useful network backup, examine your network configuration from stem to stern and also look at the backup logs made by your software to see what errors are being reported. Basically, if a shared volume is available for exchanging files, it should work fine for a networked backup.

> **WARNING!** If you want to back up an entire Mac OS X volume, including system files, you need software that's compatible with this operating system. Older backup software may work fine with application and document files, but it won't see the thousands of hidden or invisible files that are part of the Mac OS X installation, nor will such software work with volumes formatted in the Unix File System (UFS) format.

Doing a Folder Backup via the Command Line

You can also copy your files courtesy of Mac OS X's Terminal application, which is located in the Utilities folder. If you're accustomed to dragging and dropping files in the Finder, you are used to some of its quirks and advantages. The Finder, for example, assumes that you want to move a file when you drag its icon from one location on the same disk to another and that you want to copy (not move) a file when you drag its icon to another disk.

On the other hand, when you use a command-line interface, you have to tell the operating system specifically what you want to do, and not make assumptions.

376

Immediate Solutions

***WARNING!** Do not attempt to copy a Classic application via the command line. Unix doesn't understand the traditional Mac way of separating the elements of an application into data and resource forks; thus the file will be corrupted. But document files can be easily copied this way.*

To copy your Documents folder to a backup drive, follow these steps:

1. Launch Terminal if it's not already open.

2. In the Terminal screen, type "sudo cp –R Documents /Volumes/Backup" and press the Return key. The first time you type a **sudo** command, you'll be asked for your administrator password, because the command grants you Super User access (a sort of temporary root access); it allows you to perform basically any system command via the terminal. Such access will remain in effect for five minutes, after which you'll have to authenticate again to perform more functions.

*NOTE: In the previous command line, **cp** is the copy command. **-R** is a flag that stands for recursive, which means that you are copying a folder, not a file, named Documents. The name **Backup** in this case represents the name of your backup medium; you can use any name you want. Also bear in mind this command requires the presence of a folder or file named Documents. Chapter 20 covers the Unix command line in more detail.*

3. To copy additional folders, use the same commands, substituting the name of the folder you want to copy.

*NOTE: When you want to copy a file rather than a folder, do not use the recursive command. Specify the path or location of the file, such as **Documents/filename** for a file in your Documents folder.*

Related solutions:	Found on page:
A Short List of Popular Command-Line Features	428
Using Mac OS X's Command-Line FTP Software	431

17. Performing Backups

377

Chapter 18

Security and Mac OS X

If you need an immediate solution to:	See page:
Choosing a Mac Virus Detection Program	384
MicroMat's TechTool Pro	384
Intego's VirusBarrier	385
Network Associates' Virex	387
Symantec's Norton AntiVirus	388
Using Apple's Mac OS X's Built-in Firewall	390
Choosing Personal Firewall Software	392
Norton Personal Firewall	393
Intego's NetBarrier	393
Intego's ContentBarrier	394
Firewalk X	395
BrickHouse	395
Hardware Firewalls	396

Chapter 18 Security and Mac OS X

In Brief

Macs are not immune to computer viruses. Even if you use your Mac at home or in a small business, the danger, while not as ever-present as on the Windows platform, still exists. You've no doubt read the reports of email and macro viruses and felt that perhaps they were threatening only to users of other computing platforms and that folks who use Macs don't have to fret over such things. After all, the Windows platform has been the victim of literally thousands of computer viruses, and programs are updated frequently, sometimes as often as once a week, to combat the latest strains. Therefore, it's often believed that the pranksters who create such viruses have no time to do their dirty work with Macs.

Of course, as those who have worked on Macs for many years may realize, this just isn't so. There have been several dozen Mac viruses over the years, some just annoying, others causing crashes and possible loss of data.

NOTE: *I have seen two serious instances of mass virus infections on Macs. In the early 1990s, a virus called WDEF infected the desktops of Macs running System 6. More recently, in 1998 and 1999, many Macs were infected by the AutoStart virus, which even managed to turn up on a few commercial CDs—ones quickly withdrawn, I might add.*

Worse, the proliferation of macro viruses that affect Microsoft's Office software haven't totally left alone our favorite Mac computing platform. Although these viruses won't cause some of the dire effects that may be prevalent in the Windows variations, such things as damaged documents and problems with document templates have been legion.

NOTE: *Folks tend to be overconfident about Word macro viruses. I have seen them in documents from software publishers that ought to know better (names omitted to protect the guilty).*

In addition, the growth of high-speed or broadband Internet connections, such as cable modems and DSL, and the recent support for Internet-based file sharing, have made Macs increasingly vulnerable to direct attacks from the Internet.

An Overview of Mac Viruses

It's common for movies to portray the use of computer viruses as something that's good—a clever scheme to beat the bad guys and win the day, or even save the world, depending on a particular situation. From *Independence Day* to *The Net*, the underdog who is smart enough to write a virus manages to snatch victory from the jaws of defeat.

But in our real world, the author of a computer virus isn't the hero, and the victims of such viruses are not the villains. They are folks like you and me who just want to compute in comfort and safety, without having to concern ourselves with invasions of our privacy and of the sanctity of our personal computing experience.

Types of Computer Viruses

There are three basic types of computer viruses, but extensive variations exist in each group:

- *Virus*—The standard form of computer virus is a piece of code that's attached to a program or other file. When the file is opened, the virus is activated. It can, in turn, be spread to other files as part of its function. Such a virus may be a simple joke, putting up a silly message on the screen. Others may cause system crashes or damage files and perhaps the hard drive directory.

- *Trojan horse*—This is the worst sort of virus-related affliction, because, on the surface, it appears to be a file or program that has a useful, productive function. However, like the Trojan horse of old, embedded within that file is a malicious application that's ready to wreak havoc on your Mac once it's unleashed. A recent example was the Graphics Accelerator or SevenDust virus. It was sent as a system extension called Graphics Accelerator, which supposedly was designed to enhance video performance. The virus would actually erase files on a Mac's drive. Complicating matters is that a Graphics Accelerator extension was indeed provided with older versions of the Mac OS to support models equipped with ATI graphics chips. Later, that extension and its associated files were renamed with ATI prefixes, so they are easy to identify and there's less confusion.

- *Email virus*—In a sense, you could call this a Trojan horse as well. You receive a message from someone you know, claiming to contain the file you were expecting—except you weren't expecting any file. But, because you know the sender, you launch it anyway, and it does its dirty work. Usually the net effect is to copy an email address list and send similar

381

files to other users. Most such viruses do their thing under the Windows platform. However, the infamous Mac.Simpsons@mm virus, a macro virus that exploited AppleScript, was indeed a Mac-only variation that affected Microsoft's Entourage and Outlook Express users. The best approach to take is never to assume that it's all right to open a file you didn't expect to receive. Write to the sender and confirm what the file is and why it was sent to you. Get the OK before launching. Whenever you send a file to someone, it's a good idea to explain what kind of file is being sent and its purpose, so there is no room for error or suspicion.

NOTE: *The prevalence of email viruses has resulted in some companies setting up firewalls and mail servers to strip the .exe extension from an email attachment before delivery. Should you have a problem sending an executable file to a Windows user via email, send it as a Zip file instead.*

Viruses and Mac OS X

No doubt it will be a while before virus authors find ways to infect Macs running Mac OS X, because of its Unix underpinnings. The fact that computer viruses first started under Unix should be sufficient cause to remain on the alert. In addition, because you may still spend a reasonable portion of your day running programs in the Classic environment, the potential exists for infection of your older applications and files too. So, you can't escape the need to use an antivirus program to ensure that you're protected. Fortunately, the available Mac OS X antivirus applications will scan all the files on your computer so that you can see if they're infected.

In the "Immediate Solutions" section, I'll describe the popular virus-detection programs available for Mac users. I've concentrated on the ones available in Mac OS X form, or those for which Mac OS X support was promised when this book was written. If you are cautious in your personal computing habits, you should be able to get the maximum amount of protection with the least amount of interference.

Broadband Internet and Invaders from the Outside

Another possible threat stems from the fact that more Mac users have upgraded to high-speed Internet services. Whether it comes by way of a cable modem, DSL, or a wireless connection (such as Sprint Broadband Direct or satellite), the primary difference between this sort of connection and regular dial-up is that you spend far more time online.

In Brief

It's rare for someone to be connected via a modem 24/7, but with a broadband connection, you're almost always connected to the Internet, in the same way that you may be connected to a printer or shared Macs or Windows-based computers on a local network.

NOTE: Let me amend that. I have seen cable modems, such as one from the Motorola Surfboard line, which can be placed in a standby mode, in which you can deactivate the modem when your online session is over. That is one way to reduce the risk of being ever-present on the Internet, but it still leaves you vulnerable during the times you are online.

In addition, Macs can share files via the Internet, a feature of Mac OS 9 and Mac OS X. Such networking, combined with a high-speed connection, can, in effect, minimize or eliminate the difference between a local and Internet-based network. As a result, your Mac may be more vulnerable to another form of attack, from outsiders who try to take control of your computer via your TCP/IP-based Internet connection.

To protect yourself from such invasions, consider using Mac OS X's built-in firewall feature, or if you want a greater range of configuration options, a third party application. A firewall monitors Internet traffic and warns you or even block attempts to access your Mac from outside.

***NOTE:** In effect, a firewall program puts an armed guard on your Mac, monitoring traffic coming to and from your computer and preventing unauthorized access.*

Even before Mac OS X–savvy applications are available to seek out viruses, you can continue to use your existing software and have it function just fine in the Classic user environment. To learn more about how older programs interact with Apple's new operating system, please check Chapter 15.

The "Immediate Solutions" section profiles four programs designed to protect your Mac against computer viruses and several software firewall solutions, including the one available in Jaguar.

18. Security and Mac OS X

383

Immediate Solutions

Choosing a Mac Virus-Detection Program

In the early days of the Mac platform, a number of commercial and shareware virus-detection programs were available. Over time, many of these programs were acquired by other publishers or discontinued. Shareware antivirus offerings included VirusDetective, which was continued until the early 1990s, when its author decided that payments were too small to continue. Here are the currently available commercial Mac virus-protection applications.

NOTE: One of the early Mac antivirus programs, Rival, went abroad and was developed strictly for the European market for several years. However, the publisher's Web site was down when I checked it for this book.

MicroMat's TechTool Pro

This is an all-in-one application (see Figure 18.1) that not only checks for Mac computer viruses, but also handles hardware and hard drive diagnosis. Here's a quick look at the basic feature set of TechTool Pro 3:

WARNING! Some features of this program will not work under the Mac OS X environment until an upgrade comes from the publisher. You can check your hard drive with TechTool Pro when booting from a Classic Mac OS or from the supplied CD startup disk. Or, you can use MicroMat's Mac OS X disk diagnostic and optimizing application, Drive 10, which works strictly under Mac OS X.

- *Hardware diagnostics*—Does the problem lie in the RAM, the hard drive, or the logic board? TechTool Pro runs your Mac through a full diagnostic to determine whether all the systems on your computer and its attached peripherals are functioning properly.

- *Hard drive diagnostics and repairs*—You can check a hard drive from Mac OS 9.x or after restarting from the supplied CD. This program can also optimize a hard drive, which may, in theory at least, speed up performance somewhat.

NOTE: MicroMat assured me that the latest updates to TechTool Pro 3 (3.0.7 as of this writing) would reliably analyze an HFS+ drive running Mac OS X when booted from a Classic OS or the CD. Volumes formatted in the UFS format aren't supported. If you have an older version of the

Immediate Solutions

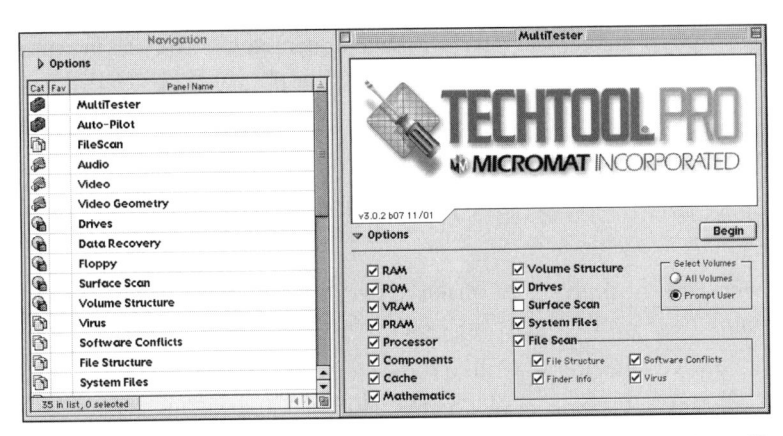

Figure 18.1 TechTool Pro performs a wide spectrum of analyses of your Mac.

program, contact the publisher about updates (any 3.x version can be updated free to a later 3.x version courtesy of a downloadable updater).

- *Software conflicts*—Although this problem is less of an issue under Mac OS X, the consequences of application or system extension conflicts have been the bane of the Mac user's experiences for years. This program can check your installation for possible problems and report on the steps you should take to eliminate them.

- *Virus scans*—This powerful component of TechTool Pro scans your Mac for the presence of viruses. As with the competition, you can opt to perform scans in the background as you use your Mac, and at scheduled intervals for more comprehensive scans. TechTool Pro can repair or move an infected file or just leave it alone (your decision). To speed performance, you can configure the program to scan only files that have not been previously checked. You can also check for online updates to address program changes and newly discovered virus strains, but this process isn't done automatically.

NOTE: *The sole feature lacking in the virus-detection component of TechTool Pro that I examined for this book was the ability to check for the presence of Word or Excel macro viruses. If you work with a reasonable number of files created in those programs, you may want to look elsewhere for virus protection.*

Intego's VirusBarrier

The newest entrant to the antivirus application arena comes from the publishers of NetBarrier, a firewall program that will be discussed later in this chapter, and several security-based utilities. VirusBarrier has a particularly unique user interface that puts configuration panels in a drawer that can be opened and closed as needed, as shown in Figure 18.2.

NOTE: Although I didn't have a chance to try a Mac OS X version of VirusBarrier in time to finish this book, the publisher assured me that the user interface and most or all of the features would run essentially the same in the Mac OS X native version.

Here are the features of VirusBarrier that will help provide the maximum degree of virus protection:

- *Simple interface*—Unlike the other programs described in this chapter, the Classic Mac OS version of VirusBarrier consists of just one file—a control panel—where all features are activated. The other programs are an amalgam of applications, control panels, system extensions, and so on. This doesn't mean they are any less effective or more complex to use, but it's something you should consider when making your purchase decision.

- *Automatic repairs*—You can opt to have infected files repaired automatically by the program, a feature that matches the capabilities of the other contenders. A system log will report on such episodes, so you can see what was fixed and why and also if the file couldn't be fixed.

- *NetUpdate*—This feature allows the program to scan the Internet for program upgrades on a regular basis, or whenever you want to do a manual check. If an update is available, it'll be downloaded automatically. Unlike other programs of this type, when new virus-detection capabilities are added, the control panel will sometimes (but not always) be updated, too.

Figure 18.2   Click a button to open a drawer that offers additional settings.

- *Doesn't intrude on software installations*—Although it's best to disable an antivirus program before performing a software installation, VirusBarrier is designed to allow such processes to run without interfering.

- *Doesn't affect boot or system performance*—Because virus scans may slow your Mac's performance, VirusBarrier promises fully transparent operation, so you won't notice its presence unless a virus infection is found. My personal experience with the Classic version showed this claim to be largely realized on the G4 hardware on which I tried it.

NOTE: *An older virus application should continue to function in the Classic environment under Mac OS X, but it will not provide automatic protection against viruses that may infect your new operating system or native applications.*

Network Associates' Virex

One of the older Mac virus-detection programs, Virex (see Figure 18.3), has had a checkered history as far as having a steady manufacturer is concerned. It has gone through several software publishers, finally ending up in the hands of the McAfee division of Network Associates. This should not, of course, deter you from buying Virex; it continues to be developed and supported with regular program and detection string updaters. The version shipping at the time this book was printed was 7.1, fully native to Mac OS X, which is being bundled with Apple's .Mac subscription service.

Here are the basic features of Virex:

- *Drag-and-drop scanning and cleaning*—Just select a file, folder, or disk icon, and drag it to the Virex application icon, and the scanning process will commence in short order. Depending on the preferences you set in the application, you'll be able to see which files might be infected, or automatically repair them to the limits of the technology.

- *Advanced cleaning*—This feature essentially tries to remove the infection from a file and restore it to its normal condition. Once again, it's not a feature that differs materially from the competition.

- *Checks for virus-like activities*—In addition to using detection strings to detect the presence of known virus strains, Virex can scan for what it considers to be virus-like activity. This way, Virex can help protect you against virus strains not already discovered.

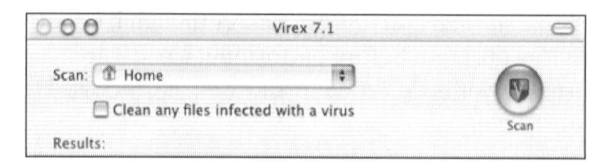

Figure 18.3 Virex continues to be updated to support newly discovered virus strains.

NOTE: *Virex 7 was released without a big publicity flourish from its publisher and may be difficult to find at the company's Web site. The easiest way to acquire a copy appears to be as part of Apple's .Mac subscription program.*

- *Frequent updates*—Virex is updated on a monthly basis, or more frequently if the need arises, to detect and repair the latest virus strains.

- *Command-line scanner*—If you want to get deeply involved with the Unix command line of Mac OS X, you can use the Terminal application to run on-demand scans or configure scheduled scanning runs.

- *Missing features*—Unfortunately, some of the features present in the Classic version of Virex are not part of Virex 7.. The most useful is background scanning, where the act of mounting a disk or launching a file causes Virex to check it for the presence of a virus. The scan-at-download feature, which checks files that you retrieve from the Internet or a network file share, also is not available, nor is a graphical interface for the scheduling operation. Background scanning can, if you're so inclined, be enabled via the Terminal application, as a *chron* task, but it's not a process for the faint of heart. The program's documentation explains how it's done.

Symantec's Norton AntiVirus

Once upon a time, the most popular Mac antivirus program was SAM, short for Symantec Anti-Virus Utilities for Macintosh. To keep the naming similar to the Windows version, the publisher reinvented the program as Norton AntiVirus. The version shipping when this book was printed, 8.0.2 (see Figure 18.4), runs fully native under Mac OS X.

The following is a brief list of the major features of Norton AntiVirus. If you're familiar with the Classic versions of this application, you'll find that many, but not all, of the key features are intact with the Mac OS X native release available at the time this book was written.

Immediate Solutions

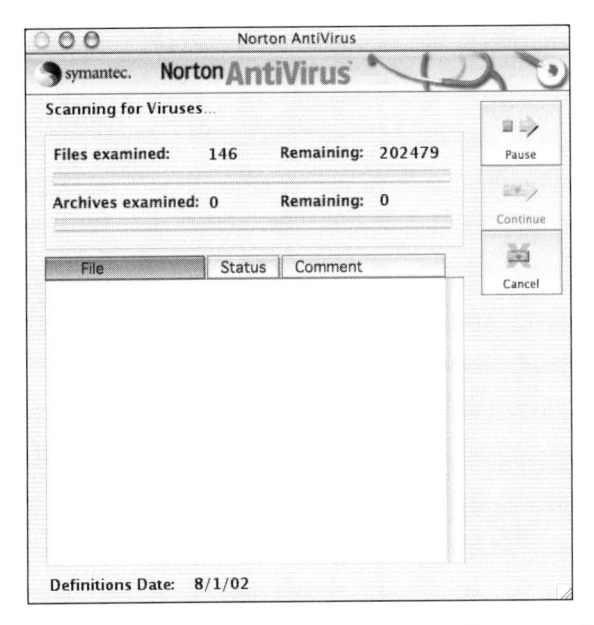

[Screenshot of Norton AntiVirus window showing "Scanning for Viruses..." Files examined: 146, Remaining: 202479, Archives examined: 0, Remaining: 0, Definitions Date: 8/1/02]

Figure 18.4 Norton AntiVirus in action, looking at my drive for potential virus infections.

- *Startup CD*—You can run Norton AntiVirus from its startup disk, which includes a bootable System Folder. This is the ultimate protection against a possible virus, because an infection can't contaminate a CD.

NOTE: As Apple releases new hardware, you'll need to order updated startup CDs for Symantec's utility products, so that they will start your Mac.

- *Automatic repair of infected files*—This option is in the program's preferences dialog box and is on by default. The application will automatically attempt to repair any file that's infected. The downside to such a feature is that it's not always perfect, and the removal of the virus strain may also damage the file so that it's not usable. This is always a good argument for having recent backups of all your critical files.
- *Checks of suspicious files*—This feature appeared first in SAM, the predecessor to Norton AntiVirus. It lets the program check for system activities that may indicate the presence of a computer virus. Several levels of protection can be configured in the program's preferences. Keep in mind, however, that if made too robust, this feature can cause a number of annoying error messages for tasks that really don't appear virus-like at all, such as

389

expanding a compressed file that contains a system extension that is not infected.

- *Checks of compressed files*—Even though a virus in a compressed file cannot infect your Mac unless the file is opened, Norton AntiVirus gives you the added ounce of protection to scan the files anyway. An ounce of protection, and all that.

- *Scans e-mail for potential virus infections*—Even though only one notable Mac e-mail virus has appeared as of the time this book was written, if you regularly communicate with Windows users, it's easy to accidentally transfer a virus that will infect their computers. This is your protection against that possibility.

- *LiveUpdate*—This feature is shared with another Symantec program, Norton Utilities. As a result, it will seek out updates for both programs in a single operation. You can configure it to access the Internet regularly in search of the updates or only when you want. This feature can be a godsend if you don't have the time to constantly monitor the Internet in search of the latest updates.

- *Missing in action*—As with Virex, certain features that were part and parcel of the Classic Mac OS version of Norton AntiVirus were not available in the first Mac OS X release. The most important of these features is scheduled scans, the ability to run a scanning operation at the times you select.

Using Apple's Mac OS X's Built-in Firewall

With so many folks getting always-on Internet services, it stands to reason that there is a far greater vulnerability to potential invasions from the Internet. Although this would seem a fairly unlikely source of trouble, there have been some well-publicized instances of so-called *denial of service* attacks, where personal computers are commandeered by Internet vandals and used to flood popular Web sites with meaningless data, which prevents real access by visitors to those sites.

Until now, those problems haven't affected Macs, but that doesn't mean our preferred computing platform is immune. Although large companies often seek hardware solutions to such problems in the form of network routers or dedicated hardware-based firewalls, some relatively inexpensive Mac programs can offer good protection for homes and small-business users.

Immediate Solutions

NOTE: *How bad is the risk? Well, many cable systems support equipment (including cable modems) that support the Data Over Cable Service Interface Specification (DOCSIS). Not only does it allow these services to use conventional cable modems you can buy at a computer or consumer electronics store, but also it encrypts the data flow from customers. This doesn't mean you are totally safe from Internet vandals, but it does reduce and usually eliminate the possibility that those who share your cable ISP's node can see your shared printers and disks. Vulnerability to denial of service attacks or similar invasions, however, still exists.*

Related solution:	Found on page:
Protecting Your Network from the Internet	209

Whether you use a cable or a DSL modem, you'll want to think seriously about enabling Jaguar's own firewall. Although this feature has always been available in Mac OS X, only with the 10.2 release did Apple offer an on/off switch. To enable the feature, simply follow these steps:

1. Launch System Preferences, and click on the Sharing preference panel.
2. Click the Firewall tab (see Figure 18.5).
3. If you want to allow a service to run despite the firewall, such as Mac or Windows file sharing and FTP access, click the appropriate On checkbox.

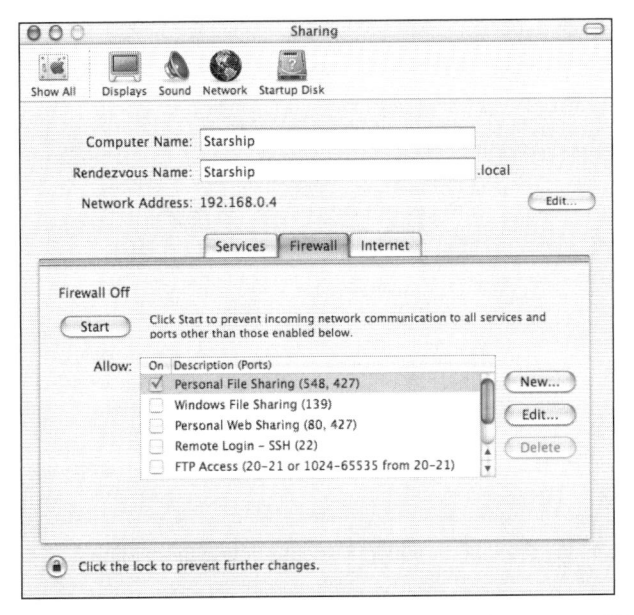

Figure 18.5   Configure Apple's firewall protection on your Mac.

18. Security and Mac OS X

391

4. Once configured, click the Start button to activate the firewall.

5. If you want to allow additional network access, such as instant messaging, networked backups via Retrospect or other functions, click the New button to configure the port to which you want to receive network traffic (see Figure 18.6).

6. Once a particular port name is chosen, the appropriate port will be selected. Click OK to store your settings.

7. If you want to turn off Jaguar's firewall, click the Stop button (it toggles to Start for the next activation).

8. To leave the System Preferences application, choose Quit from the File menu.

Choosing Personal Firewall Software

Although Mac OS X's firewall should provide good protection for most purposes, you may want more options to configure the service, such as logging intrusion attempts. If you want these advanced features, you'll find that several applications are available that will more than fulfill this need, and they are described in this section.

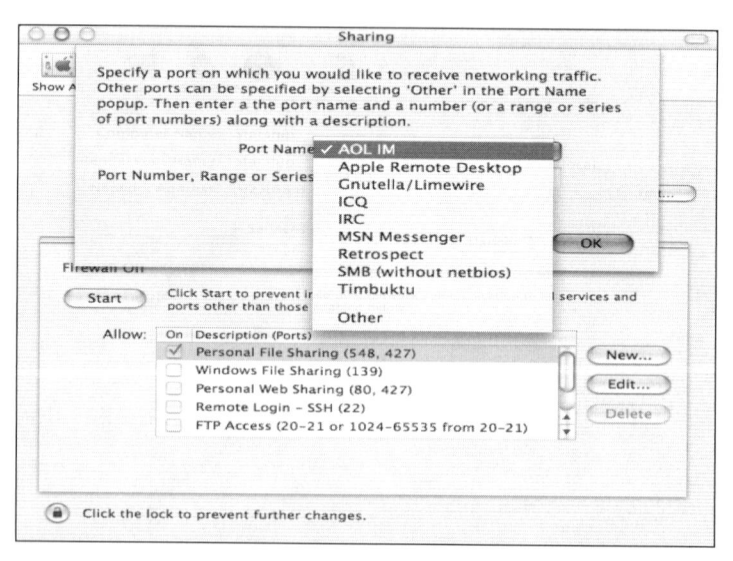

Figure 18.6   Choose the kind of network access you want to allow.

Immediate Solutions

Norton Personal Firewall

Open Door Networks, publisher of the Shareway IP software used by Apple Computer in Mac OS 9 to offer Internet-based file sharing, licensed its DoorStop software to Symantec. The result is Norton Personal Firewall (see Figure 18.7), a Mac OS X–native firewall application that offers simple, solid protection against attacks from Internet vandals. You can configure several elements of protection, from Internet-based connections to your Mac, to FTP file transfers. The program displays a warning if an attempt is made to connect to your Mac via the Internet (I get several of these a day when I'm connected via cable modem), and it logs all access attempts.

NOTE: Norton Personal Firewall is also available in bundled form as Norton Internet Security. The package also includes Norton AntiVirus and Aladdin Systems's iClean; the latter is a program that can clear cache files, cookies, and other files you may want to discard from your Mac's hard drive.

Intego's NetBarrier X

This program made Intego's reputation. NetBarrier (see Figure 18.8) shares a uniquely different interface with VirusBarrier. It lets you set

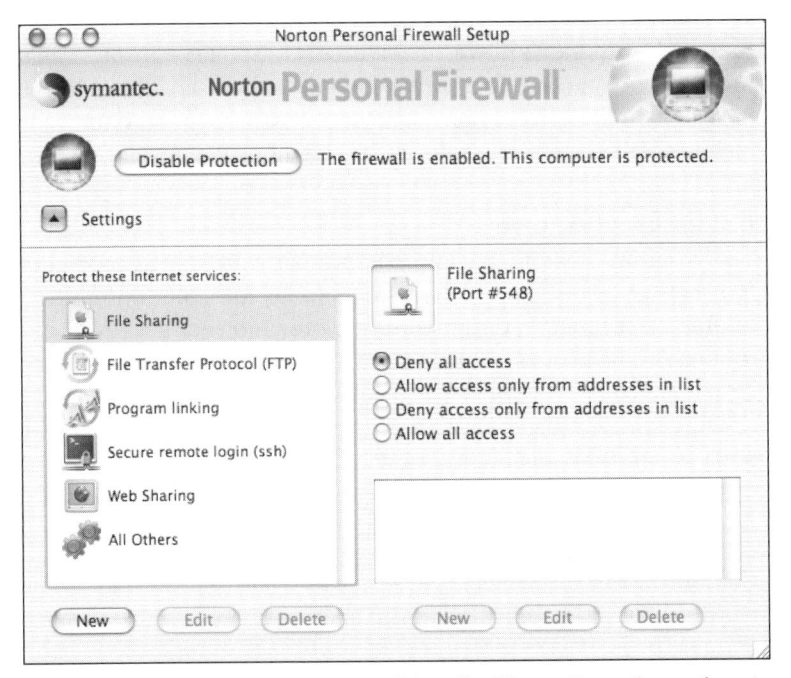

Figure 18.7 Norton Personal Firewall has flexible configuration options to ensure that you get the maximum level of protection against Net intruders.

18. Security and Mac OS X

393

Chapter 18   Security and Mac OS X

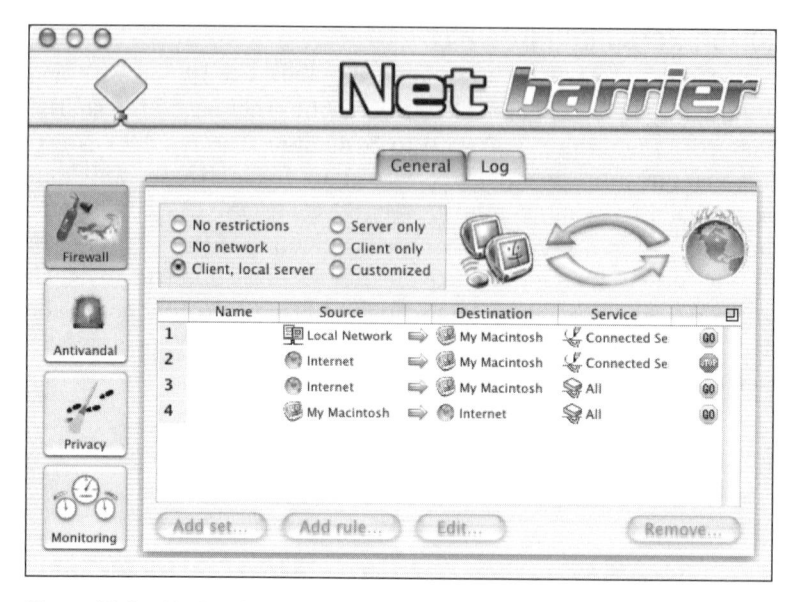

Figure 18.8   NetBarrier offers several levels of firewall protection

several levels of protection, depending on the level to which you want to limit access to and from your Mac via the Internet.

Among the program's powerful features is the ability to protect against browser plug-ins and Java applets that may house hostile code. It also provides built-in protections against access of personal information on your Mac, such as passwords and credit card information.

Intego's ContentBarrier

The programs described so far will protect your Mac against outside Internet-based invasions or virus infections. Intego's ContentBarrier, on the other hand, is designed to monitor Internet access. It works for both home users and businesses, by allowing you to filter content that might be unacceptable to those using your Mac. Additionally, you can block Internet access at specific times of the day so that children don't waste time surfing rather than doing their homework assignments and household chores. It also helps increase employee productivity, because less time is wasted on unproductive pursuits.

ContentBarrier also logs Internet access, and settings can be password protected, so only those with access privileges can change program settings.

Immediate Solutions

NOTE: *At the time this book was written, a Mac OS X compatible version of ContentBarrier wasn't available, but delivery was promised for the latter part of 2002.*

Firewalk X

Another option I'll mention, Firewalk X, a shareware application, is similar in concept to the other commercial programs, because it doesn't use Mac OS X's internal firewall. . Firewalk X offers a sophisticated range of configuration choices.

Like the commercial products, Firewalk X directs access to your Mac's ports and keep logs of attempts to penetrate your Mac's defenses. Setting up Firewalk X is quite easy, courtesy of its convenient setup assistant (see Figure 18.7), where you can select the level of protection you want.

As this book was written, the author, Mike Vannorsdel, assures us that the program will continue to be updated despite the presence of basic firewall access in Jaguar.

BrickHouse

Brian Hill's BrickHouse, also shareware, takes a somewhat more modest approach to firewall protection, by harnessing the built-in protection features of Mac OS X. However, its ability to keep tracking logs and built-in support for Mac OS X's Network Locations feature, makes it far more flexible. The author informs use that he expects to continue to update the program.

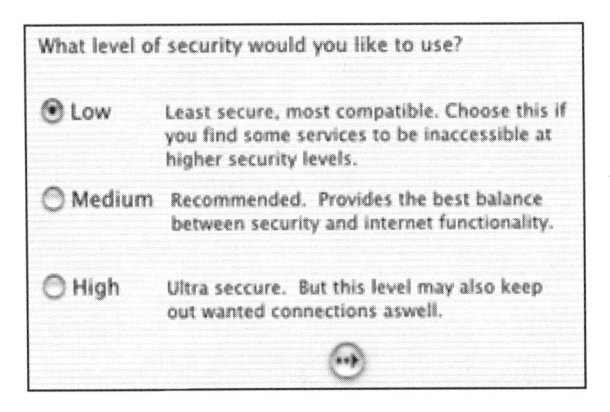

Figure 18.9   Firewalk X is a shareware firewall manager that helps you protect your Mac from Internet vandals.

395

Hardware Firewalls

Another route to firewall protection is hardware-based. Several Internet sharing hubs or switches work with your DSL or cable modem and distribute an ISP connection across your network. These products, from such companies as Asante, D-Link, MacSense, NetGear, and Proxim (formerly Farallon), and even the latest version of Apple's AirPort Base Station, include a feature called network address translation (NAT) firewall protection. With NAT activate, the IP numbers of the computers on your network are hidden, and thus outsiders cannot see them. This provides a high level of security.

Such routers offer other features, such as one or more ports for Ethernet hookups (Asante and Proxim have models with four ports, sufficient for most home office networks). Some even include a wireless capability, supporting the very same 802.11b protocol used by Apple's AirPort wireless networking system (which also includes NAT support in its latest software release).

---

*TIP: One way to test the resiliency of your firewall protection is to use a set of Web-based tools from Gibson Research called Shields Up. You can access the tools via **www.grc.com**. Although the company makes software primarily for the Windows platform, its Web-based firewall tests will function with the Classic Mac OS and Mac OS X.*

Chapter 19

Troubleshooting Mac OS X

If you need an immediate solution to:	See page:
Solving Mac OS X Installation Problems	402
Solving System Crashes and Freezes	405
The Application Won't Quit	405
Applications Refuse to Launch	406
The Classic Environment Fails to Run	407
Solving Network Access Failure	408
Login Window Shakes	408
Desktop Folder Contents Aren't Visible Under Mac OS 9.x	409
Mac OS X Can't Boot After You Deleted a File by Mistake	410
Solving Other Common Mac OS X Problems	411
Performing System-Level Disk Diagnostics	414
Setting Root Access	416
Monitoring System Use to Check for Conflicts	417

Chapter 19   Troubleshooting Mac OS X

In Brief

Unfortunate but true. Personal computers are a far cry from appliances, despite what the manufactures may tell you. It's a normal part of the life of every personal computer owner to have a program suddenly quit or to find the entire computer frozen, totally unable to function. Such problems are not restricted to users of either Macs or Windows-based PCs. They are both quite capable of failing at unexpected moments, usually when you need to complete an important document and time is short. In fact, it has been said that if your everyday automobile had the same reliability as your computer, you could barely make it to the supermarket without brakes failing or the car randomly stopping.

Long-term experience on a personal computer is littered with system troubleshooting, reinstallations, and endless searches for program updates that address one problem or another. Beginning with Mac OS 9, Apple introduced a System Update control panel that was designed to periodically check the company's support Web site in search of necessary system updates. Even third-party publishers have gotten into the act. Programs from Intego, Network Associates, and Symantec have built-in features to seek out updates.

NOTE: Another solution to the software update dilemma is UpdateAgent X from Insider Software (**www.insidersoftware.com/**), which is designed to locate all the updates you need and make them available to you in a simple user interface. Another file update alternative is VersionTracker Pro, an application provided by the folks who run the popular versiontracker.com Web site, a popular source of software upgrade information.

Mac OS X comes with the promise to liberate Mac users from regular diets of system-related troubles. Like Unix servers, which can run for days, weeks, or months (and sometimes years) without suffering breakdowns, the revolutionary new version of the Mac operating system is designed to be as resilient as possible to the trials and tribulations of daily computing.

Mac OS X's Crash-Resistant Features

Whether you surf the Internet, use heavy-duty graphics programs such as Adobe Photoshop or InDesign, or use database software that must perform a lot of sorting and organizing, sometimes your Mac will be susceptible to problems. Here's a look at what Mac OS X has to offer to provide greater reliability:

In Brief

- *Protected memory*—Every time you run a native application under Mac OS X, it gets its own memory partition, dynamically allocated by the operating system and walled off from other programs. Should that program quit or crash, the memory allocated to it is reallocated as part of the memory available to your Mac. You can continue to run your Mac safely without having to restart; try that under any previous version of the Mac OS without risking a serious crash. Although a Restart command is still available, now in the Apple menu, you will find yourself using Force Quit more often. Apple doesn't expect you to have to restart except when installing a new program or leaving Mac OS X to return to your Classic Mac OS.

NOTE: *As a matter of fact, shutdowns are seldom necessary with the newer Macs. You can use the Sleep command to have the Mac run in a super-low-power mode (using less power than a normal light bulb), ready to awaken in a second or two by a simple click of the mouse or by pressing any key on your keyboard.*

- *Advanced memory management*—Under previous versions of the Mac OS, an application received a specific portion of available memory. If this wasn't enough to run the program efficiently, you had to quit, open the Finder's Get Info window, and allocate more. In addition, if you didn't have enough free RAM to open a program, it would not run, or it would run so inefficiently that you risked poor performance, an out-of-memory error, or perhaps a system crash. Mac OS X dynamically allocates the memory a program needs and, if need be, provides virtual memory. Therefore, in theory, a program can never run out of memory.

NOTE: *Don't assume that a Unix-style virtual memory system is a panacea that has no downside. It's always better to have enough RAM to run a program—if the operating system has to use virtual memory instead, performance slows down and you'll see a spinning cursor when data has to be retrieved from your hard drive. Even though Apple recommends a minimum of 128MB of RAM for Mac OS X, having at least twice that amount delivers noticeably better performance. There's no free ride.*

- *Preemptive multitasking*—Can a superior way to manage multiple applications improve reliability? Very possibly. Some applications hog available processor time, making it difficult for other programs to run efficiently. Too many programs competing with one another can create the potential for a system crash. With Mac OS X, the operating system is the task or traffic manager, making performance better—sometimes much better—when multiple programs are performing complex tasks, such as downloading files, rendering a multimedia presentation, and printing at the same time.

NOTE: *One of the clever demonstrations Apple sometimes uses to show how resilient Mac OS X is involves running a special application that repeatedly attempts to crash the operating system while a movie trailer continues to play flawlessly.*

Keep in mind, however, that although Mac OS X is resilient and reliable, this doesn't mean that your Mac will never crash, or that programs will never quit. As long as software is written by human beings, the potential for conflicts exists. In the Immediate Solutions section, I'll show you how to cope with common problems and how to get the most reliable performance from your Mac.

The Software Update Application

Beginning with Mac OS 9, Apple added a useful new feature, Software Update. Similar to some third-party applications that search for updates, such as the LiveUpdate utility that ships with Symantec's Mac utility programs, Norton AntiVirus, Norton Utilities, and Norton SystemWorks, Apple's utility checks the system-related files on your hard drive and seeks out updates at Apple's support sites on the Internet.

This utility continues in essentially the same form under Mac OS X (see Figure 19.1), but has migrated to the System Preferences application. When you activate this pane, just click the Update Now button to have

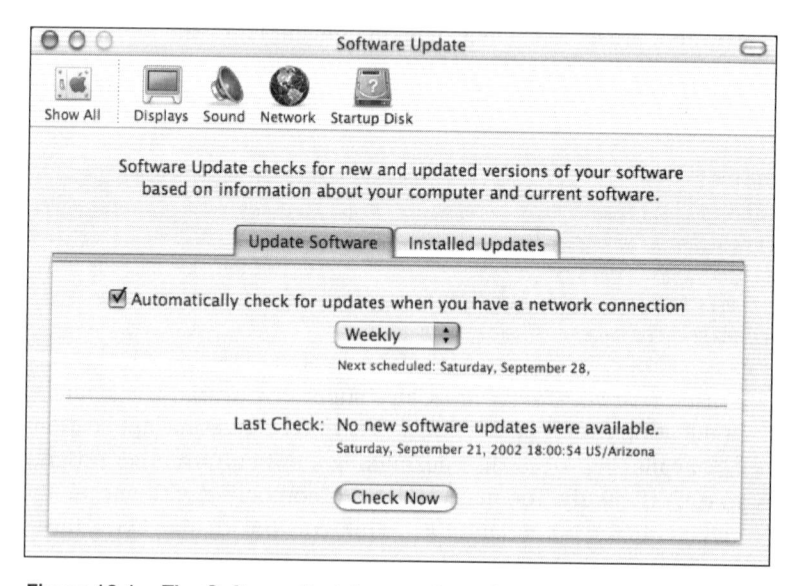

Figure 19.1 The Software Update pane from System Preferences will find needed Mac OS X updates for you.

In Brief

Software Update check Apple's Web site for updates. If they're available, they'll be listed in a dialog box. Check the ones you want, click the Install button, and the program takes care of the rest, from downloading to installing. Depending on whether an update is system related or application related, you may have to restart your Mac for the changes to take effect.

TIP: *It's a good idea to save a copy of the update installer. Right after an update has been downloaded and installed, while the System Update application is on your screen, click the Update menu, choose Save As, and select a location in the Save As dialog box for a copy of the update. Another method is to use the option to save the file to the desktop before you install it. Either way, you can easily access it in case of a system reinstallation and avoid a trip to the Internet to get it again.*

---

19. Troubleshooting Mac OS X

401

Chapter 19 Troubleshooting Mac OS X

Immediate Solutions

Solving Mac OS X Installation Problems

In Chapter 2, I covered the simple installation process for Mac OS X. For most users, everything should proceed normally. In some situations, you will encounter problems, warnings, or errors that prevent the process from continuing.

The following is a list of potential problems and solutions:

- *The firmware isn't up-to-date.* Recent Macs have a small updatable boot ROM that's used to start your computer and perform small diagnostic checks (on older Macs, upgrading isn't possible). This firmware is updated from time to time to address hardware-related problems. If you receive a warning that the Mac OS X installation cannot proceed until you install the update, visit Apple's support Web site and see which updates apply to your model. The update site is located at **www.info.apple.com/support/downloads.html**.

- *The hard drive cannot be repaired.* At the very start of the installation process, the Installer examines the target volume (the one on which you're installing Mac OS X). Minor directory damage will be fixed before the installation starts. If the damage cannot be fixed, you'll see a prompt on your screen about the problem. If this happens, the installation will stop dead in its tracks. At this point, you can try other options to repair the drive. After you restart in your Classic Mac OS environment, you can try using the version of Disk First Aid that came with the Classic Mac OS or one of the hard-drive diagnostic programs described in Chapter 2. Should none of these remedies succeed, your remaining choice is to consider backing up your files and formatting the drive. Unless the drive has a hardware problem, that final drastic step ought to take care of the trouble and allow you to install Mac OS X.

- *The hard drive cannot be updated.* During the installation process, the Installer attempts to update the hard disk device driver. If the drive is already formatted with Apple's Drive Setup utility, this step should not present a problem. Drive Setup works with any ATA-based drive and many SCSI drives. But if you have a hard drive that didn't come from Apple, it's highly likely that the drive was formatted with a different program, such as FWB's Hard Disk ToolKit or LaCie's Silverlining. You only need to make sure that the program used is compatible with Mac OS X. Otherwise, you should update the drive with the right version of your disk-formatting program. In these two cases, the message can be ignored.

WARNING! *It's not a good idea to ignore messages about drive problems or to allow installation on a drive not formatted with a Mac OS X–compatible utility. The consequences can be serious—damage to your hard drive's directory and possible loss of data.*

- *Your drive is not formatted correctly.* As I explained in Chapter 2, on a number of older Macs, such as the early iMacs and beige G3, you must put Mac OS X on a partition that occupies the first 8GB of the drive (it will appear first in your list of available volumes in the Mac OS X installer). If you've purchased a larger hard drive and divided up differently, you'll have to back up your files and reformat with the proper partition scheme. This is a hardware limitation of the models in question, so you're stuck. You have to obey the rules; I don't make them, I just report them.

- *Your Mac can't be restarted after installation fails.* When you run the Mac OS X Installer, it changes the Startup Disk selection so that it will boot from the new operating system. Should something happen to abort the installation, you need to change the setup manually. You can do so by starting your Mac with your Mac OS X CD. Just restart and hold down the C key to boot from the CD. Once you're running from the CD, the first installation screen will appear. Go to the Installer's application menu and choose Open Disk Utility. With Disk Utility launched, click the name of your target volume, and then click the Repair button. Let Disk Utility examine your Mac's hard drive for disk-related problems. If you get a clean bill of health or any drive problems are fixed, go ahead and reinstall Mac OS X. Should that installation fail, restart with your Mac OS 9.x CD, again holding down the C key. Locate the Startup Disk control panel (in the Utilities folder) and select your Classic Mac OS System Folder to restart your computer. At this point, you should consider backing up and reformatting your Mac's hard drive before attempting a new installation.

Chapter 19 Troubleshooting Mac OS X

WARNING! *I am assuming that before you began the installation, you verified that your Mac is compatible with Mac OS X and that it has the right amount of memory and storage space. Although it is possible to install Mac OS X on a non-supported model, and many users manage to do it successfully using such applications as XpostFacto, Apple will not provide any help if you attempt this method.*

- *You can't log in.* This is not as difficult as it may seem at first glance. Being a Unix-based operating system, Mac OS X expects you to enter the correct username and password unless the option to bypass the login panel is left selected in the Login pane of the System Preferences Application (this is the system default). If the problem affects an individual user of your Mac, you can log in as administrator, open the Users System Preferences panel, click the Password tab, and change the user's password. Should you be unable to access the administrator's account, restart with your Mac OS X CD by holding down the C key. When the Installer launches, go to the Installer's application menu and choose Reset Password. In the Password Reset application window, click the drive for which you want to reset the password, and then choose the name of the user whose password you want to reset from the pop-up menu. Type the new password in the first text field, and then verify it in the second. Click Save to store the new password and then quit the application. You'll be returned to the Installer application, where you can restart by quitting Installer and clicking the Restart button in the "Are you sure?" prompt. When you reboot your Mac, the new password should be in effect.

NOTE: *It's not uncommon for someone to activate the Caps Lock key by error, which means that the password would be typed in all caps. Look at the Caps Lock light on the keyboard to be sure when you're typing or creating a password.*

Related solution:	Found on page:
Installing Mac OS X	32

WARNING! *Since it is easy to restore a password with the installer disk, you should keep it locked and safe if you're in an office where security is important.*

- *Finder won't load at startup.* I ran into a situation such as this after restoring files from a first-generation iMac to a flat-panel model. Even Apple's experts at the "Genius Bar" at one of their own stores were stumped, although I discovered a Knowledge Base note about the solution later on (after I solved it). Mac OS X loads not only the fonts in the various Mac OS X Fonts folders, but the ones in the Classic Fonts folder as well. One of the fonts transferred from the old iMac to the Classic Fonts folder was damaged, somehow (although it worked on the old computer). When I rebooted under Mac OS 9 and removed the non-Apple fonts from the Fonts folder inside the Classic System Folder, I was able to restart under Mac OS X without further incident.

- *Installer quits at startup.* This problem has been reported may be caused by RAM that's defective our out of spec. The solution is to remove third-party memory and restore the RAM that shipped with the computer. Once Mac OS X is installed, you can restore the additional RAM. If you run into a problem with frequent system crashes, consider contacting the dealer or manufacturer from whom you bought the RAM about replacements. High quality memory upgrades usually come with a lifetime warranty.

Solving System Crashes and Freezes

You may have hoped that Mac OS X would represent salvation from constant system crashes, but in the real world, it doesn't work that way. From time to time, you will encounter programs that behave as badly as they did under Classic system versions, but you'll be able to exit far more safely under Mac OS X.

The following sections address some common problems and solutions.

The Application Won't Quit

Whether the Quit command is in its accustomed place in the application menu or in the File menu, as in Mac OS versions of old, you've hit a blank wall. The application won't quit. It seems to be active, and you may even be able to open, edit, and save documents, but you cannot quit the program.

The solution is the Mac OS Force Quit feature, done as follows:

1. Choose Force Quit from the Apple menu or press Command+Option+Escape.

2. On the Force Quit Applications dialog box that appears (see Figure 19.2), scroll to the application you want to quit. A non-responsive application will sometimes be listed in red.

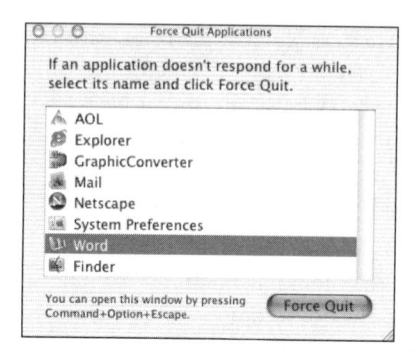

Figure 19.2 You can force quit one or more applications when this screen appears.

NOTE: *The new Force Quit feature, with its ability to selectively choose any open application, is not unique to Mac OS X. Even Windows works this way, with its End Task feature.*

3. Click Force Quit. The selected application will proceed to quit (well, usually).

After the application is forced to quit, you can continue to use your Mac in the normal fashion. Mac OS X's protected memory allows programs to crash or be forced to quit without affecting system stability. Now you can try running the application again and see if it works all right. If it still misbehaves, you should contact the publisher for technical assistance.

NOTE: *On some rare occasions, you may need to force quit an application twice before the action "takes." Such are the vagaries of software bugs even with an industrial-strength operating system.*

WARNING! *If a Classic application freezes, it's best to force quit the Classic environment instead, because it is apt to become unstable otherwise. Classic applications do not take advantage of Mac OS X's robust system protection features. When you launch your next Classic application, Classic will come along for the ride. If you have open documents from a Classic application, however, you'll want to close those applications first before attempting to force quit Classic. Otherwise, you'll lose any unsaved changes to those documents.*

Applications Refuse to Launch

If the problem you encounter involves just a single application, try launching it again. If that doesn't work, you might need to reinstall the application.

Immediate Solutions

If all your applications fail to run, however, restart your Mac and try again. Usually the restart will fix the problem. If the problems persist, contact the publisher of the software updates for Mac OS X.

NOTE: *If a number of applications that are supposed to be compatible with Mac OS X fail to launch, you should consider reinstalling Mac OS X. You can do this without losing your existing system settings or installed documents and software. Just use Jaguar's Archive and Install option, and check Preserve Users and Network Settings to keep your configuration essentially intact. I cover the entire installation process in glorious detail in Chapter 2.*

The Classic Environment Fails to Run

Do you have Mac OS 9.1 or later installed? The Classic feature simply doesn't support any earlier version of the Mac OS. In addition, many third-party system enhancements won't run in this setting. The best way to run a Classic System Folder is to configure it to be lean and mean. I cover the subject in more detail in Chapter 15.

NOTE: *The Classic environment works best with Mac OS 9.2.1 or later (9.2.2 was the version shipping at the time this book was written). In addition to offering better performance, improved boot time, and improved stability, some of the Classic quirks (such as the missing-cursor symptom) are eliminated, so it's worth updating from, say, 9.1.*

If setting up an Apple-only System Folder fails to resolve the startup problem, consider reinstalling your Classic Mac OS using the original system CD that came with Mac OS X (the most recent full Installer) or your Mac. If you have applied a system update, you'll need to do a clean installation (click Option on the first Installer screen), and then apply any system updates you've received. Don't forget that when you do a clean installation of your Classic Mac OS, you'll also have to transfer your system settings (for your ISP and Internet software) and third-party software from your older or previous System Folder to your newly installed System Folder.

NOTE: *Beginning with the Power Macs that shipped in August, 2002, there is no custom installer for Mac OS 9. It's strictly a part of the System Restore application that is used with your Restore CDs.*

Related solution:	Found on page:
Getting Reliable Performance from Classic Applications	328

407

Solving Network Access Failure

Although Mac OS X has enhanced networking capability, that doesn't mean everything will work perfectly all the time. Here are some ways to handle common network problems:

- *Settings don't change.* You do not have to restart your Mac whenever you switch network configurations, but doing so doesn't hurt. In addition, you may want to redo the settings in the Network pane of the System Preferences application, just in case you missed something the first time out. Chapter 8 has more information on this subject.

- *Networked Macs and printers are not available.* Reopen your Network pane and make sure AppleTalk is turned on and you've given your Mac a name that's unique on your network. If everything is properly configured, check your network cables and hub configuration. Also make sure the other Macs on the network can recognize your Mac or other devices on the network. If other Macs encounter similar problems, complete network troubleshooting is in order. For a large system, you should contact your network administrator for further assistance.

- *Windows networking software doesn't run.* If you're using such programs as Thursby Systems' DAVE or MacSOHO, you should contact the publisher directly about support for Mac OS X. Or just use Jaguar's built-in Windows networking features, which are described further in Chapter 8.

Related solution:	Found on page:
Correcting Network Access Problems	207

Login Window Shakes

If you enter a username and password and the window shakes when you try to log in, it means the name or password you entered is not correct. The solution is to reenter the login information and make sure each keystroke is accurate. If the symptom happens with another user, you may need to reset his or her password.

Here's how to do it:

Immediate Solutions

1. Login under your Administrator's account.
2. Launch System Preferences, and then open the Accounts pane.
3. If it's closed, click the padlock icon and enter your administrator username and password.
4. Click the name of the user whose password you want to change, click the Edit User button. The dialog shown in Figure 19.3 appears.
5. Enter the new password, and click Save to store the settings.
6. Choose Quit from the System Preferences Application menu, or press Command+Q.
7. If necessary, log out again and log in under that user's new password.

Desktop Folder Contents Aren't Visible Under Mac OS 9.x

You place a file or folder on Mac OS X's desktop, but when you reboot under Mac OS 9.x, the item is not there. What's wrong?

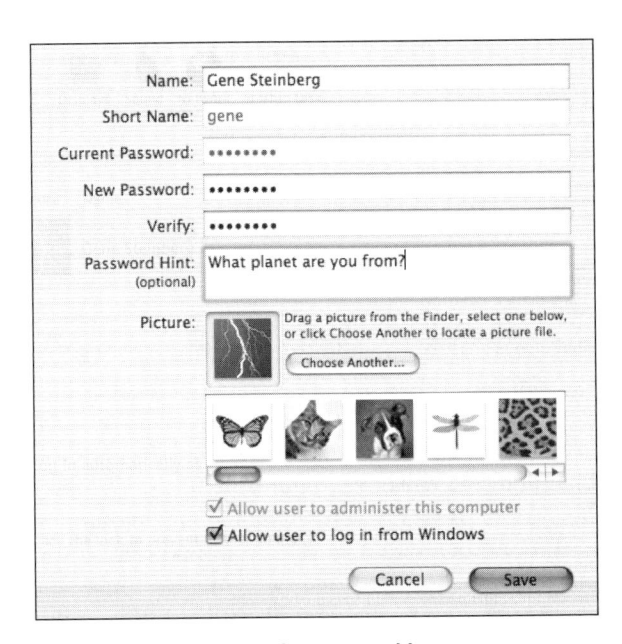

Figure 19.3   Edit a user's password here.

409

The answer is that the desktops for the two operating systems are totally separate. The contents of one are not mirrored on the other.

If you've installed Mac OS X on the same volume as Mac OS 9.1, you'll find a workable solution. There's an alias on your Mac's hard drive labeled Desktop (Mac OS 9). When you open that folder, you'll see a folder that contains all of your Classic Mac OS desktop items. If the desktop is on another drive, just access that drive from a Finder window, and you'll see a folder labeled Desktop that contains the items you want.

Mac OS X Can't Boot after You Deleted a File by Mistake

When you run your Mac under Mac OS 9, by default you'll see the following files at the top or root level of the hard drive on which Mac OS X is installed (plus any additional files or folders you've placed on the top level of the drive):

- Applications
- Applications (Mac OS 9)
- Library
- mach
- mach.sym
- mach_kernel
- System
- System Folder
- Users

If you delete something from the Mac OS X Applications folder, that application is no longer available. In addition, deleting a user's folder removes that user from the system. Do not attempt to remove any of the files labeled *mach*, or the files in the folder labeled *Library* or *System*, because removal will probably keep Mac OS X from running. Should the worst happen, you will have to run your Mac OS X Installer CD to reinstall the system. If you haven't installed any maintenance updates (such as the one from 10.2 to 10.2.1, and so on), you can perform a 'regular installation to preserve your system-related settings. Otherwise use the Archive & Install option. I cover all this in complete detail in Chapter 2.

Immediate Solutions

NOTE: No Archive & Install option? If you have an "Upgrade" rather than an "Installer" CD set for Mac OS X, the kind usually provided when you order an "Up-To-Date" package from Apple, you will have to upgrade from an earlier version of Mac OS X. You won't be able to do a clean install.

Solving Other Common Mac OS X Problems

Here are other problems you might encounter with Mac OS X. They usually have solutions, but some may not be as easy as you'd prefer:

- *Your Mac experiences kernel panic.* Shortly after your Mac starts, you see a message in English and several other languages, stating "A problem has occurred and you need to restart your computer. To do this, hold down the Power key for several seconds." What's wrong? This is due to a system-level crash of some sort, and you've been exposed to what is known as a kernel panic, since it affects the core of the operating system. Usually things will be all right after restart. If not, you'll need to force a second restart, using the appropriate reset key on your Mac or by following the direction to hold down the power key.

- *The screen remains dark when booting from the Installer CD.* Mac OS X only supports graphics cards and chips from ATI Technologies, IX Micro, and NVIDIA. If you're using a graphics card from a company such as Formac, contact the manufacturer directly about a Mac OS X–compatible version.

NOTE: If you are using a Voodoo graphic card from 3dfx Interactive, you may be out of luck. With the departure of the company after selling its assets to rival NVIDIA, the likelihood that driver updates will be produced are very slim, although several independent developers were working on drivers when this book was written. Fortunately, Mac OS X–compatible graphics cards are not terribly expensive. The ATI Radeon 7000, which outdoes the fastest Voodoo card in virtually all respects, was selling for less than $129 when this book was written. In addition, Formac informs me that their ProFormance3 card is compatible with Mac OS X, although it doesn't provide 3D acceleration (which is, in essence, the core of the Mac OS X graphical experience).

- *The printer isn't recognized.* Mac OS X should recognize most laser printers. However, ink jet printers and some USB-based laser printers may require special drivers to work. Drivers for such makes as Canon, Epson, HP, and Lexmark ink jets are provided with Mac OS X. You'll need to contact the manufacturer about the availability of driver updates for unsupported models. If none are available, the devices will work only for Classic applications.

411

- *The scanner doesn't scan.* This issue is the same as the printer not being recognized. It is up to the manufacturer to deliver a device driver that will function. Out of the box, Jaguar's Image Capture application supports a small number of consumer and SOHO models from Epson. If you cannot locate a Mac OS X–compatible version for a specific make and model, you should see if the software for a similar product in the manufacturer's line runs. Quite often, scanner drivers recognize a number of different models.

TIP: *One possible solution if your scanner maker doesn't have a Mac OS X driver is a shareware program, VueScan, from Hamrick Software (**www.hamrick.com**). This nifty application comes in versions for the Classic Mac OS, Mac OS X, Windows, and even Linux, and supports dozens of flatbed and slide scanners from all the major makers, such as Agfa, Epson, HP, Microtek, and Umax.*

- *You cannot burn a CD.* Mac OS X supports a number of third-party FireWire and USB CD burners in addition to Apple's own drives. This support allows you to use the Finder-level CD burning feature with a number of mechanisms. But a number of drives aren't supported (and this is especially true for SCSI-based CD burners), in which case, you'll have to ask the manufacturer of the product about Mac OS X–savvy software. Or, just reboot under your Classic Mac OS.

TIP: *Roxio's Toast 5.2 and CharisMac's Discribe 5 both support CD burning under Mac OS X. These product will recognize most any CD or DVD burner, including Apple's.*

- *Documents won't print.* You send a document to the printer, and the Print Center icon appears in the Dock. But it disappears just as quickly, and your document hasn't printed. The first thing to check is your print queue. To do that, launch Print Center (it's in the Utilities folder), and double-click on the printer's name from the Printer List window. If you see a toolbar icon labeled Start Jobs in the print queue window, the one that bears the name of your printer, click it. It means that the print queue was stopped for some reason. Usually this will fix the problem (it has to be checked for each printer you use). If this doesn't work, try turning the printer off and on, recheck printer cables and, if all else fails, check with the maker's Web site or versiontracker.com for updated drivers.
- *You can't use a digital camera.* Apple's Image Capture and iPhoto applications support a wide variety of cameras from most major makers. If your device isn't supported, check with the manufacturer about what options you might have with regard to image capture software.

Immediate Solutions

- *Input device features are not recognized.* Mac OS X has built-in support for the second button and the scroll wheel on some input devices, but others require special software. You'll need to contact the publisher about compatibility issues.

- *Not all drives are recognized.* Mac OS X provides standard support for many popular removable and fixed storage devices, such as Imation and Iomega drives and devices from EZQuest, LaCie, Maxtor, OWC, QPS and SmartDisk. If the product you want to use won't run, the manufacturer is your best resource for assistance.

NOTE: *If your storage device is connected courtesy of a SCSI adapter card, contact the maker of the card about Mac OS X support. Not all products will run, and some may require the installation of a new ROM chip to function properly.*

- *You can't install Classic applications.* If you get a message that you don't have the proper access privileges for such an installation, you will need to log in as administrator of your Mac to perform such an installation. Another route is to restart under your Classic Mac OS.

- *The Dock freezes.* On occasion, the Dock may fail to work, or open applications will not have the telltale arrow beneath their icon. Unfortunately, the Dock isn't recognized in the Force Quit window, so you can't quit it that way. The solution is to locate the Process Viewer application in the Utilities folder. With Process Viewer launched (see Figure 19.4), locate and select Dock. Now choose Quit Process from the Processes menu, and then choose Quit in the Quit Process dialog box. Within seconds, the Dock will disappear and relaunch itself, after which it should run normally. If it doesn't, restart your Mac.

- *You can't delete a file.* When you try to empty the trash, you get a message that the trash is in use, or that you don't have permission to zap a file. If this happens, remove the item from the Trash, and, with the item selected, call up the Finder's Get Info window. Use the Ownership & Permissions feature to make sure that your user name is listed as owner of the file. You may have to OK a password prompt first, though. If that doesn't work, put the item back in the trash, locate the Terminal application in the Utilities folder and launch it. With Terminal open, type "sudo rm –rf .Trash" and press Return. Enter your administrator's password and press Return again. All the files in the Trash will be discarded (although you may have to open and close a Trash window to see the empty icon).

413

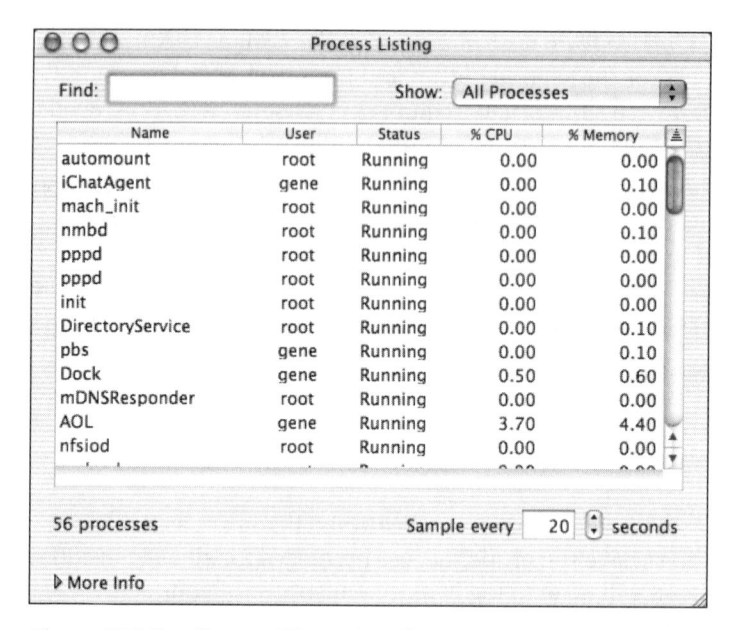

Name	User	Status	% CPU	% Memory	
automount	root	Running	0.00	0.00	
iChatAgent	gene	Running	0.00	0.10	
mach_init	root	Running	0.00	0.00	
nmbd	root	Running	0.00	0.10	
pppd	root	Running	0.00	0.00	
pppd	root	Running	0.00	0.00	
init	root	Running	0.00	0.00	
DirectoryService	root	Running	0.00	0.10	
pbs	gene	Running	0.00	0.10	
Dock	gene	Running	0.50	0.60	
mDNSResponder	root	Running	0.00	0.00	
AOL	gene	Running	3.70	4.40	
nfsiod	root	Running	0.00	0.00	

Figure 19.4 Use Process Viewer to quit a system process that isn't recognized by the Force Quit function, such as the Dock.

TIP: A quick way to fix permissions problems with Mac OS X files is to use Disk Utility. With the program open, click on the First Aid tab, select your startup drive, and click on Repair Disk Permissions. In almost every case, you'll see a few permissions fixed, but sometimes there will be a long list. Regardless, with permissions fixed, you should no longer run into problems deleting and moving files that are not in Mac OS X's System folder. It doesn't hurt to restart after permissions are repaired, but it isn't required.

WARNING! As with any Terminal action, there's no opting out. When you engage a command, the Unix core of Mac OS X will do the deed—and that, as they say, is that. Also, be sure to allow a short time for all files to be deleted before quitting Terminal; otherwise some files may still be there when you recheck the Trash.

Performing System-Level Disk Diagnostics

The arrival of Mac OS X brings with it a tremendous number of changes in the way your Mac runs. Although some functionality will no doubt change further as Mac OS X continues to be developed, there will be some constants, such as the underlying Unix core, which are just waiting to be explored by power users who want to see what makes the new system tick.

Immediate Solutions

Hard-disk management is done with a new, combined application called Disk Utility, found in the Utilities folder. It combines Disk First Aid and Drive Setup. Unfortunately, the version offered with Mac OS X cannot examine or repair damage to your startup drive. Although your drives are checked every time you boot your Mac, as an ounce of prevention, you can also perform a disk diagnostic by rebooting with your Mac OS X CD and accessing Disk Utility from the Installer's application menu. If you don't have your system CD readily at hand, here's another alternative—a disk-checking process that allows you to explore the depths of Mac OS X and have your Mac run in a fashion you never expected.

Here's what to do:

NOTE: *There's no way to provide illustrations of this process with the standard screen shot. The information provided, however, should be clear enough. Don't be alarmed by what you see; this is the way Mac OS X is designed. Just bear in mind that doing a disk repair from the command line is no more effective than running Disk Utility on a drive. However, it is a useful exercise if you want to explore the depths of Mac OS X.*

1. Restart your Mac.
2. As soon as the restart process begins, press Command+S. What you see is only vaguely reminiscent of the DOS prompt accessed under Microsoft Windows. You see a true Unix command line, and if you thought DOS looked different, it doesn't hold a candle to what you see here.
3. With the command line displayed, a mélange of text appears. At the bottom of the text is a **localhost#** prompt. Type the following command (and don't forget the space before the hyphen [-]):

```
fsck -y
```

4. Press Return. Over the next minute or two, a series of status messages appear that are not dissimilar from those you'd see in Disk First Aid. These messages indicate the progress of the disk check. You'll also see an indication that the disk is being repaired, if this is necessary. When the disk check is finished, the **localhost#** prompt returns.
5. It's time to restart and return to the comfort of the familiar Aqua interface. Type the following:

```
reboot
```

415

Chapter 19 Troubleshooting Mac OS X

6. Press Return. The screen darkens, and the Mac's startup chord sounds. Then the familiar Mac OS X startup screen appears.

NOTE: *I remember a line that Sean Connery uttered in one of the early James Bond movies when he was shown something unexpected during one of his save-the-world trips: "Shocking."*

Setting Root Access

Some Mac OS X installations may require that you access the root or top level of your system under the Terminal application. Usually the administrator's password is sufficient to gain this access, but the password will be rejected unless you enable this feature.

To solve this problem, follow these steps:

1. Go to the Utilities folder and launch the NetInfo Manager application (see Figure 19.5).

2. Go to the Domain menu, choose Security, and select Authenticate from the submenu.

3. In the password prompt, enter the administrator's username and password and then click OK.

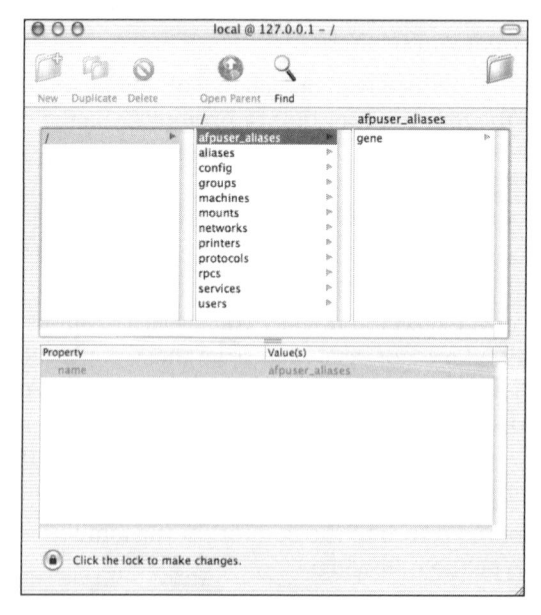

Figure 19.5   The NetInfo Manager is a useful network administrator's tool.

Immediate Solutions

4. With access gained, return to the Security command in the Domain menu and choose Enable Root User from the submenu.

5. Enter the password for the root user in the password prompt and then reenter it when requested. When it's entered, root access will be enabled or reset for your Mac, and you'll be able to use the full scope of available administration tools.

WARNING! Some Unix mavens say enabling root access presents a security risk, so use this process only as a last resort. Most users of Mac OS X will never need to use this feature.

Monitoring System Use to Check for Conflicts

Although Mac OS X may is an extremely robust operating system, it isn't perfect, and many applications are less so. From time to time you'll need to examine how your Mac is running to help a software publisher find the source of a conflict.

Here's a way to see how programs are using system and memory resources, using the Terminal application:

1. Go to the Utilities folder and launch Terminal.

2. With Terminal open, type the command "top""and press the Return key. You'll see an interactive display showing how resources may be using CPU or RAM on your Mac (see Figure 19.6). This information can help a software publisher see if there's the potential for trouble.

3. Launch Console, also located in the Utilities folder. This program will display a log of system activities (see Figure 19.7) that a publisher can use to trace the possible cause of a crash or other performance problem. The log can be saved or printed for later review.

NOTE: If your Mac is the victim of a kernel panic, information about it and what brought it about will appear in the log.

TIP: Like other Unix-based operating systems, Mac OS X is designed to perform system maintenance and update processes between 3:00 A.M. and 5:00 A.M. each day. The process includes updating and cleaning out system database and log files. If your Mac isn't running at that hour, you may find that performance dips over time, or the logs become huge. One solution to this dilemma is a freeware application, MacJanitor, which can

Chapter 19 Troubleshooting Mac OS X

manually run all those maintenance processes. You can download a copy from the author's Web site at **http://personalpages.tds.net/~brian_hill**. The author assures us that Mac OS X, through version 10.2, still performs these basic maintenance operations.

```
Terminal — tcsh (ttyp2)
Processes:  60 total, 2 running, 58 sleeping... 159 threads        09:58:25
Load Avg:  0.77, 0.52, 0.40    CPU usage:  11.1% user, 5.1% sys, 83.8% idle
SharedLibs: num =    7, resident = 1.82M code, 196K data, 548K LinkEdit
MemRegions: num = 8093, resident =   194M + 9.96M private,    229M shared
PhysMem:  84.2M wired,  369M active,  395M inactive,  848M used,  176M free
VM: 4.18G + 3.62M   48158(3) pageins, 42879(0) pageouts

  PID COMMAND      %CPU   TIME     #TH #PRTS #MREGS RPRVT   RSHRD   RSIZE   VSIZE
 8672 top          6.9%  0:00.23    1    14     18  284K+   288K+   580K+   13.6M
 8671 tcsh         0.0%  0:00.02    1    10     15  340K    540K    784K    5.73M
 8670 login        0.0%  0:00.27    1    12     33  240K    340K    564K    13.7M
 8669 Terminal     0.8%  0:00.55    3    59    133  1.22M+  9.55M+  6.20M+  111M
 8664 writeconfi   0.0%  0:00.07    1    16     19  236K    556K    1.16M   14.0M
 8663 Image Capt   0.0%  0:00.06    1    38     35  276K    1.05M   1.05M   78.8M
 8662 TWAINBridg   0.0%  0:00.86    2    49    108  840K    8.07M   3.44M   107M
 8660 SystemUISe   0.8%  0:01.88    2   150    141  1.23M   7.49M   3.44M   107M
 8659 Snapz Pro    0.8%  0:09.14    2   122    155  10.4M   21.1M   23.0M   141M
 8648 System Pre   0.0%  0:03.45    3    86    169  3.27M   10.6M   8.25M   113M
 8647 GraphicCon   0.0%  0:03.23    1    55    134  3.52M+  12.9M   7.59M   116M
 8606 Microsoft    0.0%  0:01.17    2    71    124  2.08M+  9.16M   4.43M+  110M
 8605 Microsoft    9.5%  3:55.72    6   141    372  20.4M+  68.0M   36.7M   216M
 8453 pppd         0.0%  0:00.22    1     8     16   60K    468K    156K    13.7M
 8452 pppd         0.0%  0:00.06    1    14     16   72K    468K    480K    13.7M
```

Figure 19.6 Terminal is used to access Mac OS X's Unix core directly.

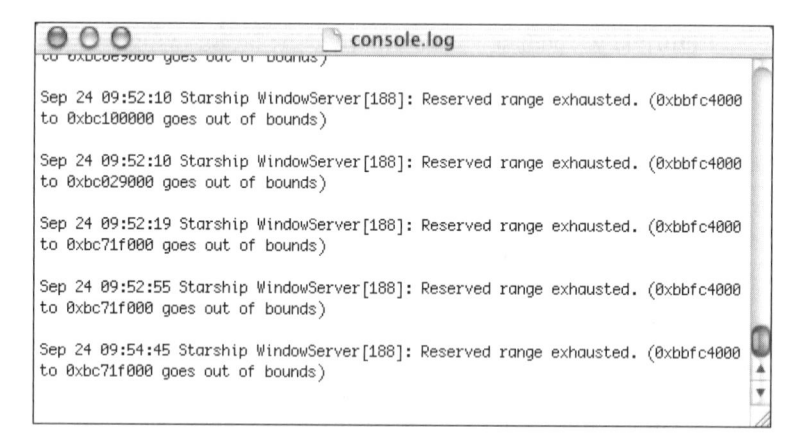

```
console.log
to 0xbc0e9000 goes out of bounds)

Sep 24 09:52:10 Starship WindowServer[188]: Reserved range exhausted. (0xbbfc4000
to 0xbc100000 goes out of bounds)

Sep 24 09:52:10 Starship WindowServer[188]: Reserved range exhausted. (0xbbfc4000
to 0xbc029000 goes out of bounds)

Sep 24 09:52:19 Starship WindowServer[188]: Reserved range exhausted. (0xbbfc4000
to 0xbc71f000 goes out of bounds)

Sep 24 09:52:55 Starship WindowServer[188]: Reserved range exhausted. (0xbbfc4000
to 0xbc71f000 goes out of bounds)

Sep 24 09:54:45 Starship WindowServer[188]: Reserved range exhausted. (0xbbfc4000
to 0xbc71f000 goes out of bounds)
```

Figure 19.7 Console logs system operations and is a useful tool to diagnose software conflicts.

Part IV
Taking Mac OS X Online

Chapter 20

A Fast Introduction to Mac OS X's Unix Environment

If you need an immediate solution to:	See page:
A Short List of Popular Command-Line Features	428
Using Mac OS X's Command-Line FTP Software	431

Chapter 20　A Fast Introduction to Mac OS X's Unix Environment

In Brief

Believe it or not, deep within the bowels of Mac OS X exists what some might regard as another universe. To enter this Twilight Zone of the operating system, you need only launch a simple application and enter a few text-based commands.

NOTE: *I'd like to give special thanks to my friend, and colleague, Pieter Paulson, for his immense help in writing this chapter.*

So far in this book, you've seen a glimmer of this strange new world, as I've shown you command line solutions to a few vexing problems with Mac OS X. For the most part, however, access to Darwin, the Unix core of Mac OS X, is optional. Apple includes a rich set of graphical tools that you can use to access many of the features you need to configure and manage your Mac. In addition, Unix mavens the world over have been toiling day and night to provide pretty Aqua front ends to hidden features and present them as system extras that can add additional Dock positioning choices, text smoothing and other interesting possibilities.

Although previous versions of the Mac OS have limited command line excursions to such utilities as ResEdit, the Terminal application (see Figure 20.1) located in the Utilities folder is far more powerful and encompassing. Terminal gives anyone with administrative access to a Mac direct control of the command line interface and the ability to harness the power of Unix to move files, manage services, and tell the computer how to function.

NOTE: *Even if you don't have administrator's access, you'll be able to do some things in Terminal, but you will be limited to commands that encompass your limited access level.*

When you first launch Terminal, you may think for a moment that you've entered the world of that other command-line operating system, DOS. No, you are seeing Unix in all its glory. With Terminal open, you'll see your username followed by a percent sign (%). This is the first stop on your voyage into the world of the command-line interface (CLI). If you've lived your life in the graphical user interface world, a CLI takes some getting used to. More to the point, it is far less forgiving than the safe, graphical world Aqua provides. When you engage a command, there

In Brief

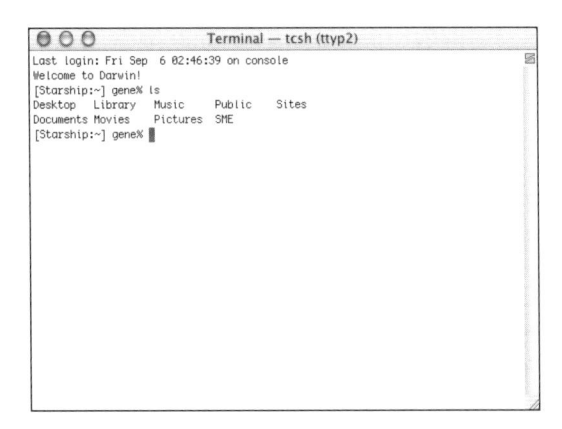

Figure 20.1 Apple's Terminal application is your "star gate" to the world of Unix.

will be no turning back—no prompt giving you the chance to opt out. So, until you learn the lay of the land, proceed with caution.

When you get used to typing a command rather than pointing and clicking, you may find that the using the CLI is far faster for some functions. However, it requires a lot more attention to detail, because every keystroke you type is a literal request to do something.

NOTE: *This section is strictly meant as a UNIX primer for readers who haven't explored the other side of Mac OS X. If you are already well-versed in UNIX terminology and commands, you'll have no trouble adapting to Mac OS X's command line.*

Looking at the Nuts and Bolts of Darwin

Terminal is a shell interface. A shell program offers a set of utilities and commands that let you write executable scripts to automate certain tasks, much like AppleScript. Shells also act as the buffer between you and the bare operating system, making your life a bit easier.

When you launch Terminal, you access the tcsh shell. This is one of the more popular shell programs and is a good choice for most users. If you're experienced in the Unix environment, you'll be pleased to know that such shells as zsh, csh, bash, and plain old sh are also available in Mac OS X. Each of these shells has its fans and detractors, but a description of the plusses and minuses of these programs is way beyond the scope of this book. If you are interested in exploring the Unix environment in more detail, you should read a library reference work on Unix.

423

Chapter 20   A Fast Introduction to Mac OS X's Unix Environment

The first thing you'll see in Terminal is the ubiquitous % that indicates you are running tcsh. From this prompt, you can type in the first command. We'll start with a command that lets you examine the contents of your personal Users file and folder directory: **ls**.

> **WARNING!** When I say that Unix is literal minded, I'm very serious. You need to be careful when you type commands and filenames, because every character must be accurate. Unix is also case sensitive. An extreme example of the consequences of a mistake was Apple's original release of iTunes 2 in 2001. A basic syntax error resulted in the loss of data from a small number of hard drives belonging to folks who installed the software. Fortunately, Apple realized its mistake and released a fixed installer, and also provided help (and sometimes reimbursement for drive recovery) to folks who lost data. However, it's just as easy for you to wipe out the contents of your drive if you do the wrong thing, so the watchwords are "be careful."

When you have typed "ls-", press the Return key to execute the command. Looking at the results, you should see a list of all the files and folders in the current directory.

OK, that's a good start. Now, to take things a bit further, perhaps you'd like to see a list of all the files, their security settings, and such interesting data as file size and commercial and modification dates. To do so, add the –l switch or modifier to the **ls** command, just as we did in Figure 20.2.

Just type "ls –l" and press Return. You should now see an expanded list showing the number of files in each folder.

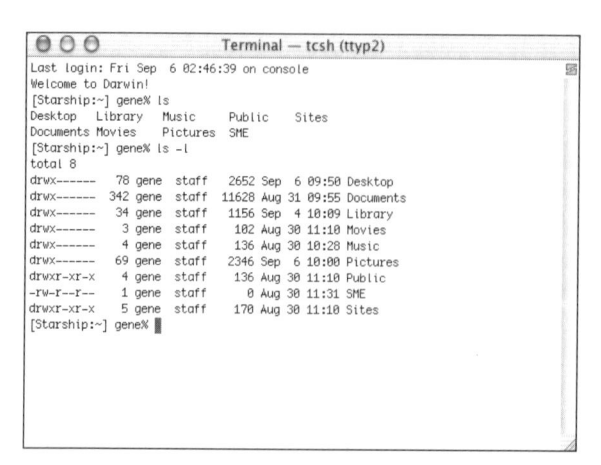

```
Last login: Fri Sep  6 02:46:39 on console
Welcome to Darwin!
[Starship:~] gene% ls
Desktop    Library   Music     Public    Sites
Documents  Movies    Pictures  SME
[Starship:~] gene% ls -l
total 8
drwx------   78 gene  staff   2652 Sep  6 09:50 Desktop
drwx------  342 gene  staff  11628 Aug 31 09:55 Documents
drwx------   34 gene  staff   1156 Sep  4 10:09 Library
drwx------    3 gene  staff    102 Aug 30 11:10 Movies
drwx------    4 gene  staff    136 Aug 30 10:28 Music
drwx------   69 gene  staff   2346 Sep  6 10:00 Pictures
drwxr-xr-x    4 gene  staff    136 Aug 30 11:10 Public
-rw-r--r--    1 gene  staff      0 Aug 30 11:31 SME
drwxr-xr-x    5 gene  staff    170 Aug 30 11:10 Sites
[Starship:~] gene%
```

Figure 20.2   A simple Unix command, in this case **ls -l**, delivers this long folder listing.

424

In Brief

TIP: *To repeat the command you just activated, press the up arrow so that* **ls –l** *appears once again at the command prompt, and press Return. The tcsh shell is smart, and it retains a history of most or all of the commands you've entered since you began your Terminal session (the number depends on its configuration). In addition, you can save the session as a text file for later access if you want to review what you did.*

By using the up and down arrows, you can scroll back and forth through all the commands you've used. This is a very useful feature if you've entered a particularly long and complex command and you'd like to use it again. It's also helpful in the event you made a mistake and want to fix the error rather than repeat the command. With all the modifications, some Unix commands can be long and complex; an easy fix is often the best way to proceed.

Introducing the Autocomplete Feature

In addition, the tcsh shell offers a really nice feature (also present in some of the other Unix shells) known as *Autocomplete*. This feature—reminiscent of the one you find in such applications as Microsoft Entourage, Internet Explorer, and Apple's Mail—lets you simply type in the first few letters of a filename or folder name or directory path and press Tab; Autocomplete then attempts to fill in the rest of the name. If two or more names match the letters you've typed, Autocomplete fills in the remaining letters to the point where the different versions diverge; then it beeps.

Here's an example: Suppose I want to go to a directory that contains the files for my latest science fiction novel. I type something like "cd /Users/gene/Ro" and then press the Tab key. The tcsh shell fills in the remaining characters so that I see **cd /Users/gene/Rockoids**. As soon as I press Return, I'm taken to the proper directory. On the other hand, if more than one file or folder name begins with *Ro* in my home directory (such as Rockoids and Rockoids2_the_coming_of_the_protectors), pressing Tab makes Autocomplete fill in everything up to *Rockoids* and then beep to let me know it has found two or more files or folders that match my criteria.

NOTE: *See anything strange here? Unix doesn't believe in word spaces. If you need one in a file or directory name, use an underscore instead, just as I've done here.*

20. A Fast Introduction to Mac OS X's Unix Environment

Chapter 20 A Fast Introduction to Mac OS X's Unix Environment

What do I do next? To go to the Rockoids2_the_coming_of_the_ protectors directory, I type "2" so that the names are no longer ambiguous, and then press Tab again. Autocomplete shows **cd /Users/ gene/Rockoids2_the_coming_of_the_protectors**, and I can press Return to jump to that directory.

Running Software from the Command Line

You are no doubt accustomed to simply double-clicking on a document or application to launch it. In contrast, running programs from the command line can be a bit of a trick if you've never used a CLI before. When you type a command name and press Return, Unix searches the directories specified in its path to see if they contain a file whose name matches what you typed in. If it finds such a file, it will launch the application.

However, Unix doesn't search the directory you are currently in, and thus it is common for users to mistakenly launch or execute the wrong application. To launch a file in the directory you are currently in, you can preface the command with a period followed by a slash (**./**) to force Unix to execute only files in the local directory; or, you can preface the filename with the whole path. For example, to launch the setup or installation program for a game you downloaded, you would switch to the directory that holds the file using a command similar to **cd /Users/gene/downloads/reallycoolgame**.

NOTE: Don't forget to press Return each time you want to engage a command. Also, don't use the period at the end of the sentence. It's just there in the interests of good grammar (otherwise my publisher's copy editors would object).

Once you're in that directory, you could use the command **./setup** or **/Users/gene/downloads/reallycoolgame/setup** to execute the setup utility.

WARNING! Most experienced Unix users prefer to use the full path when executing applications rather than the ./ shortcut, because doing so is more reliable and less prone to error. In addition, you will sometimes find that you cannot execute a file even if you are the owner and have full control of it. The problem is that you have not set the permissions on the file to allow execution. To fix this situation, use the **chmod** command to set the execute rights. The full command is **chmod +x** followed by the filename.

426

In Brief

Backing Up Files and Folders

It is possible to back up files via the Unix command line, using the copy and move commands mentioned in the "Immediate Solutions" portion of this chapter. But this process has limitations. For one thing, many Mac files have two parts—a data fork and a resource—but Unix doesn't recognize the latter. So, if you copy a file via the command line using the **cp** (Copy) or **mv** (Move) command, you'll end up with a file that is not quite the sum of its parts.

This result presents no problem if you're just copying regular document files or Mac OS X native applications. However, if you need to copy a Classic application or file related to your Classic system software, you are best advised to use the Finder and let it do its thing.

Suggested Reading

If you're curious about learning more details of Mac OS X's Unix environment, you'll want to check this material for further information:

- To learn more about the tcsh shell, point your browser to **www.cnr.berkeley.edu/~casterln/tcsh/The_commandline_editor.html**.

- If you enjoyed trying the Terminal tips listed here, you'll find additional information at **http://homepage.mac.com/x_freedom/tips/terminal.html**.

Chapter 20   A Fast Introduction to Mac OS X's Unix Environment

Immediate Solutions

A Short List of Popular Command-Line Features

To further acclimate you to Mac OS X's Unix environment, here are some common and very useful commands and the functions they perform. To make them easier to use, I've grouped similar commands together, even though they are not in alphabetical order:

NOTE: *A number of the commands I use here require that you first enter your administrator password in the Terminal command line. After you do that and press Return, you'll be able to activate these functions.*

- **cd** *(change directory)*—The **cd** command lets you switch directories, provided of course that you have the rights needed to access that directory. For example, **cd /Users/gene/Rockoids** will take you to the Rockoids directory located inside the my home directory (to use an example on my own Mac). Likewise, **cd ..** will move you to the directory one level above the one you're currently in.

- **cp** *(copy)*—This command allows you to copy a file or directory from one location to another. You can also use the **cp** command with wildcards (an asterisk) to move only those file(s) that match certain criteria. For example, the command **cp cd /Users/gene/Rockoids/Chap* /Users/gene/Rockoids_backup** will copy (not move) all files that start with *Chap* from my Rockoids directory to my backup folder.

- **mv** *(move)*—This command is used to move (not just copy) files from one location to another. The command **mv /Users/gene/Rockoids/Chap* /Users/gene/Rockoids_backup** will transfer and not copy files that begin with the word *Chap* to the target directory.

TIP: *The **mv** command is also used to rename files. For example, to rename a file named Chapter40 to Chapter41, use the command **mv Chapter40 Chapter41**.*

WARNING! A good caution is worth repeating. Don't forget that Unix doesn't recognize the resource fork of a Mac file. So, restrict your copying and moving efforts to document files or Mac OS X applications. Stay away from Classic applications or system files, and you'll stay out of trouble.

- **chgrp**—This command changes the group associated with a file. For example, as administrator, you can change the group listed for a file or directory from one user to another. To change a file's group to authors, if the file is currently assigned to a different group, use **chgrp authors [*file or directory in question*]**.

- **chmod** *(change file permissions)*—This is an extremely powerful command that you use to set the access rights for your files and directories. Although this is easy to do in the Finder's Show Info window, in the Privileges category, **chmod** is far more encompassing. What's more, it can be a saving grace in the event you encounter problems with permissions on a file or folder—a dreaded warning that you don't have the right to access, change, or copy a file (a not-uncommon event in Mac OS X). You can also use **chmod** to change the permissions on a large number of files and directories quickly, using wildcards.

    For example, you can limit the ability of others in the authors group to change certain files, but still let them read the files. Here's the command I would use to modify those file permissions: **chmod o=r / Users/gene/Rockoids/Chap***. The end result? This command sets the file permissions for all files that start with "Chap" in the directory **/Users/gene/Rockoids** to read-only status, for everyone but me as owner of the file and those in the group associated with the file or directory. You can use this command in the same fashion to let others read but not executive or modify your files.

- **chown**—This command changes the ownership of a file. As administrator of your Mac, you can use this command to switch ownership of a file or folder from one user to another. Say you wanted to switch ownership of a file created by another user. Just type the command **chown [*username*] [*name of file*]**. A press of the Return key makes you, or the person named in the command, the owner of that file or folder.

NOTE: If you must change permissions for a file or folder, you aren't confined to the command line. The Finder's Get Info has a very capable Ownership & Permissions feature that will provide easy access to all or most of the changes you need to make within a simple-to-use graphical interface. But doing it by the command line is probably more fun.

- **ln** *(link)*—The Unix variant of an alias is known as a *symbolic link*. This command, when used with the name of a file, creates a symbolic link to that file. You can use it in much the same fashion as an alias to access that particular file. For example, suppose I want to create a symbolic link to a file named Rockoids in my root or top directory. To begin with, I use the command **cd /** to switch to the root directory.

Now, I type "ln /Users/gene/Rockoids Rockoids". The result is a symbolic link named Rockoids that will access the folder named Rockoids on the root directory of my Mac's hard drive.

- **ls** *(list directory)*—In combination with the **ln** command, you can use this function to create a link to a specific directory.

- **less**—Enter this command plus the file name, and you'll be able to browse the contents of a file without modifying it.

NOTE: *If the file isn't a text file, you will be informed that the file may be binary and asked if you want to view it anyway.*

- **pwd**—This simple command displays the directory you are currently in.

- **mkdir**—This is the command line equivalent of the New Folder command in the Finder and in Open and Save dialog boxes. To create a folder called Rockoids2 in my home directory, I enter this command: **mkdir /Users/gene/Rockoids2**. When I open a Finder window, a folder appears in the location in which I established it via this command.

NOTE: *To use a word space for your new folder, you would, for example, specify the name* **Rockoids_2** *in your* **mkdir** *command line. When you view the new folder in the Folder, it will have a normal word space.*

- **rmdir** *(remove directory)*—This command is rather destructive, because it removes whole directories. Fortunately, it can delete a directory only if it has no files in it; Unix does offer some protection against deleting the wrong files.

- **rm** *(remove)*—Use this command with extreme care, because, as I said before, there's no turning back in Unix, no "Are you sure you want to erase your hard drive?" prompt if you go to far. The **rm** command deletes files. There is no corresponding undelete command. For example, to remove a file named ooops from my home directory, I'd use the command **rm /Users/gene/ooops**.

- **more**—This is a command similar to **less** that allows you to look at the contents of a file without changing it. You will not be warned, however, if you're trying to view a binary file. The command **q** can be used to exit the file.

- **passwd**—Want to change your password? Type this command, and you'll be prompted for your current password. Once you've entered that, you can enter your new password (but type it carefully, because you won't even see the number of characters displayed in the Terminal prompt).

Immediate Solutions

Using Mac OS X's Command-Line FTP Software

Several flexible Aqua-based FTP applications are available, such as Fetch and Interarchy, and you can perform a limited range of FTP access via the Connect to Server feature in the Finder's Go menu. However, the tools in Mac OS X's command line are quite flexible.

TIP: For a comprehensive list of available Mac OS X FTP software, check out www.versiontracker.com.

In this exercise, you will have a chance to check Apple's FTP site for available updates. Here's how it's done:

1. Launch Terminal from the Applications folder.
2. When you download files from the FTP site, no doubt you'll want them on your desktop for easy access (otherwise they go to the root level of your Users or Home directory). Type "cd desktop" in the Terminal window to change the location.
3. To connect to the remote site, enter the command **ftp** followed by the name of the site, in this case **ftp.apple.com**. The result, shown in Figure 20.3, will be a request for you to enter your name.
4. Enter "anonymous" to gain guest access. In the password prompt, enter your email address.

NOTE: Not all sites allow anonymous or guest access. If you cannot enter a site in this fashion, you will need to contact the company or administrator for the proper access credentials.

5. To see a list of available files, enter the command **ls** or **dir**. Use the **cd** command, as needed, to burrow through the file directory.

*NOTE: If you know the entire path to get to the directory you want, you can type it instead, separating each directory in the hierarchy with a slash—for example, **pub/software**.*

TIP: Because the name of the file or directory must be entered exactly, using upper- and lowercase as needed, you can copy the name from the Terminal window and paste it when needed to be sure it's accurate.

6. When you've located the file you want to retrieve, enter the command **get** followed by the name of the file. In the example shown in Figure 20.4, I wanted to retrieve a firmware revision for my Power Mac G4. Thus, I entered the command **get G4_FW-**

431

Chapter 20 A Fast Introduction to Mac OS X's Unix Environment

```
Terminal — tcsh (ttyp2)
Last login: Fri Sep  6 10:00:13 on ttyp2
Welcome to Darwin!
[Starship:~] gene% ftp ftp.apple.com
Trying 17.254.0.26...
Connected to ftp.apple.com.
220 ProFTPD 1.2.1 Server (Apple Computer Anonymous FTP Server) [ftp06]
Name (ftp.apple.com:gene): anonymous
331 Anonymous login ok, send your complete email address as your password.
Password:
230 Anonymous access granted, restrictions apply.
Remote system type is UNIX.
Using binary mode to transfer files.
ftp>
```

Figure 20.3   Access an FTP site via Mac OS X's command line interface.

Update_4.2.8.smi.bin. After the command has been given, file retrieval will take a few seconds to begin. When it's finished, a Transfer Complete message will appear, including both the time it took to retrieve the file and the speed (bytes per second).

TIP: Sending and receiving files to a remote FTP site is one way to test the speed of your Internet connection, free of the constraints of the Web. However, if a site becomes busy, the speed ratings may not reflect the potential. If you can access a site that allows both file uploads and downloads, it's best to test performance during the wee hours of the morning.

---

7. To send a file, you use the command **put** followed by the location and name of the file. Bear in mind, though, that commercial FTP sites usually do not allow uploads without permission, except where special folders are set up for those files.

8. When you're finished checking and retrieving files, you can quit Terminal or run a different FTP session.

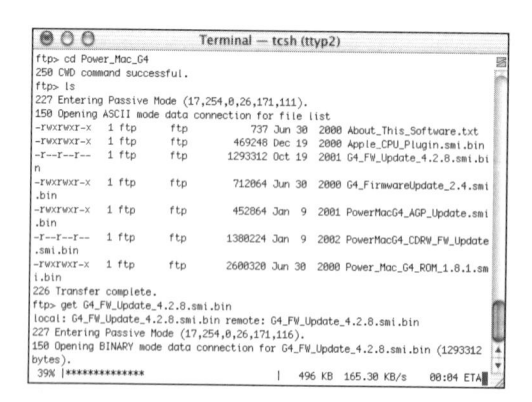

```
Terminal — tcsh (ttyp2)
ftp> cd Power_Mac_G4
250 CWD command successful.
ftp> ls
227 Entering Passive Mode (17,254,0,26,171,111).
150 Opening ASCII mode data connection for file list
-rwxrwxr-x   1 ftp      ftp           737 Jun 30  2000 About_This_Software.txt
-rwxrwxr-x   1 ftp      ftp        469248 Dec 19  2000 Apple_CPU_Plugin.smi.bin
-r--r--r--   1 ftp      ftp       1293312 Oct 19  2001 G4_FW_Update_4.2.8.smi.bi
n
-rwxrwxr-x   1 ftp      ftp        712064 Jun 30  2000 G4_FirmwareUpdate_2.4.smi
.bin
-rwxrwxr-x   1 ftp      ftp        452864 Jan  9  2001 PowerMacG4_AGP_Update.smi
.bin
-r--r--r--   1 ftp      ftp       1380224 Jan  9  2002 PowerMacG4_CDRW_FW_Update
.smi.bin
-rwxrwxr-x   1 ftp      ftp       2600320 Jun 30  2000 Power_Mac_G4_ROM_1.8.1.sm
i.bin
226 Transfer complete.
ftp> get G4_FW_Update_4.2.8.smi.bin
local: G4_FW_Update_4.2.8.smi.bin remote: G4_FW_Update_4.2.8.smi.bin
227 Entering Passive Mode (17,254,0,26,171,116).
150 Opening BINARY mode data connection for G4_FW_Update_4.2.8.smi.bin (1293312
bytes).
39% |**************            |   496 KB  165.30 KB/s    00:04 ETA
```

Figure 20.4   Here the download is still in progress.

Chapter 21

Surfing the Net

If you need an immediate solution to:	See page:
Deleting Browser Caches	446
Killing the Cache in Internet Explorer	446
Killing the Cache in iCab	447
Killing the Cache in Netscape	448
Killing the Cache in OmniWeb	448
Killing the Cache in Opera	449
Determining Whether a Larger Cache Is Necessary	449
Using Bookmarks to Get There Faster	450
Solving Internet Connection Problems	451

Chapter 21 Surfing the Net

In Brief

According to a survey of iMac users in the months following its introduction in 1998, more than 90% of them used the original pear-shaped consumer computer for Internet access. Sure enough, since Apple began coming back from the brink in 1997, it has focused more and more on the Internet, to reflect the growing number of personal computer users who need to get online. In fact, the *i* in the names iMac and iBook (but not, of course, the iPod music player) is designed to reflect the idea that these consumer computers can get you hooked up to the Internet within minutes after you install them for the very first time. Even some of the so-called "i" applications, such as iPhoto and iTunes, employ Internet access to activate some of their features.

In short, the ability to surf the Net easily and efficiently is a prime need for any personal computer, including the Mac. In this chapter, I focus on maximizing your Internet experience.

The Coming of Broadband Access

You hear it in the newspapers, on radio and TV, and when you're online: Despite plenty of bumps along the road, due to the technology industry's woes, broadband Internet access is coming to your neighborhood, and your online experience will never be the same. You've no doubt seen offer after offer filled with promises of huge speed increases over the conventional modem. Claims such as, "Experience full-motion video and high-quality stereo sound" and "Retrieve files in seconds" abound.

But when you try to have those new features installed in your home, something... well... doesn't quite match-up with the promises. For one thing, there is the fine print; perhaps such high-speed services aren't available everywhere. In fact, they may not be available at your home or office because you are too far from the telephone switching center or the upgraded cable TV lines that allow you to get onto the supercharged Internet highway.

I can't promise that I can help you get broadband any faster, but in this section, I'll cover the various technologies you'll be able to access on your Mac with Mac OS X.

In Brief

NOTE: *Getting online at high speed is only part of the equation. If you already have an ISP, you may or may not be able to continue to use the service when you switch to high speed. Some of these ISPs don't offer faster access, and others are still fighting with cable TV companies for open access. You may have to use another ISP, and end up changing your email addresses, when you move to broadband.*

Following are the technologies currently available, as well as those that may become available in the future:

- *DSL*—Short for Digital Subscriber Line, this service allows your phone line to do double duty. First, it handles phone calls and faxes just as it does now. But it can also carry high-speed digital data to and from your Mac, without affecting the use of your phone in any way. Compared to what you get with a 56Kbps modem (which actually connects at speeds from as low as 9600bps all the way up to 53Kbps—and the latter very seldom), DSL starts at around 256Kbps and generally delivers up to 1Mbps (megabits per second); speeds are higher with business-oriented services. One consumer-oriented variant, ADSL (the *A* is for *asymmetric*), throttles the upload speed to something far less—usually around 256Kbps. The reasoning is that most folks, except those who need to send large files all the time, perform far fewer upstream tasks than downstream tasks, and hence, they won't suffer much from the speed sacrifice. DSL service hooks up to a standard Mac Ethernet network, using a special device that acts like a modem to send and retrieve digital data from your phone line.

NOTE: *Another variation of DSL technology is VDSL, short for Very High Speed Digital Subscriber line. It's used by such companies as Qwest Communications to deliver cable TV and high-speed Internet to homes.*

- *Cable modem*—Via the same cable from which you receive cable TV broadcasts, you can get high-speed Internet access. Speeds are potentially even higher than DSL, up to 3Mbps and more in some situations. However, access to the cable is shared among a group of several hundred users on a single node or segment. If a lot of folks are accessing the Internet at the same time you are, expect performance to nosedive to speeds that may not be much greater than regular DSL. Upload speeds are usually throttled to 128 or 256Kbps. An interface device, the cable modem, is used to bring the signal from the cable line to your Ethernet network.

435

Chapter 21 Surfing the Net

NOTE: Some cable modem services offer a hybrid or telco service. This system uses an analog modem built into the cable modem that offers 33.6Kbps maximum uploads via a regular phone line. Although this may be the only way the service is available, other services offer the hybrid service as an intermediary step to sign up customers while they finish rewiring a neighborhood. Once the wiring is done (assuming it ever is), customers are moved to the higher-cost full service, and the preliminary service is discontinued.

- *Wireless Internet*—Do you live in a city or small town where broadband seems years away, or may never come, because the work required is too great or the population density just isn't enough to support cable modems or DSL? There's yet a third choice: wireless. Whether by satellite disk or land-based transmitters, these services offer options that are otherwise unavailable. They may cost more, and they may not give the same level of performance as a cable modem, but in some situations, they may be the only choice.

NOTE: One wireless service, Sprint Broadband Direct, once promised speeds close to what a cable modem or the fastest DSL services provide, at least for downloads. However, the service apparently didn't scale up well to large numbers of users, and new customers are no longer being accepted.

- *Future technologies*—Of course, determining the technologies of the future is a highly speculative matter, but many are betting that even faster services will emerge, using all fiber-optic cabling or other new technologies. Rewiring a city may cost billions upon billions of dollars, but if it all comes to pass, speeds on the Internet will rival those of a standard high-performance Ethernet network. If this technology is realized, you'll be able to view full-screen, full-frame video presentations via the Internet as easily as you can via cable TV and satellite. What's more, you'll be able to transfer files across the Internet at the speed of a local network. The ultimate vision of a wired generation may truly come far sooner than we expect, in keeping with the vision of a digital lifestyle espoused by Apple CEO Steve Jobs.

Mac OS X Web Browsers Profiled

The advent of Mac OS X has brought two kinds of software to surf the Net. The first is simply the Carbonized version of an existing Mac browser, as typified by Microsoft's Internet Explorer (which has been standard issue on Mac OS installations for quite some time) and such contenders as iCab, Netscape, and Opera. The second is unique to the new operating system on which Mac OS X is based, often from publishers with experience designing programs for the NeXTSTEP operating system.

In Brief

In the following pages, I'll describe five Web browsers that come from both environments. You'll learn the basic features, and then, in the "Immediate Solutions" section, you'll discover ways to maximize your online performance with these programs and others offering similar capabilities.

NOTE: *AOL's Mac OS X client software, beginning with version 10.2, used Netscape's Gecko engine as its embedded browser, and performance levels and the quality of Web page display should be similar to the standalone version. However, some of the expanded features, such as tabbed browsing, are not available.*

Microsoft Internet Explorer

Since becoming the default browser on the Mac as a result of Microsoft's $150 million investment in Apple in 1997, this application has taken over from rival Netscape as the number-one Mac browser (see Figure 21.1).

Here are the basic features of the current version of Internet Explorer:

- *Tasman browser engine*—Beginning with Internet Explorer 5, Microsoft presented a new rendering engine designed for speedier display, particularly of graphics. The Tasman engine is designed to offer full support of the Internet standards in effect when the program was created.

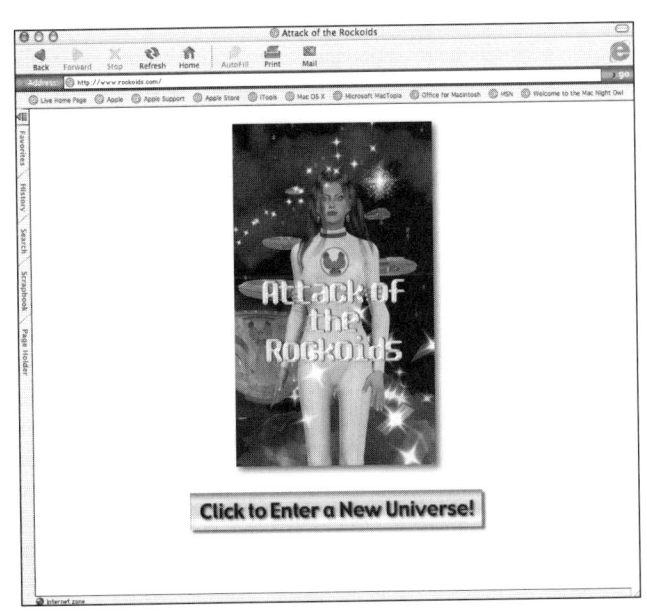

Figure 21.1   The Mac OS X version of Internet Explorer bears more than a striking resemblance to its Classic version.

437

Chapter 21 Surfing the Net

- *Search Assistant*—This feature (see Figure 21.2) takes a task-based approach to locating information on the Internet. You click the Search button, select the category of the search, and then enter the search request in the text field. You can easily switch among search engines if the first doesn't deliver the results you want.

Related solution:	*Found on page:*
Searching the Internet	172

- *Improved address auto-complete*—When you enter a site's address, a pop-up menu appears (when available) with additional choices that begin with the information you entered. Select the one you want, and you can revisit sites with the most complex addresses in minutes. Of course, adding a site to your Favorites list is the best approach.

- *Auction tracker*—If the online auctions from such services as eBay and Yahoo! interest you, this new feature (see Figure 21.3) lets you enter the information about the auctions in which you participate. If someone exceeds your bid for a particular item,

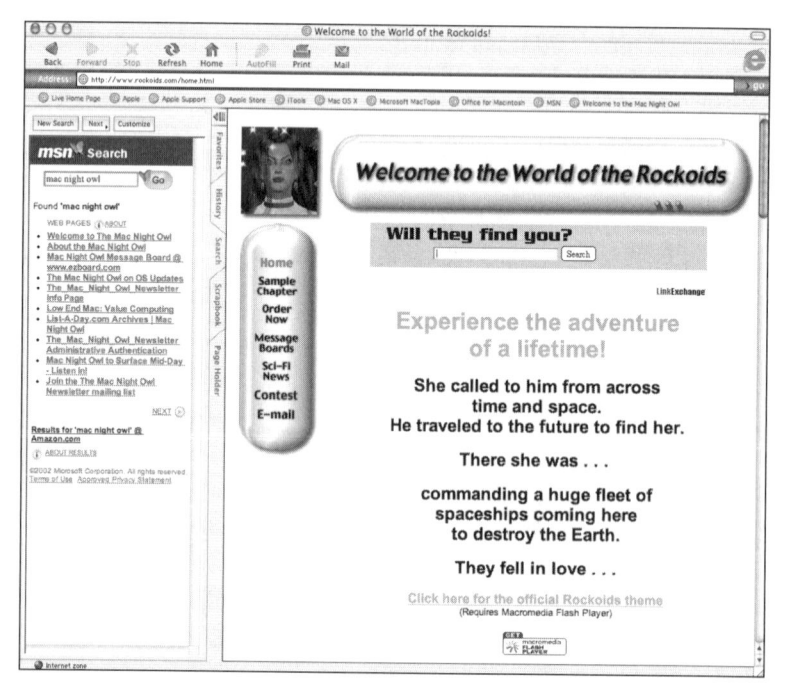

Figure 21.2 Use the Internet Explorer Search Assistant to get information from the Net more quickly.

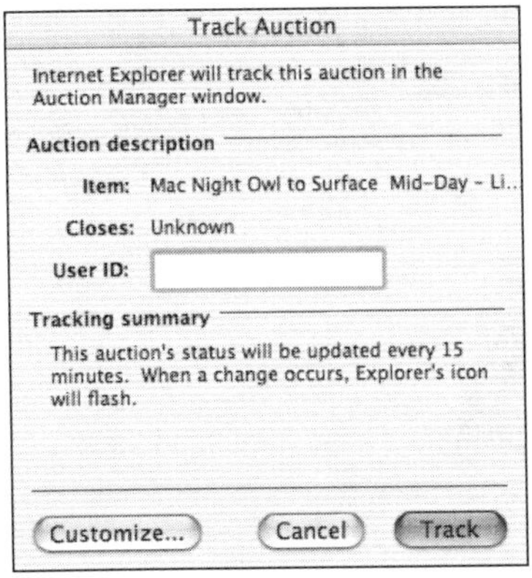

Figure 21.3 Don't let anyone outbid you. Internet Explorer's auction tracker makes it possible to know when you need to increase your bid.

you're notified via a browser display (or even by email), so you can decide whether to return and change your bid.

- *Multiple themes*—You can easily customize the browser's color scheme with your favorite Mac colors or move and replace items in the toolbar, as you prefer. This is part of the increasing concession on Microsoft's part to make its software more Mac-like.

iCab

The subject of an extended public preview program (one that was still in progress when this book was written), iCab (see Figure 21.4), the slim Web browser from a German-based software publisher, is designed to be competition for the big entrants in this product category.

TIP: You can download a copy of the latest version of iCab from **www.icab.de**.

Following is a list of major iCab features that are designed to differentiate this program from the pack:

- *Support for current Web standards*—The publisher of iCab promises support for current Web standards, including HTML 4.0 and Cascading Style Sheets Level 2 (CSS2). In addition, iCab provides extra support for specific Internet Explorer and Netscape extras, such as the Netscape **<BLINK>** command.

- *Support for older Macs*—In addition to the Mac OS X edition of iCab, another edition runs with Mac OS 7.0.1 or later with 4MB free RAM; even Macs with a 68020 processor are supported. Only Opera can match this application's support for older Macs. Such support may make it possible for you to deploy this browser on

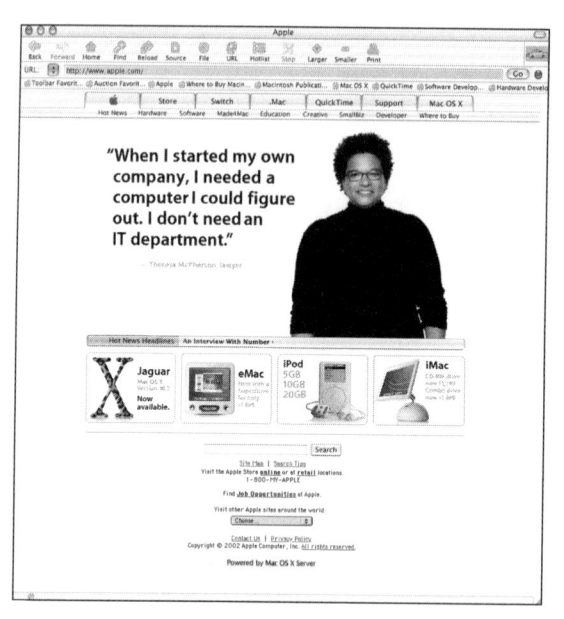

Figure 21.4 iCab is a worthy alternative to the big guys.

an entire network consisting of Macs with widely varying hardware and system setups.

- *Cookie filters*—Most Web-based cookies serve a useful purpose, such as letting you track your visits to a Web site to ease navigation. However, if you want to selectively or completely disable the cookies, you can do so in this program.

Netscape

Some time in the distant past, Netscape ruled the roost among Web browsers. Although Microsoft's Internet Explorer has long since taken over on both the Mac OS and Windows platforms, AOL Time Warner's Netscape subsidiary has been busy creating new, more feature-laden versions of the program. Netscape 7.0 for Mac OS X (see Figure 21.5) loses some of the interface oddities of the original 6.0 release while retaining its huge range of features.

Here are a few examples from the huge feature set of Netscape 6.2:

- *Gecko rendering engine*—Part of its open-source Mozilla project, Gecko is the counterpart to Internet Explorer's Tasman feature. It is supposed to provide speedier, accurate display of Web pages.
- *User-customizable sidebar*—The busy sidebar puts your favorite sites and features front and center for easy access. Additional default tabs can be added, and Netscape offers extra options at its Web site.

In Brief

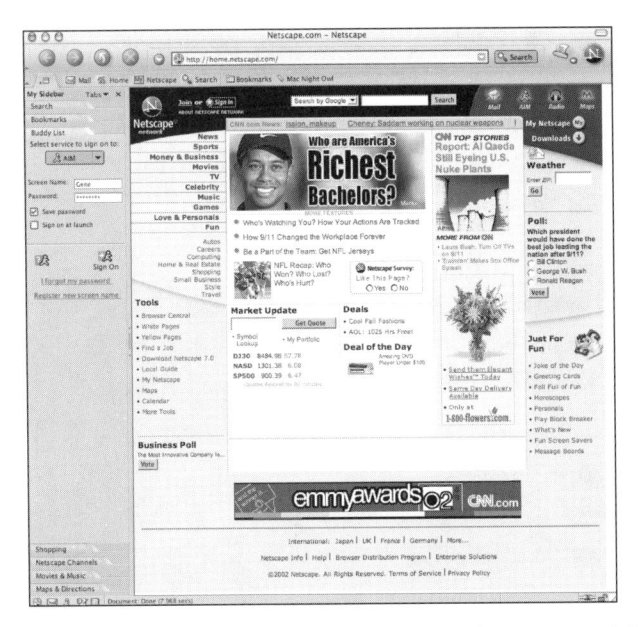

Figure 21.5   Netscape 7 remains the most feature-complete Web browser.

- *Built-in email client*—Unique among the browsers described in this chapter, Netscape includes a full-featured email client (see Figure 21.6) that can manage multiple accounts and (no surprise) even AOL email (with full support for your AOL address book).

- *Built-in Instant Messaging*—AOL's popular AIM client is also part of Netscape, so you can stay in touch with your online buddies. Support for AOL's ICQ service is also part of the package, but connections must be made separately, which means an AIM member cannot directly communicate with an ICQ member, even if you have accounts on both services.

NOTE: You can, if you prefer, use iChat to contact both AOL and AIM users, and mac.com members instead. Nothing forces you to use the chat client or any other component of Netscape if you just want to use its browser.

- *Tabbed browsing*—This nifty feature can open separate links in a single window, and you just have to click a tab to jump from one to the other.

NOTE: Those who examine feature sets may remind me that Opera had this feature first. A good feature is worth copying, I suppose.

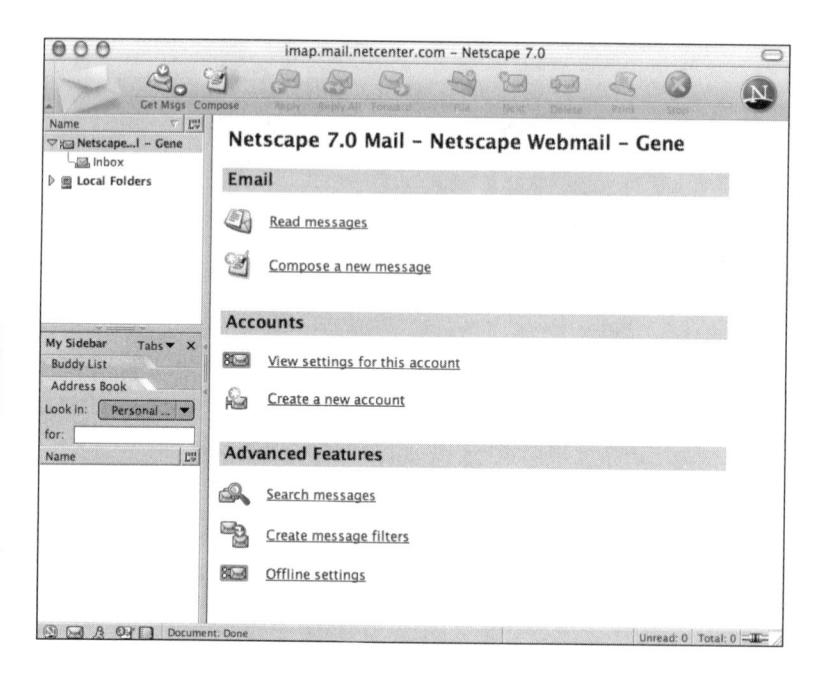

Figure 21.6 Manage your email with Netscape without the need for any other application.

OmniWeb

The major independent contender in the Mac browser wars comes from a long-time NeXTSTEP developer, The Omni Group. OmniWeb is distinguished by being developed in Apple's Cocoa programming language and featuring a decidedly different interface (see Figure 21.7).

TIP: You can easily get the latest versions of iCab, Netscape, OmniWeb, and Opera from a popular Web site that tracks and links to the latest software updates. Just point your browser to **www.versiontracker.com**. In addition to these programs, you'll find a healthy collection of software for both the Mac OS 9 and Mac OS X user environments.

Although most features simply match the other browsers, OmniWeb offers a few variations on the theme:

- *Full support of Web standards*—As with the other programs, and despite the fact that pages render differently from program to program, OmniWeb promises to deliver support for all or most current HTML standards and CSS2.

- *Slide-out drawers*—Rather than access menus, OmniWeb's bookmark and history lists are available as drawers that simply slide out from the main application window (see Figure 21.8).

In Brief

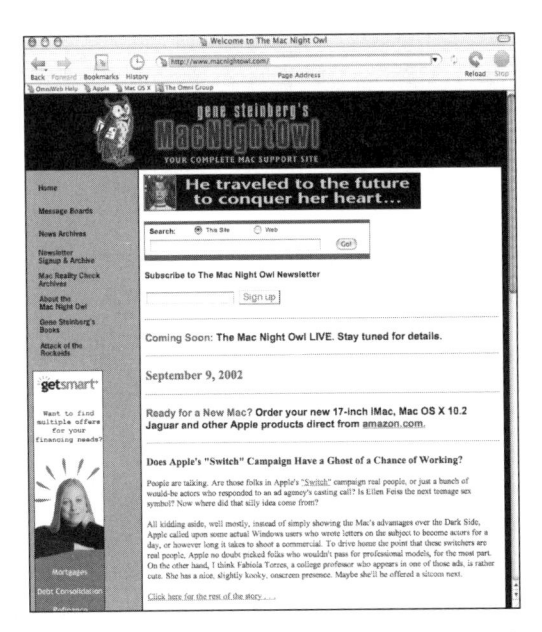

Figure 21.7   OmniWeb was created by an experienced developer of NeXTSTEP software.

This is both an advantage and a disadvantage, because the drawers can intrude on screen space.

- *Drag-and-drop bookmarks*—You can drag and drop pages to and from the bookmarks, and they'll be automatically checked for new material.
- *Easy importing of bookmarks*—Just copy the bookmarks file from either Internet Explorer or Netscape onto the bookmarks file used by OmniWeb and launch the program. The bookmarks will be automatically converted to the application's native format, so you can continue to use your existing repository of bookmarks.

NOTE: Where's that folder? With OmniWeb 4.1, it's located inside the Application Support folder within the Library folder that's placed within your personal Users folder.

Opera

From Norway comes the last and certainly not the least contender in the race to gain a foothold in the Mac Web browser marketplace. Opera for Mac OS X (see Figure 21.9) promises superior support for emerging Web standards, and speedier browser display.

NOTE: Fastest browser? I am just citing the publisher's claim. Independent tests have been inconclusive, but that's how benchmarking goes.

443

Figure 21.8   OmniWeb has a unique way to access your favorite Web sites.

The version of Opera I examined for this book wasn't complete, but it was sufficiently populated with features to get a good idea of what it does:

- *Superior Web standard support*—All Web browsers tout their support for the various World Wide Web Consortium (W3C) standards. Opera's publishers list a full range, including CSS1, CSS2, XML, HTML 4.01, and more.

- *Super-fast rendering engine*—All right, everyone claims to do it better. Opera displays the time it takes to retrieve a Web site, so you can easily do comparisons.

- *Zooming*—This feature is unique to Opera. A pull-down menu lets you select a zoom factor for a Web page (see Figure 21.10), as you would in a word processor. The settings range from 20% to 1000%. Mac OS X's smooth font rendering makes text look great, but graphics will, naturally, suffer as their size increases.

- *Direct access to search engines*—Click on a down arrow and get a list of popular search engines (which you can customize) for convenient searches for the Web-based information you want.

- *Tabbed browsing*—Sound familiar? This feature appeared in Opera first, but is also being used in Netscape 7. It allows multiple browser windows to be accessed by clicking a tab, rather than a new window. It's a great saver of screen real estate, especially on a smaller display.

In Brief

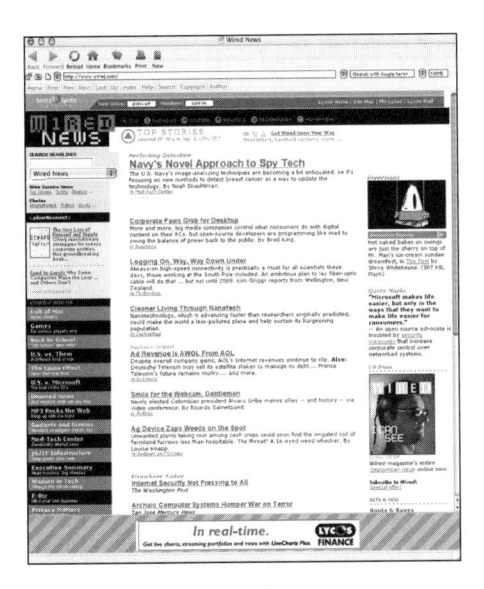

Figure 21.9 Available for a number of operating systems, Opera claims to be the fastest browser on the planet.

Mac Internet access is a highly simplified process: You launch your browser and you connect. But behind those simple actions are many more considerations to get the maximum value from your online experience and steps you can take to get the maximum stability from your surfing experience. We'll look at these issues in the next section.

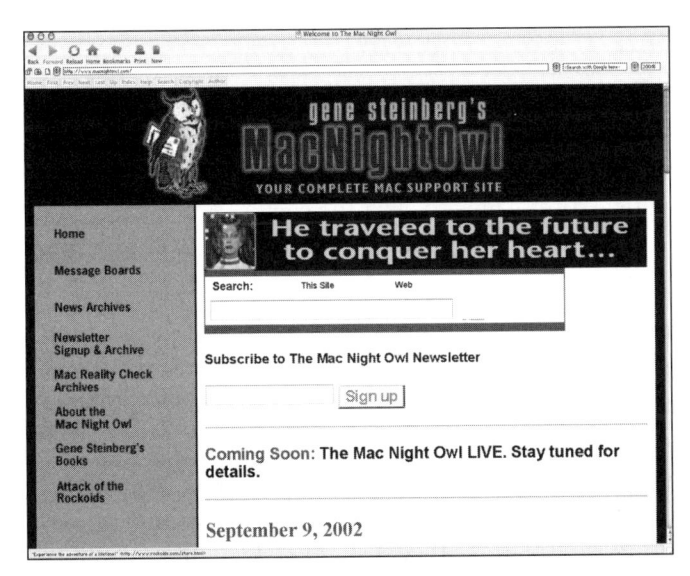

Figure 21.10 This is the author's Web site, blown up 200% courtesy of Opera.

21. Surfing the Net

445

Chapter 21 Surfing the Net

Immediate Solutions

Deleting Browser Caches

A Web browser uses a *cache*, consisting of a single file or several files, to store the artwork accessed from a Web site. Whenever you call up the site, the contents of the cache are compared with the site, and only new artwork is downloaded. This process can speed up Net performance, sometimes dramatically. But if performance bogs down or you find that your browser is crashing, the next step is to delete the cache.

WARNING! A separate set of cache files is stored in each user's Preferences folder, inside his or her Library folder. If you remove the cache files while logged in under one user account, those files won't be removed for the others. However, the administrator can do a search of all user folders with Sherlock to find and remove all the caches.

The following sections describe how to delete the caches in the five browsers described in this chapter.

TIP: When you empty a Web cache, all the artwork is gone. As a result, the browser must retrieve it again. You won't see a performance gain until the browser retrieves the site for a second time. And don't forget, the steps described here must be repeated for all users of your Mac unless the administrator performs them manually via a file search.

Killing the Cache in Internet Explorer

The user interface of the Carbon version of Internet Explorer is close enough to the Mac OS 9 version that the Preferences panels seem nearly identical. Here's how to clear the cache:

1. With Internet Explorer running, go to the Application menu and choose Preferences.

2. In the Preferences panel, scroll to Web Browser and click on the disclosure triangle to expose the settings under this category.

3. Click on the Advanced category, which produces the dialog box shown in Figure 21.11.

4. Click Empty Now to delete the contents of the cache file. Because Internet Explorer stores its entire cache in a single file, IE Cache.waf, this process should take only a second.

Immediate Solutions

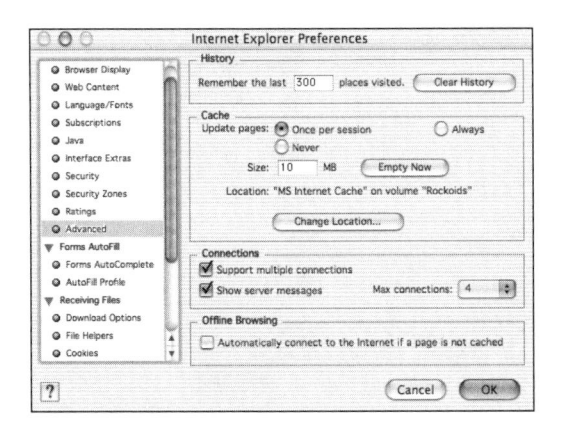

Figure 21.11 Empty the cache and perform some additional operations in this dialog box.

5. Visit your favorite sites and see if the appearance or performance improves after the site is visited for the second time.

6. If performance doesn't improve, delete the actual cache file. You'll find it in the Preferences folder inside the Library folder, which is, in turn, located in the Users folder bearing your login name. Look for a folder labeled MS Internet Cache or Explorer for this file.

Killing the Cache in iCab

The process of emptying iCab's Web cache under Mac OS X is the same as in the Classic versions. Just follow these steps:

1. With iCab running, go to the Application menu and choose Preferences.

2. Locate the category labeled Caches, and click on the disclosure triangle to show all the subcategories.

3. Locate and click Web Pages. You'll see iCab's various cache options, as shown in Figure 21.12.

4. To delete the cache, click the Clear Cache Now button. Because the cache is stored in a number of separate files, it may take a little while to remove a large cache.

5. When the cache has been removed, click OK. The Preferences dialog box closes.

6. Visit your favorite sites and see if the appearance or performance improves.

447

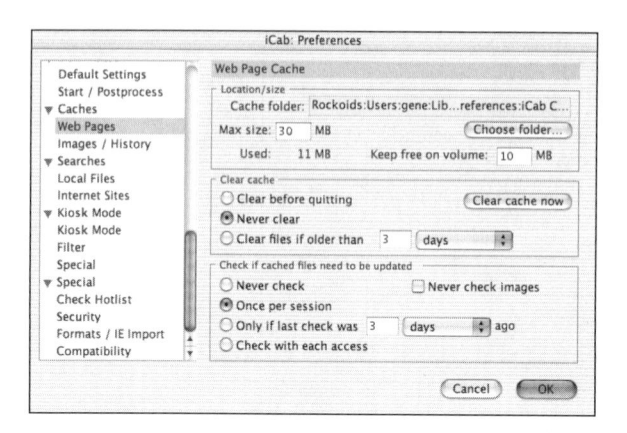

Figure 21.12 iCab's cache removal options are fairly straightforward.

Killing the Cache in Netscape

Netscape's cache-killing process is, like the others mentioned so far, pretty straightforward:

1. Launch Netscape for Mac OS X, go to the Application menu, and choose Preferences.

2. Click the arrow next to Advanced so it points downward (or leave it alone if it's already that way).

3. Click Cache to bring up the dialog box shown in Figure 21.13.

NOTE: *Despite the fact that AOL for Mac OS X uses Netscape as its browsing engine, it doesn't share the Web cache. In order to remove the cache under AOL, you need to choose Preferences from the application menu and click on the WWW icon. All that's left is to do is click the Empty Cache Now and then OK to close the dialog box.*

4. Click Clear Disk Cache to zap the cache files. As an extra ounce of prevention, you may also want to click Clear Memory Cache, which also removes the artwork cached in memory.

5. Click OK to close the Preferences dialog box.

Killing the Cache in OmniWeb

It's not just the interface that's different. There are two ways to handle the cache in OmniWeb. To actually clear the cache, simply choose Flush Cache from the Tools menu. The other cache management tool is the Cache Timeout feature, which sets the time when a cache is considered out-of-date and when a new version of the site is available. That one is in the Preferences dialog box. Talk about different!

Immediate Solutions

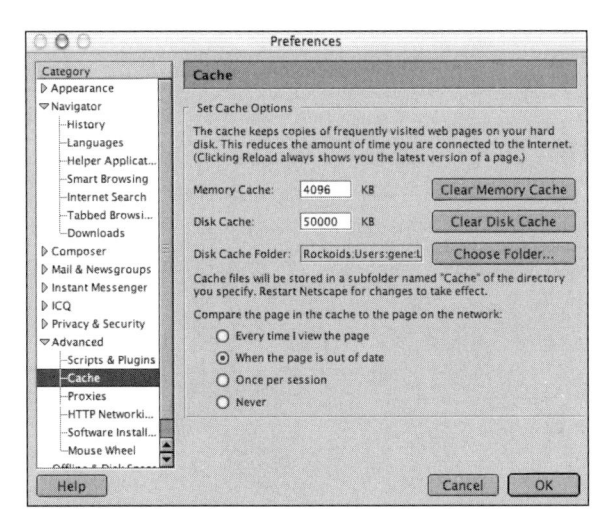

Figure 21.13 Clear Netscape's cache this dialog box

Killing the Cache in Opera

This is an early release version, so don't be surprised to see Opera's Preferences dialog box on the Edit menu. Here's how to empty the cache:

1. With Opera open, bring up the Preferences dialog box from the Application menu.
2. Click History And Cache to bring up the dialog box shown in Figure 21.14.
3. Under Disk Cache, click Empty Now to remove Opera's cache files.
4. Click OK to dismiss Opera's Preferences dialog box.

Determining Whether a Larger Cache Is Necessary

The standard Web cache is usually 5MB to 10MB (it was 2MB in the version of Opera examined for this book and 50MB for AOL and the standalone version of Netscape), but you can easily increase it to a higher figure if you prefer by accessing a browser's Preferences as described previously. Before you do so, however, consider that having a Web cache that's too large may be counterproductive. For one thing, if the browser spends additional time checking the contents of the cache before accessing an updated site from the Web, performance may actually be slower.

449

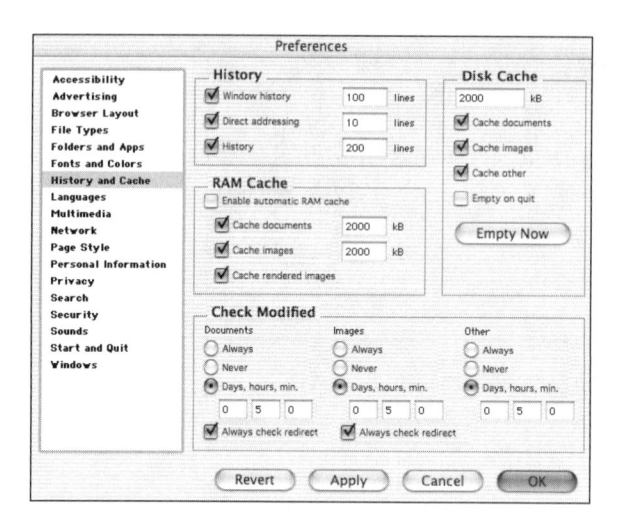

Figure 21.14 You can clear Opera's cache from this rather busy window.

However, if you frequently access a large number of Web sites with plenty of artwork, a setting of 15MB or even 20MB may be useful; iCab sets its cache at a maximum of 30MB, and no appreciable slowdown results. Your mileage may vary. If you choose to reduce the size of a cache, however, empty it first.

Using Bookmarks to Get There Faster

Over time, you'll come across Web sites you'd like to visit on a regular basis. The best way to keep track of these sites is to save them as bookmarks. Each browser has a different name for its bookmarks feature. For Internet Explorer, it's called Favorites; for iCab, it's the Hotlist; and OmniWeb uses the traditional name Bookmarks (as do Netscape and Opera).

In each case, there is a menu with the name of the bookmarks feature. To add a page to your bookmarks, access that menu and use the command to add the current page. You may see a confirmation message that you must OK in order for the page to appear on the list.

Removing a bookmark involves opening the list, selecting the bookmark, and then pressing the Delete key or choosing Delete from the Contextual menu or Edit menu (it varies from browser to browser). Again, you'll usually need to OK a prompt to delete the entry.

Immediate Solutions

Solving Internet Connection Problems

On the surface, getting on the Net with Mac OS X should be no more complicated than doing so under Mac OS 9. However, the new networking architecture may create problems from time to time, especially with programs that have only recently made the migration to the new operating system. Here's a list of some of the most frequent problems and what you can do to resolve them:

- *You cannot get online with a cable modem or DSL.* Some ISPs may require special software to connect. You'll have to contact the service to see when a Mac OS X–compatible version is available, or whether other connection options can be found. In the meantime, check whether your service will give you a static set of IP access numbers, which might get you connected when you enter them via the Network pane of the System Preferences application.

NOTE: *The need to use special software is strictly theoretical. I've not run into any services, other than AOL and CompuServe, which you cannot configure directly in the Network preference panel once you know the correct setup information.*

TIP: *Some cable providers require entering a dedicated modem ID address in your network settings to allow you to access their network. You will need to enter that information correctly in order for you to connect to that service; the Mac OS X Setup Assistant and the Network preference panels both include a place for you to put this information. Others may even require use of a special application to log in; you will have to contact the ISP directly as to what's needed to access its networks if the usual steps don't succeed.*

- *Classic applications may not run with dial-up connections.* The watchword is to try first. Aside from proprietary services, specifically AOL and CompuServe, you may not need to be concerned about this issue. There is enough Mac OS X–savvy software around to provide a satisfactory Internet experience until your favorite is updated.

NOTE: *One possible solution for this problem is a shareware utility, PortReflector, which reflects the TCP/IP connections from Mac OS 9 to Mac OS X so you can continue to use your Classic dial-up program.*

21. Surfing the Net

451

Chapter 21 Surfing the Net

> **TIP:** It's a good idea to retain a backup of your TCP/IP Preferences file before installing Mac OS X to avoid problems in case you need to use your ISP when going back to Mac OS 9.

- *Artwork changes from browser to browser.* This issue is due to the inexact nature of the way a browser interprets a page and is a chronic problem (and the source of endless headaches) for Web authors. Despite claims from each publisher that its browser supports standards better than the competition, expect differences. If you want to view a site in a particular way, you may want to stick with the browser that presents it the way you like. Another possibility is to report a display problem to the publisher of the browser application, so it can examine the situation and see if it can do anything to update the program for better display.

- *A site is not accessible.* This may be the fault of the site itself or of Internet congestion and not your browser or connection. The first possible solution is to click the Refresh or Reload button on the browser, so that the site is retrieved again from scratch. Another possible solution is to log off from your ISP and then reconnect. If neither step resolves the problem, try to access the site again at a different time.

- *A site's artwork is distorted.* One possible solution is to just refresh or reload the page, which delivers the site from scratch. If that fails to resolve the problem, follow the steps in the earlier section "Deleting Browser Caches" to empty the Web cache. If doing so doesn't resolve the issue, it may be the fault of the Web site itself, so there's nothing you can do but complain to the Webmaster.

> **TIP:** If you use the embedded version of a browser as supplied with AOL or CompuServe 2000, go to the Preferences dialog box of either application. Scroll to the WWW category and uncheck the Use Compressed Images option. This setting keeps AOL and its sister service from converting the Web artwork to a proprietary format and delivers a more accurate rendering of Web artwork and photos.

- *Download speeds vary.* It is normal for the speed of a file download to vary somewhat, whether you have a dial-up connection or broadband. This is a normal part of the process; sometimes, it's a problem with your connection or with congestion on the part of the Web server hosting the site. However, if download speed bogs down, you may want to stop the download and try again. If you have a dial-up connection, you may also want to log off and then reconnect; however, if all other services run at normal speed, there may be nothing you can do to resolve the problem.

Immediate Solutions

- *Internet Connect doesn't support your modem.* As with the Classic Mac OS, only a fixed number of popular modem makes and models are supported (although the list is quite large in Mac OS X 10.2). Most Macs that can run Mac OS X already come with an Apple internal modem, so this may not be a serious issue for you. But, if you have a different modem, feel free to experiment with a similar make or model, or just use Hayes Compatible. Most modems that support standard setups will probably function in a satisfactory manner. If you still do not get acceptable performance, contact the manufacturer of the modem directly for suggestions.

- *Dial-up connection fails.* You try to log in and don't succeed. Should this happen, verify the information you placed in the Internet Connect application. Review Chapter 8 for information on how to set up this program to work with your ISP. If the information is all right, try to connect once again. If the connection still fails, contact your ISP and see if it is doing system maintenance or can offer you alternate connection numbers.

- *The browser crashes.* With Mac OS X, you do not need to restart your Mac whenever a program freezes or suddenly quits. You can continue to work, and even try running the application again. Because some of the applications for Mac OS X are beta versions, check with the publisher's Web site for newer versions. You should also read Chapter 19, which covers a number of ways to troubleshoot Mac OS X.

- *Java applets don't run.* Although Mac OS X incorporates the very latest Java technology from Sun Microsystems, not all Web browsers were working properly with Java applets when this book was written. This was particularly true of iCab and Opera, both of which were in public beta form. If you run into a problem, first try the site in Microsoft's Internet Explorer and if it works there, check the Web site run by the publisher of your preferred browser (or VersionTracker.com) for information about an updated version that might fix the problem.

Related solutions:	Found on page:
Using Internet Connect for Dial-Up Networking	197
Solving System Crashes and Freezes	405

Chapter 22

Exploring Apple's Email Software

If you need an immediate solution to:	See page:
Setting Up Your User Account	467
Importing Your Email Messages	471
Customizing Mail's Toolbar	473
Composing a New Message	473
Responding to a Message	475
Quoting Messages	476
Spellchecking Your Messages	476
Sending Email Attachments	477
Forwarding Email	479
Adding Email Signatures	480
Formatting Email	481
Blocking Spam	481
Setting Mail Rules	482
Getting Your Email Automatically	483
Using the Address Book	484
Importing an Address Book	486
Finding a Message	487
Why Can't I Send My Email?	488
Why Are Messages Scrambled?	489
Why Doesn't Mail Check All My Accounts?	490

Chapter 22 Exploring Apple's Email Software

In Brief

When it comes to sending messages, email rules. In fact, where would we be without it? Each day, hundreds of millions of messages cross the Internet on their way to folks across the world, and email has long since supplanted postal mail in the eyes of many people for sending messages to family and business contacts.

In addition, offices use email for exchanging messages within their companies. This is becoming increasingly common, even if the recipient sits in an adjacent office or cubicle. In fact, email has sometimes replaced the practice of actually speaking with a nearby coworker.

NOTE: *Just as an example of what might be considered using email to the extreme, I have observed two coworkers seated next to each other exchanging lengthy email messages rather than simply talking it over. Another common practice is the use of instant messaging in lieu of conversation, and I'll get into that in Chapter 23, when I discuss Apple's iChat.*

All recent versions of the Mac OS have shipped with email software, usually Microsoft's Outlook Express and Netscape Communicator, both of which operate in the Classic environment. With the arrival of Mac OS X, there's a new kid on the block named, simply enough, Mail (see Figure 22.1).

Apple's new email program, based in part on the email software shipped with the NeXTSTEP operating system, the precursor to Mac OS X, started out as an essentially no-frills application. But over time it has been improved and now, in many respects, rivals the others in terms of features and performance.

Here's a brief list of its important features:

- *Junk mail filtering*—This is the number one feature, with a bullet. SPAM is the bane of the personal computer user's existence, and Mail has a sophisticated method of flagging it and getting it out of your way. Using a feature Apple calls "latent semantic analysis," both subject and content are analyzed for suspicious messages. The default "Training" mode, described later in this chapter, lets you tell Mail when it's wrong, so you can refine its accuracy.

In Brief

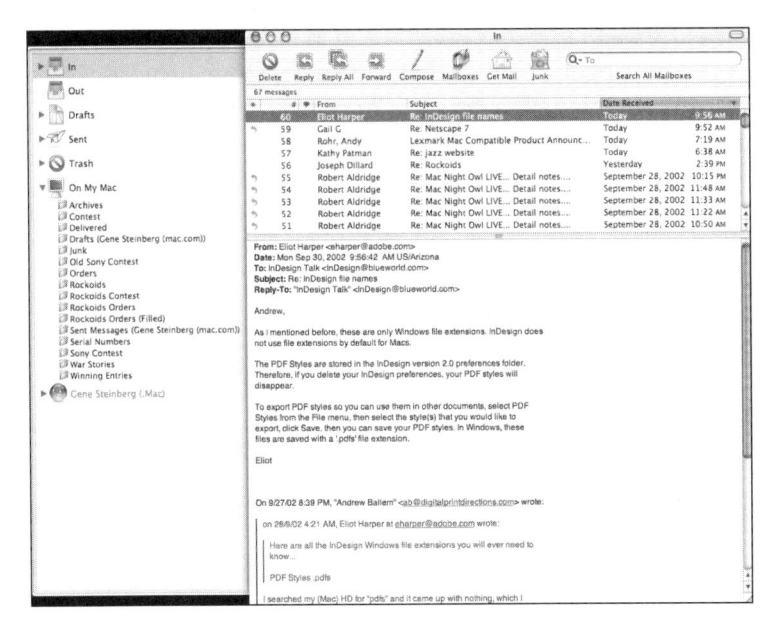

Figure 22.1 Apple's email client is clean, uncluttered, and lightning-quick.

- *Multiple user accounts*—Do you have home and office user accounts, or different email addresses for business and personal use? Mail lets you configure the program to handle all of them. You can set it to log in at specified time intervals so you're never out of touch. In addition, other users who work on your Mac can configure their own settings and store their own collections of email without having access to anyone else's mail.

- *Ability to Import Mailboxes*—No doubt, you have an email account set up with another program. With a reasonable degree of fidelity, you can import your mailboxes from Entourage, Netscape, Eudora, Outlook Express, and Claris Emailer.

NOTE: *Neither AOL nor CompuServe 2000 mailboxes are supported, and that is not expected to change. AOL Time Warner continues to use its own proprietary method of storing and processing email. All I can suggest is that you check Apple's Web site for the latest updates, but don't get too optimistic.*

- *HTML formatting supported*—You can send and receive messages with Web links and full text formatting, depending on the limits of the recipient's service. Additionally, you can place pictures within your messages, such as family photos to go with your descriptions of a family vacation.

22. Exploring Apple's Email Software

459

- *Management of stored email*—With this feature, you can set up extra folders in your personal mailbox to store the messages you receive in different categories. You can also use email rules to make sure that messages from specific sources are placed automatically in a particular folder. Rules are useful if you want to store mail for later retrieval, or if you receive lots of junk mail from a particular source and want to gather it for later disposal.

- *Automatic signatures*—You can create and store multiple signatures for personal and business messages. There's also a "rich text" option that lets you include automatic email and Web links in a signature.

- *Spellchecker*—As you write a message, if you leave on the option for interactive checking, words with potential spelling problems are flagged in red. Otherwise, you can spell-check manually before you send a message.

- *Message searching*—Messages can be searched by sender, recipient, subject, or content. This is a powerful tool that you can use to find information quickly in the messages you've stored.

NOTE: Whenever email awaits you in the Mail application, the icon for the program in the Dock will display a number specifying how many messages remain unread.

Reviewing Other Mac OS X Email Choices

Don't get me wrong. I don't want to create the impression that Mail is your only choice in Mac OS X email software. The fact that it comes free with your installation, however, and is configured when you set up Mac OS X in the System Preferences application, gets you through the initial hurdles of configuration. What's more, I have a personal affinity for its marvelous email filter, which has made my online experience far more pleasant, since I'm not bothered near as much by those pesky unsolicited messages.

But it is by no means your only choice. Here's a brief look at other options you may want to explore before you make a final decision. In each case, I'll ignore the basic email features that they all share, such as multiple user accounts, the ability to import messages from other programs, and message filtering, and move on to some of the unique attributes that are worth considering if you're looking for alternatives.

In Brief

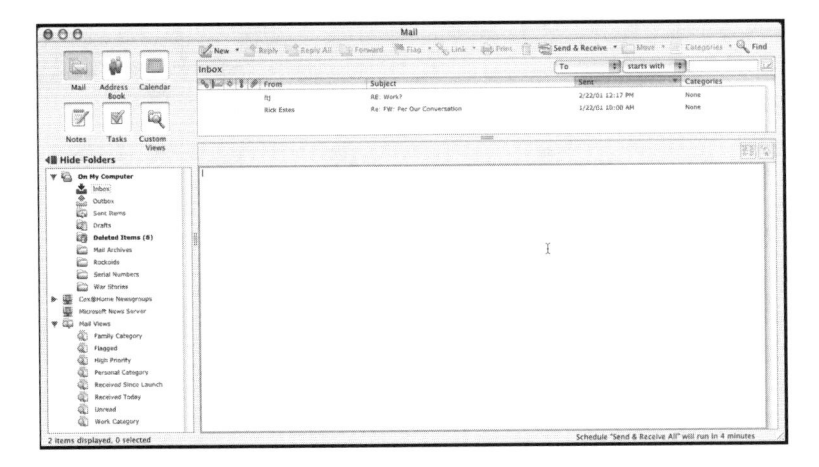

Figure 22.2 Entourage X inherits Mac OS X's Aqua user interface, plus plenty of powerful contact management features.

Entourage X

Part of Microsoft's Office v. X for Mac business application suite, Entourage X (see Figure 22.2) is descended from the free Outlook Express application. But it's not just restricted to email and newsgroup messages. This is a fully featured personal information manager that includes a calendar and task and event reminders and organization. The major features of Entourage include:

- *Rich content*—Similar to a feature that is supported in Mail and AOL's email, you are able to insert graphics and photos within the body of your message. Going further, Entourage X also works with sounds and video clips.

- *Junk mail filter*—If you're bothered and bewildered by a constant flurry of offensive or annoying sales pitches, you can set Entourage X's filter to check and flag spam. The sensitivity of the junk mail filter can be adjusted to lessen flagging of messages you do want to retrieve. In addition, you can set up exceptions, so that certain messages are not labeled as "junk." While it's not quite as sensitive as the one in Mac OS X's mail application, it is a usable alternative.

- *Address Book with international support*—Entourage X's Address Book feature includes all the basic contact information, such as name, address, email address, and so forth, plus personal information, including birthdays and anniversaries. In addition, it provides automatic support for the unique mailing address formatting used in a number of places around the world, such as Europe and Japan.

Chapter 22 Exploring Apple's Email Software

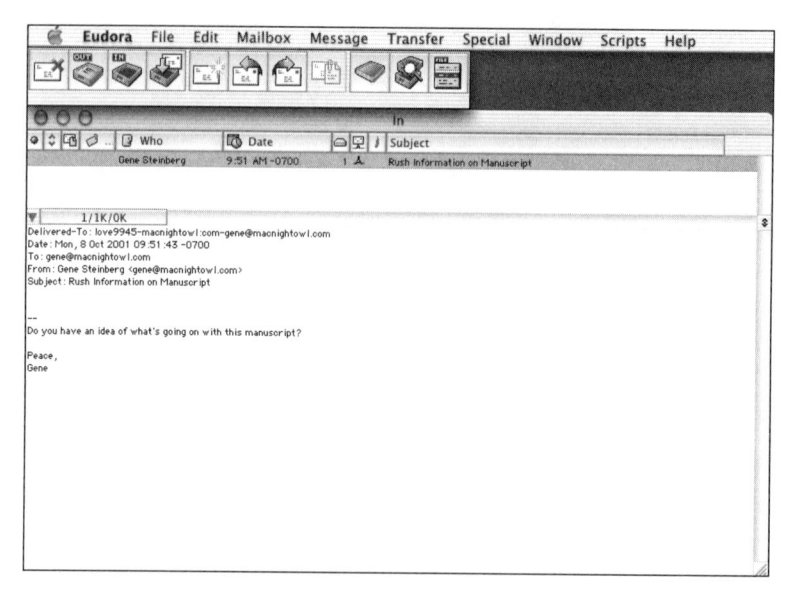

Figure 22.3 This is the Paid version of Eudora Pro, fully featured without ad banners.

- *Tri-pane calendar*—You can view your appointment and event calendar by month, week, or even workweek. You are also able to put tasks that are due or overdue in a separate pane for easy organization.

NOTE: If you prefer Apple's Mail application, you can get the calendaring functions courtesy of Apple's iCal. You'll learn more about it in the next and final chapter.

Eudora Pro

You can download and install the current version of Eudora Pro (see Figure 22.3) from the publisher's Web site (www.qualcomm.com) without paying a license fee, but the program has three modes of operation depending on whether you want to upgrade to a paid version. The first, Lite, is roughly equivalent to the Eudora Lite software used on Macs for years. You get full use of the software, but three key features, such as the ability to use Secure Sockets Layer (SSL) in logging on to an email server, placing photos in the address book, or using the MoodWatch feature (more about this feature shortly) are not available. The second free mode is called Sponsored, in which you see little ad banners on your email screen; and the final is Paid, when you pay a license fee to get full use of the software without being presented with any advertising.

In Brief

NOTE: The ad mode for Eudora is not super-intrusive, and you're not pestered with annoying pop-up windows. So if you opt for all the features but would rather let the advertisers pay the bills, this isn't a bad way to go.

Here's a brief look at some of the distinctive features of Eudora Pro:

- *SSL support*—This feature lets you gain access to email services (usually corporate and educational) that require encrypted authentication. It also lets you encrypt your email for maximum security. Apple's Mail doesn't offer this feature (although I understand it's being considered for a future version).

- *MoodWatch*—Did you ever write a message in which you expressed anger over a person or situation, and then regret what you wrote after it had been sent? The MoodWatch feature can be set to flag language that may be offensive or inflammatory, and delay sending the message to allow a cooling-off period. That way, if you decide that maybe you were just a little too over-the-top in your message, you can revise it before it's sent. It's a great way to keep friends and business contacts when the going gets tough.

- *Photos in Address Book*—AOL users have enjoyed this feature for a while: the ability to insert someone's photo in your personal address book.

NOTE: Apple's Address Book application also lets you store photos, as you'll discover later on in this chapter.

Netscape

Once upon a time, Netscape was the market leader in Web browsers, and it remains unique among the programs discussed here because it integrates the browser and the email client (see Figure 22.4) in a single application (an instant messaging client is also included).

Here are the basic features of the email component of Netscape 7's for Mac OS X:

- *AOL support*—Here's a feature that is not likely to be found in any other Mac OS X application, other than AOL's own client software. It allows you to retrieve your AOL email in the same fashion as you can retrieve email from any other online account.

- *Separate mailbox for each account*—This feature lets you easily sort messages from your various Internet accounts without having to configure an all-new mailbox for each address.

22. Exploring Apple's Email Software

463

Chapter 22 Exploring Apple's Email Software

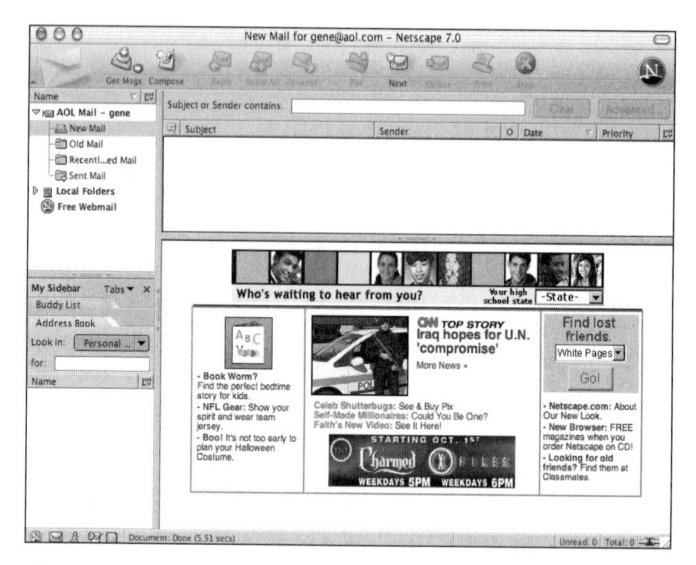

Figure 22.4 Netscape 6.1's email window is similar to the one available in prior versions of the program.

How Does Mail Rate?

Considering that some pretty powerful email programs are available for the Mac OS, just where does Mail stand when compared to Microsoft's Outlook Express and Entourage, Netscape Communicator, Qualcomm's Eudora, or even the defunct mail client, Claris Emailer? Here's a brief list of features that are lacking or only partly implemented in Mail:

> **NOTE:** Claris Emailer, which was discontinued several years ago, works well from the Classic environment. Aside from Netscape for Mac OS X, it is the only program that can handle mail from standard Internet accounts and AOL, which is one of the reasons (aside from its simple, uncluttered interface) that I continue to use it.

- *Separate address book*—Apple has provided a separate program, Address Book (see Figure 22.5), for managing your address list. It is designed to serve as the contact list not just for Mail, but for any third party program that is developed to link to it (such as SmithMicro's FAXstf X). It is linked directly with Mail and provides limited options to import the address lists from other programs.
- *Powerful message filtering*—Yes, you can establish rules for messages, but the best feature, bar none, is Mail's ability to flag possible spam email and have the messages automatically moved to a separate Junk mail filter, when in Automatic mode. The

In Brief

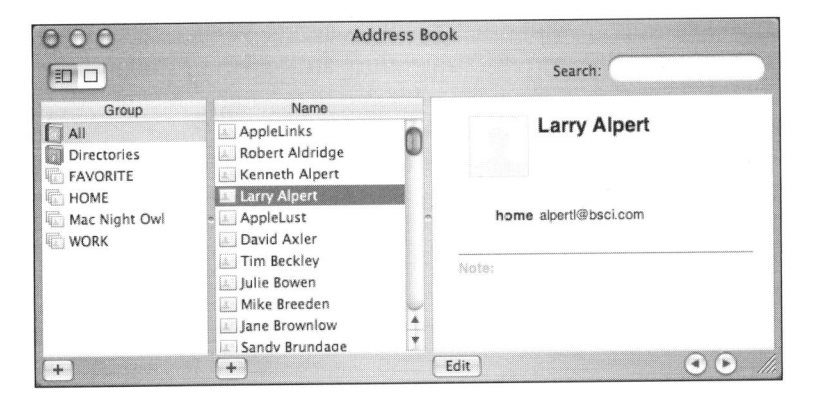

Figure 22.5 Use this program to configure an address book for messages.

contents of that folder can be deleted a regular intervals, to give you enough time to double-check for a mistake.

- *No newsgroup support*—Microsoft's Entourage and Outlook Express and Netscape can retrieve Usenet newsgroup messages. Mail doesn't support this feature. If you are interested in this option, look for a Mac OS X—savvy news-reading program to support your needs.

TIP: *Two very useful options for reading newsgroup messages are NewsWatcher-X, the Carbon update to the popular free newsgroup application; and Thoth, from Brian Clark, author of YA-NewsWatcher. The latter, however, is demoware, and the downloadable version is crippled in key functions, such as saving updates to subscribed newsgroups, unless you buy a user license. However, Thoth is worth the modest fee and is a favorite among many users. A third option, MT-NewsWatcher is favored by many, because of its superior ability to multitask. Even better, it's free.*

- *No automatic connections*—Microsoft's Outlook Express and Entourage can both be configured to check email at regular intervals, even if the program isn't open, by launching and establishing your Net connection. Mail can recheck for messages on a regular basis only when it's running.

- *No support for AOL email*—As mentioned earlier, only Netscape 6 and Claris Emailer can retrieve AOL email. If you wish to access your AOL messages otherwise, you have to log on to the AOL Web site (**www.aol.com**) with your browser and access its AOL Anywhere feature.

NOTE: *As this book was written, Mail also didn't support Microsoft's Hotmail service. You can set that up courtesy of Microsoft's own email clients, or via your Web browser.*

22. Exploring Apple's Email Software

465

Chapter 22 Exploring Apple's Email Software

If you've worked with other email programs, you'll find that setting up and using Mail is pretty straightforward, and the differences aren't all that significant. Even better, some of the initial setups, for your default email account, are done as when you configure the Mac OS X Setup Assistant. The "Immediate Solutions" section covers the basics of using this application.

Immediate Solutions

Immediate Solutions

Setting Up Your User Account

When I described how to work with the Mac OS X Setup Assistant in Chapter 3, I explained how to enter your email settings during the initial setup of the new operating system. However, if you need to change those settings or add an extra user account, just follow these steps:

NOTE: If you gave your email account information when you ran the Mac OS X Setup Assistant, it will all be here. You can edit it as needed, or add any additional ISP accounts you want.

1. Launch the Mail application.
2. Go to Mail's Application menu and choose Preferences. The dialog box shown in Figure 22.6 appears.
3. Click the Accounts icon, and then the Add Account button, shown in Figure 22.6, to bring up the Account Information dialog box (see Figure 22.7).

NOTE: If your Mac is set up with multiple user accounts, each user will be able to configure Mail separately to handle his or her accounts and email from that user account. The information isn't available to any other users, unless they log in to the same account.

4. Under the Account Type category, choose the type of email account you're establishing (usually a POP account, although

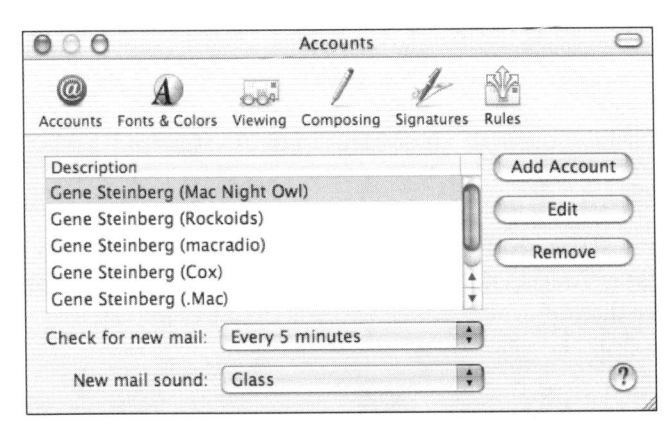

Figure 22.6 Set up and manage Mail's settings from this screen.

Chapter 22   Exploring Apple's Email Software

Figure 22.7   Enter your basic email user settings in the Account Information dialog box.

some ISPs support IMAP instead) and give a description, such as "Work", "Personal", or the name of the ISP (a default will be entered by the program otherwise). If you are setting up a .Mac account, there's a separate selection for that.

*NOTE: Not sure what account settings to use? Check with your ISP. While it may be possible to predict some settings, such as the name of a POP server (such as **pop.[ISPname].com**), even a single wrong entry will make it impossible to send or retrieve your messages.*

5. Enter your email address and full name in the first section of the dialog box.

TIP: Apple helps guide you through the type of information by pututing in gray text prompts in most of the text entry fields.

6. Under Incoming Mail Server, enter the name of the mail server from which you retrieve your email (usually your ISP's, unless you have other email accounts you want to use). Insert your username and password as needed to connect to your ISP.

7. In the final category, you need to enter the name of the Outgoing Mail Server of your ISP, if it's not already listed, and, if necessary, authentication or password account information. To store that information, simply click on the popup menu and choose Add Server.

8. In the dialog box that appears, enter the name of the server. Should authentication be required, click on the Authentication pop-up menu and specify which authentication scheme you

Immediate Solutions

want (the normal setup is Password) and then enter your username and password.

NOTE: You remaining choices are Kerberos Version 5 (GSAAPI), and MD5 Challenge-Response. Which do you need? Depends on the email server's setup, and you'll need to check with your ISP or systems administrator for that information.

9. Click OK to accept the server settings.

10. When your settings in the Account Information tab are complete, click OK to store them. Or, if you prefer, click the Special Mailboxes tab (see Figure 22.8) to further customize your settings. You have these options:

    - *Sent*—Click on the pop-up menu to select when or if sent messages are erased. The default is Never, but you can have them zapped after a day, a week or a month, or whenever you quit Mail. Your decision.

WARNING: Once a message is erased from Mail, it cannot be recovered, so choose your erase options carefully. It doesn't hurt to be conservative and have messages hang around a little longer, as they do not consume huge hunks of hard drive space.

    - *Junk*—Once you put Mail's Junk Mail filter in Automatic mode (I'll cover the subject in more detail later in this

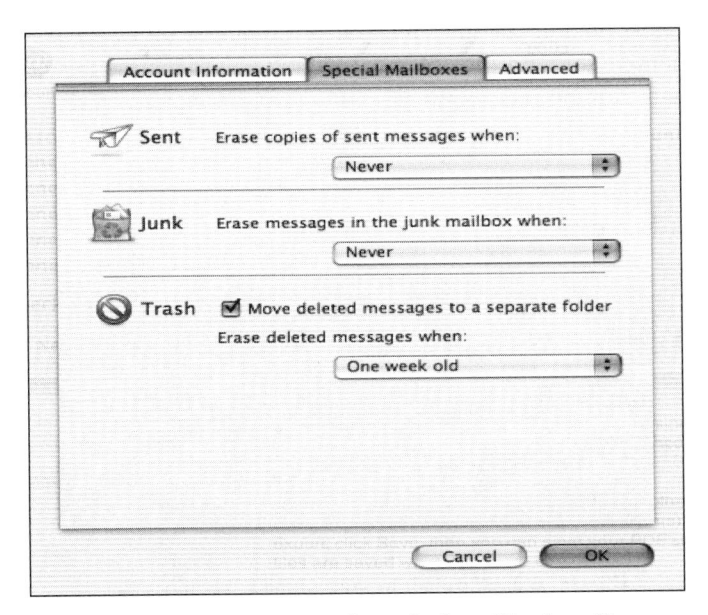

Figure 22.8   Choose how your Sent, Junk and Trash mailboxes process messages.

chapter), suspicious messages will be deposited in a Junk mailbox. You can opt to have them erased at the same intervals as your Sent mail.

- *Trash*—Once you delete messages, they are placed in a Trash folder and can be erased at the intervals you select. Your move.

NOTE: What interval should you choose? Depends on how long you need your Sent mail. For the other options, a day or a week should be sufficient to give you a chance to review and move messages that were labeled as Junk or trashed by mistake.

---

11. All done? Here's your final set of options. To see them, click on the Advanced tab (see Figure 22.9) to see setup information under these categories:

    - *Enable This Account*—Normally checked by default. You can disable a user account if you don't want to retrieve messages from it for a while.

    - *Include This Account When Checking For New Mail*—For whatever reason (perhaps the account is only used rarely), you may choose not to check for a specific email account when new mail is automatically accessed.

    - *Remove Copy from Server After Retrieving a Message*—Messages can be left on the server for a week, a month, or removed right away, when mail is retrieved via Mail. If you access email from multiple Macs, you may want to leave them be for a period of time, to allow you to access the same mail from both computers.

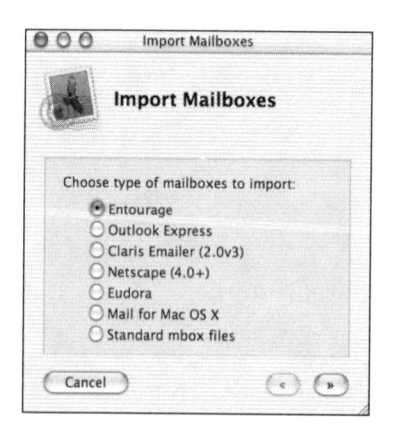

Figure 22.9 This setting controls how your email account runs.

Immediate Solutions

NOTE: The Remove now option clears messages right away. It's a useful option if you have a lot of stored mail and need to clear out your mailbox, as most ISPs have a limit on messages or storage capacity (5MB is common).

- *Prompt Me To Skip Messages Over*—Specify a size if you don't want to look at large messages or those with large attachments right away.
- *Port*—This setting is entirely based on the requirements of your ISP or network system. Normally it's best to leave the default entry. The other options, such as Use SSL (Secure Sockets Layer) and Authentication, depend entirely on the requirements of the email system you're using.

NOTE: If you're not sure what settings to enter for your email options, contact your ISP for the proper access information. It will vary considerably, depending on an individual service's setup.

12. When your settings are complete, click OK to store them.

TIP: Another useful email preference is available in the Viewing pane of the Mail Preferences dialog box. Just choose an account, click Edit and then the Account Options tab. You can use these settings to determine when messages are automatically purged from your mailbox and whether to download email images, animations, or other HTML attachments. If you don't want to view lots of clutter in your messages, particularly if most such messages are really junk mail, you'll want to turn off that option.

Related solution:	Found on page:
Setting System Preferences Under Mac OS X	46

Importing Your Email Messages

Once you've given Mail a test run, perhaps you'll decide to keep using the program. What do you do about the messages already stored in other software? Fortunately, Mail can import the contents of those mailboxes with a reasonable degree of fidelity.

Here's how to use that option:

1. With Mail open, choose Import Mailboxes from the File menu to bring up the import assistant shown in Figure 22.10. Click the right arrow to proceed or (when not grayed out) the left arrow to recheck your settings.

Chapter 22 Exploring Apple's Email Software

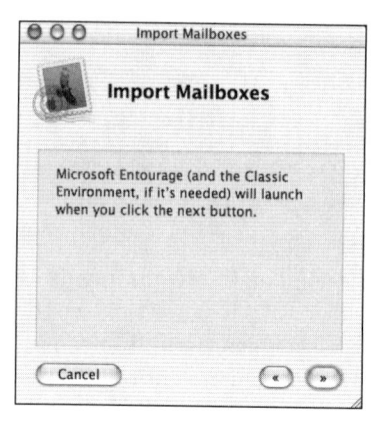

Figure 22.10 Mail notifies you that the selected email client—Entourage, in this case—will be launched as part of the import process.

2. Choose the email client from which you want to import messages. The Standard mbox files option is used to import mail from unsupported programs, so long as you can save those messages in this industry standard format. You'll want to check the export features for your e-mail program to see if mbox is supported. As you progress through the dialog boxes, click the right or "next" arrow to proceed. When you select an email client, you'll see an acknowledgment such as the one shown in Figure 22.11.

NOTE: *This process must be done separately for each email program you're using. In addition, the mailboxes will all be placed in separate message folders; there's no way to put them together except by manually dragging and dropping them into the proper location.*

3. After you've selected the mailboxes that apply to the email application (see Figure 22.11), select the ones you want to convert and click the right arrow to proceed. By default, all of the folders in the email application that you're importing will be checked.

4. You'll see a progress bar showing the number of messages being retrieved. When the import process is complete, click Done to wrap up the process and dismiss the dialog box.

5. If the list of mailboxes isn't displayed, choose Show Mailboxes from the View menu. You'll see additional folders in your Mail drawer that match the ones in your email program. Click on any of them to finish the process: Mail will update its database to incorporate the messages you've imported.

Immediate Solutions

Figure 22.11　Once you've selected mailboxes, a click of the right arrow will begin the import process.

TIP: If you have an email application not supported in Mail's Import feature, or if the import process goes badly, you may want to try AppleScript import tools that promise better-quality imports. The files are available in your AppleScript folder, in the Mail Scripts folder under Helper Scripts.

Customizing Mail's Toolbar

Extending the Finder-like display of Mail, you can easily customize the toolbar in the same fashion as the Mac OS X Finder. To make these changes, follow these steps:

1. With Mail open, choose Customize Toolbar from the View menu. The display shown in Figure 22.12 will appear.
2. To add icons to the toolbar, click and drag them to the desired location in the toolbar.
3. To remove an icon, just drag it off the toolbar, and it will disappear.
4. To restore the default set of icons, click and drag the Default Set icons to the toolbar.
5. Click Done to store your settings.

Composing a New Message

To write a brand-new message in Mail, just follow these steps:

473

Chapter 22 Exploring Apple's Email Software

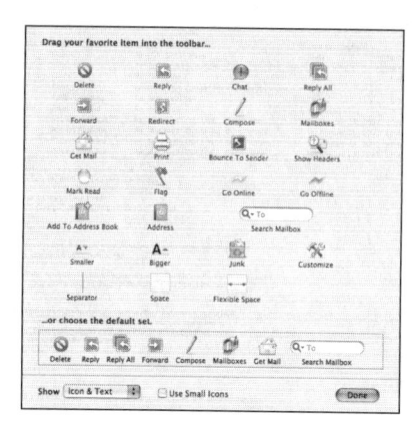

Figure 22.12 Click and drag the items you want to the toolbar.

1. Click on the Compose button, which brings up a blank email screen, shown in Figure 22.13.
2. Type the recipient's email address in the To field (such as mine, **gene@macnightowl.com**). If you enter the name of more than one recipient, separate the names with a comma. If the email address you're looking for is in your Address Book, click the Address button to bring up that program so you can add the names you want.

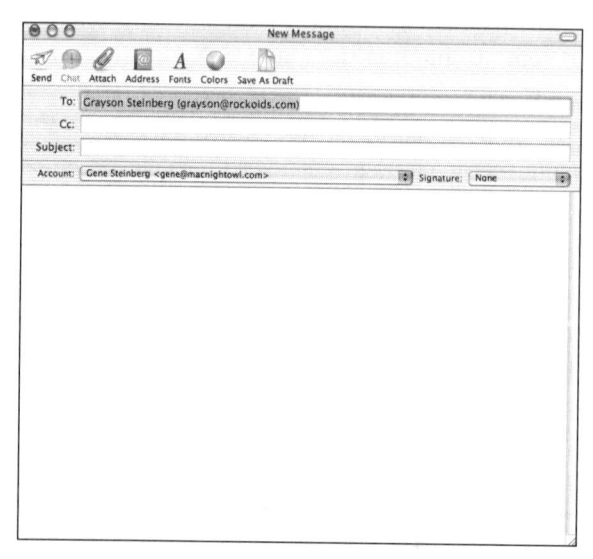

Figure 22.13 Begin writing your message here.

474

Immediate Solutions

NOTE: *A third addressing option, BCC, sends a blind carbon copy to recipients. None of the recipients will see the names of those in the BCC field. By default, this option is turned off, but you can activate it by going to the Message menu and choosing Add BCC Header, or press Command+Shift+B. Unfortunately, the BCC field can only be added on an individual message basis. There is no global setting to include this option.*

3. To send courtesy or carbon copies to other recipients, place their addresses in the CC field, separated by commas.

NOTE: *A third addressing option, BCC, sends a blind carbon copy to recipients. None of the recipients will see the names of those in the BCC field. By default, this option is turned off, but you can activate it by going to the Message menu and choosing Add BCC Header. Unfortunately, the BCC field can only be added on an individual message basis. There is no global setting to include this option.*

4. Enter a topic for your message in the Subject field. You can move through fields with the Tab key, or reverse the motion with Shift+Tab. This is the same behavior you find in any email program.
5. Type the text of your message. If the spellcheck feature is turned on (and it is by default), you'll see spelling errors flagged in red.
6. When you've completed your message, click the Send button to speed it on its way.
7. To work on the message again at a later time, go to the File menu and choose Save As Draft. The message will be stored in your Drafts mailbox for later updating.

NOTE: *By default, the messages you send are saved in the Sent folder in your personal mailbox. This and other settings for the messages you write are saved under Mail Preferences, when you click the Compose button. In this settings panel, you can also specify a different location for sent messages.*

Responding to a Message

When you receive messages, they'll show up in your Inbox, and just clicking on a title is sufficient to see the contents in the bottom pane of the Mail application window. New messages are signified by a blue button at the left of the message's title.

Once you've finished reading a message, you might want to write a reply. To do so, click the Reply button to bring up a response window, shown in Figure 22.14.

475

NOTE: If the message went to more than one recipient, you have the option to reply to the original sender or, by clicking Reply All, to everyone who received the message, including those listed in the CC field.

When you've finished writing your message, click Send to whisk it on its way (you have to be connected to your ISP for this to work, of course).

Quoting Messages

When you respond to a message, it's customary to quote relevant portions of the message to which you're responding. The normal way to do this is to first select the material that you wish to quote, and then click Reply. The quoted portion will show up in your response window.

WARNING! By default, if you don't select the portions of a message to be quoted, the entire message will appear in the response window. If you're responding to a long message, seeing so much material can be irritating for the recipient. It's better to quote just enough of the message so the recipient knows precisely what your response is about.

Spellchecking Your Messages

Mail excels in its ability to automatically check your spelling as you type, marking words with questionable spelling in red (see Figure 22.15).

Here's how you can handle Mail's powerful spellcheck features:

1. When Mail flags a word whose spelling is in question, you can either make your correction as you proceed, or Control+click the word to see a contextual menu with your spellcheck options (see Figure 22.16).

2. From the contextual menu, you can choose a different spelling from the list of suggestions, or have the spellchecker ignore or learn the word as it's spelled. When you specify a different spelling for the word, it will be replaced automatically.

3. To perform a batch spellcheck, simply choose Spelling from the Edit menu, and then Spelling from the submenu. Or, press Command+:.

Immediate Solutions

Figure 22.14 Write your answer in the response window.

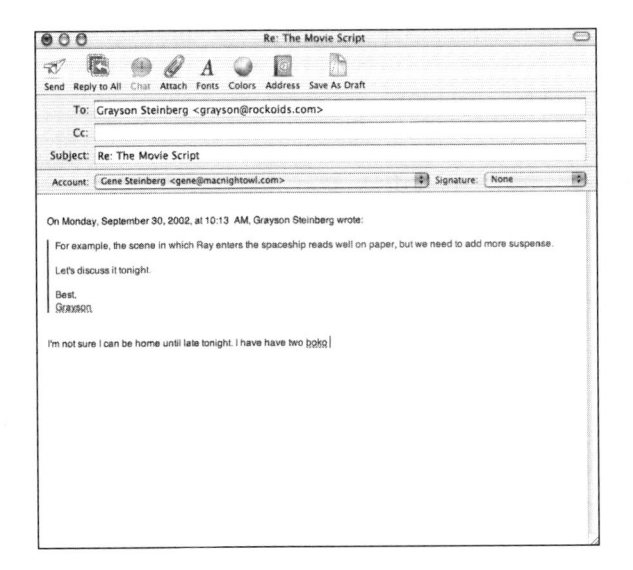

Figure 22.15 Where would your long-suffering author be without the ability to fix his spelling errors?

Sending Email Attachments

To send one or more files with your email, you'll find the process is at once simple and complex. To attach a file to your email, follow these steps:

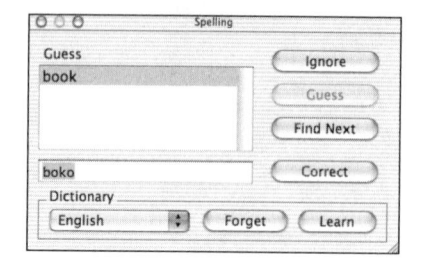

Figure 22.16 Correct the word or leave it as is.

1. Open a New Message window.
2. Click the Attach button to produce an Open dialog box, shown in Figure 22.17.
3. Select one or more files to send, and click the Open button.
4. Continue to prepare to send your message, and then click Send. If the Activity Viewer window is displayed (it's a command in the Window menu), you'll see a progress indicator showing how much of your message has been sent. The time it takes to transfer depends on the size of the file you wish to send and the speed of your Net connection.

When sending attachments, you'll need to consider a few items to make sure your files reach their destination intact:

- *Make sure your recipient can open it.* If your attachment was created in a particular application, you should check whether the recipient has the same program, or a program that can handle that type of document. For example, if you're using Microsoft Word, a Windows user with a recent version of the program can read the document. In addition, many other programs can read Word documents. However, more specialized software, such as QuarkXPress, requires that the recipient have the same program on hand.

- *Name Windows files properly.* Whereas the Mac OS, both old and new, doesn't need a file extension to identify the type of file, Windows does. The file types are entered as three-letter extensions. Common names include .doc for a Word document, .jpg for a JPEG file, and .gif for a GIF picture.

TIP: Some programs, such as Word and recent versions of Adobe Photoshop, can be set to automatically append the proper extension for a file. The Mac OS X Finder and native programs are savvy about proper file extensions, but it never hurts to double-check.

Immediate Solutions

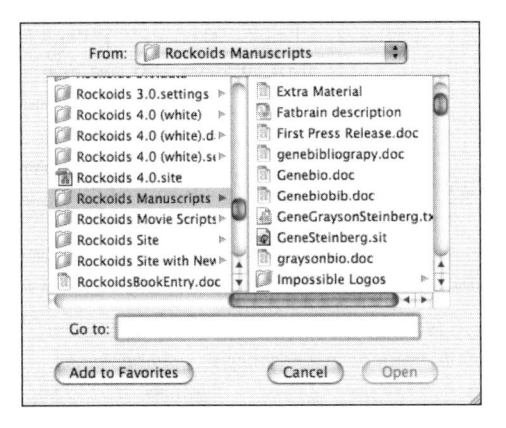

Figure 22.17 Select a file to accompany your email.

- *Be careful about compressing files.* Whereas Mac users can handle files compressed in the industry-standard StuffIt format, users of Microsoft Windows generally use Zip files (although there is a StuffIt version for Windows, as well). If you know your files will be read by both Mac and Windows users, consider the DropZip utility that comes with the latest versions of Aladdin Systems' StuffIt Deluxe. That's what I used to handle the cross-platform needs of my publisher while writing this book.

- *Don't send multiple attachments to AOL users.* AOL's email servers have problems decoding email with more than a single attachment. Just send one attachment with each message. Or, for convenience, consider using a compression program to combine the attachments into a single file. You'll also get the added benefit of being able to send a smaller file.

- *Watch out for file-size limits.* You may run into problems with large attachments. As mentioned, some services, such as AOL, limit attachments to 2MB from sources outside the service. Others can be as high as 10MB (EarthLink) or 5MB for such broadband services as Cox High Speed Internet.

Forwarding Email

Have you ever received a message that you really wanted to send to a third party, whether a friend or business contact? To send that message intact, or with some annotations of your own, just follow these steps:

Chapter 22 Exploring Apple's Email Software

1. With your new message open, click Forward. A new message window will appear with all the text in the original message quoted.
2. Address the message in the appropriate field.
3. Add text before or after the message you're forwarding, if necessary.
4. Click Send.

WARNING! *It's bad form to forward to a third party a message that the original sender might not want to disseminate. If you have any concerns about doing so, contact the original sender and ask if it's all right to send it elsewhere; if need be, specify the names of the intended recipients.*

Adding Email Signatures

Just as you put a signature on a regular letter, it's a good idea to use a signature on email as well. Although you can easily enter a signature manually, if you want to use it regularly, you can store it in Mail.

Here is how to set up a list of stored signatures:

1. With the Mail application open, go to the Application menu and choose Preferences.
2. Click the Signatures button.
3. In the Signatures dialog box, click Create Signature and type the text for the signature you want to use.
4. Enter the signature's description in the Description box (see Figure 22.18).
5. Follow the preceding steps to add extra signatures as needed.
6. With all your new signatures set up, click OK. Then, click the Active column next to the name of the signature to make it active. From here on, you can specify the signature to use from the Signature pop-up menu.

TIP: *If you are sending a message to a recipient who might not be able to see email formatted with rich text, which will show Web links and formatted text, click the Composing icon and select Plain Text from the Default Message Format pop-up menu. Doing so will affect not just your signatures, but your entire message until the setting is changed.*

Formatting Email

Mail gives you a fairly decent set of formatting controls to handle the style of your messages. With a message window open, click the Format menu to choose font style and size, and text orientation, such as left or centered. If the recipient may not be able to see a styled message, choose Make Plain Text from the Format menu.

Blocking SPAM

It's not a lunch meat, but a problem that troubles everyone with an e-mail account. While some services do have their own junk message blocking features, such as BrightMail's Spaminator, which is used by EarthLink, many services don't. You don't have to bother setting complicated rules to filter them out. Mail's powerful Junk Mail filtering feature lets you rid yourself of these annoying pitches.

Here's how to use this feature:

1. When you first run mail, Junk mail handling is in Training mode, which means messages that are questionable are flagged and listed in light brown. Without going into the significance of the color choice, this lets you separate the real from the suspicious.

2. If you see a message that isn't junk, just click on it to open the message in Mail's bottom pane, where you'll see a Not Junk button. Click that button to tell Mail that the message is not to be flagged that way, and it'll store the change in its database.

3. If Mail misses a SPAM message, select it and choose Mark as Junk Mail from the Message menu or just press Command+Shift+J.

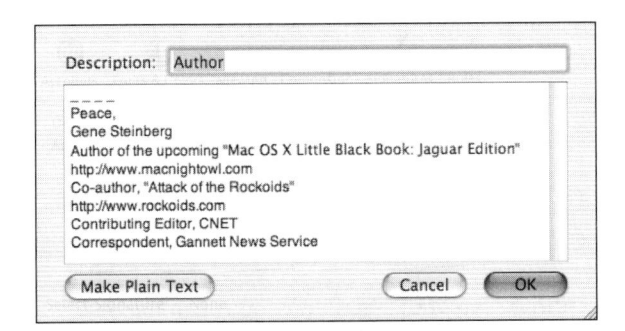

Figure 22.18   This is the author's actual signature.

4. After a week or two or when you feel Mail has gotten the idea and is correct identifying the right messages, go to Mail's application menu, choose Junk Mail and select Automatic from the sub-menu. From here on, all the Junk Mail filter will deposit all of these messages in the Junk folder.

5. You can use Mail's preferences to specify when or if the contents of the Junk mailbox are going to be deleted, as I described in the section above, entitled "Setting Up Your User Account."

WARNING! *No filter is perfect. Mail will make a mistake from time to time, so it's a good idea to check the Junk folder every day or so to make sure that messages you want aren't being improperly labeled as Junk. If you find such a message, just open it, and click Not Junk to keep it from being flagged incorrectly again. You can then drag the message into another mailbox so it isn't deleted by mistake. If Mail fails to flag a SPAM message, follow the steps in Step 3 above. The training process is never complete, even when in Automatic mode.*

Setting Mail Rules

In addition to using Mail's Junk Mail filter, you can specify custom rules to store and sort email messages. Such rules will help you organize messages for later review or disposal. Although this feature isn't as powerful as the filtering options provided by other programs mentioned in the "In Brief" section of this chapter, it's nonetheless quite useful.

Here's how to establish a mail rule:

1. With the Mail application open, choose Preferences from the Mail Application menu.

2. Click the Rules button. In the setup pane that appears, click Add Rule to bring up the setup dialog box shown in Figure 22.19.

NOTE: *By default, email rules are created for Apple's own information services. You can click the Remove buttons in the Mail preference box to dispose of them, or just uncheck the Active buttons to make them hibernate until you need them.*

---

3. Under Description, give your email-sorting rule a name. By default, it will be Rule #1, Rule #2, and so on.

Immediate Solutions

4. In the Criteria pop-up menu, select the field that applies to that specific rule, such as To, From, Subject, and so on.

5. If you need to add another category, click the plus sign, for each additional criteria you want to add. You can, for example, use the second pop-up menu to select the criteria that triggers the rule, such as whether the message Contains, Does Not Contain, Includes, and so on.

6. Type the word or phrase that field must contain to trigger the rule. For example, if all messages from someone named **grayson@rockoids.com** are to be stored, you'll enter that information for this particular rule.

7. Perform the Following Actions, check the items that determine how your rule will be applied.

8. Click the plus sign to add actions to fine-tune what happens when the criteria is met. You will be able to do such things as change the color of a flagged message, play a sound, transfer it to another mailbox or, if need be, delete it.

11. When you're finished, click OK to store the rule and then close the Mail Preferences window. From here on, any email that matches the rule criteria will be stored as you've selected. You can create different rules for different messages to provide a full range of options for storing your messages.

Getting Your Email Automatically

When you first use Mail, it automatically checks for your email on all active accounts at regular intervals. You can change this option if you want only to retrieve email manually.

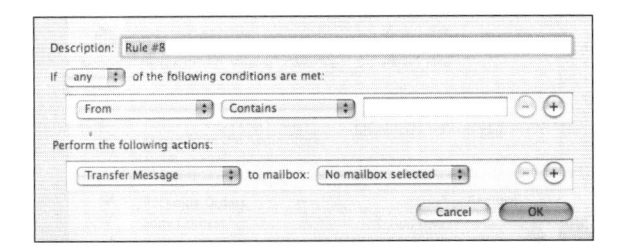

Figure 22.19   Create an email rule here.

483

Here's how to adjust the option:

1. With Mail open, go to the Application menu and choose Preferences.
2. Click Accounts and select the account for which you want to change the setting.
3. In the resulting setup window, click the Advanced tab, and then check or uncheck the Enable This Account (it's checked by default).
4. Click OK to store the settings. You'll be returned to the main Accounts setup window. From here, you can choose the Check For New Mail pop-up menu to look for new messages in your active accounts at a given interval (normal is five minutes) or manually.
5. The last setting allows you to select a sound from the pop-up menu that will notify you when a new message is received (I like Glass, but you can select None if you don't want to be disturbed). Click the close box after you've made your changes to complete the process.

Using the Address Book

No doubt you have regular contacts you'd like to send messages to without having to enter the names'manually'in an email message window. Mac OS X includes a powerful Address Book application (see Figure 22.20) that you can use to store your commonly used email addresses, or just to keep a record of your regular contacts. In addition, you can import your contacts from other email programs, if you decide to migrate from another program.

NOTE: Address Book is compatible with programs that use the vCard format. It is also used for SmithMicro's FAXstf X, the faxing software provided with many new Macs, and is available for third parties who want to use a central repository for handling contact lists.

To use this program, perform the following steps:

1. Choose Addresses from Mail's Window menu. If Mail isn't open, you'll find the Address Book application in the Dock or the Applications folder.
2. In the Group menu, click on the category that describes your contact: All, Buddy, Home, Favorite, or Work.

Immediate Solutions

3. To create a new contact, click New Card in the File menu. Enter the information in the appropriate contact fields in the Address Card window (See Figure 22.21). Each contact category is clearly labeled, so you know where to put the information.

NOTE: *The fields identified by up and down arrows can be changed. Just click on the arrows to choose another category or Custom to build a new information category from scratch.*

4. When the address card is filled in, it will automatically be stored in the All group, with your other contacts. If you want to put it in another group too, just drag it into that group, as shown in Figure 22.22.

5. If you want to create a custom group, just select New Group in the File menu and give the category a name.

NOTE: *You can attach one address card to multiple groups, or even create new groups as needed to organize your contact list.*

6. Click OK, and click Save to store the settings.
7. Repeat the preceding steps for each individual or group you wish to store.

NOTE: *To delete an address book entry, just click on it and press Delete. You'll see an acknowledgement dialog box, where you have to click Yes to remove the contact.*

8. Once you've completed an address card for a contact, you can click on the name and see the basic contents in the Preview window at the bottom of the Address Book window.

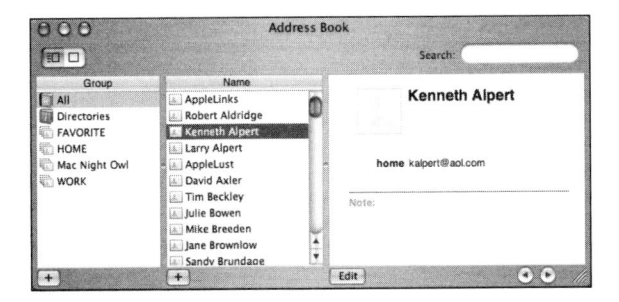

Figure 22.20   The Address Book application is a central storage repository for your regular contacts.

Chapter 22 Exploring Apple's Email Software

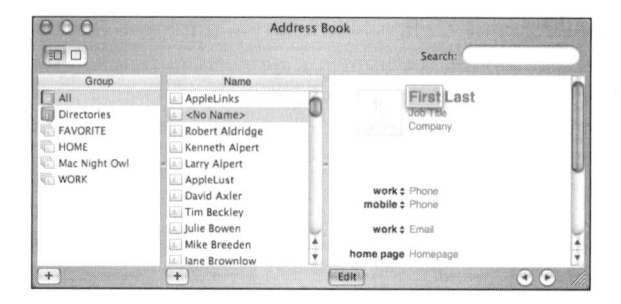

Figure 22.21 Fill in the blanks to set up a new contact.

Importing an Address Book

You do not have to redo your entire address book once you've moved on to Mail. A reasonably adept Import feature will let you import basic information from other email programs. To use the feature, follow these steps:

1. Go to your email program and use the options available (if any) to export your address book as vCards or an LDIF file.

NOTE: *Address Book only works in one direction as far as getting address information from other programs is concerned. It cannot export the address book you create in the program so you can use it in another program. I wanted to bring them into Microsoft's Entourage X, but neither Apple nor Microsoft had a way to do it beyond the standard cut and paste routine.*

2. With Address Book open, choose Import from the File menu and either vCard or LDIF from the submenu to bring up an Open dialog box shown in Figure 22.23.

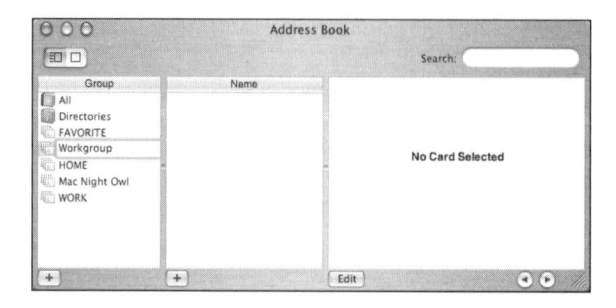

Figure 22.22 You can drag-and-drop your address cards into different groups.

Immediate Solutions

3. Select the exported address book file you want and click Open. The list you selected will be added to your Address Book, using nearly the same fields as the original.

NOTE: *If Address Book can't parse the fields, a dialog box will open in which you can select the proper destination fields for your data from a pop-up menu. If the address book entries don't come through accurately, you will need to select them in Address Book, click the Edit button, and adjust them as necessary.*

Finding a Message

Did you ever wonder what you said in that message you sent to a client a week earlier? Or, perhaps you want to find out if you sent your aunt a birthday gift, or you just need to recheck the acknowledgment letter you got from a dealer so you can track the progress of an order. Mail provides a decent set of search options so you can easily locate the message you want.

You can search by the message's header, such as the From and To information; by its subject; or by content. An individual mailbox, which you select, can be searched, or you can opt to search all your mailboxes. Here's how to run a search:

1. With Mail running, locate the mailbox you want to search, and click on its name in the Mailboxes drawer.

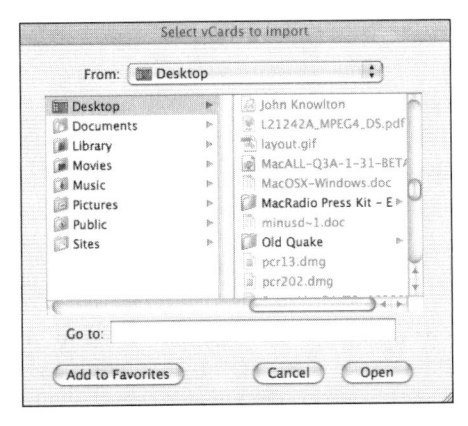

Figure 22.23   Choose the address book file from the Open dialog box.

22. Exploring Apple's Email Software

487

> **NOTE:** Mail indexes the contents of text messages, but you cannot search for text within an image or a file attachment of any kind.

2. Click the pop-up menu next to the magnifying glass icon to choose the category of the search. Entire Message covers headers, subject, and body.
3. Enter the word or phrase that describes your search in the Search field of Mail's Edit menu.
4. If a match is found, you'll see it displayed in a results window.
5. If your search ends up with the wrong result or no result, consider these options to refine your search request:
   - *Include All Words*—A search request that reads "Cars and Ford", for example, will look for email that contains these words. Use the word "and" between each word in your search.
   - *Include One Word Or The Other*—If you enter "Cars and Ford", Mail will look for matches that contain either word.
   - *Use Either Or*—If you enter "Cars and (Ford or Cadillac)", material in the first category will be located, as well as either of the items entered within the parentheses.

Why Can't I Send My Email?

Although Mail is a fairly robust application, at times it simply won't work properly. If you encounter any difficulties getting your email to go out to its recipient, consider these remedies:

- *Are you connected?* Make sure that you are actually connected to your ISP. If you're using Internet Connect for a dial-up connection, open that application and look at the status screen to make sure a connection has been made. If you've activated a system status icon for Internet Connect on your menu bar, the connection bar above the phone icon should remain solid. If it flashes, a connection hasn't been achieved. If you're connected but your email still won't work, click Disconnect to log off. Then, when the button changes to Connect, click it again to log in. If you're using a broadband connection to the Internet, such as a cable modem or DSL, you may want to try accessing a Web site to see if you have a connection. If you are connected via dial-up, or see no indication that your broadband connection is offline, contact the ISP directly for further help.

- *Message saved as a draft?* Maybe you clicked the wrong button when you wrote your message. To handle this problem, click on the Drafts mailbox, double-click the message to double check its content and then click Send.
- *E-mail sent via wrong account?* If you have several e-mail accounts, you'll have an Account pop-up menu in your message that will allow you to select the account that will send your message. The account listed will always be the one listed first in your preferences, or the one used in any message you have selected in your mailbox. If you want to change the default account, just open Mail's preferences, and drag the account you want to become the default to the top of the list. It will also be first in the pop-up menu.
- *POP server's port number is incorrect.* Open Mail's Preferences window and click the Account button. Click on the name of the account you're using, and click Edit Account. With the account information displayed, click the Advanced tab. Then, remove the entry at the bottom of the dialog box next to Port. Once you OK all the settings, Mail sets the proper number automatically when you again make your connection (assuming your ISP follows standard email protocols).
- *It's your ISP's fault.* Sometimes the fault lies with the service that provides your Internet connection. Check its Web site or call the ISP for information about maintenance or system-related problems.

NOTE: *On one occasion, I was unable to access the mail servers for one of my accounts. The technical support people gave me a different setting for its mail servers, and, once the changes were made, I was able to retrieve my email without further trouble. In addition, sometimes an ISP will change its server settings without proper notice to its subscribers (that is, in fact, what happened to me).*

Why Are Messages Scrambled?

With your regular setup, Mail formats all your messages in Multipurpose Internet Mail Extensions (MIME) or Rich Text Format. That way, you can use text styles, color, embedded graphics, and Web links in your messages. Keep in mind, however, that not all email programs can read these added frills.

To remove the formatting option, just open a new message window, and then go to the Format menu and select Make Plain Text. That should take care of this problem.

NOTE: *Although such older e-mail clients as Claris Emailer won't interpret Rich Text in messages, it usually provides the text along with the core HTML code (the latter sometimes as an attached file). As a result the messages are, at least, readable.*

Why Doesn't Mail Check All My Accounts?

If you want Mail to automatically check for email from a specific email account, you must make sure the account is active and that it is accessed when you check for email. Here's how to confirm these settings:

1. Open Mail's Preferences window by choosing that option from the Application menu.

2. Click on the Accounts icon, select the email account, click Edit, and then click the Account tab.

3. Make sure the Enable This Account option is checked. It is that way by default, but you might have unchecked it to test a preference or to temporarily disable the account.

4. Click OK to store the account changes, and then close the Mail Preferences window.

With the settings configured properly, Mail should be able to retrieve your messages automatically from all active accounts.

Related solution:	Found on page:
Using Internet Connect for Dial-Up Networking	197

Chapter 23

Exploring Apple's Digital Hub Applications

If you need an immediate solution to:	See page:
Using iCal	497
Creating New Calendar Events	497
Creating a New Calendar	498
More iCal Features Summarized	498
Setting Up iChat	499
Using iChat	501
Using iPhoto	503
Using the iDisk Feature	505

Chapter 23 Exploring Apple's iTools

In Brief

A Mac is not just the hardware and the operating system. Beginning a trend that was later echoed by other companies in the PC industry, Apple CEO Steve Jobs offered a visionary look at taking the company beyond the box during his Macworld Expo keynote in January 2000 in San Francisco. Instead of just selling computers, displays, peripherals, and the Mac OS, Apple wants to deliver additional user experiences that make the platform more compelling. This vision was later refined as a "digital hub" strategy, in which the personal computer was meant to be the hub of your digital lifestyle, which extended to such devices as camcorders, handheld computers, music players and mobile phones. Mac OS X 10.2 Jaguar is designed to easily mate with such devices.

Over time, Apple introduced a slew of so-called "i" (or digital hub) applications that range from a simple video editing application, iMovie, to iSync, a program that works with your iPod music player, Palm Pilot, cell phone and even another Mac, to keep your calendar and contact information current.

In addition, Apple introduced a suite of Web services to help expand your digital lifestyle to the Internet. These services were first introduced as iTools, a collection of special features that could only be accessed by users with Mac OS 9 or later installed (although some features can be used by folks who have older versions of the Mac OS or computers with other operating systems installed). However, free Web services are rapidly biting the dust, and by the summer of 2002, Apple morphed iTools into .Mac, a subscription-based service.

NOTE: *Another of Apple's "beyond the box" efforts is a different sort of box, the iPod. Introduced in November 2001, the iPod is a miniature jukebox player that mates with iTunes to help you take your tunes on the road. This clever little device also does double-duty as a small FireWire backup drive for your Mac. There's even a Windows version.*

The core features of .Mac include a Mac.com email address, 100MB of online storage, and backup and virus protection software. When you buy a new Mac or install Jaguar, you get a 60-day free trial.

In Brief

An Overview of Apple's Digital Hub

At the heart of Apple's digital hub offerings are a number of applications with a consistent look and feel that allow you to organize and simplify your lifestyle. Here's a brief look at what they do. I'll cover them in more detail in the Immediate Solutions section of this chapter.

- *iCal*—Help manage your busy schedule with this simple desktop calendar (see Figure 23.1). Whether you need a reminder about that doctor's appointment next week, or that critical conference with a business associate, iCal can help. The calendars can be printed or shared, if you have a .Mac membership or have access to a web server with WebDAV enabled. In case you're wondering, WebDAV is short for "Web-based Distributed Authoring and Versioning," and it's a method for handling files on remote Web servers.

NOTE: At the time this book was written, both iCal and iSync were only available as separate downloads from Apple's Web site, but it is expected that future releases of Mac OS X will include both products.

- *iChat*—Have a one-on-one online conversation with users of AOL, CompuServe or AOL Instant Messenger, or with folks who subscribe to .Mac. The coolest features of this instant messaging application include the ability to put chat text in bubbles and use custom "buddy" icons, even your own photo, to identify yourself when you're online (see Figure 23.2).

NOTE: Since popular services such as MSN and Yahoo use different instant messaging systems, you cannot access users of these services via iChat. Some day we might see compatibility among the various messaging services, but there was no solution on the horizon when I wrote this book.

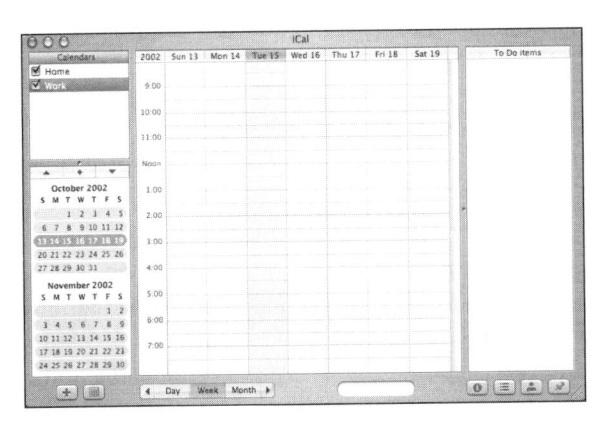

Figure 23.1   Organize your digital life with iCal.

Figure 23.2 Chat bubbles and photos fill your iChat window.

- *iDVD*—If you are among the millions who own a DVD player, no doubt you've wondered whether you can use it to show your family videos. Using Apple's iDVD solution, you can. Edit your movie in iMovie, then build a custom navigation menu in iDVD and in a short while, you'll have a high-quality DVD that can be played in almost any player (except the really old models).

- *iMovie*—One of Apple's original digital hub applications, this is a smooth-as-silk video editing program that give your movie a professional spit-and-polish without a steep learning curve. Just drag and drop a clip here, add a title and transitions (special effects that smooth the passage from one scene to another), and you have a video ready to save as a QuickTime movie, copy back to your camcorder, or save in a form that can be used by iDVD.

- *iPhoto*—Organize the photos you've taken on your digital camera or uploaded from your scanner. iPhoto (see Figure 23.3) lets you perform simple editing functions. You can resize, rotate, and remove that red eye effect (so you don't look as though you've had one too many or been up all night)). Your pictures can be printed on your color printer, or you can order up professional prints and even high-quality photo albums that will fit beautifully on any cocktail table. You can also post your photo album on your .Mac Web site.

- *iTunes*—Rip (import) songs from your music CDs, assemble tracks from music downloads, and compile them into custom music mixes to play on your Mac, dub onto a CD, or download to your iPod or other music player. iTunes also includes the ability to rate your music and sort your play list by how frequently the music is played. You can also listen to a number of Internet-based radio stations and talking books through Audible.com.

Figure 23.3 iPhoto helps you fix up and organize your digital photo library.

An overview of .Mac Features

When you sign up for .Mac, you get a fairly extensive suite of Web-based features and software. Here's a brief look at what's available.

- *Email*—Create an e-mail address with a mac.com domain. You can use any e-mail application, other than AOL and CompuServe 2000, and you'll receive a prestigious mac.com email address, reflecting your commitment to your favorite computing platform. A great feature of this e-mail service is a 15MB storage limit, higher than you get from most ISPs. So if you need to send a large file to a business contact, this may be the way to do it (I had to use my mac.com account to send some of the larger files for this book to my publisher).

NOTE: Apple's .Mac is not meant to replace your ISP; you still need an Internet account to access these services. In addition, AOL's proprietary email system makes it impossible to send email via the Mac.com address.

- *iDisk*—Apple gives you 100MB of storage space at its Web site when you opt for a full subscription; it's limited to 20MB during the free trial period. You can use iDisk for backups, your personal Web sites, or to make files available to friends, family, and business contacts. Apple also lets you purchase extra storage space (up to 1GB) for an annual fee.

- *HomePage*—Would you like to build a Web site, but don't want to learn a new application or hassle with HTML coding? No problem. Apple's HomePage feature lets you build your personal Web site with an iCal calendar, iPhoto album, iMovie home videos, rÈsumÈs, and more in just three convenient steps, all in a matter of minutes. Once your site is set up, it is hosted by Apple's Web site. The feature is similar to those offered by such services as AOL and EarthLink. And, like other free Web sites, it can be accessed by anyone with Internet access; it's not restricted to .Mac users or even to Mac users.

> **NOTE:** Such free no-hassle Web builders as HomePage aren't designed for a full-fledged business site. They are fine for a personal page, a family photo album, or even for posting your rÈsumÈ. But if you wish to do business on the Web, the best way is to use a professional Web-authoring program (such as Adobe's GoLive or Macromedia's Dreamweaver) and then get a regular "dot.com"-style custom domain name via a commercial Web hosting service.

- *iCards*—Send personal greeting cards or business announcements using a convenient array of photos and artwork. iCards also features a fairly decent selection of fonts and color styles.
- *Backup*—As I said in Chapter 17, regular backups are crucial if you want to recover your files in the event something goes wrong with your Mac. Backup works with your Mac's optical drive, or can use your iDisk for offsite, online storage.
- *Virex*—A long-time favorite of many Mac users, McAfee's Virex, which is covered in more detail in Chapter 18, is bundled with a .Mac account.

Immediate Solutions

Some of Apple's digital hub applications (such as iDVD and iMovie) are worth a full chapter by themselves. Fortunately, both programs come with complete Help menus (and sometimes a tutorial) that will easily guide you through the basics of using these applications.

In this section, I'll cover some of the other digital hub features offered with Jaguar:

Using iCal

Are you ready to get organized? Apple's iCal makes it simple, even for folks like me whose Mac display is covered with little, yellow sticky-notes and reminders.

Here's a brief overview of how iCal works:

Creating New Calendar Events

1. Launch iCal, which will open in the default month view.
2. Click on Day or Week at the bottom of the calendar window (sorry, this doesn't work when you view your calendar by the month).
3. First, click on the name of the calendar to select it. The default styles are Home and Work.
4. Point the mouse at the time an event will begin, and click and drag to the end of your event, as I've done in Figure 23.4.

NOTE: If you mess up and set the wrong time, you can click and drag your event to a different location. Double-click on the event's start time, or click on the "i" or Info icon at the bottom right of the calendar window, to bring up the Event Info window. Here you can change the duration, or its status, such as whether the event is tentative, confirmed, or cancelled, and, if you wish, to move the event to a different calendar.

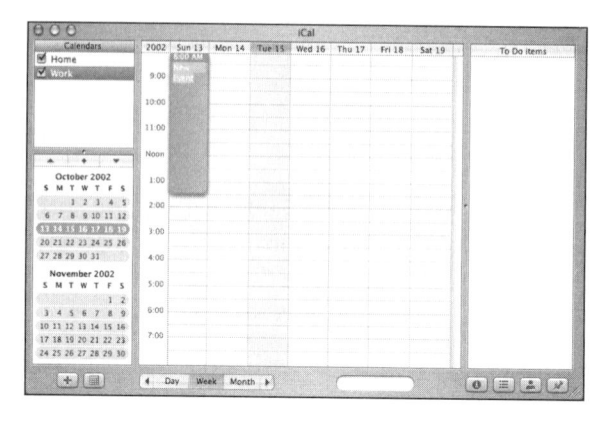

Figure 23.4 Click and drag and instantly create a calendar event.

Creating a New Calendar

1. With iCal open, double-click on the white area below the list of calendars, or just click on the plus symbol ("+") at the bottom left of the calendar window.

2. Name your calendar in the way that suits your needs, such as school or club reminders, or whatever applies.

3. Following the instructions above, you can now populate your new calendar with events.

More iCal Features Summarized

I can only give you the bare essentials of iCal's capabilities in this chapter. You'll find the application intuitive and easy to master. Here's the short list:

- *Guest Invites:* To invite your family, friends, or business associates to an event, just click on the People icon at the bottom right of the calendar window. Your Address Book contacts list will appear. Once you've brought up the list, drag the names of your contacts to the actual event in your calendar. You can use the Event Info window, available by double-clicking on the event time, to send invitations, after clicking on the People icon.

- *To Do Lists:* In addition to event reminders, you can also create a To Do list to help organize and prioritize daily tasks, , such as your shopping list or cleaning up that messy office. The feature is available via the pushpin button at the bottom right of the calendar window. Click on the button and enter your tasks in the To Do Items window. You can also rate To Do items in order of importance, courtesy of the Priority pop-up menu.

Immediate Solutions

- *Navigation Arrows:* Click the navigation arrows to move back and forth through a calendar. The diamond button is used to display today's date, in case the rush of events has made you momentarily forget.
- *Calendar Sharing:* Once you've set up a calendar, choose Publish from the calendar menu to share it on your .Mac Web site or another Web server.

Setting Up iChat

Instant messaging has become a world unto itself. Teens use it to "talk" to their friends, and the rest of us use it for relaxation or to stay in touch with business contacts. Businesses use them for inter-office communication.

NOTE: Several years ago, I visited AOL's headquarters in Dulles, Virginia. While talking with some of my friends there, I noticed they used instant messaging to talk with co-workers instead of using phones. Here is a case of a company using its own product to interact.

You can use iChat to communicate with other Jaguar users on your network. In order to use iChat for Internet-based communication, you need an account with AOL or AOL Instant Messenger (AIM or a mac.com e-mail address. The latter comes with a .Mac subscription. If you don't subscribe to .Mac or AOL, you can set up an AIM account at AOL's web site at: **http://www.aim.com/index.adp?promo=208884&aolperm=h**. Once you have a user name for iChat, you can set up the software in just a few seconds, following these instructions:

NOTE: Rendezvous chats and regular iChat conversations are totally separate. They show up in separate chat windows, and the participants in one cannot participate using the other chat method unless it's supported on their computers, and/or they have a supported online account.

1. Launch iChat from the Dock or from the Applications folder.
2. When the Welcome To iChat screen appears (see Figure 23.5), enter your name, the type of account (Mac.com or AIM), and the account name and password.

NOTE: If you don't have an AOL or AIM account, you can sign up for Mac.com right from the iChat Welcome dialog.

499

Chapter 23   Exploring Apple's iTools

Figure 23.5   Tell iChat which account you want to use for instant messaging.

3. Click OK when you're finished.

4. If you want to access Jaguar's Rendezvous networking feature to communicate with other Mac OS X 10.2 users on your network, click yes at the Rendezvous prompt (see Figure 23.6).

NOTE: Rendezvous messaging only works with other Macs running Mac OS X 10.2 or later. It will not let you network with users of early Mac operating systems.

5. Once your setup is done, your personal Buddy List will appear. If you already have an active AOL or AIM account, it'll be populated by your full list of online contacts (see Figure 23.7).

6. To add another name to your Buddy List, click the plus symbol at the bottom of the Buddy List window, choose the contact's AOL, AIM or Mac.com user name from your Address Book window and click on Select Buddy.

7. If the name isn't stored in your Address Book list, click New Person to bring up a dialog box. You can now enter the

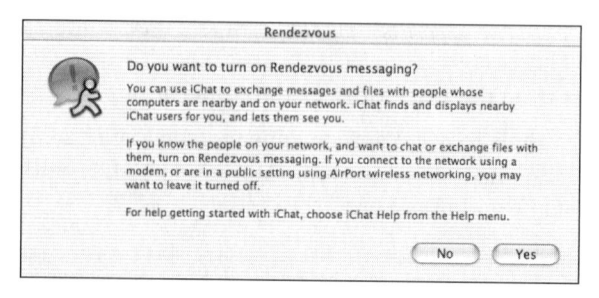

Figure 23.6   Click yes only if you have other Jaguar users on your network.

500

Immediate Solutions

Figure 23.7 Double click on a name to send that person a message.

member's user name, and, if you wish, enter additional information, including a photo, to store in the Address Book.

8. Click Add to put the name in your Buddy List and repeat the above steps to add more contacts to your Buddy List.

WARNING! *Be careful about entering the name of a new contact in your Buddy List. You must use the actual online or, as AOL calls it, screen name, and not a person's real name. If you enter the wrong name, it will point to the wrong person. You cannot rename someone to make them easier to identify, for otherwise it will point to the wrong person. Since my AOL screen name is Gene, you can understand I'm often the victim of mistaken identity because many members overlook these simple requirements.*

Using iChat

Once iChat is configured, you'll see the name darken in your Buddy List when your online contact logs in. Once the contact appears, just double click on the name to bring up an iChat window.

Just enter your chat text in the bottom text field, and press Return or Enter to send it on its way. Chat text will appear in little cartoon-like balloons (as you see in Figure 23.8).

The little icons at the bottom of the chat window allow you to show or hide a Buddy, change text to bold or italic, add a smiley or other emoticon (a little symbol that express emotion) or send a file attachment to your online contact.

501

Chapter 23 Exploring Apple's iTools

Figure 23.8 It's not Donald Duck or Bugs Bunny, but your author and an online friend having a friendly conversation.

iChat also includes the following features:

- *Automatic chat logging*—Just open iChat's Preferences box from its application menu, click the Messages icon, and choose Automatically Save Chat Transcripts. That way you can have an online business meeting.

- *Set up a chat room*—If you want to speak with several people at once, just select New Chat from the File menu. With the chat window opened, click the plus or Add button at the bottom of the list of chat participants, and select the buddies you want to invite. When you press Return they'll receive a chat invitation. If they accept your invitation, their names will appear among the Participants in your chat room.

- *Custom buddy photos*—Use your photo to identify yourself, as I've done in Figure 23.8. The feature is supported in Apple's Address Book, where you can easily drop in a contact's picture.

- *Configure chat balloons*—The Messages preference panel in iChat also lets you change the color of your chat balloons or pick a different typeface to display chat text.

- *Protect your privacy*—It's not uncommon to get online solicitations from folks you didn't want to contact. If you get offensive or irritating messages, or just don't want someone to know when you're online, click the Privacy icon in iChat's preferences window and enter the name of those users you want to block. You also have the option of only allowing those users you specify to see when you're online. That provides the utmost in online privacy.

Immediate Solutions

Using iPhoto

Digital cameras are fast becoming a staple in the home or office of both amateur and professional photographers. It's now possible to get a high quality picture without spending a king's ransom on a camera. If you take lots of digital pictures, wouldn't it be nice to have a convenient way to organize your libraries? That's the logic behind Apple's iPhoto (see Figure 23.9).

When you install Jaguar, iTools comes along for the ride, and it's placed, like other applications, in the Applications folder (there's also a Dock icon for it when you do a clean install). When you first launch iPhoto (see Figure 23.10), you'll have the option to decide whether iPhoto will open whenever you connect a digital camera to your Mac. If you say No, Image Capture will run instead.

Here's a brief look at iPhoto's features:

- *Simple editing*—While it won't replace a dedicated image editing program, such as Adobe Photoshop, you can handle a few basic touch-ups in iTools (see Figure 23.11). You can adjust brightness

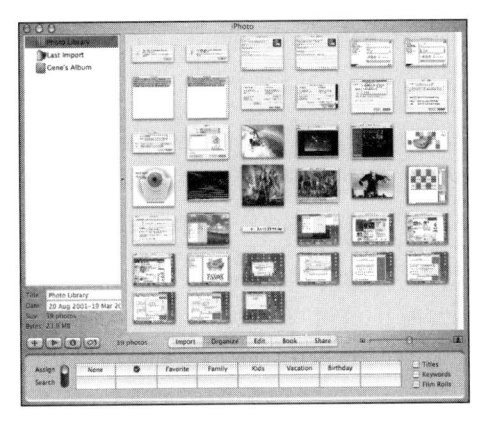

Figure 23.9 iPhoto lets you organize and edit your digital photo library.

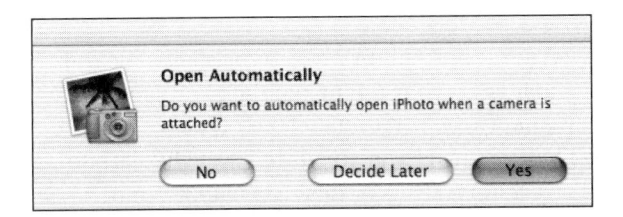

Figure 23.10 Would you like iPhoto to open whenever you connect your camera?

503

Figure 23.11   Handle simple touch-ups in iPhoto.

and contrast, resize and crop, convert to black and white, or eliminate the red-eye effect. These features are sufficient for most family photos.

- *Organize your library*—You don't have to confront a confusing mess of pictures. Create custom albums for family functions, vacations, corporate events, and so on. You can import photos from the most popular digital cameras (check **http://www.apple.com/iphoto/compatibility/** for the latest listing), or use your scanner to handle photo prints.

- *Create a printed photo album*—You can create high-quality, professionally bound and printed, coffee table-style photo albums at a modest price, through Apple's publishing partner. This is a great way to catalog important family or corporate events.

NOTE: You can, if you prefer, make your own album, using a color inkjet printer. Just take your prints to the local copy center, and select a custom binding. But Album's photo album solution is so elegant you might prefer it.

- *Extra features*—Your iPhoto library can be published at your .Mac Web site, e-mailed to your online contacts, or sent out for professional, lab-quality photo prints via an online retailer. A finished photo library can also be converted to a QuickTime movie or used as a screen saver or desktop background.

Immediate Solutions

Using the iDisk Feature

One of the more useful functions of .Mac is iDisk, which, when you become a paid subscriber, gives you 100MB of online storage space to use as you wish, for backups, for documents you need to exchange with your business contacts, or to post your personal Web site. Here's how to use the feature.

From the Mac OS X Finder, choose iDisk from the Go menu or press Command+Option+I. Within a few seconds, the icon for your personal iDisk will appear on the desktop and be listed under Computer in the Finder. You can now access this disk in the same fashion as any other—you can share, view files, send and retrieve files, and so on.

NOTE: *The speed of iDisk access depends on several factors, not the least of which is the speed of your ISP connection. It's slow going with a dial-up connection, but reasonably swift with a broadband hookup. In addition, network congestion at Apple's Web site may contribute to performance slowdowns.*

TIP: *You can also add the iDisk icon to the Finder's toolbar. Choose Customize Toolbar from the View menu, and when the list of icons appears, drag the iTools icon to the position you want in the toolbar. Click Done to make it so.*

However, your iDisk isn't exclusive to your Mac running Mac OS 9 or X. You can access your files from any PC running the Linux or Windows operating system if it uses a WebDAV client application.

Here's how it's done:

1. From the PC, launch your Web browser and enter the following URL: **http://idisk.mac.com/*username*** (where you enter your iTools account name).
2. Enter the password from the login prompt.

NOTE: *Other users can access your Public folder on your iDisk without having to know your password. Have them point their browsers to **http://idisk.mac.com/username/Public**. Any file placed in your Public folder can be retrieved in this fashion by anyone with Internet access, so be careful what you put there.*

If you need more storage space, you can click on the Upgrade button at Apple's iDisk page and increase disk storage from 100MB all the way to 1GB. You'll want to consult the Upgrade Storage page for current pricing information.

505

Chapter 23 Exploring Apple's iTools

TIP: *If you don't want others to see your Public folder, it can be password-protected via the Internet panel in System Preferences. With this panel open, click the iDisk tab, and check the option labeled Use a Password to Protect Your Public Folder. Once this option is selected, you can enter the appropriate password to restrict access.*

Glossary

10BaseT—The designation for standard 10Mbps Ethernet run over twisted-pair network cable. 10BaseT is the most common form of Ethernet available today and has largely supplanted the other forms of Ethernet: ThickNet and ThinNet (which use coaxial cable). 10BaseT utilizes either Category 3 or Category 5 four-pair twisted-pair wire to send data up to 100 meters without the need for a repeater. The follow-up to 10BaseT is the newer 100BaseTX, which sends data at 100Mbps over Category 5 twisted-pair cable. As the cost of 100BaseT network adapters and the associated hubs and switches continues to drop, expect that 100BaseTX will replace 10BaseT. Other variations include 100BaseFx and 100BaseVG. The latest generation, supported by Apple's current line of desktop Power Macs and recent versions of the PowerBook G4, is 1000BaseT, also known as Gigabit Ethernet.

active (focus) window—The Finder or document window that you are presently using. The Finder lets you work in single-window mode, where the nonactive Finder and document windows are collapsed and moved to the Dock.

Address Book—A Mac OS X application that contains a database of contact information that can be accessed by Apple's iChat, Mail and any other application that is designed to tap this data.

alias—A pointer or reference to an original file that is accessed in the same fashion as the original. An alias allows you to more easily access a file, regardless of whether it is located on your Mac's drive, on a networked drive, or on the Internet; the Unix version is the Symbolic Link.

America Online (AOL)—The largest Internet Service Provider (ISP) in the world, with more than 34 million members and increasing as fast as we speak. Headquartered in Vienna, Virginia, AOL (part of the AOL Time Warner conglomerate) provides Internet access to users worldwide.

AOL Instant Messenger (AIM)—A popular instant messaging technology that has tens of millions of members, and is supported by Apple's iChat application.

Apache—The world-famous Web hosting software is built into Mac OS X, and is activated simply by starting Web Sharing in the Sharing preference panel. Once activated, you can host your own Web site on your Mac.

Apple menu—The menu that sits in its accustomed spot at the left side of the menu bar. Apple has revised the Apple menu to include system-wide commands formerly reserved for the Special menu. These include the ability to restart and shut down the computer.

AppleScript—Apple's scripting language, a natural language programming feature that lets you automate repetitive or complex routines by running a small application (or applet).

AppleTalk—A network protocol developed by Apple Computer in the mid-1980s to provide networking services for Macintosh operating system (OS) computers. AppleTalk is available in two forms: AppleTalk Phase 1, which was developed in 1984, and AppleTalk Phase 2, which was released in 1988 to address many of the issues that plagued AppleTalk Phase 1. AppleTalk is available on all Macintosh-based computers and provides a quick and simple workgroup networking solution that can be set up in minutes.

AppleTalk zones—The segments into which a network is divided. This method allows more AppleTalk devices on the same network segment than would normally be permitted by the limit of 254 AppleTalk devices per network. AppleTalk zones are also used in a manner somewhat like an office workgroup or department, in which all the computers in a specific AppleTalk zone have access to all the resources that are available on that zone.

AppleWorks—Apple's business application suite, supplied free on consumer models, such as the iBook and iMac. AppleWorks 6 was one of the first programs Carbonized to run native under Mac OS X.

application—The program that actually lets you do work on a Mac. An application may handle word processing or page layout chores, allow you to access the Internet, or perform preventive maintenance on your Mac by checking your hard drive.

Application menu—Represented by the application icon or name at the left side of Mac OS X's menu bar, the Application menu lets you access additional features, such as quitting an application or accessing its preferences. In some programs, particularly ones not fully ported to the new operating system, the File menu provides some of these features.

application programming interface (API)—The set of tools programmers use to develop software for a specific operating system. See also *Carbon* and *Cocoa*.

assistants—Special programs, such as the Setup Assistant, that are used to configure settings for your Mac operating system or to perform a complex function in software. Examples of the latter include the assistants provided with programs such as AppleWorks to set up a template for a specific type of document.

attachment—One or more files that are connected to your email message, in effect going along for the ride. You can attach a document, graphics, or program file, but your ISP may restrict the maximum size of the file.

back up—The process of making one or more extra copies of your files as a protective measure to guard against the possibility that your original file may become lost or damaged.

binary numbers—The 1s and 0s that make up computer language.

Blind carbon copy (BCC)—This is a copy of an email message sent to recipients without displaying the names of others who might receive the message.

bookmarks—See *Favorites*.

boot—Short for *bootstrap*, the process of starting a computer. During the boot process, your Mac's hardware is checked, and then the operating system components load.

browser—A program that's used to view files. This term is generally used for a Web browser, a program that accesses and interprets documents on the World Wide Web and converts them to a form that reflects their original content.

byte—The basic object of data that a computer uses. In a modern computer, a byte consists of 8 bits—that is, 1s or 0s that represent a binary number. See also *binary numbers*.

cable modem—A device that works with a standard cable television connection to provide high-speed Internet access.

cache—Usually, a small amount of memory allocated for frequently used data. You'll find a cache in such places as a hard drive, a CPU, and a logic (or mother) board.

Calculator—A Mac application that mimics the function of a regular calculator. The version included with Jaguar sports a Basic interface for simple calculations and an Advanced interface that matches the functions of a scientific calculator.

Carbon—A set of application programming interfaces that allows a software publisher to update its existing programs to support the Aqua interface and most other features of Mac OS X. See also *application programming interface (API)*.

carbon copy (CC)—The process of sending one or more extra copies of email messages to other recipients.

CD-ROM—Stands for compact disc read-only memory; a variant of the music CD that stores computer data. CD-ROMs are also used for software installations. The departure of floppy drives from Macs, the lower cost of pressing CDs, and the larger space taken up by software have all contributed to the switchover.

checkbox—A small, square box that's used to toggle a specific program function. You may, for example, click on a checkbox to insert a checkmark that activates a feature; then you click again to remove the checkmark and turn off the feature.

checksum—A number that is calculated based upon the data in a packet or file. Checksums are reviewed as the data is being examined after transmission to see if the checksum calculated before transmission and the checksum calculated after transmission are identical, indicating that the data was not corrupted.

Chooser—In Mac operating systems prior to Mac OS X, a program that controls the Macintosh's networking and printer connections.

click—The process of moving your pointing device (mouse, trackball, and so on) over an item, and then pressing the mouse button one time.

clipboard

clipboard—A memory-resident area onto which you copy or cut data from a document. The present iteration of the Mac OS clipboard stores just one item, so when you copy a second, it replaces the first. However, some programs (such as recent versions of Microsoft Word) have their own clipboard-handling features, which give you additional storage areas.

Clock—A Mac OS X application that displays an analog or digital clock on the Dock or, optionally, as a floating window.

close button—The small red button with an *X* in its center when the mouse moves over it, located at the top of a Finder or document window (it's gray when you access the optional Graphite interface). Clicking on the box closes the window but may not necessarily result in quitting the application.

Cocoa—An application programming interface for Mac OS X applications. Cocoa is descended from the NeXTSTEP programming environment, called Objective C, which is designed to make it easier to build complete applications using a set of predefined components called objects.

collapse button—The yellow Finder button (with a – in it when the mouse passes over it) that is used to minimize a window and move it to the Dock (under the optional Graphite interface, it's just gray).

ColorSync—A settings pane in the System Preferences application that allows you to configure color-matching options. ColorSync is a component of the Mac OS that allows input devices, computer monitors, and output devices, such as printers, to be more accurately calibrated.

command—A means of telling your computer how to perform a function. Commands may be entered by text or by selecting a menu item.

command-line interface (CLI)—A way of interacting with a computer or other intelligent devices using commands that you type in via a keyboard. Mac OS X includes an application known as Terminal that allows you to interact with the operating system the same as you do with any Unix-based system.

Common UNIX Printing System (CUPS)—A portable printing system for Unix-based systems that Apple licensed for Mac OS X 10.2 from Easy Software Products.

compression—A means of reducing the size of a file using mathematical algorithms that check for redundant data. Compression programs include such products as the StuffIt family from Aladdin Systems.

computer name—A name assigned to your Mac when you install Mac OS X, allowing it to be properly located and identified on your network. The name can also be modified in the Sharing panel of the System Preferences application.

contextual menu—A pop-up menu accessed by a Control+click. It displays a set of commands that relate specifically to the selected item, such as file management functions. For example, Control+clicking on a folder or disk icon will bring up a contextual menu of file management functions.

cooperative multitasking—The inefficient multitasking scheme of the Classic version of the Mac operating system in which programs are designed to work together to share CPU time. See also *preemptive multitasking*.

creator type—A 4-byte code assigned to a Macintosh file that tells the Finder the application program that created it. The traditional Macintosh operating system (OS) uses creator codes to determine which application should be launched when a user attempts to open a specific file. In addition, Mac OS X can interpret file extensions, such as .doc for a Word document, to determine which application may be used to open a document (this is also done under the Classic Mac OS by way of the File Exchange Control Panel).

Darwin—The core of Mac OS X, incorporating a Unix microkernel that consists of Mach 3.0 and FreeBSD. Making this element of the operating system open source (meaning the programming code is available for use by anyone signing Apple's legal document) allows third-party programmers to develop updates and improvements that can then be shared. These changes may be used by Apple for updates and improvements to Mac OS X.

Date & Time—A settings panel in the System Preferences application that lets you set the time and date and whether your Mac's clock is automatically synchronized to a network or Internet-based time server.

DAVE—A tool from Thursby Software Systems, Inc., which allows the Macintosh to communicate using the Network Basic Input Output System (NetBIOS) protocol used on Windows-based networks. DAVE also provides Macintosh users with a variety of tools to access resources on the Windows-based network. See also *NetBIOS*.

desktop—The backdrop or background artwork that appears behind your Finder or file windows on your Mac. Icons representing files or disks may be placed upon the desktop for convenient access.

DHCP—Stands for Dynamic Host Configuration Protocol. A network protocol that automates the process of assigning an Internet Protocol (IP) address and other network-specific information to computers that request it on the network. A DHCP server on the network responds to requests from a computer on the network and then assigns an IP address to computers for a specified time. By only leasing the IP address to each computer, DHCP allows the IP addresses of computers that are no longer using them to be reclaimed and redistributed to other computers on the network. See also *IP*.

dialog box—A window that contains items you must click or enter data into to activate a particular function.

directory—See *folder*.

Dock—Mac OS X's taskbar, consisting of a row of colorful icons at the bottom of the screen (or, optionally, at the sides) that are used for one-click access to applications, files, and folders. It's meant as a replacement for the application switcher and Control Strip features of previous versions of the Mac OS.

domain—The organization to which servers and computers belong. For example, **www.apple.com** is a computer in the **apple.com** domain. Like the

Domain Name Service (DNS), which controls domain information on the Internet and your local network, Microsoft Active Directory is based on the domain structure. See also *Domain Name Service (DNS)*.

Domain Name Service (DNS)—The service on the network that matches up a computer's host name with its Internet Protocol (IP) address. DNS servers receive requests from computers on the network that request the IP address of a server using a specific Internet domain name. For example, when you type in **www.apple.com**, your computer contacts a DNS server to get the IP address assigned to the computer named **www.apple.com**. It then takes the IP address it receives from the DNS server and uses it to connect to the remote computer. See also *IP* and *computer name*.

double-click—An action whereby you point at an item, and then press the mouse button twice in rapid succession to open or activate the item.

double-click speed—The rate or rhythm of a double-click required to activate a function. This setting is user-dependent and can be configured as a mouse setting in the Preferences application.

download—Receiving a file from another computer, whether on your network or via the Internet.

drag—Moving a selected item from one place to another. You can drag such things as picture objects, text, disk, and file icons.

drag-and-drop—Clicking on an item to select it, and then dragging it to a new location and releasing the mouse button, thereby dropping it into its new locale.

driver—A program that allows your Mac to work with a peripheral device, such as a printer, removable hard drive, scanner, or digital camera.

DSL—Short for Digital Subscriber Line. A method designed to deliver high-speed Internet connections to a home or office using standard telephone lines. A variation, ADSL, will throttle upload speeds to a fraction of download speeds, and is usually available at a lower monthly charge.

duplex—The way a computer transmits and receives traffic on the network. Half-duplex mode means a computer must wait for all transmissions to it to cease before it begins sending out data. Full-duplex means a computer can send and receive data at the same time. 10Mbps Ethernet is normally half-duplex (full-duplex mode is not often implemented). 100Mbps Ethernet, also called Fast Ethernet, supports full-duplex mode; it allows a computer to send and receive data at 100Mbps each way, bringing the actual throughput up to 200Mbps. See also *Ethernet* and *Fast Ethernet*.

duplexing—A feature offered by some printers that allows you to automatically print on both sides of the page. If the option is available, you can configure it in Mac OS X's Print Center application and then the Print dialog box. Where the feature is offered, the printed page goes through a special paper path in which the paper is reversed so that the back side is printed after the front side.

DVD drive—A device using an updated version of CD technology that allows it to store a much greater amount of data. DVD-ROM drives can read regular CDs, plus those based on DVD technology (including videos). A DVD-R drive, such as the Apple SuperDrive, can burn both CDs and DVDs. DVD stands for Digital Versatile Disc (not Video, as commonly believed) because of the variety of formats it supports.

Edit menu—A menu used for text and picture editing functions, such as copying and pasting.

Eject—A Finder command that has two functions, depending on the kind of drive selected when it's accessed. It either dismounts a drive from your Mac or, if the drive is removable, ejects the disk media from the drive.

email—Short for electronic mail. One of the most popular forms of online communication. It's the process of sending messages across a network within an online service or across the Internet. See also *attachment*.

email address—The identity of the person you're contacting. The email address consists of two parts: the username, followed by an @ symbol, and then the location or domain that hosts the user's account. AOL and CompuServe members, on the other hand, use just their username (called a screen name) without a domain to communicate to other members of the service.

Empty Trash—A Finder command that removes any items placed in the Trash.

Energy Saver—A settings pane in the System Preferences application that lets you set an idle time interval for a Mac system to shut down or sleep.

Erase—A function in Mac OS X's Disk Utility application that deletes the contents of a selected disk and creates a new directory (the same as the Initialize function in a disk formatting program). This function is disabled on the startup disk.

Ethernet—A network standard developed in the 1970s by Bob Metcalfe at Xerox PARC as a way to provide a high-speed connection between computers and printers. Over the years, Ethernet has become the principal network technology that links computers and other network-based devices on a local area network (LAN). Ethernet is most commonly seen in two varieties these days: standard Ethernet, which moves data at 10Mbps, and Fast Ethernet, which moves data at 100Mbps. Gigabit Ethernet, which moves data at 1 billion bits of data a second, is starting to become more widespread since its introduction in the desktop Power Macintosh line in the summer of 2000. See also *Fast Ethernet*.

Fast Ethernet—The version of Ethernet that transfers data at 100Mbps in half-duplex mode. Fast Ethernet can operate in full-duplex mode as well, so actual throughput using Fast Ethernet can reach 200Mbps.

Favorites—A feature of Mac OS X that lets you store aliases to items you wish to revisit on a regular basis. A similar feature is provided with a Web browser, where links are stored in a menu for quick access to the sites to which you want to return. However, the names of this feature vary. Although it's Favorites with Internet Explorer, Netscape calls it Bookmarks instead. See also *history*.

file extensions—The three-character suffixes on MS-DOS, Unix, and Windows files that tell the operating system what type of data the file contains. For example, a .doc file extension tells Windows that the file in question is a Microsoft Word document. Mac OS X recognizes a file either by its creator and type information (as with previous Mac OS versions) or by its file extension.

File menu—The menu that accesses file-related functions, such as opening and saving documents.

File Sharing—A feature of the Mac OS that allows you to easily share your Mac's files with other computers on a network or over the Internet.

file system—The fashion in which files are stored on your Mac.

file type—The 4-byte code that tells the Macintosh operating system (OS) what type of data is contained in the file. For example, a file type of TEXT indicates that the file contains text.

Finder—An application that manages the file viewing and transfer process for the items available to your Mac, either locally or via a network. The Finder displays the list of available files, allowing you to open or transfer them to another location (such as a different drive volume or a networked volume).

firewall—A computer or router configured to act as a gateway between your local area network (LAN) and the Internet. Firewalls can be anything from a Cisco router with some access lists applied to the interface that is connected to the Internet, to special software you set up on your Mac. By limiting the access that computers on the Internet have to your LAN, the firewall protects you from attack and intrusion by hackers and other unfriendly elements. Mac OS X has a built-in command line firewall that can be enabled via the Sharing panel of the System Preferences application.

FireWire—A high-speed peripheral bus that is now featured on all Macs but the entry-level iMac. It provides plug-and-play capability, a potential throughput of 400Mbps (higher for later FireWire versions), and support for up to 63 daisy-chained devices for each FireWire port. See also *USB*.

floppy disk—An older magnetic storage medium consisting of a small square object, inside of which is a flexible sheet of magnetic material. Because of the limitations of this storage medium, newer Macs have dispensed with such drives. However, a later generation of storage devices called SuperDisk uses floppy-based media with up to 240MB of storage capacity. The Iomega Zip drive, with 100MB and 250MB capacities, also uses some floppy disk–based technology.

folder—A container-like item on your Mac identified by a folder-like icon that holds other folders and files; also referred to as a directory.

formatting—(1) The process of erasing the contents of a drive and preparing it for use or reuse. (2) The characteristics of the text in your document, which include font, size, style, and color, along with the layout of the document.

fragmentation—In terms of disk storage, the separation of the various segments of files, which are placed on different parts of a drive. Fragmentation happens when larger files are frequently copied and removed from a drive. Computer memory may also become fragmented, but Mac OS X is designed to control the situation by allocating memory dynamically as needed by an application.

FTP—Stands for File Transfer Protocol. A protocol used to move files across the Internet, usually from a remote server to your desktop computer. FTP is commonly used to move files larger than 1MB because it is a more efficient protocol for moving data than Hypertext Transfer Protocol (HTTP). FTP uses Transmission Control Protocol (TCP) port 21 to send FTP commands between the sending and receiving computers, and a randomly assigned TCP port above 1024 to transfer the data. The most common FTP application on the Macintosh is known as Fetch. See also *HTTP* and *TCP*.

gateway—A computer or router that directs traffic off the current network segment and out to the rest of the network.

General—A settings pane in the System Preferences application. It's a throwback to the General Control Panel of Mac System 6 and earlier, where appearance options for titles, highlighting, and such options as text smoothing thresholds and styles are set. By default, you can choose the Blue Aqua interface or a more subtle Graphite (Gray) option.

gigabyte (GB)—A term that refers to 1,024 megabytes.

Go menu—A menu, new for Mac OS X, that offers access to frequently used document folders, networked computers, and the Finder's toolbar buttons.

Grab—An application that performs screen captures. Mac OS X 10.1 and later also support the traditional Mac method, Command+Shift+3, to capture a picture of your screen.

hard disk—A storage mechanism that consists of an assembly of rapidly spinning disks placed inside a sealed, rectangular enclosure. Data is read and written by one or more heads that access the data stored on the spinning disks. Also known as a fixed hard drive or just as a hard drive or fixed disk.

Help menu—A menu that, when accessed from the Finder or desktop, provides immediate access to the Mac OS Help menu. Most other applications also offer a Help menu of one sort or another.

hexadecimal numbers—Another method of describing the numeric value of a byte. Hexadecimal values are based upon base 16 math, where numbers range from 0 through F. To display the full value of a byte, you use two hexadecimal numbers. For example, to represent a byte with the value of 255, type "FF". See also *binary numbers*.

HFS+—A version of the Macintosh file system that increases the number of files that can be supported on a Mac drive, thus reducing the minimum file size on larger devices. Similar to FAT32 under Windows. Sometimes known as Mac OS Extended.

Hierarchical File System (HFS)—The standard system for organizing files on the Macintosh operating system (OS). Similar to FAT16 on the Windows platform. Sometimes known as Mac OS Standard.

history

history—A feature of a Web browser that displays a list of recently visited sites. In contrast to a Bookmarks or Favorites feature (which includes the links you actually store), the history constantly updates as newer sites are accessed. The history list is normally cleared when you quit the application. See also *Favorites*.

home page—The introductory or index page of a Web site. A home page usually contains information about the site's purpose, along with links to its popular features. You can specify a default home page in your Web browser so that you always visit that site upon launching the browser.

HTML—Stands for Hypertext Markup Language. A text-based formatting language used to describe the elements of a Web page.

HTTP—Stands for Hypertext Transfer Protocol, the Internet Protocol (IP) network protocol that is used to move data from Web servers to your Web browser. HTTP utilizes Transmission Control Protocol (TCP) to send and receive information from a Web server and then to send back information to the Web server, allowing you to interact with it. It is a connectionless protocol, meaning that it sends or receives one piece of information and then closes down the connection. Although this approach made sense with small amounts of data, as on early Web pages, as Web pages grew, performance was apt to suffer. To improve HTTP's performance, HTTP version 1.1, which allows whole Web pages to be downloaded without breaking the connection, was developed. See also *HTTPS*, *IP*, and *TCP*.

HTTPS—The version of Hypertext Transfer Protocol (HTTP) that uses Secure Sockets Layer (SSL) encryption when you are sending and receiving data from secure Web servers. HTTPS normally uses Transmission Control Protocol (TCP) port 443 to send and receive information. HTTPS can use either 40- or 128-bit encryption, depending on where the browser or the server is located. See also *HTTP* and *TCP*.

hub—A connection device that forms the center of an Ethernet network; also used to extend the ports available via FireWire or USB.

hyperlink—An item in a document or on a Web page that, when you click it once, takes you to another page or site.

ICal—One of Apple's digital hub applications, used to create a calendar that illustrates to-do tasks that can be printed, shared, or published on the Internet.

iChat—Apple's instant messaging client, which supports AOL's instant messaging system, users of Apple's .Mac Web services and direct network connections between fellow iChat users.

icons—One of the key features of a graphical computer operating system, such as Mac OS X. Icons are pictures used as metaphors for real-world items, such as folders, files, documents, or disks.

ICQ—The original instant-message protocol that is used to send instant messages across the Internet. ICQ is now owned by AOL Time Warner (see *Instant Messenger*). A related protocol, ICQW, also allows users to see when others are connected to the Internet and to set up multiperson conversations across the Internet.

516

Inkwell—Apple didn't just toss out all the technology it developed for the failed Newton handheld. Inkwell provides system-wide handwriting recognition that works with any input device that can read the written word, such as a drawing tablet.

iMovie—A desktop video editing program from Apple that is included with Mac OS X. It allows for simple drag-and-drop editing from a digital or DV camcorder, or from a multimedia file.

iPhoto—Bundled with Mac OS X, this application is used to import and organize a digital photo library, and offer the ability to make simple photo editing, such as removal of the red eye effects.

insertion point—A thin vertical bar in a text box that indicates where text is being entered.

Instant Messenger—A program from America Online (AOL) that sends instant messages across the Internet. This program also allows users to see when others are connected to the Internet and to set up one-on-one conversations with them. Special "branded" versions of Instant Messenger are provided by such companies as EarthLink and Netscape (a subsidiary of AOL). Microsoft's variation on the instant messaging theme is called MSN Messenger. See also *MSN Messenger* and *ICQ*.

International—A settings pane in the System Preferences application where you can specify system languages and currency conversion options, in addition to date and time formats unique to a specific part of the world.

Internet—(1) A worldwide computer network consisting of hundreds of millions of computers, used to spread data from computer to computer. The Internet has become the focal point for such enterprises as email, shopping, and mass communication. (2) A settings pane in the System Preferences application that lets you enter settings for hooking up to your ISP.

Internet Connect—An application used to make dial-up connections to your ISP. It combines functions from both the Remote Access and TCP/IP control panels of previous versions of the Mac OS.

Internet Relay Chat (IRC)—A set of client software and servers that allows groups of users from all across the world to have interactive conversations in real-time. Users who want to join an IRC use an IRC client to connect to server networks on the Internet. Once connected to one of the many IRC networks, users can create or join conversations on just about every subject known to humans.

Internet Service Provider (ISP)—A company that provides users with a connection to the Internet. From huge ISPs such as America Online (AOL) and EarthLink to small local operations such as FastQ and Aracnets.com, an ISP allows users to dial up and connect to the Internet from their home or office.

IP—Stands for Internet Protocol. The network protocol that is used to send information over the Internet. IP was developed in the 1970s by Vincent Cerf and others to provide a reliable method of transferring data over the Internet. IP can send network traffic over many network media, from low-speed serial connections to multigigabit fiber connections.

iPod—A tiny jukebox player from Apple Computer that mates with iTunes and uses a Mac's FireWire port to synchronize your playlists, run as a backup storage device, and to receive electrical power.

iSync—An application from Apple that is designed to synchronize contact and calendar information with a cell phone or handheld device, such as a Palm Pilot.

iTunes—A jukebox program from Apple Computer, descended from Casady & Greene's SoundJam. It comes with Mac OS X and allows you to encode (rip) music from an audio CD, create playlists, play music and Internet radio, and burn music CDs.

Java—A cross-platform programming language that allows applications (or mini applications called applets) to execute or run on computers running a variety of operating systems. Mac OS X's Cocoa component includes native support for Java. Java is the brainchild of Sun Microsystems.

Jaz drive—A removable storage product from Iomega that uses standard hard drive technology and supports storage of 1GB or 2GB, depending on the drive and media used.

JetDirect—The trade name of a series of network interface cards and their associated software created by Hewlett-Packard for use with its DeskJet and LaserJet printers. JetDirect cards provide the printer with an Ethernet port and allow it to send and receive data from a server or workstation that is configured to host the printer.

Junk Mail Filter—A feature of Apple's Mail application, Microsoft Entourage X and other programs, which is designed to filter out so-called SPAM e-mail.

Keyboard—A settings pane in the System Preferences application that is used for keyboard speed and repeat rates.

kilobyte (KB)—The equivalent of 1,024 bytes of data.

kbps—Short for kilobits (thousands of bits) per second; typically a measurement of data transfer rate.

link—(1) See *hyperlink*. (2) The Unix equivalent of an alias. See *alias*.

local area network (LAN)—A high-speed network, either in a single building or multiple buildings at a single site. LANs are almost always connected by some sort of high-speed networking infrastructure such as Ethernet.

LocalTalk—The Mac's original networking method, a slow but usable way to transfer data. Over time, Ethernet support was added; native LocalTalk was removed from new Macs beginning in 1998, with the introduction of the iMac. See also *network adapter*.

log in—The process of entering your username and password to access a specific computer or network service.

Login—A settings pane in the System Preferences application where you can also specify whether a login prompt appears at startup and which applications are turned on with your system. In that way, it provides a function similar to the Startup Items folder in previous versions of the Mac OS.

log off

log off—The process of ending your session with a computer or network service.

Macintosh HD—The common name Apple gives to the hard drive on your new computer. This name can be easily changed, as long as the drive itself is not being shared over a network.

Mail—The email application that Apple provides with Mac OS X. It provides simple management of user accounts and also offers timed retrieval of messages.

mailbox—In email programs, a folder that contains the email messages you've stored or received.

maximize—The act of expanding a Finder or application window to its largest possible size. The maximize function under Mac OS X is controlled by a green button (with a plus sign inside when a mouse passes over it) at the left side of a window's title bar (it stays gray in the optional Graphite view).

Mbps—Short for megabits (millions of bits) per second; typically a measurement of data transfer rate.

megabyte (MB)—The name for 1,024 kilobytes of computer data.

menu—A small window without title or control bars or buttons that contains a list of commands you can access to perform a function on your computer.

menu bar—A horizontal bar that extends across the top of your Mac's display, containing a list of labels of functions relevant to the Mac OS or the program you're using. Clicking any of those labels produces a menu with commands that relate to that label.

minimize—The act of reducing a Finder or application window to an icon that appears on the Dock. The minimize function under Mac OS X is activated by a yellow button (with a minus symbol within as the mouse passes over it) at the left of a window's title bar. See also *collapse button* and *Dock*.

modem—A device that is used to transfer digital computer data across analog telephone lines.

Monitors—Similar to the Control Panel under Mac OS 9; the settings pane available from the System Preferences application that lets you change screen depth and resolution. For some Apple-brand displays, geometry adjustments are also present.

Mouse—Part of the System Preferences application; the settings pane used to set mouse clicking and tracking rates.

MSN Messenger—Microsoft's version of an instant messaging program. See also *Instant Messenger*.

multitasking—A computer's performing more than a single function or running more than a single program at the same time. See also *cooperative multitasking* and *preemptive multitasking*.

NetBIOS—A networking scheme that allows applications and network services to communicate in a more or less transparent way. It is used by such programs as Thursby Software's DAVE and Connectix's DoubleTalk to provide

519

network

networking between Mac and Windows-based personal computers. SAMBA, a NetBIOS client for Linux and Unix, became part of Mac OS X beginning with version 10.1.

network—A system consisting of two or more computers or a computer with shared printers. A network may be connected by wires or by such wireless features as Apple Computer's AirPort products.

Network—A settings pane in the System Preferences application used for your network options.

network adapter—The piece of electronics that connects a computer to the local area network (LAN). One example of a network adapter is the Ethernet port that is included on all current Apple computers (such as the iBook, iMac, PowerBook, and Power Macintosh) and many modern Windows-based PCs. Other types of network adapters include Token Ring, an older IBM network system; and LocalTalk, the original network solution that Apple developed for inclusion with the Macintosh. See also *LocalTalk*.

network hub—A small electrical device that connects several network connections. To prevent signal loss, Ethernet hubs, for example, amplify the network signal so that it does not become degraded as it goes through the hub to its destination. The downside to hubs is that they connect all the computers on the network together and thus frequently cause performance degradation because of packet collisions. See also *hub*, *network switch*, and *packets*.

network segment—The portion of the network that is connected to a router. Network segments can range from a small two- or three-host network connected to an interface on a router to a large switched network with hundreds of computers all connected to a series of switches and then a router.

network switch—A small network device that connects several network connections together. To prevent signal loss, network switches amplify the network signal so that it does not become degraded as it goes through the switch to its destination. Switches, unlike hubs, do not connect all the computers on the network together, except as a virtual circuit. Thus they avoid performance degradation caused by packet collisions, because they create a connection directly between the source and the destination. See also *network hub*.

newsgroups—Internet-based bulletin boards where users from all over the world can converse and share information regarding a variety of topics. For instance, if you are looking for technical information about a problem you are having with a computer or your network, checking the appropriate newsgroups or posting a message may well get you an answer. Also called Usenet. You can use such programs as Microsoft's Entourage X, NewsWatcher X and MT-NewsWatcher (freeware applications), or Thoth (shareware) to access newsgroup messages.

online service—The outgrowth of the original bulletin board systems (BBS) in the early days of personal computing. An online

service consists of such features as message boards, email service, information centers, files for download, and chat rooms. The popular online services of the present day, including AOL, CompuServe, and Prodigy Internet, also include Internet access.

Open dialog box—A dialog box used to select a document to open from within an open application.

Open GL—An industry standard 3D technology commonly used for games, such as Quake 3 Arena from id Software. It is also used for 3D rendering programs, such as Maya, an animation program from Alias/Wavefront widely used in the motion picture industry.

packets—Little pieces of data formed when larger data is divided for efficient transfer over a network.

password—A set of characters (consisting of letters and/or numbers) that is used to gain access to a protected feature. You use a password for such functions as logging in to your Mac, to a network, or to your ISP.

point—The act of directing the mouse cursor above a specific item.

pop-up window—A menu listing various commands that is accessed by a Control+click (Apple's contextual menus feature) or from a dialog box.

port—(1) A connection jack used to attach peripherals to your Mac. These include such staples as your keyboard and mouse, as well as printers, removable drives, digital cameras, and other items. Current-model Macs include Ethernet and USB ports, and some include FireWire. (2) A reference to the connection points used for Internet access.

Post Office Protocol (POP)—The primary network protocol that mail servers use to distribute email to users across the network. Programs such as Eudora, Microsoft Outlook Express, Microsoft Entourage X, and Apple's Mail connect to the central email server using POP. Once they have logged on to the mail server, they can receive email that has been stored on the server waiting for the user to retrieve it.

PostScript—A page-description language developed by Adobe Systems in the early 1980s to improve the print quality of documents. In PostScript, the contents of a page are reduced to mathematical calculations, and as such, PostScript is commonly regarded as being device-independent. This means the quality of the printed document depends on the capabilities of the output device. Over the last 15 years, PostScript has evolved into the primary printer description language. Portable Document Format (PDF), which is the basis of Mac OS X's imaging technology, is based on PostScript. See also *TrueType*.

PostScript Printer Description (PPD) file—A file that tells your computer how to communicate with a specific PostScript printer to support its special features. For example, a PPD may tell your computer that the printer has multiple paper trays and allow you to select among them.

preemptive multitasking—A feature of Mac OS X and other operating systems in which the operating system serves as the task manager or traffic cop, parceling out CPU time to the various programs you are running. Compare with *cooperative multitasking*, a feature of older versions of the Mac OS in which the programs themselves shared CPU time.

preferences—A Mac OS X application or dialog box in which you make a set of configuration settings.

Print Center

Print Center—An application used to select printers, manage printer options, and track and control printer job queues.

printer driver—A program that tells your computer how to communicate with the printers on your network. A LaserWriter printer drive ships with Mac OS X. Some laser printers require special, custom drivers to deliver specific features. Other kinds of printers, such as ink jet models, come with their own software that must be installed for them to work with your Mac.

print queue—The service on the computer or server hosting the printer that stores print jobs as they are getting ready for the printer. Setting access rights on the print queue is very important so that you do not allow inappropriate users to delete another user's print jobs.

Process Viewer—An application that lets you see how much RAM and processor power the system and opened applications are using. It can also be accessed via the Terminal when you do an ADMIN login and type the command "TOP".

protected memory—A feature of Mac OS X and other operating systems in which the programs you run each have a separate memory space. If the program crashes for any reason, it will be shut down and the memory address space cleared. This approach prevents that program from affecting other functions on your Mac and helps prevent a system-wide crash.

pull-down menu—A list of commands that appears when you click on an item in the menu bar.

Quartz—The new imaging technology used for Mac OS X. It combines several standards, such as Open GL, PDF, and QuickTime, to provide the stunning visual effects that are part of the Aqua user interface.

Quartz Extreme—An enhanced version of Quartz that offloads 2D and 3D graphics and QuickTime images to high-performance graphic chips, using AGP, to provide superior performance.

QuickTime—Apple Computer's multimedia protocol, which supports a variety of audio and video compression methods to create and play back such productions. QuickTime is available in both Macintosh operating system (OS), Linux, and Windows versions. Preferences for Apple's QuickTime software can be set with the panel available from the System Preferences application.

QuickTime TV—A service of QuickTime, similar to RealAudio and its competitor, in which streaming audio and video presentations can be viewed from the Internet.

radio button—A small button, usually in a dialog box, that functions similarly to a checkbox. However, whereas more than one checkbox may sometimes be selected, a radio button toggles a function when clicked.

RAM—Stands for Random Access Memory. A computer chip designed to hold temporary memory, used by your Mac OS software and the application software you are running.

RAM Disk—A portion of RAM allocated to simulate a hard drive.

RealAudio—A popular Internet-based multimedia streaming protocol that allows users with a RealAudio or RealVideo player to hear audio and video productions direct from a Web site. It competes with QuickTime TV, which offers a similar capability.

Rendezvous—Based on a proposed open networking standard, it's a feature of Jaguar that allows for automatic recognition of networked devices, including computers, printers, cell phones and PDAs.

reset switch—A small button (sometimes recessed) with a triangular-shaped icon above it or inside it. This button is used to force your Mac to restart in the event of a system crash. Mac OS X is designed to minimize the prospects of such problems.

router—A specialized computer whose sole purpose is to move network traffic from one network segment to another.

Save—The command you access to continue saving the contents of a document that has already been named and stored via the Save As dialog box.

Save As—A dialog box that drops down as a sheet in the appropriate document window. It's used to name your file and to specify such items as file format and the location where the file is to be stored.

scalable font—A font that can be viewed or printed in any available point size. Both PostScript and TrueType fonts are scalable font formats.

Screen Saver—A pane available via the System Preferences application. It lets you activate Apple's new screen saver and set the idle time interval. This is a feature that more or less mimics the one previously available under Windows.

scrollbar—A vertical or horizontal bar that you drag to navigate a Finder or document window.

seed routing—The seeding of an AppleTalk network with a network number, also known as a cable range. By seeding the AppleTalk network's cable range, you can create zones on AppleTalk Phase 2 networks.

serial port—A connection jack used for such devices as modems, some printers, and digital cameras. Serial ports send data 1 bit at a time to the printer. Until Apple switched to USB for low-speed serial devices, all Macs had separate modem and printer ports for these functions (although they were combined in some PowerBooks).

Services—A feature of the application menu that displays links to programs that work with the one you have open to provide additional features.

Sharing—A pane under the System Preferences application where you can activate file sharing. The Mac OS X version also allows you to log into your Mac via Telnet and FTP.

Sheet—Mac OS X's revised Open and Save dialog box, which drops down from the window of the document to which the operation applies.

Sherlock 3—Apple's search program, a Web search tool divided into channels or categories, providing such content as Internet search results, flight information, phone numbers and other information.

SMTP—Stands for Simple Mail Transfer Protocol. The network protocol that transfers mail between mail servers over the Internet. SMTP is a text-based protocol that runs over Transmission Control Protocol/Internet Protocol (TCP/IP) on port 25.

Sound—The settings pane in the System Preferences application that lets you set system and alert volumes, and choose from the repository of alert sounds.

Special menu—No longer included with Mac OS X. This menu's functions have been moved to the Apple menu.

Speech—The settings pane in the System Preferences application that is used to select alert voices and speech rates for applications that support text-to-speech translation.

spooler—A program on a printer or on a server controlling the printer that stores print jobs until the printer is ready to print them. A printer spooler allows multiple people to print to the printer at the same time and then have each printer job stored and printed in the order that it came in. Some spooler programs prioritize the order in which print jobs are printed, based on who sent them and the priority assigned to them. The Mac OSX print spooler is the Print Center application. See *print queue*.

spring-loaded folders—A feature in Jaguar and the Classic Mac OS in which a folder automatically jumps open when an item is placed above it.

Startup Disk—The settings pane in the System Preferences application used to choose the disk from which your Mac starts. It can also be used to select between Mac OS X and older Mac OS environments.

StuffIt—A data-compression program from Aladdin Systems commonly used on Macintosh-based computers. Stuffed files are compressed using mathematical algorithms to reduce the space that the files take up on the computer. Stuffed files are commonly sent over the Internet because they can check themselves for consistency when the file is being unstuffed. Similar to the Zip protocol on the DOS and Windows platforms. See also *ZIP*.

SuperDisk—A removable device format that reads both regular

HD (1.4MB) floppy disks and special 120MB and 240MB floppy-disk media. Not to be confused with SuperDrive.

SuperDrive—An optical drive that can write and write to both CDs and DVDs.

surf—The act of browsing through Web sites in search of the ones that interest you.

System Menu—A type of application that puts up a display on the menu bar showing the status of a system setting. Mac OS X's System Preferences application lets you turn on a system menu for such functions as display resolution and color depth, volume, modem connection status, and AirPort networking.

Systems Preferences

System Preferences—An application that, in part, replaces the Control Panels folder. It offers direct access to Mac OS X system preferences, such as date and time, monitor resolution, and network configuration.

TCP—Stands for Transmission Control Protocol. A connection-oriented network protocol that moves data over the local area network (LAN) or the Internet safely and reliably using Internet Protocol (IP). TCP relies on a built-in error-correction system to identify problems in the transmission of data and then retransmit them, ensuring that the data is transferred properly. TCP can also dynamically alter the speed of transmission to reflect changing network conditions or the load on either the sending or receiving computer. See also *IP*.

Telnet—A text-based network protocol that operates on Transmission Control Protocol (TCP) port 23. Telnet is frequently used when you want to communicate with a computer or router on the network that uses a command-line interface (CLI). Telnet is a popular tool used when you are connecting to routers on the network because it allows you to connect to any router on the network from one workstation. You can also use Telnet programs to connect to other TCP ports, such as port 25—Simple Mail Transfer Protocol (SMTP)—to probe them, and see whether the programs that use these ports are functioning as expected. See also *command-line interface (CLI)*, *SMTP*, and *TCP*.

Terminal—A Mac OS X application used to access the Unix command-line interface.

title bar—A rectangular area at the top of a Finder or document window that contains its name and navigation buttons.

toolbar—A row of icons or buttons that, when clicked once, activate a specific command in a program.

TrueType—A printer technology developed in the 1980s and 1990s, first by Apple Computer and later with the help of Microsoft, as an alternative to Adobe's PostScript fonts. Like PostScript, TrueType describes fonts as mathematical expressions so that they can be scaled or manipulated without destroying the original font's proportions. Although originally designed for the Macintosh operating system (OS), TrueType has become more popular on the Windows platform. See also *PostScript*.

typeface—A specific design for a set of printed letters and other characters. An example of a typeface is Helvetica Bold.

type size—The size of letters and numbers, measured in points (approximately 1/72 of an inch). The point size is measured from the top of a capital letter to the bottom of a descender, such as appears in the letter *y*, plus a little space for air.

type style—The altered look of a typeface in various forms, such as italic, bold, bold italic, and underlined.

UFS—Stands for Unix File System. A file system available under Mac OS X. A UFS-formatted disk is free of disk fragmentation problems and is a good environment for developing Unix and Mac OS X applications, but isn't compatible with the Classic Mac OS.

Universal Access—A feature of Jaguar that provides a superior user experience for the physically handicapped. It includes text-to-speech, enlarged text, the ability to navigate the desktop and applications without a mouse and other features.

Unix—A popular industrial-strength multitasking operating system that was developed at AT&T Bell Laboratories. Originally intended for minicomputers, it has been modified for use on personal computers. Various flavors of Unix are available. Popular variations include Linux and Mac OS X.

upload—The process of transferring a file from your Mac to another computer on a network or via the Internet.

URL—Stands for Uniform Resource Locator. The information used to locate and access a site on the Internet or on your local network.

USB—Stands for universal serial bus. A low- to moderate-speed plug-and-play peripheral standard developed by Intel that is used on Macs for the keyboard, mouse, digital cameras, drives, and printers. A high-speed variation, USB 2.0, debuted early in 2001 but had not been supported by Apple at the time this book was written. Compare with *FireWire*, which handles high-speed peripheral devices.

View menu—A menu available from the desktop or Finder that sets Finder viewing options, such as icon or column view, and whether the toolbar buttons should appear.

virtual memory—A method used to extend the memory available to your Mac by allocating a portion of your hard drive as a swap file. When built-in memory is not sufficient to meet operating system or program needs, Mac OS X uses the file to swap unneeded data. Beginning with Mac OS X, the memory needs of an application are established dynamically as needed.

virus—Computer code that attaches itself to a program or document and causes an unsavory side effect (a silly message or, at worst, damage to the file or drive) or that just replicates itself and passes itself on to another program or document. All personal computers are vulnerable to viruses, and it's a good idea to purchase up-to-date software to protect your Mac.

Web (World Wide Web)—The preeminent Internet feature that provides animation and graphical and text displays of information. The Web is read by using a program called a browser. See also *Web browser*.

Web browser—A program designed to view documents created for display on the Web. The most popular Web browsers are Microsoft Internet Explorer and Netscape Navigator (or Communicator). A third Web program, OmniWeb, supports only Mac OS X.

Web page—A single document designed for display on the Web.

Web site—A location on the Web that contains one or more Web pages and is designed for business or personal use (or both).

window—A rectangular (or square) object that displays the contents of a document or directory.

Window menu—The window used to select from open document or folder windows.

Wireless Internet—Technologies that use either satellite transmissions or fixed wireless transmission systems to deliver high-speed Internet to a home or office without the need for a wired connection. An example of such a service is Sprint Broadband Direct (a service being phased out due to high costs and network bottlenecks).

ZIP—A compression format that works on PCs, Macintoshes, and Unix-based computers (although it's primarily oriented towards the DOS/Windows markets). The ZIP file format employs mathematical algorithms to reduce the space that the files take up on the computer. Zipped files are also frequently sent over the Internet because they can check themselves for consistency when the file is being expanded. See also *StuffIt*.

Zip drive—A removable storage device from Iomega Corporation. This drive uses media that look like thick floppy disks and store either 100MB or 250MB of data (depending on the kind of drive and media type you use).

Index

.Mac features, 495–496
10.2 *versus* 10.1, 16–18

A

About This Mac feature, 89
Access privileges, 188–189
Acrobat Reader, 299
ADB, 263
ADB-to-USB adapter, 267
Address Book, 17, 299
    importing another, 486–487
    using, 484–486
Administrator
    you as, 142–143
Adobe Systems, 309
Adobe Type Manager. *See* ATM
Advanced virtual memory, 7–8
AirPort, 29. *See also* Wireless networking
Alias
    creating, 103
Alias/Wavefront, 309
Amelio, Gil, 3
AOL
    software, 311
API, 9–10
Apple
    Backup, 362
    email software, 457–490
    Internet resource, 306
    software, 298–308
Apple Desktop Bus.
See ADB
Apple Type Solution. *See* ATS

AppleCare, 164
AppleScript, 212–214
    features, 214
    locating the collection, 217
    making or editing your first, 220–223
    tools for using, 215–216
AppleWorks, 312–315
    tables, using, 313–315
Application features
    complex installations, 233
    exploring new, 229–232
    folder, 87–88
    menu, 91
Application program interfaces.
See API
Aqua, 3, 10–12
ATM, 8
    font management, 338
ATS, 339–340
Audio MIDI Setup, 299
Autocomplete feature, 425–426
Awake mode, 279

B

Background, 99
Backup, 27–28, 357–377, 496
    commercial programs, 359–364
    files and folders, 427
    for daily plan, 371–372
    for special software, 372–374
    freeware and shareware, 364
    Internet-based, 364–366
    media, 366–370
    via the command line, 376–377

Basic scripts, 217
Battery life, 283–286
    optimizing, tips for, 285–286
Beige PowerMac G3, 28
BeOS, 3–4
Bitmap fonts, 336
BlackJack
    Internet resource, 365
Bluetooth File Exchange, 299
Bookmarks
    using, 450
BrickHouse, 395
Broadband access, 434–436
Browsers, 436–445
    deleting caches, 446–449
Built-in firewall, 390–392
Burning CDs and DVDs, 108–110

C

Cable modem, 435–436
Carbon, 9–10, 296–297
Castlewood ORB drive, 368
CD & DVD
    setting preferences, 53–54
CD writer or burner, 269–270
CD-R, 369
CD-RW, 369
Chess, 299
Classic
    compatibility environment, 320–324
    getting reliable performance from, 328–331
    limitations of, 321–324
    restoring, 110–111
    setting preferences, 48–49
    startup application, running as, 326–328
    troubleshooting, 332–333
Clock, 299
Cocoa, 9, 297
ColorSync, 300
    scripts, 218
    setting preferences, 55–56
    support for, 8
Column view, 84

resizing, 101
Combo cards, 266
Command-line interface, 7
    features, 427–430
    FTP software, 431–432
Computer icon, 86
Conflict Catcher
    Internet resource, 330
Connectivity
    verifying, 202–203
Console, 300
ContentBarrier, 394–395
Contextual menus
    accessing, 104
Control Panel
    settings, 40–42
Copland, 3
Copying a file, 103
Copying setups
    Internet and networking, 31
Corel, 309
CPU Monitor, 300
Create, 316–318
    inspector, 317
    web pages, starting, 318
Creating favorites, 104

D

Darwin, 5–8, 423–425
    Internet resource, 6
Data
    backup, 27–28
Date & Time
    setting preferences, 56–58
Dedicated security software, 145
Deneba, 310
Desktop, 16
    setting preferences, 58–59, 132–134
Desktop management, 121–140
Dictionary, 164
Digital cameras, 268–269
    installing, 274–275
Digital hub applications, 491–506
Digital music players, 271. *See also* iTunes
Digital subscriber line. *See* DSL
Disk First Aid, 23–24

Go menu

Disk image
    using, 233–234
Disk Utility, 301
DiskWarrior, 26–27
Display
    setting preferences, 59–65
Display Calibrator, 302
Dock, 14–16, 90, 122–128
    setting preferences, 65, 129–132
    using, 135–137
Drive 10, 24–25. *See also* TechTool Pro
Drop box
    access problems, 207
DSL, 435
DVD Player, 302
DVD-R, 369
DVD-RW, 369

E

eBay, 164
eBook readers
    installing, 274–275
Edit menu, 92–93
Ejecting a disk, 105
Energy-Saver, 284
    setting preferences, 65–67
Entourage X, 461–462
Ethernet, 264
Eudora Pro, 462–463
    Internet resource, 462
Excel X
    auto recover feature, 316
Expansion cards, 267
Extensis Suitcase, 339

F

Favorites
    creating, 104
    folder, 87
Features, new, 3–20
FileMaker, 309
Files
    advanced searching techniques, 167
    content, searching for, 167–169
    copying, 103

menu, 91–92
    searching for, 104, 166
Finder, 12–14, 17
    burning CDs and DVDs, 108–110
    customizing toolbar, 101–102
    keyboard shortcuts, 108
    new menus, 88–94
    scripts, 218
    setting preferences, 95–102, 134–135
    toolbar icons, 86–88
Finding a file, 104
Firewalk, 395
FireWire, 29, 265
FireWire Target Disk Mode, 292
Firmware
    Internet resource, 28
Flights, 164
Floppy drive, 366–367
Folder Action scripts, 218, 223–224
Font management, 335–356
    formats defined, 336–337, 337–339
    troubleshooting, 355–356
Font Panel, 231–232, 341–343
    adding and using favorites, 346–347
    checking characters, 349–350
    creating a collection, 347–349
    installing fonts, 344
    special features, 343
    using, 345
Font Reserve, 339
    managing library, 351–353
FontSync scripts, 218
Force Quit command, 90
Freeware
    software backup, 364
FWB Backup ToolKit, 363

G

Gassee, Jean Louis, 3
General preferences
    setting, 61–62
Genie effect, 15–16
Get Info window
    using, 105–107
Get Mac OS X Software command, 89
Go menu, 93

531

Grab, 302
Graphic cards, 270
Greg's Browser, 83

H

Handheld computers, 271
Hard drives, 269
Hardware
　deciding to buy new, 255–256
　extended warranties, 256–257
　firewalls, 396
　installing, 251–252
　maintaining, 252–255
　management, 247–260
　special features, 248–250
　troubleshooting, 257–260
Help menu, 94
High-speed ethernet, 266
Home folder, 86–87
HomePage, 495–496

I

iCab, 439–440
　deleting cache, 447–448
　Internet resource, 439
iCal, 493, 497–498
iCards, 496
iChat, 16–17, 302, 493, 501–502
　setting up, 499–500
Icon
　arrangement, 98
　size, 98
Icon View, 83
iDisk, 495, 505–506
　Internet resource, 365
iDVD, 494
iMac, 28
Image Capture, 303
iMovie, 280–281, 303, 494.
See also Video editing
Info scripts, 218
Inkwell, 18
Installer
　using, 233
Installing
　determining where to, 31
　instructions, 32–36
　Mac OS 9.2 or later, 31
　programs, 227–244
　unsupported, 36–38
Instant messaging, AOL-compatible.
　See iChat
Insurance, 289
Intego Personal Backup X, 360–362
　Internet resource, 360
International preferences
　setting, 62
Internet, 164
　connection problems, solving, 451–453
　searching, 172–174
　setting preferences, 70–72
Internet Connect, 303
　using for dial-up networking, 197–202
Internet Explorer, 304
Internet preferences
　setting, 62–64
Internet Services scripts, 218
Iomega Peerless drive, 368
Iomega's QuikSync 3, 363
iPhoto, 304, 494, 503–504
iPod, 271
iTunes, 305, 494. *See also* Digital music players

J

Jaguar, 8–9
　and Unix environment, 412–432
Jaz drive, 368
Jobs, Steve, 3
Junk mail filtering, 17

K

Key Caps, 305
Keyboard
　setting preferences, 72–73

Netscape

Keychain access application, 143–144, 305–306
  changing settings, 155–157
  checking and using, 155
  for children, 159–160
  multiple users, problems with, 157–159
  running on another Mac, 157
  setting up, 153–155

L

Label position, 98
Laptops
  airport x-rays, 290
  battery life, 283–286
  expansion, 282
  insurance for, 289
  online performance, 290–292
  portable printer for, 289
  tools for, 278–281
  travel kit, creating, 286–289
  traveling bag, 286
Launching
  older programs, 325–326
Lisa, 5
List view columns, 83–84
  changing, 100–101
Local talk-to-ethernet bridge, 266–267
Location feature, 90
Location Manager
  creating custom setups, 204–205
Log Out command, 90
Login application
  creating, 234–237
Login Items
  setting preferences, 73–74
Loudspeakers, 271

M

Mac OS X
  crashes and freezes, solving, 405–407
  features, crash-resistant, 398–400
  installation problems, solving, 402–405
  multiple users, 141–160

  peripheral compatibility, 19
  preparing for, 18–20, 22–28
  printer and serial devices, 19–20
  software compatibility, 19
  system requirements, 18–19
  vs. Classic, 44–45
Macromedia, 310
Mail
  adding signatures, 480
  address book, using, 484–486
  automatic delivery, 483–484
  blocking spam, 481–482
  comparison with other email programs, 464–466
  composing new messages, 473–475
  finding a message, 487–488
  formatting, 481
  forwarding, 479–480
  importing messages, 471–473
  quoting messages, 476
  responding to a message, 475–476
  sending attachments, 477–479
  setting rules, 482–483
  spellchecking, 476–477
  toolbar, customizing, 473
  troubleshooting, 488–490
  user account, setting up, 467–471
Mail scripts, 218
MasterJuggler
  font management, 339
Microsoft
  software, 297–298
Microsoft Internet Explorer, 437–439
  deleting cache, 446–447
Mouse
  setting preferences, 74–75
Movies, 164
Moving files, 103
Multiple user setup, 141–160
  instructions, 147–149

N

Navigation scripts, 218
NetBarrier X, 393–394
NetInfo Manager, 306
Netscape, 440–442, 463–464
  deleting cache, 448

533

Network
  access failure, solving, 408
  connection problems, 207–209
  identity, 190
  protecting from the Internet, 209–210
  setting preferences, 75–77
  utility, 306
  volume, 370
Networking, 179–210
  accessing networked Macs, 182–185
  enhanced, 18
NeXSTEP, 3
NeXT Inc., 3
Norton AntiVirus, 388–390
Norton Personal Firewall, 393
Norton Utilities, 24

O

Office v.X, 315–316
Older programs
  launching, 325–326
OmniWeb, 442–443
  deleting cache, 448
Open dialog box, 230
  using, 237–239
Open With command, 92
OpenType fonts, 336
Opera, 443–445
  deleting cache, 449
OS 9.x
  returning to, 334
  system folder, 331–332

P

Package, 228–229
Palm OS handhelds
  installing, 274–275
Passwords
  using strong, 146
Path icon, 102
PDF, 8
  support for, 8
Peripheral ports, 262–267
  adding missing, 265–267
Peripherals, 267–271
  installation of, troubleshooting, 275–276
Personal firewall software
  choosing, 392–395
Pictures, 164
Portable Document Format. *See* PDF
Portable hard drive, 368
Portable printer, 289
PostScript fonts, 336
Power On Software's Rewind, 363
PowerBook G3, 28
Preemptive multitasking, 7
Preferences
  general, 67–69
  setting Accounts, 53
  setting CD & DVD, 53–54
  setting Classic, 54–55
  setting ColorSync, 55–56
  setting Date & Time, 56–58
  setting Desktop, 58–59
  setting Display, 59–65
  setting Dock, 65
  setting International, 69–70
  setting Internet, 70–72
  setting Keyboard, 72–73
  setting Login Items, 73–74
  setting Mouse, 74–75
  setting Network, 75–77
  setting QuickTime, 77–78
  setting Screen Effects, 78
  setting Sharing, 78–80
  setting Software Update, 80–81
  setting Sound, 81–83
  setting Startup Disk, 84
  setting Universal Access, 84–86
Preview, 306
Printers
  configuring, 86–88
  selecting without a chooser, 42–43
Processor upgrade cards, 30
Project Gallery, 316
Protected memory, 6–7

Software

Q

Quartz, 8–9
Quartz 2D, 8
Quartz Extreme, 8–9, 18
QuickDraw, 8
QuickTime Player, 306
    setting preferences, 77–78
Quit command
    new location, 231

R

Recent Items feature, 90
Removable drives, 269
Rendezvous, 17, 181
Restart command, 90
Retrospect, 359–360
    Desktop Backup, 360
    Express Backup, 359–360
    Internet resource, 359
    Workgroup Backup, 360
Rhapsody, 3, 269–297
Root access
    setting, 416–417

S

Safeware
    Internet resource, 289
Sample scripts
    choosing, 217–219
Save As dialog box, 231
    using, 239–241
Scalable fonts, 336–337
Scanners, 268
    installing new, 272
Screen Effects
    setting preferences, 78
Screenshots
    creating, 107–108
Scripts
    editor, 219
    running from the Unix command line, 224
    using menu, 219–220
SCSI cards, 266
SCSI port, 263–264
SCSI-to-FireWire converter, 266
SCSI-to-USB converters, 266
Search feature, 161–178. *See also* Sherlock 3
    installing additional modules, 177
Security, 379–396
    features, 142–145
Serial port, 263
Serial-to-USB converters, 266
Services command, 229–230
Setup Assistant
    configuring, steps for, 46–51
Shared folders, 144–145
Shared Macs
    connecting to, 193–195
Shared volumes
    accessing with network browser, 191–192
    accessing with the Chooser, 192–193
Shared Windows and Unix servers
    connecting to, 195–197
Shareware
    software backup, 364
Sharing
    files, 183–193
    setting preferences, 71–72, 78–80
Sherlock 3, 17
    customizing Internet search request, 174–177
    setting preferences, 171–172
Sherlock scripts, 219
Shut Down command, 90
Sleep mode, 90, 279
SmartDisk
    Internet resource, 368
Software, 297–311
    running from the command line, 426
    troubleshooting, 242–244, 257–260

535

Software Update, 400–401
  setting preferences, 80–81
Sonnet Technology, 30
Sound
  setting preferences, 81–83
Speech
  setting preferences, 74–75
Spring Cleaning, 228
Spring-loaded folders, 14
Starting Points, 312–315
Startup application
  creating, 234–237
Startup Disk
  setting preferences, 84
Stickies, 307
Stocks, 164
Stone Design, 310–311
Storage devices
  installing new, 273–274
Suitcase
  managing font library, 354–355
SuperDisk drive, 367
System logins, 145
System preferences, 18, 307
  folder, 90
System-level disk diagnostics
  performing, 414–416

T

Tape drives, 369–370
TechTool Pro, 24–25, 384–385. See also Drive 10
TeleAdapt
  Internet resource, 289
Terminal, 307
Text size, 98
TextEdit, 308
  avoiding too-small fonts, 350–351
Third-party graphics cards, 29
Third-party SCSI cards, 29
TinkerTool, 138–139
Toolbarscripts
  Internet resource, 225
  using, 225

Translation, 164
Trojan Horse, 381
Troubleshooting, 397–418
TrueType fonts, 336

U

Universal Access
  setting preferences, 84–86
Universal Serial Bus.
See USB
Unix, 307–308
  Internet resource, 307
Unsupported installation, 36–38
UpdateAgent X, 398
URL scripts, 219
USB, 264, 265
  drives, 29
User accounts
  customizing, 149–151
  editing, 152–153

V

VersionTracker
  Internet resource, 124
Video editing, 280–281. See also iMovie
View menu, 93
Viewing preferences, setting, 97–100
Virex, 387–388, 496
Virtual Private Network. See VPN
Virus Barrier, 385–387
Virus-detection programs, 384–390
Viruses
  and broadband Internet, 382–383
  email, 381
  types of, 381
VPN
  connecting via, 203–204
VueScan
  Internet resource, 268

W

Watson
  Internet resource, 178
Wavefront, 309
Web or FTP server
  setting up, 206–207
Window menu, 94
Wireless Internet, 436
Wireless networking, 270. *See also* AirPort
Word X
  multiple selection feature, 316
Wozniak, Steve, 3

X

XPostFacto, 36–38
  Internet resource, 22

Y

Yellow Pages, 164

Z

Zip drive, 367

Mac® OS X v. 10.2 Jaguar Little Black Book
Quick Reference *(continued)*

5. Choose a password of at least four characters, consisting of random upper and lower case letters and numbers to make it difficult to guess. If you want, also write a hint, a phrase or word that'll remind you of the password if you forget it.
6. Choose your Internet access option. Depending on your connection method, which runs the gamut from a dial-up modem to a cable modem, you will be presented with a different set of setup screens.
7. Enter your TCP/IP settings information for Internet access via cable modem or DSL or local area network.
8. If you want to set up an iTools account, enter the setup information where requested, then click Continue to send your registration to Apple and move on to the next step of setup process.
9. Enter your email settings, including your email address, and the incoming and outgoing email servers required by your ISP. You will have to refer to the settings provided by your ISP or your previous Mac OS installation as to what needs to be entered here.
10. Select your proper geographic location, so the time display of the menu bar clock is accurate. In addition to moving the slider to the right area, you may have to select another option via the pop-up menu (such as for the state of Arizona).
11. Review you settings. You can click the back arrow to redo an earlier setting.
12. Once your settings are finished, click the Go Ahead button to continue the startup process and bring you to the Mac OS X desktop.

How to Make System Settings

Use the System Preferences application, and select a settings panel from the icon list. Preferences are divided into four categories: Personal, Hardware, Internet & Network and System. Third party preference panels are placed in the Other category (which only shows up if additional preferences are installed). Some settings may require that the administrator for the Mac login if another user accesses your Mac; these will be identified by a padlock icon.

Key System Settings described in alphabetical order:

- *Accounts Preferences:* Bring up this screen if you want to change your login password or add additional users to your Mac, to take advantage of its multiple users features. You can also attach a picture to apply to each user, which will be available when you login to your Mac. To make a change, click on your user name, then click the Edit User button and enter the new password twice in the appropriate text fields and then the appropriate hint, if you want a reminder. Once you click the OK button, your new password goes into effect. The Cancel button undoes the changes you've made.
- *Classic Preferences:* The Classic Preferences panel lets you specify the startup volume for the Classic operating system. The Advanced preference panel is used to configure additional options, such as whether or not to rebuild the Classic Mac OS system's desktop or restart with extensions off or to bring Extensions Manager up when Classic opens.
- *ColorSync Preferences:* Apple's ColorSync technology is tightly integrated into Mac OS X. You can use this settings panel to choose a ColorSync profile for input devices, such as a scanner, your Mac's display, output devices (a printer), or a proofing device.
- *Date & Time Preferences:* These settings mirror the ones you've already done in the Setup Assistant. There is, however, a new wrinkle to these settings. At the bottom left of the settings screen, you'll notice a button labeled Click The Lock To Prevent Further Changes. This means you can protect this panel and any other panel with a padlock icon so that only users with administrator's access.
- *Desktop:* Use these settings to configure what kind of desktop backdrop you will have on your Mac.
- *Display Preferences:* This settings panel is used to configure the size (resolution) of the images on your Mac's display and the color depth setting. If you wish to change color depth, click on the Colors pop-up menu. Click the Color tab if you want to adjust the color balance or calibration of your display. On some Macs, such as the iMac, you will also find a Geometry option that lets you configure your CRT display for the most accurate appearance.
- *Dock Preferences:* Apple's famous Mac OS X taskbar can be configured in a several ways to adjust display. The settings include Dock size, magnification and whether the Dock will be hidden unless you move the mouse cursor to the bottom of the screen. You can also pin the Dock at the left or right ends of your Mac's display.

- *Energy Saver Preferences:* These settings perform such functions as putting the system into sleep mode after a preset period of time. There are also separate settings for display and hard drive sleep modes. The Options tab gives you more settings, such as whether to wake the computer as a result of network access and, on some models, whether to automatically restart in the event of a power failure.
- *General Preferences:* In part, Aqua equivalent of the Appearance control panel, which lets you choose from Aqua or Graphite color themes and highlight color. You can also configure scroll arrows, the number of recent items displayed for applications and documents in the Apple menu and the text smoothing threshold.
- *International Preferences:* Select the preferred keyboard layout from the list, and then choose how date, time, and numbers will appear. The Keyboard Menu feature puts up a menu bar icon to allow for fast keyboard layout switches.
- *Internet Preferences:* Mirrors the Internet Control Panel of earlier Mac OS versions. Set up your iTools user account and then configure your regular email, Web and newsgroup access and the applications you want to use.
- *Keyboard Preferences:* These settings affect your Mac keyboard's Automatic Repeat modes. The Full Keyboard Access tab gives you the ability to use the keyboard for fast access to menu bar items, Finder windows and the Dock.
- *Login Items Preferences:* This setting works the same as the Startup Items folder under previous versions of the Mac OS. The programs that appear in this window launch when you log in. Click on the Add button to locate and select startup applications that will open when you boot or login to your Mac, and click on the Remove button to delete a selected items.
- *Mouse Preferences:* Move the Mouse Speed slider to adjust the tracking speed. The Double-Click Delay setting is used to configure the ideal interval for a double-click to activate a Mac OS function. On some Apple laptops, there will be a separate Trackpad tab for additional settings.
- *Network Preferences:* This configuration screen is used for setting up Internet access and LAN hookups. Settings include network type, PPoE for DSL hookups, AppleTalk, plus configuring your modem for dial-up access. It combines the functions of the Classic Mac OS's Modem, Remote Access and TCP/IP Control Panels.
- *QuickTime Preferences:* This settings panel is used to set how QuickTime works on your Mac. You can choose connection speed to optimize performance, depending on your Internet connection, and automatically update QuickTime software.
- *Screen Saver:* Apple's built-in screen saver offers cool, liquid images of icons, beaches, the cosmos, forests, and more. It is on by default. You can also activate a password feature to defeat the screen saver, change the interval under which it activates, or turn it off all together.
- *Sharing Preferences:* Peer-to-peer file sharing is one of the delights of the Mac OS. Open this panel (and click on the Start button for such services as Personal File Sharing Windows File Sharing Personal Web sharing (which uses the Apache Web Server software to let you host a site) and Printer Sharing. You also have the option to allow remote login (Telnet) or FTP access to your Mac. The Sharing panel is also used to rename your Macintosh.

NOTE: File sharing under Mac OS X supports both AppleTalk and TCP/IP, so you can network with any Mac or a Windows network with Services for Macintosh installed. There's also an SMB client that allows you to directly connect to Windows and Unix file shares using their native networking protocol.

- *Software Update Preferences:* Regular updates will be available to make Mac OS X run better, and to add new features. You can update your software manually, whenever you want or click the Automatically button to have Apple's Web site checked on a Daily, Weekly or Monthly basis for needed updates. The status display will show the last time you attempted the update. Click Update Now whenever you want to recheck for updates.

NOTE: Depending on the size of the update, Apple may opt to distribute that update via CD instead of online. This was true in the upgrade from Mac OS X 10.1 to 10.2, or will also be true for subsequent major upgrades, which are sometimes called "reference releases."

- *Sound Preferences:* The Sound settings control overall system volume, alert volume and you also have the option to pick from a selection of alert sounds. Some computer speakers or multimedia hardware may place additional settings on this panel, such as a choice of input sources.

- *Speech Preferences:* Some Mac programs support Mac OS X's Speech Manager, which allows you to activate Mac functions via spoken commands and have text to be read back to you. In this settings pane, you can decide whether to activate the speech recognition feature. Click On and then click Listening to specify whether you can speak a command with or without a listening key (a keyboard shortcut that precedes the speech command. The Text-to-Speech tab brings up a screen you can choose a voice from the list, then specify the rate at which the voice is played back.
- *Startup Disk Preferences:* This setting lets you switch startup disks, if you have additional volumes with system software on them on your Mac. The change is usually made will be made to switch from Mac OS X back to your Classic Mac OS.
- *Universal Access:* For those with injuries or disabilities, this preference panel gives you an assortment of options to reduce the need to use the mouse, and to allow the keyboard to emulate mouse functions, or to simplify multiple keystroke shortcuts.

Setting Up Printers Under Mac OS X

Use the Print Center application to add and configure the printers connected to your Mac or to your network. When printing, the Print Center application will automatically appear in the Dock and display a visual indicator of the amount of pages remaining in a print job, or a warning icon in case there's a problem. You can also click on the icon to bring up a screen showing the status of your print queue.

NOTE: *A number of printer drivers are included as standard issue with Mac OS X. In addition, Mac OS X automatically recognizes USB printers without needing to go to Print Center except to change a default printer, so long as the correct printer drivers are installed. Adding an output device under Print Center is generally confined to a network printer (one that connects to your Ethernet or AirPort network).*

To add a printer:
1. Go to the Utilities folder and locate and double-click on the Print Center application icon to launch it.
2. If you have no printers selected, you'll see a dialog box asking if you wish to add a printer. Click on the Add button. If you already have printers selected, click on the Add Printer button in the Printers window. If your printer uses AppleTalk, make sure the feature is turned on in the Network panel of System Preferences (you'll be notified of this and taken to the Network panel if necessary).
3. On the next screen, click on the Connection pop-up menu and select the network or peripheral connection on which you want to check for printers. Depending on the kind of Mac you have, you can choose from several connection protocols, including AppleTalk, IP Printing, or USB. The Directory Services option can locate an enterprise printer located on your network.

NOTE: *Some network printers will run via the IP printing mode, but you need to retrieve the IP number for your printer to access this mode. For most situations, choosing AppleTalk ought to be sufficient for good performance. You also find custom port lists for specific model printers from Epson, HP and Lexmark.*

---

4. If your printer is located in another network zone, click on the second pop-up menu to pick that zone.
5. Continue browsing for printers until they are all displayed.

NOTE: *Apple provides PPD files for a number of popular printers. Such files, which add support for special printer features, such as extra paper trays and special paper sizes, can be obtained from the manufacturer or from Adobe's Web site, at http://www.adobe.com/products/printerdrivers/macppd.html. PPD files are placed on your startup drive in the following location: Library>Printers>PPDs>Contents>Resources>en.lproj (or whatever language you're using).*

---

6. Click on the red button to close the window. At this point, all of your available printers should appear in the main Printer window.